Mortgage Payment Handbook

Monthly Payment Tables
and
Annual Amortization Schedules
for Fixed-Rate Mortgages

Eric Wiener

BARNES
&NOBLE
BOOKS
NEW YORK

This edition published by Barnes & Noble Inc.
1992 Barnes & Noble Books

ISBN 0-88029-715-8

Printed and bound in the United States of America

M 9 8 7 6 5 4 3 2 1

Contents

Introduction

The financial tables in this book are intended for anyone who borrows, lends, or invests money. You don't need to be a economist, mathematician, or financial expert to use them—you'll find simple explanations and examples right here in the introduction. Because these tables have been designed to be read easily, any investor or borrower should find them to be an excellent tool. They were not intended for professionals, and no pre-calculated formulas or mathematical proofs are needed to use them (such information is not necessary for the use of the tables). It is highly recommended that anyone not familiar with mortgage payment tables take the time needed to read the entire introduction.

Before we go any further, let's cover some of the basic definitions used:

Principal—The amount of money borrowed or lent.

Interest Rate—A percentage based upon some period of time (typically a year) which, when multiplied by the principal, determines either the fee charged to the borrower or the amount of money earned by the principal over time.

Term—The time between the delivery of the principal funds to the borrower and the complete payback of the principal to the lender.

Amortization—The method of repaying a principal through a schedule of installment payments. Every installment pays the interest to date and a portion of the principal.

A glossary of other relevant terms is provided at the end of the book.

All of these tables are based upon fixed-interest borrowing (common mortgages). This means that the interest rate is set at the beginning of the term and does not change. *Do not use these tables for any transactions which are not fixed-interest transactions—i.e., they should not be used for variable-rate or adjustable-rate mortgages.*

The monthly payment tables cover fixed-interest loans with interest rates ranging from 5% to 23% at ¼% intervals over terms from 1 to 40 years and principals from $10,000 to $1,000,000. In addition, coefficients can be used to determine any monthly payment for principals less than $10,000,000. These coefficients can also be used to calculate smaller principals such as car loans. The amortization tables cover fixed-interest loans of $10,000 with interest rates ranging from 5% to 23% at ¼% intervals for terms of 15 and 30 years.

The decision to purchase a home or secure financing for a small business is usually very complicated. It may, in fact, be one of the most important financial decisions anyone can make. Because this kind of decision is so important, it is essential that potential borrowers and investors understand how mortgage financing works.

Basically, one party, the lender (usually a bank), agrees to lend another party, the borrower (usually a car or home buyer, or business owner), a sum of money for a specified length of time. The borrower agrees to pay back the lender in regular monthly payments beginning 1 month after the loan is made and ending when the entire principal and interest is paid. The principal is amortized over the term of the loan to determine the monthly payment.

For larger principals, quite often the loan is secured with some sort of collateral. This collateral usually consists of the assets being purchased with the borrowed money. This means that if the borrower cannot repay the loan according to the terms of the agreement, the lender has the right to seize these assets, since he possesses a lien against the borrower's property according to the terms of the loan agreement. In the common case of home mortgages, the mortgage is secured by the property being purchased; in effect, the lender "owns" the borrower's property until the debt (or lien) has been fully paid off (and the lien is removed from the property).

In the case where no assets are being purchased, as in a commercial loan for operating capital, the loan can be secured by the borrowing entity's existing assets (furniture, equipment, property, etc.) or by the assets of one of the principals of the borrowing entity. For example, one or more of the shareowners in a corporation can secure a loan for the corporation by putting up personal assets as collateral.

Monthly Payment Tables

How to Use the Monthly Payment Tables:

The monthly payment tables are simple to use. To find a specific monthly payment, first locate the facing pages for the interest rate of your loan. Next, use the left-hand column to find the row showing the amount of your principal. Continue along that row until you reach the column showing the correct term of your mortgage. The sum shown indicates the monthly payment for your mortgage—consisting of both the interest and the payment (amortization) on the principal of the loan.

Example 1—Early Stages of Home Buying

Mr. and Mrs. Appleton would like to buy a house, but they are not sure what they can afford to spend. They think that they could probably handle mortgage payments of around $1,000 a month. After checking with several banks, they find out that they can get an interest rate of 9.25% over 25 years or 8% over 30 years. What price range should they be looking at for their house? Turn to the page listing the monthly payment table at a 9.25% rate of interest. Now, move down the 25-year column until you find payments in the range that they can afford. Looking across the column you will see that the Appletons can afford to look for houses requiring between $110,000 and $120,000 of financing. Examining the table at 8% interest over a 30-year term shows that they can afford to look at houses requiring between $130,000 and $140,000 of financing. Remember that the Appletons will still need from $30,000 to $50,000 to cover the down payment and closing costs on their house.

Example 2—Late Stages of Home Buying

The Appletons find a house that will cost $157,000 to purchase. The bank will require a 20% ($31,400) down payment on the purchase. This will leave the Appletons with $125,600 to finance. After careful consideration, they decide to get their mortgage from a bank which offers to lend them the money at a rate of 8% over 30 years. Turn to the page with the 8% monthly payment table and cross-reference a 30-year term with the principal to determine that their monthly payments will be between $880.52 and $953.89.

Example 3—Small Business Investment Opportunity

A local restauranteur wishes to rebuild the dining room and install new kitchen facilities in his business. He will need $300,000 to make these improvements. A group of doctors looking for an investment agrees to lend the restauranteur the money over 5 years at 12.5% interest. What will the monthly payments be to the doctors and how much will they make over 5 years? Turn to the 12.5% monthly payment table, cross-reference a term of 5 years with a principal of $300,000 to determine that the monthly payments will be $6,749.38. Multiply $6,749.38 by 60 (12 payments per year for 5 years) and determine that the doctors will collect $404,962.80—a profit of $104,962.80.

How to Use the Coefficients:

The bottom row of every monthly payment table contains a coefficient. This number is used to determine the precise monthly payment for a loan that is not an exact match with the principals given in the table, or a loan exceeding $1,000,000. Look up the coefficient based upon the desired interest rate and term, then multiply the principal by the coefficient. The following example shows how to use a coefficient. (Note: coefficients cannot be used to determine monthly payments for principals above $10,000,000.)

Example 1—Late Stages of Home Buying

In example 2 of the previous section, the Appletons determined that they would require $125,600.00 in financing from the bank to buy their dream house. They used the tables to figure out that their monthly payments would be between $880.52 and $953.89. At this point, the Appletons want to know exactly how much their monthly payments are going to be so they can project their new monthly budget. Turn to the 8% monthly payment table and cross-reference a 30-year term with the coefficient row at the bottom of the page. The table lists the 30-year coefficient as 0.007337646. Multiply the coefficient (0.007337646) by the principal ($125,600.00) to determine that their monthly payments will be $921.61.

Example 2—Purchasing a Car

Ms. Dryden is buying an economy automobile. The dealer offers to sell her the car for $6,754.00. He also offers her 9.5% financing over 5 years if she can come up with $500.00 as a down payment. What will her monthly payments be if she decides to buy the car under these terms? First, look up the 5-year coefficient from the 9.5% monthly payment table. The coefficient is 0.021001861. Now, subtract the $500.00 Ms. Dryden will be using as a down payment from the $6,754.00 to determine that the amount being financed for this purchase will be $6,254.00. Multiply the principal ($6,254.00) by the coefficient (0.021001861) to determine that Ms. Dryden's monthly payments will be $131.35.

In determining the total cost of your loan, be sure to take into account the additional money needed to pay any points on the mortgage. Points (also known as discount points) are a fee charged by a lender to originate a loan. Points are payable over and above your monthly interest payments and refer to a specific percentage of the original amount of the principal (i.e., one percent is the equivalent of one point).

Amortization Schedules

An amortization schedule is very useful to have on hand after a loan has been made, since it outlines the important aspects of the loan over time. This table shows how much of the interest and principal on a loan were paid over the course of each year, and how much of the principal is left to be paid at the end of that year. This information is valuable for many reasons. First of all, the interest paid may be tax deductible. Second, you may want to know how much of the principal is still owed. Finally, the total amount of all payments made and all interest paid appears at the bottom of each of these tables. Remember that only in rare instances does a monthly payment result in the exact payoff of a loan. Most institutions disregard the final balance, as it is always *assumed* to be zero.

As a final note, you will see that a larger portion of the payments over a year goes toward interest at the beginning of the term of the loan than at the end of the term. At the beginning of a loan, payments are mostly towards interest, whereas, at the end of a loan, payments are mostly on the principal. Many lenders permit a borrower to prepay the principal on a loan. Prepayments can effectively shorten the term of a loan without placing the borrower under the obligation to pay any more than the monthly payment should his or her financial situation change for the worse.

Amortization schedules are listed separately for 15-year and 30-year conventional mortgages, and are arranged sequentially by interest rate. Each entry has four columns. The first column lists the year of the term, the second column shows the amount of principal still owed at the end of each year, and the third and fourth columns show the amount of interest and principal paid over the year. The monthly payment is shown at the top of each schedule and the total payout and total interest paid is shown at the bottom.

How to Use the Amortization Tables:

Since these tables have been developed using principals of $10,000, they can only be used for purposes of estimation. If you require exact numbers see your banker or accountant.

Example 1—Estimation of Interest Paid

The Appletons are now in the 14th year of their 30-year conventional mortgage at an 8% rate of interest. The initial principal of the mortgage was $125,600. This is about 12.5 x $10,000. They wish to know how much interest they paid during the last year. Turn to the page with the 8% amortization schedule and find the 30-year table. Last year was the 13th year of their loan, so go to the row beginning with the number 13. Moving over two columns to the right you will find $688.38. Multiply $688.38 by 12.5 to determine that the total interest the Appletons paid was $8,605. It is important to remember that this amount is only an approximation of the interest paid.

Example 2—Estimation of Equity

The Appletons are now finishing their 20th year of the loan just described. Their only child, Sarah, is ready to attend college. They believe that they might be able to pay for part of her tuition by taking out a loan on the equity they have built up in their home. An appraiser tells them that their home is now worth $285,000 on the market. The Appletons must now determine how much they still owe on their mortgage to see what their equity is in the house. Turn to the page with the 8% amortization schedule and find the 30-year table. Look for the row beginning with the number 20. The number in the first column to the right is $6,125.16. Multiply $6,125.16 by 12.5 to determine that the Appletons still owe about $76,565 on their house. This means that they have about $208,435 of equity in their house against which they can borrow.

Example 3—Buying Out of a Mortgage

The Appletons were lucky. Their daughter Sarah won a full academic scholarship to college. She is now a sophomore, and Mr. Appleton is retiring from his job. The Appletons decide that they no longer need to live in a big house in the city and want purchase a new home in the country. Although they will be able to live comfortably on Mr. Appleton's pension, they do not wish to take out another mortgage. A young couple, the Servises, have offered to purchase the Appleton's house in the city for $280,000. However, the Appletons still have 9 years to pay on their current mortgage. If they sell the house they will have to pay the bank the remaining principal. Turn to the page with the 8% amortization schedule and find the 30-year table. Go to the row beginning with the number 21. The number in the first column to the right is $5,636.23. Multiply $5,636.23 by 12.5 (remember that the original principal of the mortgage was about 12.5 x $10,000) to determine that the Appletons still owe about $70,452.88 on their house. This means that they will have about $209,547.12 in cash remaining from the sale of their house to the Servises. They can now go shopping for a house in the country and pay cash—providing that they keep all their costs under $209,547.12.

In conclusion, credit is a cornerstone of capitalist societies and there is no getting around it. Countries, states, cities, counties, townships, businesses, banks, associations, and non- profit organizations—as well as individuals—extend credit toward the purchase of goods and services all over the world. Some transactions are done on a handshake, while others are covered by meticulously crafted agreements hundreds of pages long. Regardless of their size or nature, they all have one thing in common—*trust*. Basic trust means that both parties involved are honest and will earnestly fulfill the original agreement toward a mutual advantage. Both sides of the agreement must gain something from the agreement for it to be ethical and sound.

On the part of the borrower, it is expected that the principal will be paid back according to the conditions of the agreement. It is therefore expected that the borrower can truly accomplish this. In the case of formal loans with lending institutions it is often necessary for the borrower to demonstrate an ability to pay back the principal. This is usually done in several different ways. As the amount of the principal and payments appears to near the maximum amount that a borrower can truly afford, other means of gaining trust, such as collateral or co-signers, are sometimes required. Co-signers are individuals or entities (such as corporations or government entities like the Small Business Association or the Veteran's Administration) who will guarantee that if the borrower fails to meet the letter of the agreement, they will. Young people getting settled in life typically rely on parents as co-signers in assisting to establish credit. Start-up businesses can sometimes get state economic development authorities to guarantee a loan. There are almost as many ways to establish credit as there are goods and services to purchase with it—so don't be discouraged.

On the part of the lender, it is expected that the borrower is guaranteed the undisturbed enjoyment or use of the goods and services being purchased with the principal, and that the borrower is not charged an unreasonable rate of interest for the use of the principal. It is therefore very important that the borrower explore all of the financing options available before entering into an agreement. There are many lending institutions to consider. It is in the best interests of the borrower to realize that he or she is effectively "purchasing" the temporary use of funds. The "purchase" price is the interest rate plus any other costs involved such as points paid to a bank when "buying" a mortgage. Borrowers should always compare interest rates and conditions of payment before agreeing to terms.

Credit is neither good nor evil—it is both a tool and a means to an end. Although credit can be misused or abused, it can also be used to attain the things we need to function and survive, as well as a means to put idle assets to work for us. Remember, Wimpy probably did pay on Tuesday for those hamburgers he ate today. Wimpy ate, and Popeye sold two hamburgers—the first one, and then on Tuesday . . .

Monthly
Payment
Tables

5.00% MONTHLY AMORTIZING PAYMENTS

AMOUNT	1 YEAR	2 YEARS	3 YEARS	4 YEARS	5 YEARS	6 YEARS	7 YEARS	8 YEARS
10 000	856.07	438.71	299.71	230.29	188.71	161.05	141.34	126.60
20 000	1712.15	877.43	599.42	460.59	377.42	322.10	282.68	253.20
30 000	2568.22	1316.14	899.13	690.88	566.14	483.15	424.02	379.80
40 000	3424.30	1754.86	1198.84	921.17	754.85	644.20	565.36	506.40
50 000	4280.37	2193.57	1498.54	1151.46	943.56	805.25	706.70	633.00
60 000	5136.45	2632.28	1798.25	1381.76	1132.27	966.30	848.03	759.60
70 000	5992.52	3071.00	2097.96	1612.05	1320.99	1127.35	989.37	886.19
80 000	6848.60	3509.71	2397.67	1842.34	1509.70	1288.39	1130.71	1012.79
90 000	7704.67	3948.42	2697.38	2072.64	1698.41	1449.44	1272.05	1139.39
100 000	8560.75	4387.14	2997.09	2302.93	1887.12	1610.49	1413.39	1265.99
110 000	9416.82	4825.85	3296.80	2533.22	2075.84	1771.54	1554.73	1392.59
120 000	10272.90	5264.57	3596.51	2763.52	2264.55	1932.59	1696.07	1519.19
130 000	11128.97	5703.28	3896.22	2993.81	2453.26	2093.64	1837.41	1645.79
140 000	11985.05	6141.99	4195.93	3224.10	2641.97	2254.69	1978.75	1772.39
150 000	12841.12	6580.71	4495.63	3454.39	2830.68	2415.74	2120.09	1898.99
160 000	13697.20	7019.42	4795.34	3684.69	3019.40	2576.79	2261.43	2025.59
170 000	14553.27	7458.14	5095.05	3914.98	3208.11	2737.84	2402.76	2152.19
180 000	15409.35	7896.85	5394.76	4145.27	3396.82	2898.89	2544.10	2278.79
190 000	16265.43	8335.56	5694.47	4375.57	3585.53	3059.94	2685.44	2405.38
200 000	17121.50	8774.28	5994.18	4605.86	3774.25	3220.99	2826.78	2531.98
210 000	17977.57	9212.99	6293.89	4836.15	3962.96	3382.04	2968.12	2658.58
220 000	18833.65	9651.71	6593.60	5066.44	4151.67	3543.09	3109.46	2785.18
230 000	19689.72	10090.42	6893.31	5296.74	4340.38	3704.13	3250.80	2911.78
240 000	20545.80	10529.13	7193.02	5527.03	4529.10	3865.18	3392.14	3038.38
250 000	21401.87	10967.85	7492.72	5757.32	4717.81	4026.23	3533.48	3164.98
260 000	22257.95	11406.56	7792.43	5987.62	4906.52	4187.28	3674.82	3291.58
270 000	23114.02	11845.27	8092.14	6217.91	5095.23	4348.33	3816.16	3418.18
280 000	23970.10	12283.99	8391.85	6448.20	5283.95	4509.38	3957.49	3544.78
290 000	24826.17	12722.70	8691.56	6678.49	5472.66	4670.43	4098.83	3671.38
300 000	25682.25	13161.42	8991.27	6908.79	5661.37	4831.48	4240.17	3797.98
320 000	27394.40	14038.84	9590.69	7369.37	6038.79	5153.58	4522.85	4051.17
340 000	29106.55	14916.27	10190.11	7829.96	6416.22	5475.68	4805.53	4304.37
360 000	30818.69	15793.70	10789.52	8290.55	6793.64	5797.78	5088.21	4557.57
380 000	32530.84	16671.13	11388.94	8751.13	7171.07	6119.87	5370.89	4810.77
400 000	34242.99	17548.56	11988.36	9211.72	7548.49	6441.97	5653.56	5063.97
420 000	35955.14	18425.98	12587.78	9672.30	7925.92	6764.07	5936.24	5317.17
440 000	37667.29	19303.41	13187.20	10132.89	8303.34	7086.17	6218.92	5570.36
460 000	39379.44	20180.84	13786.61	10593.47	8680.77	7408.27	6501.60	5823.56
480 000	41091.59	21058.27	14386.03	11054.06	9058.19	7730.37	6784.28	6076.76
500 000	42803.74	21935.69	14985.45	11514.65	9435.62	8052.47	7066.95	6329.96
520 000	44515.89	22813.12	15584.87	11975.23	9813.04	8374.56	7349.63	6583.16
540 000	46228.04	23690.55	16184.29	12435.82	10190.47	8696.66	7632.31	6836.36
560 000	47940.19	24567.98	16783.70	12896.40	10567.89	9018.76	7914.99	7089.55
580 000	49652.34	25445.41	17383.12	13356.99	10945.32	9340.86	8197.67	7342.75
600 000	51364.49	26322.83	17982.54	13817.58	11322.74	9662.96	8480.34	7595.95
620 000	53076.64	27200.26	18581.96	14278.16	11700.16	9985.06	8763.02	7849.15
640 000	54788.79	28077.69	19181.38	14738.75	12077.59	10307.16	9045.70	8102.35
660 000	56500.94	28955.12	19780.79	15199.33	12455.01	10629.26	9328.38	8355.55
680 000	58213.09	29832.54	20380.21	15659.92	12832.44	10951.35	9611.06	8608.74
700 000	59925.24	30709.97	20979.63	16120.50	13209.86	11273.45	9893.74	8861.94
720 000	61637.39	31587.40	21579.05	16581.09	13587.29	11595.55	10176.41	9115.14
740 000	63349.54	32464.83	22178.47	17041.68	13964.71	11917.65	10459.09	9368.34
760 000	65061.69	33342.25	22777.88	17502.26	14342.14	12239.75	10741.77	9621.54
780 000	66773.84	34219.68	23377.30	17962.85	14719.56	12561.85	11024.45	9874.74
800 000	68485.99	35097.11	23976.72	18423.43	15096.99	12883.95	11307.13	10127.94
820 000	70198.14	35974.54	24576.14	18884.02	15474.41	13206.04	11589.80	10381.13
840 000	71910.29	36851.97	25175.56	19344.61	15851.84	13528.14	11872.48	10634.33
860 000	73622.44	37729.39	25774.97	19805.19	16229.26	13850.24	12155.16	10887.53
880 000	75334.59	38606.82	26374.39	20265.78	16606.69	14172.34	12437.84	11140.73
900 000	77046.74	39484.25	26973.81	20726.36	16984.11	14494.44	12720.52	11393.93
920 000	78758.89	40361.68	27573.23	21186.95	17361.53	14816.54	13003.20	11647.13
940 000	80471.04	41239.10	28172.65	21647.53	17738.96	15138.64	13285.87	11900.32
960 000	82183.19	42116.53	28772.06	22108.12	18116.38	15460.73	13568.55	12153.52
980 000	83895.34	42993.96	29371.48	22568.71	18493.81	15782.83	13851.23	12406.72
1000 000	85607.49	43871.39	29970.90	23029.29	18871.23	16104.93	14133.91	12659.92
Coefficient	.085607486	.043871388	.029970899	.023029292	.018871233	.016104932	.014133908	.012659919

MONTHLY AMORTIZING PAYMENTS 5.00%

AMOUNT	9 YEARS	10 YEARS	15 YEARS	20 YEARS	25 YEARS	30 YEARS	35 YEARS	40 YEARS
10 000	115.17	106.07	79.08	66.00	58.46	53.68	50.47	48.22
20 000	230.35	212.13	158.16	131.99	116.92	107.36	100.94	96.44
30 000	345.52	318.20	237.24	197.99	175.38	161.05	151.41	144.66
40 000	460.69	424.26	316.32	263.98	233.84	214.73	201.88	192.88
50 000	575.86	530.33	395.40	329.98	292.30	268.41	252.34	241.10
60 000	691.04	636.39	474.48	395.97	350.75	322.09	302.81	289.32
70 000	806.21	742.46	553.56	461.97	409.21	375.78	353.28	337.54
80 000	921.38	848.52	632.63	527.96	467.67	429.46	403.75	385.76
90 000	1036.55	954.59	711.71	593.96	526.13	483.14	454.22	433.98
100 000	1151.73	1060.66	790.79	659.96	584.59	536.82	504.69	482.20
110 000	1266.90	1166.72	869.87	725.95	643.05	590.50	555.16	530.42
120 000	1382.07	1272.79	948.95	791.95	701.51	644.19	605.63	578.64
130 000	1497.25	1378.85	1028.03	857.94	759.97	697.87	656.09	626.86
140 000	1612.42	1484.92	1107.11	923.94	818.43	751.55	706.56	675.08
150 000	1727.59	1590.98	1186.19	989.93	876.89	805.23	757.03	723.29
160 000	1842.76	1697.05	1265.27	1055.93	935.34	858.91	807.50	771.51
170 000	1957.94	1803.11	1344.35	1121.92	993.80	912.60	857.97	819.73
180 000	2073.11	1909.18	1423.43	1187.92	1052.26	966.28	908.44	867.95
190 000	2188.28	2015.24	1502.51	1253.92	1110.72	1019.96	958.91	916.17
200 000	2303.45	2121.31	1581.59	1319.91	1169.18	1073.64	1009.38	964.39
210 000	2418.63	2227.38	1660.67	1385.91	1227.64	1127.33	1059.84	1012.61
220 000	2533.80	2333.44	1739.75	1451.90	1286.10	1181.01	1110.31	1060.83
230 000	2648.97	2439.51	1818.83	1517.90	1344.56	1234.69	1160.78	1109.05
240 000	2764.15	2545.57	1897.90	1583.89	1403.02	1288.37	1211.25	1157.27
250 000	2879.32	2651.64	1976.98	1649.89	1461.48	1342.05	1261.72	1205.49
260 000	2994.49	2757.70	2056.06	1715.89	1519.93	1395.74	1312.19	1253.71
270 000	3109.66	2863.77	2135.14	1781.88	1578.39	1449.42	1362.66	1301.93
280 000	3224.84	2969.83	2214.22	1847.88	1636.85	1503.10	1413.13	1350.15
290 000	3340.01	3075.90	2293.30	1913.87	1695.31	1556.78	1463.59	1398.37
300 000	3455.18	3181.97	2372.38	1979.87	1753.77	1610.46	1514.06	1446.59
320 000	3685.53	3394.10	2530.54	2111.86	1870.69	1717.83	1615.00	1543.03
340 000	3915.87	3606.23	2688.70	2243.85	1987.61	1825.19	1715.94	1639.47
360 000	4146.22	3818.36	2846.86	2375.84	2104.52	1932.56	1816.88	1735.91
380 000	4376.56	4030.49	3005.02	2507.83	2221.44	2039.92	1917.81	1832.35
400 000	4606.91	4242.62	3163.17	2639.82	2338.36	2147.29	2018.75	1928.79
420 000	4837.25	4454.75	3321.33	2771.81	2455.28	2254.65	2119.69	2025.23
440 000	5067.60	4666.88	3479.49	2903.81	2572.20	2362.02	2220.63	2121.67
460 000	5297.95	4879.01	3637.65	3035.80	2689.11	2469.38	2321.56	2218.10
480 000	5528.29	5091.14	3795.81	3167.79	2806.03	2576.74	2422.50	2314.54
500 000	5758.64	5303.28	3953.97	3299.78	2922.95	2684.11	2523.44	2410.98
520 000	5988.98	5515.41	4112.13	3431.77	3039.87	2791.47	2624.38	2507.42
540 000	6219.33	5727.54	4270.29	3563.76	3156.79	2898.84	2725.31	2603.86
560 000	6449.67	5939.67	4428.44	3695.75	3273.70	3006.20	2826.25	2700.30
580 000	6680.02	6151.80	4586.60	3827.74	3390.62	3113.57	2927.19	2796.74
600 000	6910.36	6363.93	4744.76	3959.73	3507.54	3220.93	3028.13	2893.18
620 000	7140.71	6576.06	4902.92	4091.73	3624.46	3328.29	3129.06	2989.62
640 000	7371.05	6788.19	5061.08	4223.72	3741.38	3435.66	3230.00	3086.06
660 000	7601.40	7000.32	5219.24	4355.71	3858.29	3543.02	3330.94	3182.50
680 000	7831.75	7212.46	5377.40	4487.70	3975.21	3650.39	3431.88	3278.94
700 000	8062.09	7424.59	5535.56	4619.69	4092.13	3757.75	3532.81	3375.38
720 000	8292.44	7636.72	5693.71	4751.68	4209.05	3865.12	3633.75	3471.82
740 000	8522.78	7848.85	5851.87	4883.67	4325.97	3972.48	3734.69	3568.25
760 000	8753.13	8060.98	6010.03	5015.66	4442.88	4079.84	3835.63	3664.69
780 000	8983.47	8273.11	6168.19	5147.66	4559.80	4187.21	3936.56	3761.13
800 000	9213.82	8485.24	6326.35	5279.65	4676.72	4294.57	4037.50	3857.57
820 000	9444.16	8697.37	6484.51	5411.64	4793.64	4401.94	4138.44	3954.01
840 000	9674.51	8909.50	6642.67	5543.63	4910.56	4509.30	4239.38	4050.45
860 000	9904.85	9121.63	6800.83	5675.62	5027.47	4616.67	4340.31	4146.89
880 000	10135.20	9333.77	6958.98	5807.61	5144.39	4724.03	4441.25	4243.33
900 000	10365.55	9545.90	7117.14	5939.60	5261.31	4831.39	4542.19	4339.77
920 000	10595.89	9758.03	7275.30	6071.59	5378.23	4938.76	4643.13	4436.21
940 000	10826.24	9970.16	7433.46	6203.58	5495.15	5046.12	4744.06	4532.65
960 000	11056.58	10182.29	7591.62	6335.58	5612.06	5153.49	4845.00	4629.09
980 000	11286.93	10394.42	7749.78	6467.57	5728.98	5260.85	4945.94	4725.53
1000 000	11517.27	10606.55	7907.94	6599.56	5845.90	5368.22	5046.88	4821.97
Coefficient	.011517273	.010606552	.007907937	.006599558	.005845901	.005368216	.005046877	.004821966

3

5.25% MONTHLY AMORTIZING PAYMENTS

AMOUNT	1 YEAR	2 YEARS	3 YEARS	4 YEARS	5 YEARS	6 YEARS	7 YEARS	8 YEARS
10 000	857.22	439.83	300.83	231.43	189.86	162.21	142.52	127.79
20 000	1714.44	879.67	601.67	462.85	379.72	324.42	285.03	255.59
30 000	2571.66	1319.50	902.50	694.28	569.58	486.63	427.55	383.38
40 000	3428.88	1759.34	1203.33	925.71	759.44	648.85	570.07	511.17
50 000	4286.10	2199.17	1504.16	1157.14	949.30	811.06	712.58	638.96
60 000	5143.33	2639.01	1805.00	1388.56	1139.16	973.27	855.10	766.76
70 000	6000.55	3078.84	2105.83	1619.99	1329.02	1135.48	997.62	894.55
80 000	6857.77	3518.68	2406.66	1851.42	1518.88	1297.69	1140.13	1022.34
90 000	7714.99	3958.51	2707.49	2082.84	1708.74	1459.90	1282.65	1150.14
100 000	8572.21	4398.34	3008.33	2314.27	1898.60	1622.12	1425.17	1277.93
110 000	9429.43	4838.18	3309.16	2545.70	2088.46	1784.33	1567.68	1405.72
120 000	10286.65	5278.01	3609.99	2777.13	2278.32	1946.54	1710.20	1533.51
130 000	11143.87	5717.85	3910.82	3008.55	2468.18	2108.75	1852.72	1661.31
140 000	12001.09	6157.68	4211.66	3239.98	2658.04	2270.96	1995.23	1789.10
150 000	12858.31	6597.52	4512.49	3471.41	2847.90	2433.17	2137.75	1916.89
160 000	13715.54	7037.35	4813.32	3702.83	3037.76	2595.38	2280.27	2044.69
170 000	14572.76	7477.18	5114.16	3934.26	3227.62	2757.60	2422.79	2172.48
180 000	15429.98	7917.02	5414.99	4165.69	3417.48	2919.81	2565.30	2300.27
190 000	16287.20	8356.85	5715.82	4397.12	3607.34	3082.02	2707.82	2428.06
200 000	17144.42	8796.69	6016.65	4628.54	3797.20	3244.23	2850.34	2555.86
210 000	18001.64	9236.52	6317.49	4859.97	3987.06	3406.44	2992.85	2683.65
220 000	18858.86	9676.36	6618.32	5091.40	4176.92	3568.65	3135.37	2811.44
230 000	19716.08	10116.19	6919.15	5322.82	4366.78	3730.87	3277.89	2939.23
240 000	20573.30	10556.03	7219.98	5554.25	4556.64	3893.08	3420.40	3067.03
250 000	21430.52	10995.86	7520.82	5785.68	4746.50	4055.29	3562.92	3194.82
260 000	22287.75	11435.69	7821.65	6017.10	4936.36	4217.50	3705.44	3322.61
270 000	23144.97	11875.53	8122.48	6248.53	5126.22	4379.71	3847.95	3450.41
280 000	24002.19	12315.36	8423.32	6479.96	5316.08	4541.92	3990.47	3578.20
290 000	24859.41	12755.20	8724.15	6711.39	5505.94	4704.13	4132.99	3705.99
300 000	25716.63	13195.03	9024.98	6942.81	5695.79	4866.35	4275.50	3833.78
320 000	27431.07	14074.70	9626.65	7405.67	6075.51	5190.77	4560.54	4089.37
340 000	29145.51	14954.37	10228.31	7868.52	6455.23	5515.19	4845.57	4344.96
360 000	30859.95	15834.04	10829.98	8331.38	6834.95	5839.62	5130.60	4600.54
380 000	32574.40	16713.71	11431.64	8794.23	7214.67	6164.04	5415.64	4856.13
400 000	34288.84	17593.38	12033.31	9257.08	7594.39	6488.46	5700.67	5111.71
420 000	36003.28	18473.04	12634.97	9719.94	7974.11	6812.88	5985.70	5367.30
440 000	37717.72	19352.71	13236.64	10182.79	8353.83	7137.31	6270.74	5622.88
460 000	39432.16	20232.38	13838.30	10645.65	8733.55	7461.73	6555.77	5878.47
480 000	41146.61	21112.05	14439.97	11108.50	9113.27	7786.15	6840.80	6134.06
500 000	42861.05	21991.72	15041.63	11571.36	9492.99	8110.58	7125.84	6389.64
520 000	44575.49	22871.39	15643.30	12034.21	9872.71	8435.00	7410.87	6645.23
540 000	46289.93	23751.06	16244.97	12497.06	10252.43	8759.42	7695.91	6900.81
560 000	48004.37	24630.73	16846.63	12959.92	10632.15	9083.85	7980.94	7156.40
580 000	49718.82	25510.39	17448.30	13422.77	11011.87	9408.27	8265.97	7411.98
600 000	51433.26	26390.06	18049.96	13885.63	11391.59	9732.69	8551.01	7667.57
620 000	53147.70	27269.73	18651.63	14348.48	11771.31	10057.11	8836.04	7923.15
640 000	54862.14	28149.40	19253.29	14811.34	12151.03	10381.54	9121.07	8178.74
660 000	56576.58	29029.07	19854.96	15274.19	12530.75	10705.96	9406.11	8434.33
680 000	58291.03	29908.74	20456.62	15737.04	12910.47	11030.38	9691.14	8689.91
700 000	60005.47	30788.41	21058.29	16199.90	13290.19	11354.81	9976.17	8945.50
720 000	61719.91	31668.08	21659.95	16662.75	13669.91	11679.23	10261.21	9201.08
740 000	63434.35	32547.74	22261.62	17125.61	14049.63	12003.65	10546.24	9456.67
760 000	65148.79	33427.41	22863.28	17588.46	14429.35	12328.08	10831.27	9712.25
780 000	66863.24	34307.08	23464.95	18051.31	14809.07	12652.50	11116.31	9967.84
800 000	68577.68	35186.75	24066.62	18514.17	15188.79	12976.92	11401.34	10223.43
820 000	70292.12	36066.42	24668.28	18977.02	15568.51	13301.35	11686.38	10479.01
840 000	72006.56	36946.09	25269.95	19439.88	15948.23	13625.77	11971.41	10734.60
860 000	73721.00	37825.76	25871.61	19902.73	16327.95	13950.19	12256.44	10990.18
880 000	75435.45	38705.43	26473.28	20365.59	16707.67	14274.61	12541.48	11245.77
900 000	77149.89	39585.09	27074.94	20828.44	17087.38	14599.04	12826.51	11501.35
920 000	78864.33	40464.76	27676.61	21291.29	17467.10	14923.46	13111.54	11756.94
940 000	80578.77	41344.43	28278.27	21754.15	17846.82	15247.88	13396.58	12012.53
960 000	82293.21	42224.10	28879.94	22217.00	18226.54	15572.31	13681.61	12268.11
980 000	84007.66	43103.77	29481.60	22679.86	18606.26	15896.73	13966.64	12523.70
1000 000	85722.10	43983.44	30083.27	23142.71	18985.98	16221.15	14251.68	12779.28
Coefficient	.085722097	.043983438	.030083269	.023142711	.018985983	.016221153	.014251677	.012779282

4

MONTHLY AMORTIZING PAYMENTS — 5.25%

AMOUNT	9 YEARS	10 YEARS	15 YEARS	20 YEARS	25 YEARS	30 YEARS	35 YEARS	40 YEARS
10 000	116.38	107.29	80.39	67.38	59.92	55.22	52.07	49.89
20 000	232.77	214.58	160.78	134.77	119.85	110.44	104.15	99.77
30 000	349.15	321.88	241.16	202.15	179.77	165.66	156.22	149.66
40 000	465.53	429.17	321.55	269.54	239.70	220.88	208.30	199.55
50 000	581.91	536.46	401.94	336.92	299.62	276.10	260.37	249.44
60 000	698.30	643.75	482.33	404.31	359.55	331.32	312.45	299.32
70 000	814.68	751.04	562.71	471.69	419.47	386.54	364.52	349.21
80 000	931.06	858.33	643.10	539.08	479.40	441.76	416.59	399.10
90 000	1047.44	965.63	723.49	606.46	539.32	496.98	468.67	448.98
100 000	1163.83	1072.92	803.88	673.84	599.25	552.20	520.74	498.87
110 000	1280.21	1180.21	884.27	741.23	659.17	607.42	572.82	548.76
120 000	1396.59	1287.50	964.65	808.61	719.10	662.64	624.89	598.64
130 000	1512.97	1394.79	1045.04	876.00	779.02	717.86	676.97	648.53
140 000	1629.36	1502.08	1125.43	943.38	838.95	773.09	729.04	698.42
150 000	1745.74	1609.38	1205.82	1010.77	898.87	828.31	781.11	748.31
160 000	1862.12	1716.67	1286.20	1078.15	958.80	883.53	833.19	798.19
170 000	1978.50	1823.96	1366.59	1145.54	1018.72	938.75	885.26	848.08
180 000	2094.89	1931.25	1446.98	1212.92	1078.65	993.97	937.34	897.97
190 000	2211.27	2038.54	1527.37	1280.30	1138.57	1049.19	989.41	947.85
200 000	2327.65	2145.83	1607.76	1347.69	1198.50	1104.41	1041.49	997.74
210 000	2444.03	2253.13	1688.14	1415.07	1258.42	1159.63	1093.56	1047.63
220 000	2560.42	2360.42	1768.53	1482.46	1318.34	1214.85	1145.63	1097.51
230 000	2676.80	2467.71	1848.92	1549.84	1378.27	1270.07	1197.71	1147.40
240 000	2793.18	2575.00	1929.31	1617.23	1438.19	1325.29	1249.78	1197.29
250 000	2909.56	2682.29	2009.69	1684.61	1498.12	1380.51	1301.86	1247.18
260 000	3025.95	2789.58	2090.08	1751.99	1558.04	1435.73	1353.93	1297.06
270 000	3142.33	2896.88	2170.47	1819.38	1617.97	1490.95	1406.01	1346.95
280 000	3258.71	3004.17	2250.86	1886.76	1677.89	1546.17	1458.08	1396.84
290 000	3375.09	3111.46	2331.25	1954.15	1737.82	1601.39	1510.15	1446.72
300 000	3491.48	3218.75	2411.63	2021.53	1797.74	1656.61	1562.23	1496.61
320 000	3724.24	3433.33	2572.41	2156.30	1917.59	1767.05	1666.38	1596.38
340 000	3957.01	3647.92	2733.18	2291.07	2037.44	1877.49	1770.53	1696.16
360 000	4189.77	3862.50	2893.96	2425.84	2157.29	1987.93	1874.67	1795.93
380 000	4422.54	4077.08	3054.74	2560.61	2277.14	2098.37	1978.82	1895.71
400 000	4655.30	4291.67	3215.51	2695.38	2396.99	2208.81	2082.97	1995.48
420 000	4888.07	4506.25	3376.29	2830.15	2516.84	2319.26	2187.12	2095.26
440 000	5120.83	4720.83	3537.06	2964.91	2636.69	2429.70	2291.27	2195.03
460 000	5353.60	4935.42	3697.84	3099.68	2756.54	2540.14	2395.42	2294.80
480 000	5586.36	5150.00	3858.61	3234.45	2876.39	2650.58	2499.57	2394.58
500 000	5819.13	5364.59	4019.39	3369.22	2996.24	2761.02	2603.72	2494.35
520 000	6051.89	5579.17	4180.16	3503.99	3116.09	2871.46	2707.86	2594.13
540 000	6284.66	5793.75	4340.94	3638.76	3235.94	2981.90	2812.01	2693.90
560 000	6517.42	6008.34	4501.72	3773.53	3355.79	3092.34	2916.16	2793.67
580 000	6750.19	6222.92	4662.49	3908.30	3475.64	3202.78	3020.31	2893.45
600 000	6982.95	6437.50	4823.27	4043.07	3595.49	3313.22	3124.46	2993.22
620 000	7215.72	6652.09	4984.04	4177.83	3715.34	3423.66	3228.61	3093.00
640 000	7448.48	6866.67	5144.82	4312.60	3835.19	3534.10	3332.76	3192.77
660 000	7681.25	7081.25	5305.59	4447.37	3955.03	3644.54	3436.90	3292.54
680 000	7914.01	7295.84	5466.37	4582.14	4074.88	3754.99	3541.05	3392.32
700 000	8146.78	7510.42	5627.14	4716.91	4194.73	3865.43	3645.20	3492.09
720 000	8379.54	7725.00	5787.92	4851.68	4314.58	3975.87	3749.35	3591.87
740 000	8612.31	7939.59	5948.69	4986.45	4434.43	4086.31	3853.50	3691.64
760 000	8845.07	8154.17	6109.47	5121.22	4554.28	4196.75	3957.65	3791.41
780 000	9077.84	8368.75	6270.25	5255.98	4674.13	4307.19	4061.80	3891.19
800 000	9310.60	8583.34	6431.02	5390.75	4793.98	4417.63	4165.94	3990.96
820 000	9543.37	8797.92	6591.80	5525.52	4913.83	4528.07	4270.09	4090.74
840 000	9776.14	9012.50	6752.57	5660.29	5033.68	4638.51	4374.24	4190.51
860 000	10008.90	9227.09	6913.35	5795.06	5153.53	4748.95	4478.39	4290.28
880 000	10241.67	9441.67	7074.12	5929.83	5273.38	4859.39	4582.54	4390.06
900 000	10474.43	9656.25	7234.90	6064.60	5393.23	4969.83	4686.69	4489.83
920 000	10707.20	9870.84	7395.67	6199.37	5513.08	5080.27	4790.84	4589.61
940 000	10939.96	10085.42	7556.45	6334.14	5632.93	5190.71	4894.98	4689.38
960 000	11172.73	10300.00	7717.23	6468.90	5752.78	5301.16	4999.13	4789.15
980 000	11405.49	10514.59	7878.00	6603.67	5872.63	5411.60	5103.28	4888.93
1000 000	11638.26	10729.17	8038.78	6738.44	5992.48	5522.04	5207.43	4988.70
Coefficient	.011638256	.010729170	.008038777	.006738442	.005992477	.005522037	.005207430	.004988703

5

AMOUNT	1 YEAR	2 YEARS	3 YEARS	4 YEARS	5 YEARS	6 YEARS	7 YEARS	8 YEARS
10 000	858.37	440.96	301.96	232.56	191.01	163.38	143.70	128.99
20 000	1716.74	881.91	603.92	465.13	382.02	326.76	287.40	257.99
30 000	2575.10	1322.87	905.88	697.69	573.03	490.14	431.10	386.98
40 000	3433.47	1763.83	1207.84	930.26	764.05	653.52	574.80	515.97
50 000	4291.84	2204.78	1509.80	1162.82	955.06	816.89	718.50	644.97
60 000	5150.21	2645.74	1811.75	1395.39	1146.07	980.27	862.20	773.96
70 000	6008.57	3086.70	2113.71	1627.95	1337.08	1143.65	1005.90	902.95
80 000	6866.94	3527.65	2415.67	1860.52	1528.09	1307.03	1149.60	1031.95
90 000	7725.31	3968.61	2717.63	2093.08	1719.10	1470.41	1293.30	1160.94
100 000	8583.68	4409.57	3019.59	2325.65	1910.12	1633.79	1437.00	1289.93
110 000	9442.05	4850.52	3321.55	2558.21	2101.13	1797.17	1580.70	1418.93
120 000	10300.41	5291.48	3623.51	2790.78	2292.14	1960.55	1724.41	1547.92
130 000	11158.78	5732.44	3925.47	3023.34	2483.15	2123.93	1868.11	1676.91
140 000	12017.15	6173.39	4227.43	3255.91	2674.16	2287.30	2011.81	1805.91
150 000	12875.52	6614.35	4529.39	3488.47	2865.17	2450.68	2155.51	1934.90
160 000	13733.88	7055.31	4831.34	3721.04	3056.19	2614.06	2299.21	2063.89
170 000	14592.25	7496.26	5133.30	3953.60	3247.20	2777.44	2442.91	2192.88
180 000	15450.62	7937.22	5435.26	4186.17	3438.21	2940.82	2586.61	2321.88
190 000	16308.99	8378.18	5737.22	4418.73	3629.22	3104.20	2730.31	2450.87
200 000	17167.36	8819.13	6039.18	4651.29	3820.23	3267.58	2874.01	2579.86
210 000	18025.72	9260.09	6341.14	4883.86	4011.24	3430.96	3017.71	2708.86
220 000	18884.09	9701.04	6643.10	5116.42	4202.26	3594.33	3161.41	2837.85
230 000	19742.46	10142.00	6945.06	5348.99	4393.27	3757.71	3305.11	2966.84
240 000	20600.83	10582.96	7247.02	5581.55	4584.28	3921.09	3448.81	3095.84
250 000	21459.19	11023.91	7548.98	5814.12	4775.29	4084.47	3592.51	3224.83
260 000	22317.56	11464.87	7850.93	6046.68	4966.30	4247.85	3736.21	3353.82
270 000	23175.93	11905.83	8152.89	6279.25	5157.31	4411.23	3879.91	3482.82
280 000	24034.30	12346.78	8454.85	6511.81	5348.33	4574.61	4023.61	3611.81
290 000	24892.67	12787.74	8756.81	6744.38	5539.34	4737.99	4167.31	3740.80
300 000	25751.03	13228.70	9058.77	6976.94	5730.35	4901.37	4311.01	3869.80
320 000	27467.77	14110.61	9662.69	7442.07	6112.37	5228.12	4598.41	4127.78
340 000	29184.50	14992.52	10266.61	7907.20	6494.40	5554.88	4885.81	4385.77
360 000	30901.24	15874.44	10870.53	8372.33	6876.42	5881.64	5173.22	4643.76
380 000	32617.98	16756.35	11474.44	8837.46	7258.44	6208.40	5460.62	4901.74
400 000	34334.71	17638.26	12078.36	9302.59	7640.46	6535.15	5748.02	5159.73
420 000	36051.45	18520.18	12682.28	9767.72	8022.49	6861.91	6035.42	5417.72
440 000	37768.18	19402.09	13286.20	10232.85	8404.51	7188.67	6322.82	5675.70
460 000	39484.92	20284.00	13890.12	10697.98	8786.53	7515.43	6610.22	5933.69
480 000	41201.65	21165.92	14494.03	11163.11	9168.56	7842.19	6897.62	6191.67
500 000	42918.39	22047.83	15097.95	11628.24	9550.58	8168.94	7185.02	6449.66
520 000	44635.12	22929.74	15701.87	12093.37	9932.60	8495.70	7472.42	6707.65
540 000	46351.86	23811.66	16305.79	12558.50	10314.63	8822.46	7759.82	6965.63
560 000	48068.60	24693.57	16909.71	13023.62	10696.65	9149.22	8047.22	7223.62
580 000	49785.33	25575.48	17513.62	13488.75	11078.67	9475.97	8334.62	7481.61
600 000	51502.07	26457.40	18117.54	13953.88	11460.70	9802.73	8622.03	7739.59
620 000	53218.80	27339.31	18721.46	14419.01	11842.72	10129.49	8909.43	7997.58
640 000	54935.54	28221.22	19325.38	14884.14	12224.74	10456.25	9196.83	8255.57
660 000	56652.27	29103.13	19929.30	15349.27	12606.77	10783.00	9484.23	8513.55
680 000	58369.01	29985.05	20533.21	15814.40	12988.79	11109.76	9771.63	8771.54
700 000	60085.74	30866.96	21137.13	16279.53	13370.81	11436.52	10059.03	9029.53
720 000	61802.48	31748.87	21741.05	16744.66	13752.84	11763.28	10346.43	9287.51
740 000	63519.22	32630.79	22344.97	17209.79	14134.86	12090.04	10633.83	9545.50
760 000	65235.95	33512.70	22948.89	17674.92	14516.88	12416.79	10921.23	9803.48
780 000	66952.69	34394.61	23552.80	18140.05	14898.91	12743.55	11208.63	10061.47
800 000	68669.42	35276.53	24156.72	18605.18	15280.93	13070.31	11496.03	10319.46
820 000	70386.16	36158.44	24760.64	19070.31	15662.95	13397.07	11783.43	10577.44
840 000	72102.89	37040.35	25364.56	19535.44	16044.98	13723.82	12070.84	10835.43
860 000	73819.63	37922.27	25968.48	20000.57	16427.00	14050.58	12358.24	11093.42
880 000	75536.36	38804.18	26572.39	20465.70	16809.02	14377.34	12645.64	11351.40
900 000	77253.10	39686.09	27176.31	20930.83	17191.05	14704.10	12933.04	11609.39
920 000	78969.84	40568.01	27780.23	21395.96	17573.07	15030.86	13220.44	11867.38
940 000	80686.57	41449.92	28384.15	21861.08	17955.09	15357.61	13507.84	12125.36
960 000	82403.31	42331.83	28988.07	22326.21	18337.12	15684.37	13795.24	12383.35
980 000	84120.04	43213.75	29591.98	22791.34	18719.14	16011.13	14082.64	12641.34
1000 000	85836.78	44095.66	30195.90	23256.47	19101.16	16337.89	14370.04	12899.32
Coefficient	.085836778	.044095659	.030195903	.023256473	.019101162	.016337886	.014370042	.012899322

AMOUNT	9 YEARS	10 YEARS	15 YEARS	20 YEARS	25 YEARS	30 YEARS	35 YEARS	40 YEARS
10 000	117.60	108.53	81.71	68.79	61.41	56.78	53.70	51.58
20 000	235.20	217.05	163.42	137.58	122.82	113.56	107.40	103.15
30 000	352.80	325.58	245.13	206.37	184.23	170.34	161.10	154.73
40 000	470.40	434.11	326.83	275.15	245.64	227.12	214.81	206.31
50 000	588.00	542.63	408.54	343.94	307.04	283.89	268.51	257.89
60 000	705.60	651.16	490.25	412.73	368.45	340.67	322.21	309.46
70 000	823.20	759.68	571.96	481.52	429.86	397.45	375.91	361.04
80 000	940.80	868.21	653.67	550.31	491.27	454.23	429.61	412.62
90 000	1058.40	976.74	735.38	619.10	552.68	511.01	483.31	464.19
100 000	1176.00	1085.26	817.08	687.89	614.09	567.79	537.02	515.77
110 000	1293.60	1193.79	898.79	756.68	675.50	624.57	590.72	567.35
120 000	1411.20	1302.32	980.50	825.46	736.91	681.35	644.42	618.92
130 000	1528.80	1410.84	1062.21	894.25	798.31	738.13	698.12	670.50
140 000	1646.40	1519.37	1143.92	963.04	859.72	794.90	751.82	722.08
150 000	1764.00	1627.89	1225.63	1031.83	921.13	851.68	805.52	773.66
160 000	1881.60	1736.42	1307.33	1100.62	982.54	908.46	859.23	825.23
170 000	1999.20	1844.95	1389.04	1169.41	1043.95	965.24	912.93	876.81
180 000	2116.80	1953.47	1470.75	1238.20	1105.36	1022.02	966.63	928.39
190 000	2234.40	2062.00	1552.46	1306.99	1166.77	1078.80	1020.33	979.96
200 000	2352.00	2170.53	1634.17	1375.77	1228.18	1135.58	1074.03	1031.54
210 000	2469.60	2279.05	1715.88	1444.56	1289.58	1192.36	1127.73	1083.12
220 000	2587.20	2387.58	1797.58	1513.35	1350.99	1249.14	1181.44	1134.69
230 000	2704.80	2496.10	1879.29	1582.14	1412.40	1305.91	1235.14	1186.27
240 000	2822.40	2604.63	1961.00	1650.93	1473.81	1362.69	1288.84	1237.85
250 000	2940.00	2713.16	2042.71	1719.72	1535.22	1419.47	1342.54	1289.43
260 000	3057.60	2821.68	2124.42	1788.51	1596.63	1476.25	1396.24	1341.00
270 000	3175.20	2930.21	2206.13	1857.30	1658.04	1533.03	1449.94	1392.58
280 000	3292.80	3038.74	2287.83	1926.08	1719.45	1589.81	1503.65	1444.16
290 000	3410.40	3147.26	2369.54	1994.87	1780.85	1646.59	1557.35	1495.73
300 000	3528.00	3255.79	2451.25	2063.66	1842.26	1703.37	1611.05	1547.31
320 000	3763.20	3472.84	2614.67	2201.24	1965.08	1816.92	1718.45	1650.46
340 000	3998.40	3689.89	2778.08	2338.82	2087.90	1930.48	1825.86	1753.62
360 000	4233.60	3906.95	2941.50	2476.39	2210.71	2044.04	1933.26	1856.77
380 000	4468.80	4124.00	3104.92	2613.97	2333.53	2157.60	2040.66	1959.93
400 000	4704.00	4341.05	3268.33	2751.55	2456.35	2271.16	2148.07	2063.08
420 000	4939.20	4558.10	3431.75	2889.13	2579.17	2384.71	2255.47	2166.24
440 000	5174.40	4775.16	3595.17	3026.70	2701.98	2498.27	2362.87	2269.39
460 000	5409.60	4992.21	3758.58	3164.28	2824.80	2611.83	2470.27	2372.54
480 000	5644.80	5209.26	3922.00	3301.86	2947.62	2725.39	2577.68	2475.70
500 000	5880.00	5426.31	4085.42	3439.44	3070.44	2838.95	2685.08	2578.85
520 000	6115.20	5643.37	4248.83	3577.01	3193.25	2952.50	2792.48	2682.01
540 000	6350.40	5860.42	4412.25	3714.59	3316.07	3066.06	2899.89	2785.16
560 000	6585.60	6077.47	4575.67	3852.17	3438.89	3179.62	3007.29	2888.31
580 000	6820.80	6294.52	4739.08	3989.75	3561.71	3293.18	3114.69	2991.47
600 000	7056.00	6511.58	4902.50	4127.32	3684.52	3406.73	3222.10	3094.62
620 000	7291.20	6728.63	5065.92	4264.90	3807.34	3520.29	3329.50	3197.78
640 000	7526.40	6945.68	5229.33	4402.48	3930.16	3633.85	3436.90	3300.93
660 000	7761.60	7162.73	5392.75	4540.06	4052.98	3747.41	3544.31	3404.08
680 000	7996.80	7379.79	5556.17	4677.63	4175.80	3860.97	3651.71	3507.24
700 000	8232.00	7596.84	5719.58	4815.21	4298.61	3974.52	3759.11	3610.39
720 000	8467.20	7813.89	5883.00	4952.79	4421.43	4088.08	3866.52	3713.55
740 000	8702.40	8030.94	6046.42	5090.37	4544.25	4201.64	3973.92	3816.70
760 000	8937.60	8248.00	6209.83	5227.94	4667.06	4315.20	4081.32	3919.85
780 000	9172.80	8465.05	6373.25	5365.52	4789.88	4428.75	4188.73	4023.01
800 000	9408.00	8682.10	6536.67	5503.10	4912.70	4542.31	4296.13	4126.16
820 000	9643.20	8899.15	6700.08	5640.68	5035.52	4655.87	4403.53	4229.32
840 000	9878.40	9116.21	6863.50	5778.25	5158.34	4769.43	4510.94	4332.47
860 000	10113.60	9333.26	7026.92	5915.83	5281.15	4882.99	4618.34	4435.62
880 000	10348.80	9550.31	7190.33	6053.41	5403.97	4996.54	4725.74	4538.78
900 000	10584.00	9767.37	7353.75	6190.99	5526.79	5110.10	4833.15	4641.93
920 000	10819.20	9984.42	7517.17	6328.56	5649.61	5223.66	4940.55	4745.09
940 000	11054.40	10201.47	7680.58	6466.14	5772.42	5337.22	5047.95	4848.24
960 000	11289.60	10418.52	7844.00	6603.72	5895.24	5450.77	5155.36	4951.39
980 000	11524.80	10635.58	8007.42	6741.30	6018.06	5564.33	5262.76	5054.55
1000 000	11760.00	10852.63	8170.84	6878.87	6140.88	5677.89	5370.16	5157.70
Coefficient	.011759998	.010852628	.008170835	.006878873	.00614 0875	.005677890	.005370163	.005157703

MONTHLY AMORTIZING PAYMENTS

AMOUNT	1 YEAR	2 YEARS	3 YEARS	4 YEARS	5 YEARS	6 YEARS	7 YEARS	8 YEARS
10 000	859.52	442.08	303.09	233.71	192.17	164.55	144.89	130.20
20 000	1719.03	884.16	606.18	467.41	384.34	329.10	289.78	260.40
30 000	2578.55	1326.24	909.26	701.12	576.50	493.65	434.67	390.60
40 000	3438.06	1768.32	1212.35	934.82	768.67	658.21	579.56	520.80
50 000	4297.58	2210.40	1515.44	1168.53	960.84	822.76	724.45	651.00
60 000	5157.09	2652.48	1818.53	1402.23	1153.01	987.31	869.34	781.20
70 000	6016.61	3094.56	2121.62	1635.94	1345.17	1151.86	1014.23	911.40
80 000	6876.13	3536.64	2424.70	1869.65	1537.34	1316.41	1159.12	1041.60
90 000	7735.64	3978.72	2727.79	2103.35	1729.51	1480.96	1304.01	1171.80
100 000	8595.16	4420.80	3030.88	2337.06	1921.68	1645.51	1448.90	1302.00
110 000	9454.67	4862.89	3333.97	2570.76	2113.84	1810.06	1593.79	1432.20
120 000	10314.19	5304.97	3637.05	2804.47	2306.01	1974.62	1738.68	1562.40
130 000	11173.70	5747.05	3940.14	3038.18	2498.18	2139.17	1883.57	1692.60
140 000	12033.22	6189.13	4243.23	3271.88	2690.35	2303.72	2028.46	1822.81
150 000	12892.74	6631.21	4546.32	3505.59	2882.52	2468.27	2173.35	1953.01
160 000	13752.25	7073.29	4849.41	3739.29	3074.68	2632.82	2318.24	2083.21
170 000	14611.77	7515.37	5152.49	3973.00	3266.85	2797.37	2463.13	2213.41
180 000	15471.28	7957.45	5455.58	4206.70	3459.02	2961.92	2608.02	2343.61
190 000	16330.80	8399.53	5758.67	4440.41	3651.19	3126.48	2752.91	2473.81
200 000	17190.31	8841.61	6061.76	4674.12	3843.35	3291.03	2897.80	2604.01
210 000	18049.83	9283.69	6364.85	4907.82	4035.52	3455.58	3042.69	2734.21
220 000	18909.35	9725.77	6667.93	5141.53	4227.69	3620.13	3187.58	2864.41
230 000	19768.86	10167.85	6971.02	5375.23	4419.86	3784.68	3332.47	2994.61
240 000	20628.38	10609.93	7274.11	5608.94	4612.02	3949.23	3477.36	3124.81
250 000	21487.89	11052.01	7577.20	5842.65	4804.19	4113.78	3622.25	3255.01
260 000	22347.41	11494.09	7880.29	6076.35	4996.36	4278.33	3767.14	3385.21
270 000	23206.92	11936.17	8183.37	6310.06	5188.53	4442.89	3912.03	3515.41
280 000	24066.44	12378.25	8486.46	6543.76	5380.70	4607.44	4056.92	3645.61
290 000	24925.96	12820.33	8789.55	6777.47	5572.86	4771.99	4201.81	3775.81
300 000	25785.47	13262.41	9092.64	7011.17	5765.03	4936.54	4346.70	3906.01
320 000	27504.50	14146.58	9698.81	7478.59	6149.37	5265.64	4636.48	4166.41
340 000	29223.53	15030.74	10304.99	7946.00	6533.70	5594.74	4926.26	4426.81
360 000	30942.56	15914.90	10911.16	8413.41	6918.04	5923.85	5216.04	4687.21
380 000	32661.60	16799.06	11517.34	8880.82	7302.37	6252.95	5505.82	4947.61
400 000	34380.63	17683.22	12123.52	9348.23	7686.71	6582.05	5795.60	5208.02
420 000	36099.66	18567.38	12729.69	9815.64	8071.04	6911.16	6085.38	5468.42
440 000	37818.69	19451.54	13335.87	10283.06	8455.38	7240.26	6375.16	5728.82
460 000	39537.72	20335.70	13942.04	10750.47	8839.71	7569.36	6664.94	5989.22
480 000	41256.75	21219.86	14548.22	11217.88	9224.05	7898.46	6954.72	6249.62
500 000	42975.78	22104.02	15154.40	11685.29	9608.38	8227.57	7244.50	6510.02
520 000	44694.82	22988.19	15760.57	12152.70	9992.72	8556.67	7534.28	6770.42
540 000	46413.85	23872.35	16366.75	12620.11	10377.05	8885.77	7824.06	7030.82
560 000	48132.88	24756.51	16972.92	13087.52	10761.39	9214.87	8113.84	7291.22
580 000	49851.91	25640.67	17579.10	13554.94	11145.73	9543.98	8403.62	7551.62
600 000	51570.94	26524.83	18185.27	14022.35	11530.06	9873.08	8693.40	7812.02
620 000	53289.97	27408.99	18791.45	14489.76	11914.40	10202.18	8983.18	8072.42
640 000	55009.00	28293.15	19397.63	14957.17	12298.73	10531.28	9272.96	8332.82
660 000	56728.04	29177.31	20003.80	15424.58	12683.07	10860.39	9562.74	8593.23
680 000	58447.07	30061.47	20609.98	15891.99	13067.40	11189.49	9852.52	8853.63
700 000	60166.10	30945.63	21216.15	16359.41	13451.74	11518.59	10142.30	9114.03
720 000	61885.13	31829.80	21822.33	16826.82	13836.07	11847.70	10432.08	9374.43
740 000	63604.16	32713.96	22428.50	17294.23	14220.41	12176.80	10721.86	9634.83
760 000	65323.19	33598.12	23034.68	17761.64	14604.74	12505.90	11011.64	9895.23
780 000	67042.22	34482.28	23640.86	18229.05	14989.08	12835.00	11301.42	10155.63
800 000	68761.26	35366.44	24247.03	18696.46	15373.41	13164.11	11591.20	10416.03
820 000	70480.29	36250.60	24853.21	19163.88	15757.75	13493.21	11880.98	10676.43
840 000	72199.32	37134.76	25459.38	19631.29	16142.09	13822.31	12170.76	10936.83
860 000	73918.35	38018.92	26065.56	20098.70	16526.42	14151.41	12460.54	11197.23
880 000	75637.38	38903.08	26671.74	20566.11	16910.76	14480.52	12750.32	11457.63
900 000	77356.41	39787.24	27277.91	21033.52	17295.09	14809.62	13040.10	11718.03
920 000	79075.44	40671.41	27884.09	21500.93	17679.43	15138.72	13329.88	11978.43
940 000	80794.47	41555.57	28490.26	21968.35	18063.76	15467.82	13619.66	12238.84
960 000	82513.51	42439.73	29096.44	22435.76	18448.10	15796.93	13909.44	12499.24
980 000	84232.54	43323.89	29702.61	22903.17	18832.43	16126.03	14199.22	12759.64
1000 000	85951.57	44208.05	30308.79	23370.58	19216.77	16455.13	14489.00	13020.04
Coefficient	.085951569	.044208049	.030308790	.023370580	.019216768	.016455132	.014489002	.013020038

AMOUNT	9 YEARS	10 YEARS	15 YEARS	20 YEARS	25 YEARS	30 YEARS	35 YEARS	40 YEARS
10 000	118.82	109.77	83.04	70.21	62.91	58.36	55.35	53.29
20 000	237.65	219.54	166.08	140.42	125.82	116.71	110.70	106.58
30 000	356.47	329.31	249.12	210.63	188.73	175.07	166.05	159.87
40 000	475.30	439.08	332.16	280.83	251.64	233.43	221.40	213.16
50 000	594.12	548.85	415.21	351.04	314.55	291.79	276.75	266.44
60 000	712.95	658.62	498.25	421.25	377.46	350.14	332.10	319.73
70 000	831.77	768.38	581.29	491.46	440.37	408.50	387.45	373.02
80 000	950.60	878.15	664.33	561.67	503.29	466.86	442.80	426.31
90 000	1069.42	987.92	747.37	631.88	566.20	525.22	498.15	479.60
100 000	1188.25	1097.69	830.41	702.08	629.11	583.57	553.50	532.89
110 000	1307.07	1207.46	913.45	772.29	692.02	641.93	608.85	586.18
120 000	1425.90	1317.23	996.49	842.50	754.93	700.29	664.20	639.47
130 000	1544.72	1427.00	1079.53	912.71	817.84	758.64	719.55	692.75
140 000	1663.55	1536.77	1162.57	982.92	880.75	817.00	774.90	746.04
150 000	1782.37	1646.54	1245.62	1053.13	943.66	875.36	830.25	799.33
160 000	1901.20	1756.31	1328.66	1123.33	1006.57	933.72	885.60	852.62
170 000	2020.02	1866.08	1411.70	1193.54	1069.48	992.07	940.95	905.91
180 000	2138.85	1975.85	1494.74	1263.75	1132.39	1050.43	996.30	959.20
190 000	2257.67	2085.62	1577.78	1333.96	1195.30	1108.79	1051.65	1012.49
200 000	2376.50	2195.38	1660.82	1404.17	1258.21	1167.15	1107.00	1065.78
210 000	2495.32	2305.15	1743.86	1474.38	1321.12	1225.50	1162.35	1119.06
220 000	2614.15	2414.92	1826.90	1544.58	1384.03	1283.86	1217.70	1172.35
230 000	2732.97	2524.69	1909.94	1614.79	1446.94	1342.22	1273.05	1225.64
240 000	2851.80	2634.46	1992.98	1685.00	1509.86	1400.57	1328.40	1278.93
250 000	2970.62	2744.23	2076.03	1755.21	1572.77	1458.93	1383.75	1332.22
260 000	3089.45	2854.00	2159.07	1825.42	1635.68	1517.29	1439.10	1385.51
270 000	3208.27	2963.77	2242.11	1895.63	1698.59	1575.65	1494.45	1438.80
280 000	3327.10	3073.54	2325.15	1965.83	1761.50	1634.00	1549.80	1492.09
290 000	3445.92	3183.31	2408.19	2036.04	1824.41	1692.36	1605.15	1545.37
300 000	3564.75	3293.08	2491.23	2106.25	1887.32	1750.72	1660.50	1598.66
320 000	3802.40	3512.62	2657.31	2246.67	2013.14	1867.43	1771.20	1705.24
340 000	4040.05	3732.15	2823.39	2387.08	2138.96	1984.15	1881.90	1811.82
360 000	4277.70	3951.69	2989.48	2527.50	2264.78	2100.86	1992.60	1918.40
380 000	4515.35	4171.23	3155.56	2667.92	2390.60	2217.58	2103.30	2024.97
400 000	4753.00	4390.77	3321.64	2808.33	2516.43	2334.29	2214.00	2131.55
420 000	4990.65	4610.31	3487.72	2948.75	2642.25	2451.01	2324.70	2238.13
440 000	5228.30	4829.85	3653.80	3089.17	2768.07	2567.72	2435.40	2344.71
460 000	5465.95	5049.38	3819.89	3229.58	2893.89	2684.44	2546.10	2451.28
480 000	5703.60	5268.92	3985.97	3370.00	3019.71	2801.15	2656.80	2557.86
500 000	5941.25	5488.46	4152.05	3510.42	3145.53	2917.86	2767.50	2664.44
520 000	6178.90	5708.00	4318.13	3650.83	3271.35	3034.58	2878.20	2771.02
540 000	6416.55	5927.54	4484.21	3791.25	3397.17	3151.29	2988.90	2877.59
560 000	6654.20	6147.08	4650.30	3931.67	3523.00	3268.01	3099.60	2984.17
580 000	6891.85	6366.61	4816.38	4072.08	3648.82	3384.72	3210.30	3090.75
600 000	7129.50	6586.15	4982.46	4212.50	3774.64	3501.44	3321.00	3197.33
620 000	7367.15	6805.69	5148.54	4352.92	3900.46	3618.15	3431.70	3303.90
640 000	7604.80	7025.23	5314.62	4493.33	4026.28	3734.87	3542.40	3410.48
660 000	7842.45	7244.77	5480.71	4633.75	4152.10	3851.58	3653.10	3517.06
680 000	8080.10	7464.31	5646.79	4774.17	4277.92	3968.30	3763.80	3623.64
700 000	8317.75	7683.85	5812.87	4914.58	4403.74	4085.01	3874.50	3730.21
720 000	8555.40	7903.38	5978.95	5055.00	4529.57	4201.72	3985.20	3836.79
740 000	8793.05	8122.92	6145.03	5195.42	4655.39	4318.44	4095.91	3943.37
760 000	9030.70	8342.46	6311.12	5335.83	4781.21	4435.15	4206.61	4049.95
780 000	9268.35	8562.00	6477.20	5476.25	4907.03	4551.87	4317.31	4156.52
800 000	9506.00	8781.54	6643.28	5616.67	5032.85	4668.58	4428.01	4263.10
820 000	9743.65	9001.08	6809.36	5757.08	5158.67	4785.30	4538.71	4369.68
840 000	9981.30	9220.61	6975.44	5897.50	5284.49	4902.01	4649.41	4476.26
860 000	10218.95	9440.15	7141.53	6037.92	5410.32	5018.73	4760.11	4582.83
880 000	10456.60	9659.69	7307.61	6178.33	5536.14	5135.44	4870.81	4689.41
900 000	10694.25	9879.23	7473.69	6318.75	5661.96	5252.16	4981.51	4795.99
920 000	10931.90	10098.77	7639.77	6459.17	5787.78	5368.87	5092.21	4902.57
940 000	11169.55	10318.31	7805.85	6599.58	5913.60	5485.59	5202.91	5009.14
960 000	11407.20	10537.85	7971.94	6740.00	6039.42	5602.30	5313.61	5115.72
980 000	11644.85	10757.38	8138.02	6880.42	6165.24	5719.01	5424.31	5222.30
1000 000	11882.50	10976.92	8304.10	7020.84	6291.06	5835.73	5535.01	5328.88
Coefficient	.011882496	.010976922	.008304101	.007020835	.006291064	.005835729	.005535007	.005328876

9

MONTHLY AMORTIZING PAYMENTS

AMOUNT	1 YEAR	2 YEARS	3 YEARS	4 YEARS	5 YEARS	6 YEARS	7 YEARS	8 YEARS
10 000	860.66	443.21	304.22	234.85	193.33	165.73	146.09	131.41
20 000	1721.33	886.41	608.44	469.70	386.66	331.46	292.17	262.83
30 000	2581.99	1329.62	912.66	704.55	579.98	497.19	438.26	394.24
40 000	3442.66	1772.82	1216.88	939.40	773.31	662.92	584.34	525.66
50 000	4303.32	2216.03	1521.10	1174.25	966.64	828.64	730.43	657.07
60 000	5163.99	2659.24	1825.32	1409.10	1159.97	994.37	876.51	788.49
70 000	6024.65	3102.44	2129.54	1643.95	1353.30	1160.10	1022.60	919.90
80 000	6885.31	3545.65	2433.75	1878.80	1546.62	1325.83	1168.68	1051.31
90 000	7745.98	3988.85	2737.97	2113.65	1739.95	1491.56	1314.77	1182.73
100 000	8606.64	4432.06	3042.19	2348.50	1933.28	1657.29	1460.86	1314.14
110 000	9467.31	4875.27	3346.41	2583.35	2126.61	1823.02	1606.94	1445.56
120 000	10327.97	5318.47	3650.63	2818.20	2319.94	1988.75	1753.03	1576.97
130 000	11188.64	5761.68	3954.85	3053.05	2513.26	2154.48	1899.11	1708.39
140 000	12049.30	6204.89	4259.07	3287.90	2706.59	2320.20	2045.20	1839.80
150 000	12909.96	6648.09	4563.29	3522.75	2899.92	2485.93	2191.28	1971.21
160 000	13770.63	7091.30	4867.51	3757.60	3093.25	2651.66	2337.37	2102.63
170 000	14631.29	7534.50	5171.73	3992.46	3286.58	2817.39	2483.45	2234.04
180 000	15491.96	7977.71	5475.95	4227.31	3479.90	2983.12	2629.54	2365.46
190 000	16352.62	8420.92	5780.17	4462.16	3673.23	3148.85	2775.63	2496.87
200 000	17213.29	8864.12	6084.39	4697.01	3866.56	3314.58	2921.71	2628.29
210 000	18073.95	9307.33	6388.61	4931.86	4059.89	3480.31	3067.80	2759.70
220 000	18934.61	9750.53	6692.83	5166.71	4253.22	3646.04	3213.88	2891.11
230 000	19795.28	10193.74	6997.05	5401.56	4446.54	3811.76	3359.97	3022.53
240 000	20655.94	10636.95	7301.26	5636.41	4639.87	3977.49	3506.05	3153.94
250 000	21516.61	11080.15	7605.48	5871.26	4833.20	4143.22	3652.14	3285.36
260 000	22377.27	11523.36	7909.70	6106.11	5026.53	4308.95	3798.22	3416.77
270 000	23237.94	11966.56	8213.92	6340.96	5219.86	4474.68	3944.31	3548.19
280 000	24098.60	12409.77	8518.14	6575.81	5413.18	4640.41	4090.40	3679.60
290 000	24959.26	12852.98	8822.36	6810.66	5606.51	4806.14	4236.48	3811.01
300 000	25819.93	13296.18	9126.58	7045.51	5799.84	4971.87	4382.57	3942.43
320 000	27541.26	14182.60	9735.02	7515.21	6186.50	5303.32	4674.74	4205.26
340 000	29262.59	15069.01	10343.46	7984.91	6573.15	5634.78	4966.91	4468.09
360 000	30983.91	15955.42	10951.90	8454.61	6959.81	5966.24	5259.08	4730.91
380 000	32705.24	16841.83	11560.34	8924.31	7346.46	6297.70	5551.25	4993.74
400 000	34426.57	17728.24	12168.77	9394.01	7733.12	6629.15	5843.42	5256.57
420 000	36147.90	18614.66	12777.21	9863.71	8119.78	6960.61	6135.59	5519.40
440 000	37869.23	19501.07	13385.65	10333.41	8506.43	7292.07	6427.76	5782.23
460 000	39590.56	20387.48	13994.09	10803.11	8893.09	7623.53	6719.93	6045.06
480 000	41311.89	21273.89	14602.53	11272.81	9279.74	7954.99	7012.11	6307.89
500 000	43033.22	22160.30	15210.97	11742.52	9666.40	8286.44	7304.28	6570.71
520 000	44754.54	23046.72	15819.41	12212.22	10053.06	8617.90	7596.45	6833.54
540 000	46475.87	23933.13	16427.85	12681.92	10439.71	8949.36	7888.62	7096.37
560 000	48197.20	24819.54	17036.28	13151.62	10826.37	9280.82	8180.79	7359.20
580 000	49918.53	25705.95	17644.72	13621.32	11213.02	9612.27	8472.96	7622.03
600 000	51639.86	26592.37	18253.16	14091.02	11599.68	9943.73	8765.13	7884.86
620 000	53361.19	27478.78	18861.60	14560.72	11986.34	10275.19	9057.30	8147.69
640 000	55082.52	28365.19	19470.04	15030.42	12372.99	10606.65	9349.47	8410.52
660 000	56803.84	29251.60	20078.48	15500.12	12759.65	10938.11	9641.65	8673.34
680 000	58525.17	30138.01	20686.92	15969.82	13146.30	11269.56	9933.82	8936.17
700 000	60246.50	31024.43	21295.36	16439.52	13532.96	11601.02	10225.99	9199.00
720 000	61967.83	31910.84	21903.79	16909.22	13919.62	11932.48	10518.16	9461.83
740 000	63689.16	32797.25	22512.23	17378.92	14306.27	12263.94	10810.33	9724.66
760 000	65410.49	33683.66	23120.67	17848.62	14692.93	12595.39	11102.50	9987.49
780 000	67131.82	34570.08	23729.11	18318.32	15079.58	12926.85	11394.67	10250.32
800 000	68853.14	35456.49	24337.55	18788.02	15466.24	13258.31	11686.84	10513.14
820 000	70574.47	36342.90	24945.99	19257.72	15852.90	13589.77	11979.01	10775.97
840 000	72295.80	37229.31	25554.43	19727.43	16239.55	13921.23	12271.19	11038.80
860 000	74017.13	38115.72	26162.87	20197.13	16626.21	14252.68	12563.36	11301.63
880 000	75738.46	39002.14	26771.30	20666.83	17012.86	14584.14	12855.53	11564.46
900 000	77459.79	39888.55	27379.74	21136.53	17399.52	14915.60	13147.70	11827.29
920 000	79181.12	40774.96	27988.18	21606.23	17786.18	15247.06	13439.87	12090.12
940 000	80902.44	41661.37	28596.62	22075.93	18172.83	15578.51	13732.04	12352.94
960 000	82623.77	42547.79	29205.06	22545.63	18559.49	15909.97	14024.21	12615.77
980 000	84345.10	43434.20	29813.50	23015.33	18946.14	16241.43	14316.38	12878.60
1000 000	86066.43	44320.61	30421.94	23485.03	19332.80	16572.89	14608.55	13141.43
Coefficient	.086066430	.044320610	.030421937	.023485030	.019332801	.016572887	.014608554	.013141430

10

MONTHLY AMORTIZING PAYMENTS 6.00%

AMOUNT	9 YEARS	10 YEARS	15 YEARS	20 YEARS	25 YEARS	30 YEARS	35 YEARS	40 YEARS
10 000	120.06	111.02	84.39	71.64	64.43	59.96	57.02	55.02
20 000	240.12	222.04	168.77	143.29	128.86	119.91	114.04	110.04
30 000	360.17	333.06	253.16	214.93	193.29	179.87	171.06	165.06
40 000	480.23	444.08	337.54	286.57	257.72	239.82	228.08	220.09
50 000	600.29	555.10	421.93	358.22	322.15	299.78	285.09	275.11
60 000	720.35	666.12	506.31	429.86	386.58	359.73	342.11	330.13
70 000	840.40	777.14	590.70	501.50	451.01	419.69	399.13	385.15
80 000	960.46	888.16	675.09	573.14	515.44	479.64	456.15	440.17
90 000	1080.52	999.18	759.47	644.79	579.87	539.60	513.17	495.19
100 000	1200.58	1110.21	843.86	716.43	644.30	599.55	570.19	550.21
110 000	1320.63	1221.23	928.24	788.07	708.73	659.51	627.21	605.23
120 000	1440.69	1332.25	1012.63	859.72	773.16	719.46	684.23	660.26
130 000	1560.75	1443.27	1097.01	931.36	837.59	779.42	741.25	715.28
140 000	1680.81	1554.29	1181.40	1003.00	902.02	839.37	798.27	770.30
150 000	1800.86	1665.31	1265.79	1074.65	966.45	899.33	855.28	825.32
160 000	1920.92	1776.33	1350.17	1146.29	1030.88	959.28	912.30	880.34
170 000	2040.98	1887.35	1434.56	1217.93	1095.31	1019.24	969.32	935.36
180 000	2161.04	1998.37	1518.94	1289.58	1159.74	1079.19	1026.34	990.38
190 000	2281.09	2109.39	1603.33	1361.22	1224.17	1139.15	1083.36	1045.41
200 000	2401.15	2220.41	1687.71	1432.86	1288.60	1199.10	1140.38	1100.43
210 000	2521.21	2331.43	1772.10	1504.51	1353.03	1259.06	1197.40	1155.45
220 000	2641.27	2442.45	1856.48	1576.15	1417.46	1319.01	1254.42	1210.47
230 000	2761.32	2553.47	1940.87	1647.79	1481.89	1378.97	1311.44	1265.49
240 000	2881.38	2664.49	2025.26	1719.43	1546.32	1438.92	1368.46	1320.51
250 000	3001.44	2775.51	2109.64	1791.08	1610.75	1498.88	1425.47	1375.53
260 000	3121.50	2886.53	2194.03	1862.72	1675.18	1558.83	1482.49	1430.56
270 000	3241.55	2997.55	2278.41	1934.36	1739.61	1618.79	1539.51	1485.58
280 000	3361.61	3108.57	2362.80	2006.01	1804.04	1678.74	1596.53	1540.60
290 000	3481.67	3219.59	2447.18	2077.65	1868.47	1738.70	1653.55	1595.62
300 000	3601.73	3330.62	2531.57	2149.29	1932.90	1798.65	1710.57	1650.64
320 000	3841.84	3552.66	2700.34	2292.58	2061.76	1918.56	1824.61	1760.68
340 000	4081.96	3774.70	2869.11	2435.87	2190.62	2038.47	1938.64	1870.73
360 000	4322.07	3996.74	3037.88	2579.15	2319.49	2158.38	2052.68	1980.77
380 000	4562.19	4218.78	3206.66	2722.44	2448.35	2278.29	2166.72	2090.81
400 000	4802.30	4440.82	3375.43	2865.72	2577.21	2398.20	2280.76	2200.85
420 000	5042.42	4662.86	3544.20	3009.01	2706.07	2518.11	2394.80	2310.90
440 000	5282.53	4884.90	3712.97	3152.30	2834.93	2638.02	2508.83	2420.94
460 000	5522.65	5106.94	3881.74	3295.58	2963.79	2757.93	2622.87	2530.98
480 000	5762.76	5328.98	4050.51	3438.87	3092.65	2877.84	2736.91	2641.03
500 000	6002.88	5551.03	4219.28	3582.16	3221.51	2997.75	2850.95	2751.07
520 000	6242.99	5773.07	4388.06	3725.44	3350.37	3117.66	2964.99	2861.11
540 000	6483.11	5995.11	4556.83	3868.73	3479.23	3237.57	3079.02	2971.15
560 000	6723.22	6217.15	4725.60	4012.01	3608.09	3357.48	3193.06	3081.20
580 000	6963.34	6439.19	4894.37	4155.30	3736.95	3477.39	3307.10	3191.24
600 000	7203.45	6661.23	5063.14	4298.59	3865.81	3597.30	3421.14	3301.28
620 000	7443.57	6883.27	5231.91	4441.87	3994.67	3717.21	3535.18	3411.32
640 000	7683.68	7105.31	5400.68	4585.16	4123.53	3837.12	3649.21	3521.37
660 000	7923.80	7327.35	5569.45	4728.45	4252.39	3957.03	3763.25	3631.41
680 000	8163.91	7549.39	5738.23	4871.73	4381.25	4076.94	3877.29	3741.45
700 000	8404.03	7771.44	5907.00	5015.02	4510.11	4196.85	3991.33	3851.50
720 000	8644.14	7993.48	6075.77	5158.30	4638.97	4316.76	4105.37	3961.54
740 000	8884.26	8215.52	6244.54	5301.59	4767.83	4436.67	4219.40	4071.58
760 000	9124.37	8437.56	6413.31	5444.88	4896.69	4556.58	4333.44	4181.62
780 000	9364.49	8659.60	6582.08	5588.16	5025.55	4676.49	4447.48	4291.67
800 000	9604.60	8881.64	6750.85	5731.45	5154.41	4796.40	4561.52	4401.71
820 000	9844.72	9103.68	6919.63	5874.74	5283.27	4916.31	4675.56	4511.75
840 000	10084.83	9325.72	7088.40	6018.02	5412.13	5036.22	4789.59	4621.79
860 000	10324.95	9547.76	7257.17	6161.31	5540.99	5156.13	4903.63	4731.84
880 000	10565.06	9769.80	7425.94	6304.59	5669.85	5276.04	5017.67	4841.88
900 000	10805.18	9991.85	7594.71	6447.88	5798.71	5395.95	5131.71	4951.92
920 000	11045.29	10213.89	7763.48	6591.17	5927.57	5515.86	5245.75	5061.97
940 000	11285.41	10435.93	7932.25	6734.45	6056.43	5635.77	5359.78	5172.01
960 000	11525.52	10657.97	8101.03	6877.74	6185.29	5755.68	5473.82	5282.05
980 000	11765.64	10880.01	8269.80	7021.02	6314.15	5875.59	5587.86	5392.09
1000 000	12005.75	11102.05	8438.57	7164.31	6443.01	5995.50	5701.90	5502.14
Coefficient	.012005750	.011102050	.008438568	.007164311	.006443014	.005995505	.005701897	.005502136

11

6.25% MONTHLY AMORTIZING PAYMENTS

AMOUNT	1 YEAR	2 YEARS	3 YEARS	4 YEARS	5 YEARS	6 YEARS	7 YEARS	8 YEARS
10 000	861.81	444.33	305.35	236.00	194.49	166.91	147.29	132.63
20 000	1723.63	888.67	610.71	472.00	388.99	333.82	294.57	265.27
30 000	2585.44	1333.00	916.06	707.99	583.48	500.73	441.86	397.90
40 000	3447.26	1777.33	1221.41	943.99	777.97	667.65	589.15	530.54
50 000	4309.07	2221.67	1526.77	1179.99	972.46	834.56	736.43	663.17
60 000	5170.88	2666.00	1832.12	1415.99	1166.96	1001.47	883.72	795.81
70 000	6032.70	3110.33	2137.47	1651.99	1361.45	1168.38	1031.01	928.44
80 000	6894.51	3554.67	2442.83	1887.99	1555.94	1335.29	1178.30	1061.08
90 000	7756.32	3999.00	2748.18	2123.98	1750.43	1502.20	1325.58	1193.71
100 000	8618.14	4443.33	3053.53	2359.98	1944.93	1669.12	1472.87	1326.35
110 000	9479.95	4887.67	3358.89	2595.98	2139.42	1836.03	1620.16	1458.98
120 000	10341.77	5332.00	3664.24	2831.98	2333.91	2002.94	1767.44	1591.62
130 000	11203.58	5776.33	3969.59	3067.98	2528.40	2169.85	1914.73	1724.25
140 000	12065.39	6220.67	4274.95	3303.97	2722.90	2336.76	2062.02	1856.89
150 000	12927.21	6665.00	4580.30	3539.97	2917.39	2503.67	2209.30	1989.52
160 000	13789.02	7109.33	4885.66	3775.97	3111.88	2670.58	2356.59	2122.16
170 000	14650.83	7553.67	5191.01	4011.97	3306.37	2837.50	2503.88	2254.79
180 000	15512.65	7998.00	5496.36	4247.97	3500.87	3004.41	2651.17	2387.43
190 000	16374.46	8442.33	5801.72	4483.97	3695.36	3171.32	2798.45	2520.06
200 000	17236.28	8886.67	6107.07	4719.96	3889.85	3338.23	2945.74	2652.70
210 000	18098.09	9331.00	6412.42	4955.96	4084.35	3505.14	3093.03	2785.33
220 000	18959.90	9775.34	6717.78	5191.96	4278.84	3672.05	3240.31	2917.97
230 000	19821.72	10219.67	7023.13	5427.96	4473.33	3838.97	3387.60	3050.60
240 000	20683.53	10664.00	7328.48	5663.96	4667.82	4005.88	3534.89	3183.24
250 000	21545.35	11108.34	7633.84	5899.96	4862.32	4172.79	3682.17	3315.87
260 000	22407.16	11552.67	7939.19	6135.95	5056.81	4339.70	3829.46	3448.51
270 000	23268.97	11997.00	8244.54	6371.95	5251.30	4506.61	3976.75	3581.14
280 000	24130.79	12441.34	8549.90	6607.95	5445.79	4673.52	4124.04	3713.78
290 000	24992.60	12885.67	8855.25	6843.95	5640.29	4840.43	4271.32	3846.41
300 000	25854.41	13330.00	9160.60	7079.95	5834.78	5007.35	4418.61	3979.05
320 000	27578.04	14218.67	9771.31	7551.94	6223.76	5341.17	4713.18	4244.32
340 000	29301.67	15107.34	10382.02	8023.94	6612.75	5674.99	5007.76	4509.59
360 000	31025.30	15996.00	10992.72	8495.94	7001.73	6008.82	5302.33	4774.86
380 000	32748.92	16884.67	11603.43	8967.93	7390.72	6342.64	5596.91	5040.13
400 000	34472.55	17773.34	12214.14	9439.93	7779.70	6676.46	5891.48	5305.40
420 000	36196.18	18662.00	12824.84	9911.92	8168.69	7010.28	6186.05	5570.67
440 000	37919.81	19550.67	13435.55	10383.92	8557.68	7344.11	6480.63	5835.94
460 000	39643.44	20439.34	14046.26	10855.92	8946.66	7677.93	6775.20	6101.21
480 000	41367.06	21328.00	14656.97	11327.91	9335.65	8011.75	7069.78	6366.48
500 000	43090.69	22216.67	15267.67	11799.91	9724.63	8345.58	7364.35	6631.75
520 000	44814.32	23105.34	15878.38	12271.91	10113.62	8679.40	7658.92	6897.02
540 000	46537.95	23994.00	16489.09	12743.90	10502.60	9013.22	7953.50	7162.29
560 000	48261.57	24882.67	17099.79	13215.90	10891.59	9347.05	8248.07	7427.56
580 000	49985.20	25771.34	17710.50	13687.90	11280.57	9680.87	8542.65	7692.83
600 000	51708.83	26660.01	18321.21	14159.89	11669.56	10014.69	8837.22	7958.10
620 000	53432.46	27548.67	18931.91	14631.89	12058.54	10348.51	9131.79	8223.37
640 000	55156.08	28437.34	19542.62	15103.88	12447.53	10682.34	9426.37	8488.64
660 000	56879.71	29326.01	20153.33	15575.88	12836.51	11016.16	9720.94	8753.91
680 000	58603.34	30214.67	20764.03	16047.88	13225.50	11349.98	10015.52	9019.18
700 000	60326.97	31103.34	21374.74	16519.87	13614.48	11683.81	10310.09	9284.45
720 000	62050.59	31992.01	21985.45	16991.87	14003.47	12017.63	10604.66	9549.72
740 000	63774.22	32880.67	22596.15	17463.87	14392.45	12351.45	10899.24	9814.99
760 000	65497.85	33769.34	23206.86	17935.86	14781.44	12685.28	11193.81	10080.26
780 000	67221.48	34658.01	23817.57	18407.86	15170.42	13019.10	11488.39	10345.53
800 000	68945.10	35546.67	24428.28	18879.86	15559.41	13352.92	11782.96	10610.80
820 000	70668.73	36435.34	25038.98	19351.85	15948.39	13686.75	12077.53	10876.07
840 000	72392.36	37324.01	25649.69	19823.85	16337.38	14020.57	12372.11	11141.34
860 000	74115.99	38212.67	26260.40	20295.85	16726.37	14354.39	12666.68	11406.61
880 000	75839.62	39101.34	26871.10	20767.84	17115.35	14688.21	12961.26	11671.88
900 000	77563.24	39990.01	27481.81	21239.84	17504.34	15022.04	13255.83	11937.15
920 000	79286.87	40878.67	28092.52	21711.83	17893.32	15355.86	13550.40	12202.42
940 000	81010.50	41767.34	28703.22	22183.83	18282.31	15689.68	13844.98	12467.69
960 000	82734.13	42656.01	29313.93	22655.83	18671.29	16023.51	14139.55	12732.96
980 000	84457.75	43544.68	29924.64	23127.82	19060.28	16357.33	14434.13	12998.23
1000 000	86181.38	44433.34	30535.34	23599.82	19449.26	16691.15	14728.70	13263.50
Coefficient	.086181381	.044433342	.030535344	.023599820	.019449262	.016691153	.014728699	.013263495

12

MONTHLY AMORTIZING PAYMENTS 6.25%

AMOUNT	9 YEARS	10 YEARS	15 YEARS	20 YEARS	25 YEARS	30 YEARS	35 YEARS	40 YEARS
10 000	121.30	112.28	85.74	73.09	65.97	61.57	58.71	56.77
20 000	242.60	224.56	171.48	146.19	131.93	123.14	117.42	113.55
30 000	363.89	336.84	257.23	219.28	197.90	184.72	176.12	170.32
40 000	485.19	449.12	342.97	292.37	263.87	246.29	234.83	227.10
50 000	606.49	561.40	428.71	365.46	329.83	307.86	293.54	283.87
60 000	727.79	673.68	514.45	438.56	395.80	369.43	352.25	340.64
70 000	849.08	785.96	600.20	511.65	461.77	431.00	410.95	397.42
80 000	970.38	898.24	685.94	584.74	527.74	492.57	469.66	454.19
90 000	1091.68	1010.52	771.68	657.84	593.70	554.15	528.37	510.97
100 000	1212.98	1122.80	857.42	730.93	659.67	615.72	587.08	567.74
110 000	1334.27	1235.08	943.17	804.02	725.64	677.29	645.78	624.51
120 000	1455.57	1347.36	1028.91	877.11	791.60	738.86	704.49	681.29
130 000	1576.87	1459.64	1114.65	950.21	857.57	800.43	763.20	738.06
140 000	1698.17	1571.92	1200.39	1023.30	923.54	862.00	821.91	794.84
150 000	1819.46	1684.20	1286.13	1096.39	989.50	923.58	880.61	851.61
160 000	1940.76	1796.48	1371.88	1169.49	1055.47	985.15	939.32	908.38
170 000	2062.06	1908.76	1457.62	1242.58	1121.44	1046.72	998.03	965.16
180 000	2183.36	2021.04	1543.36	1315.67	1187.40	1108.29	1056.74	1021.93
190 000	2304.65	2133.32	1629.10	1388.76	1253.37	1169.86	1115.45	1078.71
200 000	2425.95	2245.60	1714.85	1461.86	1319.34	1231.43	1174.15	1135.48
210 000	2547.25	2357.88	1800.59	1534.95	1385.31	1293.01	1232.86	1192.25
220 000	2668.55	2470.16	1886.33	1608.04	1451.27	1354.58	1291.57	1249.03
230 000	2789.84	2582.44	1972.07	1681.13	1517.24	1416.15	1350.28	1305.80
240 000	2911.14	2694.72	2057.81	1754.23	1583.21	1477.72	1408.98	1362.58
250 000	3032.44	2807.00	2143.56	1827.32	1649.17	1539.29	1467.69	1419.35
260 000	3153.74	2919.28	2229.30	1900.41	1715.14	1600.86	1526.40	1476.12
270 000	3275.03	3031.56	2315.04	1973.51	1781.11	1662.44	1585.11	1532.90
280 000	3396.33	3143.84	2400.78	2046.60	1847.07	1724.01	1643.81	1589.67
290 000	3517.63	3256.12	2486.53	2119.69	1913.04	1785.58	1702.52	1646.44
300 000	3638.93	3368.40	2572.27	2192.78	1979.01	1847.15	1761.23	1703.22
320 000	3881.52	3592.96	2743.75	2338.97	2110.94	1970.30	1878.64	1816.77
340 000	4124.12	3817.52	2915.24	2485.16	2242.88	2093.44	1996.06	1930.31
360 000	4366.71	4042.08	3086.72	2631.34	2374.81	2216.58	2113.48	2043.86
380 000	4609.31	4266.64	3258.21	2777.53	2506.75	2339.73	2230.89	2157.41
400 000	4851.90	4491.20	3429.69	2923.71	2638.68	2462.87	2348.31	2270.96
420 000	5094.50	4715.76	3601.18	3069.90	2770.61	2586.01	2465.72	2384.51
440 000	5337.09	4940.32	3772.66	3216.08	2902.55	2709.16	2583.14	2498.05
460 000	5579.69	5164.88	3944.15	3362.27	3034.48	2832.30	2700.55	2611.60
480 000	5822.28	5389.44	4115.63	3508.46	3166.41	2955.44	2817.97	2725.15
500 000	6064.88	5614.00	4287.11	3654.64	3298.35	3078.59	2935.38	2838.70
520 000	6307.47	5838.56	4458.60	3800.83	3430.28	3201.73	3052.80	2952.25
540 000	6550.07	6063.12	4630.08	3947.01	3562.21	3324.87	3170.21	3065.79
560 000	6792.66	6287.69	4801.57	4093.20	3694.15	3448.02	3287.63	3179.34
580 000	7035.26	6512.25	4973.05	4239.38	3826.08	3571.16	3405.04	3292.89
600 000	7277.85	6736.81	5144.54	4385.57	3958.02	3694.30	3522.46	3406.44
620 000	7520.45	6961.37	5316.02	4531.75	4089.95	3817.45	3639.87	3519.99
640 000	7763.04	7185.93	5487.51	4677.94	4221.88	3940.59	3757.29	3633.53
660 000	8005.64	7410.49	5658.99	4824.13	4353.82	4063.73	3874.70	3747.08
680 000	8248.23	7635.05	5830.48	4970.31	4485.75	4186.88	3992.12	3860.63
700 000	8490.83	7859.61	6001.96	5116.50	4617.69	4310.02	4109.54	3974.18
720 000	8733.43	8084.17	6173.44	5262.68	4749.62	4433.16	4226.95	4087.73
740 000	8976.02	8308.73	6344.93	5408.87	4881.55	4556.31	4344.37	4201.27
760 000	9218.62	8533.29	6516.41	5555.05	5013.49	4679.45	4461.78	4314.82
780 000	9461.21	8757.85	6687.90	5701.24	5145.42	4802.59	4579.20	4428.37
800 000	9703.81	8982.41	6859.38	5847.43	5277.36	4925.74	4696.61	4541.92
820 000	9946.40	9206.97	7030.87	5993.61	5409.29	5048.88	4814.03	4655.46
840 000	10189.00	9431.53	7202.35	6139.80	5541.22	5172.02	4931.44	4769.01
860 000	10431.59	9656.09	7373.84	6285.98	5673.16	5295.17	5048.86	4882.56
880 000	10674.19	9880.65	7545.32	6432.17	5805.09	5418.31	5166.27	4996.11
900 000	10916.78	10105.21	7716.81	6578.35	5937.02	5541.45	5283.69	5109.66
920 000	11159.38	10329.77	7888.29	6724.54	6068.96	5664.60	5401.10	5223.20
940 000	11401.97	10554.33	8059.78	6870.73	6200.89	5787.74	5518.52	5336.75
960 000	11644.57	10778.89	8231.26	7016.91	6332.83	5910.89	5635.93	5450.30
980 000	11887.16	11003.45	8402.74	7163.10	6464.76	6034.03	5753.35	5563.85
1000 000	12129.76	11228.01	8574.23	7309.28	6596.69	6157.17	5870.77	5677.40
Coefficient	.012129757	.011228009	.008574229	.007309282	.006596694	.006157172	.005870765	.005677396

13

MONTHLY AMORTIZING PAYMENTS

AMOUNT	1 YEAR	2 YEARS	3 YEARS	4 YEARS	5 YEARS	6 YEARS	7 YEARS	8 YEARS
10 000	862.96	445.46	306.49	237.15	195.66	168.10	148.49	133.86
20 000	1725.93	890.93	612.98	474.30	391.32	336.20	296.99	267.72
30 000	2588.89	1336.39	919.47	711.45	586.98	504.30	445.48	401.59
40 000	3451.86	1781.85	1225.96	948.60	782.65	672.40	593.98	535.45
50 000	4314.82	2227.31	1532.45	1185.75	978.31	840.50	742.47	669.31
60 000	5177.79	2672.78	1838.94	1422.90	1173.97	1008.60	890.97	803.17
70 000	6040.75	3118.24	2145.43	1660.05	1369.63	1176.70	1039.46	937.04
80 000	6903.71	3563.70	2451.92	1897.20	1565.29	1344.79	1187.95	1070.90
90 000	7766.68	4009.16	2758.41	2134.35	1760.95	1512.89	1336.45	1204.76
100 000	8629.64	4454.63	3064.90	2371.50	1956.61	1680.99	1484.94	1338.62
110 000	9492.61	4900.09	3371.39	2608.64	2152.28	1849.09	1633.44	1472.49
120 000	10355.57	5345.55	3677.88	2845.79	2347.94	2017.19	1781.93	1606.35
130 000	11218.53	5791.01	3984.37	3082.94	2543.60	2185.29	1930.43	1740.21
140 000	12081.50	6236.48	4290.86	3320.09	2739.26	2353.39	2078.92	1874.07
150 000	12944.46	6681.94	4597.35	3557.24	2934.92	2521.49	2227.42	2007.93
160 000	13807.43	7127.40	4903.84	3794.39	3130.58	2689.59	2375.91	2141.80
170 000	14670.39	7572.86	5210.33	4031.54	3326.24	2857.69	2524.40	2275.66
180 000	15533.36	8018.33	5516.82	4268.69	3521.91	3025.79	2672.90	2409.52
190 000	16396.32	8463.79	5823.31	4505.84	3717.57	3193.89	2821.39	2543.38
200 000	17259.28	8909.25	6129.80	4742.99	3913.23	3361.99	2969.89	2677.25
210 000	18122.25	9354.71	6436.29	4980.14	4108.89	3530.09	3118.38	2811.11
220 000	18985.21	9800.18	6742.78	5217.29	4304.55	3698.18	3266.88	2944.97
230 000	19848.18	10245.64	7049.27	5454.44	4500.21	3866.28	3415.37	3078.83
240 000	20711.14	10691.10	7355.76	5691.59	4695.88	4034.38	3563.86	3212.70
250 000	21574.11	11136.56	7662.25	5928.74	4891.54	4202.48	3712.36	3346.56
260 000	22437.07	11582.03	7968.74	6165.89	5087.20	4370.58	3860.85	3480.42
270 000	23300.03	12027.49	8275.23	6403.04	5282.86	4538.68	4009.35	3614.28
280 000	24163.00	12472.95	8581.72	6640.19	5478.52	4706.78	4157.84	3748.14
290 000	25025.96	12918.41	8888.21	6877.34	5674.18	4874.88	4306.34	3882.01
300 000	25888.93	13363.88	9194.70	7114.49	5869.84	5042.98	4454.83	4015.87
320 000	27614.86	14254.80	9807.68	7588.78	6261.17	5379.18	4751.82	4283.59
340 000	29340.78	15145.73	10420.66	8063.08	6652.49	5715.38	5048.81	4551.32
360 000	31066.71	16036.65	11033.64	8537.38	7043.81	6051.57	5345.80	4819.04
380 000	32792.64	16927.58	11646.62	9011.68	7435.14	6387.77	5642.79	5086.77
400 000	34518.57	17818.50	12259.60	9485.98	7826.46	6723.97	5939.77	5354.49
420 000	36244.50	18709.43	12872.58	9960.28	8217.78	7060.17	6236.76	5622.22
440 000	37970.43	19600.35	13485.56	10434.58	8609.10	7396.37	6533.75	5889.94
460 000	39696.35	20491.28	14098.54	10908.88	9000.43	7732.57	6830.74	6157.67
480 000	41422.28	21382.20	14711.52	11383.18	9391.75	8068.77	7127.73	6425.39
500 000	43148.21	22273.13	15324.50	11857.48	9783.07	8404.96	7424.72	6693.12
520 000	44874.14	23164.05	15937.48	12331.78	10174.40	8741.16	7721.71	6960.84
540 000	46600.07	24054.98	16550.46	12806.07	10565.72	9077.36	8018.70	7228.57
560 000	48326.00	24945.90	17163.44	13280.37	10957.04	9413.56	8315.68	7496.29
580 000	50051.92	25836.83	17776.42	13754.67	11348.37	9749.76	8612.67	7764.01
600 000	51777.85	26727.75	18389.40	14228.97	11739.69	10085.96	8909.66	8031.74
620 000	53503.78	27618.68	19002.38	14703.27	12131.01	10422.16	9206.65	8299.46
640 000	55229.71	28509.60	19615.36	15177.57	12522.33	10758.36	9503.64	8567.19
660 000	56955.64	29400.53	20228.34	15651.87	12913.66	11094.55	9800.63	8834.91
680 000	58681.57	30291.45	20841.32	16126.17	13304.98	11430.75	10097.62	9102.64
700 000	60407.50	31182.38	21454.30	16600.47	13696.30	11766.95	10394.61	9370.36
720 000	62133.42	32073.30	22067.28	17074.77	14087.63	12103.15	10691.59	9638.09
740 000	63859.35	32964.23	22680.26	17549.06	14478.95	12439.35	10988.58	9905.81
760 000	65585.28	33855.15	23293.24	18023.36	14870.27	12775.55	11285.57	10173.54
780 000	67311.21	34746.08	23906.22	18497.66	15261.59	13111.75	11582.56	10441.26
800 000	69037.14	35637.00	24519.20	18971.96	15652.92	13447.94	11879.55	10708.99
820 000	70763.07	36527.93	25132.18	19446.26	16044.24	13784.14	12176.54	10976.71
840 000	72488.99	37418.85	25745.16	19920.56	16435.56	14120.34	12473.53	11244.43
860 000	74214.92	38309.78	26358.14	20394.86	16826.89	14456.54	12770.51	11512.16
880 000	75940.85	39200.70	26971.12	20869.16	17218.21	14792.74	13067.50	11779.88
900 000	77666.78	40091.63	27584.10	21343.46	17609.53	15128.94	13364.49	12047.61
920 000	79392.71	40982.55	28197.08	21817.76	18000.86	15465.14	13661.48	12315.33
940 000	81118.64	41873.48	28810.06	22292.05	18392.18	15801.33	13958.47	12583.06
960 000	82844.57	42764.40	29423.04	22766.35	18783.50	16137.53	14255.46	12850.78
980 000	84570.49	43655.33	30036.02	23240.65	19174.82	16473.73	14552.45	13118.51
1000 000	86296.42	44546.25	30649.00	23714.95	19566.15	16809.93	14849.44	13386.23
Coefficient	.086296422	.044546251	.030649001	.023714952	.019566147	.016809930	.014849436	.013386232

AMOUNT	9 YEARS	10 YEARS	15 YEARS	20 YEARS	25 YEARS	30 YEARS	35 YEARS	40 YEARS
10 000	122.55	113.55	87.11	74.56	67.52	63.21	60.42	58.55
20 000	245.09	227.10	174.22	149.11	135.04	126.41	120.83	117.09
30 000	367.64	340.64	261.33	223.67	202.56	189.62	181.25	175.64
40 000	490.18	454.19	348.44	298.23	270.08	252.83	241.66	234.18
50 000	612.73	567.74	435.55	372.79	337.60	316.03	302.08	292.73
60 000	735.27	681.29	522.66	447.34	405.12	379.24	362.49	351.27
70 000	857.82	794.84	609.78	521.90	472.65	442.45	422.91	409.82
80 000	980.36	908.38	696.89	596.46	540.17	505.65	483.32	468.37
90 000	1102.91	1021.93	784.00	671.02	607.69	568.86	543.74	526.91
100 000	1225.45	1135.48	871.11	745.57	675.21	632.07	604.15	585.46
110 000	1348.00	1249.03	958.22	820.13	742.73	695.27	664.57	644.00
120 000	1470.54	1362.58	1045.33	894.69	810.25	758.48	724.99	702.55
130 000	1593.09	1476.12	1132.44	969.25	877.77	821.69	785.40	761.09
140 000	1715.63	1589.67	1219.55	1043.80	945.29	884.90	845.82	819.64
150 000	1838.18	1703.22	1306.66	1118.36	1012.81	948.10	906.23	878.19
160 000	1960.72	1816.77	1393.77	1192.92	1080.33	1011.31	966.65	936.73
170 000	2083.27	1930.32	1480.88	1267.47	1147.85	1074.52	1027.06	995.28
180 000	2205.81	2043.86	1567.99	1342.03	1215.37	1137.72	1087.48	1053.82
190 000	2328.36	2157.41	1655.10	1416.59	1282.89	1200.93	1147.89	1112.37
200 000	2450.90	2270.96	1742.21	1491.15	1350.41	1264.14	1208.31	1170.91
210 000	2573.45	2384.51	1829.33	1565.70	1417.94	1327.34	1268.72	1229.46
220 000	2695.99	2498.06	1916.44	1640.26	1485.46	1390.55	1329.14	1288.00
230 000	2818.54	2611.60	2003.55	1714.82	1552.98	1453.76	1389.55	1346.55
240 000	2941.08	2725.15	2090.66	1789.38	1620.50	1516.96	1449.97	1405.10
250 000	3063.63	2838.70	2177.77	1863.93	1688.02	1580.17	1510.39	1463.64
260 000	3186.17	2952.25	2264.88	1938.49	1755.54	1643.38	1570.80	1522.19
270 000	3308.72	3065.80	2351.99	2013.05	1823.06	1706.58	1631.22	1580.73
280 000	3431.26	3179.34	2439.10	2087.60	1890.58	1769.79	1691.63	1639.28
290 000	3553.81	3292.89	2526.21	2162.16	1958.10	1833.00	1752.05	1697.82
300 000	3676.35	3406.44	2613.32	2236.72	2025.62	1896.20	1812.46	1756.37
320 000	3921.44	3633.54	2787.54	2385.83	2160.66	2022.62	1933.29	1873.46
340 000	4166.54	3860.63	2961.77	2534.95	2295.70	2149.03	2054.12	1990.55
360 000	4411.63	4087.73	3135.99	2684.06	2430.75	2275.44	2174.96	2107.64
380 000	4656.72	4314.82	3310.21	2833.18	2565.79	2401.86	2295.79	2224.74
400 000	4901.81	4541.92	3484.43	2982.29	2700.83	2528.27	2416.62	2341.83
420 000	5146.90	4769.01	3658.65	3131.41	2835.87	2654.69	2537.45	2458.92
440 000	5391.99	4996.11	3832.87	3280.52	2970.91	2781.10	2658.28	2576.01
460 000	5637.08	5223.21	4007.09	3429.64	3105.95	2907.51	2779.11	2693.10
480 000	5882.17	5450.30	4181.32	3578.75	3240.99	3033.93	2899.94	2810.19
500 000	6127.26	5677.40	4355.54	3727.87	3376.04	3160.34	3020.77	2927.28
520 000	6372.35	5904.49	4529.76	3876.98	3511.08	3286.75	3141.60	3044.38
540 000	6617.44	6131.59	4703.98	4026.10	3646.12	3413.17	3262.43	3161.47
560 000	6862.53	6358.69	4878.20	4175.21	3781.16	3539.58	3383.26	3278.56
580 000	7107.62	6585.78	5052.42	4324.32	3916.20	3665.99	3504.09	3395.65
600 000	7352.71	6812.88	5226.64	4473.44	4051.24	3792.41	3624.93	3512.74
620 000	7597.80	7039.97	5400.87	4622.55	4186.28	3918.82	3745.76	3629.83
640 000	7842.89	7267.07	5575.09	4771.67	4321.33	4045.24	3866.59	3746.92
660 000	8087.98	7494.17	5749.31	4920.78	4456.37	4171.65	3987.42	3864.01
680 000	8333.07	7721.26	5923.53	5069.90	4591.41	4298.06	4108.25	3981.11
700 000	8578.16	7948.36	6097.75	5219.01	4726.45	4424.48	4229.08	4098.20
720 000	8823.25	8175.45	6271.97	5368.13	4861.49	4550.89	4349.91	4215.29
740 000	9068.34	8402.55	6446.19	5517.24	4996.53	4677.30	4470.74	4332.38
760 000	9313.43	8629.65	6620.42	5666.36	5131.57	4803.72	4591.57	4449.47
780 000	9558.52	8856.74	6794.64	5815.47	5266.62	4930.13	4712.40	4566.56
800 000	9803.61	9083.84	6968.86	5964.59	5401.66	5056.54	4833.23	4683.65
820 000	10048.70	9310.93	7143.08	6113.70	5536.70	5182.96	4954.07	4800.75
840 000	10293.79	9538.03	7317.30	6262.81	5671.74	5309.37	5074.90	4917.84
860 000	10538.88	9765.13	7491.52	6411.93	5806.78	5435.78	5195.73	5034.93
880 000	10783.97	9992.22	7665.75	6561.04	5941.82	5562.20	5316.56	5152.02
900 000	11029.06	10219.32	7839.97	6710.16	6076.86	5688.61	5437.39	5269.11
920 000	11274.15	10446.41	8014.19	6859.27	6211.91	5815.03	5558.22	5386.20
940 000	11519.24	10673.51	8188.41	7008.39	6346.95	5941.44	5679.05	5503.29
960 000	11764.33	10900.61	8362.63	7157.50	6481.99	6067.85	5799.88	5620.39
980 000	12009.42	11127.70	8536.85	7306.62	6617.03	6194.27	5920.71	5737.48
1000 000	12254.52	11354.80	8711.07	7455.73	6752.07	6320.68	6041.54	5854.57
Coefficient	.012254515	.011354797	.008711074	.007455732	.006752072	.006320680	.006041543	.005854568

MONTHLY AMORTIZING PAYMENTS

AMOUNT	1 YEAR	2 YEARS	3 YEARS	4 YEARS	5 YEARS	6 YEARS	7 YEARS	8 YEARS
10 000	864.12	446.59	307.63	238.30	196.83	169.29	149.71	135.10
20 000	1728.23	893.19	615.26	476.61	393.67	338.58	299.42	270.19
30 000	2592.35	1339.78	922.89	714.91	590.50	507.88	449.12	405.29
40 000	3456.46	1786.37	1230.52	953.22	787.34	677.17	598.83	540.39
50 000	4320.58	2232.97	1538.15	1191.52	984.17	846.46	748.54	675.48
60 000	5184.69	2679.56	1845.78	1429.83	1181.01	1015.75	898.25	810.58
70 000	6048.81	3126.15	2153.40	1668.13	1377.84	1185.04	1047.95	945.67
80 000	6912.92	3572.75	2461.03	1906.43	1574.68	1354.34	1197.66	1080.77
90 000	7777.04	4019.34	2768.66	2144.74	1771.51	1523.63	1347.37	1215.87
100 000	8641.15	4465.93	3076.29	2383.04	1968.35	1692.92	1497.08	1350.96
110 000	9505.27	4912.53	3383.92	2621.35	2165.18	1862.21	1646.78	1486.06
120 000	10369.39	5359.12	3691.55	2859.65	2362.02	2031.51	1796.49	1621.16
130 000	11233.50	5805.71	3999.18	3097.96	2558.85	2200.80	1946.20	1756.25
140 000	12097.62	6252.31	4306.81	3336.26	2755.68	2370.09	2095.91	1891.35
150 000	12961.73	6698.90	4614.44	3574.56	2952.52	2539.38	2245.61	2026.45
160 000	13825.85	7145.49	4922.07	3812.87	3149.35	2708.67	2395.32	2161.54
170 000	14689.96	7592.09	5229.70	4051.17	3346.19	2877.97	2545.03	2296.64
180 000	15554.08	8038.68	5537.33	4289.48	3543.02	3047.26	2694.74	2431.74
190 000	16418.19	8485.27	5844.95	4527.78	3739.86	3216.55	2844.44	2566.83
200 000	17282.31	8931.87	6152.58	4766.09	3936.69	3385.84	2994.15	2701.93
210 000	18146.42	9378.46	6460.21	5004.39	4133.53	3555.13	3143.86	2837.02
220 000	19010.54	9825.05	6767.84	5242.69	4330.36	3724.43	3293.57	2972.12
230 000	19874.65	10271.65	7075.47	5481.00	4527.20	3893.72	3443.28	3107.22
240 000	20738.77	10718.24	7383.10	5719.30	4724.03	4063.01	3592.98	3242.31
250 000	21602.89	11164.83	7690.73	5957.61	4920.87	4232.30	3742.69	3377.41
260 000	22467.00	11611.43	7998.36	6195.91	5117.70	4401.60	3892.40	3512.51
270 000	23331.12	12058.02	8305.99	6434.22	5314.53	4570.89	4042.11	3647.60
280 000	24195.23	12504.61	8613.62	6672.52	5511.37	4740.18	4191.81	3782.70
290 000	25059.35	12951.21	8921.25	6910.82	5708.20	4909.47	4341.52	3917.80
300 000	25923.46	13397.80	9228.88	7149.13	5905.04	5078.76	4491.23	4052.89
320 000	27651.69	14290.99	9844.13	7625.74	6298.71	5417.35	4790.64	4323.08
340 000	29379.92	15184.17	10459.39	8102.35	6692.38	5755.93	5090.06	4593.28
360 000	31108.16	16077.36	11074.65	8578.95	7086.05	6094.52	5389.47	4863.47
380 000	32836.39	16970.55	11689.91	9055.56	7479.71	6433.10	5688.89	5133.66
400 000	34564.62	17863.73	12305.17	9532.17	7873.38	6771.69	5988.31	5403.86
420 000	36292.85	18756.92	12920.43	10008.78	8267.05	7110.27	6287.72	5674.05
440 000	38021.08	19650.11	13535.68	10485.39	8660.72	7448.85	6587.14	5944.24
460 000	39749.31	20543.29	14150.94	10962.00	9054.39	7787.44	6886.55	6214.43
480 000	41477.54	21436.48	14766.20	11438.60	9448.06	8126.02	7185.97	6484.63
500 000	43205.77	22329.67	15381.46	11915.21	9841.73	8464.61	7485.38	6754.82
520 000	44934.00	23222.85	15996.72	12391.82	10235.40	8803.19	7784.80	7025.01
540 000	46662.23	24116.04	16611.98	12868.43	10629.07	9141.78	8084.21	7295.21
560 000	48390.46	25009.23	17227.24	13345.04	11022.74	9480.36	8383.63	7565.40
580 000	50118.69	25902.41	17842.49	13821.65	11416.41	9818.94	8683.04	7835.59
600 000	51846.93	26795.60	18457.75	14298.26	11810.08	10157.53	8982.46	8105.78
620 000	53575.16	27688.79	19073.01	14774.86	12203.75	10496.11	9281.87	8375.98
640 000	55303.39	28581.97	19688.27	15251.47	12597.41	10834.70	9581.29	8646.17
660 000	57031.62	29475.16	20303.53	15728.08	12991.08	11173.28	9880.70	8916.36
680 000	58759.85	30368.35	20918.79	16204.69	13384.75	11511.87	10180.12	9186.56
700 000	60488.08	31261.53	21534.04	16681.30	13778.42	11850.45	10479.53	9456.75
720 000	62216.31	32154.72	22149.30	17157.91	14172.09	12189.03	10778.95	9726.94
740 000	63944.54	33047.91	22764.56	17634.52	14565.76	12527.62	11078.36	9997.13
760 000	65672.77	33941.09	23379.82	18111.12	14959.43	12866.20	11377.78	10267.33
780 000	67401.00	34834.28	23995.08	18587.73	15353.10	13204.79	11677.20	10537.52
800 000	69129.23	35727.47	24610.34	19064.34	15746.77	13543.37	11976.61	10807.71
820 000	70857.47	36620.65	25225.59	19540.95	16140.44	13881.96	12276.03	11077.90
840 000	72585.70	37513.84	25840.85	20017.56	16534.11	14220.54	12575.44	11348.10
860 000	74313.93	38407.03	26456.11	20494.17	16927.78	14559.12	12874.86	11618.29
880 000	76042.16	39300.21	27071.37	20970.78	17321.44	14897.71	13174.27	11888.48
900 000	77770.39	40193.40	27686.63	21447.38	17715.11	15236.29	13473.69	12158.68
920 000	79498.62	41086.59	28301.89	21923.99	18108.78	15574.88	13773.10	12428.87
940 000	81226.85	41979.77	28917.14	22400.60	18502.45	15913.46	14072.52	12699.06
960 000	82955.08	42872.96	29532.40	22877.21	18896.12	16252.05	14371.93	12969.25
980 000	84683.31	43766.15	30147.66	23353.82	19289.79	16590.63	14671.35	13239.45
1000 000	86411.54	44659.33	30762.92	23830.43	19683.46	16929.21	14970.76	13509.64
Coefficient	.086411543	.044659332	.030762920	.023830427	.019683460	.016929214	.014970763	.013509640

AMOUNT	9 YEARS	10 YEARS	15 YEARS	20 YEARS	25 YEARS	30 YEARS	35 YEARS	40 YEARS
10 000	123.80	114.82	88.49	76.04	69.09	64.86	62.14	60.34
20 000	247.60	229.65	176.98	152.07	138.18	129.72	124.28	120.67
30 000	371.40	344.47	265.47	228.11	207.27	194.58	186.42	181.01
40 000	495.20	459.30	353.96	304.15	276.36	259.44	248.57	241.34
50 000	619.00	574.12	442.45	380.18	345.46	324.30	310.71	301.68
60 000	742.80	688.94	530.95	456.22	414.55	389.16	372.85	362.01
70 000	866.60	803.77	619.44	532.25	483.64	454.02	434.99	422.35
80 000	990.40	918.59	707.93	608.29	552.73	518.88	497.13	482.69
90 000	1114.20	1033.42	796.42	684.33	621.82	583.74	559.27	543.02
100 000	1238.00	1148.24	884.91	760.36	690.91	648.60	621.42	603.36
110 000	1361.80	1263.07	973.40	836.40	760.00	713.46	683.56	663.69
120 000	1485.60	1377.89	1061.89	912.44	829.09	778.32	745.70	724.03
130 000	1609.40	1492.71	1150.38	988.47	898.18	843.18	807.84	784.36
140 000	1733.20	1607.54	1238.87	1064.51	967.28	908.04	869.98	844.70
150 000	1857.00	1722.36	1327.36	1140.55	1036.37	972.90	932.12	905.04
160 000	1980.80	1837.19	1415.86	1216.58	1105.46	1037.76	994.27	965.37
170 000	2104.60	1952.01	1504.35	1292.62	1174.55	1102.62	1056.41	1025.71
180 000	2228.40	2066.83	1592.84	1368.66	1243.64	1167.48	1118.55	1086.04
190 000	2352.20	2181.66	1681.33	1444.69	1312.73	1232.34	1180.69	1146.38
200 000	2476.00	2296.48	1769.82	1520.73	1381.82	1297.20	1242.83	1206.71
210 000	2599.80	2411.31	1858.31	1596.76	1450.91	1362.06	1304.97	1267.05
220 000	2723.61	2526.13	1946.80	1672.80	1520.01	1426.92	1367.12	1327.38
230 000	2847.41	2640.95	2035.29	1748.84	1589.10	1491.78	1429.26	1387.72
240 000	2971.21	2755.78	2123.78	1824.87	1658.19	1556.64	1491.40	1448.06
250 000	3095.01	2870.60	2212.27	1900.91	1727.28	1621.50	1553.54	1508.39
260 000	3218.81	2985.43	2300.76	1976.95	1796.37	1686.36	1615.68	1568.73
270 000	3342.61	3100.25	2389.26	2052.98	1865.46	1751.21	1677.82	1629.06
280 000	3466.41	3215.08	2477.75	2129.02	1934.55	1816.07	1739.97	1689.40
290 000	3590.21	3329.90	2566.24	2205.06	2003.64	1880.93	1802.11	1749.73
300 000	3714.01	3444.72	2654.73	2281.09	2072.73	1945.79	1864.25	1810.07
320 000	3961.61	3674.37	2831.71	2433.16	2210.92	2075.51	1988.53	1930.74
340 000	4209.21	3904.02	3008.69	2585.24	2349.10	2205.23	2112.82	2051.41
360 000	4456.81	4133.67	3185.67	2737.31	2487.28	2334.95	2237.10	2172.08
380 000	4704.41	4363.32	3362.66	2889.38	2625.46	2464.67	2361.38	2292.76
400 000	4952.01	4592.96	3539.64	3041.46	2763.65	2594.39	2485.67	2413.43
420 000	5199.61	4822.61	3716.62	3193.53	2901.83	2724.11	2609.95	2534.10
440 000	5447.21	5052.26	3893.60	3345.60	3040.01	2853.83	2734.23	2654.77
460 000	5694.81	5281.91	4070.58	3497.67	3178.19	2983.55	2858.52	2775.44
480 000	5942.41	5511.56	4247.57	3649.75	3316.38	3113.27	2982.80	2896.11
500 000	6190.00	5741.21	4424.55	3801.82	3454.56	3242.99	3107.00	3016.78
520 000	6437.61	5970.85	4601.53	3953.89	3592.74	3372.71	3231.37	3137.46
540 000	6685.21	6200.50	4778.51	4105.97	3730.92	3502.43	3355.65	3258.13
560 000	6932.81	6430.15	4955.49	4258.04	3869.10	3632.15	3479.93	3378.80
580 000	7180.41	6659.80	5132.48	4410.11	4007.29	3761.87	3604.22	3499.47
600 000	7428.01	6889.45	5309.46	4562.18	4145.47	3891.59	3728.50	3620.14
620 000	7675.61	7119.09	5486.44	4714.26	4283.65	4021.31	3852.78	3740.81
640 000	7923.21	7348.74	5663.42	4866.33	4421.83	4151.03	3977.07	3861.48
660 000	8170.82	7578.39	5840.40	5018.40	4560.02	4280.75	4101.35	3982.15
680 000	8418.42	7808.04	6017.38	5170.48	4698.20	4410.47	4225.63	4102.83
700 000	8666.02	8037.69	6194.37	5322.55	4836.38	4540.19	4349.92	4223.50
720 000	8913.62	8267.34	6371.35	5474.62	4974.56	4669.91	4474.20	4344.17
740 000	9161.22	8496.98	6548.33	5626.69	5112.75	4799.63	4598.48	4464.84
760 000	9408.82	8726.63	6725.31	5778.77	5250.93	4929.35	4722.77	4585.51
780 000	9656.42	8956.28	6902.29	5930.84	5389.11	5059.07	4847.05	4706.18
800 000	9904.02	9185.93	7079.28	6082.91	5527.29	5188.78	4971.33	4826.85
820 000	10151.62	9415.58	7256.26	6234.98	5665.47	5318.50	5095.62	4947.53
840 000	10399.22	9645.23	7433.24	6387.06	5803.66	5448.22	5219.90	5068.20
860 000	10646.82	9874.87	7610.22	6539.13	5941.84	5577.94	5344.18	5188.87
880 000	10894.42	10104.52	7787.20	6691.20	6080.02	5707.66	5468.47	5309.54
900 000	11142.02	10334.17	7964.19	6843.28	6218.20	5837.38	5592.75	5430.21
920 000	11389.62	10563.82	8141.17	6995.35	6356.39	5967.10	5717.03	5550.88
940 000	11637.22	10793.47	8318.15	7147.42	6494.57	6096.82	5841.32	5671.55
960 000	11884.82	11023.11	8495.13	7299.49	6632.75	6226.54	5965.60	5792.23
980 000	12132.42	11252.76	8672.11	7451.57	6770.93	6356.26	6089.88	5912.90
1000 000	12380.02	11482.41	8849.09	7603.64	6909.12	6485.98	6214.17	6033.57
Coefficient	.012380023	.011482411	.008849095	.007603640	.006909115	.006485981	.006214165	.006033568

adk #205 (house) pay 185 - dp(37) ≈ 150K = 1K month

7.00% MONTHLY AMORTIZING PAYMENTS

AMOUNT	1 YEAR	2 YEARS	3 YEARS	4 YEARS	5 YEARS	6 YEARS	7 YEARS	8 YEARS
10 000	865.27	447.73	308.77	239.46	198.01	170.49	150.93	136.34
20 000	1730.53	895.45	617.54	478.92	396.02	340.98	301.85	272.67
30 000	2595.80	1343.18	926.31	718.39	594.04	511.47	452.78	409.01
40 000	3461.07	1790.90	1235.08	957.85	792.05	681.96	603.71	545.35
50 000	4326.34	2238.63	1543.85	1197.31	990.06	852.45	754.63	681.69
60 000	5191.60	2686.35	1852.63	1436.77	1188.07	1022.94	905.56	818.02
70 000	6056.87	3134.08	2161.40	1676.24	1386.08	1193.43	1056.49	954.36
80 000	6922.14	3581.81	2470.17	1915.70	1584.10	1363.92	1207.41	1090.70
90 000	7787.41	4029.53	2778.94	2155.16	1782.11	1534.41	1358.34	1227.03
100 000	8652.67	4477.26	3087.71	2394.62	1980.12	1704.90	1509.27	1363.37
110 000	9517.94	4924.98	3396.48	2634.09	2178.13	1875.39	1660.19	1499.71
120 000	10383.21	5372.71	3705.25	2873.55	2376.14	2045.88	1811.12	1636.05
130 000	11248.48	5820.44	4014.02	3113.01	2574.16	2216.37	1962.05	1772.38
140 000	12113.74	6268.16	4322.79	3352.47	2772.17	2386.86	2112.98	1908.72
150 000	12979.01	6715.89	4631.56	3591.94	2970.18	2557.35	2263.90	2045.06
160 000	13844.28	7163.61	4940.34	3831.40	3168.19	2727.84	2414.83	2181.39
170 000	14709.55	7611.34	5249.11	4070.86	3366.20	2898.33	2565.76	2317.73
180 000	15574.81	8059.06	5557.88	4310.32	3564.22	3068.82	2716.68	2454.07
190 000	16440.08	8506.79	5866.65	4549.79	3762.23	3239.31	2867.61	2590.41
200 000	17305.35	8954.52	6175.42	4789.25	3960.24	3409.80	3018.54	2726.74
210 000	18170.62	9402.24	6484.19	5028.71	4158.25	3580.29	3169.46	2863.08
220 000	19035.88	9849.97	6792.96	5268.17	4356.26	3750.78	3320.39	2999.42
230 000	19901.15	10297.69	7101.73	5507.64	4554.28	3921.27	3471.32	3135.75
240 000	20766.42	10745.42	7410.50	5747.10	4752.29	4091.76	3622.24	3272.09
250 000	21631.69	11193.15	7719.27	5986.56	4950.30	4262.25	3773.17	3408.43
260 000	22496.95	11640.87	8028.04	6226.02	5148.31	4432.74	3924.10	3544.77
270 000	23362.22	12088.60	8336.82	6465.49	5346.32	4603.23	4075.02	3681.10
280 000	24227.49	12536.32	8645.59	6704.95	5544.34	4773.72	4225.95	3817.44
290 000	25092.76	12984.05	8954.36	6944.41	5742.35	4944.21	4376.88	3953.78
300 000	25958.02	13431.77	9263.13	7183.87	5940.36	5114.70	4527.80	4090.12
320 000	27688.56	14327.23	9880.67	7662.80	6336.38	5455.68	4829.66	4362.79
340 000	29419.09	15222.68	10498.21	8141.72	6732.41	5796.66	5131.51	4635.46
360 000	31149.63	16118.13	11115.75	8620.65	7128.43	6137.64	5433.36	4908.14
380 000	32880.16	17013.58	11733.30	9099.57	7524.46	6478.62	5735.22	5180.81
400 000	34610.70	17909.03	12350.84	9578.50	7920.48	6819.60	6037.07	5453.49
420 000	36341.23	18804.48	12968.38	10057.42	8316.50	7160.58	6338.93	5726.16
440 000	38071.77	19699.94	13585.92	10536.35	8712.53	7501.56	6640.78	5998.84
460 000	39802.30	20595.39	14203.46	11015.27	9108.55	7842.54	6942.63	6271.51
480 000	41532.84	21490.84	14821.01	11494.20	9504.58	8183.52	7244.49	6544.18
500 000	43263.37	22386.29	15438.55	11973.12	9900.60	8524.50	7546.34	6816.86
520 000	44993.91	23281.74	16056.09	12452.05	10296.62	8865.48	7848.19	7089.53
540 000	46724.44	24177.19	16673.63	12930.97	10692.65	9206.46	8150.05	7362.21
560 000	48454.98	25072.65	17291.17	13409.90	11088.67	9547.44	8451.90	7634.88
580 000	50185.51	25968.10	17908.72	13888.82	11484.70	9888.42	8753.75	7907.56
600 000	51916.05	26863.55	18526.26	14367.75	11880.72	10229.40	9055.61	8180.23
620 000	53646.58	27759.00	19143.80	14846.67	12276.74	10570.38	9357.46	8452.90
640 000	55377.12	28654.45	19761.34	15325.60	12672.77	10911.36	9659.31	8725.58
660 000	57107.65	29549.90	20378.88	15804.52	13068.79	11252.34	9961.17	8998.25
680 000	58838.19	30445.36	20996.42	16283.45	13464.82	11593.32	10263.02	9270.93
700 000	60568.72	31340.81	21613.97	16762.37	13860.84	11934.30	10564.88	9543.60
720 000	62299.26	32236.26	22231.51	17241.29	14256.86	12275.29	10866.73	9816.28
740 000	64029.79	33131.71	22849.05	17720.22	14652.89	12616.27	11168.58	10088.95
760 000	65760.33	34027.16	23466.59	18199.14	15048.91	12957.25	11470.44	10361.62
780 000	67490.86	34922.61	24084.13	18678.07	15444.94	13298.23	11772.29	10634.30
800 000	69221.40	35818.07	24701.68	19156.99	15840.96	13639.21	12074.14	10906.97
820 000	70951.93	36713.52	25319.22	19635.92	16236.98	13980.19	12376.00	11179.65
840 000	72682.46	37608.97	25936.76	20114.84	16633.01	14321.17	12677.85	11452.32
860 000	74413.00	38504.42	26554.30	20593.77	17029.03	14662.15	12979.70	11725.00
880 000	76143.53	39399.87	27171.84	21072.69	17425.06	15003.13	13281.56	11997.67
900 000	77874.07	40295.32	27789.39	21551.62	17821.08	15344.11	13583.41	12270.35
920 000	79604.60	41190.78	28406.93	22030.54	18217.10	15685.09	13885.26	12543.02
940 000	81335.14	42086.23	29024.47	22509.47	18613.13	16026.07	14187.12	12815.69
960 000	83065.67	42981.68	29642.01	22988.39	19009.15	16367.05	14488.97	13088.37
980 000	84796.21	43877.13	30259.55	23467.32	19405.18	16708.03	14790.83	13361.04
1000 000	86526.74	44772.58	30877.10	23946.24	19801.20	17049.01	15092.68	13633.72
Coefficient	.086526744	.044772582	.030877095	.023946243	.019801199	.017049007	.015092679	.013633717

MONTHLY AMORTIZING PAYMENTS — 7.00%

AMOUNT	9 YEARS	10 YEARS	15 YEARS	20 YEARS	25 YEARS	30 YEARS	35 YEARS	40 YEARS
10 000	125.06	116.11	89.88	77.53	70.68	66.53	63.89	62.14
20 000	250.13	232.22	179.77	155.06	141.36	133.06	127.77	124.29
30 000	375.19	348.33	269.65	232.59	212.03	199.59	191.66	186.43
40 000	500.25	464.43	359.53	310.12	282.71	266.12	255.54	248.57
50 000	625.31	580.54	449.41	387.65	353.39	332.65	319.43	310.72
60 000	750.38	696.65	539.30	465.18	424.07	399.18	383.31	372.86
70 000	875.44	812.76	629.18	542.71	494.75	465.71	447.20	435.00
80 000	1000.50	928.87	719.06	620.24	565.42	532.24	511.09	497.15
90 000	1125.56	1044.98	808.95	697.77	636.10	598.77	574.97	559.29
100 000	1250.63	1161.08	898.83	775.30	706.78	665.30	638.86	621.43
110 000	1375.69	1277.19	988.71	852.83	777.46	731.83	702.74	683.57
120 000	1500.75	1393.30	1078.59	930.36	848.14	798.36	766.63	745.72
130 000	1625.82	1509.41	1168.48	1007.89	918.81	864.89	830.51	807.86
140 000	1750.88	1625.52	1258.36	1085.42	989.49	931.42	894.40	870.00
150 000	1875.94	1741.63	1348.24	1162.95	1060.17	997.95	958.28	932.15
160 000	2001.00	1857.74	1438.13	1240.48	1130.85	1064.48	1022.17	994.29
170 000	2126.07	1973.84	1528.01	1318.01	1201.52	1131.01	1086.06	1056.43
180 000	2251.13	2089.95	1617.89	1395.54	1272.20	1197.54	1149.94	1118.58
190 000	2376.19	2206.06	1707.77	1473.07	1342.88	1264.07	1213.83	1180.72
200 000	2501.26	2322.17	1797.66	1550.60	1413.56	1330.61	1277.71	1242.86
210 000	2626.32	2438.28	1887.54	1628.13	1484.24	1397.14	1341.60	1305.01
220 000	2751.38	2554.39	1977.42	1705.66	1554.91	1463.67	1405.48	1367.15
230 000	2876.44	2670.49	2067.31	1783.19	1625.59	1530.20	1469.37	1429.29
240 000	3001.51	2786.60	2157.19	1860.72	1696.27	1596.73	1533.26	1491.44
250 000	3126.57	2902.71	2247.07	1938.25	1766.95	1663.26	1597.14	1553.58
260 000	3251.63	3018.82	2336.95	2015.78	1837.63	1729.79	1661.03	1615.72
270 000	3376.69	3134.93	2426.84	2093.31	1908.30	1796.32	1724.91	1677.86
280 000	3501.76	3251.04	2516.72	2170.84	1978.98	1862.85	1788.80	1740.01
290 000	3626.82	3367.15	2606.60	2248.37	2049.66	1929.38	1852.68	1802.15
300 000	3751.88	3483.25	2696.48	2325.90	2120.34	1995.91	1916.57	1864.29
320 000	4002.01	3715.47	2876.25	2480.96	2261.69	2128.97	2044.34	1988.58
340 000	4252.13	3947.69	3056.02	2636.02	2403.05	2262.03	2172.11	2112.87
360 000	4502.26	4179.90	3235.78	2791.08	2544.41	2395.09	2299.88	2237.15
380 000	4752.39	4412.12	3415.55	2946.14	2685.76	2528.15	2427.65	2361.44
400 000	5002.51	4644.34	3595.31	3101.20	2827.12	2661.21	2555.43	2485.73
420 000	5252.64	4876.56	3775.08	3256.26	2968.47	2794.27	2683.20	2610.01
440 000	5502.76	5108.77	3954.84	3411.32	3109.83	2927.33	2810.97	2734.30
460 000	5752.89	5340.99	4134.61	3566.37	3251.18	3060.39	2938.74	2858.58
480 000	6003.01	5573.21	4314.38	3721.43	3392.54	3193.45	3066.51	2982.87
500 000	6253.14	5805.42	4494.14	3876.49	3533.90	3326.51	3194.28	3107.16
520 000	6503.26	6037.64	4673.91	4031.55	3675.25	3459.57	3322.05	3231.44
540 000	6753.39	6269.86	4853.67	4186.61	3816.61	3592.63	3449.82	3355.73
560 000	7003.52	6502.07	5033.44	4341.67	3957.96	3725.69	3577.60	3480.02
580 000	7253.64	6734.29	5213.20	4496.73	4099.32	3858.75	3705.37	3604.30
600 000	7503.77	6966.51	5392.97	4651.79	4240.68	3991.82	3833.14	3728.59
620 000	7753.89	7198.73	5572.74	4806.85	4382.03	4124.88	3960.91	3852.87
640 000	8004.02	7430.94	5752.50	4961.91	4523.39	4257.94	4088.68	3977.16
660 000	8254.14	7663.16	5932.27	5116.97	4664.74	4391.00	4216.45	4101.45
680 000	8504.27	7895.38	6112.03	5272.03	4806.10	4524.06	4344.22	4225.73
700 000	8754.39	8127.59	6291.80	5427.09	4947.45	4657.12	4471.99	4350.02
720 000	9004.52	8359.81	6471.56	5582.15	5088.81	4790.18	4599.77	4474.31
740 000	9254.64	8592.03	6651.33	5737.21	5230.17	4923.24	4727.54	4598.59
760 000	9504.77	8824.24	6831.10	5892.27	5371.52	5056.30	4855.31	4722.88
780 000	9754.90	9056.46	7010.86	6047.33	5512.88	5189.36	4983.08	4847.16
800 000	10005.02	9288.68	7190.63	6202.39	5654.23	5322.42	5110.85	4971.45
820 000	10255.15	9520.89	7370.39	6357.45	5795.59	5455.48	5238.62	5095.74
840 000	10505.27	9753.11	7550.16	6512.51	5936.95	5588.54	5366.39	5220.02
860 000	10755.40	9985.33	7729.92	6667.57	6078.30	5721.60	5494.17	5344.31
880 000	11005.52	10217.55	7909.69	6822.63	6219.66	5854.66	5621.94	5468.60
900 000	11255.65	10449.76	8089.45	6977.69	6361.01	5987.72	5749.71	5592.88
920 000	11505.77	10681.98	8269.22	7132.75	6502.37	6120.78	5877.48	5717.17
940 000	11755.90	10914.20	8448.99	7287.81	6643.72	6253.84	6005.25	5841.45
960 000	12006.03	11146.41	8628.75	7442.87	6785.08	6386.90	6133.02	5965.74
980 000	12256.15	11378.63	8808.52	7597.93	6926.44	6519.96	6260.79	6090.03
1000 000	12506.28	11610.85	8988.28	7752.99	7067.79	6653.03	6388.56	6214.31
Coefficient	.012506277	.011610847	.008988283	.007752989	.007067792	.006653025	.006388564	.006214313

MONTHLY AMORTIZING PAYMENTS

AMOUNT	1 YEAR	2 YEARS	3 YEARS	4 YEARS	5 YEARS	6 YEARS	7 YEARS	8 YEARS
10 000	866.42	448.86	309.92	240.62	199.19	171.69	152.15	137.58
20 000	1732.84	897.72	619.83	481.25	398.39	343.39	304.30	275.17
30 000	2599.26	1346.58	929.75	721.87	597.58	515.08	456.46	412.75
40 000	3465.68	1795.44	1239.66	962.50	796.77	686.77	608.61	550.34
50 000	4332.10	2244.30	1549.58	1203.12	995.97	858.47	760.76	687.92
60 000	5198.52	2693.16	1859.49	1443.74	1195.16	1030.16	912.91	825.51
70 000	6064.94	3142.02	2169.41	1684.37	1394.36	1201.85	1065.06	963.09
80 000	6931.36	3590.88	2479.32	1924.99	1593.55	1373.54	1217.21	1100.68
90 000	7797.78	4039.74	2789.24	2165.62	1792.74	1545.24	1369.37	1238.26
100 000	8664.20	4488.60	3099.15	2406.24	1991.94	1716.93	1521.52	1375.85
110 000	9530.63	4937.46	3409.07	2646.86	2191.13	1888.62	1673.67	1513.43
120 000	10397.05	5386.32	3718.98	2887.49	2390.32	2060.32	1825.82	1651.02
130 000	11263.47	5835.18	4028.90	3128.11	2589.52	2232.01	1977.97	1788.60
140 000	12129.89	6284.04	4338.81	3368.74	2788.71	2403.70	2130.13	1926.18
150 000	12996.31	6732.90	4648.73	3609.36	2987.90	2575.40	2282.28	2063.77
160 000	13862.73	7181.76	4958.64	3849.98	3187.10	2747.09	2434.43	2201.35
170 000	14729.15	7630.62	5268.56	4090.61	3386.29	2918.78	2586.58	2338.94
180 000	15595.57	8079.48	5578.47	4331.23	3585.48	3090.48	2738.73	2476.52
190 000	16461.99	8528.34	5888.39	4571.86	3784.68	3262.17	2890.89	2614.11
200 000	17328.41	8977.20	6198.31	4812.48	3983.87	3433.86	3043.04	2751.69
210 000	18194.83	9426.06	6508.22	5053.10	4183.07	3605.55	3195.19	2889.28
220 000	19061.25	9874.92	6818.14	5293.73	4382.26	3777.25	3347.34	3026.86
230 000	19927.67	10323.78	7128.05	5534.35	4581.45	3948.94	3499.49	3164.45
240 000	20794.09	10772.64	7437.97	5774.98	4780.65	4120.63	3651.64	3302.03
250 000	21660.51	11221.50	7747.88	6015.60	4979.84	4292.33	3803.80	3439.62
260 000	22526.93	11670.36	8057.80	6256.22	5179.03	4464.02	3955.95	3577.20
270 000	23393.35	12119.22	8367.71	6496.85	5378.23	4635.71	4108.10	3714.78
280 000	24259.77	12568.08	8677.63	6737.47	5577.42	4807.41	4260.25	3852.37
290 000	25126.19	13016.94	8987.54	6978.10	5776.61	4979.10	4412.40	3989.95
300 000	25992.61	13465.80	9297.46	7218.72	5975.81	5150.79	4564.56	4127.54
320 000	27725.45	14363.52	9917.29	7699.97	6374.20	5494.18	4868.86	4402.71
340 000	29458.30	15261.24	10537.12	8181.22	6772.58	5837.56	5173.16	4677.88
360 000	31191.14	16158.96	11156.95	8662.46	7170.97	6180.95	5477.47	4953.05
380 000	32923.98	17056.68	11776.78	9143.71	7569.36	6524.34	5781.77	5228.22
400 000	34656.82	17954.40	12396.61	9624.96	7967.74	6867.72	6086.07	5503.38
420 000	36389.66	18852.12	13016.44	10106.21	8366.13	7211.11	6390.38	5778.55
440 000	38122.50	19749.84	13636.27	10587.46	8764.52	7554.49	6694.68	6053.72
460 000	39855.34	20647.56	14256.10	11068.70	9162.91	7897.88	6998.99	6328.89
480 000	41588.18	21545.28	14875.93	11549.95	9561.29	8241.27	7303.29	6604.06
500 000	43321.02	22443.00	15495.76	12031.20	9959.68	8584.65	7607.59	6879.23
520 000	45053.86	23340.72	16115.59	12512.45	10358.07	8928.04	7911.90	7154.40
540 000	46786.70	24238.44	16735.42	12993.70	10756.45	9271.43	8216.20	7429.57
560 000	48519.55	25136.16	17355.26	13474.94	11154.84	9614.81	8520.50	7704.74
580 000	50252.39	26033.88	17975.09	13956.19	11553.23	9958.20	8824.81	7979.91
600 000	51985.23	26931.60	18594.92	14437.44	11951.62	10301.58	9129.11	8255.08
620 000	53718.07	27829.32	19214.75	14918.69	12350.00	10644.97	9433.41	8530.25
640 000	55450.91	28727.04	19834.58	15399.94	12748.39	10988.36	9737.72	8805.42
660 000	57183.75	29624.76	20454.41	15881.18	13146.78	11331.74	10042.02	9080.58
680 000	58916.59	30522.48	21074.24	16362.43	13545.17	11675.13	10346.33	9355.75
700 000	60649.43	31420.20	21694.07	16843.68	13943.55	12018.51	10650.63	9630.92
720 000	62382.27	32317.92	22313.90	17324.93	14341.94	12361.90	10954.93	9906.09
740 000	64115.11	33215.64	22933.73	17806.18	14740.33	12705.29	11259.24	10181.26
760 000	65847.95	34113.36	23553.56	18287.42	15138.71	13048.67	11563.54	10456.43
780 000	67580.80	35011.08	24173.39	18768.67	15537.10	13392.06	11867.84	10731.60
800 000	69313.64	35908.80	24793.22	19249.92	15935.49	13735.44	12172.15	11006.77
820 000	71046.48	36806.52	25413.05	19731.17	16333.88	14078.83	12476.45	11281.94
840 000	72779.32	37704.24	26032.88	20212.42	16732.26	14422.22	12780.76	11557.11
860 000	74512.16	38601.96	26652.71	20693.66	17130.65	14765.60	13085.06	11832.28
880 000	76245.00	39499.68	27272.54	21174.91	17529.04	15108.99	13389.36	12107.45
900 000	77977.84	40397.40	27892.37	21656.16	17927.42	15452.38	13693.67	12382.61
920 000	79710.68	41295.12	28512.20	22137.41	18325.81	15795.76	13997.97	12657.78
940 000	81443.52	42192.84	29132.04	22618.66	18724.20	16139.15	14302.27	12932.95
960 000	83176.36	43090.56	29751.87	23099.90	19122.59	16482.53	14606.58	13208.12
980 000	84909.21	43988.28	30371.70	23581.15	19520.97	16825.92	14910.88	13483.29
1000 000	86642.05	44886.00	30991.53	24062.40	19919.36	17169.31	15215.19	13758.46
Coefficient	.086642046	.044886003	.030991527	.024062401	.019919361	.017169306	.015215185	.013758461

MONTHLY AMORTIZING PAYMENTS 7.25%

AMOUNT	9 YEARS	10 YEARS	15 YEARS	20 YEARS	25 YEARS	30 YEARS	35 YEARS	40 YEARS
10 000	126.33	117.40	91.29	79.04	72.28	68.22	65.65	63.97
20 000	252.67	234.80	182.57	158.08	144.56	136.44	131.29	127.93
30 000	379.00	352.20	273.86	237.11	216.84	204.65	196.94	191.90
40 000	505.33	469.60	365.15	316.15	289.12	272.87	262.59	255.87
50 000	631.66	587.01	456.43	395.19	361.40	341.09	328.23	319.84
60 000	758.00	704.41	547.72	474.23	433.68	409.31	393.88	383.80
70 000	884.33	821.81	639.00	553.26	505.96	477.52	459.53	447.77
80 000	1010.66	939.21	730.29	632.30	578.25	545.74	525.17	511.74
90 000	1136.99	1056.61	821.58	711.34	650.53	613.96	590.82	575.70
100 000	1263.33	1174.01	912.86	790.38	722.81	682.18	656.47	639.67
110 000	1389.66	1291.41	1004.15	869.41	795.09	750.39	722.11	703.64
120 000	1515.99	1408.81	1095.44	948.45	867.37	818.61	787.76	767.61
130 000	1642.33	1526.21	1186.72	1027.49	939.65	886.83	853.41	831.57
140 000	1768.66	1643.61	1278.01	1106.53	1011.93	955.05	919.05	895.54
150 000	1894.99	1761.02	1369.29	1185.56	1084.21	1023.26	984.70	959.51
160 000	2021.32	1878.42	1460.58	1264.60	1156.49	1091.48	1050.35	1023.48
170 000	2147.66	1995.82	1551.87	1343.64	1228.77	1159.70	1115.99	1087.44
180 000	2273.99	2113.22	1643.15	1422.68	1301.05	1227.92	1181.64	1151.41
190 000	2400.32	2230.62	1734.44	1501.71	1373.33	1296.13	1247.29	1215.38
200 000	2526.66	2348.02	1825.73	1580.75	1445.61	1364.35	1312.93	1279.34
210 000	2652.99	2465.42	1917.01	1659.79	1517.89	1432.57	1378.58	1343.31
220 000	2779.32	2582.82	2008.30	1738.83	1590.18	1500.79	1444.23	1407.28
230 000	2905.65	2700.22	2099.58	1817.86	1662.46	1569.01	1509.87	1471.25
240 000	3031.99	2817.62	2190.87	1896.90	1734.74	1637.22	1575.52	1535.21
250 000	3158.32	2935.03	2282.16	1975.94	1807.02	1705.44	1641.17	1599.18
260 000	3284.65	3052.43	2373.44	2054.98	1879.30	1773.66	1706.81	1663.15
270 000	3410.98	3169.83	2464.73	2134.02	1951.58	1841.88	1772.46	1727.11
280 000	3537.32	3287.23	2556.02	2213.05	2023.86	1910.09	1838.11	1791.08
290 000	3663.65	3404.63	2647.30	2292.09	2096.14	1978.31	1903.76	1855.05
300 000	3789.98	3522.03	2738.59	2371.13	2168.42	2046.53	1969.40	1919.02
320 000	4042.65	3756.83	2921.16	2529.20	2312.98	2182.96	2100.70	2046.95
340 000	4295.31	3991.64	3103.73	2687.28	2457.54	2319.40	2231.99	2174.88
360 000	4547.98	4226.44	3286.31	2845.35	2602.10	2455.83	2363.28	2302.82
380 000	4800.64	4461.24	3468.88	3003.43	2746.67	2592.27	2494.58	2430.75
400 000	5053.31	4696.04	3651.45	3161.50	2891.23	2728.71	2625.87	2558.69
420 000	5305.98	4930.84	3834.02	3319.58	3035.79	2865.14	2757.16	2686.62
440 000	5558.64	5165.65	4016.60	3477.65	3180.35	3001.58	2888.46	2814.56
460 000	5811.31	5400.45	4199.17	3635.73	3324.91	3138.01	3019.75	2942.49
480 000	6063.97	5635.25	4381.74	3793.80	3469.47	3274.45	3151.04	3070.43
500 000	6316.64	5870.05	4564.31	3951.88	3614.03	3410.88	3282.34	3198.36
520 000	6569.30	6104.85	4746.89	4109.96	3758.60	3547.32	3413.63	3326.29
540 000	6821.97	6339.66	4929.46	4268.03	3903.16	3683.75	3544.92	3454.23
560 000	7074.63	6574.46	5112.03	4426.11	4047.72	3820.19	3676.22	3582.16
580 000	7327.30	6809.26	5294.60	4584.18	4192.28	3956.62	3807.51	3710.10
600 000	7579.97	7044.06	5477.18	4742.26	4336.84	4093.06	3938.80	3838.03
620 000	7832.63	7278.86	5659.75	4900.33	4481.40	4229.49	4070.10	3965.97
640 000	8085.30	7513.67	5842.32	5058.41	4625.96	4365.93	4201.39	4093.90
660 000	8337.96	7748.47	6024.90	5216.48	4770.53	4502.36	4332.68	4221.83
680 000	8590.63	7983.27	6207.47	5374.56	4915.09	4638.80	4463.98	4349.77
700 000	8843.29	8218.07	6390.04	5532.63	5059.65	4775.23	4595.27	4477.70
720 000	9095.96	8452.87	6572.61	5690.71	5204.21	4911.67	4726.56	4605.64
740 000	9348.62	8687.68	6755.19	5848.78	5348.77	5048.10	4857.86	4733.57
760 000	9601.29	8922.48	6937.76	6006.86	5493.33	5184.54	4989.15	4861.51
780 000	9853.96	9157.28	7120.33	6164.93	5637.89	5320.98	5120.44	4989.44
800 000	10106.62	9392.08	7302.90	6323.01	5782.46	5457.41	5251.74	5117.38
820 000	10359.29	9626.89	7485.48	6481.08	5927.02	5593.85	5383.03	5245.31
840 000	10611.95	9861.69	7668.05	6639.16	6071.58	5730.28	5514.33	5373.24
860 000	10864.62	10096.49	7850.62	6797.23	6216.14	5866.72	5645.62	5501.18
880 000	11117.28	10331.29	8033.19	6955.31	6360.70	6003.15	5776.91	5629.11
900 000	11369.95	10566.09	8215.77	7113.38	6505.26	6139.59	5908.21	5757.05
920 000	11622.61	10800.90	8398.34	7271.46	6649.82	6276.02	6039.50	5884.98
940 000	11875.28	11035.70	8580.91	7429.53	6794.38	6412.46	6170.79	6012.92
960 000	12127.94	11270.50	8763.48	7587.61	6938.95	6548.89	6302.09	6140.85
980 000	12380.61	11505.30	8946.06	7745.68	7083.51	6685.33	6433.38	6268.78
1000 000	12633.28	11740.10	9128.63	7903.76	7228.07	6821.76	6564.67	6396.72
Coefficient	.012653276	.011740104	.009128629	.007903760	.007228069	.006821763	.006564673	.006396719

21

7.50%   MONTHLY AMORTIZING PAYMENTS

AMOUNT	1 YEAR	2 YEARS	3 YEARS	4 YEARS	5 YEARS	6 YEARS	7 YEARS	8 YEARS
10 000	867.57	450.00	311.06	241.79	200.38	172.90	153.38	138.84
20 000	1735.15	899.99	622.12	483.58	400.76	345.80	306.77	277.68
30 000	2602.72	1349.99	933.19	725.37	601.14	518.70	460.15	416.52
40 000	3470.30	1799.98	1244.25	967.16	801.52	691.60	613.53	555.35
50 000	4337.87	2249.98	1555.31	1208.95	1001.90	864.51	766.91	694.19
60 000	5205.45	2699.98	1866.37	1450.73	1202.28	1037.41	920.30	833.03
70 000	6073.02	3149.97	2177.44	1692.52	1402.66	1210.31	1073.68	971.87
80 000	6940.59	3599.97	2488.50	1934.31	1603.04	1383.21	1227.06	1110.71
90 000	7808.17	4049.96	2799.56	2176.10	1803.42	1556.11	1380.44	1249.55
100 000	8675.74	4499.96	3110.62	2417.89	2003.79	1729.01	1533.83	1388.39
110 000	9543.32	4949.96	3421.68	2659.68	2204.17	1901.91	1687.21	1527.23
120 000	10410.89	5399.95	3732.75	2901.47	2404.55	2074.81	1840.59	1666.06
130 000	11278.46	5849.95	4043.81	3143.26	2604.93	2247.71	1993.98	1804.90
140 000	12146.04	6299.94	4354.87	3385.05	2805.31	2420.62	2147.36	1943.74
150 000	13013.61	6749.94	4665.93	3626.84	3005.69	2593.52	2300.74	2082.58
160 000	13881.19	7199.93	4977.00	3868.63	3206.07	2766.42	2454.12	2221.42
170 000	14748.76	7649.93	5288.06	4110.41	3406.45	2939.32	2607.51	2360.26
180 000	15616.34	8099.93	5599.12	4352.20	3606.83	3112.22	2760.89	2499.10
190 000	16483.91	8549.92	5910.18	4593.99	3807.21	3285.12	2914.27	2637.94
200 000	17351.48	8999.92	6221.24	4835.78	4007.59	3458.02	3067.66	2776.77
210 000	18219.06	9449.91	6532.31	5077.57	4207.97	3630.92	3221.04	2915.61
220 000	19086.63	9899.91	6843.37	5319.36	4408.35	3803.82	3374.42	3054.45
230 000	19954.21	10349.91	7154.43	5561.15	4608.73	3976.73	3527.80	3193.29
240 000	20821.78	10799.90	7465.49	5802.94	4809.11	4149.63	3681.19	3332.13
250 000	21689.35	11249.90	7776.55	6044.73	5009.49	4322.53	3834.57	3470.97
260 000	22556.93	11699.89	8087.62	6286.51	5209.87	4495.43	3987.95	3609.81
270 000	23424.50	12149.89	8398.68	6528.30	5410.25	4668.33	4141.33	3748.65
280 000	24292.08	12599.89	8709.74	6770.09	5610.63	4841.23	4294.72	3887.48
290 000	25159.65	13049.88	9020.80	7011.88	5811.00	5014.13	4448.10	4026.32
300 000	26027.23	13499.88	9331.87	7253.67	6011.38	5187.03	4601.48	4165.16
320 000	27762.37	14399.87	9953.99	7737.25	6412.14	5532.84	4908.25	4442.84
340 000	29497.52	15299.86	10576.11	8220.83	6812.90	5878.64	5215.01	4720.52
360 000	31232.67	16199.85	11198.24	8704.40	7213.66	6224.44	5521.78	4998.19
380 000	32967.82	17099.85	11820.36	9187.98	7614.42	6570.24	5828.55	5275.87
400 000	34702.97	17999.84	12442.49	9671.56	8015.18	6916.04	6135.31	5553.55
420 000	36438.12	18899.83	13064.61	10155.14	8415.94	7261.85	6442.08	5831.23
440 000	38173.26	19799.82	13686.74	10638.72	8816.70	7607.65	6748.84	6108.90
460 000	39908.41	20699.81	14308.86	11122.29	9217.46	7953.45	7055.61	6386.58
480 000	41643.56	21599.80	14930.99	11605.87	9618.21	8299.25	7362.37	6664.26
500 000	43378.71	22499.80	15553.11	12089.45	10018.97	8645.06	7669.14	6941.94
520 000	45113.86	23399.79	16175.23	12573.03	10419.73	8990.86	7975.90	7219.61
540 000	46849.01	24299.78	16797.36	13056.61	10820.49	9336.66	8282.67	7497.29
560 000	48584.15	25199.77	17419.48	13540.19	11221.25	9682.46	8589.44	7774.97
580 000	50319.30	26099.76	18041.61	14023.76	11622.01	10028.26	8896.20	8052.65
600 000	52054.45	26999.76	18663.73	14507.34	12022.77	10374.07	9202.97	8330.32
620 000	53789.60	27899.75	19285.86	14990.92	12423.53	10719.87	9509.73	8608.00
640 000	55524.75	28799.74	19907.98	15474.50	12824.29	11065.67	9816.50	8885.68
660 000	57259.90	29699.73	20530.10	15958.08	13225.05	11411.47	10123.26	9163.35
680 000	58995.04	30599.72	21152.23	16441.65	13625.80	11757.28	10430.03	9441.03
700 000	60730.19	31499.72	21774.35	16925.23	14026.56	12103.08	10736.79	9718.71
720 000	62465.34	32399.71	22396.48	17408.81	14427.32	12448.88	11043.56	9996.39
740 000	64200.49	33299.70	23018.60	17892.39	14828.08	12794.68	11350.32	10274.06
760 000	65935.64	34199.69	23640.73	18375.97	15228.84	13140.48	11657.09	10551.74
780 000	67670.79	35099.68	24262.85	18859.54	15629.60	13486.29	11963.86	10829.42
800 000	69405.93	35999.67	24884.98	19343.12	16030.36	13832.09	12270.62	11107.10
820 000	71141.08	36899.67	25507.10	19826.70	16431.12	14177.89	12577.39	11384.77
840 000	72876.23	37799.66	26129.22	20310.28	16831.88	14523.69	12884.15	11662.45
860 000	74611.38	38699.65	26751.35	20793.86	17232.63	14869.50	13190.92	11940.13
880 000	76346.53	39599.64	27373.47	21277.43	17633.39	15215.30	13497.68	12217.81
900 000	78081.68	40499.63	27995.60	21761.01	18034.15	15561.10	13804.45	12495.48
920 000	79816.82	41399.63	28617.72	22244.59	18434.91	15906.90	14111.21	12773.16
940 000	81551.97	42299.62	29239.85	22728.17	18835.67	16252.70	14417.98	13050.84
960 000	83287.12	43199.61	29861.97	23211.75	19236.43	16598.51	14724.75	13328.52
980 000	85022.27	44099.60	30484.09	23695.32	19637.19	16944.31	15031.51	13606.19
1000 000	86757.42	44999.59	31106.22	24178.90	20037.95	17290.11	15338.28	13883.87
Coefficient	.086757417	.044999593	.031106219	.024178902	.020037947	.017290111	.015338277	.013883871

22

AMOUNT	9 YEARS	10 YEARS	15 YEARS	20 YEARS	25 YEARS	30 YEARS	35 YEARS	40 YEARS
10 000	127.61	118.70	92.70	80.56	73.90	69.92	67.42	65.81
20 000	255.22	237.40	185.40	161.12	147.80	139.84	134.85	131.61
30 000	382.83	356.11	278.10	241.68	221.70	209.76	202.27	197.42
40 000	510.44	474.81	370.80	322.24	295.60	279.69	269.70	263.23
50 000	638.05	593.51	463.51	402.80	369.50	349.61	337.12	329.04
60 000	765.66	712.21	556.21	483.36	443.39	419.53	404.55	394.84
70 000	893.27	830.91	648.91	563.92	517.29	489.45	471.97	460.65
80 000	1020.88	949.61	741.61	644.47	591.19	559.37	539.39	526.46
90 000	1148.49	1068.32	834.31	725.03	665.09	629.29	606.82	592.26
100 000	1276.10	1187.02	927.01	805.59	738.99	699.21	674.24	658.07
110 000	1403.71	1305.72	1019.71	886.15	812.89	769.14	741.67	723.88
120 000	1531.32	1424.42	1112.41	966.71	886.79	839.06	809.09	789.68
130 000	1658.93	1543.12	1205.12	1047.27	960.69	908.98	876.52	855.49
140 000	1786.54	1661.82	1297.82	1127.83	1034.59	978.90	943.94	921.30
150 000	1914.15	1780.53	1390.52	1208.39	1108.49	1048.82	1011.36	987.11
160 000	2041.76	1899.23	1483.22	1288.95	1182.39	1118.74	1078.79	1052.91
170 000	2169.37	2017.93	1575.92	1369.51	1256.29	1188.66	1146.21	1118.72
180 000	2296.98	2136.63	1668.62	1450.07	1330.18	1258.59	1213.64	1184.53
190 000	2424.59	2255.33	1761.32	1530.63	1404.08	1328.51	1281.06	1250.33
200 000	2552.20	2374.04	1854.03	1611.19	1477.98	1398.43	1348.49	1316.14
210 000	2679.81	2492.74	1946.73	1691.75	1551.88	1468.35	1415.91	1381.95
220 000	2807.42	2611.44	2039.43	1772.31	1625.78	1538.27	1483.33	1447.76
230 000	2935.03	2730.14	2132.13	1852.86	1699.68	1608.19	1550.76	1513.56
240 000	3062.64	2848.84	2224.83	1933.42	1773.58	1678.11	1618.18	1579.37
250 000	3190.25	2967.54	2317.53	2013.98	1847.48	1748.04	1685.61	1645.18
260 000	3317.86	3086.25	2410.23	2094.54	1921.38	1817.96	1753.03	1710.98
270 000	3445.47	3204.95	2502.93	2175.10	1995.28	1887.88	1820.46	1776.79
280 000	3573.08	3323.65	2595.63	2255.66	2069.18	1957.80	1887.88	1842.60
290 000	3700.69	3442.35	2688.34	2336.22	2143.07	2027.72	1955.30	1908.41
300 000	3828.30	3561.05	2781.04	2416.78	2216.97	2097.64	2022.73	1974.21
320 000	4083.53	3798.46	2966.44	2577.90	2364.77	2237.49	2157.58	2105.83
340 000	4338.75	4035.86	3151.84	2739.02	2512.57	2377.33	2292.42	2237.44
360 000	4593.97	4273.26	3337.24	2900.14	2660.37	2517.17	2427.27	2369.05
380 000	4849.19	4510.67	3522.65	3061.25	2808.17	2657.02	2562.12	2500.67
400 000	5104.41	4748.07	3708.05	3222.37	2955.96	2796.86	2696.97	2632.28
420 000	5359.63	4985.47	3893.45	3383.49	3103.76	2936.70	2831.82	2763.90
440 000	5614.85	5222.88	4078.85	3544.61	3251.56	3076.54	2966.67	2895.51
460 000	5870.07	5460.28	4264.26	3705.73	3399.36	3216.39	3101.52	3027.13
480 000	6125.29	5697.68	4449.66	3866.85	3547.16	3356.23	3236.36	3158.74
500 000	6380.51	5935.09	4635.06	4027.97	3694.96	3496.07	3371.21	3290.35
520 000	6635.73	6172.49	4820.46	4189.08	3842.75	3635.92	3506.06	3421.97
540 000	6890.95	6409.90	5005.87	4350.20	3990.55	3775.76	3640.91	3553.58
560 000	7146.17	6647.30	5191.27	4511.32	4138.35	3915.60	3775.76	3685.20
580 000	7401.39	6884.70	5376.67	4672.44	4286.15	4055.44	3910.61	3816.81
600 000	7656.61	7122.11	5562.07	4833.56	4433.95	4195.29	4045.46	3948.42
620 000	7911.83	7359.51	5747.48	4994.68	4581.75	4335.13	4180.30	4080.04
640 000	8167.05	7596.91	5932.88	5155.80	4729.54	4474.97	4315.15	4211.65
660 000	8422.27	7834.32	6118.28	5316.92	4877.34	4614.82	4450.00	4343.27
680 000	8677.49	8071.72	6303.68	5478.03	5025.14	4754.66	4584.85	4474.88
700 000	8932.71	8309.12	6489.09	5639.15	5172.94	4894.50	4719.70	4606.49
720 000	9187.93	8546.53	6674.49	5800.27	5320.74	5034.34	4854.55	4738.11
740 000	9443.15	8783.93	6859.89	5961.39	5468.53	5174.19	4989.40	4869.72
760 000	9698.37	9021.33	7045.29	6122.51	5616.33	5314.03	5124.24	5001.34
780 000	9953.59	9258.74	7230.70	6283.63	5764.13	5453.87	5259.09	5132.95
800 000	10208.81	9496.14	7416.10	6444.75	5911.93	5593.72	5393.94	5264.57
820 000	10464.03	9733.55	7601.50	6605.86	6059.73	5733.56	5528.79	5396.18
840 000	10719.25	9970.95	7786.90	6766.98	6207.53	5873.40	5663.64	5527.79
860 000	10974.47	10208.35	7972.31	6928.10	6355.32	6013.24	5798.49	5659.41
880 000	11229.69	10445.76	8157.71	7089.22	6503.12	6153.09	5933.33	5791.02
900 000	11484.91	10683.16	8343.11	7250.34	6650.92	6292.93	6068.18	5922.64
920 000	11740.13	10920.56	8528.51	7411.46	6798.72	6432.77	6203.03	6054.25
940 000	11995.36	11157.97	8713.92	7572.58	6946.52	6572.62	6337.88	6185.86
960 000	12250.58	11395.37	8899.32	7733.69	7094.32	6712.46	6472.73	6317.48
980 000	12505.80	11632.77	9084.72	7894.81	7242.11	6852.30	6607.58	6449.09
1000 000	12761.02	11870.18	9270.12	8055.93	7389.91	6992.15	6742.43	6580.71
Coefficient	.012761016	.011870177	.009270124	.008055932	.007389912	.006992145	.006742426	.006580707

23

MONTHLY AMORTIZING PAYMENTS

AMOUNT	1 YEAR	2 YEARS	3 YEARS	4 YEARS	5 YEARS	6 YEARS	7 YEARS	8 YEARS
10 000	868.73	451.13	312.21	242.96	201.57	174.11	154.62	140.10
20 000	1737.46	902.27	624.42	485.91	403.14	348.23	309.24	280.20
30 000	2606.19	1353.40	936.63	728.87	604.71	522.34	463.86	420.30
40 000	3474.92	1804.53	1248.85	971.83	806.28	696.46	618.48	560.40
50 000	4343.64	2255.67	1561.06	1214.79	1007.85	870.57	773.10	700.50
60 000	5212.37	2706.80	1873.27	1457.74	1209.42	1044.69	927.72	840.60
70 000	6081.10	3157.93	2185.48	1700.70	1410.99	1218.80	1082.34	980.70
80 000	6949.83	3609.07	2497.69	1943.66	1612.56	1392.91	1236.96	1120.80
90 000	7818.56	4060.20	2809.90	2186.62	1814.13	1567.03	1391.58	1260.89
100 000	8687.29	4511.34	3122.12	2429.57	2015.70	1741.14	1546.20	1400.99
110 000	9556.02	4962.47	3434.33	2672.53	2217.27	1915.26	1700.81	1541.09
120 000	10424.75	5413.60	3746.54	2915.49	2418.84	2089.37	1855.43	1681.19
130 000	11293.48	5864.74	4058.75	3158.45	2620.40	2263.49	2010.05	1821.29
140 000	12162.20	6315.87	4370.96	3401.40	2821.97	2437.60	2164.67	1961.39
150 000	13030.93	6767.00	4683.17	3644.36	3023.54	2611.71	2319.29	2101.49
160 000	13899.66	7218.14	4995.39	3887.32	3225.11	2785.83	2473.91	2241.59
170 000	14768.39	7669.27	5307.60	4130.28	3426.68	2959.94	2628.53	2381.69
180 000	15637.12	8120.40	5619.81	4373.23	3628.25	3134.06	2783.15	2521.79
190 000	16505.85	8571.54	5932.02	4616.19	3829.82	3308.17	2937.77	2661.89
200 000	17374.58	9022.67	6244.23	4859.15	4031.39	3482.28	3092.39	2801.99
210 000	18243.31	9473.80	6556.44	5102.11	4232.96	3656.40	3247.01	2942.09
220 000	19112.04	9924.94	6868.66	5345.06	4434.53	3830.51	3401.63	3082.19
230 000	19980.76	10376.07	7180.87	5588.02	4636.10	4004.63	3556.25	3222.29
240 000	20849.49	10827.20	7493.08	5830.98	4837.67	4178.74	3710.87	3362.39
250 000	21718.22	11278.34	7805.29	6073.94	5039.24	4352.86	3865.49	3502.49
260 000	22586.95	11729.47	8117.50	6316.89	5240.81	4526.97	4020.11	3642.59
270 000	23455.68	12180.61	8429.71	6559.85	5442.38	4701.08	4174.73	3782.68
280 000	24324.41	12631.74	8741.93	6802.81	5643.95	4875.20	4329.35	3922.78
290 000	25193.14	13082.87	9054.14	7045.77	5845.52	5049.31	4483.97	4062.88
300 000	26061.87	13534.01	9366.35	7288.72	6047.09	5223.43	4638.59	4202.98
320 000	27799.32	14436.27	9990.77	7774.64	6450.23	5571.66	4947.82	4483.18
340 000	29536.78	15338.54	10615.20	8260.55	6853.37	5919.88	5257.06	4763.38
360 000	31274.24	16240.81	11239.62	8746.47	7256.51	6268.11	5566.30	5043.58
380 000	33011.70	17143.07	11864.04	9232.38	7659.64	6616.34	5875.54	5323.78
400 000	34749.16	18045.34	12488.47	9718.30	8062.78	6964.57	6184.78	5603.98
420 000	36486.61	18947.61	13112.89	10204.21	8465.92	7312.80	6494.02	5884.18
440 000	38224.07	19849.88	13737.31	10690.13	8869.06	7661.03	6803.26	6164.38
460 000	39961.53	20752.14	14361.74	11176.04	9272.20	8009.26	7112.50	6444.57
480 000	41698.99	21654.41	14986.16	11661.96	9675.34	8357.48	7421.74	6724.77
500 000	43436.44	22556.68	15610.58	12147.87	10078.48	8705.71	7730.98	7004.97
520 000	45173.90	23458.94	16235.01	12633.79	10481.62	9053.94	8040.22	7285.17
540 000	46911.36	24361.21	16859.43	13119.70	10884.76	9402.17	8349.45	7565.37
560 000	48648.82	25263.48	17483.85	13605.62	11287.90	9750.40	8658.69	7845.57
580 000	50386.28	26165.75	18108.28	14091.53	11691.04	10098.63	8967.93	8125.77
600 000	52123.73	27068.01	18732.70	14577.45	12094.18	10446.85	9277.17	8405.97
620 000	53861.19	27970.28	19357.12	15063.36	12497.31	10795.08	9586.41	8686.17
640 000	55598.65	28872.55	19981.55	15549.27	12900.45	11143.31	9895.65	8966.36
660 000	57336.11	29774.81	20605.97	16035.19	13303.59	11491.54	10204.89	9246.56
680 000	59073.56	30677.08	21230.39	16521.10	13706.73	11839.77	10514.13	9526.76
700 000	60811.02	31579.35	21854.82	17007.02	14109.87	12188.00	10823.37	9806.96
720 000	62548.48	32481.61	22479.24	17492.93	14513.01	12536.23	11132.61	10087.16
740 000	64285.94	33383.88	23103.66	17978.85	14916.15	12884.45	11441.85	10367.36
760 000	66023.39	34286.15	23728.09	18464.76	15319.29	13232.68	11751.08	10647.56
780 000	67760.85	35188.42	24352.51	18950.68	15722.43	13580.91	12060.32	10927.76
800 000	69498.31	36090.68	24976.93	19436.59	16125.57	13929.14	12369.56	11207.96
820 000	71235.77	36992.95	25601.36	19922.51	16528.71	14277.37	12678.80	11488.15
840 000	72973.23	37895.22	26225.78	20408.42	16931.85	14625.60	12988.04	11768.35
860 000	74710.68	38797.48	26850.20	20894.34	17334.98	14973.82	13297.28	12048.55
880 000	76448.14	39699.75	27474.63	21380.25	17738.12	15322.05	13606.52	12328.75
900 000	78185.60	40602.02	28099.05	21866.17	18141.26	15670.28	13915.76	12608.95
920 000	79923.06	41504.29	28723.47	22352.08	18544.40	16018.51	14225.00	12889.15
940 000	81660.51	42406.55	29347.90	22838.00	18947.54	16366.74	14534.24	13169.35
960 000	83397.97	43308.82	29972.32	23323.91	19350.68	16714.97	14843.47	13449.55
980 000	85135.43	44211.09	30596.74	23809.83	19753.82	17063.20	15152.71	13729.75
1000 000	86872.89	45113.35	31221.17	24295.74	20156.96	17411.42	15461.95	14009.94
Coefficient	.086872888	.045113354	.031221166	.024295742	.020156959	.017411424	.015461953	.014009944

MONTHLY AMORTIZING PAYMENTS — 7.75%

AMOUNT	9 YEARS	10 YEARS	15 YEARS	20 YEARS	25 YEARS	30 YEARS	35 YEARS	40 YEARS
10 000	128.89	120.01	94.13	82.09	75.53	71.64	69.22	67.66
20 000	257.79	240.02	188.26	164.19	151.07	143.28	138.44	135.32
30 000	386.68	360.03	282.38	246.28	226.60	214.92	207.65	202.99
40 000	515.58	480.04	376.51	328.38	302.13	286.56	276.87	270.65
50 000	644.47	600.05	470.64	410.47	377.66	358.21	346.09	338.31
60 000	773.37	720.06	564.77	492.57	453.20	429.85	415.31	405.97
70 000	902.26	840.07	658.89	574.66	528.73	501.49	484.52	473.63
80 000	1031.16	960.09	753.02	656.76	604.26	573.13	553.74	541.30
90 000	1160.05	1080.10	847.15	738.85	679.80	644.77	622.96	608.96
100 000	1288.95	1200.11	941.28	820.95	755.33	716.41	692.18	676.62
110 000	1417.84	1320.12	1035.40	903.04	830.86	788.05	761.39	744.28
120 000	1546.74	1440.13	1129.53	985.14	906.39	859.69	830.61	811.94
130 000	1675.63	1560.14	1223.66	1067.23	981.93	931.34	899.83	879.61
140 000	1804.53	1680.15	1317.79	1149.33	1057.46	1002.98	969.05	947.27
150 000	1933.42	1800.16	1411.91	1231.42	1132.99	1074.62	1038.26	1014.93
160 000	2062.32	1920.17	1506.04	1313.52	1208.53	1146.26	1107.48	1082.59
170 000	2191.21	2040.18	1600.17	1395.61	1284.06	1217.90	1176.70	1150.25
180 000	2320.11	2160.19	1694.30	1477.71	1359.59	1289.54	1245.92	1217.92
190 000	2449.00	2280.20	1788.42	1559.80	1435.12	1361.18	1315.13	1285.58
200 000	2577.90	2400.21	1882.55	1641.90	1510.66	1432.82	1384.35	1353.24
210 000	2706.79	2520.22	1976.68	1723.99	1586.19	1504.47	1453.57	1420.90
220 000	2835.69	2640.23	2070.81	1806.09	1661.72	1576.11	1522.79	1488.56
230 000	2964.58	2760.24	2164.93	1888.18	1737.26	1647.75	1592.00	1556.23
240 000	3093.48	2880.26	2259.06	1970.28	1812.79	1719.39	1661.22	1623.89
250 000	3222.37	3000.27	2353.19	2052.37	1888.32	1791.03	1730.44	1691.55
260 000	3351.27	3120.28	2447.32	2134.47	1963.85	1862.67	1799.66	1759.21
270 000	3480.16	3240.29	2541.44	2216.56	2039.39	1934.31	1868.87	1826.87
280 000	3609.06	3360.30	2635.57	2298.66	2114.92	2005.95	1938.09	1894.54
290 000	3737.95	3480.31	2729.70	2380.75	2190.45	2077.60	2007.31	1962.20
300 000	3866.85	3600.32	2823.83	2462.85	2265.99	2149.24	2076.53	2029.86
320 000	4124.64	3840.34	3012.08	2627.04	2417.05	2292.52	2214.96	2165.18
340 000	4382.43	4080.36	3200.34	2791.23	2568.12	2435.80	2353.40	2300.51
360 000	4640.22	4320.38	3388.59	2955.41	2719.18	2579.08	2491.83	2435.83
380 000	4898.01	4560.40	3576.85	3119.60	2870.25	2722.37	2630.27	2571.16
400 000	5155.80	4800.43	3765.10	3283.79	3021.32	2865.65	2768.70	2706.48
420 000	5413.59	5040.45	3953.36	3447.98	3172.38	3008.93	2907.14	2841.80
440 000	5671.38	5280.47	4141.61	3612.17	3323.45	3152.21	3045.57	2977.13
460 000	5929.17	5520.49	4329.87	3776.36	3474.51	3295.50	3184.01	3112.45
480 000	6186.96	5760.51	4518.12	3940.55	3625.58	3438.78	3322.44	3247.78
500 000	6444.75	6000.53	4706.38	4104.74	3776.64	3582.06	3460.88	3383.10
520 000	6702.54	6240.55	4894.63	4268.93	3927.71	3725.34	3599.31	3518.42
540 000	6960.33	6480.57	5082.89	4433.12	4078.78	3868.63	3737.75	3653.75
560 000	7218.12	6720.60	5271.14	4597.31	4229.84	4011.91	3876.19	3789.07
580 000	7475.91	6960.62	5459.40	4761.50	4380.91	4155.19	4014.62	3924.40
600 000	7733.70	7200.64	5647.65	4925.69	4531.97	4298.47	4153.06	4059.72
620 000	7991.49	7440.66	5835.91	5089.88	4683.04	4441.76	4291.49	4195.04
640 000	8249.28	7680.68	6024.17	5254.07	4834.10	4585.04	4429.93	4330.37
660 000	8507.07	7920.70	6212.42	5418.26	4985.17	4728.32	4568.36	4465.69
680 000	8764.86	8160.72	6400.68	5582.45	5136.24	4871.60	4706.80	4601.02
700 000	9022.65	8400.74	6588.93	5746.64	5287.30	5014.89	4845.23	4736.34
720 000	9280.44	8640.77	6777.19	5910.83	5438.37	5158.17	4983.67	4871.66
740 000	9538.23	8880.79	6965.44	6075.02	5589.43	5301.45	5122.10	5006.99
760 000	9796.02	9120.81	7153.70	6239.21	5740.50	5444.73	5260.54	5142.31
780 000	10053.81	9360.83	7341.95	6403.40	5891.56	5588.02	5398.97	5277.64
800 000	10311.60	9600.85	7530.21	6567.59	6042.63	5731.30	5537.41	5412.96
820 000	10569.39	9840.87	7718.46	6731.78	6193.70	5874.58	5675.84	5548.28
840 000	10827.18	10080.89	7906.72	6895.97	6344.76	6017.86	5814.28	5683.61
860 000	11084.97	10320.91	8094.97	7060.16	6495.83	6161.14	5952.71	5818.93
880 000	11342.76	10560.94	8283.23	7224.35	6646.89	6304.43	6091.15	5954.26
900 000	11600.55	10800.96	8471.48	7388.54	6797.96	6447.71	6229.58	6089.58
920 000	11858.34	11040.98	8659.74	7552.73	6949.02	6590.99	6368.02	6224.90
940 000	12116.13	11281.00	8847.99	7716.92	7100.09	6734.27	6506.45	6360.23
960 000	12373.92	11521.02	9036.25	7881.11	7251.16	6877.56	6644.89	6495.55
980 000	12631.71	11761.04	9224.50	8045.30	7402.22	7020.84	6783.32	6630.88
1000 000	12889.50	12001.06	9412.76	8209.49	7553.29	7164.12	6921.76	6766.20
Coefficient	.012889497	.012001063	.009412758	.008209486	.007553288	.007164122	.006921759	.006766199

AMOUNT	1 YEAR	2 YEARS	3 YEARS	4 YEARS	5 YEARS	6 YEARS	7 YEARS	8 YEARS
10 000	869.88	452.27	313.36	244.13	202.76	175.33	155.86	141.37
20 000	1739.77	904.55	626.73	488.26	405.53	350.66	311.72	282.73
30 000	2609.65	1356.82	940.09	732.39	608.29	526.00	467.59	424.10
40 000	3479.54	1809.09	1253.45	976.52	811.06	701.33	623.45	565.47
50 000	4349.42	2261.36	1566.82	1220.65	1013.82	876.66	779.31	706.83
60 000	5219.31	2713.64	1880.18	1464.78	1216.58	1051.99	935.17	848.20
70 000	6089.19	3165.91	2193.55	1708.90	1419.35	1227.33	1091.03	989.57
80 000	6959.07	3618.18	2506.91	1953.03	1622.11	1402.66	1246.90	1130.93
90 000	7828.96	4070.46	2820.27	2197.16	1824.88	1577.99	1402.76	1272.30
100 000	8698.84	4522.73	3133.64	2441.29	2027.64	1753.32	1558.62	1413.67
110 000	9568.73	4975.00	3447.00	2685.42	2230.40	1928.66	1714.48	1555.03
120 000	10438.61	5427.28	3760.36	2929.55	2433.17	2103.99	1870.35	1696.40
130 000	11308.50	5879.55	4073.73	3173.68	2635.93	2279.32	2026.21	1837.77
140 000	12178.38	6331.82	4387.09	3417.81	2838.70	2454.65	2182.07	1979.14
150 000	13048.26	6784.09	4700.45	3661.94	3041.46	2629.99	2337.93	2120.50
160 000	13918.15	7236.37	5013.82	3906.07	3244.22	2805.32	2493.79	2261.87
170 000	14788.03	7688.64	5327.18	4150.20	3446.99	2980.65	2649.66	2403.24
180 000	15657.92	8140.91	5640.55	4394.33	3649.75	3155.98	2805.52	2544.60
190 000	16527.80	8593.19	5953.91	4638.46	3852.51	3331.32	2961.38	2685.97
200 000	17397.69	9045.46	6267.27	4882.58	4055.28	3506.65	3117.24	2827.34
210 000	18267.57	9497.73	6580.64	5126.71	4258.04	3681.98	3273.10	2968.70
220 000	19137.45	9950.00	6894.00	5370.84	4460.81	3857.31	3428.97	3110.07
230 000	20007.34	10402.28	7207.36	5614.97	4663.57	4032.65	3584.83	3251.44
240 000	20877.22	10854.55	7520.73	5859.10	4866.33	4207.98	3740.69	3392.80
250 000	21747.11	11306.82	7834.09	6103.23	5069.10	4383.31	3896.55	3534.17
260 000	22616.99	11759.10	8147.45	6347.36	5271.86	4558.64	4052.42	3675.54
270 000	23486.88	12211.37	8460.82	6591.49	5474.63	4733.98	4208.28	3816.90
280 000	24356.76	12663.64	8774.18	6835.62	5677.39	4909.31	4364.14	3958.27
290 000	25226.64	13115.92	9087.55	7079.75	5880.15	5084.64	4520.00	4099.64
300 000	26096.53	13568.19	9400.91	7323.88	6082.92	5259.97	4675.86	4241.00
320 000	27836.30	14472.73	10027.64	7812.14	6488.45	5610.64	4987.59	4523.74
340 000	29576.07	15377.28	10654.36	8300.39	6893.97	5961.30	5299.31	4806.47
360 000	31315.83	16281.83	11281.09	8788.65	7299.50	6311.97	5611.04	5089.20
380 000	33055.60	17186.37	11907.82	9276.91	7705.03	6662.63	5922.76	5371.94
400 000	34795.37	18090.92	12534.55	9765.17	8110.56	7013.30	6234.49	5654.67
420 000	36535.14	18995.46	13161.27	10253.43	8516.09	7363.96	6546.21	5937.41
440 000	38274.91	19900.01	13788.00	10741.69	8921.61	7714.63	6857.93	6220.14
460 000	40014.68	20804.56	14414.73	11229.94	9327.14	8065.29	7169.66	6502.87
480 000	41754.45	21709.10	15041.45	11718.20	9732.67	8415.96	7481.38	6785.61
500 000	43494.21	22613.65	15668.18	12206.46	10138.20	8766.62	7793.11	7068.34
520 000	45233.98	23518.19	16294.91	12694.72	10543.72	9117.29	8104.83	7351.07
540 000	46973.75	24422.74	16921.64	13182.98	10949.25	9467.95	8416.56	7633.81
560 000	48713.52	25327.28	17548.36	13671.24	11354.78	9818.61	8728.28	7916.54
580 000	50453.29	26231.83	18175.09	14159.49	11760.31	10169.28	9040.00	8199.27
600 000	52193.06	27136.38	18801.82	14647.75	12165.84	10519.94	9351.73	8482.01
620 000	53932.83	28040.92	19428.55	15136.01	12571.36	10870.61	9663.45	8764.74
640 000	55672.59	28945.47	20055.27	15624.27	12976.89	11221.27	9975.18	9047.47
660 000	57412.36	29850.01	20682.00	16112.53	13382.42	11571.94	10286.90	9330.21
680 000	59152.13	30754.56	21308.73	16600.79	13787.95	11922.60	10598.63	9612.94
700 000	60891.90	31659.11	21935.45	17089.05	14193.48	12273.27	10910.35	9895.68
720 000	62631.67	32563.65	22562.18	17577.30	14599.00	12623.93	11222.07	10178.41
740 000	64371.44	33468.20	23188.91	18065.56	15004.53	12974.60	11533.80	10461.14
760 000	66111.21	34372.74	23815.64	18553.82	15410.06	13325.26	11845.52	10743.88
780 000	67850.97	35277.29	24442.36	19042.08	15815.59	13675.93	12157.25	11026.61
800 000	69590.74	36181.84	25069.09	19530.34	16221.12	14026.59	12468.97	11309.34
820 000	71330.51	37086.38	25695.82	20018.60	16626.64	14377.26	12780.70	11592.08
840 000	73070.28	37990.93	26322.55	20506.85	17032.17	14727.92	13092.42	11874.81
860 000	74810.05	38895.47	26949.27	20995.11	17437.70	15078.59	13404.14	12157.54
880 000	76549.82	39800.02	27576.00	21483.37	17843.23	15429.25	13715.87	12440.28
900 000	78289.59	40704.56	28202.73	21971.63	18248.75	15779.92	14027.59	12723.01
920 000	80029.35	41609.11	28829.45	22459.89	18654.28	16130.58	14339.32	13005.74
940 000	81769.12	42513.66	29456.18	22948.15	19059.81	16481.25	14651.04	13288.48
960 000	83508.89	43418.20	30082.91	23436.41	19465.34	16831.91	14962.77	13571.21
980 000	85248.66	44322.75	30709.64	23924.66	19870.87	17182.58	15274.49	13853.95
1000 000	86988.43	45227.29	31336.36	24412.92	20276.39	17533.24	15586.21	14136.68
Coefficient	.086988429	.045227294	.031336364	.024412922	.020276394	.017533241	.015586214	.014136679

AMOUNT	9 YEARS	10 YEARS	15 YEARS	20 YEARS	25 YEARS	30 YEARS	35 YEARS	40 YEARS
10 000	130.19	121.33	95.57	83.64	77.18	73.38	71.03	69.53
20 000	260.37	242.66	191.13	167.29	154.36	146.75	142.05	139.06
30 000	390.56	363.98	286.70	250.93	231.54	220.13	213.08	208.59
40 000	520.75	485.31	382.26	334.58	308.73	293.51	284.10	278.12
50 000	650.94	606.64	477.83	418.22	385.91	366.88	355.13	347.66
60 000	781.12	727.97	573.39	501.86	463.09	440.26	426.16	417.19
70 000	911.31	849.29	668.96	585.51	540.27	513.64	497.18	486.72
80 000	1041.50	970.62	764.52	669.15	617.45	587.01	568.21	556.25
90 000	1171.68	1091.95	860.09	752.80	694.63	660.39	639.23	625.78
100 000	1301.87	1213.28	955.65	836.44	771.82	733.76	710.26	695.31
110 000	1432.06	1334.60	1051.22	920.08	849.00	807.14	781.29	764.84
120 000	1562.25	1455.93	1146.78	1003.73	926.18	880.52	852.31	834.37
130 000	1692.43	1577.26	1242.35	1087.37	1003.36	953.89	923.34	903.91
140 000	1822.62	1698.59	1337.91	1171.02	1080.54	1027.27	994.37	973.44
150 000	1952.81	1819.91	1433.48	1254.66	1157.72	1100.65	1065.39	1042.97
160 000	2082.99	1941.24	1529.04	1338.30	1234.91	1174.02	1136.42	1112.50
170 000	2213.18	2062.57	1624.61	1421.95	1312.09	1247.40	1207.44	1182.03
180 000	2343.37	2183.90	1720.17	1505.59	1389.27	1320.78	1278.47	1251.56
190 000	2473.56	2305.22	1815.74	1589.24	1466.45	1394.15	1349.50	1321.09
200 000	2603.74	2426.55	1911.30	1672.88	1543.63	1467.53	1420.52	1390.62
210 000	2733.93	2547.88	2006.87	1756.52	1620.81	1540.91	1491.55	1460.15
220 000	2864.12	2669.21	2102.43	1840.17	1698.00	1614.28	1562.57	1529.69
230 000	2994.30	2790.53	2198.00	1923.81	1775.18	1687.66	1633.60	1599.22
240 000	3124.49	2911.86	2293.57	2007.46	1852.36	1761.04	1704.63	1668.75
250 000	3254.68	3033.19	2389.13	2091.10	1929.54	1834.41	1775.65	1738.28
260 000	3384.87	3154.52	2484.70	2174.74	2006.72	1907.79	1846.68	1807.81
270 000	3515.05	3275.85	2580.26	2258.39	2083.90	1981.16	1917.70	1877.34
280 000	3645.24	3397.17	2675.83	2342.03	2161.09	2054.54	1988.73	1946.87
290 000	3775.43	3518.50	2771.39	2425.68	2238.27	2127.92	2059.76	2016.40
300 000	3905.61	3639.83	2866.96	2509.32	2315.45	2201.29	2130.78	2085.94
320 000	4165.99	3882.48	3058.09	2676.61	2469.81	2348.05	2272.83	2225.00
340 000	4426.36	4125.14	3249.22	2843.90	2624.18	2494.80	2414.89	2364.06
360 000	4686.74	4367.79	3440.35	3011.18	2778.54	2641.55	2556.94	2503.12
380 000	4947.11	4610.45	3631.48	3178.47	2932.90	2788.31	2698.99	2642.18
400 000	5207.49	4853.10	3822.61	3345.76	3087.26	2935.06	2841.04	2781.25
420 000	5467.86	5095.76	4013.74	3513.05	3241.63	3081.81	2983.10	2920.31
440 000	5728.23	5338.41	4204.87	3680.34	3395.99	3228.56	3125.15	3059.37
460 000	5988.61	5581.07	4396.00	3847.62	3550.35	3375.32	3267.20	3198.43
480 000	6248.98	5823.72	4587.13	4014.91	3704.72	3522.07	3409.25	3337.50
500 000	6509.36	6066.38	4778.26	4182.20	3859.08	3668.82	3551.30	3476.56
520 000	6769.73	6309.04	4969.39	4349.49	4013.44	3815.58	3693.36	3615.62
540 000	7030.11	6551.69	5160.52	4516.78	4167.81	3962.33	3835.41	3754.68
560 000	7290.48	6794.35	5351.65	4684.06	4322.17	4109.08	3977.46	3893.75
580 000	7550.85	7037.00	5542.78	4851.35	4476.53	4255.83	4119.51	4032.81
600 000	7811.23	7279.66	5733.91	5018.64	4630.90	4402.59	4261.57	4171.87
620 000	8071.60	7522.31	5925.04	5185.93	4785.26	4549.34	4403.62	4310.93
640 000	8331.98	7764.97	6116.17	5353.22	4939.62	4696.09	4545.67	4449.99
660 000	8592.35	8007.62	6307.30	5520.50	5093.99	4842.85	4687.72	4589.06
680 000	8852.73	8250.28	6498.43	5687.79	5248.35	4989.60	4829.77	4728.12
700 000	9113.10	8492.93	6689.56	5855.08	5402.71	5136.35	4971.83	4867.18
720 000	9373.47	8735.59	6880.70	6022.37	5557.08	5283.11	5113.88	5006.24
740 000	9633.85	8978.24	7071.83	6189.66	5711.44	5429.86	5255.93	5145.31
760 000	9894.22	9220.90	7262.96	6356.94	5865.80	5576.61	5397.98	5284.37
780 000	10154.60	9463.55	7454.09	6524.23	6020.17	5723.36	5540.04	5423.43
800 000	10414.97	9706.21	7645.22	6691.52	6174.53	5870.12	5682.09	5562.49
820 000	10675.35	9948.86	7836.35	6858.81	6328.89	6016.87	5824.14	5701.56
840 000	10935.72	10191.52	8027.48	7026.10	6483.26	6163.62	5966.19	5840.62
860 000	11196.09	10434.17	8218.61	7193.38	6637.62	6310.38	6108.24	5979.68
880 000	11456.47	10676.83	8409.74	7360.67	6791.98	6457.13	6250.30	6118.74
900 000	11716.84	10919.48	8600.87	7527.96	6946.35	6603.88	6392.35	6257.81
920 000	11977.22	11162.14	8792.00	7695.25	7100.71	6750.63	6534.40	6396.87
940 000	12237.59	11404.79	8983.13	7862.54	7255.07	6897.39	6676.45	6535.93
960 000	12497.97	11647.45	9174.26	8029.82	7409.44	7044.14	6818.50	6674.99
980 000	12758.34	11890.10	9365.39	8197.11	7563.80	7190.89	6960.56	6814.05
1000 000	13018.72	12132.76	9556.52	8364.40	7718.16	7337.65	7102.61	6953.12
Coefficient	.013018715	.012132760	.009556521	.008364401	.007718162	.007337646	.007102609	.006953117

Monthly Amortizing Payments

AMOUNT	1 YEAR	2 YEARS	3 YEARS	4 YEARS	5 YEARS	6 YEARS	7 YEARS	8 YEARS
10 000	871.04	453.41	314.52	245.30	203.96	176.56	157.11	142.64
20 000	1742.08	906.83	629.04	490.61	407.93	353.11	314.22	285.28
30 000	2613.12	1360.24	943.55	735.91	611.89	529.67	471.33	427.92
40 000	3484.16	1813.66	1258.07	981.22	815.85	706.22	628.44	570.56
50 000	4355.20	2267.07	1572.59	1226.52	1019.81	882.78	785.55	713.20
60 000	5226.24	2720.48	1887.11	1471.83	1223.78	1059.33	942.66	855.84
70 000	6097.28	3173.90	2201.63	1717.13	1427.74	1235.89	1099.77	998.49
80 000	6968.33	3627.31	2516.15	1962.44	1631.70	1412.44	1256.88	1141.13
90 000	7839.37	4080.73	2830.66	2207.74	1835.66	1589.00	1414.00	1283.77
100 000	8710.41	4534.14	3145.18	2453.04	2039.63	1765.56	1571.11	1426.41
110 000	9581.45	4987.55	3459.70	2698.35	2243.59	1942.11	1728.22	1569.05
120 000	10452.49	5440.97	3774.22	2943.65	2447.55	2118.67	1885.33	1711.69
130 000	11323.53	5894.38	4088.74	3188.96	2651.51	2295.22	2042.44	1854.33
140 000	12194.57	6347.80	4403.25	3434.26	2855.48	2471.78	2199.55	1996.97
150 000	13065.61	6801.21	4717.77	3679.57	3059.44	2648.33	2356.66	2139.61
160 000	13936.65	7254.62	5032.29	3924.87	3263.40	2824.89	2513.77	2282.25
170 000	14807.69	7708.04	5346.81	4170.18	3467.36	3001.45	2670.88	2424.89
180 000	15678.73	8161.45	5661.33	4415.48	3671.33	3178.00	2827.99	2567.53
190 000	16549.77	8614.87	5975.85	4660.78	3875.29	3354.56	2985.10	2710.17
200 000	17420.81	9068.28	6290.36	4906.09	4079.25	3531.11	3142.21	2852.81
210 000	18291.85	9521.69	6604.88	5151.39	4283.21	3707.67	3299.32	2995.46
220 000	19162.90	9975.11	6919.40	5396.70	4487.18	3884.22	3456.43	3138.10
230 000	20033.94	10428.52	7233.92	5642.00	4691.14	4060.78	3613.54	3280.74
240 000	20904.98	10881.93	7548.44	5887.31	4895.10	4237.33	3770.65	3423.38
250 000	21776.02	11335.35	7862.96	6132.61	5099.06	4413.89	3927.76	3566.02
260 000	22647.06	11788.76	8177.47	6377.92	5303.03	4590.45	4084.88	3708.66
270 000	23518.10	12242.18	8491.99	6623.22	5506.99	4767.00	4241.99	3851.30
280 000	24389.14	12695.59	8806.51	6868.52	5710.95	4943.56	4399.10	3993.94
290 000	25260.18	13149.00	9121.03	7113.83	5914.91	5120.11	4556.21	4136.58
300 000	26131.22	13602.42	9435.55	7359.13	6118.88	5296.67	4713.32	4279.22
320 000	27873.30	14509.25	10064.58	7849.74	6526.80	5649.78	5027.54	4564.50
340 000	29615.38	15416.07	10693.62	8340.35	6934.73	6002.89	5341.76	4849.79
360 000	31357.47	16322.90	11322.66	8830.96	7342.65	6356.00	5655.98	5135.07
380 000	33099.55	17229.73	11951.69	9321.57	7750.58	6709.11	5970.20	5420.35
400 000	34841.63	18136.56	12580.73	9812.18	8158.50	7062.22	6284.42	5705.63
420 000	36583.71	19043.39	13209.76	10302.79	8566.43	7415.34	6598.64	5990.91
440 000	38325.79	19950.21	13838.80	10793.39	8974.35	7768.45	6912.87	6276.19
460 000	40067.87	20857.04	14467.84	11284.00	9382.28	8121.56	7227.09	6561.47
480 000	41809.95	21763.87	15096.87	11774.61	9790.20	8474.67	7541.31	6846.76
500 000	43552.04	22670.70	15725.91	12265.22	10198.13	8827.78	7855.53	7132.04
520 000	45294.12	23577.53	16354.95	12755.83	10606.05	9180.89	8169.75	7417.32
540 000	47036.20	24484.35	16983.98	13246.44	11013.98	9534.00	8483.97	7702.60
560 000	48778.28	25391.18	17613.02	13737.05	11421.90	9887.11	8798.19	7987.88
580 000	50520.36	26298.01	18242.06	14227.66	11829.83	10240.23	9112.41	8273.16
600 000	52262.44	27204.84	18871.09	14718.27	12237.75	10593.34	9426.63	8558.44
620 000	54004.52	28111.66	19500.13	15208.87	12645.68	10946.45	9740.86	8843.73
640 000	55746.60	29018.49	20129.17	15699.48	13053.60	11299.56	10055.08	9129.01
660 000	57488.69	29925.32	20758.20	16190.09	13461.53	11652.67	10369.30	9414.29
680 000	59230.77	30832.15	21387.24	16680.70	13869.45	12005.78	10683.52	9699.57
700 000	60972.85	31738.98	22016.27	17171.31	14277.38	12358.89	10997.74	9984.85
720 000	62714.93	32645.80	22645.31	17661.92	14685.30	12712.00	11311.96	10270.13
740 000	64457.01	33552.63	23274.35	18152.53	15093.23	13065.12	11626.18	10555.41
760 000	66199.09	34459.46	23903.38	18643.14	15501.15	13418.23	11940.40	10840.70
780 000	67941.17	35366.29	24532.42	19133.75	15909.08	13771.34	12254.63	11125.98
800 000	69683.26	36273.12	25161.46	19624.35	16317.00	14124.45	12568.85	11411.26
820 000	71425.34	37179.94	25790.49	20114.96	16724.93	14477.56	12883.07	11696.54
840 000	73167.42	38086.77	26419.53	20605.57	17132.85	14830.67	13197.29	11981.82
860 000	74909.50	38993.60	27048.57	21096.18	17540.78	15183.78	13511.51	12267.10
880 000	76651.58	39900.43	27677.60	21586.79	17948.70	15536.89	13825.73	12552.39
900 000	78393.66	40807.26	28306.64	22077.40	18356.63	15890.00	14139.95	12837.67
920 000	80135.74	41714.08	28935.68	22568.01	18764.55	16243.12	14454.17	13122.95
940 000	81877.83	42620.91	29564.71	23058.62	19172.48	16596.23	14768.39	13408.23
960 000	83619.91	43527.74	30193.75	23549.23	19580.40	16949.34	15082.62	13693.51
980 000	85361.99	44434.57	30822.78	24039.83	19988.33	17302.45	15396.84	13978.79
1000 000	87104.07	45341.40	31451.82	24530.44	20396.25	17655.56	15711.06	14264.07
Coefficient	.087104070	.045341395	.031451821	.024530443	.020396251	.017655561	.015711058	.014264074

28

AMOUNT	9 YEARS	10 YEARS	15 YEARS	20 YEARS	25 YEARS	30 YEARS	35 YEARS	40 YEARS
10 000	131.49	122.65	97.01	85.21	78.85	75.13	72.85	71.41
20 000	262.97	245.31	194.03	170.41	157.69	150.25	145.70	142.83
30 000	394.46	367.96	291.04	255.62	236.54	225.38	218.55	214.24
40 000	525.95	490.61	388.06	340.83	315.38	300.51	291.40	285.66
50 000	657.43	613.26	485.07	426.03	394.23	375.63	364.25	357.07
60 000	788.92	735.92	582.08	511.24	473.07	450.76	437.09	428.48
70 000	920.41	858.57	679.10	596.45	551.92	525.89	509.94	499.90
80 000	1051.89	981.22	776.11	681.65	630.76	601.01	582.79	571.31
90 000	1183.38	1103.87	873.13	766.86	709.61	676.14	655.64	642.72
100 000	1314.87	1226.53	970.14	852.07	788.45	751.27	728.49	714.14
110 000	1446.35	1349.18	1067.15	937.27	867.30	826.39	801.34	785.55
120 000	1577.84	1471.83	1164.17	1022.48	946.14	901.52	874.19	856.97
130 000	1709.33	1594.48	1261.18	1107.69	1024.99	976.65	947.04	928.38
140 000	1840.81	1717.14	1358.20	1192.89	1103.83	1051.77	1019.89	999.79
150 000	1972.30	1839.79	1455.21	1278.10	1182.68	1126.90	1092.74	1071.21
160 000	2103.79	1962.44	1552.22	1363.30	1261.52	1202.03	1165.59	1142.62
170 000	2235.27	2085.09	1649.24	1448.51	1340.37	1277.15	1238.43	1214.04
180 000	2366.76	2207.75	1746.25	1533.72	1419.21	1352.28	1311.28	1285.45
190 000	2498.25	2330.40	1843.27	1618.92	1498.06	1427.41	1384.13	1356.86
200 000	2629.73	2453.05	1940.28	1704.13	1576.90	1502.53	1456.98	1428.28
210 000	2761.22	2575.71	2037.29	1789.34	1655.75	1577.66	1529.83	1499.69
220 000	2892.71	2698.36	2134.31	1874.54	1734.59	1652.79	1602.68	1571.11
230 000	3024.19	2821.01	2231.32	1959.75	1813.44	1727.91	1675.53	1642.52
240 000	3155.68	2943.66	2328.34	2044.96	1892.28	1803.04	1748.38	1713.93
250 000	3287.17	3066.32	2425.35	2130.16	1971.13	1878.17	1821.23	1785.35
260 000	3418.65	3188.97	2522.37	2215.37	2049.97	1953.29	1894.08	1856.76
270 000	3550.14	3311.62	2619.38	2300.58	2128.82	2028.42	1966.93	1928.17
280 000	3681.63	3434.27	2716.39	2385.78	2207.66	2103.55	2039.78	1999.59
290 000	3813.11	3556.93	2813.41	2470.99	2286.51	2178.67	2112.62	2071.00
300 000	3944.60	3679.58	2910.42	2556.20	2365.35	2253.80	2185.47	2142.42
320 000	4207.57	3924.88	3104.45	2726.61	2523.04	2404.05	2331.17	2285.24
340 000	4470.55	4170.19	3298.48	2897.02	2680.73	2554.31	2476.87	2428.07
360 000	4733.52	4415.49	3492.51	3067.44	2838.42	2704.56	2622.57	2570.90
380 000	4996.49	4660.80	3686.53	3237.85	2996.11	2854.81	2768.27	2713.73
400 000	5259.47	4906.10	3880.56	3408.26	3153.80	3005.07	2913.96	2856.56
420 000	5522.44	5151.41	4074.59	3578.68	3311.49	3155.32	3059.66	2999.38
440 000	5785.41	5396.72	4268.62	3749.09	3469.18	3305.57	3205.36	3142.21
460 000	6048.39	5642.02	4462.65	3919.50	3626.87	3455.83	3351.06	3285.04
480 000	6311.36	5887.33	4656.67	4089.91	3784.56	3606.08	3496.76	3427.87
500 000	6574.33	6132.63	4850.70	4260.33	3942.25	3756.33	3642.46	3570.69
520 000	6837.31	6377.94	5044.73	4430.74	4099.94	3906.59	3788.15	3713.52
540 000	7100.28	6623.24	5238.76	4601.15	4257.63	4056.84	3933.85	3856.35
560 000	7363.25	6868.55	5432.79	4771.57	4415.32	4207.09	4079.55	3999.18
580 000	7626.23	7113.85	5626.81	4941.98	4573.01	4357.35	4225.25	4142.01
600 000	7889.20	7359.16	5820.84	5112.39	4730.70	4507.60	4370.95	4284.83
620 000	8152.17	7604.46	6014.87	5282.81	4888.39	4657.85	4516.64	4427.66
640 000	8415.15	7849.77	6208.90	5453.22	5046.08	4808.11	4662.34	4570.49
660 000	8678.12	8095.07	6402.93	5623.63	5203.77	4958.36	4808.04	4713.32
680 000	8941.09	8340.38	6596.95	5794.05	5361.46	5108.61	4953.74	4856.14
700 000	9204.07	8585.68	6790.98	5964.46	5519.15	5258.87	5099.44	4998.97
720 000	9467.04	8830.99	6985.01	6134.87	5676.84	5409.12	5245.14	5141.80
740 000	9730.01	9076.29	7179.04	6305.29	5834.53	5559.37	5390.83	5284.63
760 000	9992.99	9321.60	7373.07	6475.70	5992.22	5709.63	5536.53	5427.45
780 000	10255.96	9566.90	7567.10	6646.11	6149.91	5859.88	5682.23	5570.28
800 000	10518.93	9812.21	7761.12	6816.52	6307.60	6010.13	5827.93	5713.11
820 000	10781.91	10057.51	7955.15	6986.94	6465.29	6160.39	5973.63	5855.94
840 000	11044.88	10302.82	8149.18	7157.35	6622.98	6310.64	6119.33	5998.77
860 000	11307.85	10548.13	8343.21	7327.76	6780.67	6460.89	6265.02	6141.59
880 000	11570.83	10793.43	8537.24	7498.18	6938.36	6611.15	6410.72	6284.42
900 000	11833.80	11038.74	8731.26	7668.59	7096.05	6761.40	6556.42	6427.25
920 000	12096.77	11284.04	8925.29	7839.00	7253.74	6911.65	6702.12	6570.08
940 000	12359.75	11529.35	9119.32	8009.42	7411.43	7061.91	6847.82	6712.90
960 000	12622.72	11774.65	9313.35	8179.83	7569.12	7212.16	6993.51	6855.73
980 000	12885.69	12019.96	9507.38	8350.24	7726.81	7362.41	7139.21	6998.56
1000 000	13148.67	12265.26	9701.40	8520.66	7884.50	7512.67	7284.91	7141.39
Coefficient	.013148668	.012265262	.009701404	.008520656	.007884501	.007512666	.007284911	.007141388

AMOUNT	1 YEAR	2 YEARS	3 YEARS	4 YEARS	5 YEARS	6 YEARS	7 YEARS	8 YEARS
10 000	872.20	454.56	315.68	246.48	205.17	177.78	158.36	143.92
20 000	1744.40	909.11	631.35	492.97	410.33	355.57	316.73	287.84
30 000	2616.59	1363.67	947.03	739.45	615.50	533.35	475.09	431.76
40 000	3488.79	1818.23	1262.70	985.93	820.66	711.14	633.46	575.69
50 000	4360.99	2272.78	1578.38	1232.42	1025.83	888.92	791.82	719.61
60 000	5233.19	2727.34	1894.05	1478.90	1230.99	1066.70	950.19	863.53
70 000	6105.38	3181.90	2209.73	1725.38	1436.16	1244.49	1108.55	1007.45
80 000	6977.58	3636.45	2525.40	1971.86	1641.32	1422.27	1266.92	1151.37
90 000	7849.78	4091.01	2841.08	2218.35	1846.49	1600.05	1425.28	1295.29
100 000	8721.98	4545.57	3156.75	2464.83	2051.65	1777.84	1583.65	1439.21
110 000	9594.18	5000.12	3472.43	2711.31	2256.82	1955.62	1742.01	1583.13
120 000	10466.37	5454.68	3788.10	2957.80	2461.98	2133.41	1900.38	1727.06
130 000	11338.57	5909.24	4103.78	3204.28	2667.15	2311.19	2058.74	1870.98
140 000	12210.77	6363.79	4419.46	3450.76	2872.31	2488.97	2217.11	2014.90
150 000	13082.97	6818.35	4735.13	3697.25	3077.48	2666.76	2375.47	2158.82
160 000	13955.16	7272.91	5050.81	3943.73	3282.65	2844.54	2533.84	2302.74
170 000	14827.36	7727.46	5366.48	4190.21	3487.81	3022.33	2692.20	2446.66
180 000	15699.56	8182.02	5682.16	4436.69	3692.98	3200.11	2850.57	2590.58
190 000	16571.76	8636.58	5997.83	4683.18	3898.14	3377.89	3008.93	2734.50
200 000	17443.96	9091.14	6313.51	4929.66	4103.31	3555.68	3167.30	2878.43
210 000	18316.15	9545.69	6629.18	5176.14	4308.47	3733.46	3325.66	3022.35
220 000	19188.35	10000.25	6944.86	5422.63	4513.64	3911.24	3484.03	3166.27
230 000	20060.55	10454.81	7260.53	5669.11	4718.80	4089.03	3642.39	3310.19
240 000	20932.75	10909.36	7576.21	5915.59	4923.97	4266.81	3800.76	3454.11
250 000	21804.95	11363.92	7891.88	6162.08	5129.13	4444.60	3959.12	3598.03
260 000	22677.14	11818.48	8207.56	6408.56	5334.30	4622.38	4117.49	3741.95
270 000	23549.34	12273.03	8523.23	6655.04	5539.46	4800.16	4275.85	3885.87
280 000	24421.54	12727.59	8838.91	6901.52	5744.63	4977.95	4434.22	4029.80
290 000	25293.74	13182.15	9154.59	7148.01	5949.79	5155.73	4592.58	4173.72
300 000	26165.93	13636.70	9470.26	7394.49	6154.96	5333.52	4750.95	4317.64
320 000	27910.33	14545.82	10101.61	7887.46	6565.29	5689.08	5067.68	4605.48
340 000	29654.73	15454.93	10732.96	8380.42	6975.62	6044.65	5384.40	4893.32
360 000	31399.12	16364.04	11364.31	8873.39	7385.95	6400.22	5701.13	5181.17
380 000	33143.52	17273.16	11995.66	9366.36	7796.28	6755.79	6017.86	5469.01
400 000	34887.91	18182.27	12627.01	9859.32	8206.61	7111.35	6334.59	5756.85
420 000	36632.31	19091.38	13258.37	10352.29	8616.94	7466.92	6651.32	6044.69
440 000	38376.70	20000.50	13889.72	10845.25	9027.27	7822.49	6968.05	6332.54
460 000	40121.10	20909.61	14521.07	11338.22	9437.60	8178.06	7284.78	6620.38
480 000	41865.49	21818.72	15152.42	11831.19	9847.94	8533.62	7601.51	6908.22
500 000	43609.89	22727.84	15783.77	12324.15	10258.27	8889.19	7918.24	7196.06
520 000	45354.29	23636.95	16415.12	12817.12	10668.60	9244.76	8234.97	7483.91
540 000	47098.68	24546.07	17046.47	13310.08	11078.93	9600.33	8551.70	7771.75
560 000	48843.08	25455.18	17677.82	13803.05	11489.26	9955.90	8868.43	8059.59
580 000	50587.47	26364.29	18309.17	14296.02	11899.59	10311.46	9185.16	8347.43
600 000	52331.87	27273.41	18940.52	14788.98	12309.92	10667.03	9501.89	8635.28
620 000	54076.26	28182.52	19571.87	15281.95	12720.25	11022.60	9818.62	8923.12
640 000	55820.66	29091.63	20203.22	15774.91	13130.58	11378.17	10135.35	9210.96
660 000	57565.06	30000.75	20834.57	16267.88	13540.91	11733.73	10452.08	9498.80
680 000	59309.45	30909.86	21465.93	16760.85	13951.24	12089.30	10768.81	9786.65
700 000	61053.85	31818.97	22097.28	17253.81	14361.57	12444.87	11085.54	10074.49
720 000	62798.24	32728.09	22728.63	17746.78	14771.90	12800.44	11402.27	10362.33
740 000	64542.64	33637.20	23359.98	18239.74	15182.23	13156.00	11719.00	10650.17
760 000	66287.03	34546.31	23991.33	18732.71	15592.56	13511.57	12035.73	10938.02
780 000	68031.43	35455.43	24622.68	19225.68	16002.89	13867.14	12352.46	11225.86
800 000	69775.82	36364.54	25254.03	19718.64	16413.23	14222.71	12669.19	11513.70
820 000	71520.22	37273.65	25885.38	20211.61	16823.56	14578.28	12985.92	11801.54
840 000	73264.62	38182.77	26516.73	20704.57	17233.89	14933.84	13302.65	12089.39
860 000	75009.01	39091.88	27148.08	21197.54	17644.22	15289.41	13619.38	12377.23
880 000	76753.41	40000.99	27779.43	21690.51	18054.55	15644.98	13936.11	12665.07
900 000	78497.80	40910.11	28410.78	22183.47	18464.88	16000.55	14252.84	12952.92
920 000	80242.20	41819.22	29042.13	22676.44	18875.21	16356.11	14569.57	13240.76
940 000	81986.59	42728.34	29673.48	23169.40	19285.54	16711.68	14886.30	13528.60
960 000	83730.99	43637.45	30304.84	23662.37	19695.87	17067.25	15203.03	13816.44
980 000	85475.39	44546.56	30936.19	24155.34	20106.20	17422.82	15519.76	14104.29
1000 000	87219.78	45455.68	31567.54	24648.30	20516.53	17778.39	15836.49	14392.13
Coefficient	.087219781	.045455676	.031567537	.024648303	.020516532	.017778385	.015836485	.014392128

AMOUNT	9 YEARS	10 YEARS	15 YEARS	20 YEARS	25 YEARS	30 YEARS	35 YEARS	40 YEARS
10 000	132.79	123.99	98.47	86.78	80.52	76.89	74.69	73.31
20 000	265.59	247.97	196.95	173.56	161.05	153.78	149.37	146.62
30 000	398.38	371.96	295.42	260.35	241.57	230.67	224.06	219.93
40 000	531.17	495.94	393.90	347.13	322.09	307.57	298.74	293.24
50 000	663.97	619.93	492.37	433.91	402.61	384.46	373.43	366.55
60 000	796.76	743.91	590.84	520.69	483.14	461.35	448.12	439.86
70 000	929.55	867.90	689.32	607.48	563.66	538.24	522.80	513.17
80 000	1062.35	991.89	787.79	694.26	644.18	615.13	597.49	586.48
90 000	1195.14	1115.87	886.27	781.04	724.70	692.02	672.17	659.78
100 000	1327.94	1239.86	984.74	867.82	805.23	768.91	746.86	733.09
110 000	1460.73	1363.84	1083.21	954.61	885.75	845.80	821.55	806.40
120 000	1593.52	1487.83	1181.69	1041.39	966.27	922.70	896.23	879.71
130 000	1726.32	1611.81	1280.16	1128.17	1046.80	999.59	970.92	953.02
140 000	1859.11	1735.80	1378.64	1214.95	1127.32	1076.48	1045.60	1026.33
150 000	1991.90	1859.79	1477.11	1301.73	1207.84	1153.37	1120.29	1099.64
160 000	2124.70	1983.77	1575.58	1388.52	1288.36	1230.26	1194.98	1172.95
170 000	2257.49	2107.76	1674.06	1475.30	1368.89	1307.15	1269.66	1246.26
180 000	2390.28	2231.74	1772.53	1562.08	1449.41	1384.04	1344.35	1319.57
190 000	2523.08	2355.73	1871.01	1648.86	1529.93	1460.94	1419.04	1392.88
200 000	2655.87	2479.71	1969.48	1735.65	1610.45	1537.83	1493.72	1466.19
210 000	2788.66	2603.70	2067.95	1822.43	1690.98	1614.72	1568.41	1539.50
220 000	2921.46	2727.69	2166.43	1909.21	1771.50	1691.61	1643.09	1612.81
230 000	3054.25	2851.67	2264.90	1995.99	1852.02	1768.50	1717.78	1686.12
240 000	3187.04	2975.66	2363.37	2082.78	1932.55	1845.39	1792.47	1759.43
250 000	3319.84	3099.64	2461.85	2169.56	2013.07	1922.28	1867.15	1832.74
260 000	3452.63	3223.63	2560.32	2256.34	2093.59	1999.18	1941.84	1906.04
270 000	3585.43	3347.61	2658.80	2343.12	2174.11	2076.07	2016.52	1979.35
280 000	3718.22	3471.60	2757.27	2429.90	2254.64	2152.96	2091.21	2052.66
290 000	3851.01	3595.58	2855.74	2516.69	2335.16	2229.85	2165.90	2125.97
300 000	3983.81	3719.57	2954.22	2603.47	2415.68	2306.74	2240.58	2199.28
320 000	4249.39	3967.54	3151.17	2777.03	2576.73	2460.52	2389.95	2345.90
340 000	4514.98	4215.51	3348.11	2950.60	2737.77	2614.31	2539.33	2492.52
360 000	4780.57	4463.48	3545.06	3124.16	2898.82	2768.09	2688.70	2639.14
380 000	5046.15	4711.46	3742.01	3297.73	3059.86	2921.87	2838.07	2785.76
400 000	5311.74	4959.43	3938.96	3471.29	3220.91	3075.65	2987.44	2932.38
420 000	5577.33	5207.40	4135.91	3644.86	3381.95	3229.44	3136.81	3079.00
440 000	5842.92	5455.37	4332.85	3818.42	3543.00	3383.22	3286.19	3225.61
460 000	6108.50	5703.34	4529.80	3991.99	3704.04	3537.00	3435.56	3372.23
480 000	6374.09	5951.31	4726.75	4165.55	3865.09	3690.78	3584.93	3518.85
500 000	6639.68	6199.28	4923.70	4339.12	4026.14	3844.57	3734.30	3665.47
520 000	6905.26	6447.26	5120.65	4512.68	4187.18	3998.35	3883.68	3812.09
540 000	7170.85	6695.23	5317.59	4686.25	4348.23	4152.13	4033.05	3958.71
560 000	7436.44	6943.20	5514.54	4859.81	4509.27	4305.92	4182.42	4105.33
580 000	7702.02	7191.17	5711.49	5033.37	4670.32	4459.70	4331.79	4251.95
600 000	7967.61	7439.14	5908.44	5206.94	4831.36	4613.48	4481.16	4398.56
620 000	8233.20	7687.11	6105.38	5380.50	4992.41	4767.26	4630.54	4545.18
640 000	8498.79	7935.08	6302.33	5554.07	5153.45	4921.05	4779.91	4691.80
660 000	8764.37	8183.06	6499.28	5727.63	5314.50	5074.83	4929.28	4838.42
680 000	9029.96	8431.03	6696.23	5901.20	5475.54	5228.61	5078.65	4985.04
700 000	9295.55	8679.00	6893.18	6074.76	5636.59	5382.39	5228.02	5131.66
720 000	9561.13	8926.97	7090.12	6248.33	5797.64	5536.18	5377.40	5278.28
740 000	9826.72	9174.94	7287.07	6421.89	5958.68	5689.96	5526.77	5424.90
760 000	10092.31	9422.91	7484.02	6595.46	6119.73	5843.74	5676.14	5571.52
780 000	10357.90	9670.88	7680.97	6769.02	6280.77	5997.53	5825.51	5718.13
800 000	10623.48	9918.86	7877.92	6942.59	6441.82	6151.31	5974.88	5864.75
820 000	10889.07	10166.83	8074.86	7116.15	6602.86	6305.09	6124.26	6011.37
840 000	11154.66	10414.80	8271.81	7289.71	6763.91	6458.87	6273.63	6157.99
860 000	11420.24	10662.77	8468.76	7463.28	6924.95	6612.66	6423.00	6304.61
880 000	11685.83	10910.74	8665.71	7636.84	7086.00	6766.44	6572.37	6451.23
900 000	11951.42	11158.71	8862.66	7810.41	7247.04	6920.22	6721.75	6597.85
920 000	12217.00	11406.68	9059.60	7983.97	7408.09	7074.00	6871.12	6744.47
940 000	12482.59	11654.65	9256.55	8157.54	7569.13	7227.79	7020.49	6891.08
960 000	12748.18	11902.63	9453.50	8331.10	7730.18	7381.57	7169.86	7037.70
980 000	13013.77	12150.60	9650.45	8504.67	7891.23	7535.35	7319.23	7184.32
1000 000	13279.35	12398.57	9847.40	8678.23	8052.27	7689.14	7468.61	7330.94
Coefficient	.013279353	.012398569	.009847395	.008678232	.008052271	.007689135	.007468606	.007330941

31

AMOUNT	1 YEAR	2 YEARS	3 YEARS	4 YEARS	5 YEARS	6 YEARS	7 YEARS	8 YEARS
10 000	873.36	455.70	316.84	247.67	206.37	179.02	159.62	145.21
20 000	1746.71	911.40	633.67	495.33	412.74	358.03	319.25	290.42
30 000	2620.07	1367.10	950.51	743.00	619.12	537.05	478.87	435.63
40 000	3493.42	1822.81	1267.34	990.66	825.49	716.07	638.50	580.83
50 000	4366.78	2278.51	1584.18	1238.33	1031.86	895.09	798.12	726.04
60 000	5240.14	2734.21	1901.01	1485.99	1238.23	1074.10	957.75	871.25
70 000	6113.49	3189.91	2217.85	1733.66	1444.61	1253.12	1117.37	1016.46
80 000	6986.85	3645.61	2534.68	1981.32	1650.98	1432.14	1277.00	1161.67
90 000	7860.20	4101.31	2851.52	2228.99	1857.35	1611.15	1436.62	1306.88
100 000	8733.56	4557.01	3168.35	2476.65	2063.72	1790.17	1596.25	1452.08
110 000	9606.92	5012.71	3485.19	2724.32	2270.10	1969.19	1755.87	1597.29
120 000	10480.27	5468.42	3802.02	2971.98	2476.47	2148.21	1915.50	1742.50
130 000	11353.63	5924.12	4118.86	3219.65	2682.84	2327.22	2075.12	1887.71
140 000	12226.98	6379.82	4435.69	3467.31	2889.21	2506.24	2234.75	2032.92
150 000	13100.34	6835.52	4752.53	3714.98	3095.58	2685.26	2394.37	2178.13
160 000	13973.69	7291.22	5069.36	3962.64	3301.96	2864.27	2554.00	2323.33
170 000	14847.05	7746.92	5386.20	4210.31	3508.33	3043.29	2713.62	2468.54
180 000	15720.41	8202.62	5703.03	4457.97	3714.70	3222.31	2873.25	2613.75
190 000	16593.76	8658.32	6019.87	4705.64	3921.07	3401.32	3032.87	2758.96
200 000	17467.12	9114.03	6336.70	4953.30	4127.45	3580.34	3192.50	2904.17
210 000	18340.47	9569.73	6653.54	5200.97	4333.82	3759.36	3352.12	3049.38
220 000	19213.83	10025.43	6970.37	5448.63	4540.19	3938.38	3511.75	3194.58
230 000	20087.19	10481.13	7287.21	5696.30	4746.56	4117.39	3671.37	3339.79
240 000	20960.54	10936.83	7604.04	5943.96	4952.94	4296.41	3831.00	3485.00
250 000	21833.90	11392.53	7920.88	6191.63	5159.31	4475.43	3990.62	3630.21
260 000	22707.25	11848.23	8237.71	6439.29	5365.68	4654.44	4150.25	3775.42
270 000	23580.61	12303.93	8554.55	6686.96	5572.05	4833.46	4309.87	3920.63
280 000	24453.97	12759.64	8871.38	6934.62	5778.42	5012.48	4469.50	4065.83
290 000	25327.32	13215.34	9188.22	7182.29	5984.80	5191.50	4629.12	4211.04
300 000	26200.68	13671.04	9505.05	7429.95	6191.17	5370.51	4788.75	4356.25
320 000	27947.39	14582.44	10138.72	7925.28	6603.91	5728.55	5108.00	4646.67
340 000	29694.10	15493.84	10772.39	8420.61	7016.66	6086.58	5427.25	4937.09
360 000	31440.81	16405.25	11406.06	8915.94	7429.40	6444.62	5746.50	5227.50
380 000	33187.52	17316.65	12039.73	9411.27	7842.15	6802.65	6065.75	5517.92
400 000	34934.24	18228.05	12673.40	9906.60	8254.89	7160.68	6385.00	5808.34
420 000	36680.95	19139.45	13307.07	10401.93	8667.64	7518.72	6704.25	6098.75
440 000	38427.66	20050.86	13940.74	10897.26	9080.38	7876.75	7023.50	6389.17
460 000	40174.37	20962.26	14574.41	11392.59	9493.13	8234.79	7342.75	6679.59
480 000	41921.08	21873.66	15208.08	11887.92	9905.87	8592.82	7662.00	6970.00
500 000	43667.80	22785.06	15841.75	12383.25	10318.62	8950.86	7981.25	7260.42
520 000	45414.51	23696.47	16475.42	12878.58	10731.36	9308.89	8300.50	7550.84
540 000	47161.22	24607.87	17109.09	13373.91	11144.10	9666.92	8619.75	7841.25
560 000	48907.93	25519.27	17742.76	13869.24	11556.85	10024.96	8938.99	8131.67
580 000	50654.64	26430.67	18376.43	14364.57	11969.59	10382.99	9258.24	8422.09
600 000	52401.36	27342.08	19010.10	14859.90	12382.34	10741.03	9577.49	8712.50
620 000	54148.07	28253.48	19643.77	15355.23	12795.08	11099.06	9896.74	9002.92
640 000	55894.78	29164.88	20277.44	15850.56	13207.83	11457.09	10215.99	9293.34
660 000	57641.49	30076.28	20911.11	16345.89	13620.57	11815.13	10535.24	9583.75
680 000	59388.20	30987.69	21544.78	16841.22	14033.32	12173.16	10854.49	9874.17
700 000	61134.91	31899.09	22178.45	17336.55	14446.06	12531.20	11173.74	10164.59
720 000	62881.63	32810.49	22812.12	17831.88	14858.81	12889.23	11492.99	10455.00
740 000	64628.34	33721.89	23445.79	18327.21	15271.55	13247.27	11812.24	10745.42
760 000	66375.05	34633.30	24079.46	18822.54	15684.30	13605.30	12131.49	11035.84
780 000	68121.76	35544.70	24713.13	19317.87	16097.04	13963.33	12450.74	11326.25
800 000	69868.47	36456.10	25346.80	19813.20	16509.78	14321.37	12769.99	11616.67
820 000	71615.19	37367.50	25980.47	20308.53	16922.53	14679.40	13089.24	11907.09
840 000	73361.90	38278.91	26614.14	20803.86	17335.27	15037.44	13408.49	12197.50
860 000	75108.61	39190.31	27247.81	21299.19	17748.02	15395.47	13727.74	12487.92
880 000	76855.32	40101.71	27881.48	21794.52	18160.76	15753.50	14046.99	12778.34
900 000	78602.03	41013.11	28515.15	22289.85	18573.51	16111.54	14366.24	13068.76
920 000	80348.74	41924.52	29148.82	22785.18	18986.25	16469.57	14685.49	13359.17
940 000	82095.46	42835.92	29782.49	23280.51	19399.00	16827.61	15004.74	13649.59
960 000	83842.17	43747.32	30416.16	23775.84	19811.74	17185.64	15323.99	13940.01
980 000	85588.88	44658.72	31049.83	24271.17	20224.49	17543.68	15643.24	14230.42
1000 000	87335.59	45570.13	31683.51	24766.50	20637.23	17901.71	15962.49	14520.84
Coefficient	.087335592	.045570126	.031683505	.024766503	.020637231	.017901710	.015962491	.014520839

MONTHLY AMORTIZING PAYMENTS 8.75%

AMOUNT	9 YEARS	10 YEARS	15 YEARS	20 YEARS	25 YEARS	30 YEARS	35 YEARS	40 YEARS
10 000	134.11	125.33	99.94	88.37	82.21	78.67	76.54	75.22
20 000	268.22	250.65	199.89	176.74	164.43	157.34	153.07	150.43
30 000	402.32	375.98	299.83	265.11	246.64	236.01	229.61	225.65
40 000	536.43	501.31	399.78	353.48	328.86	314.68	306.15	300.87
50 000	670.54	626.63	499.72	441.86	411.07	393.35	382.68	376.09
60 000	804.65	751.96	599.67	530.23	493.29	472.02	459.22	451.30
70 000	938.75	877.29	699.61	618.60	575.50	550.69	535.75	526.52
80 000	1072.86	1002.61	799.56	706.97	657.71	629.36	612.29	601.74
90 000	1206.97	1127.94	899.50	795.34	739.93	708.03	688.83	676.95
100 000	1341.08	1253.27	999.45	883.71	822.14	786.70	765.36	752.17
110 000	1475.18	1378.59	1099.39	972.08	904.36	865.37	841.90	827.39
120 000	1609.29	1503.92	1199.34	1060.45	986.57	944.04	918.44	902.60
130 000	1743.40	1629.25	1299.28	1148.82	1068.79	1022.71	994.97	977.82
140 000	1877.51	1754.57	1399.23	1237.19	1151.00	1101.38	1071.51	1053.04
150 000	2011.62	1879.90	1499.17	1325.57	1233.22	1180.05	1148.04	1128.26
160 000	2145.72	2005.23	1599.12	1413.94	1315.43	1258.72	1224.58	1203.47
170 000	2279.83	2130.55	1699.06	1502.31	1397.64	1337.39	1301.12	1278.69
180 000	2413.94	2255.88	1799.01	1590.68	1479.86	1416.06	1377.65	1353.91
190 000	2548.05	2381.21	1898.95	1679.05	1562.07	1494.73	1454.19	1429.12
200 000	2682.15	2506.54	1998.90	1767.42	1644.29	1573.40	1530.73	1504.34
210 000	2816.26	2631.86	2098.84	1855.79	1726.50	1652.07	1607.26	1579.56
220 000	2950.37	2757.19	2198.79	1944.16	1808.72	1730.74	1683.80	1654.78
230 000	3084.48	2882.52	2298.73	2032.53	1890.93	1809.41	1760.34	1729.99
240 000	3218.58	3007.84	2398.68	2120.91	1973.14	1888.08	1836.87	1805.21
250 000	3352.69	3133.17	2498.62	2209.28	2055.36	1966.75	1913.41	1880.43
260 000	3486.80	3258.50	2598.57	2297.65	2137.57	2045.42	1989.94	1955.64
270 000	3620.91	3383.82	2698.51	2386.02	2219.79	2124.09	2066.48	2030.86
280 000	3755.01	3509.15	2798.46	2474.39	2302.00	2202.76	2143.02	2106.08
290 000	3889.12	3634.48	2898.40	2562.76	2384.22	2281.43	2219.55	2181.29
300 000	4023.23	3759.80	2998.35	2651.13	2466.43	2360.10	2296.09	2256.51
320 000	4291.45	4010.46	3198.24	2827.87	2630.86	2517.44	2449.16	2406.95
340 000	4559.66	4261.11	3398.13	3004.62	2795.29	2674.78	2602.23	2557.38
360 000	4827.88	4511.76	3598.02	3181.36	2959.72	2832.12	2755.31	2707.81
380 000	5096.09	4762.42	3797.91	3358.10	3124.15	2989.46	2908.38	2858.25
400 000	5364.31	5013.07	3997.79	3534.84	3288.57	3146.80	3061.45	3008.68
420 000	5632.52	5263.72	4197.68	3711.58	3453.00	3304.14	3214.53	3159.12
440 000	5900.74	5514.38	4397.57	3888.33	3617.43	3461.48	3367.60	3309.55
460 000	6168.95	5765.03	4597.46	4065.07	3781.86	3618.82	3520.67	3459.98
480 000	6437.17	6015.68	4797.35	4241.81	3946.29	3776.16	3673.74	3610.42
500 000	6705.38	6266.34	4997.24	4418.55	4110.72	3933.50	3826.82	3760.85
520 000	6973.60	6516.99	5197.13	4595.30	4275.15	4090.84	3979.89	3911.29
540 000	7241.81	6767.64	5397.02	4772.04	4439.58	4248.18	4132.96	4061.72
560 000	7510.03	7018.30	5596.91	4948.78	4604.00	4405.52	4286.03	4212.15
580 000	7778.24	7268.95	5796.80	5125.52	4768.43	4562.86	4439.11	4362.59
600 000	8046.46	7519.61	5996.69	5302.26	4932.86	4720.20	4592.18	4513.02
620 000	8314.68	7770.26	6196.58	5479.01	5097.29	4877.54	4745.25	4663.46
640 000	8582.89	8020.91	6396.47	5655.75	5261.72	5034.88	4898.32	4813.89
660 000	8851.11	8271.57	6596.36	5832.49	5426.15	5192.22	5051.40	4964.33
680 000	9119.32	8522.22	6796.25	6009.23	5590.58	5349.56	5204.47	5114.76
700 000	9387.54	8772.87	6996.14	6185.97	5755.01	5506.90	5357.54	5265.19
720 000	9655.75	9023.53	7196.03	6362.72	5919.43	5664.24	5510.61	5415.63
740 000	9923.97	9274.18	7395.92	6539.46	6083.86	5821.58	5663.69	5566.06
760 000	10192.18	9524.83	7595.81	6716.20	6248.29	5978.92	5816.76	5716.50
780 000	10460.40	9775.49	7795.70	6892.94	6412.72	6136.26	5969.83	5866.93
800 000	10728.61	10026.14	7995.59	7069.69	6577.15	6293.60	6122.90	6017.36
820 000	10996.83	10276.79	8195.48	7246.43	6741.58	6450.94	6275.98	6167.80
840 000	11265.04	10527.45	8395.37	7423.17	6906.01	6608.28	6429.05	6318.23
860 000	11533.26	10778.10	8595.26	7599.91	7070.43	6765.62	6582.12	6468.67
880 000	11801.47	11028.75	8795.15	7776.66	7234.86	6922.96	6735.20	6619.10
900 000	12069.69	11279.41	8995.04	7953.40	7399.29	7080.30	6888.27	6769.53
920 000	12337.91	11530.06	9194.93	8130.14	7563.72	7237.64	7041.34	6919.97
940 000	12606.12	11780.71	9394.82	8306.88	7728.15	7394.98	7194.41	7070.40
960 000	12874.34	12031.37	9594.71	8483.62	7892.58	7552.32	7347.49	7220.84
980 000	13142.55	12282.02	9794.60	8660.36	8057.01	7709.66	7500.56	7371.27
1000 000	13410.77	12532.68	9994.49	8837.11	8221.44	7867.00	7653.63	7521.71
Coefficient	.013410767	.012532675	.009994487	.008837107	.008221436	.007867004	.007653631	.007521705

33

MONTHLY AMORTIZING PAYMENTS

AMOUNT	1 YEAR	2 YEARS	3 YEARS	4 YEARS	5 YEARS	6 YEARS	7 YEARS	8 YEARS
10 000	874.51	456.85	318.00	248.85	207.58	180.26	160.89	146.50
20 000	1749.03	913.69	635.99	497.70	415.17	360.51	321.78	293.00
30 000	2623.54	1370.54	953.99	746.55	622.75	540.77	482.67	439.51
40 000	3498.06	1827.39	1271.99	995.40	830.33	721.02	643.56	586.01
50 000	4372.57	2284.24	1589.99	1244.25	1037.92	901.28	804.45	732.51
60 000	5247.09	2741.08	1907.98	1493.10	1245.50	1081.53	965.34	879.01
70 000	6121.60	3197.93	2225.98	1741.95	1453.08	1261.79	1126.24	1025.51
80 000	6996.12	3654.78	2543.98	1990.80	1660.67	1442.04	1287.13	1172.02
90 000	7870.63	4111.63	2861.98	2239.65	1868.25	1622.30	1448.02	1318.52
100 000	8745.15	4568.47	3179.97	2488.50	2075.84	1802.55	1608.91	1465.02
110 000	9619.66	5025.32	3497.97	2737.35	2283.42	1982.81	1769.80	1611.52
120 000	10494.18	5482.17	3815.97	2986.21	2491.00	2163.06	1930.69	1758.02
130 000	11368.69	5930.02	4133.97	3235.06	2698.59	2343.32	2091.58	1904.53
140 000	12243.21	6395.86	4451.96	3483.91	2906.17	2523.58	2252.47	2051.03
150 000	13117.72	6852.71	4769.96	3732.76	3113.75	2703.83	2413.36	2197.53
160 000	13992.24	7309.56	5087.96	3981.61	3321.34	2884.09	2574.25	2344.03
170 000	14866.75	7766.41	5405.95	4230.46	3528.92	3064.34	2735.14	2490.53
180 000	15741.27	8223.25	5723.95	4479.31	3736.50	3244.60	2896.03	2637.04
190 000	16615.78	8680.10	6041.95	4728.16	3944.09	3424.85	3056.92	2783.54
200 000	17490.30	9136.95	6359.95	4977.01	4151.67	3605.11	3217.82	2930.04
210 000	18364.81	9593.80	6677.94	5225.86	4359.25	3785.36	3378.71	3076.54
220 000	19239.33	10050.64	6995.94	5474.71	4566.84	3965.62	3539.60	3223.04
230 000	20113.84	10507.49	7313.94	5723.56	4774.42	4145.87	3700.49	3369.55
240 000	20988.36	10964.34	7631.94	5972.41	4982.01	4326.13	3861.38	3516.05
250 000	21862.87	11421.18	7949.93	6221.26	5189.59	4506.38	4022.27	3662.55
260 000	22737.39	11878.03	8267.93	6470.11	5397.17	4686.64	4183.16	3809.05
270 000	23611.90	12334.88	8585.93	6718.96	5604.76	4866.89	4344.05	3955.55
280 000	24486.42	12791.73	8903.92	6967.81	5812.34	5047.15	4504.94	4102.06
290 000	25360.93	13248.57	9221.92	7216.66	6019.92	5227.41	4665.83	4248.56
300 000	26235.44	13705.42	9539.92	7465.51	6227.51	5407.66	4826.72	4395.06
320 000	27984.47	14619.12	10175.91	7963.21	6642.67	5768.17	5148.50	4688.06
340 000	29733.50	15532.81	10811.91	8460.91	7057.84	6128.68	5470.29	4981.07
360 000	31482.53	16446.51	11447.90	8958.62	7473.01	6489.19	5792.07	5274.07
380 000	33231.56	17360.20	12083.90	9456.32	7888.17	6849.70	6113.85	5567.08
400 000	34980.59	18273.90	12719.89	9954.02	8303.34	7210.21	6435.63	5860.08
420 000	36729.62	19187.59	13355.89	10451.72	8718.51	7570.73	6757.41	6153.09
440 000	38478.65	20101.29	13991.88	10949.42	9133.68	7931.24	7079.19	6446.09
460 000	40227.68	21014.98	14627.88	11447.12	9548.84	8291.75	7400.98	6739.09
480 000	41976.71	21928.67	15263.87	11944.82	9964.01	8652.26	7722.76	7032.10
500 000	43725.74	22842.37	15899.87	12442.52	10379.18	9012.77	8044.54	7325.10
520 000	45474.77	23756.06	16535.86	12940.22	10794.34	9373.28	8366.32	7618.11
540 000	47223.80	24669.76	17171.85	13437.92	11209.51	9733.79	8688.10	7911.11
560 000	48972.83	25583.45	17807.85	13935.62	11624.68	10094.30	9009.88	8204.11
580 000	50721.86	26497.15	18443.84	14433.32	12039.85	10454.81	9331.67	8497.12
600 000	52470.89	27410.84	19079.84	14931.03	12455.01	10815.32	9653.45	8790.12
620 000	54219.92	28324.54	19715.83	15428.73	12870.18	11175.83	9975.23	9083.13
640 000	55968.95	29238.23	20351.83	15926.43	13285.35	11536.34	10297.01	9376.13
660 000	57717.98	30151.93	20987.82	16424.13	13700.51	11896.85	10618.79	9669.13
680 000	59467.01	31065.62	21623.82	16921.83	14115.68	12257.37	10940.57	9962.14
700 000	61216.04	31979.32	22259.81	17419.53	14530.85	12617.88	11262.35	10255.14
720 000	62965.07	32893.01	22895.81	17917.23	14946.02	12978.39	11584.14	10548.15
740 000	64714.10	33806.71	23531.80	18414.93	15361.18	13338.90	11905.92	10841.15
760 000	66463.13	34720.40	24167.80	18912.63	15776.35	13699.41	12227.70	11134.15
780 000	68212.16	35634.10	24803.79	19410.33	16191.52	14059.92	12549.48	11427.16
800 000	69961.19	36547.79	25439.78	19908.03	16606.68	14420.43	12871.26	11720.16
820 000	71710.22	37461.49	26075.78	20405.74	17021.85	14780.94	13193.04	12013.17
840 000	73459.25	38375.18	26711.77	20903.44	17437.02	15141.45	13514.83	12306.17
860 000	75208.28	39288.88	27347.77	21401.14	17852.19	15501.96	13836.61	12599.17
880 000	76957.31	40202.57	27983.76	21898.84	18267.35	15862.47	14158.39	12892.18
900 000	78706.33	41116.27	28619.76	22396.54	18682.52	16222.98	14480.17	13185.18
920 000	80455.36	42029.96	29255.75	22894.24	19097.69	16583.49	14801.95	13478.19
940 000	82204.39	42943.65	29891.75	23391.94	19512.85	16944.00	15123.73	13771.19
960 000	83953.42	43857.35	30527.74	23889.64	19928.02	17304.52	15445.51	14064.19
980 000	85702.45	44771.04	31163.74	24387.34	20343.19	17665.03	15767.30	14357.20
1000 000	87451.48	45684.74	31799.73	24885.04	20758.36	18025.54	16089.08	14650.20
Coefficient	.087451483	.045684739	.031799731	.024885043	.020758355	.018025537	.016089078	.014650203

34

MONTHLY AMORTIZING PAYMENTS 9.00%

AMOUNT	9 YEARS	10 YEARS	15 YEARS	20 YEARS	25 YEARS	30 YEARS	35 YEARS	40 YEARS
10 000	135.43	126.68	101.43	89.97	83.92	80.46	78.40	77.14
20 000	270.86	253.35	202.85	179.95	167.84	160.92	156.80	154.27
30 000	406.29	380.03	304.28	269.92	251.76	241.39	235.20	231.41
40 000	541.72	506.70	405.71	359.89	335.68	321.85	313.60	308.54
50 000	677.15	633.38	507.13	449.86	419.60	402.31	392.00	385.68
60 000	812.57	760.05	608.56	539.84	503.52	482.77	470.40	462.82
70 000	948.00	886.73	709.99	629.81	587.44	563.24	548.80	539.95
80 000	1083.43	1013.41	811.41	719.78	671.36	643.70	627.19	617.09
90 000	1218.86	1140.08	912.84	809.75	755.28	724.16	705.59	694.23
100 000	1354.29	1266.76	1014.27	899.73	839.20	804.62	783.99	771.36
110 000	1489.72	1393.43	1115.69	989.70	923.12	885.08	862.39	848.50
120 000	1625.15	1520.11	1217.12	1079.67	1007.04	965.55	940.79	925.63
130 000	1760.58	1646.79	1318.55	1169.64	1090.96	1046.01	1019.19	1002.77
140 000	1896.01	1773.46	1419.97	1259.62	1174.87	1126.47	1097.59	1079.91
150 000	2031.44	1900.14	1521.40	1349.59	1258.79	1206.93	1175.99	1157.04
160 000	2166.87	2026.81	1622.83	1439.56	1342.71	1287.40	1254.39	1234.18
170 000	2302.29	2153.49	1724.25	1529.53	1426.63	1367.86	1332.79	1311.31
180 000	2437.72	2280.16	1825.68	1619.51	1510.55	1448.32	1411.19	1388.45
190 000	2573.15	2406.84	1927.11	1709.48	1594.47	1528.78	1489.59	1465.59
200 000	2708.58	2533.52	2028.53	1799.45	1678.39	1609.25	1567.99	1542.72
210 000	2844.01	2660.19	2129.96	1889.42	1762.31	1689.71	1646.39	1619.86
220 000	2979.44	2786.87	2231.39	1979.40	1846.23	1770.17	1724.78	1697.00
230 000	3114.87	2913.54	2332.81	2069.37	1930.15	1850.63	1803.18	1774.13
240 000	3250.30	3040.22	2434.24	2159.34	2014.07	1931.09	1881.58	1851.27
250 000	3385.73	3166.89	2535.67	2249.32	2097.99	2011.56	1959.98	1928.40
260 000	3521.16	3293.57	2637.09	2339.29	2181.91	2092.02	2038.38	2005.54
270 000	3656.59	3420.25	2738.52	2429.26	2265.83	2172.48	2116.78	2082.68
280 000	3792.01	3546.92	2839.95	2519.23	2349.75	2252.94	2195.18	2159.81
290 000	3927.44	3673.60	2941.37	2609.21	2433.67	2333.41	2273.58	2236.95
300 000	4062.87	3800.27	3042.80	2699.18	2517.59	2413.87	2351.98	2314.08
320 000	4333.73	4053.62	3245.65	2879.12	2685.43	2574.79	2508.78	2468.36
340 000	4604.59	4306.98	3448.51	3059.07	2853.27	2735.72	2665.58	2622.63
360 000	4875.45	4560.33	3651.36	3239.01	3021.11	2896.64	2822.37	2776.90
380 000	5146.31	4813.68	3854.21	3418.96	3188.95	3057.57	2979.17	2931.17
400 000	5417.16	5067.03	4057.07	3598.90	3356.79	3218.49	3135.97	3085.45
420 000	5688.02	5320.38	4259.92	3778.85	3524.62	3379.41	3292.77	3239.72
440 000	5958.88	5573.73	4462.77	3958.79	3692.46	3540.34	3449.57	3393.99
460 000	6229.74	5827.09	4665.63	4138.74	3860.30	3701.26	3606.37	3548.26
480 000	6500.60	6080.44	4868.48	4318.68	4028.14	3862.19	3763.17	3702.54
500 000	6771.45	6333.79	5071.33	4498.63	4195.98	4023.11	3919.97	3856.81
520 000	7042.31	6587.14	5274.19	4678.58	4363.82	4184.04	4076.76	4011.08
540 000	7313.17	6840.49	5477.04	4858.52	4531.66	4344.96	4233.56	4165.35
560 000	7584.03	7093.84	5679.89	5038.47	4699.50	4505.89	4390.36	4319.62
580 000	7854.89	7347.19	5882.75	5218.41	4867.34	4666.81	4547.16	4473.90
600 000	8125.75	7600.55	6085.60	5398.36	5035.18	4827.74	4703.96	4628.17
620 000	8396.60	7853.90	6288.45	5578.30	5203.02	4988.66	4860.76	4782.44
640 000	8667.46	8107.25	6491.31	5758.25	5370.86	5149.58	5017.56	4936.71
660 000	8938.32	8360.60	6694.16	5938.19	5538.70	5310.51	5174.35	5090.99
680 000	9209.18	8613.95	6897.01	6118.14	5706.54	5471.43	5331.15	5245.26
700 000	9480.04	8867.30	7099.87	6298.08	5874.37	5632.36	5487.95	5399.53
720 000	9750.89	9120.66	7302.72	6478.03	6042.21	5793.28	5644.75	5553.80
740 000	10021.75	9374.01	7505.57	6657.97	6210.05	5954.21	5801.55	5708.08
760 000	10292.61	9627.36	7708.43	6837.92	6377.89	6115.13	5958.35	5862.35
780 000	10563.47	9880.71	7911.28	7017.86	6545.73	6276.06	6115.15	6016.62
800 000	10834.33	10134.06	8114.13	7197.81	6713.57	6436.98	6271.94	6170.89
820 000	11105.19	10387.41	8316.99	7377.75	6881.41	6597.91	6428.74	6325.16
840 000	11376.04	10640.76	8519.84	7557.70	7049.25	6758.83	6585.54	6479.44
860 000	11646.90	10894.12	8722.69	7737.64	7217.09	6919.75	6742.34	6633.71
880 000	11917.76	11147.47	8925.55	7917.59	7384.93	7080.68	6899.14	6787.98
900 000	12188.62	11400.82	9128.40	8097.53	7552.77	7241.60	7055.94	6942.25
920 000	12459.48	11654.17	9331.25	8277.48	7720.61	7402.53	7212.74	7096.53
940 000	12730.33	11907.52	9534.11	8457.42	7888.45	7563.45	7369.53	7250.80
960 000	13001.19	12160.87	9736.96	8637.37	8056.29	7724.38	7526.33	7405.07
980 000	13272.05	12414.23	9939.81	8817.31	8224.12	7885.30	7683.13	7559.34
1000 000	13542.91	12667.58	10142.67	8997.26	8391.96	8046.23	7839.93	7713.61
Coefficient	.013542909	.012667577	.010142666	.008997260	.008391964	.008046226	.007839930	.007713615

35

AMOUNT	1 YEAR	2 YEARS	3 YEARS	4 YEARS	5 YEARS	6 YEARS	7 YEARS	8 YEARS
10 000	875.67	458.00	319.16	250.04	208.80	181.50	162.16	147.80
20 000	1751.35	915.99	638.32	500.08	417.60	363.00	324.32	295.60
30 000	2627.02	1373.99	957.49	750.12	626.40	544.50	486.49	443.41
40 000	3502.70	1831.98	1276.65	1000.16	835.20	725.99	648.65	591.21
50 000	4378.37	2289.98	1595.81	1250.20	1043.99	907.49	810.81	739.01
60 000	5254.05	2747.97	1914.97	1500.24	1252.79	1088.99	972.97	886.81
70 000	6129.72	3205.97	2234.13	1750.27	1461.59	1270.49	1135.14	1034.62
80 000	7005.40	3663.96	2553.30	2000.31	1670.39	1451.99	1297.30	1182.42
90 000	7881.07	4121.96	2872.46	2250.35	1879.19	1633.49	1459.46	1330.22
100 000	8756.75	4579.95	3191.62	2500.39	2087.99	1814.99	1621.62	1478.02
110 000	9632.42	5037.95	3510.78	2750.43	2296.79	1996.49	1783.79	1625.82
120 000	10508.09	5495.94	3829.95	3000.47	2505.59	2177.98	1945.95	1773.63
130 000	11383.77	5953.94	4149.11	3250.51	2714.39	2359.48	2108.11	1921.43
140 000	12259.44	6411.93	4468.27	3500.55	2923.19	2540.98	2270.27	2069.23
150 000	13135.12	6869.93	4787.43	3750.59	3131.98	2722.48	2432.44	2217.03
160 000	14010.79	7327.92	5106.59	4000.63	3340.78	2903.98	2594.60	2364.84
170 000	14886.47	7785.92	5425.76	4250.67	3549.58	3085.48	2756.76	2512.64
180 000	15762.14	8243.92	5744.92	4500.71	3758.38	3266.98	2918.92	2660.44
190 000	16637.82	8701.91	6064.08	4750.74	3967.18	3448.47	3081.09	2808.24
200 000	17513.49	9159.91	6383.24	5000.78	4175.98	3629.97	3243.25	2956.04
210 000	18389.17	9617.90	6702.40	5250.82	4384.78	3811.47	3405.41	3103.85
220 000	19264.84	10075.90	7021.57	5500.86	4593.58	3992.97	3567.57	3251.65
230 000	20140.51	10533.89	7340.73	5750.90	4802.38	4174.47	3729.74	3399.45
240 000	21016.19	10991.89	7659.89	6000.94	5011.18	4355.97	3891.90	3547.25
250 000	21891.86	11449.88	7979.05	6250.98	5219.97	4537.47	4054.06	3695.06
260 000	22767.54	11907.88	8298.21	6501.02	5428.77	4718.96	4216.22	3842.86
270 000	23643.21	12365.87	8617.38	6751.06	5637.57	4900.46	4378.39	3990.66
280 000	24518.89	12823.87	8936.54	7001.10	5846.37	5081.96	4540.55	4138.46
290 000	25394.56	13281.86	9255.70	7251.14	6055.17	5263.46	4702.71	4286.26
300 000	26270.24	13739.86	9574.86	7501.18	6263.97	5444.96	4864.87	4434.07
320 000	28021.59	14655.85	10213.19	8001.25	6681.57	5807.96	5189.20	4729.67
340 000	29772.93	15571.84	10851.51	8501.33	7099.17	6170.95	5513.52	5025.27
360 000	31524.28	16487.83	11489.84	9001.41	7516.76	6533.95	5837.85	5320.88
380 000	33275.63	17403.82	12128.16	9501.49	7934.36	6896.95	6162.17	5616.48
400 000	35026.98	18319.81	12766.48	10001.57	8351.96	7259.95	6486.50	5912.09
420 000	36778.33	19235.80	13404.81	10501.65	8769.56	7622.94	6810.82	6207.69
440 000	38529.68	20151.79	14043.13	11001.72	9187.16	7985.94	7135.15	6503.30
460 000	40281.03	21067.78	14681.46	11501.80	9604.75	8348.94	7459.47	6798.90
480 000	42032.38	21983.77	15319.78	12001.88	10022.35	8711.93	7783.80	7094.51
500 000	43783.73	22899.76	15958.11	12501.96	10439.95	9074.93	8108.12	7390.11
520 000	45535.08	23815.76	16596.43	13002.04	10857.55	9437.93	8432.45	7685.71
540 000	47286.43	24731.75	17234.75	13502.12	11275.15	9800.93	8756.77	7981.32
560 000	49037.77	25647.74	17873.08	14002.19	11692.74	10163.92	9081.10	8276.92
580 000	50789.12	26563.73	18511.40	14502.27	12110.34	10526.92	9405.42	8572.53
600 000	52540.47	27479.72	19149.73	15002.35	12527.94	10889.92	9729.75	8868.13
620 000	54291.82	28395.71	19788.05	15502.43	12945.54	11252.92	10054.07	9163.74
640 000	56043.17	29311.70	20426.38	16002.51	13363.14	11615.91	10378.39	9459.34
660 000	57794.52	30227.69	21064.70	16502.59	13780.73	11978.91	10702.72	9754.95
680 000	59545.87	31143.68	21703.02	17002.66	14198.33	12341.91	11027.04	10050.55
700 000	61297.22	32059.67	22341.35	17502.74	14615.93	12704.90	11351.37	10346.15
720 000	63048.57	32975.66	22979.67	18002.82	15033.53	13067.90	11675.69	10641.76
740 000	64799.92	33891.65	23618.00	18502.90	15451.13	13430.90	12000.02	10937.36
760 000	66551.27	34807.64	24256.32	19002.98	15868.72	13793.90	12324.34	11232.97
780 000	68302.61	35723.63	24894.64	19503.06	16286.32	14156.89	12648.67	11528.57
800 000	70053.96	36639.62	25532.97	20003.14	16703.92	14519.89	12972.99	11824.18
820 000	71805.31	37555.61	26171.29	20503.21	17121.52	14882.89	13297.32	12119.78
840 000	73556.66	38471.60	26809.62	21003.29	17539.12	15245.89	13621.64	12415.38
860 000	75308.01	39387.59	27447.94	21503.37	17956.71	15608.88	13945.97	12710.99
880 000	77059.36	40303.59	28086.27	22003.45	18374.31	15971.88	14270.29	13006.59
900 000	78810.71	41219.58	28724.59	22503.53	18791.91	16334.88	14594.62	13302.20
920 000	80562.06	42135.57	29362.91	23003.61	19209.51	16697.87	14918.94	13597.80
940 000	82313.41	43051.56	30001.24	23503.68	19627.11	17060.87	15243.27	13893.41
960 000	84064.76	43967.55	30639.56	24003.76	20044.70	17423.87	15567.59	14189.01
980 000	85816.10	44883.54	31277.89	24503.84	20462.30	17786.87	15891.92	14484.62
1000 000	87567.45	45799.53	31916.21	25003.92	20879.90	18149.86	16216.24	14780.22
Coefficient	.087567454	.045799529	.031916211	.025003919	.020879899	.018149864	.016216242	.014780220

AMOUNT	9 YEARS	10 YEARS	15 YEARS	20 YEARS	25 YEARS	30 YEARS	35 YEARS	40 YEARS
10 000	136.76	128.03	102.92	91.59	85.64	82.27	80.27	79.07
20 000	273.52	256.07	205.84	183.17	171.28	164.54	160.55	158.13
30 000	410.27	384.10	308.76	274.76	256.91	246.80	240.82	237.20
40 000	547.03	512.13	411.68	366.35	342.55	329.07	321.10	316.26
50 000	683.79	640.16	514.60	457.93	428.19	411.34	401.37	395.33
60 000	820.55	768.20	617.52	549.52	513.83	493.61	481.65	474.40
70 000	957.30	896.23	720.43	641.11	599.47	575.87	561.92	553.46
80 000	1094.06	1024.26	823.35	732.69	685.11	658.14	642.20	632.53
90 000	1230.82	1152.29	926.27	824.28	770.74	740.41	722.47	711.59
100 000	1367.58	1280.33	1029.19	915.87	856.38	822.68	802.74	790.66
110 000	1504.34	1408.36	1132.11	1007.45	942.02	904.94	883.02	869.73
120 000	1641.09	1536.39	1235.03	1099.04	1027.66	987.21	963.29	948.79
130 000	1777.85	1664.43	1337.95	1190.63	1113.30	1069.48	1043.57	1027.86
140 000	1914.61	1792.46	1440.87	1282.21	1198.93	1151.75	1123.84	1106.92
150 000	2051.37	1920.49	1543.79	1373.80	1284.57	1234.01	1204.12	1185.99
160 000	2188.12	2048.52	1646.71	1465.39	1370.21	1316.28	1284.39	1265.06
170 000	2324.88	2176.56	1749.63	1556.97	1455.85	1398.55	1364.67	1344.12
180 000	2461.64	2304.59	1852.55	1648.56	1541.49	1480.82	1444.94	1423.19
190 000	2598.40	2432.62	1955.47	1740.15	1627.13	1563.08	1525.21	1502.26
200 000	2735.15	2560.65	2058.38	1831.73	1712.76	1645.35	1605.49	1581.32
210 000	2871.91	2688.69	2161.30	1923.32	1798.40	1727.62	1685.76	1660.39
220 000	3008.67	2816.72	2264.22	2014.91	1884.04	1809.89	1766.04	1739.45
230 000	3145.43	2944.75	2367.14	2106.49	1969.68	1892.15	1846.31	1818.52
240 000	3282.19	3072.79	2470.06	2198.08	2055.32	1974.42	1926.59	1897.59
250 000	3418.94	3200.82	2572.98	2289.67	2140.95	2056.69	2006.86	1976.65
260 000	3555.70	3328.85	2675.90	2381.25	2226.59	2138.96	2087.14	2055.72
270 000	3692.46	3456.88	2778.82	2472.84	2312.23	2221.22	2167.41	2134.78
280 000	3829.22	3584.92	2881.74	2564.43	2397.87	2303.49	2247.68	2213.85
290 000	3965.97	3712.95	2984.66	2656.01	2483.51	2385.76	2327.96	2292.92
300 000	4102.73	3840.98	3087.58	2747.60	2569.15	2468.03	2408.23	2371.98
320 000	4376.25	4097.05	3293.42	2930.77	2740.42	2632.56	2568.78	2530.11
340 000	4649.76	4353.11	3499.25	3113.95	2911.70	2797.10	2729.33	2688.25
360 000	4923.28	4609.18	3705.09	3297.12	3082.97	2961.63	2889.88	2846.38
380 000	5196.79	4865.24	3910.93	3480.29	3254.25	3126.17	3050.43	3004.51
400 000	5470.31	5121.31	4116.77	3663.47	3425.53	3290.70	3210.98	3162.64
420 000	5743.83	5377.37	4322.61	3846.64	3596.80	3455.24	3371.53	3320.77
440 000	6017.34	5633.44	4528.45	4029.81	3768.08	3619.77	3532.07	3478.91
460 000	6290.86	5889.51	4734.28	4212.99	3939.36	3784.31	3692.62	3637.04
480 000	6564.37	6145.57	4940.12	4396.16	4110.63	3948.84	3853.17	3795.17
500 000	6837.89	6401.64	5145.96	4579.33	4281.91	4113.38	4013.72	3953.30
520 000	7111.40	6657.70	5351.80	4762.51	4453.19	4277.91	4174.27	4111.44
540 000	7384.92	6913.77	5557.64	4945.68	4624.46	4442.45	4334.82	4269.57
560 000	7658.43	7169.83	5763.48	5128.85	4795.74	4606.98	4495.37	4427.70
580 000	7931.95	7425.90	5969.32	5312.03	4967.01	4771.52	4655.92	4585.83
600 000	8205.46	7681.96	6175.15	5495.20	5138.29	4936.05	4816.47	4743.96
620 000	8478.98	7938.03	6380.99	5678.37	5309.57	5100.59	4977.01	4902.10
640 000	8752.50	8194.09	6586.83	5861.55	5480.84	5265.12	5137.56	5060.23
660 000	9026.01	8450.16	6792.67	6044.72	5652.12	5429.66	5298.11	5218.36
680 000	9299.53	8706.22	6998.51	6227.89	5823.40	5594.19	5458.66	5376.49
700 000	9573.04	8962.29	7204.35	6411.07	5994.67	5758.73	5619.21	5534.62
720 000	9846.56	9218.36	7410.18	6594.24	6165.95	5923.26	5779.76	5692.76
740 000	10120.07	9474.42	7616.02	6777.41	6337.23	6087.80	5940.31	5850.89
760 000	10393.59	9730.49	7821.86	6960.59	6508.50	6252.33	6100.86	6009.02
780 000	10667.10	9986.55	8027.70	7143.76	6679.78	6416.87	6261.41	6167.15
800 000	10940.62	10242.62	8233.54	7326.93	6851.05	6581.40	6421.95	6325.28
820 000	11214.13	10498.68	8439.38	7510.11	7022.33	6745.94	6582.50	6483.42
840 000	11487.65	10754.75	8645.22	7693.28	7193.61	6910.47	6743.05	6641.55
860 000	11761.17	11010.81	8851.05	7876.45	7364.88	7075.01	6903.60	6799.68
880 000	12034.68	11266.88	9056.89	8059.63	7536.16	7239.54	7064.15	6957.81
900 000	12308.20	11522.94	9262.73	8242.80	7707.44	7404.08	7224.70	7115.95
920 000	12581.71	11779.01	9468.57	8425.97	7878.71	7568.61	7385.25	7274.08
940 000	12855.23	12035.08	9674.41	8609.15	8049.99	7733.15	7545.80	7432.21
960 000	13128.74	12291.14	9880.25	8792.32	8221.27	7897.68	7706.35	7590.34
980 000	13402.26	12547.21	10086.08	8975.49	8392.54	8062.22	7866.89	7748.47
1000 000	13675.77	12803.27	10291.92	9158.67	8563.82	8226.75	8027.44	7906.61
Coefficient	.013675774	.012803272	.010291923	.009158668	.008563818	.008226754	.008027443	.007906606

MONTHLY AMORTIZING PAYMENTS

AMOUNT	1 YEAR	2 YEARS	3 YEARS	4 YEARS	5 YEARS	6 YEARS	7 YEARS	8 YEARS
10 000	876.84	459.14	320.33	251.23	210.02	182.75	163.44	149.11
20 000	1753.67	918.29	640.66	502.46	420.04	365.49	326.88	298.22
30 000	2630.51	1377.43	960.99	753.69	630.06	548.24	490.32	447.33
40 000	3507.34	1836.58	1281.32	1004.93	840.07	730.99	653.76	596.44
50 000	4384.18	2295.72	1601.65	1256.16	1050.09	913.73	817.20	745.54
60 000	5261.01	2754.87	1921.98	1507.39	1260.11	1096.48	980.64	894.65
70 000	6137.85	3214.01	2242.31	1758.62	1470.13	1279.23	1144.08	1043.76
80 000	7014.68	3673.16	2562.64	2009.85	1680.15	1461.98	1307.52	1192.87
90 000	7891.52	4132.30	2882.97	2261.08	1890.17	1644.72	1470.96	1341.98
100 000	8768.35	4591.45	3203.29	2512.31	2100.19	1827.47	1634.40	1491.09
110 000	9645.19	5050.59	3523.62	2763.54	2310.20	2010.22	1797.84	1640.20
120 000	10522.02	5509.74	3843.95	3014.78	2520.22	2192.96	1961.28	1789.31
130 000	11398.86	5968.88	4164.28	3266.01	2730.24	2375.71	2124.72	1938.42
140 000	12275.69	6428.03	4484.61	3517.24	2940.26	2558.46	2288.16	2087.52
150 000	13152.53	6887.17	4804.94	3768.47	3150.28	2741.20	2451.60	2236.63
160 000	14029.36	7346.32	5125.27	4019.70	3360.30	2923.95	2615.04	2385.74
170 000	14906.20	7805.46	5445.60	4270.93	3570.32	3106.70	2778.48	2534.85
180 000	15783.03	8264.61	5765.93	4522.16	3780.33	3289.44	2941.92	2683.96
190 000	16659.87	8723.75	6086.26	4773.40	3990.35	3472.19	3105.36	2833.07
200 000	17536.70	9182.90	6406.59	5024.63	4200.37	3654.94	3268.80	2982.18
210 000	18413.54	9642.04	6726.92	5275.86	4410.39	3837.69	3432.24	3131.29
220 000	19290.37	10101.19	7047.25	5527.09	4620.41	4020.43	3595.68	3280.40
230 000	20167.21	10560.33	7367.58	5778.32	4830.43	4203.18	3759.12	3429.50
240 000	21044.04	11019.48	7687.91	6029.55	5040.45	4385.93	3922.56	3578.61
250 000	21920.88	11478.62	8008.24	6280.78	5250.47	4568.67	4086.00	3727.72
260 000	22797.71	11937.77	8328.57	6532.00	5460.48	4751.42	4249.44	3876.83
270 000	23674.55	12396.91	8648.90	6783.25	5670.50	4934.17	4412.87	4025.94
280 000	24551.38	12856.06	8969.23	7034.48	5880.52	5116.91	4576.31	4175.05
290 000	25428.22	13315.20	9289.55	7285.71	6090.54	5299.66	4739.75	4324.16
300 000	26305.05	13774.35	9609.88	7536.94	6300.56	5482.41	4903.19	4473.27
320 000	28058.73	14692.64	10250.54	8039.40	6720.60	5847.90	5230.07	4771.48
340 000	29812.40	15610.93	10891.20	8541.87	7140.63	6213.39	5556.95	5069.70
360 000	31566.07	16529.22	11531.86	9044.33	7560.67	6578.89	5883.83	5367.92
380 000	33319.74	17447.51	12172.52	9546.79	7980.71	6944.38	6210.71	5666.14
400 000	35073.41	18365.80	12813.18	10049.25	8400.74	7309.88	6537.59	5964.35
420 000	36827.08	19284.09	13453.84	10551.72	8820.78	7675.37	6864.47	6262.57
440 000	38580.75	20202.38	14094.50	11054.18	9240.82	8040.86	7191.35	6560.79
460 000	40334.42	21120.67	14735.16	11556.64	9660.86	8406.36	7518.23	6859.01
480 000	42088.09	22038.96	15375.82	12059.11	10080.89	8771.85	7845.11	7157.23
500 000	43841.76	22957.25	16016.47	12561.57	10500.93	9137.35	8171.99	7455.44
520 000	45595.43	23875.53	16657.13	13064.03	10920.97	9502.84	8498.87	7753.66
540 000	47349.10	24793.82	17297.79	13566.49	11341.00	9868.33	8825.75	8051.88
560 000	49102.77	25712.11	17938.45	14068.96	11761.04	10233.83	9152.63	8350.10
580 000	50856.44	26630.40	18579.11	14571.42	12181.08	10599.32	9479.51	8648.31
600 000	52610.11	27548.69	19219.77	15073.88	12601.12	10964.81	9806.39	8946.53
620 000	54363.78	28466.98	19860.43	15576.34	13021.15	11330.31	10133.27	9244.75
640 000	56117.45	29385.27	20501.09	16078.81	13441.19	11695.80	10460.15	9542.97
660 000	57871.12	30303.56	21141.75	16581.27	13861.23	12061.30	10787.03	9841.19
680 000	59624.79	31221.85	21782.40	17083.73	14281.27	12426.79	11113.91	10139.40
700 000	61378.46	32140.14	22423.06	17586.20	14701.30	12792.28	11440.79	10437.62
720 000	63132.13	33058.43	23063.72	18088.66	15121.34	13157.78	11767.67	10735.84
740 000	64885.80	33976.72	23704.38	18591.12	15541.38	13523.27	12094.55	11034.06
760 000	66639.47	34895.01	24345.04	19093.58	15961.41	13888.77	12421.43	11332.27
780 000	68393.14	35813.30	24985.70	19596.05	16381.45	14254.26	12748.31	11630.49
800 000	70146.81	36731.59	25626.36	20098.51	16801.49	14619.75	13075.18	11928.71
820 000	71900.48	37649.88	26267.02	20600.97	17221.53	14985.25	13402.06	12226.93
840 000	73654.15	38568.17	26907.68	21103.43	17641.56	15350.74	13728.94	12525.15
860 000	75407.82	39486.46	27548.34	21605.90	18061.60	15716.23	14055.82	12823.36
880 000	77161.49	40404.75	28189.99	22108.36	18481.64	16081.73	14382.70	13121.58
900 000	78915.16	41323.04	28829.65	22610.82	18901.67	16447.22	14709.58	13419.80
920 000	80668.83	42241.33	29470.31	23113.29	19321.71	16812.72	15036.46	13718.02
940 000	82422.51	43159.62	30110.97	23615.75	19741.75	17178.21	15363.34	14016.23
960 000	84176.18	44077.91	30751.63	24118.21	20161.79	17543.70	15690.22	14314.45
980 000	85929.85	44996.20	31392.29	24620.67	20581.82	17909.20	16017.10	14612.67
1000 000	87683.52	45914.49	32032.95	25123.14	21001.86	18274.69	16343.98	14910.89
Coefficient	.087683516	.045914490	.032032948	.025123136	.021001861	.018274691	.016343981	.014910887

38

MONTHLY AMORTIZING PAYMENTS 9.50%

AMOUNT	9 YEARS	10 YEARS	15 YEARS	20 YEARS	25 YEARS	30 YEARS	35 YEARS	40 YEARS
10 000	138.09	129.40	104.42	93.21	87.37	84.09	82.16	81.01
20 000	276.19	258.80	208.84	186.43	174.74	168.17	164.32	162.01
30 000	414.28	388.19	313.27	279.64	262.11	252.26	246.48	243.02
40 000	552.37	517.59	417.69	372.85	349.48	336.34	328.64	324.02
50 000	690.47	646.99	522.11	466.07	436.85	420.43	410.81	405.03
60 000	828.56	776.39	626.53	559.28	524.22	504.51	492.97	486.04
70 000	966.66	905.78	730.96	652.49	611.59	588.60	575.13	567.04
80 000	1104.75	1035.18	835.38	745.70	698.96	672.68	657.29	648.05
90 000	1242.84	1164.58	939.80	838.92	786.33	756.77	739.45	729.06
100 000	1380.94	1293.98	1044.22	932.13	873.70	840.85	821.61	810.06
110 000	1519.03	1423.37	1148.65	1025.34	961.07	924.94	903.77	891.07
120 000	1657.12	1552.77	1253.07	1118.56	1048.44	1009.03	985.93	972.07
130 000	1795.22	1682.17	1357.49	1211.77	1135.81	1093.11	1068.10	1053.08
140 000	1933.31	1811.57	1461.91	1304.98	1223.18	1177.20	1150.26	1134.09
150 000	2071.40	1940.96	1566.34	1398.20	1310.55	1261.28	1232.42	1215.09
160 000	2209.50	2070.36	1670.76	1491.41	1397.91	1345.37	1314.58	1296.10
170 000	2347.59	2199.76	1775.18	1584.62	1485.28	1429.45	1396.74	1377.10
180 000	2485.68	2329.16	1879.60	1677.84	1572.65	1513.54	1478.90	1458.11
190 000	2623.78	2458.55	1984.03	1771.05	1660.02	1597.62	1561.06	1539.12
200 000	2761.87	2587.95	2088.45	1864.26	1747.39	1681.71	1643.22	1620.12
210 000	2899.97	2717.35	2192.87	1957.48	1834.76	1765.79	1725.38	1701.13
220 000	3038.06	2846.75	2297.29	2050.69	1922.13	1849.88	1807.55	1782.14
230 000	3176.15	2976.14	2401.72	2143.90	2009.50	1933.96	1889.71	1863.14
240 000	3314.25	3105.54	2506.14	2237.11	2096.87	2018.05	1971.87	1944.15
250 000	3452.34	3234.94	2610.56	2330.33	2184.24	2102.14	2054.03	2025.15
260 000	3590.43	3364.34	2714.98	2423.54	2271.61	2186.22	2136.19	2106.16
270 000	3728.53	3493.73	2819.41	2516.75	2358.98	2270.31	2218.35	2187.17
280 000	3866.62	3623.13	2923.83	2609.97	2446.35	2354.39	2300.51	2268.17
290 000	4004.71	3752.53	3028.25	2703.18	2533.72	2438.48	2382.67	2349.18
300 000	4142.81	3881.93	3132.67	2796.39	2621.09	2522.56	2464.83	2430.18
320 000	4419.00	4140.72	3341.52	2982.82	2795.83	2690.73	2629.16	2592.20
340 000	4695.18	4399.52	3550.36	3169.25	2970.57	2858.90	2793.48	2754.21
360 000	4971.37	4658.31	3759.21	3355.67	3145.31	3027.08	2957.80	2916.22
380 000	5247.56	4917.11	3968.05	3542.10	3320.05	3195.25	3122.12	3078.23
400 000	5523.74	5175.90	4176.90	3728.52	3494.79	3363.42	3286.45	3240.25
420 000	5799.93	5434.70	4385.74	3914.95	3669.53	3531.59	3450.77	3402.26
440 000	6076.12	5693.49	4594.59	4101.38	3844.27	3699.76	3615.09	3564.27
460 000	6352.31	5952.29	4803.43	4287.80	4019.00	3867.93	3779.41	3726.28
480 000	6628.49	6211.08	5012.28	4474.23	4193.74	4036.10	3943.74	3888.30
500 000	6904.68	6469.88	5221.12	4660.66	4368.48	4204.27	4108.06	4050.31
520 000	7180.87	6728.67	5429.97	4847.08	4543.22	4372.44	4272.38	4212.32
540 000	7457.05	6987.47	5638.81	5033.51	4717.96	4540.61	4436.70	4374.33
560 000	7733.24	7246.26	5847.66	5219.93	4892.70	4708.78	4601.02	4536.34
580 000	8009.43	7505.06	6056.50	5406.36	5067.44	4876.95	4765.35	4698.36
600 000	8285.62	7763.85	6265.35	5592.79	5242.18	5045.13	4929.67	4860.37
620 000	8561.80	8022.65	6474.19	5779.21	5416.92	5213.30	5093.99	5022.38
640 000	8837.99	8281.44	6683.04	5965.64	5591.66	5381.47	5258.31	5184.39
660 000	9114.18	8540.24	6891.88	6152.07	5766.40	5549.64	5422.64	5346.41
680 000	9390.37	8799.03	7100.73	6338.49	5941.14	5717.81	5586.96	5508.42
700 000	9666.55	9057.83	7309.57	6524.92	6115.88	5885.98	5751.28	5670.43
720 000	9942.74	9316.62	7518.42	6711.34	6290.62	6054.15	5915.60	5832.44
740 000	10218.93	9575.42	7727.26	6897.77	6465.36	6222.32	6079.93	5994.46
760 000	10495.11	9834.21	7936.11	7084.20	6640.09	6390.49	6244.25	6156.47
780 000	10771.30	10093.01	8144.95	7270.62	6814.83	6558.66	6408.57	6318.48
800 000	11047.49	10351.80	8353.80	7457.05	6989.57	6726.83	6572.89	6480.49
820 000	11323.68	10610.60	8562.64	7643.48	7164.31	6895.00	6737.22	6642.51
840 000	11599.86	10869.40	8771.49	7829.90	7339.05	7063.18	6901.54	6804.52
860 000	11876.05	11128.19	8980.33	8016.33	7513.79	7231.35	7065.86	6966.53
880 000	12152.24	11386.99	9189.18	8202.75	7688.53	7399.52	7230.18	7128.54
900 000	12428.42	11645.78	9398.02	8389.18	7863.27	7567.69	7394.50	7290.55
920 000	12704.61	11904.58	9606.87	8575.61	8038.01	7735.86	7558.83	7452.57
940 000	12980.80	12163.37	9815.71	8762.03	8212.75	7904.03	7723.15	7614.58
960 000	13256.99	12422.17	10024.56	8948.46	8387.49	8072.20	7887.47	7776.59
980 000	13533.17	12680.96	10233.40	9134.89	8562.23	8240.37	8051.79	7938.60
1000 000	13809.36	12939.76	10442.25	9321.31	8736.97	8408.54	8216.12	8100.62
Coefficient	.013809361	.012939756	.010442247	.009321312	.008736967	.008408542	.008216116	.008100616

39

MONTHLY AMORTIZING PAYMENTS

AMOUNT	1 YEAR	2 YEARS	3 YEARS	4 YEARS	5 YEARS	6 YEARS	7 YEARS	8 YEARS
10 000	878.00	460.30	321.50	252.43	211.24	184.00	164.72	150.42
20 000	1755.99	920.59	643.00	504.85	422.48	368.00	329.45	300.84
30 000	2633.99	1380.89	964.50	757.28	633.73	552.00	494.17	451.27
40 000	3511.99	1841.18	1286.00	1009.71	844.97	736.00	658.89	601.69
50 000	4389.98	2301.48	1607.50	1262.13	1056.21	920.00	823.61	752.11
60 000	5267.98	2761.78	1929.00	1514.56	1267.45	1104.00	988.34	902.53
70 000	6145.98	3222.07	2250.50	1766.99	1478.70	1288.00	1153.06	1052.95
80 000	7023.97	3682.37	2572.00	2019.42	1689.94	1472.00	1317.78	1203.38
90 000	7901.97	4142.67	2893.49	2271.84	1901.18	1656.00	1482.51	1353.80
100 000	8779.97	4602.96	3214.99	2524.27	2112.42	1840.00	1647.23	1504.22
110 000	9657.96	5063.26	3536.49	2776.70	2323.67	2024.00	1811.95	1654.64
120 000	10535.96	5523.55	3857.99	3029.12	2534.91	2208.00	1976.68	1805.06
130 000	11413.96	5983.85	4179.49	3281.55	2746.15	2392.00	2141.40	1955.49
140 000	12291.95	6444.15	4500.99	3533.98	2957.39	2576.00	2306.12	2105.91
150 000	13169.95	6904.44	4822.49	3786.40	3168.64	2760.00	2470.84	2256.33
160 000	14047.95	7364.74	5143.99	4038.83	3379.88	2944.00	2635.57	2406.75
170 000	14925.94	7825.04	5465.49	4291.26	3591.12	3128.00	2800.29	2557.17
180 000	15803.94	8285.33	5786.99	4543.68	3802.36	3312.00	2965.01	2707.60
190 000	16681.93	8745.63	6108.49	4796.11	4013.61	3496.00	3129.74	2858.02
200 000	17559.93	9205.92	6429.99	5048.54	4224.85	3680.00	3294.46	3008.44
210 000	18437.93	9666.22	6751.49	5300.96	4436.09	3864.00	3459.18	3158.86
220 000	19315.92	10126.52	7072.99	5553.39	4647.33	4048.00	3623.91	3309.28
230 000	20193.92	10586.81	7394.49	5805.82	4858.58	4232.00	3788.63	3459.71
240 000	21071.92	11047.11	7715.99	6058.25	5069.82	4416.00	3953.35	3610.13
250 000	21949.91	11507.41	8037.49	6310.67	5281.06	4600.00	4118.07	3760.55
260 000	22827.91	11967.70	8358.98	6563.10	5492.30	4784.00	4282.80	3910.97
270 000	23705.91	12428.00	8680.48	6815.53	5703.55	4968.00	4447.52	4061.39
280 000	24583.90	12888.29	9001.98	7067.95	5914.79	5152.00	4612.24	4211.82
290 000	25461.90	13348.59	9323.48	7320.38	6126.03	5336.00	4776.97	4362.24
300 000	26339.90	13808.89	9644.98	7572.81	6337.27	5520.00	4941.69	4512.66
320 000	28095.89	14729.48	10287.98	8077.66	6759.76	5888.01	5271.13	4813.50
340 000	29851.88	15650.07	10930.98	8582.51	7182.24	6256.01	5600.58	5114.35
360 000	31607.88	16570.66	11573.98	9087.37	7604.73	6624.01	5930.03	5415.19
380 000	33363.87	17491.26	12216.98	9592.22	8027.21	6992.01	6259.47	5716.04
400 000	35119.86	18411.85	12859.98	10097.08	8449.70	7360.01	6588.92	6016.88
420 000	36875.86	19332.44	13502.98	10601.93	8872.18	7728.01	6918.36	6317.72
440 000	38631.85	20253.03	14145.97	11106.78	9294.67	8096.01	7247.81	6618.57
460 000	40387.84	21173.63	14788.97	11611.64	9717.15	8464.01	7577.26	6919.41
480 000	42143.84	22094.22	15431.97	12116.49	10139.64	8832.01	7906.70	7220.26
500 000	43899.83	23014.81	16074.97	12621.35	10562.12	9200.01	8236.15	7521.10
520 000	45655.82	23935.40	16717.97	13126.20	10984.61	9568.01	8565.59	7821.95
540 000	47411.81	24856.00	17360.97	13631.05	11407.09	9936.01	8895.04	8122.79
560 000	49167.81	25776.59	18003.97	14135.91	11829.58	10304.01	9224.49	8423.63
580 000	50923.80	26697.18	18646.97	14640.76	12252.05	10672.01	9553.93	8724.48
600 000	52679.79	27617.77	19289.97	15145.61	12674.55	11040.01	9883.38	9025.32
620 000	54435.79	28538.37	19932.96	15650.47	13097.03	11408.01	10212.82	9326.17
640 000	56191.78	29458.96	20575.96	16155.32	13519.52	11776.01	10542.27	9627.01
660 000	57947.77	30379.55	21218.96	16660.18	13942.00	12144.01	10871.72	9927.85
680 000	59703.77	31300.14	21861.96	17165.03	14364.49	12512.01	11201.16	10228.70
700 000	61459.76	32220.73	22504.96	17669.88	14786.97	12880.01	11530.61	10529.54
720 000	63215.75	33141.33	23147.96	18174.74	15209.45	13248.01	11860.05	10830.39
740 000	64971.75	34061.92	23790.96	18679.59	15631.94	13616.01	12189.50	11131.23
760 000	66727.74	34982.51	24433.96	19184.44	16054.42	13984.01	12518.94	11432.07
780 000	68483.73	35903.10	25076.95	19689.30	16476.91	14352.01	12848.39	11732.92
800 000	70239.73	36823.70	25719.95	20194.15	16899.39	14720.01	13177.84	12033.76
820 000	71995.72	37744.29	26362.95	20699.01	17321.88	15088.01	13507.28	12334.61
840 000	73751.71	38664.88	27005.95	21203.86	17744.36	15456.01	13836.73	12635.45
860 000	75507.71	39585.47	27648.95	21708.71	18166.85	15824.01	14166.17	12936.29
880 000	77263.70	40506.07	28291.95	22213.57	18589.33	16192.01	14495.62	13237.14
900 000	79019.69	41426.66	28934.95	22718.42	19011.82	16560.01	14825.07	13537.98
920 000	80775.68	42347.25	29577.95	23223.27	19434.30	16928.01	15154.51	13838.83
940 000	82531.68	43267.84	30220.95	23728.13	19856.79	17296.02	15483.96	14139.67
960 000	84287.67	44188.44	30863.94	24232.98	20279.27	17664.02	15813.40	14440.51
980 000	86043.66	45109.03	31506.94	24737.84	20701.76	18032.02	16142.85	14741.36
1000 000	87799.66	46029.62	32149.94	25242.69	21124.24	18400.02	16472.30	15042.20
Coefficient	.087799657	.046029621	.032149942	.025242690	.021124243	.018400016	.016472296	.015042202

40

MONTHLY AMORTIZING PAYMENTS 9.75%

AMOUNT	9 YEARS	10 YEARS	15 YEARS	20 YEARS	25 YEARS	30 YEARS	35 YEARS	40 YEARS
10 000	139.44	130.77	105.94	94.85	89.11	85.92	84.06	82.96
20 000	278.87	261.54	211.87	189.70	178.23	171.83	168.12	165.91
30 000	418.31	392.31	317.81	284.56	267.34	257.75	252.18	248.87
40 000	557.75	523.08	423.75	379.41	356.45	343.66	336.24	331.82
50 000	697.18	653.85	529.68	474.26	445.57	429.58	420.29	414.78
60 000	836.62	784.62	635.62	569.11	534.68	515.49	504.35	497.74
70 000	976.05	915.39	741.55	663.96	623.80	601.41	588.41	580.69
80 000	1115.49	1046.16	847.49	758.81	712.91	687.32	672.47	663.65
90 000	1254.93	1176.93	953.43	853.67	802.02	773.24	756.53	746.60
100 000	1394.37	1307.70	1059.36	948.52	891.14	859.15	840.59	829.56
110 000	1533.80	1438.47	1165.30	1043.37	980.25	945.07	924.65	912.51
120 000	1673.24	1569.24	1271.24	1138.22	1069.36	1030.99	1008.71	995.47
130 000	1812.68	1700.01	1377.17	1233.07	1158.48	1116.90	1092.77	1078.43
140 000	1952.11	1830.78	1483.11	1327.92	1247.59	1202.82	1176.83	1161.38
150 000	2091.55	1961.55	1589.04	1422.78	1336.71	1288.73	1260.88	1244.34
160 000	2230.99	2092.32	1694.98	1517.63	1425.82	1374.65	1344.94	1327.29
170 000	2370.42	2223.09	1800.92	1612.48	1514.93	1460.56	1429.00	1410.25
180 000	2509.86	2353.86	1906.85	1707.33	1604.05	1546.48	1513.06	1493.21
190 000	2649.30	2484.63	2012.79	1802.18	1693.16	1632.39	1597.12	1576.16
200 000	2788.73	2615.41	2118.73	1897.03	1782.27	1718.31	1681.18	1659.12
210 000	2928.17	2746.18	2224.66	1991.89	1871.39	1804.22	1765.24	1742.07
220 000	3067.61	2876.95	2330.60	2086.74	1960.50	1890.14	1849.30	1825.03
230 000	3207.04	3007.72	2436.53	2181.59	2049.62	1976.06	1933.36	1907.98
240 000	3346.48	3138.49	2542.47	2276.44	2138.73	2061.97	2017.41	1990.94
250 000	3485.92	3269.26	2648.41	2371.29	2227.84	2147.89	2101.47	2073.90
260 000	3625.35	3400.03	2754.34	2466.14	2316.96	2233.80	2185.53	2156.85
270 000	3764.79	3530.80	2860.28	2561.00	2406.07	2319.72	2269.59	2239.81
280 000	3904.23	3661.57	2966.22	2655.85	2495.18	2405.63	2353.65	2322.76
290 000	4043.66	3792.34	3072.15	2750.70	2584.30	2491.55	2437.71	2405.72
300 000	4183.10	3923.11	3178.09	2845.55	2673.41	2577.46	2521.77	2488.68
320 000	4461.97	4184.65	3389.96	3035.25	2851.64	2749.29	2689.89	2654.59
340 000	4740.85	4446.19	3601.83	3224.96	3029.87	2921.12	2858.00	2820.50
360 000	5019.72	4707.73	3813.71	3414.66	3208.09	3092.96	3026.12	2986.41
380 000	5298.59	4969.27	4025.58	3604.36	3386.32	3264.79	3194.24	3152.32
400 000	5577.47	5230.81	4237.45	3794.07	3564.55	3436.62	3362.36	3318.23
420 000	5856.34	5492.35	4449.32	3983.77	3742.78	3608.45	3530.48	3484.15
440 000	6135.21	5753.89	4661.20	4173.47	3921.00	3780.28	3698.59	3650.06
460 000	6414.09	6015.43	4873.07	4363.18	4099.23	3952.11	3866.71	3815.97
480 000	6692.96	6276.97	5084.94	4552.88	4277.46	4123.94	4034.83	3981.88
500 000	6971.83	6538.51	5296.81	4742.58	4455.69	4295.77	4202.95	4147.79
520 000	7250.71	6800.05	5508.69	4932.29	4633.91	4467.60	4371.06	4313.70
540 000	7529.58	7061.59	5720.56	5121.99	4812.14	4639.43	4539.18	4479.62
560 000	7808.45	7323.13	5932.43	5311.69	4990.37	4811.26	4707.30	4645.53
580 000	8087.33	7584.67	6144.30	5501.40	5168.60	4983.10	4875.42	4811.44
600 000	8366.20	7846.22	6356.18	5691.10	5346.82	5154.93	5043.54	4977.35
620 000	8645.07	8107.76	6568.05	5880.80	5525.05	5326.76	5211.65	5143.26
640 000	8923.95	8369.30	6779.92	6070.51	5703.28	5498.59	5379.77	5309.18
660 000	9202.82	8630.84	6991.79	6260.21	5881.51	5670.42	5547.89	5475.09
680 000	9481.69	8892.38	7203.67	6449.91	6059.73	5842.25	5716.01	5641.00
700 000	9760.57	9153.92	7415.54	6639.62	6237.96	6014.08	5884.13	5806.91
720 000	10039.44	9415.46	7627.41	6829.32	6416.19	6185.91	6052.24	5972.82
740 000	10318.31	9677.00	7839.28	7019.03	6594.42	6357.74	6220.36	6138.73
760 000	10597.19	9938.54	8051.16	7208.73	6772.64	6529.57	6388.48	6304.65
780 000	10876.06	10200.08	8263.03	7398.43	6950.87	6701.40	6556.60	6470.56
800 000	11154.93	10461.62	8474.90	7588.14	7129.10	6873.24	6724.72	6636.47
820 000	11433.81	10723.16	8686.77	7777.84	7307.33	7045.07	6892.83	6802.38
840 000	11712.68	10984.70	8898.65	7967.54	7485.55	7216.90	7060.95	6968.29
860 000	11991.55	11246.24	9110.52	8157.25	7663.78	7388.73	7229.07	7134.20
880 000	12270.43	11507.78	9322.39	8346.95	7842.01	7560.56	7397.19	7300.12
900 000	12549.30	11769.32	9534.26	8536.65	8020.24	7732.39	7565.30	7466.03
920 000	12828.17	12030.86	9746.14	8726.36	8198.46	7904.22	7733.42	7631.94
940 000	13107.05	12292.40	9958.01	8916.06	8376.69	8076.05	7901.54	7797.85
960 000	13385.92	12553.94	10169.88	9105.76	8554.92	8247.88	8069.66	7963.76
980 000	13664.79	12815.48	10381.75	9295.47	8733.15	8419.71	8237.78	8129.67
1000 000	13943.67	13077.03	10593.63	9485.17	8911.37	8591.54	8405.89	8295.59
Coefficient	.013943666	.013077025	.010593626	.009485169	.008911374	.008591544	.008405894	.008295586

41

MONTHLY AMORTIZING PAYMENTS

AMOUNT	1 YEAR	2 YEARS	3 YEARS	4 YEARS	5 YEARS	6 YEARS	7 YEARS	8 YEARS
10 000	879.16	461.45	322.67	253.63	212.47	185.26	166.01	151.74
20 000	1758.32	922.90	645.34	507.25	424.94	370.52	332.02	303.48
30 000	2637.48	1384.35	968.02	760.88	637.41	555.78	498.04	455.22
40 000	3516.64	1845.80	1290.69	1014.50	849.88	741.03	664.05	606.97
50 000	4395.79	2307.25	1613.36	1268.13	1062.35	926.29	830.06	758.71
60 000	5274.95	2768.70	1936.03	1521.76	1274.82	1111.55	996.07	910.45
70 000	6154.11	3230.15	2258.70	1775.38	1487.29	1296.81	1162.08	1062.19
80 000	7033.27	3691.59	2581.38	2029.01	1699.76	1482.07	1328.09	1213.93
90 000	7912.43	4153.04	2904.05	2282.63	1912.23	1667.33	1494.11	1365.67
100 000	8791.59	4614.49	3226.72	2536.26	2124.70	1852.58	1660.12	1517.42
110 000	9670.75	5075.94	3549.39	2789.88	2337.18	2037.84	1826.13	1669.16
120 000	10549.91	5537.39	3872.06	3043.51	2549.65	2223.10	1992.14	1820.90
130 000	11429.07	5998.84	4194.73	3297.14	2762.12	2408.36	2158.15	1972.64
140 000	12308.22	6460.29	4517.41	3550.76	2974.59	2593.62	2324.17	2124.38
150 000	13187.38	6921.74	4840.08	3804.39	3187.06	2778.88	2490.18	2276.12
160 000	14066.54	7383.19	5162.75	4058.01	3399.53	2964.13	2656.19	2427.87
170 000	14945.70	7844.64	5485.42	4311.64	3612.00	3149.39	2822.20	2579.61
180 000	15824.86	8306.09	5808.09	4565.27	3824.47	3334.65	2988.21	2731.35
190 000	16704.02	8767.54	6130.77	4818.89	4036.94	3519.91	3154.22	2883.09
200 000	17583.18	9228.99	6453.44	5072.52	4249.41	3705.17	3320.24	3034.83
210 000	18462.34	9690.44	6776.11	5326.14	4461.88	3890.43	3486.25	3186.57
220 000	19341.50	10151.88	7098.78	5579.77	4674.35	4075.68	3652.26	3338.32
230 000	20220.65	10613.33	7421.45	5833.39	4886.82	4260.94	3818.27	3490.06
240 000	21099.81	11074.78	7744.13	6087.02	5099.29	4446.20	3984.28	3641.80
250 000	21978.97	11536.23	8066.80	6340.65	5311.76	4631.46	4150.30	3793.54
260 000	22858.13	11997.68	8389.47	6594.27	5524.23	4816.72	4316.31	3945.28
270 000	23737.29	12459.13	8712.14	6847.90	5736.70	5001.98	4482.32	4097.02
280 000	24616.45	12920.58	9034.81	7101.52	5949.17	5187.23	4648.33	4248.77
290 000	25495.61	13382.03	9357.48	7355.15	6161.64	5372.49	4814.34	4400.51
300 000	26374.77	13843.48	9680.16	7608.78	6374.11	5557.75	4980.35	4552.25
320 000	28133.08	14766.38	10325.50	8116.03	6799.05	5928.27	5312.38	4855.73
340 000	29891.40	15689.28	10970.84	8623.28	7224.00	6298.78	5644.40	5159.22
360 000	31649.72	16612.17	11616.19	9130.53	7648.94	6669.30	5976.43	5462.70
380 000	33408.04	17535.07	12261.53	9637.78	8073.88	7039.82	6308.45	5766.18
400 000	35166.36	18457.97	12906.88	10145.03	8498.82	7410.34	6640.47	6069.67
420 000	36924.67	19380.87	13552.22	10652.29	8923.76	7780.85	6972.50	6373.15
440 000	38682.99	20303.77	14197.56	11159.54	9348.70	8151.37	7304.52	6676.63
460 000	40441.31	21226.67	14842.91	11666.79	9773.64	8521.89	7636.54	6980.12
480 000	42199.63	22149.57	15488.25	12174.04	10198.58	8892.40	7968.57	7283.60
500 000	43957.94	23072.46	16133.59	12681.29	10623.52	9262.92	8300.59	7587.08
520 000	45716.26	23995.36	16778.94	13188.54	11048.46	9633.44	8632.62	7890.57
540 000	47474.58	24918.26	17424.28	13695.80	11473.40	10003.95	8964.64	8194.05
560 000	49232.90	25841.16	18069.63	14203.05	11898.35	10374.47	9296.66	8497.53
580 000	50991.22	26764.06	18714.97	14710.30	12323.29	10744.99	9628.69	8801.02
600 000	52749.53	27686.96	19360.31	15217.55	12748.23	11115.50	9960.71	9104.50
620 000	54507.85	28609.86	20005.66	15724.80	13173.17	11486.02	10292.73	9407.98
640 000	56266.17	29532.75	20651.00	16232.05	13598.11	11856.54	10624.76	9711.46
660 000	58024.49	30455.65	21296.34	16739.31	14023.05	12227.05	10956.78	10014.95
680 000	59782.80	31378.55	21941.69	17246.56	14447.99	12597.57	11288.80	10318.43
700 000	61541.12	32301.45	22587.03	17753.81	14872.93	12968.09	11620.83	10621.91
720 000	63299.44	33224.35	23232.38	18261.06	15297.87	13338.60	11952.85	10925.40
740 000	65057.76	34147.25	23877.72	18768.31	15722.81	13709.12	12284.88	11228.88
760 000	66816.07	35070.15	24523.06	19275.56	16147.75	14079.64	12616.90	11532.36
780 000	68574.39	35993.04	25168.41	19782.82	16572.70	14450.15	12948.92	11835.85
800 000	70332.71	36915.94	25813.75	20290.07	16997.64	14820.67	13280.95	12139.33
820 000	72091.03	37838.84	26459.09	20797.32	17422.58	15191.19	13612.97	12442.81
840 000	73849.35	38761.74	27104.44	21304.57	17847.52	15561.70	13944.99	12746.30
860 000	75607.66	39684.64	27749.78	21811.82	18272.46	15932.22	14277.02	13049.78
880 000	77365.98	40607.54	28395.13	22319.07	18697.40	16302.74	14609.04	13353.26
900 000	79124.30	41530.44	29040.47	22826.33	19122.34	16673.25	14941.06	13656.75
920 000	80882.62	42453.33	29685.81	23333.58	19547.28	17043.77	15273.09	13960.23
940 000	82640.93	43376.23	30331.16	23840.83	19972.22	17414.29	15605.11	14263.71
960 000	84399.25	44299.13	30976.50	24348.08	20397.16	17784.80	15937.14	14567.20
980 000	86157.57	45222.03	31621.85	24855.33	20822.11	18155.32	16269.16	14870.68
1000 000	87915.89	46144.93	32267.19	25362.58	21247.05	18525.84	16601.183	15174.16
Coefficient	.087915888	.046144929	.032267189	.025362584	.021247046	.018525838	.016601183	.015174164

42

AMOUNT	9 YEARS	10 YEARS	15 YEARS	20 YEARS	25 YEARS	30 YEARS	35 YEARS	40 YEARS
10 000	140.79	132.15	107.46	96.50	90.87	87.76	85.97	84.91
20 000	281.57	264.30	214.92	193.00	181.74	175.51	171.93	169.83
30 000	422.36	396.45	322.38	289.51	272.61	263.27	257.90	254.74
40 000	563.15	528.60	429.84	386.01	363.48	351.03	343.87	339.66
50 000	703.93	660.75	537.30	482.51	454.35	438.79	429.84	424.57
60 000	844.72	792.90	644.76	579.01	545.22	526.54	515.80	509.49
70 000	985.51	925.06	752.22	675.52	636.09	614.30	601.77	594.40
80 000	1126.29	1057.21	859.68	772.02	726.96	702.06	687.74	679.32
90 000	1267.08	1189.36	967.14	868.52	817.83	789.81	773.71	764.23
100 000	1407.87	1321.51	1074.61	965.02	908.70	877.57	859.67	849.15
110 000	1548.66	1453.66	1182.07	1061.52	999.57	965.33	945.64	934.06
120 000	1689.44	1585.81	1289.53	1158.03	1090.44	1053.09	1031.61	1018.98
130 000	1830.23	1717.96	1396.99	1254.53	1181.31	1140.84	1117.57	1103.89
140 000	1971.02	1850.11	1504.45	1351.03	1272.18	1228.60	1203.54	1188.80
150 000	2111.80	1982.26	1611.91	1447.53	1363.05	1316.36	1289.51	1273.72
160 000	2252.59	2114.41	1719.37	1544.03	1453.92	1404.11	1375.48	1358.63
170 000	2393.38	2246.56	1826.83	1640.54	1544.79	1491.87	1461.44	1443.55
180 000	2534.16	2378.71	1934.29	1737.04	1635.66	1579.63	1547.41	1528.46
190 000	2674.95	2510.86	2041.75	1833.54	1726.53	1667.39	1633.38	1613.38
200 000	2815.74	2643.01	2149.21	1930.04	1817.40	1755.14	1719.34	1698.29
210 000	2956.52	2775.17	2256.67	2026.55	1908.27	1842.90	1805.31	1783.21
220 000	3097.31	2907.32	2364.13	2123.05	1999.14	1930.66	1891.28	1868.12
230 000	3238.10	3039.47	2471.59	2219.55	2090.01	2018.41	1977.25	1953.04
240 000	3378.88	3171.62	2579.05	2316.05	2180.88	2106.17	2063.21	2037.95
250 000	3519.67	3303.77	2686.51	2412.55	2271.75	2193.93	2149.18	2122.86
260 000	3660.46	3435.92	2793.97	2509.06	2362.62	2281.69	2235.15	2207.78
270 000	3801.25	3568.07	2901.43	2605.56	2453.49	2369.44	2321.12	2292.69
280 000	3942.03	3700.22	3008.89	2702.06	2544.36	2457.20	2407.08	2377.61
290 000	4082.82	3832.37	3116.35	2798.56	2635.23	2544.96	2493.05	2462.52
300 000	4223.61	3964.52	3223.82	2895.06	2726.10	2632.71	2579.02	2547.44
320 000	4505.18	4228.82	3438.74	3088.07	2907.84	2808.23	2750.95	2717.27
340 000	4786.75	4493.13	3653.66	3281.07	3089.58	2983.74	2922.89	2887.10
360 000	5068.33	4757.43	3868.58	3474.08	3271.32	3159.26	3094.82	3056.93
380 000	5349.90	5021.73	4083.50	3667.08	3453.06	3334.77	3266.76	3226.75
400 000	5631.47	5286.03	4298.42	3860.09	3634.80	3510.29	3438.69	3396.58
420 000	5913.05	5550.33	4513.34	4053.09	3816.54	3685.80	3610.62	3566.41
440 000	6194.62	5814.63	4728.26	4246.10	3998.28	3861.32	3782.56	3736.24
460 000	6476.20	6078.93	4943.18	4439.10	4180.02	4036.83	3954.49	3906.07
480 000	6757.77	6343.24	5158.10	4632.10	4361.76	4212.34	4126.43	4075.90
500 000	7039.34	6607.54	5373.03	4825.11	4543.50	4387.86	4298.36	4245.73
520 000	7320.92	6871.84	5587.95	5018.11	4725.24	4563.37	4470.30	4415.56
540 000	7602.49	7136.14	5802.87	5211.12	4906.98	4738.89	4642.23	4585.39
560 000	7884.06	7400.44	6017.79	5404.12	5088.72	4914.40	4814.17	4755.22
580 000	8165.64	7664.74	6232.71	5597.13	5270.46	5089.92	4986.10	4925.05
600 000	8447.21	7929.04	6447.63	5790.13	5452.20	5265.43	5158.03	5094.88
620 000	8728.79	8193.35	6662.55	5983.13	5633.94	5440.94	5329.97	5264.70
640 000	9010.36	8457.65	6877.47	6176.14	5815.69	5616.46	5501.90	5434.53
660 000	9291.93	8721.95	7092.39	6369.14	5997.43	5791.97	5673.84	5604.36
680 000	9573.51	8986.25	7307.31	6562.15	6179.17	5967.49	5845.77	5774.19
700 000	9855.08	9250.55	7522.24	6755.15	6360.91	6143.00	6017.71	5944.02
720 000	10136.65	9514.85	7737.16	6948.16	6542.65	6318.52	6189.64	6113.85
740 000	10418.23	9779.15	7952.08	7141.16	6724.39	6494.03	6361.58	6283.68
760 000	10699.80	10043.46	8167.00	7334.16	6906.13	6669.54	6533.51	6453.51
780 000	10981.38	10307.76	8381.92	7527.17	7087.87	6845.06	6705.44	6623.34
800 000	11262.95	10572.06	8596.84	7720.17	7269.61	7020.57	6877.38	6793.17
820 000	11544.52	10836.36	8811.76	7913.18	7451.35	7196.09	7049.31	6963.00
840 000	11826.10	11100.66	9026.68	8106.18	7633.09	7371.60	7221.25	7132.83
860 000	12107.67	11364.96	9241.60	8299.19	7814.83	7547.12	7393.18	7302.65
880 000	12389.24	11629.27	9456.52	8492.19	7996.57	7722.63	7565.12	7472.48
900 000	12670.82	11893.57	9671.45	8685.19	8178.31	7898.14	7737.05	7642.31
920 000	12952.39	12157.87	9886.37	8878.20	8360.05	8073.66	7908.99	7812.14
940 000	13233.96	12422.17	10101.29	9071.20	8541.79	8249.17	8080.92	7981.97
960 000	13515.54	12686.47	10316.21	9264.21	8723.53	8424.69	8252.86	8151.80
980 000	13797.11	12950.77	10531.13	9457.21	8905.27	8600.20	8424.79	8321.63
1000 000	14078.69	13215.07	10746.05	9650.22	9087.01	8775.72	8596.72	8491.46
Coefficient	.014078686	.013215074	.010746051	.009650216	.009087008	.008775716	.008596724	.008491459

MONTHLY AMORTIZING PAYMENTS

AMOUNT	1 YEAR	2 YEARS	3 YEARS	4 YEARS	5 YEARS	6 YEARS	7 YEARS	8 YEARS
10 000	880.32	462.60	323.85	254.83	213.70	186.52	167.31	153.07
20 000	1760.64	925.21	647.69	509.66	427.41	373.04	334.61	306.14
30 000	2640.97	1387.81	971.54	764.48	641.11	559.56	501.92	459.20
40 000	3521.29	1850.42	1295.39	1019.31	854.81	746.09	669.23	612.27
50 000	4401.61	2313.02	1619.23	1274.14	1068.51	932.61	836.53	765.34
60 000	5281.93	2775.62	1943.08	1528.97	1282.22	1119.13	1003.84	918.41
70 000	6162.25	3238.23	2266.93	1783.80	1495.92	1305.65	1171.15	1071.47
80 000	7042.58	3700.83	2590.77	2038.63	1709.62	1492.17	1338.45	1224.54
90 000	7922.90	4163.44	2914.62	2293.45	1923.32	1678.69	1505.76	1377.61
100 000	8803.22	4626.04	3238.47	2548.28	2137.03	1865.22	1673.06	1530.68
110 000	9683.54	5088.64	3562.32	2803.11	2350.73	2051.74	1840.37	1683.74
120 000	10563.87	5551.25	3886.16	3057.94	2564.43	2238.26	2007.68	1836.81
130 000	11444.19	6013.85	4210.01	3312.77	2778.13	2424.78	2174.98	1989.88
140 000	12324.51	6476.46	4533.86	3567.59	2991.84	2611.30	2342.29	2142.95
150 000	13204.83	6939.06	4857.70	3822.42	3205.54	2797.82	2509.60	2296.02
160 000	14085.15	7401.66	5181.55	4077.25	3419.24	2984.34	2676.90	2449.08
170 000	14965.48	7864.27	5505.40	4332.08	3632.94	3170.87	2844.21	2602.15
180 000	15845.80	8326.87	5829.24	4586.91	3846.65	3357.39	3011.52	2755.22
190 000	16726.12	8789.48	6153.09	4841.73	4060.35	3543.91	3178.82	2908.29
200 000	17606.44	9252.08	6476.94	5096.56	4274.05	3730.43	3346.13	3061.35
210 000	18486.76	9714.68	6800.78	5351.39	4487.76	3916.95	3513.44	3214.42
220 000	19367.09	10177.29	7124.63	5606.22	4701.46	4103.47	3680.74	3367.49
230 000	20247.41	10639.89	7448.48	5861.05	4915.16	4290.00	3848.05	3520.56
240 000	21127.73	11102.50	7772.32	6115.88	5128.86	4476.52	4015.35	3673.62
250 000	22008.05	11565.10	8096.17	6370.70	5342.57	4663.04	4182.66	3826.69
260 000	22888.37	12027.70	8420.02	6625.53	5556.27	4849.56	4349.97	3979.76
270 000	23768.70	12490.31	8743.87	6880.36	5769.97	5036.08	4517.27	4132.83
280 000	24649.02	12952.91	9067.71	7135.19	5983.67	5222.60	4684.58	4285.90
290 000	25529.34	13415.52	9391.56	7390.02	6197.38	5409.13	4851.89	4438.96
300 000	26409.66	13878.12	9715.41	7644.84	6411.08	5595.65	5019.19	4592.03
320 000	28170.31	14803.33	10363.10	8154.50	6838.48	5968.69	5353.81	4898.17
340 000	29930.95	15728.54	11010.79	8664.16	7265.89	6341.73	5688.42	5204.30
360 000	31691.60	16653.74	11658.49	9173.81	7693.29	6714.78	6023.03	5510.44
380 000	33452.24	17578.95	12306.18	9683.47	8120.70	7087.82	6357.64	5816.57
400 000	35212.88	18504.16	12953.87	10193.13	8548.11	7460.86	6692.26	6122.71
420 000	36973.53	19429.37	13601.57	10702.78	8975.51	7833.91	7026.87	6428.84
440 000	38734.17	20354.58	14249.26	11212.44	9402.92	8206.95	7361.48	6734.98
460 000	40494.82	21279.78	14896.96	11722.09	9830.32	8579.99	7696.10	7041.11
480 000	42255.46	22204.99	15544.65	12231.75	10257.73	8953.03	8030.71	7347.25
500 000	44016.10	23130.20	16192.34	12741.41	10685.13	9326.08	8365.32	7653.38
520 000	45776.75	24055.41	16840.04	13251.06	11112.54	9699.12	8699.93	7959.52
540 000	47537.39	24980.62	17487.73	13760.72	11539.94	10072.16	9034.55	8265.66
560 000	49298.04	25905.82	18135.42	14270.38	11967.35	10445.21	9369.16	8571.79
580 000	51058.68	26831.03	18783.12	14780.03	12394.75	10818.25	9703.77	8877.93
600 000	52819.33	27756.24	19430.81	15289.69	12822.16	11191.29	10038.39	9184.06
620 000	54579.97	28681.45	20078.51	15799.35	13249.56	11564.34	10373.00	9490.20
640 000	56340.61	29606.66	20726.20	16309.00	13676.97	11937.38	10707.61	9796.33
660 000	58101.26	30531.86	21373.89	16818.66	14104.37	12310.42	11042.22	10102.47
680 000	59861.90	31457.07	22021.59	17328.31	14531.78	12683.47	11376.84	10408.60
700 000	61622.55	32382.28	22669.28	17837.97	14959.18	13056.51	11711.45	10714.74
720 000	63383.19	33307.49	23316.97	18347.63	15386.59	13429.55	12046.06	11020.87
740 000	65143.83	34232.70	23964.67	18857.28	15813.99	13802.60	12380.68	11327.01
760 000	66904.48	35157.90	24612.36	19366.94	16241.40	14175.64	12715.29	11633.14
780 000	68665.12	36083.11	25260.06	19876.60	16668.81	14548.68	13049.90	11939.28
800 000	70425.77	37008.32	25907.75	20386.25	17096.21	14921.72	13384.51	12245.42
820 000	72186.41	37933.53	26555.44	20895.91	17523.62	15294.77	13719.13	12551.55
840 000	73947.06	38858.74	27203.14	21405.56	17951.02	15667.81	14053.74	12857.69
860 000	75707.70	39783.94	27850.83	21915.22	18378.43	16040.85	14388.35	13163.82
880 000	77468.34	40709.15	28498.52	22424.88	18805.83	16413.90	14722.97	13469.96
900 000	79228.99	41634.36	29146.22	22934.53	19233.24	16786.94	15057.58	13776.09
920 000	80989.63	42559.57	29793.91	23444.19	19660.64	17159.98	15392.19	14082.23
940 000	82750.28	43484.78	30441.60	23953.85	20088.05	17533.03	15726.80	14388.36
960 000	84510.92	44409.98	31089.30	24463.50	20515.45	17906.07	16061.42	14694.50
980 000	86271.56	45335.19	31736.99	24973.16	20942.86	18279.11	16396.03	15000.63
1000 000	88032.21	46260.40	32384.69	25482.82	21370.26	18652.16	16730.64	15306.77
Coefficient	.088032209	.046260399	.032384686	.025482815	.021370263	.018652156	.016730643	.015306769

44

AMOUNT	9 YEARS	10 YEARS	15 YEARS	20 YEARS	25 YEARS	30 YEARS	35 YEARS	40 YEARS
10 000	142.14	133.54	109.00	98.16	92.64	89.61	87.89	86.88
20 000	284.29	267.08	217.99	196.33	185.28	179.22	175.77	173.76
30 000	426.43	400.62	326.99	294.49	277.91	268.83	263.66	260.65
40 000	568.58	534.16	435.98	392.66	370.55	358.44	351.54	347.53
50 000	710.72	667.70	544.98	490.82	463.19	448.05	439.43	434.41
60 000	852.87	801.23	653.97	588.99	555.83	537.66	527.31	521.29
70 000	995.01	934.77	762.97	687.15	648.47	627.27	615.20	608.17
80 000	1137.15	1068.31	871.96	785.31	741.11	716.88	703.08	695.05
90 000	1279.30	1201.85	980.96	883.48	833.74	806.49	790.97	781.94
100 000	1421.44	1335.39	1089.95	981.64	926.38	896.10	878.86	868.82
110 000	1563.59	1468.93	1198.95	1079.81	1019.02	985.71	966.74	955.70
120 000	1705.73	1602.47	1307.94	1177.97	1111.66	1075.32	1054.63	1042.58
130 000	1847.87	1736.01	1416.94	1276.14	1204.30	1164.93	1142.51	1129.46
140 000	1990.02	1869.55	1525.93	1374.30	1296.94	1254.54	1230.40	1216.35
150 000	2132.16	2003.09	1634.93	1472.47	1389.57	1344.15	1318.28	1303.23
160 000	2274.31	2136.62	1743.92	1570.63	1482.21	1433.76	1406.17	1390.11
170 000	2416.45	2270.16	1852.92	1668.79	1574.85	1523.37	1494.05	1476.99
180 000	2558.60	2403.70	1961.91	1766.96	1667.49	1612.98	1581.94	1563.87
190 000	2700.74	2537.24	2070.91	1865.12	1760.13	1702.59	1669.83	1650.75
200 000	2842.88	2670.78	2179.90	1963.29	1852.77	1792.20	1757.71	1737.64
210 000	2985.03	2804.32	2288.90	2061.45	1945.40	1881.81	1845.60	1824.52
220 000	3127.17	2937.86	2397.89	2159.62	2038.04	1971.42	1933.48	1911.40
230 000	3269.32	3071.40	2506.89	2257.78	2130.68	2061.03	2021.37	1998.28
240 000	3411.46	3204.94	2615.88	2355.94	2223.32	2150.64	2109.25	2085.16
250 000	3553.60	3338.48	2724.88	2454.11	2315.96	2240.25	2197.14	2172.05
260 000	3695.75	3472.01	2833.87	2552.27	2408.60	2329.86	2285.02	2258.93
270 000	3837.89	3605.55	2942.87	2650.44	2501.23	2419.47	2372.91	2345.81
280 000	3980.04	3739.09	3051.86	2748.60	2593.87	2509.08	2460.80	2432.69
290 000	4122.18	3872.63	3160.86	2846.77	2686.51	2598.69	2548.68	2519.57
300 000	4264.33	4006.17	3269.85	2944.93	2779.15	2688.30	2636.57	2606.45
320 000	4548.61	4273.25	3487.84	3141.26	2964.43	2867.52	2812.34	2780.22
340 000	4832.90	4540.33	3705.83	3337.59	3149.70	3046.74	2988.11	2953.98
360 000	5117.19	4807.40	3923.82	3533.92	3334.98	3225.96	3163.88	3127.75
380 000	5401.48	5074.48	4141.81	3730.24	3520.26	3405.18	3339.65	3301.51
400 000	5685.77	5341.56	4359.80	3926.57	3705.53	3584.41	3515.42	3475.27
420 000	5970.06	5608.64	4577.79	4122.90	3890.81	3763.63	3691.19	3649.04
440 000	6254.34	5875.72	4795.78	4319.23	4076.09	3942.85	3866.96	3822.80
460 000	6538.63	6142.79	5013.77	4515.56	4261.36	4122.07	4042.74	3996.56
480 000	6822.92	6409.87	5231.76	4711.89	4446.64	4301.29	4218.51	4170.33
500 000	7107.21	6676.95	5449.75	4908.22	4631.92	4480.51	4394.28	4344.09
520 000	7391.50	6944.03	5667.74	5104.55	4817.19	4659.73	4570.05	4517.85
540 000	7675.79	7211.11	5885.73	5300.87	5002.47	4838.95	4745.82	4691.62
560 000	7960.07	7478.18	6103.73	5497.20	5187.75	5018.17	4921.59	4865.38
580 000	8244.36	7745.26	6321.72	5693.53	5373.02	5197.39	5097.36	5039.15
600 000	8528.65	8012.34	6539.71	5889.86	5558.30	5376.61	5273.13	5212.91
620 000	8812.94	8279.42	6757.70	6086.19	5743.58	5555.83	5448.90	5386.67
640 000	9097.23	8546.50	6975.69	6282.52	5928.85	5735.05	5624.68	5560.44
660 000	9381.52	8813.57	7193.68	6478.85	6114.13	5914.27	5800.45	5734.20
680 000	9665.80	9080.65	7411.67	6675.18	6299.41	6093.49	5976.22	5907.96
700 000	9950.09	9347.73	7629.66	6871.50	6484.68	6272.71	6151.99	6081.73
720 000	10234.38	9614.81	7847.65	7067.83	6669.96	6451.93	6327.76	6255.49
740 000	10518.67	9881.89	8065.64	7264.16	6855.24	6631.15	6503.53	6429.25
760 000	10802.96	10148.96	8283.63	7460.49	7040.51	6810.37	6679.30	6603.02
780 000	11087.25	10416.04	8501.62	7656.82	7225.79	6989.59	6855.07	6776.78
800 000	11371.54	10683.12	8719.61	7853.15	7411.07	7168.81	7030.84	6950.55
820 000	11655.82	10950.20	8937.60	8049.48	7596.34	7348.03	7206.62	7124.31
840 000	11940.11	11217.28	9155.59	8245.80	7781.62	7527.25	7382.39	7298.07
860 000	12224.40	11484.35	9373.58	8442.13	7966.90	7706.47	7558.16	7471.84
880 000	12508.69	11751.43	9591.57	8638.46	8152.17	7885.69	7733.93	7645.60
900 000	12792.98	12018.51	9809.56	8834.79	8337.45	8064.91	7909.70	7819.36
920 000	13077.27	12285.59	10027.55	9031.12	8522.73	8244.13	8085.47	7993.13
940 000	13361.55	12552.67	10245.54	9227.45	8708.00	8423.35	8261.24	8166.89
960 000	13645.84	12819.74	10463.53	9423.78	8893.28	8602.57	8437.01	8340.65
980 000	13930.13	13086.82	10681.52	9620.11	9078.56	8781.79	8612.78	8514.42
1000 000	14214.42	13353.90	10899.51	9816.43	9263.83	8961.01	8788.56	8688.18
Coefficient	.014214419	.013353900	.010899509	.009816434	.009263833	.008961013	.008788556	.008688182

10.50% MONTHLY AMORTIZING PAYMENTS

AMOUNT	1 YEAR	2 YEARS	3 YEARS	4 YEARS	5 YEARS	6 YEARS	7 YEARS	8 YEARS
10 000	881.49	463.76	325.02	256.03	214.94	187.79	168.61	154.40
20 000	1762.97	927.52	650.05	512.07	429.88	375.58	337.21	308.80
30 000	2644.46	1391.28	975.07	768.10	644.82	563.37	505.82	463.20
40 000	3525.94	1855.04	1300.10	1024.14	859.76	751.16	674.43	617.60
50 000	4407.43	2318.80	1625.12	1280.17	1074.70	938.95	843.03	772.00
60 000	5288.92	2782.56	1950.15	1536.20	1289.63	1126.74	1011.64	926.40
70 000	6170.40	3246.32	2275.17	1792.24	1504.57	1314.53	1180.25	1080.80
80 000	7051.89	3710.08	2600.20	2048.27	1719.51	1502.32	1348.85	1235.20
90 000	7933.37	4173.84	2925.22	2304.30	1934.45	1690.11	1517.46	1389.60
100 000	8814.86	4637.60	3250.24	2560.34	2149.39	1877.90	1686.07	1544.00
110 000	9696.35	5101.36	3575.27	2816.37	2364.33	2065.69	1854.67	1698.40
120 000	10577.83	5565.12	3900.29	3072.41	2579.27	2253.48	2023.28	1852.80
130 000	11459.32	6028.89	4225.32	3328.44	2794.21	2441.27	2191.89	2007.20
140 000	12340.80	6492.65	4550.34	3584.47	3009.15	2629.06	2360.49	2161.60
150 000	13222.29	6956.41	4875.37	3840.51	3224.09	2816.85	2529.10	2316.00
160 000	14103.78	7420.17	5200.39	4096.54	3439.02	3004.64	2697.71	2470.40
170 000	14985.26	7883.93	5525.42	4352.57	3653.96	3192.42	2866.31	2624.80
180 000	15866.75	8347.69	5850.44	4608.61	3868.90	3380.21	3034.92	2779.20
190 000	16748.23	8811.45	6175.46	4864.64	4083.84	3568.00	3203.53	2933.60
200 000	17629.72	9275.21	6500.49	5120.68	4298.78	3755.79	3372.13	3088.00
210 000	18511.21	9738.97	6825.51	5376.71	4513.72	3943.58	3540.74	3242.40
220 000	19392.69	10202.73	7150.54	5632.74	4728.66	4131.37	3709.35	3396.80
230 000	20274.18	10666.49	7475.56	5888.78	4943.60	4319.16	3877.95	3551.20
240 000	21155.66	11130.25	7800.59	6144.81	5158.54	4506.95	4046.56	3705.60
250 000	22037.15	11594.01	8125.61	6400.84	5373.48	4694.74	4215.17	3860.00
260 000	22918.64	12057.77	8450.64	6656.88	5588.41	4882.53	4383.77	4014.40
270 000	23800.12	12521.53	8775.66	6912.91	5803.35	5070.32	4552.38	4168.80
280 000	24681.61	12985.29	9100.68	7168.95	6018.29	5258.11	4720.99	4323.20
290 000	25563.09	13449.06	9425.71	7424.98	6233.23	5445.90	4889.60	4477.60
300 000	26444.58	13912.82	9750.73	7681.01	6448.17	5633.69	5058.20	4632.01
320 000	28207.55	14840.33	10400.78	8193.08	6878.05	6009.27	5395.42	4940.81
340 000	29970.52	15767.85	11050.83	8705.15	7307.93	6384.85	5732.63	5249.61
360 000	31733.50	16695.37	11700.88	9217.22	7737.80	6760.43	6069.84	5558.41
380 000	33496.47	17622.90	12350.93	9729.28	8167.68	7136.01	6407.06	5867.21
400 000	35259.44	18550.42	13000.98	10241.35	8597.56	7511.59	6744.27	6176.01
420 000	37022.41	19477.94	13651.03	10753.42	9027.44	7887.17	7081.48	6484.81
440 000	38785.38	20405.46	14301.07	11265.49	9457.32	8262.75	7418.70	6793.61
460 000	40548.36	21332.98	14951.12	11777.55	9887.19	8638.33	7755.91	7102.41
480 000	42311.33	22260.50	15601.17	12289.62	10317.07	9013.91	8093.12	7411.21
500 000	44074.30	23188.02	16251.22	12801.69	10746.95	9389.49	8430.34	7720.01
520 000	45837.27	24115.54	16901.27	13313.76	11176.83	9765.06	8767.55	8028.81
540 000	47600.24	25043.06	17551.32	13825.82	11606.71	10140.64	9104.76	8337.61
560 000	49363.22	25970.58	18201.37	14337.89	12036.58	10516.22	9441.98	8646.41
580 000	51126.19	26898.10	18851.42	14849.96	12466.46	10891.80	9779.19	8955.21
600 000	52889.16	27825.62	19501.47	15362.03	12896.34	11267.38	10116.40	9264.01
620 000	54652.13	28753.14	20151.51	15874.09	13326.22	11642.96	10453.62	9572.81
640 000	56415.10	29680.67	20801.56	16386.16	13756.10	12018.54	10790.83	9881.61
660 000	58178.08	30608.19	21451.61	16898.23	14185.97	12394.12	11128.04	10190.41
680 000	59941.05	31535.71	22101.66	17410.30	14615.85	12769.70	11465.26	10499.21
700 000	61704.02	32463.23	22751.71	17922.37	15045.73	13145.28	11802.47	10808.01
720 000	63466.99	33390.75	23401.76	18434.43	15475.61	13520.86	12139.68	11116.81
740 000	65229.96	34318.27	24051.81	18946.50	15905.49	13896.44	12476.90	11425.61
760 000	66992.94	35245.79	24701.86	19458.57	16335.36	14272.02	12814.11	11734.41
780 000	68755.91	36173.31	25351.91	19970.64	16765.24	14647.60	13151.32	12043.21
800 000	70518.88	37100.83	26001.95	20482.70	17195.12	15023.18	13488.54	12352.01
820 000	72281.85	38028.35	26652.00	20994.77	17625.00	15398.76	13825.75	12660.81
840 000	74044.82	38955.87	27302.05	21506.84	18054.88	15774.33	14162.97	12969.61
860 000	75807.80	39883.39	27952.10	22018.91	18484.75	16149.91	14500.18	13278.41
880 000	77570.77	40810.92	28602.15	22530.97	18914.63	16525.49	14837.39	13587.21
900 000	79333.74	41738.44	29252.20	23043.04	19344.51	16901.07	15174.61	13896.02
920 000	81096.71	42665.96	29902.25	23555.11	19774.39	17276.65	15511.82	14204.82
940 000	82859.68	43593.48	30552.30	24067.18	20204.27	17652.23	15849.03	14513.62
960 000	84622.66	44521.00	31202.35	24579.24	20634.14	18027.81	16186.25	14822.42
980 000	86385.63	45448.52	31852.39	25091.31	21064.02	18403.39	16523.46	15131.22
1000 000	88148.60	46376.04	32502.44	25603.38	21493.90	18778.97	16860.67	15440.02
Coefficient	.088148600	.046376040	.032502443	.025603379	.021493900	.018778970	.016860673	.015440017

46

AMOUNT	9 YEARS	10 YEARS	15 YEARS	20 YEARS	25 YEARS	30 YEARS	35 YEARS	40 YEARS
10 000	143.51	134.94	110.54	99.84	94.42	91.47	89.81	88.86
20 000	287.02	269.87	221.08	199.68	188.84	182.95	179.63	177.71
30 000	430.53	404.81	331.62	299.51	283.25	274.42	269.44	266.57
40 000	574.03	539.74	442.16	399.35	377.67	365.90	359.25	355.43
50 000	717.54	674.68	552.70	499.19	472.09	457.37	449.07	444.29
60 000	861.05	809.61	663.24	599.03	566.51	548.84	538.88	533.14
70 000	1004.56	944.55	773.78	698.87	660.93	640.32	628.69	622.00
80 000	1148.07	1079.48	884.32	798.70	755.35	731.79	718.51	710.86
90 000	1291.58	1214.42	994.86	898.54	849.76	823.27	808.32	799.71
100 000	1435.09	1349.35	1105.40	998.38	944.18	914.74	898.13	888.57
110 000	1578.59	1484.29	1215.94	1098.22	1038.60	1006.21	987.95	977.43
120 000	1722.10	1619.22	1326.48	1198.06	1133.02	1097.69	1077.76	1066.28
130 000	1865.61	1754.16	1437.02	1297.89	1227.44	1189.16	1167.57	1155.14
140 000	2009.12	1889.09	1547.56	1397.73	1321.85	1280.64	1257.39	1244.00
150 000	2152.63	2024.03	1658.10	1497.57	1416.27	1372.11	1347.20	1332.86
160 000	2296.14	2158.96	1768.64	1597.41	1510.69	1463.58	1437.01	1421.71
170 000	2439.65	2293.90	1879.18	1697.25	1605.11	1555.06	1526.83	1510.57
180 000	2583.15	2428.83	1989.72	1797.08	1699.53	1646.53	1616.64	1599.43
190 000	2726.66	2563.77	2100.26	1896.92	1793.95	1738.00	1706.45	1688.28
200 000	2870.17	2698.70	2210.80	1996.76	1888.36	1829.48	1796.27	1777.14
210 000	3013.68	2833.64	2321.34	2096.60	1982.78	1920.95	1886.08	1866.00
220 000	3157.19	2968.57	2431.88	2196.44	2077.20	2012.43	1975.89	1954.85
230 000	3300.70	3103.51	2542.42	2296.27	2171.62	2103.90	2065.71	2043.71
240 000	3444.21	3238.44	2652.96	2396.11	2266.04	2195.37	2155.52	2132.57
250 000	3587.72	3373.38	2763.50	2495.95	2360.45	2286.85	2245.33	2221.43
260 000	3731.22	3508.31	2874.04	2595.79	2454.87	2378.32	2335.15	2310.28
270 000	3874.73	3643.25	2984.58	2695.63	2549.29	2469.80	2424.96	2399.14
280 000	4018.24	3778.18	3095.12	2795.46	2643.71	2561.27	2514.78	2488.00
290 000	4161.75	3913.12	3205.66	2895.30	2738.13	2652.74	2604.59	2576.85
300 000	4305.26	4048.05	3316.20	2995.14	2832.55	2744.22	2694.40	2665.71
320 000	4592.28	4317.92	3537.28	3194.82	3021.38	2927.17	2874.03	2843.42
340 000	4879.29	4587.79	3758.36	3394.49	3210.22	3110.11	3053.66	3021.14
360 000	5166.31	4857.66	3979.44	3594.17	3399.05	3293.06	3233.28	3198.85
380 000	5453.33	5127.53	4200.52	3793.84	3587.89	3476.01	3412.91	3376.57
400 000	5740.34	5397.40	4421.60	3993.52	3776.73	3658.96	3592.54	3554.28
420 000	6027.36	5667.27	4642.68	4193.20	3965.56	3841.91	3772.16	3732.00
440 000	6314.38	5937.14	4863.76	4392.87	4154.40	4024.85	3951.79	3909.71
460 000	6601.40	6207.01	5084.83	4592.55	4343.24	4207.80	4131.42	4087.42
480 000	6888.41	6476.88	5305.91	4792.22	4532.07	4390.75	4311.04	4265.14
500 000	7175.43	6746.75	5526.99	4991.90	4720.91	4573.70	4490.67	4442.85
520 000	7462.45	7016.62	5748.07	5191.58	4909.74	4756.64	4670.30	4620.57
540 000	7749.46	7286.49	5969.15	5391.25	5098.58	4939.59	4849.92	4798.28
560 000	8036.48	7556.36	6190.23	5590.93	5287.42	5122.54	5029.55	4975.99
580 000	8323.50	7826.23	6411.31	5790.60	5476.25	5305.49	5209.18	5153.71
600 000	8610.52	8096.10	6632.39	5990.28	5665.09	5488.44	5388.80	5331.42
620 000	8897.53	8365.97	6853.47	6189.96	5853.93	5671.38	5568.43	5509.14
640 000	9184.55	8635.84	7074.55	6389.63	6042.76	5854.33	5748.06	5686.85
660 000	9471.57	8905.71	7295.63	6589.31	6231.60	6037.28	5927.68	5864.56
680 000	9758.59	9175.58	7516.71	6788.98	6420.44	6220.23	6107.31	6042.28
700 000	10045.60	9445.45	7737.79	6988.66	6609.27	6403.18	6286.94	6219.99
720 000	10332.62	9715.32	7958.87	7188.34	6798.11	6586.12	6466.56	6397.71
740 000	10619.64	9985.19	8179.95	7388.01	6986.94	6769.07	6646.19	6575.42
760 000	10906.65	10255.06	8401.03	7587.69	7175.78	6952.02	6825.82	6753.13
780 000	11193.67	10524.93	8622.11	7787.36	7364.62	7134.97	7005.45	6930.85
800 000	11480.69	10794.80	8843.19	7987.04	7553.45	7317.91	7185.07	7108.56
820 000	11767.71	11064.67	9064.27	8186.72	7742.29	7500.86	7364.70	7286.28
840 000	12054.72	11334.54	9285.35	8386.39	7931.13	7683.81	7544.33	7463.99
860 000	12341.74	11604.41	9506.43	8586.07	8119.96	7866.76	7723.95	7641.70
880 000	12628.76	11874.28	9727.51	8785.74	8308.80	8049.71	7903.58	7819.42
900 000	12915.77	12144.15	9948.59	8985.42	8497.64	8232.65	8083.21	7997.13
920 000	13202.79	12414.02	10169.67	9185.10	8686.47	8415.60	8262.83	8174.85
940 000	13489.81	12683.89	10390.75	9384.77	8875.31	8598.55	8442.46	8352.56
960 000	13776.83	12953.76	10611.83	9584.45	9064.14	8781.50	8622.09	8530.27
980 000	14063.84	13223.63	10832.91	9784.12	9252.98	8964.45	8801.71	8707.99
1000 000	14350.86	13493.50	11053.99	9983.80	9441.82	9147.39	8981.34	8885.70
Coefficient	.014350861	.013493500	.011053989	.009983799	.009441817	.009147393	.008981340	.008885703

47

MONTHLY AMORTIZING PAYMENTS

AMOUNT	1 YEAR	2 YEARS	3 YEARS	4 YEARS	5 YEARS	6 YEARS	7 YEARS	8 YEARS
10 000	882.65	464.92	326.20	257.24	216.18	189.06	169.91	155.74
20 000	1765.30	929.84	652.41	514.49	432.36	378.13	339.83	311.48
30 000	2647.95	1394.76	978.61	771.73	648.54	567.19	509.74	467.22
40 000	3530.60	1859.67	1304.82	1028.97	864.72	756.25	679.65	622.96
50 000	4413.25	2324.59	1631.02	1286.21	1080.90	945.31	849.56	778.70
60 000	5295.91	2789.51	1957.23	1543.46	1297.08	1134.38	1019.48	934.43
70 000	6178.56	3254.43	2283.43	1800.70	1513.26	1323.44	1189.39	1090.17
80 000	7061.21	3719.35	2609.64	2057.94	1729.44	1512.50	1359.30	1245.91
90 000	7943.86	4184.27	2935.84	2315.19	1945.62	1701.56	1529.21	1401.65
100 000	8826.51	4649.19	3262.05	2572.43	2161.80	1890.63	1699.13	1557.39
110 000	9709.16	5114.10	3588.25	2829.67	2377.97	2079.69	1869.04	1713.13
120 000	10591.81	5579.02	3914.45	3086.91	2594.15	2268.75	2038.95	1868.87
130 000	11474.46	6043.94	4240.66	3344.16	2810.33	2457.82	2208.87	2024.61
140 000	12357.11	6508.86	4566.86	3601.40	3026.51	2646.88	2378.78	2180.35
150 000	13239.76	6973.78	4893.07	3858.64	3242.69	2835.94	2548.69	2336.09
160 000	14122.41	7438.70	5219.27	4115.89	3458.87	3025.00	2718.60	2491.82
170 000	15005.07	7903.61	5545.48	4373.13	3675.05	3214.07	2888.52	2647.56
180 000	15887.72	8368.53	5871.68	4630.37	3891.23	3403.13	3058.43	2803.30
190 000	16770.37	8833.45	6197.89	4887.61	4107.41	3592.19	3228.34	2959.04
200 000	17653.02	9298.37	6524.09	5144.86	4323.59	3781.26	3398.25	3114.78
210 000	18535.67	9763.29	6850.29	5402.10	4539.77	3970.32	3568.17	3270.52
220 000	19418.32	10228.21	7176.50	5659.34	4755.95	4159.38	3738.08	3426.26
230 000	20300.97	10693.13	7502.70	5916.58	4972.13	4348.44	3907.99	3582.00
240 000	21183.62	11158.04	7828.91	6173.83	5188.31	4537.51	4077.91	3737.74
250 000	22066.27	11622.96	8155.11	6431.07	5404.49	4726.57	4247.82	3893.48
260 000	22948.92	12087.88	8481.32	6688.31	5620.67	4915.63	4417.73	4049.21
270 000	23831.57	12552.80	8807.52	6945.56	5836.85	5104.69	4587.64	4204.95
280 000	24714.23	13017.72	9133.73	7202.80	6053.03	5293.76	4757.56	4360.69
290 000	25596.88	13482.64	9459.93	7460.04	6269.21	5482.82	4927.47	4516.43
300 000	26479.53	13947.56	9786.14	7717.28	6485.39	5671.88	5097.38	4672.17
320 000	28244.83	14877.39	10438.54	8231.77	6917.74	6050.01	5437.21	4983.65
340 000	30010.13	15807.23	11090.95	8746.26	7350.10	6428.13	5777.03	5295.13
360 000	31775.43	16737.07	11743.36	9260.74	7782.46	6806.26	6116.86	5606.61
380 000	33540.73	17666.90	12395.77	9775.23	8214.82	7184.39	6456.68	5918.08
400 000	35306.04	18596.74	13048.18	10289.71	8647.18	7562.51	6796.51	6229.56
420 000	37071.34	19526.58	13700.59	10804.20	9079.54	7940.64	7136.33	6541.04
440 000	38836.64	20456.41	14353.00	11318.68	9511.90	8318.76	7476.16	6852.52
460 000	40601.94	21386.25	15005.41	11833.17	9944.26	8696.89	7815.98	7164.00
480 000	42367.24	22316.09	15657.82	12347.66	10376.62	9075.01	8155.81	7475.47
500 000	44132.55	23245.93	16310.23	12862.14	10808.98	9453.14	8495.64	7786.95
520 000	45897.85	24175.76	16962.63	13376.63	11241.34	9831.26	8835.46	8098.43
540 000	47663.15	25105.60	17615.04	13891.11	11673.69	10209.39	9175.29	8409.91
560 000	49428.45	26035.44	18267.45	14405.60	12106.05	10587.52	9515.11	8721.39
580 000	51193.75	26965.27	18919.86	14920.08	12538.41	10965.64	9854.94	9032.86
600 000	52959.05	27895.11	19572.27	15434.57	12970.77	11343.77	10194.76	9344.34
620 000	54724.36	28824.95	20224.68	15949.05	13403.13	11721.89	10534.59	9655.82
640 000	56489.66	29754.79	20877.09	16463.54	13835.49	12100.02	10874.41	9967.30
660 000	58254.96	30684.62	21529.50	16978.03	14267.85	12478.14	11214.24	10278.78
680 000	60020.26	31614.46	22181.91	17492.51	14700.21	12856.27	11554.06	10590.25
700 000	61785.56	32544.30	22834.32	18007.00	15132.57	13234.39	11893.89	10901.73
720 000	63550.87	33474.13	23486.72	18521.48	15564.93	13612.52	12233.72	11213.21
740 000	65316.17	34403.97	24139.13	19035.97	15997.29	13990.64	12573.54	11524.69
760 000	67081.47	35333.81	24791.54	19550.45	16429.64	14368.77	12913.37	11836.17
780 000	68846.77	36263.64	25443.95	20064.94	16862.00	14746.90	13253.19	12147.64
800 000	70612.07	37193.48	26096.36	20579.43	17294.36	15125.02	13593.02	12459.12
820 000	72377.37	38123.32	26748.77	21093.91	17726.72	15503.15	13932.84	12770.60
840 000	74142.68	39053.16	27401.18	21608.40	18159.08	15881.27	14272.67	13082.08
860 000	75907.98	39982.99	28053.59	22122.88	18591.44	16259.40	14612.49	13393.56
880 000	77673.28	40912.83	28706.00	22637.37	19023.80	16637.52	14952.32	13705.03
900 000	79438.58	41842.67	29358.41	23151.85	19456.16	17015.65	15292.14	14016.51
920 000	81203.88	42772.50	30010.81	23666.34	19888.52	17393.77	15631.97	14327.99
940 000	82969.19	43702.34	30663.22	24180.83	20320.88	17771.90	15971.79	14639.47
960 000	84734.49	44632.18	31315.63	24695.31	20753.23	18150.03	16311.62	14950.95
980 000	86499.79	45562.01	31968.04	25209.80	21185.59	18528.15	16651.45	15262.42
1000 000	88265.09	46491.85	32620.45	25724.28	21617.95	18906.28	16991.27	15573.90
Coefficient	.088265091	.046491852	.032620451	.025724282	.021617953	.018906277	.016991271	.015573903

AMOUNT	9 YEARS	10 YEARS	15 YEARS	20 YEARS	25 YEARS	30 YEARS	35 YEARS	40 YEARS
10 000	144.88	136.34	112.09	101.52	96.21	93.35	91.75	90.84
20 000	289.76	272.68	224.19	203.05	192.42	186.70	183.50	181.68
30 000	434.64	409.02	336.28	304.57	288.63	280.04	275.25	272.52
40 000	579.52	545.35	448.38	406.09	384.84	373.39	367.00	363.36
50 000	724.40	681.69	560.47	507.61	481.05	466.74	458.75	454.20
60 000	869.28	818.03	672.57	609.14	577.26	560.09	550.50	545.04
70 000	1014.16	954.37	784.66	710.66	673.46	653.44	642.25	635.88
80 000	1159.04	1090.71	896.76	812.18	769.67	746.79	734.00	726.72
90 000	1303.92	1227.05	1008.85	913.71	865.88	840.13	825.75	817.56
100 000	1448.80	1363.39	1120.95	1015.23	962.09	933.48	917.50	908.40
110 000	1593.68	1499.73	1233.04	1116.75	1058.30	1026.83	1009.25	999.24
120 000	1738.56	1636.06	1345.14	1218.27	1154.51	1120.18	1101.00	1090.08
130 000	1883.44	1772.40	1457.23	1319.80	1250.72	1213.53	1192.75	1180.92
140 000	2028.32	1908.74	1569.33	1421.32	1346.93	1306.87	1284.50	1271.76
150 000	2173.20	2045.08	1681.42	1522.84	1443.14	1400.22	1376.25	1362.60
160 000	2318.08	2181.42	1793.52	1624.37	1539.35	1493.57	1468.00	1453.44
170 000	2462.96	2317.76	1905.61	1725.89	1635.56	1586.92	1559.75	1544.28
180 000	2607.84	2454.10	2017.71	1827.41	1731.77	1680.27	1651.51	1635.11
190 000	2752.72	2590.43	2129.80	1928.94	1827.98	1773.61	1743.26	1725.95
200 000	2897.60	2726.77	2241.90	2030.46	1924.19	1866.96	1835.01	1816.79
210 000	3042.48	2863.11	2353.99	2131.98	2020.39	1960.31	1926.76	1907.63
220 000	3187.36	2999.45	2466.09	2233.50	2116.60	2053.66	2018.51	1998.47
230 000	3332.24	3135.79	2578.18	2335.03	2212.81	2147.01	2110.26	2089.31
240 000	3477.12	3272.13	2690.28	2436.55	2309.02	2240.36	2202.01	2180.15
250 000	3622.00	3408.47	2802.37	2538.07	2405.23	2333.70	2293.76	2270.99
260 000	3766.88	3544.81	2914.46	2639.60	2501.44	2427.05	2385.51	2361.83
270 000	3911.76	3681.14	3026.56	2741.12	2597.65	2520.40	2477.26	2452.67
280 000	4056.64	3817.48	3138.65	2842.64	2693.86	2613.75	2569.01	2543.51
290 000	4201.52	3953.82	3250.75	2944.16	2790.07	2707.10	2660.76	2634.35
300 000	4346.40	4090.16	3362.84	3045.69	2886.28	2800.44	2752.51	2725.19
320 000	4636.16	4362.84	3587.03	3248.73	3078.70	2987.14	2936.01	2906.87
340 000	4925.92	4635.52	3811.22	3451.78	3271.12	3173.84	3119.51	3088.55
360 000	5215.68	4908.19	4035.41	3654.82	3463.53	3360.53	3303.01	3270.23
380 000	5505.44	5180.87	4259.60	3857.87	3655.95	3547.23	3486.51	3451.91
400 000	5795.20	5453.55	4483.79	4060.92	3848.37	3733.93	3670.01	3633.59
420 000	6084.96	5726.22	4707.98	4263.96	4040.79	3920.62	3853.51	3815.27
440 000	6374.72	5998.90	4932.17	4467.01	4233.21	4107.32	4037.01	3996.95
460 000	6664.48	6271.58	5156.36	4670.05	4425.63	4294.01	4220.51	4178.63
480 000	6954.24	6544.26	5380.55	4873.10	4618.04	4480.71	4404.01	4360.31
500 000	7244.01	6816.93	5604.74	5076.14	4810.46	4667.41	4587.51	4541.99
520 000	7533.77	7089.61	5828.93	5279.19	5002.88	4854.10	4771.02	4723.67
540 000	7823.53	7362.29	6053.12	5482.24	5195.30	5040.80	4954.52	4905.34
560 000	8113.29	7634.97	6277.31	5685.28	5387.72	5227.50	5138.02	5087.02
580 000	8403.05	7907.64	6501.50	5888.33	5580.14	5414.19	5321.52	5268.70
600 000	8692.81	8180.32	6725.69	6091.37	5772.56	5600.89	5505.02	5450.38
620 000	8982.57	8453.00	6949.88	6294.42	5964.97	5787.58	5688.52	5632.06
640 000	9272.33	8725.68	7174.07	6497.47	6157.39	5974.28	5872.02	5813.74
660 000	9562.09	8998.35	7398.26	6700.51	6349.81	6160.98	6055.52	5995.42
680 000	9851.85	9271.03	7622.45	6903.56	6542.23	6347.67	6239.02	6177.10
700 000	10141.61	9543.71	7846.64	7106.60	6734.65	6534.37	6422.52	6358.78
720 000	10431.37	9816.38	8070.83	7309.65	6927.07	6721.07	6606.02	6540.46
740 000	10721.13	10089.06	8295.02	7512.69	7119.49	6907.76	6789.52	6722.14
760 000	11010.89	10361.74	8519.20	7715.74	7311.90	7094.46	6973.02	6903.82
780 000	11300.65	10634.42	8743.39	7918.79	7504.32	7281.15	7156.52	7085.50
800 000	11590.41	10907.09	8967.58	8121.83	7696.74	7467.85	7340.02	7267.18
820 000	11880.17	11179.77	9191.77	8324.88	7889.16	7654.55	7523.52	7448.86
840 000	12169.93	11452.45	9415.96	8527.92	8081.58	7841.24	7707.02	7630.54
860 000	12459.69	11725.13	9640.15	8730.97	8274.00	8027.94	7890.52	7812.22
880 000	12749.45	11997.80	9864.34	8934.02	8466.42	8214.64	8074.03	7993.90
900 000	13039.21	12270.48	10088.53	9137.06	8658.83	8401.33	8257.53	8175.57
920 000	13328.97	12543.16	10312.72	9340.11	8851.25	8588.03	8441.03	8357.25
940 000	13618.73	12815.84	10536.91	9543.15	9043.67	8774.73	8624.53	8538.93
960 000	13908.49	13088.51	10761.10	9746.20	9236.09	8961.42	8808.03	8720.61
980 000	14198.25	13361.19	10985.29	9949.24	9428.51	9148.12	8991.53	8902.29
1000 000	14488.01	13633.87	11209.48	10152.29	9620.93	9334.81	9175.03	9083.97
Coefficient	.014488010	.013633868	.011209480	.010152290	.009620927	.009334814	.009175029	.009083972

11.00% MONTHLY AMORTIZING PAYMENTS

AMOUNT	1 YEAR	2 YEARS	3 YEARS	4 YEARS	5 YEARS	6 YEARS	7 YEARS	8 YEARS
10 000	883.82	466.08	327.39	258.46	217.42	190.34	171.22	157.08
20 000	1767.63	932.16	654.77	516.91	434.85	380.68	342.45	314.17
30 000	2651.45	1398.24	982.16	775.37	652.27	571.02	513.67	471.25
40 000	3535.27	1864.31	1309.55	1033.82	869.70	761.36	684.90	628.34
50 000	4419.08	2330.39	1636.94	1292.28	1087.12	951.70	856.12	785.42
60 000	5302.90	2796.47	1964.32	1550.73	1304.55	1142.04	1027.35	942.51
70 000	6186.72	3262.55	2291.71	1809.19	1521.97	1332.39	1198.57	1099.59
80 000	7070.53	3728.63	2619.10	2067.64	1739.39	1522.73	1369.79	1256.67
90 000	7954.35	4194.71	2946.48	2326.10	1956.82	1713.07	1541.02	1413.76
100 000	8838.17	4660.78	3273.87	2584.55	2174.24	1903.41	1712.24	1570.84
110 000	9721.98	5126.86	3601.26	2843.01	2391.67	2093.75	1883.47	1727.93
120 000	10605.80	5592.94	3928.65	3101.46	2609.09	2284.09	2054.69	1885.01
130 000	11489.62	6059.02	4256.03	3359.92	2826.51	2474.43	2225.92	2042.10
140 000	12373.43	6525.10	4583.42	3618.37	3043.94	2664.77	2397.14	2199.18
150 000	13257.25	6991.18	4910.81	3876.83	3261.36	2855.11	2568.37	2356.26
160 000	14141.07	7457.25	5238.19	4135.28	3478.79	3045.45	2739.59	2513.35
170 000	15024.88	7923.33	5565.58	4393.74	3696.21	3235.79	2910.81	2670.43
180 000	15908.70	8389.41	5892.97	4652.19	3913.64	3426.13	3082.04	2827.52
190 000	16792.52	8855.49	6220.36	4910.65	4131.06	3616.48	3253.26	2984.60
200 000	17676.33	9321.57	6547.74	5169.10	4348.48	3806.82	3424.49	3141.69
210 000	18560.15	9787.65	6875.13	5427.56	4565.91	3997.16	3595.71	3298.77
220 000	19443.97	10253.73	7202.52	5686.01	4783.33	4187.50	3766.94	3455.85
230 000	20327.78	10719.80	7529.90	5944.47	5000.76	4377.84	3938.16	3612.94
240 000	21211.60	11185.88	7857.29	6202.93	5218.18	4568.18	4109.38	3770.02
250 000	22095.42	11651.96	8184.68	6461.38	5435.61	4758.52	4280.61	3927.11
260 000	22979.23	12118.04	8512.07	6719.84	5653.03	4948.86	4451.83	4084.19
270 000	23863.05	12584.12	8839.45	6978.29	5870.45	5139.20	4623.06	4241.28
280 000	24746.87	13050.20	9166.84	7236.75	6087.88	5329.54	4794.28	4398.36
290 000	25630.68	13516.27	9494.23	7495.20	6305.30	5519.88	4965.51	4555.44
300 000	26514.50	13982.35	9821.62	7753.66	6522.73	5710.22	5136.73	4712.53
320 000	28282.13	14914.51	10476.39	8270.57	6957.58	6090.91	5479.18	5026.70
340 000	30049.77	15846.67	11131.16	8787.48	7392.42	6471.59	5821.63	5340.86
360 000	31817.40	16778.80	11785.94	9304.39	7827.27	6852.27	6164.08	5655.03
380 000	33585.03	17710.98	12440.71	9821.30	8262.12	7232.95	6506.53	5969.20
400 000	35352.66	18643.14	13095.49	10338.21	8696.97	7613.63	6848.97	6283.37
420 000	37120.30	19575.29	13750.26	10855.12	9131.82	7994.31	7191.42	6597.54
440 000	38887.93	20507.45	14405.04	11372.03	9566.67	8374.99	7533.87	6911.71
460 000	40655.56	21439.61	15059.81	11888.94	10001.51	8755.68	7876.32	7225.88
480 000	42423.20	22371.76	15714.58	12405.85	10436.36	9136.36	8218.77	7540.04
500 000	44190.83	23303.92	16369.36	12922.76	10871.21	9517.04	8561.22	7854.21
520 000	45958.46	24236.08	17024.13	13439.67	11306.06	9897.72	8903.67	8168.38
540 000	47726.10	25168.23	17678.91	13956.58	11740.91	10278.40	9246.12	8482.55
560 000	49493.73	26100.39	18333.68	14473.49	12175.76	10659.08	9588.56	8796.72
580 000	51261.36	27032.55	18988.46	14990.40	12610.60	11039.77	9931.01	9110.89
600 000	53029.00	27964.70	19643.23	15507.31	13045.45	11420.45	10273.46	9425.06
620 000	54796.63	28896.86	20298.00	16024.22	13480.30	11801.13	10615.91	9739.22
640 000	56564.26	29829.02	20952.78	16541.13	13915.15	12181.81	10958.36	10053.39
660 000	58331.90	30761.18	21607.55	17058.04	14350.00	12562.49	11300.81	10367.56
680 000	60099.53	31693.33	22262.33	17574.95	14784.85	12943.17	11643.26	10681.73
700 000	61867.16	32625.49	22917.10	18091.87	15219.70	13323.86	11985.71	10995.90
720 000	63634.80	33557.65	23571.88	18608.78	15654.54	13704.54	12328.15	11310.07
740 000	65402.43	34489.80	24226.65	19125.69	16089.39	14085.22	12670.60	11624.24
760 000	67170.06	35421.96	24881.42	19642.60	16524.24	14465.90	13013.05	11938.40
780 000	68937.70	36354.12	25536.20	20159.51	16959.09	14846.58	13355.50	12252.57
800 000	70705.33	37286.27	26190.97	20676.42	17393.94	15227.26	13697.95	12566.74
820 000	72472.96	38218.43	26845.75	21193.33	17828.79	15607.94	14040.40	12880.91
840 000	74240.60	39150.59	27500.52	21710.24	18263.63	15988.63	14382.85	13195.08
860 000	76008.23	40082.74	28155.30	22227.15	18698.48	16369.31	14725.29	13509.25
880 000	77775.86	41014.90	28810.07	22744.06	19133.33	16749.99	15067.74	13823.41
900 000	79543.50	41947.06	29464.85	23260.97	19568.18	17130.67	15410.19	14137.58
920 000	81311.13	42879.21	30119.62	23777.88	20003.03	17511.35	15752.64	14451.75
940 000	83078.76	43811.37	30774.39	24294.79	20437.88	17892.03	16095.09	14765.92
960 000	84846.40	44743.53	31429.17	24811.70	20872.73	18272.72	16437.54	15080.09
980 000	86614.03	45675.68	32083.94	25328.61	21307.57	18653.40	16779.99	15394.26
1000 000	88381.66	46607.84	32738.72	25845.52	21742.42	19034.08	17122.44	15708.43
Coefficient	.088381662	.046607841	.032738717	.025845522	.021742422	.019034079	.017122446	.015708426

50

AMOUNT	9 YEARS	10 YEARS	15 YEARS	20 YEARS	25 YEARS	30 YEARS	35 YEARS	40 YEARS
10 000	146.26	137.75	113.66	103.22	98.01	95.23	93.70	92.83
20 000	292.52	275.50	227.32	206.44	196.02	190.46	187.39	185.66
30 000	438.78	413.25	340.98	309.66	294.03	285.70	281.09	278.49
40 000	585.03	551.00	454.64	412.88	392.05	380.93	374.78	371.32
50 000	731.29	688.75	568.30	516.09	490.06	476.16	468.48	464.15
60 000	877.55	826.50	681.96	619.31	588.07	571.39	562.17	556.98
70 000	1023.81	964.25	795.62	722.53	686.08	666.63	655.87	649.81
80 000	1170.07	1102.00	909.28	825.75	784.09	761.86	749.57	742.64
90 000	1316.33	1239.75	1022.94	928.97	882.10	857.09	843.26	835.46
100 000	1462.59	1377.50	1136.60	1032.19	980.11	952.32	936.96	928.29
110 000	1608.84	1515.25	1250.26	1135.41	1078.12	1047.56	1030.65	1021.12
120 000	1755.10	1653.00	1363.92	1238.63	1176.14	1142.79	1124.35	1113.95
130 000	1901.36	1790.75	1477.58	1341.84	1274.15	1238.02	1218.05	1206.78
140 000	2047.62	1928.50	1591.24	1445.06	1372.16	1333.25	1311.74	1299.61
150 000	2193.88	2066.25	1704.90	1548.28	1470.17	1428.49	1405.44	1392.44
160 000	2340.14	2204.00	1818.56	1651.50	1568.18	1523.72	1499.13	1485.27
170 000	2486.40	2341.75	1932.21	1754.72	1666.19	1618.95	1592.83	1578.10
180 000	2632.65	2479.50	2045.87	1857.94	1764.20	1714.18	1686.52	1670.93
190 000	2778.91	2617.25	2159.53	1961.16	1862.21	1809.41	1780.22	1763.76
200 000	2925.17	2755.00	2273.19	2064.38	1960.23	1904.65	1873.92	1856.59
210 000	3071.43	2892.75	2386.85	2167.60	2058.24	1999.88	1967.61	1949.42
220 000	3217.69	3030.50	2500.51	2270.81	2156.25	2095.11	2061.31	2042.25
230 000	3363.95	3168.25	2614.17	2374.03	2254.26	2190.34	2155.00	2135.08
240 000	3510.21	3306.00	2727.83	2477.25	2352.27	2285.58	2248.70	2227.91
250 000	3656.47	3443.75	2841.49	2580.47	2450.28	2380.81	2342.39	2320.74
260 000	3802.72	3581.50	2955.15	2683.69	2548.29	2476.04	2436.09	2413.57
270 000	3948.98	3719.25	3068.81	2786.91	2646.31	2571.27	2529.79	2506.39
280 000	4095.24	3857.00	3182.47	2890.13	2744.32	2666.51	2623.48	2599.22
290 000	4241.50	3994.75	3296.13	2993.35	2842.33	2761.74	2717.18	2692.05
300 000	4387.76	4132.50	3409.79	3096.57	2940.34	2856.97	2810.87	2784.88
320 000	4680.28	4408.00	3637.11	3303.00	3136.36	3047.43	2998.26	2970.54
340 000	4972.79	4683.50	3864.43	3509.44	3332.38	3237.90	3185.66	3156.20
360 000	5265.31	4959.00	4091.75	3715.88	3528.41	3428.36	3373.05	3341.86
380 000	5557.83	5234.50	4319.07	3922.32	3724.43	3618.83	3560.44	3527.52
400 000	5850.34	5510.00	4546.39	4128.75	3920.45	3809.29	3747.83	3713.18
420 000	6142.86	5785.50	4773.71	4335.19	4116.48	3999.76	3935.22	3898.84
440 000	6435.38	6061.00	5001.03	4541.63	4312.50	4190.22	4122.61	4084.50
460 000	6727.90	6336.50	5228.35	4748.07	4508.52	4380.69	4310.01	4270.15
480 000	7020.41	6612.00	5455.67	4954.50	4704.54	4571.15	4497.40	4455.81
500 000	7312.93	6887.50	5682.98	5160.94	4900.57	4761.62	4684.79	4641.47
520 000	7605.45	7163.00	5910.30	5367.38	5096.59	4952.08	4872.18	4827.13
540 000	7897.96	7438.50	6137.62	5573.82	5292.61	5142.55	5059.57	5012.79
560 000	8190.48	7714.00	6364.94	5780.26	5488.63	5333.01	5246.96	5198.45
580 000	8483.00	7989.50	6592.26	5986.69	5684.66	5523.48	5434.35	5384.11
600 000	8775.52	8265.00	6819.58	6193.13	5880.68	5713.94	5621.75	5569.77
620 000	9068.03	8540.50	7046.90	6399.57	6076.70	5904.41	5809.14	5755.43
640 000	9360.55	8816.00	7274.22	6606.01	6272.72	6094.87	5996.53	5941.08
660 000	9653.07	9091.50	7501.54	6812.44	6468.75	6285.33	6183.92	6126.74
680 000	9945.59	9367.00	7728.86	7018.88	6664.77	6475.80	6371.31	6312.40
700 000	10238.10	9642.50	7956.18	7225.32	6860.79	6666.26	6558.70	6498.06
720 000	10530.62	9918.00	8183.50	7431.76	7056.81	6856.73	6746.10	6683.72
740 000	10823.14	10193.50	8410.82	7638.19	7252.84	7047.19	6933.49	6869.38
760 000	11115.65	10469.00	8638.14	7844.63	7448.86	7237.66	7120.88	7055.04
780 000	11408.17	10744.50	8865.46	8051.07	7644.88	7428.12	7308.27	7240.70
800 000	11700.69	11020.00	9092.78	8257.51	7840.90	7618.59	7495.66	7426.36
820 000	11993.20	11295.50	9320.09	8463.94	8036.93	7809.05	7683.05	7612.01
840 000	12285.72	11571.00	9547.41	8670.38	8232.95	7999.52	7870.44	7797.67
860 000	12578.24	11846.50	9774.73	8876.82	8428.97	8189.98	8057.84	7983.33
880 000	12870.76	12122.00	10002.05	9083.26	8625.00	8380.45	8245.23	8168.99
900 000	13163.27	12397.50	10229.37	9289.70	8821.02	8570.91	8432.62	8354.65
920 000	13455.79	12673.00	10456.69	9496.13	9017.04	8761.38	8620.01	8540.31
940 000	13748.31	12948.50	10684.01	9702.57	9213.06	8951.84	8807.40	8725.97
960 000	14040.83	13224.00	10911.33	9909.01	9409.09	9142.30	8994.79	8911.63
980 000	14333.34	13499.50	11138.65	10115.45	9605.11	9332.77	9182.19	9097.29
1000 000	14625.86	13775.00	11365.97	10321.88	9801.13	9523.23	9369.58	9282.94
Coefficient	.014625861	.013775001	.011365969	.010321884	.009801131	.009523234	.009369577	.009282944

51

AMOUNT	1 YEAR	2 YEARS	3 YEARS	4 YEARS	5 YEARS	6 YEARS	7 YEARS	8 YEARS
10 000	884.98	467.24	328.57	259.67	218.67	191.62	172.54	158.44
20 000	1769.97	934.48	657.14	519.34	437.35	383.25	345.08	316.87
30 000	2654.95	1401.72	985.72	779.01	656.02	574.87	517.62	475.31
40 000	3539.93	1868.96	1314.29	1038.68	874.69	766.49	690.17	633.74
50 000	4424.92	2336.20	1642.86	1298.35	1093.37	958.12	862.71	792.18
60 000	5309.90	2803.44	1971.43	1558.03	1312.04	1149.74	1035.25	950.62
70 000	6194.88	3270.68	2300.01	1817.70	1530.71	1341.37	1207.79	1109.05
80 000	7079.87	3737.92	2628.58	2077.37	1749.38	1532.99	1380.33	1267.49
90 000	7964.85	4205.16	2957.15	2337.04	1968.06	1724.61	1552.87	1425.92
100 000	8849.83	4672.40	3285.72	2596.71	2186.73	1916.24	1725.42	1584.36
110 000	9734.81	5139.64	3614.30	2856.38	2405.40	2107.86	1897.96	1742.79
120 000	10619.80	5606.88	3942.87	3116.05	2624.08	2299.48	2070.50	1901.23
130 000	11504.78	6074.12	4271.44	3375.72	2842.75	2491.11	2243.04	2059.67
140 000	12389.76	6541.36	4600.01	3635.39	3061.42	2682.73	2415.58	2218.10
150 000	13274.75	7008.60	4928.59	3895.06	3280.10	2874.36	2588.12	2376.54
160 000	14159.73	7475.84	5257.16	4154.74	3498.77	3065.98	2760.67	2534.97
170 000	15044.71	7943.08	5585.73	4414.41	3717.44	3257.60	2933.21	2693.41
180 000	15929.70	8410.32	5914.30	4674.08	3936.12	3449.23	3105.75	2851.85
190 000	16814.68	8877.56	6242.87	4933.75	4154.79	3640.85	3278.29	3010.28
200 000	17699.66	9344.80	6571.45	5193.42	4373.46	3832.47	3450.83	3168.72
210 000	18584.65	9812.04	6900.02	5453.09	4592.13	4024.10	3623.37	3327.15
220 000	19469.63	10279.28	7228.59	5712.76	4810.81	4215.72	3795.92	3485.59
230 000	20354.61	10746.52	7557.16	5972.43	5029.48	4407.35	3968.46	3644.02
240 000	21239.60	11213.76	7885.74	6232.10	5248.15	4598.97	4141.00	3802.46
250 000	22124.58	11681.00	8214.31	6491.77	5466.83	4790.59	4313.54	3960.90
260 000	23009.56	12148.24	8542.88	6751.45	5685.50	4982.22	4486.08	4119.33
270 000	23894.54	12615.48	8871.45	7011.12	5904.17	5173.84	4658.62	4277.77
280 000	24779.53	13082.72	9200.03	7270.79	6122.85	5365.46	4831.17	4436.20
290 000	25664.51	13549.96	9528.60	7530.46	6341.52	5557.09	5003.71	4594.64
300 000	26549.49	14017.20	9857.17	7790.13	6560.19	5748.71	5176.25	4753.08
320 000	28319.46	14951.68	10514.31	8309.47	6997.54	6131.96	5521.33	5069.95
340 000	30089.43	15886.16	11171.46	8828.81	7434.88	6515.21	5866.42	5386.82
360 000	31859.39	16820.64	11828.60	9348.15	7872.23	6898.45	6211.50	5703.69
380 000	33629.36	17755.12	12485.75	9867.50	8309.58	7281.70	6556.58	6020.56
400 000	35399.33	18689.60	13142.89	10386.84	8746.92	7664.95	6901.67	6337.43
420 000	37169.29	19624.08	13800.04	10906.18	9184.27	8048.20	7246.75	6654.31
440 000	38939.26	20558.56	14457.18	11425.52	9621.62	8431.44	7591.83	6971.18
460 000	40709.22	21493.04	15114.33	11944.86	10058.96	8814.69	7936.92	7288.05
480 000	42479.19	22427.52	15771.47	12464.21	10496.31	9197.94	8282.00	7604.92
500 000	44249.16	23362.00	16428.62	12983.55	10933.65	9581.19	8627.08	7921.79
520 000	46019.12	24296.48	17085.76	13502.89	11371.00	9964.43	8972.17	8238.66
540 000	47789.09	25230.96	17742.91	14022.23	11808.35	10347.68	9317.25	8555.54
560 000	49559.06	26165.44	18400.05	14541.57	12245.69	10730.93	9662.33	8872.41
580 000	51329.02	27099.92	19057.20	15060.92	12683.04	11114.18	10007.42	9189.28
600 000	53098.99	28034.40	19714.34	15580.26	13120.38	11497.42	10352.50	9506.15
620 000	54868.95	28968.88	20371.49	16099.60	13557.73	11880.67	10697.58	9823.02
640 000	56638.92	29903.35	21028.63	16618.94	13995.08	12263.92	11042.67	10139.89
660 000	58408.89	30837.83	21685.77	17138.28	14432.42	12647.16	11387.75	10456.77
680 000	60178.85	31772.31	22342.92	17657.63	14869.77	13030.41	11732.83	10773.64
700 000	61948.82	32706.79	23000.06	18176.97	15307.11	13413.66	12077.92	11090.51
720 000	63718.79	33641.27	23657.21	18696.31	15744.46	13796.91	12423.00	11407.38
740 000	65488.75	34575.75	24314.35	19215.65	16181.81	14180.15	12768.08	11724.25
760 000	67258.72	35510.23	24971.50	19734.99	16619.15	14563.40	13113.17	12041.12
780 000	69028.68	36444.71	25628.64	20254.34	17056.50	14946.65	13458.25	12358.00
800 000	70798.65	37379.19	26285.79	20773.68	17493.85	15329.90	13803.33	12674.87
820 000	72568.62	38313.67	26942.93	21293.02	17931.19	15713.14	14148.42	12991.74
840 000	74338.58	39248.15	27600.08	21812.36	18368.54	16096.39	14493.50	13308.61
860 000	76108.55	40182.63	28257.22	22331.70	18805.88	16479.64	14838.58	13625.48
880 000	77878.52	41117.11	28914.37	22851.05	19243.23	16862.89	15183.67	13942.35
900 000	79648.48	42051.59	29571.51	23370.39	19680.58	17246.13	15528.75	14259.23
920 000	81418.45	42986.07	30228.66	23889.73	20117.92	17629.38	15873.83	14576.10
940 000	83188.41	43920.55	30885.80	24409.07	20555.27	18012.63	16218.92	14892.97
960 000	84958.38	44855.03	31542.94	24928.41	20992.61	18395.88	16564.00	15209.84
980 000	86728.35	45789.51	32200.09	25447.76	21429.96	18779.12	16909.08	15526.71
1000 000	88498.31	46723.99	32857.23	25967.10	21867.31	19162.37	17254.17	15843.58
Coefficient	.088498313	.046723992	.032857234	.025967097	.021867307	.019162371	.017254166	.015843584

52

MONTHLY AMORTIZING PAYMENTS 11.25%

AMOUNT	9 YEARS	10 YEARS	15 YEARS	20 YEARS	25 YEARS	30 YEARS	35 YEARS	40 YEARS
10 000	147.64	139.17	115.23	104.93	99.82	97.13	95.65	94.83
20 000	295.29	278.34	230.47	209.85	199.65	194.25	191.30	189.65
30 000	442.93	417.51	345.70	314.78	299.47	291.38	286.95	284.48
40 000	590.58	556.68	460.94	419.70	399.30	388.50	382.60	379.30
50 000	738.22	695.84	576.17	524.63	499.12	485.63	478.25	474.13
60 000	885.86	835.01	691.41	629.55	598.94	582.76	573.90	568.95
70 000	1033.51	974.18	806.64	734.48	698.77	679.88	669.55	663.78
80 000	1181.15	1113.35	921.88	839.40	798.59	777.01	765.20	758.61
90 000	1328.80	1252.52	1037.11	944.33	898.42	874.14	860.84	853.43
100 000	1476.44	1391.69	1152.34	1049.26	998.24	971.26	956.49	948.26
110 000	1624.09	1530.86	1267.58	1154.18	1098.06	1068.39	1052.14	1043.08
120 000	1771.73	1670.03	1382.81	1259.11	1197.89	1165.51	1147.79	1137.91
130 000	1919.37	1809.20	1498.05	1364.03	1297.71	1262.64	1243.44	1232.73
140 000	2067.02	1948.37	1613.28	1468.96	1397.54	1359.77	1339.09	1327.56
150 000	2214.66	2087.53	1728.52	1573.88	1497.36	1456.89	1434.74	1422.39
160 000	2362.31	2226.70	1843.75	1678.81	1597.18	1554.02	1530.39	1517.21
170 000	2509.95	2365.87	1958.99	1783.74	1697.01	1651.14	1626.04	1612.04
180 000	2657.59	2505.04	2074.22	1888.66	1796.83	1748.27	1721.69	1706.86
190 000	2805.24	2644.21	2189.45	1993.59	1896.66	1845.40	1817.34	1801.69
200 000	2952.88	2783.38	2304.69	2098.51	1996.48	1942.52	1912.99	1896.51
210 000	3100.53	2922.55	2419.92	2203.44	2096.30	2039.65	2008.64	1991.34
220 000	3248.17	3061.72	2535.16	2308.36	2196.13	2136.78	2104.29	2086.17
230 000	3395.81	3200.89	2650.39	2413.29	2295.95	2233.90	2199.94	2180.99
240 000	3543.46	3340.05	2765.63	2518.21	2395.78	2331.03	2295.59	2275.82
250 000	3691.10	3479.22	2880.86	2623.14	2495.60	2428.15	2391.23	2370.64
260 000	3838.75	3618.39	2996.10	2728.07	2595.42	2525.28	2486.88	2465.47
270 000	3986.39	3757.56	3111.33	2832.99	2695.25	2622.41	2582.53	2560.29
280 000	4134.04	3896.73	3226.56	2937.92	2795.07	2719.53	2678.18	2655.12
290 000	4281.68	4035.90	3341.80	3042.84	2894.89	2816.66	2773.83	2749.95
300 000	4429.32	4175.07	3457.03	3147.77	2994.72	2913.78	2869.48	2844.77
320 000	4724.61	4453.41	3687.50	3357.62	3194.37	3108.04	3060.78	3034.42
340 000	5019.90	4731.74	3917.97	3567.47	3394.01	3302.29	3252.08	3224.07
360 000	5315.19	5010.08	4148.44	3777.32	3593.66	3496.54	3443.38	3413.73
380 000	5610.48	5288.42	4378.91	3987.17	3793.31	3690.79	3634.68	3603.38
400 000	5905.76	5566.76	4609.38	4197.02	3992.96	3885.05	3825.98	3793.03
420 000	6201.05	5845.10	4839.85	4406.88	4192.61	4079.30	4017.27	3982.68
440 000	6496.34	6123.43	5070.32	4616.73	4392.25	4273.55	4208.57	4172.33
460 000	6791.63	6401.77	5300.79	4826.58	4591.90	4467.80	4399.87	4361.98
480 000	7086.92	6680.11	5531.25	5036.43	4791.55	4662.05	4591.17	4551.64
500 000	7382.21	6958.45	5761.72	5246.28	4991.20	4856.31	4782.47	4741.29
520 000	7677.49	7236.78	5992.19	5456.13	5190.85	5050.56	4973.77	4930.94
540 000	7972.78	7515.12	6222.66	5665.98	5390.49	5244.81	5165.07	5120.59
560 000	8268.07	7793.46	6453.13	5875.83	5590.14	5439.06	5356.37	5310.24
580 000	8563.36	8071.80	6683.60	6085.68	5789.79	5633.32	5547.66	5499.89
600 000	8858.65	8350.14	6914.07	6295.54	5989.44	5827.57	5738.96	5689.54
620 000	9153.94	8628.47	7144.54	6505.39	6189.09	6021.82	5930.26	5879.20
640 000	9449.22	8906.81	7375.01	6715.24	6388.73	6216.07	6121.56	6068.85
660 000	9744.51	9185.15	7605.47	6925.09	6588.38	6410.33	6312.86	6258.50
680 000	10039.80	9463.49	7835.94	7134.94	6788.03	6604.58	6504.16	6448.15
700 000	10335.09	9741.83	8066.41	7344.79	6987.68	6798.83	6695.46	6637.80
720 000	10630.38	10020.16	8296.88	7554.64	7187.33	6993.08	6886.76	6827.45
740 000	10925.66	10298.50	8527.35	7764.49	7386.97	7187.33	7078.05	7017.10
760 000	11220.95	10576.84	8757.82	7974.35	7586.62	7381.59	7269.35	7206.76
780 000	11516.24	10855.18	8988.29	8184.20	7786.27	7575.84	7460.65	7396.41
800 000	11811.53	11133.52	9218.76	8394.05	7985.92	7770.09	7651.95	7586.06
820 000	12106.82	11411.85	9449.23	8603.90	8185.56	7964.34	7843.25	7775.71
840 000	12402.11	11690.19	9679.69	8813.75	8385.21	8158.60	8034.55	7965.36
860 000	12697.39	11968.53	9910.16	9023.60	8584.86	8352.85	8225.85	8155.01
880 000	12992.68	12246.87	10140.63	9233.45	8784.51	8547.10	8417.15	8344.66
900 000	13287.97	12525.20	10371.10	9443.30	8984.16	8741.35	8608.45	8534.32
920 000	13583.26	12803.54	10601.57	9653.16	9183.80	8935.60	8799.74	8723.97
940 000	13878.55	13081.88	10832.04	9863.01	9383.45	9129.86	8991.04	8913.62
960 000	14173.84	13360.22	11062.51	10072.86	9583.10	9324.11	9182.34	9103.27
980 000	14469.12	13638.56	11292.98	10282.71	9782.75	9518.36	9373.64	9292.92
1000 000	14764.41	13916.89	11523.45	10492.56	9982.40	9712.61	9564.94	9482.57
Coefficient	.014764412	.013916894	.011523446	.010492560	.009982396	.009712614	.009564939	.009482573

53

MONTHLY AMORTIZING PAYMENTS

AMOUNT	1 YEAR	2 YEARS	3 YEARS	4 YEARS	5 YEARS	6 YEARS	7 YEARS	8 YEARS
10 000	886.15	468.40	329.76	260.89	219.93	192.91	173.86	159.79
20 000	1772.30	936.81	659.52	521.78	439.85	385.82	347.73	319.59
30 000	2658.45	1405.21	989.28	782.67	659.78	578.73	521.59	479.38
40 000	3544.60	1873.61	1319.04	1043.56	879.70	771.65	695.46	639.17
50 000	4430.75	2342.02	1648.80	1304.45	1099.63	964.56	869.32	798.97
60 000	5316.90	2810.42	1978.56	1565.34	1319.56	1157.47	1043.19	958.76
70 000	6203.05	3278.82	2308.32	1826.23	1539.48	1350.38	1217.05	1118.56
80 000	7089.20	3747.22	2638.08	2087.12	1759.41	1543.29	1390.92	1278.35
90 000	7975.35	4215.63	2967.84	2348.01	1979.33	1736.20	1564.78	1438.14
100 000	8861.51	4684.03	3297.60	2608.90	2199.26	1929.12	1738.65	1597.94
110 000	9747.66	5152.43	3627.36	2869.79	2419.19	2122.03	1912.51	1757.73
120 000	10633.81	5620.84	3957.12	3130.68	2639.11	2314.94	2086.38	1917.52
130 000	11519.96	6089.24	4286.88	3391.57	2859.04	2507.85	2260.24	2077.32
140 000	12406.11	6557.64	4616.64	3652.46	3078.96	2700.76	2434.10	2237.11
150 000	13292.26	7026.05	4946.40	3913.35	3298.89	2893.67	2607.97	2396.91
160 000	14178.41	7494.45	5276.16	4174.24	3518.82	3086.58	2781.83	2556.70
170 000	15064.56	7962.85	5605.92	4435.13	3738.74	3279.50	2955.70	2716.49
180 000	15950.71	8431.26	5935.68	4696.02	3958.67	3472.41	3129.56	2876.29
190 000	16836.86	8899.66	6265.44	4956.91	4178.60	3665.32	3303.43	3036.08
200 000	17723.01	9368.06	6595.20	5217.80	4398.52	3858.23	3477.29	3195.87
210 000	18609.16	9836.47	6924.96	5478.69	4618.45	4051.14	3651.16	3355.67
220 000	19495.31	10304.87	7254.72	5739.58	4838.37	4244.05	3825.02	3515.46
230 000	20381.46	10773.27	7584.48	6000.47	5058.30	4436.97	3998.89	3675.26
240 000	21267.61	11241.67	7914.24	6261.36	5278.23	4629.88	4172.75	3835.05
250 000	22153.76	11710.08	8244.00	6522.25	5498.15	4822.79	4346.62	3994.84
260 000	23039.91	12178.48	8573.76	6783.14	5718.08	5015.70	4520.48	4154.64
270 000	23926.06	12646.88	8903.52	7044.03	5938.00	5208.61	4694.34	4314.43
280 000	24812.22	13115.29	9233.28	7304.92	6157.93	5401.52	4868.21	4474.22
290 000	25698.37	13583.69	9563.04	7565.81	6377.86	5594.44	5042.07	4634.02
300 000	26584.52	14052.09	9892.80	7826.70	6597.78	5787.35	5215.94	4793.81
320 000	28356.82	14988.90	10552.32	8348.48	7037.63	6173.17	5563.67	5113.40
340 000	30129.12	15925.71	11211.84	8870.26	7477.49	6558.99	5911.40	5432.99
360 000	31901.42	16862.51	11871.36	9392.04	7917.34	6944.82	6259.13	5752.57
380 000	33673.72	17799.32	12530.88	9913.82	8357.19	7330.64	6606.85	6072.16
400 000	35446.02	18736.12	13190.40	10435.60	8797.04	7716.46	6954.58	6391.75
420 000	37218.32	19672.93	13849.92	10957.38	9236.89	8102.29	7302.31	6711.34
440 000	38960.62	20609.74	14509.44	11479.16	9676.75	8488.11	7650.04	7030.92
460 000	40762.92	21546.54	15168.96	12000.94	10116.60	8873.93	7997.77	7350.51
480 000	42535.23	22483.35	15828.48	12522.72	10556.45	9259.75	8345.50	7670.10
500 000	44307.53	23420.16	16488.00	13044.50	10996.30	9645.58	8693.23	7989.69
520 000	46079.83	24356.96	17147.52	13566.28	11436.16	10031.40	9040.96	8309.27
540 000	47852.13	25293.77	17807.04	14088.06	11876.01	10417.22	9388.69	8628.86
560 000	49624.43	26230.57	18466.56	14609.84	12315.86	10803.05	9736.42	8948.45
580 000	51396.73	27167.38	19126.08	15131.62	12755.71	11188.87	10084.15	9268.04
600 000	53169.03	28104.19	19785.60	15653.40	13195.56	11574.69	10431.88	9587.62
620 000	54941.33	29040.99	20445.12	16175.18	13635.42	11960.52	10779.61	9907.21
640 000	56713.63	29977.80	21104.64	16696.97	14075.27	12346.34	11127.33	10226.80
660 000	58485.94	30914.61	21764.16	17218.75	14515.12	12732.16	11475.06	10546.39
680 000	60258.24	31851.41	22423.68	17740.53	14954.97	13117.99	11822.79	10865.97
700 000	62030.54	32788.22	23083.20	18262.31	15394.82	13503.81	12170.52	11185.56
720 000	63802.84	33725.02	23742.72	18784.09	15834.68	13889.63	12518.25	11505.15
740 000	65575.14	34661.83	24402.24	19305.87	16274.53	14275.46	12865.98	11824.74
760 000	67347.44	35598.64	25061.76	19827.65	16714.38	14661.28	13213.71	12144.32
780 000	69119.74	36535.44	25721.28	20349.43	17154.23	15047.10	13561.44	12463.91
800 000	70892.04	37472.25	26380.80	20871.21	17594.09	15432.92	13909.17	12783.50
820 000	72664.34	38409.06	27040.32	21392.99	18033.94	15818.75	14256.90	13103.09
840 000	74436.65	39345.86	27699.84	21914.77	18473.79	16204.57	14604.63	13422.67
860 000	76208.95	40282.67	28359.36	22436.55	18913.64	16590.39	14952.36	13742.26
880 000	77981.25	41219.47	29018.88	22958.33	19353.49	16976.22	15300.08	14061.85
900 000	79753.55	42156.28	29678.40	23480.11	19793.35	17362.04	15647.81	14381.44
920 000	81525.85	43093.09	30337.92	24001.89	20233.20	17747.86	15995.54	14701.02
940 000	83298.15	44029.89	30997.44	24523.67	20673.05	18133.69	16343.27	15020.61
960 000	85070.45	44966.70	31656.96	25045.45	21112.90	18519.51	16691.00	15340.20
980 000	86842.75	45903.51	32316.48	25567.23	21552.75	18905.33	17038.73	15659.79
1000 000	88615.05	46840.31	32976.00	26089.01	21992.61	19291.16	17386.46	15979.37
Coefficient	.088615054	.046840312	.032976004	.026089008	.021992607	.019291156	.017386460	.015979374

54

MONTHLY AMORTIZING PAYMENTS   11.50%

AMOUNT	9 YEARS	10 YEARS	15 YEARS	20 YEARS	25 YEARS	30 YEARS	35 YEARS	40 YEARS
10 000	149.04	140.60	116.82	106.64	101.65	99.03	97.61	96.83
20 000	298.07	281.19	233.64	213.29	203.29	198.06	195.22	193.66
30 000	447.11	421.79	350.46	319.93	304.94	297.09	292.83	290.48
40 000	596.15	562.38	467.28	426.57	406.59	396.12	390.44	387.31
50 000	745.18	702.98	584.09	533.21	508.23	495.15	488.05	484.14
60 000	894.22	843.57	700.91	639.86	609.88	594.17	585.66	580.97
70 000	1043.26	984.17	817.73	746.50	711.53	693.20	683.28	677.80
80 000	1192.29	1124.76	934.55	853.14	813.18	792.23	780.89	774.63
90 000	1341.33	1265.36	1051.37	959.79	914.82	891.26	878.50	871.45
100 000	1490.37	1405.95	1168.19	1066.43	1016.47	990.29	976.11	968.28
110 000	1639.40	1546.55	1285.01	1173.07	1118.12	1089.32	1073.72	1065.11
120 000	1788.44	1687.15	1401.83	1279.72	1219.76	1188.35	1171.33	1161.94
130 000	1937.48	1827.74	1518.65	1386.36	1321.41	1287.38	1268.94	1258.77
140 000	2086.51	1968.34	1635.47	1493.00	1423.06	1386.41	1366.55	1355.59
150 000	2235.55	2108.93	1752.28	1599.64	1524.70	1485.44	1464.16	1452.42
160 000	2384.59	2249.53	1869.10	1706.29	1626.35	1584.47	1561.77	1549.25
170 000	2533.62	2390.12	1985.92	1812.93	1728.00	1683.50	1659.38	1646.08
180 000	2682.66	2530.72	2102.74	1919.57	1829.64	1782.52	1756.99	1742.91
190 000	2831.70	2671.31	2219.56	2026.22	1931.29	1881.55	1854.60	1839.74
200 000	2980.73	2811.91	2336.38	2132.86	2032.94	1980.58	1952.21	1936.56
210 000	3129.77	2952.50	2453.20	2239.50	2134.58	2079.61	2049.83	2033.39
220 000	3278.81	3093.10	2570.02	2346.15	2236.23	2178.64	2147.44	2130.22
230 000	3427.84	3233.70	2686.84	2452.79	2337.88	2277.67	2245.05	2227.05
240 000	3576.88	3374.29	2803.66	2559.43	2439.53	2376.70	2342.66	2323.88
250 000	3725.92	3514.89	2920.47	2666.07	2541.17	2475.73	2440.27	2420.70
260 000	3874.95	3655.48	3037.29	2772.72	2642.82	2574.76	2537.88	2517.53
270 000	4023.99	3796.08	3154.11	2879.36	2744.47	2673.79	2635.49	2614.36
280 000	4173.02	3936.67	3270.93	2986.00	2846.11	2772.82	2733.10	2711.19
290 000	4322.06	4077.27	3387.75	3092.65	2947.76	2871.85	2830.71	2808.02
300 000	4471.10	4217.86	3504.57	3199.29	3049.41	2970.87	2928.32	2904.85
320 000	4769.17	4499.05	3738.21	3412.57	3252.70	3168.93	3123.54	3098.50
340 000	5067.24	4780.24	3971.85	3625.86	3455.99	3366.99	3318.76	3292.16
360 000	5365.32	5061.44	4205.48	3839.15	3659.29	3565.05	3513.99	3485.81
380 000	5663.39	5342.63	4439.12	4052.43	3862.58	3763.11	3709.21	3679.47
400 000	5961.46	5623.82	4672.76	4265.72	4065.88	3961.17	3904.43	3873.13
420 000	6259.54	5905.01	4906.40	4479.00	4269.17	4159.22	4099.65	4066.78
440 000	6557.61	6186.20	5140.04	4692.29	4472.46	4357.28	4294.87	4260.44
460 000	6855.68	6467.39	5373.67	4905.58	4675.76	4555.34	4490.09	4454.10
480 000	7153.76	6748.58	5607.31	5118.86	4879.05	4753.40	4685.32	4647.75
500 000	7451.83	7029.77	5840.95	5332.15	5082.34	4951.46	4880.54	4841.41
520 000	7749.90	7310.96	6074.59	5545.43	5285.64	5149.52	5075.76	5035.07
540 000	8047.98	7592.15	6308.22	5758.72	5488.93	5347.57	5270.98	5228.72
560 000	8346.05	7873.34	6541.86	5972.01	5692.23	5545.63	5466.20	5422.38
580 000	8644.12	8154.54	6775.50	6185.29	5895.52	5743.69	5661.42	5616.04
600 000	8942.20	8435.73	7009.14	6398.58	6098.81	5941.75	5856.64	5809.69
620 000	9240.27	8716.92	7242.78	6611.86	6302.11	6139.81	6051.87	6003.35
640 000	9538.34	8998.11	7476.41	6825.15	6505.40	6337.86	6247.09	6197.00
660 000	9836.42	9279.30	7710.05	7038.44	6708.70	6535.92	6442.31	6390.66
680 000	10134.49	9560.49	7943.69	7251.72	6911.99	6733.98	6637.53	6584.32
700 000	10432.56	9841.68	8177.33	7465.01	7115.28	6932.04	6832.75	6777.97
720 000	10730.64	10122.87	8410.97	7678.29	7318.58	7130.10	7027.97	6971.63
740 000	11028.71	10404.06	8644.60	7891.58	7521.87	7328.16	7223.19	7165.29
760 000	11326.78	10685.25	8878.24	8104.86	7725.16	7526.21	7418.42	7358.94
780 000	11624.85	10966.44	9111.88	8318.15	7928.46	7724.27	7613.64	7552.60
800 000	11922.93	11247.64	9345.52	8531.44	8131.75	7922.33	7808.86	7746.26
820 000	12221.00	11528.83	9579.16	8744.72	8335.05	8120.39	8004.08	7939.91
840 000	12519.07	11810.02	9812.79	8958.01	8538.34	8318.45	8199.30	8133.57
860 000	12817.15	12091.21	10046.43	9171.29	8741.63	8516.51	8394.52	8327.22
880 000	13115.22	12372.40	10280.07	9384.58	8944.93	8714.56	8589.74	8520.88
900 000	13413.29	12653.59	10513.71	9597.87	9148.22	8912.62	8784.97	8714.54
920 000	13711.37	12934.78	10747.35	9811.15	9351.51	9110.68	8980.19	8908.19
940 000	14009.44	13215.97	10980.98	10024.44	9554.81	9308.74	9175.41	9101.85
960 000	14307.51	13497.16	11214.62	10237.72	9758.10	9506.80	9370.63	9295.51
980 000	14605.59	13778.35	11448.26	10451.01	9961.40	9704.86	9565.85	9489.16
1000 000	14903.66	14059.54	11681.90	10664.30	10164.69	9902.91	9761.07	9682.82
Coefficient	.014903660	.014059544	.011681898	.010664296	.010164690	.009902914	.009761073	.009682819

55

MONTHLY AMORTIZING PAYMENTS

AMOUNT	1 YEAR	2 YEARS	3 YEARS	4 YEARS	5 YEARS	6 YEARS	7 YEARS	8 YEARS
10 000	887.32	469.57	330.95	262.11	221.18	194.20	175.19	161.16
20 000	1774.64	939.14	661.90	524.23	442.37	388.41	350.39	322.32
30 000	2661.96	1408.70	992.85	786.34	663.55	582.61	525.58	483.47
40 000	3549.28	1878.27	1323.80	1048.45	884.73	776.82	700.77	644.63
50 000	4436.59	2347.84	1654.75	1310.56	1105.92	971.02	875.97	805.79
60 000	5323.91	2817.41	1985.70	1572.68	1327.10	1165.23	1051.16	966.95
70 000	6211.23	3286.98	2316.65	1834.79	1548.28	1359.43	1226.35	1128.11
80 000	7098.55	3756.54	2647.60	2096.90	1769.47	1553.63	1401.55	1289.26
90 000	7985.87	4226.11	2978.55	2359.01	1990.65	1747.84	1576.74	1452.42
100 000	8873.19	4695.68	3309.50	2621.13	2211.83	1942.04	1751.93	1611.58
110 000	9760.51	5165.25	3640.45	2883.24	2433.02	2136.25	1927.12	1772.74
120 000	10647.83	5634.82	3971.40	3145.35	2654.20	2330.45	2102.32	1933.90
130 000	11535.15	6104.38	4302.35	3407.46	2875.38	2524.66	2277.51	2095.05
140 000	12422.46	6573.95	4633.30	3669.58	3096.56	2718.86	2452.70	2256.21
150 000	13309.78	7043.52	4964.25	3931.69	3317.75	2913.06	2627.90	2417.37
160 000	14197.10	7513.09	5295.20	4193.80	3538.93	3107.27	2803.09	2578.53
170 000	15084.42	7982.66	5626.16	4455.91	3760.11	3301.47	2978.28	2739.68
180 000	15971.74	8452.23	5957.11	4718.03	3981.30	3495.68	3153.48	2900.84
190 000	16859.06	8921.79	6288.06	4980.14	4202.48	3689.88	3328.67	3062.00
200 000	17746.38	9391.36	6619.01	5242.25	4423.66	3884.09	3503.86	3223.16
210 000	18633.70	9860.93	6949.96	5504.36	4644.85	4078.29	3679.06	3384.32
220 000	19521.01	10330.50	7280.91	5766.48	4866.03	4272.49	3854.25	3545.47
230 000	20408.33	10800.07	7611.86	6028.59	5087.21	4466.70	4029.44	3706.63
240 000	21295.65	11269.63	7942.81	6290.70	5308.40	4660.90	4204.64	3867.79
250 000	22182.97	11739.20	8273.76	6552.81	5529.58	4855.11	4379.83	4028.95
260 000	23070.29	12208.77	8604.71	6814.93	5750.76	5049.31	4555.02	4190.11
270 000	23957.61	12678.34	8935.66	7077.04	5971.95	5243.52	4730.22	4351.26
280 000	24844.93	13147.91	9266.61	7339.15	6193.13	5437.72	4905.41	4512.42
290 000	25732.25	13617.47	9597.56	7601.26	6414.31	5631.92	5080.60	4673.58
300 000	26619.57	14087.04	9928.51	7863.38	6635.50	5826.13	5255.79	4834.74
320 000	28394.27	15026.18	10590.41	8387.60	7077.86	6214.54	5606.18	5157.05
340 000	30168.84	15965.31	11252.31	8911.83	7520.23	6602.95	5956.57	5479.37
360 000	31943.48	16904.45	11914.21	9436.05	7962.60	6991.35	6306.95	5801.69
380 000	33718.12	17843.59	12576.11	9960.28	8404.96	7379.76	6657.34	6124.00
400 000	35492.75	18782.72	13238.01	10484.50	8847.33	7768.17	7007.73	6446.32
420 000	37267.39	19721.86	13899.91	11008.73	9289.69	8156.58	7358.11	6768.63
440 000	39042.03	20660.99	14561.81	11532.95	9732.06	8544.99	7708.50	7090.95
460 000	40816.67	21600.13	15223.71	12057.18	10174.43	8933.40	8058.89	7413.27
480 000	42591.31	22539.27	15885.61	12581.40	10616.79	9321.81	8409.27	7735.58
500 000	44365.94	23478.40	16547.52	13105.63	11059.16	9710.21	8759.66	8057.90
520 000	46140.58	24417.54	17209.42	13629.85	11501.53	10098.62	9110.04	8380.21
540 000	47915.22	25356.68	17871.32	14154.08	11943.89	10487.03	9460.43	8702.53
560 000	49689.86	26295.81	18533.22	14678.30	12386.26	10875.44	9810.82	9024.84
580 000	51464.49	27234.95	19195.12	15202.53	12828.63	11263.85	10161.20	9347.16
600 000	53239.13	28174.08	19857.02	15726.75	13270.99	11652.26	10511.59	9669.48
620 000	55013.77	29113.22	20518.92	16250.98	13713.36	12040.67	10861.98	9991.79
640 000	56788.41	30052.36	21180.82	16775.20	14155.73	12429.07	11212.36	10314.11
660 000	58563.04	30991.49	21842.72	17299.43	14598.09	12817.48	11562.75	10636.42
680 000	60337.68	31930.63	22504.62	17823.65	15040.46	13205.89	11913.13	10958.74
700 000	62112.32	32869.76	23166.52	18347.88	15482.82	13594.30	12263.52	11281.06
720 000	63886.96	33808.90	23828.42	18872.10	15925.19	13982.71	12613.91	11603.37
740 000	65661.60	34748.04	24490.32	19396.33	16367.56	14371.12	12964.29	11925.69
760 000	67436.23	35687.17	25152.22	19920.55	16809.92	14759.53	13314.68	12248.00
780 000	69210.87	36626.31	25814.12	20444.78	17252.29	15147.93	13665.07	12570.32
800 000	70985.51	37565.44	26476.02	20969.00	17694.66	15536.34	14015.45	12892.64
820 000	72760.15	38504.58	27137.92	21493.23	18137.02	15924.75	14365.84	13214.95
840 000	74534.78	39443.72	27799.83	22017.46	18579.39	16313.16	14716.23	13537.27
860 000	76309.42	40382.85	28461.73	22541.68	19021.76	16701.57	15066.61	13859.58
880 000	78084.06	41321.99	29123.63	23065.91	19464.12	17089.98	15417.00	14181.90
900 000	79858.70	42261.13	29785.53	23590.13	19906.49	17478.39	15767.38	14504.21
920 000	81633.34	43200.26	30447.43	24114.36	20348.86	17866.79	16117.77	14826.53
940 000	83407.97	44139.40	31109.33	24638.58	20791.22	18255.20	16468.16	15148.85
960 000	85182.61	45078.53	31771.23	25162.81	21233.59	18643.61	16818.54	15471.16
980 000	86957.25	46017.67	32433.13	25687.03	21675.95	19032.02	17168.93	15793.48
1000 000	88731.89	46956.81	33095.03	26211.26	22118.32	19420.43	17519.32	16115.79
Coefficient	.088731886	.046956806	.033095030	.026211256	.022118321	.019420429	.017519316	.016115794

AMOUNT	9 YEARS	10 YEARS	15 YEARS	20 YEARS	25 YEARS	30 YEARS	35 YEARS	40 YEARS
10 000	150.44	142.03	118.41	108.37	103.48	100.94	99.58	98.84
20 000	300.87	284.06	236.83	216.74	206.96	201.88	199.16	197.67
30 000	451.31	426.09	355.24	325.11	310.44	302.82	298.74	296.51
40 000	601.74	568.12	473.65	433.48	413.92	403.76	398.32	395.35
50 000	752.18	710.15	592.07	541.85	517.40	504.70	497.90	494.18
60 000	902.62	852.18	710.48	650.22	620.88	605.65	597.48	593.02
70 000	1053.05	994.21	828.89	758.59	724.36	706.59	697.06	691.85
80 000	1203.49	1136.24	947.31	866.97	827.84	807.53	796.64	790.69
90 000	1353.92	1278.27	1065.72	975.34	931.32	908.47	896.21	889.53
100 000	1504.36	1420.29	1184.13	1083.71	1034.80	1009.41	995.79	988.36
110 000	1654.80	1562.32	1302.54	1192.08	1138.28	1110.35	1095.37	1087.20
120 000	1805.23	1704.35	1420.96	1300.45	1241.76	1211.29	1194.95	1186.04
130 000	1955.67	1846.38	1539.37	1408.82	1345.24	1312.23	1294.53	1284.87
140 000	2106.10	1988.41	1657.78	1517.19	1448.72	1413.17	1394.11	1383.71
150 000	2256.54	2130.44	1776.20	1625.56	1552.20	1514.11	1493.69	1482.55
160 000	2406.98	2272.47	1894.61	1733.93	1655.68	1615.06	1593.27	1581.38
170 000	2557.41	2414.50	2013.02	1842.30	1759.16	1716.00	1692.85	1680.22
180 000	2707.85	2556.53	2131.44	1950.67	1862.64	1816.94	1792.43	1779.06
190 000	2858.28	2698.56	2249.85	2059.04	1966.12	1917.88	1892.01	1877.89
200 000	3008.72	2840.59	2368.26	2167.41	2069.60	2018.82	1991.59	1976.73
210 000	3159.16	2982.62	2486.68	2275.78	2173.08	2119.76	2091.17	2075.56
220 000	3309.59	3124.65	2605.09	2384.16	2276.56	2220.70	2190.75	2174.40
230 000	3460.03	3266.68	2723.50	2492.53	2380.04	2321.64	2290.33	2273.24
240 000	3610.46	3408.71	2841.92	2600.90	2483.52	2422.58	2389.91	2372.07
250 000	3760.90	3550.74	2960.33	2709.27	2587.00	2523.52	2489.48	2470.91
260 000	3911.34	3692.77	3078.74	2817.64	2690.48	2624.47	2589.06	2569.75
270 000	4061.77	3834.80	3197.15	2926.01	2793.96	2725.41	2688.64	2668.58
280 000	4212.21	3976.82	3315.57	3034.38	2897.43	2826.35	2788.22	2767.42
290 000	4362.64	4118.85	3433.98	3142.75	3000.91	2927.29	2887.80	2866.26
300 000	4513.08	4260.88	3552.39	3251.12	3104.39	3028.23	2987.38	2965.09
320 000	4813.95	4544.94	3789.22	3467.86	3311.35	3230.11	3186.54	3162.76
340 000	5114.82	4829.00	4026.05	3684.60	3518.31	3431.99	3385.70	3360.44
360 000	5415.70	5113.06	4262.87	3901.35	3725.27	3633.87	3584.86	3558.11
380 000	5716.57	5397.12	4499.70	4118.09	3932.23	3835.76	3784.02	3755.78
400 000	6017.44	5681.18	4736.53	4334.83	4139.19	4037.64	3983.18	3953.46
420 000	6318.31	5965.24	4973.35	4551.57	4346.15	4239.52	4182.33	4151.13
440 000	6619.18	6249.30	5210.18	4768.31	4553.11	4441.40	4381.49	4348.80
460 000	6920.06	6533.36	5447.00	4985.05	4760.07	4643.28	4580.65	4546.47
480 000	7220.93	6817.41	5683.83	5201.79	4967.03	4845.17	4779.81	4744.15
500 000	7521.80	7101.47	5920.66	5418.54	5173.99	5047.05	4978.97	4941.82
520 000	7822.67	7385.53	6157.48	5635.28	5380.95	5248.93	5178.13	5139.49
540 000	8123.55	7669.59	6394.31	5852.02	5587.91	5450.81	5377.29	5337.17
560 000	8424.42	7953.65	6631.14	6068.76	5794.87	5652.69	5576.45	5534.84
580 000	8725.29	8237.71	6867.96	6285.50	6001.83	5854.58	5775.60	5732.51
600 000	9026.16	8521.77	7104.79	6502.24	6208.79	6056.46	5974.76	5930.18
620 000	9327.03	8805.89	7341.61	6718.98	6415.75	6258.34	6173.92	6127.86
640 000	9627.91	9089.89	7578.44	6935.73	6622.71	6460.22	6373.08	6325.53
660 000	9928.78	9373.94	7815.27	7152.47	6829.67	6662.10	6572.24	6523.20
680 000	10229.65	9658.00	8052.09	7369.21	7036.63	6863.99	6771.40	6720.88
700 000	10530.52	9942.06	8288.92	7585.95	7243.59	7065.87	6970.56	6918.55
720 000	10831.39	10226.12	8525.75	7802.69	7450.55	7267.75	7169.72	7116.22
740 000	11132.27	10510.18	8762.57	8019.43	7657.51	7469.63	7368.87	7313.89
760 000	11433.14	10794.24	8999.40	8236.17	7864.47	7671.51	7568.03	7511.57
780 000	11734.01	11078.30	9236.22	8452.92	8071.43	7873.40	7767.19	7709.24
800 000	12034.88	11362.36	9473.05	8669.66	8278.39	8075.28	7966.35	7906.91
820 000	12335.75	11646.42	9709.88	8886.40	8485.35	8277.16	8165.51	8104.58
840 000	12636.63	11930.47	9946.70	9103.14	8692.30	8479.04	8364.67	8302.26
860 000	12937.50	12214.53	10183.53	9319.88	8899.26	8680.92	8563.83	8499.93
880 000	13238.37	12498.59	10420.36	9536.62	9106.22	8882.81	8762.99	8697.60
900 000	13539.24	12782.65	10657.18	9753.36	9313.18	9084.69	8962.15	8895.28
920 000	13840.11	13066.71	10894.01	9970.11	9520.14	9286.57	9161.30	9092.95
940 000	14140.99	13350.77	11130.84	10186.85	9727.10	9488.45	9360.46	9290.62
960 000	14441.86	13634.83	11367.66	10403.59	9934.06	9690.33	9559.62	9488.29
980 000	14742.73	13918.89	11604.49	10620.33	10141.02	9892.22	9758.78	9685.97
1000 000	15043.60	14202.95	11841.31	10837.07	10347.98	10094.10	9957.94	9883.64
Coefficient	.015043602	.014202946	.011841314	.010837071	.010347982	.010094097	.009957939	.009883640

12.00% Monthly Amortizing Payments

AMOUNT	1 YEAR	2 YEARS	3 YEARS	4 YEARS	5 YEARS	6 YEARS	7 YEARS	8 YEARS
10 000	888.49	470.73	332.14	263.34	222.44	195.50	176.53	162.53
20 000	1776.98	941.47	664.29	526.68	444.89	391.00	353.05	325.06
30 000	2665.46	1412.20	996.43	790.02	667.33	586.51	529.58	487.59
40 000	3553.95	1882.94	1328.57	1053.35	889.78	782.01	706.11	650.11
50 000	4442.44	2353.67	1660.72	1316.69	1112.22	977.51	882.64	812.64
60 000	5330.93	2824.41	1992.86	1580.03	1334.67	1173.01	1059.16	975.17
70 000	6219.42	3295.14	2325.00	1843.37	1557.11	1368.51	1235.69	1137.70
80 000	7107.90	3765.88	2657.14	2106.71	1779.56	1564.02	1412.22	1300.23
90 000	7996.39	4236.61	2989.29	2370.05	2002.00	1759.52	1588.75	1462.76
100 000	8884.88	4707.35	3321.43	2633.38	2224.44	1955.02	1765.27	1625.28
110 000	9773.37	5178.08	3653.57	2896.72	2446.89	2150.52	1941.80	1787.81
120 000	10661.85	5648.82	3985.72	3160.06	2669.33	2346.02	2118.33	1950.34
130 000	11550.34	6119.55	4317.86	3423.40	2891.78	2541.52	2294.86	2112.87
140 000	12438.83	6590.29	4650.00	3686.74	3114.22	2737.03	2471.38	2275.40
150 000	13327.32	7061.02	4982.15	3950.08	3336.67	2932.53	2647.91	2437.93
160 000	14215.81	7531.76	5314.29	4213.41	3559.11	3128.03	2824.44	2600.45
170 000	15104.29	8002.49	5646.43	4476.75	3781.56	3323.53	3000.96	2762.98
180 000	15992.78	8473.23	5978.58	4740.09	4004.00	3519.03	3177.49	2925.51
190 000	16881.27	8943.96	6310.72	5003.43	4226.44	3714.54	3354.02	3088.04
200 000	17769.76	9414.69	6642.86	5266.77	4448.89	3910.04	3530.55	3250.57
210 000	18658.25	9885.43	6975.00	5530.11	4671.33	4105.54	3707.07	3413.10
220 000	19546.73	10356.16	7307.15	5793.44	4893.78	4301.04	3883.60	3575.63
230 000	20435.22	10826.90	7639.29	6056.78	5116.22	4496.54	4060.13	3738.15
240 000	21323.71	11297.63	7971.43	6320.12	5338.67	4692.05	4236.66	3900.68
250 000	22212.20	11768.37	8303.58	6583.46	5561.11	4887.55	4413.18	4063.21
260 000	23100.68	12239.10	8635.72	6846.80	5783.56	5083.05	4589.71	4225.74
270 000	23989.17	12709.84	8967.86	7110.14	6006.00	5278.55	4766.24	4388.27
280 000	24877.66	13180.57	9300.01	7373.47	6228.45	5474.05	4942.77	4550.80
290 000	25766.15	13651.31	9632.15	7636.81	6450.89	5669.56	5119.29	4713.32
300 000	26654.64	14122.04	9964.29	7900.15	6673.33	5865.06	5295.82	4875.85
320 000	28431.61	15063.51	10628.58	8426.83	7118.22	6256.06	5648.87	5200.91
340 000	30208.59	16004.98	11292.86	8953.50	7563.11	6647.07	6001.93	5525.97
360 000	31985.66	16946.45	11957.15	9480.18	8008.00	7038.07	6354.98	5851.02
380 000	33762.54	17887.92	12621.44	10006.86	8452.89	7429.07	6708.04	6176.08
400 000	35539.51	18829.39	13285.72	10533.53	8897.78	7820.08	7061.09	6501.14
420 000	37316.49	19770.86	13950.01	11060.21	9342.67	8211.08	7414.15	6826.19
440 000	39093.47	20712.33	14614.30	11586.89	9787.56	8602.08	7767.20	7151.25
460 000	40870.44	21653.80	15278.58	12113.57	10232.45	8993.09	8120.26	7476.31
480 000	42647.42	22595.27	15942.87	12640.24	10677.33	9384.09	8473.31	7801.36
500 000	44424.39	23536.74	16607.15	13166.92	11122.22	9775.10	8826.37	8126.42
520 000	46201.37	24478.21	17271.44	13693.60	11567.11	10166.10	9179.42	8451.48
540 000	47978.34	25419.68	17935.73	14220.27	12012.00	10557.10	9532.48	8776.53
560 000	49755.32	26361.14	18600.01	14746.95	12456.89	10948.11	9885.53	9101.59
580 000	51532.30	27302.61	19264.30	15273.63	12901.78	11339.11	10238.59	9426.65
600 000	53309.27	28244.08	19928.58	15800.30	13346.67	11730.12	10591.64	9751.70
620 000	55086.25	29185.55	20592.87	16326.98	13791.56	12121.12	10944.69	10076.76
640 000	56863.22	30127.02	21257.16	16853.66	14236.45	12512.12	11297.75	10401.82
660 000	58640.20	31068.49	21921.44	17380.33	14681.34	12903.13	11650.80	10726.88
680 000	60417.18	32009.96	22585.73	17907.01	15126.22	13294.13	12003.86	11051.93
700 000	62194.15	32951.43	23250.02	18433.69	15571.11	13685.13	12356.91	11376.99
720 000	63971.13	33892.90	23914.30	18960.36	16016.00	14076.14	12709.97	11702.05
740 000	65748.10	34834.37	24578.59	19487.04	16460.89	14467.14	13063.02	12027.10
760 000	67525.08	35775.84	25242.87	20013.72	16905.78	14858.15	13416.08	12352.16
780 000	69302.05	36717.31	25907.16	20540.39	17350.67	15249.15	13769.13	12677.22
800 000	71079.03	37658.78	26571.45	21067.07	17795.56	15640.15	14122.19	13002.27
820 000	72856.01	38600.25	27235.73	21593.75	18240.45	16031.16	14475.24	13327.33
840 000	74632.98	39541.72	27900.02	22120.42	18685.34	16422.16	14828.30	13652.39
860 000	76409.96	40483.19	28564.30	22647.10	19130.22	16813.17	15181.35	13977.44
880 000	78186.93	41424.66	29228.59	23173.78	19575.11	17204.17	15534.41	14302.50
900 000	79963.91	42366.13	29892.88	23700.45	20020.00	17595.17	15887.46	14627.56
920 000	81740.88	43307.60	30557.16	24227.13	20464.89	17986.18	16240.51	14952.61
940 000	83517.86	44249.06	31221.45	24753.81	20909.78	18377.18	16593.57	15277.67
960 000	85294.84	45190.53	31885.74	25280.48	21354.67	18768.18	16946.62	15602.73
980 000	87071.81	46132.00	32550.02	25807.16	21799.56	19159.19	17299.68	15927.78
1000 000	88848.79	47073.47	33214.31	26333.84	22244.45	19550.19	17652.73	16252.84
Coefficient	.088848787	.047073473	.033214308	.026333837	.022244447	.019550192	.017652733	.016252841

58

MONTHLY AMORTIZING PAYMENTS 12.00%

AMOUNT	9 YEARS	10 YEARS	15 YEARS	20 YEARS	25 YEARS	30 YEARS	35 YEARS	40 YEARS
10 000	151.84	143.47	120.02	110.11	105.32	102.86	101.55	100.85
20 000	303.68	286.94	240.03	220.22	210.64	205.72	203.11	201.70
30 000	455.53	430.41	360.05	330.33	315.97	308.58	304.66	302.55
40 000	607.37	573.88	480.07	440.43	421.29	411.45	406.22	403.40
50 000	759.21	717.35	600.08	550.54	526.61	514.31	507.77	504.25
60 000	911.05	860.83	720.10	660.65	631.93	617.17	609.33	605.10
70 000	1062.90	1004.30	840.12	770.76	737.26	720.03	710.88	705.95
80 000	1214.74	1147.77	960.13	880.87	842.58	822.89	812.44	806.80
90 000	1366.58	1291.24	1080.15	990.98	947.90	925.75	913.99	907.65
100 000	1518.42	1434.71	1200.17	1101.09	1053.22	1028.61	1015.55	1008.50
110 000	1670.27	1578.18	1320.18	1211.19	1158.55	1131.47	1117.10	1109.35
120 000	1822.11	1721.65	1440.20	1321.30	1263.87	1234.34	1218.66	1210.20
130 000	1973.95	1865.12	1560.22	1431.41	1369.19	1337.20	1320.21	1311.05
140 000	2125.79	2008.59	1680.24	1541.52	1474.51	1440.06	1421.77	1411.90
150 000	2277.63	2152.06	1800.25	1651.63	1579.84	1542.92	1523.32	1512.75
160 000	2429.48	2295.54	1920.27	1761.74	1685.16	1645.78	1624.88	1613.60
170 000	2581.32	2439.01	2040.29	1871.85	1790.48	1748.64	1726.43	1714.45
180 000	2733.16	2582.48	2160.30	1981.95	1895.80	1851.50	1827.99	1815.30
190 000	2885.00	2725.95	2280.32	2092.06	2001.13	1954.36	1929.54	1916.15
200 000	3036.85	2869.42	2400.34	2202.17	2106.45	2057.23	2031.10	2017.00
210 000	3188.69	3012.89	2520.35	2312.28	2211.77	2160.09	2132.65	2117.85
220 000	3340.53	3156.36	2640.37	2423.39	2317.09	2262.95	2234.21	2218.70
230 000	3492.37	3299.83	2760.39	2533.50	2422.42	2365.81	2335.76	2319.55
240 000	3644.22	3443.30	2880.40	2642.61	2527.74	2468.67	2437.32	2420.40
250 000	3796.06	3586.77	3000.42	2752.72	2633.06	2571.53	2538.87	2521.25
260 000	3947.90	3730.24	3120.44	2862.82	2738.38	2674.39	2640.43	2622.10
270 000	4099.74	3873.72	3240.45	2972.93	2843.71	2777.25	2741.98	2722.95
280 000	4251.59	4017.19	3360.47	3083.04	2949.03	2880.12	2843.54	2823.80
290 000	4403.43	4160.66	3480.49	3193.15	3054.35	2982.98	2945.09	2924.65
300 000	4555.27	4304.13	3600.50	3303.26	3159.67	3085.84	3046.65	3025.50
320 000	4858.95	4591.07	3840.54	3523.48	3370.32	3291.56	3249.76	3227.20
340 000	5162.64	4878.01	4080.57	3743.69	3580.96	3497.28	3452.87	3428.90
360 000	5466.32	5164.95	4320.61	3963.91	3791.61	3703.01	3655.98	3630.60
380 000	5770.01	5451.90	4560.64	4184.13	4002.25	3908.73	3859.09	3832.30
400 000	6073.69	5738.84	4800.67	4404.34	4212.90	4114.45	4062.20	4034.00
420 000	6377.38	6025.78	5040.71	4624.56	4423.54	4320.17	4265.31	4235.70
440 000	6681.06	6312.72	5280.74	4844.78	4634.19	4525.90	4468.42	4437.40
460 000	6984.75	6599.66	5520.77	5065.00	4844.83	4731.62	4671.53	4639.10
480 000	7288.43	6886.61	5760.81	5285.21	5055.48	4937.34	4874.64	4840.80
500 000	7592.12	7173.55	6000.84	5505.43	5266.12	5143.06	5077.75	5042.50
520 000	7895.80	7460.49	6240.87	5725.65	5476.77	5348.79	5280.86	5244.20
540 000	8199.49	7747.43	6480.91	5945.86	5687.41	5554.51	5483.97	5445.90
560 000	8503.17	8034.37	6720.94	6166.08	5898.05	5760.23	5687.08	5647.60
580 000	8806.86	8321.32	6960.97	6386.30	6108.70	5965.95	5890.19	5849.30
600 000	9110.54	8608.26	7201.01	6606.52	6319.34	6171.68	6093.30	6051.00
620 000	9414.22	8895.20	7441.04	6826.73	6529.99	6377.40	6296.41	6252.70
640 000	9717.91	9182.14	7681.08	7046.95	6740.63	6583.12	6499.52	6454.40
660 000	10021.59	9469.08	7921.11	7267.17	6951.28	6788.84	6702.63	6656.10
680 000	10325.28	9756.02	8161.14	7487.39	7161.92	6994.57	6905.74	6857.80
700 000	10628.96	10042.97	8401.18	7707.60	7372.57	7200.29	7108.85	7059.50
720 000	10932.65	10329.91	8641.21	7927.82	7583.21	7406.01	7311.96	7261.20
740 000	11236.33	10616.85	8881.24	8148.04	7793.86	7611.73	7515.07	7462.90
760 000	11540.02	10903.79	9121.28	8368.25	8004.50	7817.46	7718.18	7664.60
780 000	11843.70	11190.73	9361.31	8588.47	8215.15	8023.18	7921.29	7866.30
800 000	12147.39	11477.68	9601.34	8808.69	8425.79	8228.90	8124.40	8068.00
820 000	12451.07	11764.62	9841.38	9028.91	8636.44	8434.62	8327.51	8269.70
840 000	12754.76	12051.56	10081.41	9249.12	8847.08	8640.35	8530.62	8471.40
860 000	13058.44	12338.50	10321.45	9469.34	9057.73	8846.07	8733.73	8673.10
880 000	13362.13	12625.44	10561.48	9689.56	9268.37	9051.79	8936.84	8874.80
900 000	13665.81	12912.39	10801.51	9909.77	9479.02	9257.51	9139.95	9076.50
920 000	13969.49	13199.33	11041.55	10129.99	9689.66	9463.24	9343.06	9278.20
940 000	14273.18	13486.27	11281.58	10350.21	9900.31	9668.96	9546.17	9479.90
960 000	14576.86	13773.21	11521.61	10570.43	10110.95	9874.68	9749.28	9681.60
980 000	14880.55	14060.15	11761.65	10790.64	10321.60	10080.40	9952.39	9883.30
1000 000	15184.23	14347.10	12001.68	11010.86	10532.24	10286.13	10155.50	10085.00
Coefficient	.015184233	.014347095	.012001681	.011010861	.010532241	.010286126	.010155498	.010085000

AMOUNT	1 YEAR	2 YEARS	3 YEARS	4 YEARS	5 YEARS	6 YEARS	7 YEARS	8 YEARS
10 000	889.66	471.90	333.34	264.57	223.71	196.80	177.87	163.91
20 000	1779.32	943.81	666.68	529.13	447.42	393.61	355.73	327.81
30 000	2668.97	1415.71	1000.02	793.70	671.13	590.41	533.60	491.72
40 000	3558.63	1887.61	1333.35	1058.27	894.84	787.22	711.47	655.62
50 000	4448.29	2359.52	1666.69	1322.84	1118.55	984.02	889.34	819.53
60 000	5337.95	2831.42	2000.03	1587.40	1342.26	1180.83	1067.20	983.43
70 000	6227.61	3303.32	2333.37	1851.97	1565.97	1377.63	1245.07	1147.34
80 000	7117.26	3775.22	2666.71	2116.54	1789.68	1574.44	1422.94	1311.24
90 000	8006.92	4247.13	3000.05	2381.11	2013.39	1771.24	1600.80	1475.15
100 000	8896.58	4719.03	3333.38	2645.67	2237.10	1968.04	1778.67	1639.05
110 000	9786.24	5190.93	3666.72	2910.24	2460.81	2164.85	1956.54	1802.96
120 000	10675.89	5662.84	4000.06	3174.81	2684.52	2361.65	2134.40	1966.86
130 000	11565.55	6134.74	4333.40	3439.38	2908.23	2558.46	2312.27	2130.77
140 000	12455.21	6606.64	4666.74	3703.94	3131.94	2755.26	2490.14	2294.67
150 000	13344.87	7078.55	5000.08	3968.51	3355.65	2952.07	2668.01	2458.58
160 000	14234.53	7550.45	5333.41	4233.08	3579.36	3148.87	2845.87	2622.48
170 000	15124.18	8022.35	5666.75	4497.65	3803.07	3345.68	3023.74	2786.39
180 000	16013.84	8494.25	6000.09	4762.21	4026.78	3542.48	3201.61	2950.29
190 000	16903.50	8966.16	6333.43	5026.78	4250.49	3739.28	3379.47	3114.20
200 000	17793.16	9438.06	6666.77	5291.35	4474.20	3936.09	3557.34	3278.10
210 000	18682.82	9909.96	7000.11	5555.92	4697.91	4132.89	3735.21	3442.01
220 000	19572.47	10381.87	7333.45	5820.48	4921.62	4329.70	3913.08	3605.91
230 000	20462.13	10853.77	7666.78	6085.05	5145.33	4526.50	4090.94	3769.82
240 000	21351.79	11325.67	8000.12	6349.62	5369.04	4723.31	4268.81	3933.72
250 000	22241.45	11797.58	8333.46	6614.19	5592.75	4920.11	4446.68	4097.63
260 000	23131.10	12269.48	8666.80	6878.75	5816.46	5116.91	4624.54	4261.53
270 000	24020.76	12741.38	9000.14	7143.32	6040.17	5313.72	4802.41	4425.44
280 000	24910.42	13213.29	9333.48	7407.89	6263.88	5510.52	4980.28	4589.34
290 000	25800.08	13685.19	9666.81	7672.46	6487.59	5707.33	5158.15	4753.25
300 000	26689.74	14157.09	10000.15	7937.02	6711.30	5904.13	5336.01	4917.15
320 000	28469.05	15100.90	10666.83	8466.16	7158.72	6297.74	5691.75	5244.96
340 000	30248.37	16044.70	11333.51	8995.29	7606.14	6691.35	6047.48	5572.77
360 000	32027.68	16988.51	12000.18	9524.43	8053.56	7084.96	6403.21	5900.58
380 000	33807.00	17932.32	12666.86	10053.56	8500.98	7478.57	6758.95	6228.39
400 000	35586.32	18876.12	13333.54	10582.70	8948.39	7872.18	7114.68	6556.21
420 000	37365.63	19819.93	14000.21	11111.83	9395.81	8265.79	7470.42	6884.02
440 000	39144.95	20763.73	14666.89	11640.97	9843.23	8659.39	7826.15	7211.83
460 000	40924.26	21707.54	15333.57	12170.10	10290.65	9053.00	8181.89	7539.64
480 000	42703.58	22651.35	16000.24	12699.24	10738.07	9446.61	8537.62	7867.45
500 000	44482.89	23595.15	16666.92	13228.37	11185.49	9840.22	8893.35	8195.26
520 000	46262.21	24538.96	17333.60	13757.51	11632.91	10233.83	9249.09	8523.07
540 000	48041.53	25482.76	18000.28	14286.64	12080.33	10627.44	9604.82	8850.88
560 000	49820.84	26426.57	18666.95	14815.78	12527.75	11021.05	9960.56	9178.69
580 000	51600.16	27370.38	19333.63	15344.91	12975.17	11414.66	10316.29	9506.50
600 000	53379.47	28314.18	20000.31	15874.05	13422.59	11808.27	10672.02	9834.31
620 000	55158.79	29257.99	20666.98	16403.18	13870.01	12201.87	11027.76	10162.12
640 000	56938.10	30201.79	21333.66	16932.32	14317.43	12595.48	11383.49	10489.93
660 000	58717.42	31145.60	22000.34	17461.45	14764.85	12989.09	11739.23	10817.74
680 000	60496.74	32089.41	22667.01	17990.59	15212.27	13382.70	12094.96	11145.55
700 000	62276.05	33033.21	23333.69	18519.72	15659.69	13776.31	12450.69	11473.36
720 000	64055.37	33977.02	24000.37	19048.86	16107.11	14169.92	12806.43	11801.17
740 000	65834.68	34920.82	24667.04	19577.99	16554.53	14563.53	13162.16	12128.98
760 000	67614.00	35864.63	25333.72	20107.13	17001.95	14957.14	13517.90	12456.79
780 000	69393.31	36808.44	26000.40	20636.26	17449.37	15350.74	13873.63	12784.C0
800 000	71172.63	37752.24	26667.07	21165.40	17896.79	15744.35	14229.37	13112.41
820 000	72951.95	38696.05	27333.75	21694.53	18344.21	16137.96	14585.10	13440.22
840 000	74731.26	39639.86	28000.43	22223.67	18791.63	16531.57	14940.83	13768.03
860 000	76510.58	40583.66	28667.10	22752.80	19239.05	16925.18	15296.57	14095.84
880 000	78289.89	41527.47	29333.78	23281.94	19686.47	17318.79	15652.30	14423.65
900 000	80069.21	42471.27	30000.46	23811.07	20133.89	17712.40	16008.04	14751.46
920 000	81848.52	43415.08	30667.14	24340.21	20581.31	18106.01	16363.77	15079.27
940 000	83627.84	44358.89	31333.81	24869.34	21028.73	18499.62	16719.50	15407.08
960 000	85407.16	45302.69	32000.49	25398.48	21476.15	18893.22	17075.24	15734.89
980 000	87186.47	46246.50	32667.17	25927.61	21923.57	19286.83	17430.97	16062.70
1000 000	88965.79	47190.30	33333.84	26456.75	22370.99	19680.44	17786.71	16390.51
Coefficient	.088965788	.047190304	.033333843	.026456749	.022370987	.019680442	.017786707	.016390513

AMOUNT	9 YEARS	10 YEARS	15 YEARS	20 YEARS	25 YEARS	30 YEARS	35 YEARS	40 YEARS
10 000	153.26	144.92	121.63	111.86	107.17	104.79	103.54	102.87
20 000	306.51	289.84	243.26	223.71	214.35	209.58	207.07	205.74
30 000	459.77	434.76	364.89	335.57	321.52	314.37	310.61	308.61
40 000	613.02	579.68	486.52	447.43	428.70	419.16	414.15	411.47
50 000	766.28	724.60	608.15	559.28	535.87	523.95	517.69	514.34
60 000	919.53	869.52	729.78	671.14	643.05	628.74	621.22	617.21
70 000	1072.79	1014.44	851.41	783.00	750.22	733.53	724.76	720.08
80 000	1226.04	1159.36	973.04	894.85	857.40	838.32	828.30	822.95
90 000	1379.30	1304.28	1094.67	1006.71	964.57	943.11	931.83	925.82
100 000	1532.56	1449.20	1216.30	1118.56	1071.74	1047.90	1035.37	1028.69
110 000	1685.81	1594.12	1337.93	1230.42	1178.92	1152.69	1138.91	1131.55
120 000	1839.07	1739.04	1459.56	1342.28	1286.09	1257.48	1242.45	1234.42
130 000	1992.32	1883.96	1581.19	1454.13	1393.27	1362.27	1345.98	1337.29
140 000	2145.58	2028.88	1702.82	1565.99	1500.44	1467.05	1449.52	1440.16
150 000	2298.83	2173.80	1824.45	1677.85	1607.62	1571.84	1553.06	1543.03
160 000	2452.09	2318.72	1946.08	1789.70	1714.79	1676.63	1656.59	1645.90
170 000	2605.34	2463.64	2067.71	1901.56	1821.96	1781.42	1760.13	1748.77
180 000	2758.60	2608.56	2189.34	2013.42	1929.14	1886.21	1863.67	1851.64
190 000	2911.85	2753.48	2310.97	2125.27	2036.31	1991.00	1967.21	1954.50
200 000	3065.11	2898.40	2432.60	2237.13	2143.49	2095.79	2070.74	2057.37
210 000	3218.37	3043.32	2554.23	2348.99	2250.66	2200.58	2174.28	2160.24
220 000	3371.62	3188.24	2675.86	2460.84	2357.84	2305.37	2277.82	2263.11
230 000	3524.88	3333.16	2797.49	2572.70	2465.01	2410.16	2381.35	2365.98
240 000	3678.13	3478.08	2919.12	2684.56	2572.19	2514.95	2484.89	2468.85
250 000	3831.39	3623.00	3040.75	2796.41	2679.36	2619.74	2588.43	2571.72
260 000	3984.64	3767.92	3162.38	2908.27	2786.53	2724.53	2691.96	2674.58
270 000	4137.90	3912.84	3284.01	3020.12	2893.71	2829.32	2795.50	2777.45
280 000	4291.15	4057.76	3405.64	3131.98	3000.88	2934.11	2899.04	2880.32
290 000	4444.41	4202.68	3527.27	3243.84	3108.06	3038.90	3002.58	2983.19
300 000	4597.67	4347.60	3648.90	3355.69	3215.23	3143.69	3106.11	3086.06
320 000	4904.18	4637.44	3892.16	3579.41	3429.58	3353.27	3313.19	3291.80
340 000	5210.69	4927.28	4135.42	3803.12	3643.93	3562.85	3520.26	3497.53
360 000	5517.20	5217.12	4378.68	4026.83	3858.28	3772.43	3727.34	3703.27
380 000	5823.71	5506.96	4621.94	4250.55	4072.63	3982.01	3934.41	3909.01
400 000	6130.23	5796.79	4865.19	4474.26	4286.98	4191.59	4141.48	4114.74
420 000	6436.73	6086.63	5108.45	4697.97	4501.32	4401.16	4348.56	4320.48
440 000	6743.24	6376.47	5351.71	4921.68	4715.67	4610.74	4555.63	4526.22
460 000	7049.75	6666.31	5594.97	5145.40	4930.02	4820.32	4762.71	4731.96
480 000	7356.26	6956.15	5838.23	5369.11	5144.37	5029.90	4969.78	4937.69
500 000	7662.78	7245.99	6081.49	5592.82	5358.72	5239.48	5176.86	5143.43
520 000	7969.29	7535.83	6324.75	5816.54	5573.07	5449.06	5383.93	5349.17
540 000	8275.80	7825.67	6568.01	6040.25	5787.42	5658.64	5591.00	5554.91
560 000	8582.31	8115.51	6811.27	6263.96	6001.77	5868.22	5798.08	5760.64
580 000	8888.82	8405.35	7054.53	6487.68	6216.11	6077.80	6005.15	5966.38
600 000	9195.33	8695.19	7297.79	6711.39	6430.46	6287.38	6212.23	6172.12
620 000	9501.84	8985.03	7541.05	6935.10	6644.81	6496.96	6419.30	6377.85
640 000	9808.35	9274.87	7784.31	7158.81	6859.16	6706.54	6626.38	6583.59
660 000	10114.86	9564.71	8027.57	7382.53	7073.51	6916.12	6833.45	6789.33
680 000	10421.37	9854.55	8270.83	7606.24	7287.86	7125.70	7040.52	6995.07
700 000	10727.89	10144.39	8514.09	7829.95	7502.21	7335.27	7247.60	7200.80
720 000	11034.40	10434.23	8757.35	8053.67	7716.56	7544.85	7454.67	7406.54
740 000	11340.91	10724.07	9000.61	8277.38	7930.90	7754.43	7661.75	7612.28
760 000	11647.42	11013.91	9243.87	8501.09	8145.25	7964.01	7868.82	7818.00
780 000	11953.93	11303.75	9487.13	8724.80	8359.60	8173.59	8075.89	8023.75
800 000	12260.44	11593.59	9730.39	8948.52	8573.95	8383.17	8282.97	8229.49
820 000	12566.95	11883.43	9973.65	9172.23	8788.30	8592.75	8490.04	8435.23
840 000	12873.46	12173.27	10216.91	9395.94	9002.65	8802.33	8697.12	8640.96
860 000	13179.97	12463.11	10460.17	9619.66	9217.00	9011.91	8904.19	8846.70
880 000	13486.48	12752.95	10703.43	9843.37	9431.35	9221.49	9111.27	9052.44
900 000	13793.00	13042.79	10946.69	10067.08	9645.69	9431.07	9318.34	9258.18
920 000	14099.51	13332.63	11189.95	10290.80	9860.04	9640.65	9525.41	9463.91
940 000	14406.02	13622.47	11433.21	10514.51	10074.39	9850.23	9732.49	9669.65
960 000	14712.53	13912.31	11676.47	10738.22	10288.74	10059.81	9939.56	9875.39
980 000	15019.04	14202.15	11919.73	10961.93	10503.09	10269.38	10146.64	10081.12
1000 000	15325.55	14491.99	12162.99	11185.65	10717.44	10478.96	10353.71	10286.86
Coefficient	.015325550	.014491987	.012162987	.011185647	.010717438	.010478964	.010353711	.010286862

12.50% — MONTHLY AMORTIZING PAYMENTS

AMOUNT	1 YEAR	2 YEARS	3 YEARS	4 YEARS	5 YEARS	6 YEARS	7 YEARS	8 YEARS
10 000	890.83	473.07	334.54	265.80	224.98	198.11	179.21	165.29
20 000	1781.66	946.15	669.07	531.60	449.96	396.22	358.42	330.58
30 000	2672.49	1419.22	1003.61	797.40	674.94	594.34	537.64	495.86
40 000	3563.31	1892.29	1338.14	1063.20	899.92	792.45	716.85	661.15
50 000	4454.14	2365.37	1672.68	1329.00	1124.90	990.56	896.06	826.44
60 000	5344.97	2838.44	2007.22	1594.80	1349.88	1188.67	1075.27	991.73
70 000	6235.80	3311.51	2341.75	1860.60	1574.86	1386.78	1254.49	1157.02
80 000	7126.63	3784.58	2676.29	2126.40	1799.84	1584.89	1433.70	1322.30
90 000	8017.46	4257.66	3010.83	2392.20	2024.81	1783.01	1612.91	1487.59
100 000	8908.29	4730.73	3345.36	2658.00	2249.79	1981.12	1792.12	1652.88
110 000	9799.12	5203.80	3679.90	2923.80	2474.77	2179.23	1971.34	1818.17
120 000	10689.94	5676.88	4014.43	3189.60	2699.75	2377.34	2150.55	1983.46
130 000	11580.77	6149.95	4348.97	3455.40	2924.73	2575.45	2329.76	2148.75
140 000	12471.60	6623.02	4683.51	3721.20	3149.71	2773.56	2508.97	2314.03
150 000	13362.43	7096.10	5018.04	3987.00	3374.69	2971.68	2688.19	2479.32
160 000	14253.26	7569.17	5352.58	4252.80	3599.67	3169.79	2867.40	2644.61
170 000	15144.09	8042.24	5687.12	4518.60	3824.65	3367.90	3046.61	2809.90
180 000	16034.92	8515.31	6021.65	4784.40	4049.63	3566.01	3225.82	2975.19
190 000	16925.75	8988.39	6356.19	5050.20	4274.61	3764.12	3405.04	3140.47
200 000	17816.57	9461.46	6690.72	5316.00	4499.59	3962.24	3584.25	3305.76
210 000	18707.40	9934.53	7025.26	5581.80	4724.57	4160.35	3763.46	3471.05
220 000	19598.23	10407.61	7359.80	5847.60	4949.55	4358.46	3942.67	3636.34
230 000	20489.06	10880.68	7694.33	6113.40	5174.53	4556.57	4121.88	3801.63
240 000	21379.89	11353.75	8028.87	6379.20	5399.51	4754.68	4301.10	3966.91
250 000	22270.72	11826.83	8363.41	6645.00	5624.48	4952.79	4480.31	4132.20
260 000	23161.55	12299.90	8697.94	6910.80	5849.46	5150.91	4659.52	4297.49
270 000	24052.37	12772.97	9032.48	7176.60	6074.44	5349.02	4838.73	4462.78
280 000	24943.20	13246.05	9367.01	7442.40	6299.42	5547.13	5017.95	4628.07
290 000	25834.03	13719.12	9701.55	7708.20	6524.40	5745.24	5197.16	4793.35
300 000	26724.86	14192.19	10036.09	7974.00	6749.38	5943.35	5376.37	4958.64
320 000	28506.52	15138.34	10705.16	8505.60	7199.34	6339.58	5734.80	5289.22
340 000	30288.18	16084.48	11374.23	9037.20	7649.30	6735.80	6093.22	5619.80
360 000	32069.83	17030.63	12043.30	9568.80	8099.26	7132.02	6451.65	5950.37
380 000	33851.49	17976.78	12712.38	10100.40	8549.22	7528.25	6810.07	6280.95
400 000	35633.15	18922.92	13381.45	10632.00	8999.18	7924.47	7168.50	6611.52
420 000	37414.80	19869.07	14050.52	11163.60	9449.13	8320.69	7526.92	6942.10
440 000	39196.46	20815.21	14719.59	11695.20	9899.09	8716.92	7885.34	7272.68
460 000	40978.12	21761.36	15388.67	12226.80	10349.05	9113.14	8243.77	7603.25
480 000	42759.78	22707.51	16057.74	12758.40	10799.01	9509.37	8602.19	7933.83
500 000	44541.43	23653.65	16726.81	13290.00	11248.97	9905.59	8960.62	8264.40
520 000	46323.09	24599.80	17395.88	13821.60	11698.93	10301.81	9319.04	8594.98
540 000	48104.75	25545.94	18064.96	14353.20	12148.89	10698.04	9677.47	8925.56
560 000	49886.41	26492.09	18734.03	14884.80	12598.85	11094.26	10035.89	9256.13
580 000	51668.06	27438.24	19403.10	15416.40	13048.80	11490.48	10394.32	9586.71
600 000	53449.72	28384.38	20072.17	15948.00	13498.76	11886.71	10752.74	9917.29
620 000	55231.38	29330.53	20741.25	16479.60	13948.72	12282.93	11111.17	10247.86
640 000	57013.04	30276.68	21410.32	17011.20	14398.68	12679.15	11469.59	10578.44
660 000	58794.69	31222.82	22079.39	17542.80	14848.64	13075.38	11828.02	10909.01
680 000	60576.35	32168.97	22748.46	18074.40	15298.60	13471.60	12186.44	11239.59
700 000	62358.01	33115.11	23417.54	18606.00	15748.56	13867.82	12544.87	11570.17
720 000	64139.67	34061.26	24086.61	19137.60	16198.52	14264.05	12903.29	11900.74
740 000	65921.32	35007.41	24755.68	19669.20	16648.47	14660.27	13261.72	12231.32
760 000	67702.98	35953.55	25424.75	20200.80	17098.43	15056.50	13620.14	12561.89
780 000	69484.64	36899.70	26093.83	20732.40	17548.39	15452.72	13978.57	12892.47
800 000	71266.30	37845.84	26762.90	21264.00	17998.35	15848.94	14336.99	13223.05
820 000	73047.95	38791.99	27431.97	21795.60	18448.31	16245.17	14695.42	13553.62
840 000	74829.61	39738.14	28101.04	22327.20	18898.27	16641.39	15053.84	13884.20
860 000	76611.27	40684.28	28770.12	22858.80	19348.23	17037.61	15412.26	14214.78
880 000	78392.92	41630.43	29439.19	23390.40	19798.19	17433.84	15770.69	14545.35
900 000	80174.58	42576.57	30108.26	23922.00	20248.14	17830.06	16129.11	14875.93
920 000	81956.24	43522.72	30777.33	24453.60	20698.10	18226.28	16487.54	15206.50
940 000	83737.90	44468.87	31446.41	24985.20	21148.06	18622.51	16845.96	15537.08
960 000	85519.55	45415.01	32115.48	25516.80	21598.02	19018.73	17204.39	15867.66
980 000	87301.21	46361.16	32784.55	26048.40	22047.98	19414.95	17562.81	16198.23
1000 000	89082.87	47307.31	33453.62	26580.00	22497.94	19811.18	17921.24	16528.81
Coefficient	.089082869	.047307305	.033453624	.026579998	.022497938	.019811178	.017921238	.016528809

62

AMOUNT	9 YEARS	10 YEARS	15 YEARS	20 YEARS	25 YEARS	30 YEARS	35 YEARS	40 YEARS
10 000	154.68	146.38	123.25	113.61	109.04	106.73	105.53	104.89
20 000	309.35	292.75	246.50	227.23	218.07	213.45	211.05	209.78
30 000	464.03	439.13	369.76	340.84	327.11	320.18	316.58	314.68
40 000	618.70	585.50	493.01	454.46	436.14	426.90	422.10	419.57
50 000	773.38	731.88	616.26	568.07	545.18	533.63	527.63	524.46
60 000	928.05	878.26	739.51	681.68	654.21	640.35	633.15	629.35
70 000	1082.73	1024.63	862.77	795.30	763.25	747.08	738.68	734.24
80 000	1237.40	1171.01	986.02	908.91	872.28	853.81	844.20	839.14
90 000	1392.08	1317.39	1109.27	1022.53	981.32	960.53	949.73	944.03
100 000	1546.76	1463.76	1232.52	1136.14	1090.35	1067.26	1055.25	1048.92
110 000	1701.43	1610.14	1355.77	1249.75	1199.39	1173.98	1160.78	1153.81
120 000	1856.11	1756.51	1479.03	1363.37	1308.42	1280.71	1266.31	1258.70
130 000	2010.78	1902.89	1602.28	1476.98	1417.46	1387.44	1371.83	1363.60
140 000	2165.46	2049.27	1725.53	1590.60	1526.50	1494.16	1477.36	1468.49
150 000	2320.13	2195.64	1848.78	1704.21	1635.53	1600.89	1582.88	1573.38
160 000	2474.81	2342.02	1972.04	1817.82	1744.57	1707.61	1688.41	1678.27
170 000	2629.48	2488.39	2095.29	1931.44	1853.60	1814.34	1793.93	1783.16
180 000	2784.16	2634.77	2218.54	2045.05	1962.64	1921.06	1899.46	1888.05
190 000	2938.83	2781.15	2341.79	2158.67	2071.67	2027.79	2004.98	1992.95
200 000	3093.51	2927.52	2465.04	2272.28	2180.71	2134.52	2110.51	2097.84
210 000	3248.19	3073.90	2588.30	2385.90	2289.74	2241.24	2216.03	2202.73
220 000	3402.86	3220.28	2711.55	2499.51	2398.78	2347.97	2321.56	2307.62
230 000	3557.54	3366.65	2834.80	2613.12	2507.81	2454.69	2427.09	2412.51
240 000	3712.21	3513.03	2958.05	2726.74	2616.85	2561.42	2532.61	2517.41
250 000	3866.89	3659.40	3081.31	2840.35	2725.89	2668.14	2638.14	2622.30
260 000	4021.56	3805.78	3204.56	2953.97	2834.92	2774.87	2743.66	2727.19
270 000	4176.24	3952.16	3327.81	3067.58	2943.96	2881.60	2849.19	2832.08
280 000	4330.91	4098.53	3451.06	3181.19	3052.99	2988.32	2954.71	2936.97
290 000	4485.59	4244.91	3574.31	3294.81	3162.03	3095.05	3060.24	3041.87
300 000	4640.27	4391.29	3697.57	3408.42	3271.06	3201.77	3165.76	3146.76
320 000	4949.62	4684.04	3944.07	3635.65	3489.13	3415.22	3376.81	3356.54
340 000	5258.97	4976.79	4190.58	3862.88	3707.20	3628.68	3587.86	3566.33
360 000	5568.32	5269.54	4437.08	4090.11	3925.27	3842.13	3798.92	3776.11
380 000	5877.67	5562.29	4683.58	4317.33	4143.35	4055.58	4009.97	3985.89
400 000	6187.02	5855.05	4930.09	4544.56	4361.42	4269.03	4221.02	4195.68
420 000	6496.37	6147.80	5176.59	4771.79	4579.49	4482.48	4432.07	4405.46
440 000	6805.72	6440.55	5423.10	4999.02	4797.56	4695.93	4643.12	4615.25
460 000	7115.07	6733.30	5669.60	5226.25	5015.63	4909.39	4854.17	4825.03
480 000	7424.42	7026.06	5916.11	5453.47	5233.70	5122.84	5065.22	5034.81
500 000	7733.78	7318.81	6162.61	5680.70	5451.77	5336.29	5276.27	5244.60
520 000	8043.13	7611.56	6409.11	5907.93	5669.84	5549.74	5487.32	5454.38
540 000	8352.48	7904.31	6655.62	6135.16	5887.91	5763.19	5698.37	5664.16
560 000	8661.83	8197.07	6902.12	6362.39	6105.98	5976.64	5909.42	5873.95
580 000	8971.18	8489.82	7148.63	6589.61	6324.05	6190.10	6120.48	6083.73
600 000	9280.53	8782.57	7395.13	6816.84	6542.12	6403.55	6331.53	6293.52
620 000	9589.88	9075.32	7641.64	7044.07	6760.20	6617.00	6542.58	6503.30
640 000	9899.23	9368.07	7888.14	7271.30	6978.27	6830.45	6753.63	6713.08
660 000	10208.58	9660.83	8134.65	7498.53	7196.34	7043.90	6964.68	6922.87
680 000	10517.93	9953.58	8381.15	7725.76	7414.41	7257.35	7175.73	7132.65
700 000	10827.29	10246.33	8627.65	7952.98	7632.48	7470.80	7386.78	7342.44
720 000	11136.64	10539.08	8874.16	8180.21	7850.55	7684.26	7597.83	7552.22
740 000	11445.99	10831.84	9120.66	8407.44	8068.62	7897.71	7808.88	7762.00
760 000	11755.34	11124.59	9367.17	8634.67	8286.69	8111.16	8019.93	7971.79
780 000	12064.69	11417.34	9613.67	8861.90	8504.76	8324.61	8230.98	8181.57
800 000	12374.04	11710.09	9860.18	9089.12	8722.83	8538.06	8442.04	8391.36
820 000	12683.39	12002.85	10106.68	9316.35	8940.90	8751.51	8653.09	8601.14
840 000	12992.74	12295.60	10353.19	9543.58	9158.97	8964.97	8864.14	8810.92
860 000	13302.09	12588.35	10599.69	9770.81	9377.05	9178.42	9075.19	9020.71
880 000	13611.44	12881.10	10846.19	9998.04	9595.12	9391.87	9286.24	9230.49
900 000	13920.80	13173.86	11092.70	10225.26	9813.19	9605.32	9497.29	9440.27
920 000	14230.15	13466.61	11339.20	10452.49	10031.26	9818.77	9708.34	9650.06
940 000	14539.50	13759.36	11585.71	10679.72	10249.33	10032.22	9919.39	9859.84
960 000	14848.85	14052.11	11832.21	10906.95	10467.40	10245.67	10130.44	10069.63
980 000	15158.20	14344.86	12078.72	11134.18	10685.47	10459.13	10341.49	10279.41
1000 000	15467.55	14637.62	12325.22	11361.41	10903.54	10672.58	10552.54	10489.19
Coefficient	.015467551	.014637617	.012325221	.011361405	.010903541	.010672578	.010552544	.010489194

63

MONTHLY AMORTIZING PAYMENTS

AMOUNT	1 YEAR	2 YEARS	3 YEARS	4 YEARS	5 YEARS	6 YEARS	7 YEARS	8 YEARS
10 000	892.00	474.24	335.74	267.04	226.25	199.42	180.56	166.68
20 000	1784.00	948.49	671.47	534.07	452.51	398.85	361.13	333.35
30 000	2676.00	1422.73	1007.21	801.11	678.76	598.27	541.69	500.03
40 000	3568.00	1896.98	1342.95	1068.14	905.01	797.70	722.25	666.71
50 000	4460.00	2371.22	1678.68	1335.18	1131.27	997.12	902.82	833.39
60 000	5352.00	2845.47	2014.42	1602.21	1357.52	1196.54	1083.38	1000.06
70 000	6244.00	3319.71	2350.16	1869.25	1583.77	1395.97	1263.94	1166.74
80 000	7136.00	3793.96	2685.89	2136.29	1810.02	1595.39	1444.51	1333.42
90 000	8028.00	4268.20	3021.63	2403.32	2036.28	1794.82	1625.07	1500.10
100 000	8920.00	4742.45	3357.37	2670.36	2262.53	1994.24	1805.63	1666.77
110 000	9812.00	5216.69	3693.10	2937.39	2488.78	2193.66	1986.20	1833.45
120 000	10704.00	5690.94	4028.84	3204.43	2715.04	2393.09	2166.76	2000.13
130 000	11596.00	6165.18	4364.58	3471.47	2941.29	2592.51	2347.32	2166.80
140 000	12488.00	6639.43	4700.31	3738.50	3167.54	2791.94	2527.89	2333.48
150 000	13380.00	7113.67	5036.05	4005.54	3393.80	2991.36	2708.45	2500.16
160 000	14272.01	7587.92	5371.79	4272.57	3620.05	3190.78	2889.01	2666.84
170 000	15164.01	8062.16	5707.52	4539.61	3846.30	3390.21	3069.58	2833.51
180 000	16056.01	8536.41	6043.26	4806.64	4072.55	3589.63	3250.14	3000.19
190 000	16948.01	9010.65	6379.00	5073.68	4298.81	3789.06	3430.70	3166.87
200 000	17840.01	9484.90	6714.73	5340.72	4525.06	3988.48	3611.26	3333.54
210 000	18732.01	9959.14	7050.47	5607.75	4751.31	4187.90	3791.83	3500.22
220 000	19624.01	10433.38	7386.21	5874.79	4977.57	4387.33	3972.39	3666.90
230 000	20516.01	10907.63	7721.94	6141.82	5203.82	4586.75	4152.95	3833.58
240 000	21408.01	11381.87	8057.68	6408.86	5430.07	4786.18	4333.52	4000.25
250 000	22300.01	11856.12	8393.42	6675.90	5656.33	4985.60	4514.08	4166.93
260 000	23192.01	12330.36	8729.15	6942.93	5882.58	5185.02	4694.64	4333.61
270 000	24084.01	12804.61	9064.89	7209.97	6108.83	5384.45	4875.21	4500.29
280 000	24976.01	13278.85	9400.63	7477.00	6335.08	5583.87	5055.77	4666.96
290 000	25868.01	13753.10	9736.36	7744.04	6561.34	5783.30	5236.33	4833.64
300 000	26760.01	14227.34	10072.10	8011.07	6787.59	5982.72	5416.90	5000.32
320 000	28544.01	15175.83	10743.57	8545.15	7240.10	6381.57	5778.02	5333.67
340 000	30328.01	16124.32	11415.04	9079.22	7692.60	6780.42	6139.15	5667.03
360 000	32112.01	17072.81	12086.52	9613.29	8145.11	7179.26	6500.28	6000.38
380 000	33896.01	18021.30	12757.99	10147.36	8597.61	7578.11	6861.40	6333.74
400 000	35680.01	18969.79	13429.46	10681.43	9050.12	7976.96	7222.53	6667.09
420 000	37464.01	19918.28	14100.94	11215.50	9502.63	8375.81	7583.66	7000.44
440 000	39248.01	20866.77	14772.41	11749.58	9955.13	8774.66	7944.78	7333.80
460 000	41032.01	21815.26	15443.88	12283.65	10407.64	9173.50	8305.91	7667.15
480 000	42816.01	22763.75	16115.36	12817.72	10860.14	9572.35	8667.04	8000.51
500 000	44600.02	23712.24	16786.83	13351.79	11312.65	9971.20	9028.16	8333.86
520 000	46384.02	24660.73	17458.30	13885.86	11765.16	10370.05	9389.29	8667.22
540 000	48168.02	25609.22	18129.78	14419.93	12217.66	10768.90	9750.41	9000.57
560 000	49952.02	26557.71	18801.25	14954.00	12670.17	11167.74	10111.54	9333.93
580 000	51736.02	27506.20	19472.72	15488.08	13122.67	11566.59	10472.67	9667.28
600 000	53520.02	28454.69	20144.20	16022.15	13575.18	11965.44	10833.79	10000.63
620 000	55304.02	29403.18	20815.67	16556.22	14027.69	12364.29	11194.92	10333.99
640 000	57088.02	30351.67	21487.14	17090.29	14480.19	12763.14	11556.05	10667.34
660 000	58872.02	31300.15	22158.62	17624.36	14932.70	13161.98	11917.17	11000.70
680 000	60656.02	32248.64	22830.09	18158.43	15385.20	13560.83	12278.30	11334.05
700 000	62440.02	33197.13	23501.56	18692.51	15837.71	13959.68	12639.43	11667.41
720 000	64224.02	34145.62	24173.04	19226.58	16290.22	14358.53	13000.55	12000.76
740 000	66008.02	35094.11	24844.51	19760.65	16742.72	14757.38	13361.68	12334.12
760 000	67792.02	36042.60	25515.98	20294.72	17195.23	15156.22	13722.81	12667.47
780 000	69576.02	36991.09	26187.46	20828.79	17647.73	15555.07	14083.93	13000.82
800 000	71360.02	37939.58	26858.93	21362.86	18100.24	15953.92	14445.06	13334.18
820 000	73144.02	38888.07	27530.40	21896.94	18552.75	16352.77	14806.19	13667.53
840 000	74928.03	39836.56	28201.88	22431.01	19005.25	16751.62	15167.31	14000.89
860 000	76712.03	40785.05	28873.35	22965.08	19457.76	17150.46	15528.44	14334.24
880 000	78496.03	41733.54	29544.82	23499.15	19910.26	17549.31	15889.57	14667.60
900 000	80280.03	42682.03	30216.29	24033.22	20362.77	17948.16	16250.69	15000.95
920 000	82064.03	43630.52	30887.77	24567.29	20815.28	18347.01	16611.82	15334.31
940 000	83848.03	44579.01	31559.24	25101.37	21267.78	18745.86	16972.94	15667.66
960 000	85632.03	45527.50	32230.71	25635.44	21720.29	19144.70	17334.07	16001.02
980 000	87416.03	46475.99	32902.19	26169.51	22172.79	19543.55	17695.20	16334.37
1000 000	89200.03	47424.48	33573.66	26703.58	22625.30	19942.40	18056.32	16667.72
Coefficient	.089200030	.047424477	.033573661	.026703580	.022625300	.019942399	.018056324	.016667724

64

AMOUNT	9 YEARS	10 YEARS	15 YEARS	20 YEARS	25 YEARS	30 YEARS	35 YEARS	40 YEARS
10 000	156.10	147.84	124.88	115.38	110.91	108.67	107.52	106.92
20 000	312.20	295.68	249.77	230.76	221.81	217.34	215.04	213.84
30 000	468.31	443.52	374.65	346.14	332.72	326.01	322.56	320.76
40 000	624.41	591.36	499.53	461.52	443.62	434.68	430.08	427.68
50 000	780.51	739.20	624.42	576.91	554.53	543.35	537.60	534.60
60 000	936.61	887.04	749.30	692.29	665.43	652.02	645.12	641.52
70 000	1092.72	1034.88	874.19	807.67	776.34	760.69	752.64	748.44
80 000	1248.82	1182.72	999.07	923.05	887.24	869.35	860.16	855.36
90 000	1404.92	1330.56	1123.95	1038.43	998.15	978.02	967.68	962.28
100 000	1561.02	1478.40	1248.84	1153.81	1109.05	1086.69	1075.20	1069.20
110 000	1717.13	1626.24	1373.72	1269.19	1219.96	1195.36	1182.72	1176.12
120 000	1873.23	1774.08	1498.60	1384.57	1330.86	1304.03	1290.24	1283.04
130 000	2029.33	1921.92	1623.49	1499.96	1441.77	1412.70	1397.75	1389.96
140 000	2185.43	2069.76	1748.37	1615.34	1552.67	1521.37	1505.27	1496.87
150 000	2341.53	2217.60	1873.26	1730.72	1663.58	1630.04	1612.79	1603.79
160 000	2497.64	2365.44	1998.14	1846.10	1774.48	1738.71	1720.31	1710.71
170 000	2653.74	2513.28	2123.02	1961.48	1885.39	1847.38	1827.83	1817.63
180 000	2809.84	2661.12	2247.91	2076.86	1996.29	1956.05	1935.35	1924.55
190 000	2965.94	2808.96	2372.79	2192.24	2107.20	2064.72	2042.87	2031.47
200 000	3122.05	2956.80	2497.67	2307.62	2218.10	2173.39	2150.39	2138.39
210 000	3278.15	3104.64	2622.56	2423.00	2329.01	2282.06	2257.91	2245.31
220 000	3434.25	3252.48	2747.44	2538.39	2439.92	2390.73	2365.43	2352.23
230 000	3590.35	3400.32	2872.33	2653.77	2550.82	2499.39	2472.95	2459.15
240 000	3746.46	3548.16	2997.21	2769.15	2661.73	2608.06	2580.47	2566.07
250 000	3902.56	3696.00	3122.09	2884.53	2772.63	2716.73	2687.99	2672.99
260 000	4058.66	3843.84	3246.98	2999.91	2883.54	2825.40	2795.51	2779.91
270 000	4214.76	3991.68	3371.86	3115.29	2994.44	2934.07	2903.03	2886.83
280 000	4370.86	4139.51	3496.74	3230.67	3105.35	3042.74	3010.55	2993.75
290 000	4526.97	4287.35	3621.63	3346.05	3216.25	3151.41	3118.07	3100.67
300 000	4683.07	4435.19	3746.51	3461.43	3327.16	3260.08	3225.59	3207.59
320 000	4995.27	4730.87	3996.28	3692.20	3548.97	3477.42	3440.63	3421.43
340 000	5307.48	5026.55	4246.05	3922.96	3770.78	3694.76	3655.67	3635.27
360 000	5619.68	5322.23	4495.81	4153.72	3992.59	3912.10	3870.71	3849.11
380 000	5931.89	5617.91	4745.58	4384.48	4214.40	4129.43	4085.75	4062.95
400 000	6244.09	5913.59	4995.35	4615.25	4436.21	4346.77	4300.78	4276.79
420 000	6556.30	6209.27	5245.12	4846.01	4658.02	4564.11	4515.82	4490.62
440 000	6868.50	6504.95	5494.88	5076.77	4879.83	4781.45	4730.86	4704.46
460 000	7180.71	6800.63	5744.65	5307.53	5101.64	4998.79	4945.90	4918.30
480 000	7492.91	7096.31	5994.42	5538.30	5323.45	5216.13	5160.94	5132.14
500 000	7805.12	7391.99	6244.19	5769.06	5545.26	5433.47	5375.98	5345.98
520 000	8117.32	7687.67	6493.95	5999.82	5767.07	5650.80	5591.02	5559.82
540 000	8429.52	7983.35	6743.72	6230.58	5988.88	5868.14	5806.06	5773.66
560 000	8741.73	8279.03	6993.49	6461.34	6210.69	6085.48	6021.10	5987.50
580 000	9053.93	8574.71	7243.25	6692.11	6432.50	6302.82	6236.14	6201.34
600 000	9366.14	8870.39	7493.02	6922.87	6654.31	6520.16	6451.18	6415.18
620 000	9678.34	9166.07	7742.79	7153.63	6876.12	6737.50	6666.22	6629.02
640 000	9990.55	9461.75	7992.56	7384.39	7097.93	6954.84	6881.26	6842.86
660 000	10302.75	9757.43	8242.32	7615.16	7319.75	7172.18	7096.29	7056.70
680 000	10614.96	10053.11	8492.09	7845.92	7541.56	7389.51	7311.33	7270.54
700 000	10927.16	10348.79	8741.86	8076.68	7763.37	7606.85	7526.37	7484.37
720 000	11239.37	10644.47	8991.63	8307.44	7985.18	7824.19	7741.41	7698.21
740 000	11551.57	10940.15	9241.39	8538.21	8206.99	8041.53	7956.45	7912.05
760 000	11863.78	11235.83	9491.16	8768.97	8428.80	8258.87	8171.49	8125.89
780 000	12175.98	11531.51	9740.93	8999.73	8650.61	8476.21	8386.53	8339.73
800 000	12488.18	11827.18	9990.70	9230.49	8872.42	8693.55	8601.57	8553.57
820 000	12800.39	12122.86	10240.46	9461.26	9094.23	8910.88	8816.61	8767.41
840 000	13112.59	12418.54	10490.23	9692.02	9316.04	9128.22	9031.65	8981.25
860 000	13424.80	12714.22	10740.00	9922.78	9537.85	9345.56	9246.69	9195.09
880 000	13737.00	13009.90	10989.77	10153.54	9759.66	9562.90	9461.73	9408.93
900 000	14049.21	13305.58	11239.53	10384.30	9981.47	9780.24	9676.76	9622.77
920 000	14361.41	13601.26	11489.30	10615.07	10203.28	9997.58	9891.80	9836.61
940 000	14673.62	13896.94	11739.07	10845.83	10425.09	10214.92	10106.84	10050.45
960 000	14985.82	14192.62	11988.84	11076.59	10646.90	10432.25	10321.88	10264.29
980 000	15298.03	14488.30	12238.60	11307.35	10868.71	10649.59	10536.92	10478.12
1000 000	15610.23	14783.98	12488.37	11538.12	11090.52	10866.93	10751.96	10691.96
Coefficient	.015610231	.014783981	.012488370	.011538116	.011090523	.010866932	.010751961	.010691964

MONTHLY AMORTIZING PAYMENTS

AMOUNT	1 YEAR	2 YEARS	3 YEARS	4 YEARS	5 YEARS	6 YEARS	7 YEARS	8 YEARS
10 000	893.17	475.42	336.94	268.27	227.53	200.74	181.92	168.07
20 000	1786.35	950.84	673.88	536.55	455.06	401.48	363.84	336.15
30 000	2679.52	1426.25	1010.82	804.82	682.59	602.22	545.76	504.22
40 000	3572.69	1901.67	1347.76	1073.10	910.12	802.96	727.68	672.29
50 000	4465.86	2377.09	1684.70	1341.37	1137.65	1003.71	909.60	840.36
60 000	5359.04	2852.51	2021.64	1609.65	1365.18	1204.45	1091.52	1008.44
70 000	6252.21	3327.93	2358.58	1877.92	1592.72	1405.19	1273.44	1176.51
80 000	7145.38	3803.35	2695.52	2146.20	1820.25	1605.93	1455.36	1344.58
90 000	8038.56	4278.76	3032.46	2414.47	2047.78	1806.67	1637.28	1512.65
100 000	8931.73	4754.18	3369.40	2682.75	2275.31	2007.41	1819.20	1680.73
110 000	9824.90	5229.60	3706.33	2951.02	2502.84	2208.15	2001.12	1848.80
120 000	10718.07	5705.02	4043.27	3219.30	2730.37	2408.89	2183.04	2016.87
130 000	11611.25	6180.44	4380.21	3487.57	2957.90	2609.63	2364.96	2184.94
140 000	12504.42	6655.86	4717.15	3755.85	3185.43	2810.37	2546.87	2353.02
150 000	13397.59	7131.27	5054.09	4024.12	3412.96	3011.12	2728.79	2521.09
160 000	14290.76	7606.69	5391.03	4292.40	3640.49	3211.86	2910.71	2689.16
170 000	15183.94	8082.11	5727.97	4560.67	3868.02	3412.60	3092.63	2857.23
180 000	16077.11	8557.53	6064.91	4828.95	4095.55	3613.34	3274.55	3025.31
190 000	16970.28	9032.95	6401.85	5097.22	4323.08	3814.08	3456.47	3193.38
200 000	17863.46	9508.37	6738.79	5365.50	4550.61	4014.82	3638.39	3361.45
210 000	18756.63	9983.78	7075.73	5633.77	4778.15	4215.56	3820.31	3529.52
220 000	19649.80	10459.20	7412.67	5902.05	5005.68	4416.30	4002.23	3697.60
230 000	20542.97	10934.62	7749.61	6170.32	5233.21	4617.04	4184.15	3865.67
240 000	21436.15	11410.04	8086.55	6438.60	5460.74	4817.79	4366.07	4033.74
250 000	22329.32	11885.46	8423.49	6706.87	5688.27	5018.53	4547.99	4201.81
260 000	23222.49	12360.87	8760.43	6975.15	5915.80	5219.27	4729.91	4369.89
270 000	24115.67	12836.29	9097.37	7243.42	6143.33	5420.01	4911.83	4537.96
280 000	25008.84	13311.71	9434.31	7511.70	6370.86	5620.75	5093.75	4706.03
290 000	25902.01	13787.13	9771.25	7779.97	6598.39	5821.49	5275.67	4874.10
300 000	26795.18	14262.55	10108.19	8048.25	6825.92	6022.23	5457.59	5042.18
320 000	28581.53	15213.38	10782.07	8584.80	7280.98	6423.71	5821.43	5378.32
340 000	30367.88	16164.22	11455.94	9121.35	7736.04	6825.20	6185.27	5714.47
360 000	32154.22	17115.06	12129.82	9657.90	8191.11	7226.68	6549.11	6050.61
380 000	33940.57	18065.89	12803.70	10194.45	8646.17	7628.16	6912.95	6386.76
400 000	35726.91	19016.73	13477.58	10731.00	9101.23	8029.64	7276.79	6722.90
420 000	37513.26	19967.57	14151.46	11267.55	9556.29	8431.12	7640.62	7059.05
440 000	39299.60	20918.40	14825.34	11804.10	10011.35	8832.61	8004.46	7395.19
460 000	41085.95	21869.24	15499.22	12340.65	10466.41	9234.09	8368.30	7731.34
480 000	42872.29	22820.08	16173.10	12877.20	10921.47	9635.57	8732.14	8067.48
500 000	44658.64	23770.91	16846.98	13413.75	11376.54	10037.05	9095.98	8403.63
520 000	46444.99	24721.75	17520.86	13950.30	11831.60	10438.53	9459.82	8739.77
540 000	48231.33	25672.59	18194.74	14486.85	12286.66	10840.02	9823.66	9075.92
560 000	50017.68	26623.42	18868.61	15023.40	12741.72	11241.50	10187.50	9412.06
580 000	51804.02	27574.26	19542.49	15559.95	13196.78	11642.98	10551.34	9748.21
600 000	53590.37	28525.10	20216.37	16096.50	13651.84	12044.46	10915.18	10084.35
620 000	55376.71	29475.93	20890.25	16633.05	14106.90	12445.95	11279.02	10420.50
640 000	57163.06	30426.77	21564.13	17169.60	14561.97	12847.43	11642.86	10756.64
660 000	58949.41	31377.61	22238.01	17706.15	15017.03	13248.91	12006.70	11092.79
680 000	60735.75	32328.44	22911.89	18242.70	15472.09	13650.39	12370.53	11428.93
700 000	62522.10	33279.28	23585.77	18779.25	15927.15	14051.87	12734.37	11765.08
720 000	64308.44	34230.11	24259.65	19315.80	16382.21	14453.36	13098.21	12101.22
740 000	66094.79	35180.95	24933.53	19852.35	16837.27	14854.84	13462.05	12437.37
760 000	67881.13	36131.79	25607.41	20388.90	17292.33	15256.32	13825.89	12773.51
780 000	69667.48	37082.62	26281.28	20925.45	17747.40	15657.80	14189.73	13109.66
800 000	71453.82	38033.46	26955.16	21462.00	18202.46	16059.28	14553.57	13445.80
820 000	73240.17	38984.30	27629.04	21998.55	18657.52	16460.77	14917.41	13781.95
840 000	75026.52	39935.13	28302.92	22535.10	19112.58	16862.25	15281.25	14118.09
860 000	76812.86	40885.97	28976.80	23071.65	19567.64	17263.73	15645.09	14454.24
880 000	78599.21	41836.81	29650.68	23608.20	20022.70	17665.21	16008.93	14790.38
900 000	80385.55	42787.64	30324.56	24144.75	20477.76	18066.69	16372.77	15126.53
920 000	82171.90	43738.48	30998.44	24681.30	20932.83	18468.18	16736.61	15462.67
940 000	83958.24	44689.32	31672.32	25217.85	21387.89	18869.66	17100.45	15798.82
960 000	85744.59	45640.15	32346.20	25754.40	21842.95	19271.14	17464.28	16134.96
980 000	87530.94	46590.99	33020.07	26290.95	22298.01	19672.62	17828.12	16471.11
1000 000	89317.28	47541.83	33693.95	26827.50	22753.07	20074.11	18191.96	16807.26
Coefficient	.089317281	.047541826	.033693954	.026827495	.022753072	.020074105	.018191963	.016807255

MONTHLY AMORTIZING PAYMENTS 13.00%

AMOUNT	9 YEARS	10 YEARS	15 YEARS	20 YEARS	25 YEARS	30 YEARS	35 YEARS	40 YEARS
10 000	157.54	149.31	126.52	117.16	112.78	110.62	109.52	108.95
20 000	315.07	298.62	253.05	234.32	225.57	221.24	219.04	217.90
30 000	472.61	447.93	379.57	351.47	338.35	331.86	328.56	326.85
40 000	630.14	597.24	506.10	468.63	451.13	442.48	438.08	435.81
50 000	787.68	746.55	632.62	585.79	563.92	553.10	547.60	544.76
60 000	945.22	895.86	759.15	702.95	676.70	663.72	657.12	653.71
70 000	1102.75	1045.18	885.67	820.10	789.48	774.34	766.64	762.66
80 000	1260.29	1194.49	1012.19	937.26	902.27	884.96	876.15	871.61
90 000	1417.82	1343.80	1138.72	1054.42	1015.05	995.58	985.67	980.56
100 000	1575.36	1493.11	1265.24	1171.58	1127.84	1106.20	1095.19	1089.51
110 000	1732.89	1642.42	1391.77	1288.73	1240.62	1216.82	1204.71	1198.47
120 000	1890.43	1791.73	1518.29	1405.89	1353.40	1327.44	1314.23	1307.42
130 000	2047.97	1941.04	1644.81	1523.05	1466.19	1438.06	1423.75	1416.37
140 000	2205.50	2090.35	1771.34	1640.21	1578.97	1548.68	1533.27	1525.32
150 000	2363.04	2239.66	1897.86	1757.36	1691.75	1659.30	1642.79	1634.27
160 000	2520.57	2388.97	2024.39	1874.52	1804.54	1769.92	1752.31	1743.22
170 000	2678.11	2538.28	2150.91	1991.68	1917.32	1880.54	1861.83	1852.17
180 000	2835.65	2687.59	2277.44	2108.84	2030.10	1991.16	1971.35	1961.13
190 000	2993.18	2836.90	2403.96	2225.99	2142.89	2101.78	2080.87	2070.08
200 000	3150.72	2986.21	2530.48	2343.15	2255.67	2212.40	2190.39	2179.03
210 000	3308.25	3135.53	2657.01	2460.31	2368.45	2323.02	2299.91	2287.98
220 000	3465.79	3284.84	2783.53	2577.47	2481.24	2433.64	2409.42	2396.93
230 000	3623.33	3434.15	2910.06	2694.62	2594.02	2544.26	2518.94	2505.88
240 000	3780.86	3583.46	3036.58	2811.78	2706.80	2654.88	2628.46	2614.83
250 000	3938.40	3732.77	3163.11	2928.94	2819.59	2765.50	2737.98	2723.79
260 000	4095.93	3882.08	3289.63	3046.10	2932.37	2876.12	2847.50	2832.74
270 000	4253.47	4031.39	3416.15	3163.25	3045.16	2986.74	2957.02	2941.69
280 000	4411.00	4180.70	3542.68	3280.41	3157.94	3097.36	3066.54	3050.64
290 000	4568.54	4330.01	3669.20	3397.57	3270.72	3207.98	3176.06	3159.59
300 000	4726.08	4479.32	3795.73	3514.73	3383.51	3318.60	3285.58	3268.54
320 000	5041.15	4777.94	4048.78	3749.04	3609.07	3539.84	3504.62	3486.45
340 000	5356.22	5076.57	4301.82	3983.36	3834.64	3761.08	3723.66	3704.35
360 000	5671.29	5375.19	4554.87	4217.67	4060.21	3982.32	3942.70	3922.25
380 000	5986.36	5673.81	4807.92	4451.99	4285.77	4203.56	4161.73	4140.15
400 000	6301.44	5972.43	5060.97	4686.30	4511.34	4424.80	4380.77	4358.06
420 000	6616.51	6271.05	5314.02	4920.62	4736.91	4646.04	4599.81	4575.96
440 000	6931.58	6569.67	5567.07	5154.93	4962.48	4867.28	4818.85	4793.86
460 000	7246.65	6868.29	5820.11	5389.25	5188.04	5088.52	5037.89	5011.77
480 000	7561.72	7166.92	6073.16	5623.56	5413.61	5309.76	5256.93	5229.67
500 000	7876.79	7465.54	6326.21	5857.88	5639.18	5531.00	5475.97	5447.57
520 000	8191.87	7764.16	6579.26	6092.19	5864.74	5752.24	5695.00	5665.47
540 000	8506.94	8062.78	6832.31	6326.51	6090.31	5973.48	5914.04	5883.38
560 000	8822.01	8361.40	7085.36	6560.82	6315.88	6194.72	6133.08	6101.28
580 000	9137.08	8660.02	7338.40	6795.14	6541.44	6415.96	6352.12	6319.18
600 000	9452.15	8958.64	7591.45	7029.45	6767.01	6637.20	6571.16	6537.09
620 000	9767.22	9257.27	7844.50	7263.77	6992.58	6858.44	6790.20	6754.99
640 000	10082.30	9555.89	8097.55	7498.08	7218.15	7079.68	7009.24	6972.89
660 000	10397.37	9854.51	8350.60	7732.40	7443.71	7300.92	7228.27	7190.79
680 000	10712.44	10153.13	8603.65	7966.71	7669.28	7522.16	7447.31	7408.70
700 000	11027.51	10451.75	8856.70	8201.03	7894.85	7743.40	7666.35	7626.60
720 000	11342.58	10750.37	9109.74	8435.35	8120.41	7964.64	7885.39	7844.50
740 000	11657.66	11048.99	9362.79	8669.66	8345.98	8185.88	8104.43	8062.41
760 000	11972.73	11347.62	9615.84	8903.98	8571.55	8407.12	8323.47	8280.31
780 000	12287.80	11646.24	9868.89	9138.29	8797.12	8628.36	8542.51	8498.21
800 000	12602.87	11944.86	10121.94	9372.61	9022.68	8849.60	8761.54	8716.11
820 000	12917.94	12243.48	10374.99	9606.92	9248.25	9070.84	8980.58	8934.02
840 000	13233.01	12542.10	10628.03	9841.24	9473.82	9292.08	9199.62	9151.92
860 000	13548.09	12840.72	10881.08	10075.55	9699.38	9513.32	9418.66	9369.82
880 000	13863.16	13139.35	11134.13	10309.87	9924.95	9734.56	9637.70	9587.72
900 000	14178.23	13437.97	11387.18	10544.18	10150.52	9955.80	9856.74	9805.63
920 000	14493.30	13736.59	11640.23	10778.50	10376.08	10177.04	10075.78	10023.53
940 000	14808.37	14035.21	11893.28	11012.81	10601.65	10398.28	10294.82	10241.43
960 000	15123.44	14333.83	12146.33	11247.13	10827.22	10619.52	10513.85	10459.34
980 000	15438.52	14632.45	12399.37	11481.44	11052.79	10840.76	10732.89	10677.24
1000 000	15753.59	14931.07	12652.42	11715.76	11278.35	11062.00	10951.93	10895.14
Coefficient	.015753588	.014931074	.012652422	.011715757	.011278353	.011061995	.010951931	.010895142

67

13.25% MONTHLY AMORTIZING PAYMENTS

AMOUNT	1 YEAR	2 YEARS	3 YEARS	4 YEARS	5 YEARS	6 YEARS	7 YEARS	8 YEARS
10 000	894.35	476.59	338.14	269.52	228.81	202.06	183.28	169.47
20 000	1788.69	953.19	676.29	539.03	457.63	404.13	366.56	338.95
30 000	2683.04	1429.78	1014.43	808.55	686.44	606.19	549.84	508.42
40 000	3577.38	1906.37	1352.58	1078.07	915.25	808.25	733.13	677.90
50 000	4471.73	2382.97	1690.72	1347.59	1144.06	1010.31	916.41	847.37
60 000	5366.08	2859.56	2028.87	1617.10	1372.88	1212.38	1099.69	1016.84
70 000	6260.42	3336.15	2367.01	1886.62	1601.69	1414.44	1282.97	1186.32
80 000	7154.77	3812.75	2705.16	2156.14	1830.50	1616.50	1466.25	1355.79
90 000	8049.12	4289.34	3043.30	2425.66	2059.31	1818.57	1649.53	1525.27
100 000	8943.46	4765.93	3381.45	2695.17	2288.13	2020.63	1832.82	1694.74
110 000	9837.81	5242.53	3719.59	2964.69	2516.94	2222.69	2016.10	1864.21
120 000	10732.15	5719.12	4057.74	3234.21	2745.75	2424.76	2199.38	2033.69
130 000	11626.50	6195.71	4395.88	3503.73	2974.56	2626.82	2382.66	2203.16
140 000	12520.85	6672.31	4734.03	3773.24	3203.38	2828.88	2565.94	2372.64
150 000	13415.19	7148.90	5072.17	4042.76	3432.19	3030.94	2749.22	2542.11
160 000	14309.54	7625.49	5410.32	4312.28	3661.00	3233.01	2932.50	2711.58
170 000	15203.88	8102.09	5748.46	4581.80	3889.81	3435.07	3115.79	2881.06
180 000	16098.23	8578.68	6086.61	4851.31	4118.63	3637.13	3299.07	3050.53
190 000	16992.58	9055.27	6424.75	5120.83	4347.44	3839.20	3482.35	3220.01
200 000	17886.92	9531.87	6762.90	5390.35	4576.25	4041.26	3665.63	3389.48
210 000	18781.27	10008.46	7101.04	5659.87	4805.06	4243.32	3848.91	3558.95
220 000	19675.61	10485.05	7439.19	5929.38	5033.88	4445.38	4032.19	3728.43
230 000	20569.96	10961.65	7777.33	6198.90	5262.69	4647.45	4215.48	3897.90
240 000	21464.31	11438.24	8115.48	6468.42	5491.50	4849.51	4398.76	4067.38
250 000	22358.65	11914.83	8453.62	6737.94	5720.31	5051.57	4582.04	4236.85
260 000	23253.00	12391.43	8791.77	7007.45	5949.13	5253.64	4765.32	4406.32
270 000	24147.35	12868.02	9129.91	7276.97	6177.94	5455.70	4948.60	4575.80
280 000	25041.69	13344.61	9468.06	7546.49	6406.75	5657.76	5131.88	4745.27
290 000	25936.04	13821.21	9806.20	7816.01	6635.56	5859.82	5315.16	4914.75
300 000	26830.38	14297.80	10144.35	8085.52	6864.38	6061.89	5498.45	5084.22
320 000	28619.08	15250.99	10820.64	8624.56	7322.00	6466.01	5865.01	5423.17
340 000	30407.77	16204.17	11496.93	9163.59	7779.63	6870.14	6231.57	5762.12
360 000	32196.46	17157.36	12173.22	9702.63	8237.25	7274.27	6598.14	6101.06
380 000	33985.15	18110.55	12849.51	10241.66	8694.88	7678.39	6964.70	6440.01
400 000	35773.84	19063.73	13525.80	10780.70	9152.50	8082.52	7331.26	6778.96
420 000	37562.54	20016.92	14202.09	11319.73	9610.13	8486.64	7697.82	7117.91
440 000	39351.23	20970.11	14878.38	11858.77	10067.75	8890.77	8064.39	7456.86
460 000	41139.92	21923.29	15554.67	12397.80	10525.38	9294.89	8430.95	7795.80
480 000	42928.61	22876.48	16230.96	12936.84	10983.00	9699.02	8797.51	8134.75
500 000	44717.31	23829.67	16907.25	13475.87	11440.63	10103.15	9164.08	8473.70
520 000	46506.00	24782.85	17583.54	14014.91	11898.25	10507.27	9530.64	8812.65
540 000	48294.69	25736.04	18259.83	14553.94	12355.88	10911.40	9897.20	9151.60
560 000	50083.38	26689.23	18936.12	15092.98	12813.50	11315.52	10263.77	9490.54
580 000	51872.07	27642.41	19612.41	15632.01	13271.13	11719.65	10630.33	9829.49
600 000	53660.77	28595.60	20288.70	16171.05	13728.75	12123.78	10996.89	10168.44
620 000	55449.46	29548.79	20964.99	16710.08	14186.38	12527.90	11363.45	10507.39
640 000	57238.15	30501.98	21641.27	17249.11	14644.00	12932.03	11730.02	10846.34
660 000	59026.84	31455.16	22317.56	17788.15	15101.63	13336.15	12096.58	11185.28
680 000	60815.54	32408.35	22993.85	18327.18	15559.25	13740.28	12463.14	11524.23
700 000	62604.23	33361.54	23670.14	18866.22	16016.88	14144.40	12829.71	11863.18
720 000	64392.92	34314.72	24346.43	19405.25	16474.50	14548.53	13196.27	12202.13
740 000	66181.61	35267.91	25022.72	19944.29	16932.13	14952.66	13562.83	12541.08
760 000	67970.31	36221.10	25699.01	20483.32	17389.75	15356.78	13929.40	12880.02
780 000	69759.00	37174.28	26375.30	21022.36	17847.38	15760.91	14295.96	13218.97
800 000	71547.69	38127.47	27051.59	21561.39	18305.00	16165.03	14662.52	13557.92
820 000	73336.38	39080.66	27727.88	22100.43	18762.63	16569.16	15029.09	13896.87
840 000	75125.07	40033.84	28404.17	22639.46	19220.25	16973.29	15395.65	14235.82
860 000	76913.77	40987.03	29080.46	23178.50	19677.88	17377.41	15762.21	14574.76
880 000	78702.46	41940.22	29756.75	23717.53	20135.50	17781.54	16128.77	14913.71
900 000	80491.15	42893.40	30433.04	24256.57	20593.13	18185.66	16495.34	15252.66
920 000	82279.84	43846.59	31109.33	24795.60	21050.75	18589.79	16861.90	15591.61
940 000	84068.54	44799.78	31785.62	25334.64	21508.38	18993.91	17228.46	15930.56
960 000	85857.23	45752.96	32461.91	25873.67	21966.00	19398.04	17595.03	16269.50
980 000	87645.92	46706.15	33138.20	26412.71	22423.63	19802.17	17961.59	16608.45
1000 000	89434.61	47659.34	33814.49	26951.74	22881.25	20206.29	18328.15	16947.40
Coefficient	.089434612	.047659336	.033814492	.026951742	.022881254	.020206292	.018328153	.016947401

AMOUNT	9 YEARS	10 YEARS	15 YEARS	20 YEARS	25 YEARS	30 YEARS	35 YEARS	40 YEARS
10 000	158.98	150.79	128.17	118.94	114.67	112.58	111.52	110.99
20 000	317.95	301.58	256.35	237.89	229.34	225.15	223.05	221.97
30 000	476.93	452.37	384.52	356.83	344.01	337.73	334.57	332.96
40 000	635.90	603.16	512.69	475.77	458.68	450.31	446.10	443.95
50 000	794.88	753.94	640.87	594.72	573.35	562.89	557.62	554.93
60 000	953.86	904.73	769.04	713.66	688.02	675.46	669.15	665.92
70 000	1112.83	1055.52	897.22	832.60	802.69	788.04	780.67	776.91
80 000	1271.81	1206.31	1025.39	951.54	917.36	900.62	892.19	887.90
90 000	1430.79	1357.10	1153.56	1070.49	1032.03	1013.20	1003.72	998.88
100 000	1589.76	1507.89	1281.74	1189.43	1146.70	1125.77	1115.24	1109.87
110 000	1748.74	1658.68	1409.91	1308.37	1261.37	1238.35	1226.77	1220.86
120 000	1907.71	1809.47	1538.08	1427.32	1376.04	1350.93	1338.29	1331.84
130 000	2066.69	1960.26	1666.26	1546.26	1490.71	1463.51	1449.81	1442.83
140 000	2225.67	2111.04	1794.43	1665.20	1605.38	1576.08	1561.34	1553.82
150 000	2384.64	2261.83	1922.60	1784.15	1720.05	1688.66	1672.86	1664.80
160 000	2543.62	2412.62	2050.78	1903.09	1834.72	1801.24	1784.39	1775.79
170 000	2702.59	2563.41	2178.95	2022.03	1949.39	1913.81	1895.91	1886.78
180 000	2861.57	2714.20	2307.13	2140.98	2064.06	2026.39	2007.44	1997.77
190 000	3020.55	2864.99	2435.30	2259.92	2178.73	2138.97	2118.96	2108.75
200 000	3179.52	3015.78	2563.47	2378.86	2293.40	2251.55	2230.48	2219.74
210 000	3338.50	3166.57	2691.65	2497.80	2408.07	2364.12	2342.01	2330.73
220 000	3497.48	3317.36	2819.82	2616.75	2522.74	2476.70	2453.53	2441.71
230 000	3656.45	3468.14	2947.99	2735.69	2637.41	2589.28	2565.06	2552.70
240 000	3815.43	3618.93	3076.17	2854.63	2752.08	2701.86	2676.58	2663.69
250 000	3974.40	3769.72	3204.34	2973.58	2866.75	2814.43	2788.11	2774.68
260 000	4133.38	3920.51	3332.51	3092.52	2981.42	2927.01	2899.63	2885.66
270 000	4292.36	4071.30	3460.68	3211.46	3096.09	3039.59	3011.15	2996.65
280 000	4451.33	4222.09	3588.86	3330.41	3210.76	3152.17	3122.68	3107.64
290 000	4610.31	4372.88	3717.04	3449.35	3325.43	3264.74	3234.20	3218.62
300 000	4769.29	4523.67	3845.21	3568.29	3440.10	3377.32	3345.73	3329.61
320 000	5087.24	4825.25	4101.56	3806.18	3669.44	3602.48	3568.78	3551.58
340 000	5405.19	5126.82	4357.90	4044.06	3898.78	3827.63	3791.82	3773.56
360 000	5723.14	5428.40	4614.25	4281.95	4128.12	4052.78	4014.87	3995.53
380 000	6041.09	5729.98	4870.60	4519.84	4357.46	4277.94	4237.92	4217.51
400 000	6359.05	6031.56	5126.95	4757.72	4586.80	4503.09	4460.97	4439.48
420 000	6677.00	6333.13	5383.29	4995.61	4816.14	4728.25	4684.02	4661.45
440 000	6994.95	6634.71	5639.64	5233.50	5045.48	4953.40	4907.07	4883.43
460 000	7312.90	6936.29	5895.99	5471.38	5274.82	5178.56	5130.11	5105.40
480 000	7630.86	7237.87	6152.33	5709.27	5504.16	5403.71	5353.16	5327.38
500 000	7948.81	7539.45	6408.68	5947.15	5733.50	5628.87	5576.21	5549.35
520 000	8266.76	7841.02	6665.03	6185.04	5962.84	5854.02	5799.26	5771.32
540 000	8584.71	8142.60	6921.38	6422.93	6192.18	6079.18	6022.31	5993.30
560 000	8902.67	8444.18	7177.72	6660.81	6421.52	6304.33	6245.36	6215.27
580 000	9220.62	8745.76	7434.07	6898.70	6650.86	6529.49	6468.40	6437.25
600 000	9538.57	9047.33	7690.42	7136.58	6880.20	6754.64	6691.45	6659.22
620 000	9856.52	9348.91	7946.77	7374.47	7109.54	6979.80	6914.50	6881.19
640 000	10174.47	9650.49	8203.11	7612.36	7338.88	7204.95	7137.55	7103.17
660 000	10492.43	9952.07	8459.46	7850.24	7568.22	7430.11	7360.60	7325.14
680 000	10810.38	10253.65	8715.81	8088.13	7797.56	7655.26	7583.65	7547.12
700 000	11128.33	10555.22	8972.15	8326.02	8026.90	7880.41	7806.70	7769.09
720 000	11446.28	10856.80	9228.50	8563.90	8256.24	8105.57	8029.74	7991.06
740 000	11764.24	11158.38	9484.85	8801.79	8485.58	8330.72	8252.79	8213.04
760 000	12082.19	11459.96	9741.20	9039.67	8714.92	8555.88	8475.84	8435.01
780 000	12400.14	11761.53	9997.54	9277.56	8944.26	8781.03	8698.89	8656.99
800 000	12718.09	12063.11	10253.89	9515.45	9173.60	9006.19	8921.94	8878.96
820 000	13036.05	12364.69	10510.24	9753.33	9402.94	9231.34	9144.99	9100.93
840 000	13354.00	12666.27	10766.59	9991.22	9632.28	9456.50	9368.03	9322.91
860 000	13671.95	12967.85	11022.93	10229.10	9861.62	9681.65	9591.08	9544.88
880 000	13989.90	13269.42	11279.28	10466.99	10090.96	9906.81	9814.13	9766.86
900 000	14307.86	13571.00	11535.63	10704.88	10320.30	10131.96	10037.18	9988.83
920 000	14625.81	13872.58	11791.97	10942.76	10549.64	10357.12	10260.23	10210.80
940 000	14943.76	14174.16	12048.32	11180.65	10778.98	10582.27	10483.28	10432.78
960 000	15261.71	14475.74	12304.67	11418.54	11008.32	10807.43	10706.33	10654.75
980 000	15579.66	14777.31	12561.02	11656.42	11237.66	11032.58	10929.37	10876.73
1000 000	15897.62	15078.89	12817.36	11894.31	11467.00	11257.74	11152.42	11098.70
Coefficient	.015897617	.015078891	.012817364	.011894308	.011467004	.011257735	.011152422	.011098700

MONTHLY AMORTIZING PAYMENTS

AMOUNT	1 YEAR	2 YEARS	3 YEARS	4 YEARS	5 YEARS	6 YEARS	7 YEARS	8 YEARS
10 000	895.52	477.77	339.35	270.76	230.10	203.39	184.65	170.88
20 000	1791.04	955.54	678.71	541.53	460.20	406.78	369.30	341.76
30 000	2686.56	1433.31	1018.06	812.29	690.30	610.17	553.95	512.64
40 000	3582.08	1911.08	1357.41	1083.05	920.39	813.56	738.60	683.53
50 000	4477.60	2388.85	1696.76	1353.82	1150.49	1016.95	923.24	854.41
60 000	5373.12	2866.62	2036.12	1624.58	1380.59	1220.34	1107.89	1025.29
70 000	6268.64	3344.39	2375.47	1895.34	1610.69	1423.73	1292.54	1196.17
80 000	7164.16	3822.16	2714.82	2166.11	1840.79	1627.12	1477.19	1367.05
90 000	8059.68	4299.93	3054.18	2436.87	2070.89	1830.51	1661.84	1537.93
100 000	8955.20	4777.70	3393.53	2707.63	2300.98	2033.90	1846.49	1708.82
110 000	9850.72	5255.47	3732.88	2978.40	2531.08	2237.29	2031.14	1879.70
120 000	10746.24	5733.24	4072.23	3249.16	2761.18	2440.68	2215.79	2050.58
130 000	11641.76	6211.01	4411.59	3519.92	2991.28	2644.07	2400.44	2221.46
140 000	12537.28	6688.78	4750.94	3790.69	3221.38	2847.45	2585.08	2392.34
150 000	13432.80	7166.55	5090.29	4061.45	3451.48	3050.84	2769.73	2563.22
160 000	14328.33	7644.32	5429.65	4332.21	3681.58	3254.23	2954.38	2734.11
170 000	15223.85	8122.09	5769.00	4602.97	3911.67	3457.62	3139.03	2904.99
180 000	16119.37	8599.86	6108.35	4873.74	4141.77	3661.01	3323.68	3075.87
190 000	17014.89	9077.63	6447.70	5144.50	4371.87	3864.40	3508.33	3246.75
200 000	17910.41	9555.40	6787.06	5415.26	4601.97	4067.79	3692.98	3417.63
210 000	18805.93	10033.17	7126.41	5686.03	4832.07	4271.18	3877.63	3588.51
220 000	19701.45	10510.94	7465.76	5956.79	5062.17	4474.57	4062.28	3759.39
230 000	20596.97	10988.71	7805.12	6227.55	5292.26	4677.96	4246.93	3930.28
240 000	21492.49	11466.48	8144.47	6498.32	5522.36	4881.35	4431.57	4101.16
250 000	22388.01	11944.25	8483.82	6769.08	5752.46	5084.74	4616.22	4272.04
260 000	23283.53	12422.02	8823.17	7039.84	5982.56	5288.13	4800.87	4442.92
270 000	24179.05	12899.79	9162.53	7310.61	6212.66	5491.52	4985.52	4613.80
280 000	25074.57	13377.56	9501.88	7581.37	6442.76	5694.91	5170.17	4784.68
290 000	25970.09	13855.33	9841.23	7852.13	6672.86	5898.30	5354.82	4955.57
300 000	26865.61	14333.11	10180.59	8122.90	6902.95	6101.69	5539.47	5126.45
320 000	28656.65	15288.65	10859.29	8664.42	7363.15	6508.47	5908.77	5468.21
340 000	30447.69	16244.19	11538.00	9205.95	7823.35	6915.25	6278.06	5809.97
360 000	32238.73	17199.73	12216.70	9747.48	8283.54	7322.03	6647.36	6151.74
380 000	34029.77	18155.27	12895.41	10289.00	8743.74	7728.81	7016.66	6493.50
400 000	35820.81	19110.81	13574.12	10830.53	9203.94	8135.58	7385.96	6835.26
420 000	37611.85	20066.35	14252.82	11372.06	9664.14	8542.36	7755.25	7177.03
440 000	39402.89	21021.89	14931.53	11913.58	10124.33	8949.14	8124.55	7518.79
460 000	41193.94	21977.43	15610.23	12455.11	10584.53	9355.92	8493.85	7860.55
480 000	42984.98	22932.97	16288.94	12996.63	11044.73	9762.70	8863.15	8202.32
500 000	44776.02	23888.51	16967.64	13538.16	11504.92	10169.48	9232.45	8544.08
520 000	46567.06	24844.05	17646.35	14079.69	11965.12	10576.26	9601.74	8885.84
540 000	48358.10	25799.59	18325.06	14621.21	12425.32	10983.04	9971.04	9227.61
560 000	50149.14	26755.13	19003.76	15162.74	12885.51	11389.82	10340.34	9569.37
580 000	51940.18	27710.67	19682.47	15704.27	13345.71	11796.60	10709.64	9911.13
600 000	53731.22	28666.21	20361.17	16245.79	13805.91	12203.38	11078.94	10252.90
620 000	55522.26	29621.75	21039.88	16787.32	14266.11	12610.16	11448.23	10594.66
640 000	57313.30	30577.29	21718.58	17328.85	14726.30	13016.94	11817.53	10936.42
660 000	59104.34	31532.83	22397.29	17870.37	15186.50	13423.71	12186.83	11278.18
680 000	60895.38	32488.37	23076.00	18411.90	15646.70	13830.49	12556.13	11619.95
700 000	62686.42	33443.91	23754.70	18953.43	16106.89	14237.27	12925.42	11961.71
720 000	64477.46	34399.45	24433.41	19494.95	16567.09	14644.05	13294.72	12303.47
740 000	66268.50	35354.99	25112.11	20036.48	17027.29	15050.83	13664.02	12645.24
760 000	68059.55	36310.53	25790.82	20578.00	17487.48	15457.61	14033.32	12987.00
780 000	69850.59	37266.07	26469.52	21119.53	17947.68	15864.39	14402.62	13328.76
800 000	71641.63	38221.61	27148.23	21661.06	18407.88	16271.17	14771.91	13670.53
820 000	73432.67	39177.15	27826.94	22202.58	18868.07	16677.95	15141.21	14012.29
840 000	75223.71	40132.69	28505.64	22744.11	19328.27	17084.73	15510.51	14354.05
860 000	77014.75	41088.23	29184.35	23285.64	19788.47	17491.51	15879.81	14695.82
880 000	78805.79	42043.77	29863.05	23827.16	20248.67	17898.29	16249.10	15037.58
900 000	80596.83	42999.32	30541.76	24368.69	20708.86	18305.07	16618.40	15379.34
920 000	82387.87	43954.86	31220.46	24910.22	21169.06	18711.85	16987.70	15721.11
940 000	84178.91	44910.40	31899.17	25451.74	21629.26	19118.62	17357.00	16062.87
960 000	85969.95	45865.94	32577.88	25993.27	22089.45	19525.40	17726.30	16404.63
980 000	87760.99	46821.48	33256.58	26534.80	22549.65	19932.18	18095.59	16746.40
1000 000	89552.03	47777.02	33935.29	27076.32	23009.85	20338.96	18464.89	17088.16
Coefficient	.089552033	.047777017	.033935288	.027076322	.023009847	.020338962	.018464892	.017088159

MONTHLY AMORTIZING PAYMENTS 13.50%

AMOUNT	9 YEARS	10 YEARS	15 YEARS	20 YEARS	25 YEARS	30 YEARS	35 YEARS	40 YEARS
10 000	160.42	152.27	129.83	120.74	116.56	114.54	113.53	113.03
20 000	320.85	304.55	259.66	241.47	233.13	229.08	227.07	226.05
30 000	481.27	456.82	389.50	362.21	349.69	343.62	340.60	339.08
40 000	641.69	609.10	519.33	482.95	466.26	458.16	454.14	452.10
50 000	802.12	761.37	649.16	603.69	582.82	572.71	567.67	565.13
60 000	962.54	913.65	778.99	724.42	699.39	687.25	681.20	678.16
70 000	1122.96	1065.92	908.82	845.16	815.95	801.79	794.74	791.18
80 000	1283.39	1218.19	1038.65	965.90	932.52	916.33	908.27	904.21
90 000	1443.81	1370.47	1168.49	1086.64	1049.08	1030.87	1021.81	1017.24
100 000	1604.23	1522.74	1298.32	1207.37	1165.64	1145.41	1135.34	1130.26
110 000	1764.65	1675.02	1428.15	1328.11	1282.21	1259.95	1248.87	1243.29
120 000	1925.08	1827.29	1557.98	1448.85	1398.77	1374.49	1362.41	1356.31
130 000	2085.50	1979.57	1687.81	1569.59	1515.34	1489.04	1475.94	1469.34
140 000	2245.92	2131.84	1817.65	1690.32	1631.90	1603.58	1589.48	1582.37
150 000	2406.35	2284.11	1947.48	1811.06	1748.47	1718.12	1703.01	1695.39
160 000	2566.77	2436.39	2077.31	1931.80	1865.03	1832.66	1816.54	1808.42
170 000	2727.19	2588.66	2207.14	2052.54	1981.60	1947.20	1930.08	1921.44
180 000	2887.62	2740.94	2336.97	2173.27	2098.16	2061.74	2043.61	2034.47
190 000	3048.04	2893.21	2466.81	2294.01	2214.73	2176.28	2157.15	2147.50
200 000	3208.46	3045.49	2596.64	2414.75	2331.29	2290.82	2270.68	2260.52
210 000	3368.89	3197.76	2726.47	2535.49	2447.85	2405.37	2384.22	2373.55
220 000	3529.31	3350.03	2856.30	2656.22	2564.42	2519.91	2497.75	2486.57
230 000	3689.73	3502.31	2986.13	2776.96	2680.98	2634.45	2611.28	2599.60
240 000	3850.16	3654.58	3115.96	2897.70	2797.55	2748.99	2724.82	2712.63
250 000	4010.58	3806.86	3245.80	3018.44	2914.11	2863.53	2838.35	2825.65
260 000	4171.00	3959.13	3375.63	3139.17	3030.68	2978.07	2951.89	2938.68
270 000	4331.42	4111.41	3505.46	3259.91	3147.24	3092.61	3065.42	3051.71
280 000	4491.85	4263.68	3635.29	3380.65	3263.81	3207.15	3178.95	3164.73
290 000	4652.27	4415.95	3765.12	3501.39	3380.37	3321.70	3292.49	3277.76
300 000	4812.69	4568.23	3894.96	3622.12	3496.93	3436.24	3406.02	3390.78
320 000	5133.54	4872.78	4154.62	3863.60	3730.06	3665.32	3633.09	3616.84
340 000	5454.39	5177.33	4414.28	4105.07	3963.19	3894.40	3860.16	3842.89
360 000	5775.23	5481.87	4673.95	4346.55	4196.32	4123.48	4087.23	4068.94
380 000	6096.08	5786.42	4933.61	4588.02	4429.45	4352.57	4314.29	4294.99
400 000	6416.93	6090.97	5193.27	4829.50	4662.58	4581.65	4541.36	4521.04
420 000	6737.77	6395.52	5452.94	5070.97	4895.71	4810.73	4768.43	4747.10
440 000	7058.62	6700.07	5712.60	5312.45	5128.84	5039.81	4995.50	4973.15
460 000	7379.46	7004.62	5972.27	5553.92	5361.97	5268.90	5222.57	5199.20
480 000	7700.31	7309.17	6231.93	5795.40	5595.10	5497.98	5449.63	5425.25
500 000	8021.16	7613.71	6491.59	6036.87	5828.22	5727.06	5676.70	5651.31
520 000	8342.00	7918.26	6751.26	6278.35	6061.35	5956.14	5903.77	5877.36
540 000	8662.85	8222.81	7010.92	6519.82	6294.48	6185.23	6130.84	6103.41
560 000	8983.70	8527.36	7270.58	6761.30	6527.61	6414.31	6357.91	6329.46
580 000	9304.54	8831.91	7530.25	7002.77	6760.74	6643.39	6584.97	6555.51
600 000	9625.39	9136.46	7789.91	7244.25	6993.87	6872.47	6812.04	6781.57
620 000	9946.23	9441.01	8049.58	7485.72	7227.00	7101.56	7039.11	7007.62
640 000	10267.08	9745.55	8309.24	7727.20	7460.13	7330.64	7266.18	7233.67
660 000	10587.93	10050.10	8568.90	7968.67	7693.26	7559.72	7493.25	7459.72
680 000	10908.77	10354.65	8828.57	8210.15	7926.39	7788.80	7720.32	7685.78
700 000	11229.62	10659.20	9088.23	8451.62	8159.51	8017.89	7947.38	7911.83
720 000	11550.47	10963.75	9347.89	8693.10	8392.64	8246.97	8174.45	8137.88
740 000	11871.31	11268.30	9607.56	8934.57	8625.77	8476.05	8401.52	8363.93
760 000	12192.16	11572.85	9867.22	9176.05	8858.90	8705.13	8628.59	8589.99
780 000	12513.00	11877.39	10126.89	9417.52	9092.03	8934.22	8855.66	8816.04
800 000	12833.85	12181.94	10386.55	9659.00	9325.16	9163.30	9082.72	9042.09
820 000	13154.70	12486.49	10646.21	9900.47	9558.29	9392.38	9309.79	9268.14
840 000	13475.54	12791.04	10905.88	10141.95	9791.42	9621.46	9536.86	9494.19
860 000	13796.39	13095.59	11165.54	10383.42	10024.55	9850.54	9763.93	9720.25
880 000	14117.24	13400.14	11425.20	10624.90	10257.68	10079.63	9991.00	9946.30
900 000	14438.08	13704.69	11684.87	10866.37	10490.80	10308.71	10218.06	10172.35
920 000	14758.93	14009.23	11944.53	11107.85	10723.93	10537.79	10445.13	10398.40
940 000	15079.78	14313.78	12204.19	11349.32	10957.06	10766.87	10672.20	10624.46
960 000	15400.62	14618.33	12463.86	11590.80	11190.19	10995.96	10899.27	10850.51
980 000	15721.47	14922.88	12723.52	11832.27	11423.32	11225.04	11126.34	11076.56
1000 000	16042.31	15227.43	12983.19	12073.75	11656.45	11454.12	11353.41	11302.61
Coefficient	.016042314	.015227429	.012983186	.012073747	.011656449	.011454122	.011353405	.011302612

71

AMOUNT	1 YEAR	2 YEARS	3 YEARS	4 YEARS	5 YEARS	6 YEARS	7 YEARS	8 YEARS
10 000	896.70	478.95	340.56	272.01	231.39	204.72	186.02	172.30
20 000	1793.39	957.90	681.13	544.02	462.78	409.44	372.04	344.59
30 000	2690.09	1436.85	1021.69	816.04	694.17	614.16	558.07	516.89
40 000	3586.78	1915.79	1362.25	1088.05	925.55	818.88	744.09	689.18
50 000	4483.48	2394.74	1702.82	1360.06	1156.94	1023.61	930.11	861.48
60 000	5380.17	2873.69	2043.38	1632.07	1388.33	1228.33	1116.13	1033.77
70 000	6276.87	3352.64	2383.94	1904.09	1619.72	1433.05	1302.15	1206.07
80 000	7173.56	3831.59	2724.51	2176.10	1851.11	1637.77	1488.17	1378.36
90 000	8070.26	4310.54	3065.07	2448.11	2082.50	1842.49	1674.20	1550.66
100 000	8966.95	4789.49	3405.63	2720.12	2313.88	2047.21	1860.22	1722.95
110 000	9863.65	5268.44	3746.20	2992.14	2545.27	2251.93	2046.24	1895.25
120 000	10760.34	5747.38	4086.76	3264.15	2776.66	2456.65	2232.26	2067.54
130 000	11657.04	6226.33	4427.32	3536.16	3008.05	2661.37	2418.28	2239.84
140 000	12553.73	6705.28	4767.89	3808.17	3239.44	2866.10	2604.31	2412.13
150 000	13450.43	7184.23	5108.45	4080.18	3470.83	3070.82	2790.33	2584.43
160 000	14347.13	7663.18	5449.01	4352.20	3702.22	3275.54	2976.35	2756.72
170 000	15243.82	8142.13	5789.58	4624.21	3933.60	3480.26	3162.37	2929.02
180 000	16140.52	8621.08	6130.14	4896.22	4164.99	3684.98	3348.39	3101.31
190 000	17037.21	9100.02	6470.70	5168.23	4396.38	3889.70	3534.41	3273.61
200 000	17933.91	9578.97	6811.27	5440.25	4627.77	4094.42	3720.44	3445.91
210 000	18830.60	10057.92	7151.83	5712.96	4859.16	4299.14	3906.46	3618.20
220 000	19727.30	10536.87	7492.39	5984.27	5090.55	4503.86	4092.48	3790.50
230 000	20623.99	11015.82	7832.96	6256.28	5321.93	4708.59	4278.50	3962.79
240 000	21520.69	11494.77	8173.52	6528.30	5553.32	4913.31	4464.52	4135.09
250 000	22417.38	11973.72	8514.08	6800.31	5784.71	5118.03	4650.55	4307.38
260 000	23314.08	12452.67	8854.65	7072.32	6016.10	5322.75	4836.57	4479.68
270 000	24210.77	12931.61	9195.21	7344.33	6247.49	5527.47	5022.59	4651.97
280 000	25107.47	13410.56	9535.77	7616.35	6478.88	5732.19	5208.61	4824.27
290 000	26004.16	13889.51	9876.34	7888.36	6710.26	5936.91	5394.63	4996.56
300 000	26900.86	14368.46	10216.90	8160.37	6941.65	6141.63	5580.65	5168.86
320 000	28694.25	15326.36	10898.03	8704.39	7404.43	6551.08	5952.70	5513.45
340 000	30487.64	16284.25	11579.15	9248.42	7867.21	6960.52	6324.74	5858.04
360 000	32281.03	17242.15	12260.28	9792.44	8329.98	7369.96	6696.78	6202.63
380 000	34074.42	18200.05	12941.41	10336.47	8792.76	7779.40	7068.83	6547.22
400 000	35867.81	19157.95	13622.53	10880.49	9255.54	8188.84	7440.87	6891.81
420 000	37661.20	20115.84	14303.66	11424.52	9718.31	8598.29	7812.92	7236.40
440 000	39454.59	21073.74	14984.79	11968.54	10181.09	9007.73	8184.96	7580.99
460 000	41247.99	22031.64	15665.91	12512.57	10643.87	9417.17	8557.00	7925.58
480 000	43041.38	22989.54	16347.04	13056.59	11106.65	9826.61	8929.05	8270.17
500 000	44834.77	23947.43	17028.17	13600.62	11569.42	10236.06	9301.09	8614.76
520 000	46628.16	24905.33	17709.29	14144.64	12032.20	10645.50	9673.13	8959.35
540 000	48421.55	25863.23	18390.42	14688.67	12494.98	11054.94	10045.18	9303.94
560 000	50214.94	26821.13	19071.55	15232.69	12957.75	11464.38	10417.22	9648.54
580 000	52008.33	27779.02	19752.67	15776.72	13420.53	11873.82	10789.26	9993.13
600 000	53801.72	28736.92	20433.80	16320.74	13883.31	12283.27	11161.31	10337.72
620 000	55595.11	29694.82	21114.93	16864.76	14346.08	12692.71	11533.35	10682.31
640 000	57388.50	30652.71	21796.05	17408.79	14808.86	13102.15	11905.40	11026.90
660 000	59181.89	31610.61	22477.18	17952.81	15271.64	13511.59	12277.44	11371.49
680 000	60975.28	32568.51	23158.31	18496.84	15734.41	13921.04	12649.48	11716.08
700 000	62768.67	33526.41	23839.43	19040.86	16197.19	14330.48	13021.53	12060.67
720 000	64562.06	34484.30	24520.56	19584.89	16659.97	14739.92	13393.57	12405.26
740 000	66355.46	35442.20	25201.69	20128.91	17122.74	15149.36	13765.61	12749.85
760 000	68148.85	36400.10	25882.81	20672.94	17585.52	15558.80	14137.66	13094.44
780 000	69942.24	37358.00	26563.94	21216.96	18048.30	15968.25	14509.70	13439.03
800 000	71735.63	38315.89	27245.07	21760.99	18511.08	16377.69	14881.74	13783.62
820 000	73529.02	39273.79	27926.19	22305.01	18973.85	16787.13	15253.79	14128.21
840 000	75322.41	40231.69	28607.32	22849.04	19436.63	17196.57	15625.83	14472.80
860 000	77115.80	41189.59	29288.45	23393.06	19899.41	17606.02	15997.87	14817.39
880 000	78909.19	42147.48	29969.57	23937.09	20362.18	18015.46	16369.92	15161.98
900 000	80702.58	43105.38	30650.70	24481.11	20824.96	18424.90	16741.96	15506.57
920 000	82495.97	44063.28	31331.83	25025.13	21287.74	18834.34	17114.00	15851.16
940 000	84289.36	45021.17	32012.95	25569.16	21750.51	19243.78	17486.05	16195.76
960 000	86082.75	45979.07	32694.08	26113.18	22213.29	19653.23	17858.09	16540.35
980 000	87876.14	46936.97	33375.21	26657.21	22676.07	20062.67	18230.14	16884.94
1000 000	89669.53	47894.87	34056.34	27201.23	23138.84	20472.11	18602.18	17229.53
Coefficient	.089669534	.047894867	.034056335	.027201233	.023138844	.020472111	.018602180	.017229527

MONTHLY AMORTIZING PAYMENTS 13.75%

AMOUNT	9 YEARS	10 YEARS	15 YEARS	20 YEARS	25 YEARS	30 YEARS	35 YEARS	40 YEARS
10 000	161.88	153.77	131.50	122.54	118.47	116.51	115.55	115.07
20 000	323.75	307.53	263.00	245.08	236.93	233.02	231.10	230.14
30 000	485.63	461.30	394.50	367.62	355.40	349.53	346.65	345.21
40 000	647.51	615.07	525.99	490.16	473.87	466.05	462.19	460.27
50 000	809.38	768.83	657.49	612.70	592.33	582.56	577.74	575.34
60 000	971.26	922.60	788.99	735.24	710.80	699.07	693.29	690.41
70 000	1133.14	1076.37	920.49	857.78	829.27	815.58	808.84	805.48
80 000	1295.01	1230.13	1051.99	980.32	947.73	932.09	924.39	920.55
90 000	1456.89	1383.90	1183.49	1102.86	1066.20	1048.60	1039.94	1035.62
100 000	1618.77	1537.67	1314.99	1225.41	1184.67	1165.11	1155.49	1150.69
110 000	1780.64	1691.43	1446.49	1347.95	1303.13	1281.62	1271.03	1265.75
120 000	1942.52	1845.20	1577.98	1470.49	1421.60	1398.14	1386.58	1380.82
130 000	2104.40	1998.97	1709.48	1593.03	1540.07	1514.65	1502.13	1495.89
140 000	2266.27	2152.74	1840.98	1715.57	1658.53	1631.16	1617.68	1610.96
150 000	2428.15	2306.50	1972.48	1838.11	1777.00	1747.67	1733.23	1726.03
160 000	2590.03	2460.27	2103.98	1960.65	1895.47	1864.18	1848.78	1841.10
170 000	2751.90	2614.04	2235.48	2083.19	2013.93	1980.69	1964.32	1956.17
180 000	2913.78	2767.80	2366.98	2205.73	2132.40	2097.20	2079.87	2071.23
190 000	3075.66	2921.57	2498.48	2328.27	2250.87	2213.71	2195.42	2186.30
200 000	3237.54	3075.34	2629.97	2450.82	2369.33	2330.23	2310.97	2301.37
210 000	3399.41	3229.10	2761.47	2573.35	2487.80	2446.74	2426.52	2416.44
220 000	3561.29	3382.87	2892.97	2695.89	2606.27	2563.25	2542.07	2531.51
230 000	3723.17	3536.64	3024.47	2818.43	2724.73	2679.76	2657.62	2646.58
240 000	3885.04	3690.40	3155.97	2940.97	2843.20	2796.27	2773.16	2761.64
250 000	4046.92	3844.17	3287.47	3063.51	2961.67	2912.78	2888.71	2876.71
260 000	4208.80	3997.94	3418.97	3186.05	3080.13	3029.29	3004.26	2991.78
270 000	4370.67	4151.70	3550.47	3308.59	3198.60	3145.80	3119.81	3106.85
280 000	4532.55	4305.47	3681.96	3431.14	3317.06	3262.32	3235.36	3221.92
290 000	4694.43	4459.24	3813.46	3553.68	3435.53	3378.83	3350.91	3336.99
300 000	4856.30	4613.00	3944.96	3676.22	3554.00	3495.34	3466.46	3452.06
320 000	5180.06	4920.54	4207.96	3921.30	3790.93	3728.36	3697.55	3682.19
340 000	5503.81	5228.07	4470.96	4166.38	4027.86	3961.38	3928.65	3912.33
360 000	5827.56	5535.61	4733.95	4411.46	4264.80	4194.41	4159.75	4142.47
380 000	6151.32	5843.14	4996.95	4656.54	4501.73	4427.43	4390.84	4372.60
400 000	6475.07	6150.67	5259.95	4901.62	4738.66	4660.45	4621.94	4602.74
420 000	6798.82	6458.21	5522.95	5146.70	4975.60	4893.47	4853.04	4832.88
440 000	7122.58	6765.74	5785.94	5391.78	5212.53	5126.50	5084.13	5063.02
460 000	7446.33	7073.27	6048.94	5636.86	5449.46	5359.52	5315.23	5293.15
480 000	7770.08	7380.81	6311.94	5881.95	5686.40	5592.54	5546.33	5523.29
500 000	8093.84	7688.34	6574.94	6127.03	5923.33	5825.56	5777.43	5753.43
520 000	8417.59	7995.87	6837.93	6372.11	6160.26	6058.59	6008.52	5983.56
540 000	8741.35	8303.41	7100.93	6617.19	6397.20	6291.61	6239.62	6213.70
560 000	9065.10	8610.94	7363.93	6862.27	6634.13	6524.63	6470.72	6443.84
580 000	9388.85	8918.47	7626.93	7107.35	6871.06	6757.65	6701.81	6673.97
600 000	9712.61	9226.01	7889.92	7352.43	7108.00	6990.68	6932.91	6904.11
620 000	10036.36	9533.54	8152.92	7597.51	7344.93	7223.70	7164.01	7134.25
640 000	10360.11	9841.08	8415.92	7842.59	7581.86	7456.72	7395.10	7364.39
660 000	10683.87	10148.61	8678.92	8087.68	7818.80	7689.74	7626.20	7594.52
680 000	11007.62	10456.14	8941.91	8332.76	8055.73	7922.77	7857.30	7824.66
700 000	11331.37	10763.68	9204.91	8577.84	8292.66	8155.79	8088.40	8054.80
720 000	11655.13	11071.21	9467.91	8822.92	8529.60	8388.81	8319.49	8284.93
740 000	11978.88	11378.74	9730.91	9068.00	8766.53	8621.83	8550.59	8515.07
760 000	12302.63	11686.28	9993.90	9313.08	9003.46	8854.86	8781.69	8745.21
780 000	12626.39	11993.81	10256.90	9558.16	9240.39	9087.88	9012.78	8975.35
800 000	12950.14	12301.34	10519.90	9803.24	9477.33	9320.90	9243.88	9205.48
820 000	13273.90	12608.88	10782.90	10048.32	9714.26	9553.92	9474.98	9435.62
840 000	13597.65	12916.41	11045.89	10293.41	9951.19	9786.95	9706.07	9665.76
860 000	13921.40	13223.95	11308.89	10538.49	10188.13	10019.97	9937.17	9895.89
880 000	14245.16	13531.48	11571.89	10783.57	10425.06	10252.99	10168.27	10126.03
900 000	14568.91	13839.01	11834.89	11028.65	10661.99	10486.01	10399.37	10356.17
920 000	14892.66	14146.55	12097.88	11273.73	10898.93	10719.04	10630.46	10586.30
940 000	15216.42	14454.08	12360.88	11518.81	11135.86	10952.06	10861.56	10816.44
960 000	15540.17	14761.61	12623.88	11763.89	11372.79	11185.08	11092.66	11046.58
980 000	15863.92	15069.15	12886.88	12008.97	11609.73	11418.10	11323.75	11276.72
1000 000	16187.68	15376.68	13149.87	12254.05	11846.66	11651.13	11554.85	11506.85
Coefficient	.016187677	.015376681	.013149873	.012254054	.011846660	.011651125	.011554851	.011506853

73

AMOUNT	1 YEAR	2 YEARS	3 YEARS	4 YEARS	5 YEARS	6 YEARS	7 YEARS	8 YEARS
10 000	897.87	480.13	341.78	273.26	232.68	206.06	187.40	173.72
20 000	1795.74	960.26	683.55	546.53	465.37	412.11	374.80	347.43
30 000	2693.61	1440.39	1025.33	819.79	698.05	618.17	562.20	521.15
40 000	3591.48	1920.52	1367.11	1093.06	930.73	824.23	749.60	694.86
50 000	4489.36	2400.64	1708.88	1366.32	1163.41	1030.29	937.00	868.58
60 000	5387.23	2880.77	2050.66	1639.59	1396.10	1236.34	1124.40	1042.29
70 000	6285.10	3360.90	2392.43	1912.85	1628.78	1442.40	1311.80	1216.01
80 000	7182.97	3841.03	2734.21	2186.12	1861.46	1648.46	1499.20	1389.72
90 000	8080.84	4321.16	3075.99	2459.38	2094.14	1854.52	1686.60	1563.44
100 000	8978.71	4801.29	3417.76	2732.65	2326.83	2060.57	1874.00	1737.15
110 000	9876.58	5281.42	3759.54	3005.91	2559.51	2266.63	2061.40	1910.87
120 000	10774.45	5761.55	4101.32	3279.18	2792.19	2472.69	2248.80	2084.58
130 000	11672.33	6241.67	4443.09	3552.44	3024.87	2678.75	2436.20	2258.30
140 000	12570.20	6721.80	4784.87	3825.71	3257.56	2884.80	2623.60	2432.01
150 000	13468.07	7201.93	5126.64	4098.97	3490.24	3090.86	2811.00	2605.73
160 000	14365.94	7682.06	5468.42	4372.24	3722.92	3296.92	2998.40	2779.44
170 000	15263.81	8162.19	5810.20	4645.50	3955.60	3502.98	3185.80	2953.16
180 000	16161.68	8642.32	6151.97	4918.77	4188.29	3709.03	3373.20	3126.87
190 000	17059.55	9122.45	6493.75	5192.03	4420.97	3915.09	3560.60	3300.59
200 000	17957.42	9602.58	6835.53	5465.30	4653.65	4121.15	3748.00	3474.30
210 000	18855.29	10082.70	7177.30	5738.56	4886.33	4327.21	3935.40	3648.02
220 000	19753.17	10562.83	7519.08	6011.82	5119.02	4533.26	4122.80	3821.73
230 000	20651.04	11042.96	7860.86	6285.09	5351.70	4739.32	4310.20	3995.45
240 000	21548.91	11523.09	8202.63	6558.35	5584.38	4945.38	4497.60	4169.16
250 000	22446.78	12003.22	8544.41	6831.62	5817.06	5151.43	4685.00	4342.88
260 000	23344.65	12483.35	8886.18	7104.88	6049.75	5357.49	4872.40	4516.59
270 000	24242.52	12963.48	9227.96	7378.15	6282.43	5563.55	5059.80	4690.31
280 000	25140.39	13443.61	9569.74	7651.41	6515.11	5769.61	5247.20	4864.02
290 000	26038.26	13923.74	9911.51	7924.68	6747.79	5975.66	5434.60	5037.74
300 000	26936.13	14403.86	10253.29	8197.94	6980.48	6181.72	5622.00	5211.45
320 000	28731.88	15364.12	10936.84	8744.47	7445.84	6593.84	5996.80	5558.88
340 000	30527.62	16324.38	11620.39	9291.00	7911.21	7005.95	6371.60	5906.31
360 000	32323.36	17284.64	12303.95	9837.53	8376.57	7418.07	6746.40	6253.74
380 000	34119.10	18244.89	12987.50	10384.06	8841.94	7830.18	7121.20	6601.17
400 000	35914.85	19205.15	13671.05	10930.59	9307.30	8242.30	7496.00	6948.60
420 000	37710.59	20165.41	14354.61	11477.12	9772.67	8654.41	7870.81	7296.03
440 000	39506.33	21125.67	15038.16	12023.65	10238.03	9066.53	8245.61	7643.46
460 000	41302.07	22085.92	15721.71	12570.18	10703.40	9478.64	8620.41	7990.89
480 000	43097.82	23046.18	16405.26	13116.71	11168.76	9890.75	8995.21	8338.32
500 000	44893.56	24006.44	17088.82	13663.24	11634.13	10302.87	9370.01	8685.75
520 000	46689.30	24966.70	17772.37	14209.77	12099.49	10714.98	9744.81	9033.18
540 000	48485.04	25926.96	18455.92	14756.30	12564.86	11127.10	10119.61	9380.61
560 000	50280.78	26887.21	19139.47	15302.83	13030.22	11539.21	10494.41	9728.04
580 000	52076.53	27847.47	19823.03	15849.36	13495.59	11951.33	10869.21	10075.47
600 000	53872.27	28807.73	20506.58	16395.89	13960.95	12363.44	11244.01	10422.90
620 000	55668.01	29767.99	21190.13	16942.42	14426.32	12775.56	11618.81	10770.33
640 000	57463.75	30728.24	21873.68	17488.94	14891.68	13187.67	11993.61	11117.76
660 000	59259.50	31688.50	22557.24	18035.47	15357.05	13599.79	12368.41	11465.19
680 000	61055.24	32648.76	23240.79	18582.00	15822.41	14011.90	12743.21	11812.62
700 000	62850.98	33609.02	23924.34	19128.53	16287.78	14424.02	13118.01	12160.05
720 000	64646.72	34569.27	24607.90	19675.06	16753.14	14836.13	13492.81	12507.48
740 000	66442.47	35529.53	25291.45	20221.59	17218.51	15248.25	13867.61	12854.91
760 000	68238.21	36489.79	25975.00	20768.12	17683.87	15660.36	14242.41	13202.34
780 000	70033.95	37450.05	26658.55	21314.65	18149.24	16072.48	14617.21	13549.77
800 000	71829.69	38410.30	27342.11	21861.18	18614.60	16484.59	14992.01	13897.20
820 000	73625.44	39370.56	28025.66	22407.71	19079.97	16896.71	15366.81	14244.63
840 000	75421.18	40330.82	28709.21	22954.24	19545.33	17308.82	15741.61	14592.06
860 000	77216.92	41291.08	29392.76	23500.77	20010.70	17720.94	16116.41	14939.49
880 000	79012.66	42251.33	30076.32	24047.30	20476.06	18133.05	16491.21	15286.92
900 000	80808.40	43211.59	30759.87	24593.83	20941.43	18545.17	16866.01	15634.35
920 000	82604.15	44171.85	31443.42	25140.36	21406.79	18957.28	17240.81	15981.78
940 000	84399.89	45132.11	32126.97	25686.89	21872.16	19369.39	17615.61	16329.21
960 000	86195.63	46092.36	32810.53	26233.42	22337.52	19781.51	17990.41	16676.64
980 000	87991.37	47052.62	33494.08	26779.95	22802.89	20193.62	18365.21	17024.07
1000 000	89787.12	48012.88	34177.63	27326.48	23268.25	20605.74	18740.01	17371.50
Coefficient	.089787116	.048012880	.034177632	.027326476	.023268251	.020605739	.018740012	.017371501

MONTHLY AMORTIZING PAYMENTS 14.00%

AMOUNT	9 YEARS	10 YEARS	15 YEARS	20 YEARS	25 YEARS	30 YEARS	35 YEARS	40 YEARS
10 000	163.34	155.27	133.17	124.35	120.38	118.49	117.57	117.11
20 000	326.67	310.53	266.35	248.70	240.75	236.97	235.13	234.23
30 000	490.01	465.80	399.52	373.06	361.13	355.46	352.70	351.34
40 000	653.35	621.07	532.70	497.41	481.50	473.95	470.27	468.46
50 000	816.69	776.33	665.87	621.76	601.88	592.44	587.84	585.57
60 000	980.02	931.60	799.04	746.11	722.26	710.92	705.40	702.68
70 000	1143.36	1086.87	932.22	870.46	842.63	829.41	822.97	819.80
80 000	1306.70	1242.13	1065.39	994.82	963.01	947.90	940.54	936.91
90 000	1470.03	1397.40	1198.57	1119.17	1083.38	1066.38	1058.11	1054.03
100 000	1633.37	1552.66	1331.74	1243.52	1203.76	1184.87	1175.67	1171.14
110 000	1796.71	1707.93	1464.92	1367.87	1324.14	1303.36	1293.24	1288.25
120 000	1960.04	1863.20	1598.09	1492.22	1444.51	1421.85	1410.81	1405.37
130 000	2123.38	2018.46	1731.26	1616.58	1564.89	1540.33	1528.38	1522.48
140 000	2286.72	2173.73	1864.44	1740.93	1685.27	1658.82	1645.94	1639.60
150 000	2450.06	2329.00	1997.61	1865.28	1805.64	1777.31	1763.51	1756.71
160 000	2613.39	2484.26	2130.79	1989.63	1926.02	1895.79	1881.08	1873.82
170 000	2776.73	2639.53	2263.96	2113.99	2046.39	2014.28	1998.64	1990.94
180 000	2940.07	2794.80	2397.13	2238.34	2166.77	2132.77	2116.21	2108.05
190 000	3103.40	2950.06	2530.31	2362.69	2287.15	2251.26	2233.78	2225.17
200 000	3266.74	3105.33	2663.48	2487.04	2407.52	2369.74	2351.35	2342.28
210 000	3430.08	3260.60	2796.66	2611.39	2527.90	2488.23	2468.91	2459.39
220 000	3593.41	3415.86	2929.83	2735.75	2648.27	2606.72	2586.48	2576.51
230 000	3756.75	3571.13	3063.01	2860.10	2768.65	2725.20	2704.05	2693.62
240 000	3920.09	3726.39	3196.18	2984.45	2889.03	2843.69	2821.62	2810.74
250 000	4083.43	3881.66	3329.35	3108.80	3009.40	2962.18	2939.18	2927.85
260 000	4246.76	4036.93	3462.53	3233.15	3129.78	3080.67	3056.75	3044.96
270 000	4410.10	4192.19	3595.70	3357.51	3250.15	3199.15	3174.32	3162.08
280 000	4573.44	4347.46	3728.88	3481.86	3370.53	3317.64	3291.89	3279.19
290 000	4736.77	4502.73	3862.05	3606.21	3490.91	3436.13	3409.45	3396.31
300 000	4900.11	4657.99	3995.22	3730.56	3611.28	3554.62	3527.02	3513.42
320 000	5226.78	4968.53	4261.57	3979.27	3852.04	3791.59	3762.15	3747.65
340 000	5553.46	5279.06	4527.92	4227.97	4092.79	4028.56	3997.29	3981.88
360 000	5880.13	5589.59	4794.27	4476.67	4333.54	4265.54	4232.42	4216.10
380 000	6206.81	5900.12	5060.62	4725.38	4574.29	4502.51	4467.56	4450.33
400 000	6533.48	6210.66	5326.97	4974.08	4815.04	4739.49	4702.69	4684.56
420 000	6860.15	6521.19	5593.31	5222.79	5055.80	4976.46	4937.83	4918.79
440 000	7186.83	6831.72	5859.66	5471.49	5296.55	5213.44	5172.96	5153.02
460 000	7513.50	7142.26	6126.01	5720.20	5537.30	5450.41	5408.10	5387.24
480 000	7840.18	7452.79	6392.36	5968.90	5778.05	5687.38	5643.23	5621.47
500 000	8166.85	7763.32	6658.71	6217.60	6018.81	5924.36	5878.37	5855.70
520 000	8493.52	8073.85	6925.06	6466.31	6259.56	6161.33	6113.50	6089.93
540 000	8820.20	8384.39	7191.40	6715.01	6500.31	6398.31	6348.64	6324.16
560 000	9146.87	8694.92	7457.75	6963.72	6741.06	6635.28	6583.77	6558.38
580 000	9473.55	9005.45	7724.10	7212.42	6981.81	6872.26	6818.91	6792.61
600 000	9800.22	9315.99	7990.45	7461.12	7222.57	7109.23	7054.04	7026.84
620 000	10126.89	9626.52	8256.80	7709.83	7463.32	7346.20	7289.17	7261.07
640 000	10453.57	9937.05	8523.14	7958.53	7704.07	7583.18	7524.31	7495.30
660 000	10780.24	10247.59	8789.49	8207.24	7944.82	7820.15	7759.44	7729.52
680 000	11106.92	10558.12	9055.84	8455.94	8185.57	8057.13	7994.58	7963.75
700 000	11433.59	10868.65	9322.19	8704.65	8426.33	8294.10	8229.71	8197.98
720 000	11760.26	11179.18	9588.54	8953.35	8667.08	8531.08	8464.85	8432.21
740 000	12086.94	11489.72	9854.89	9202.05	8907.83	8768.05	8699.98	8666.44
760 000	12413.61	11800.25	10121.23	9450.76	9148.58	9005.02	8935.12	8900.66
780 000	12740.29	12110.78	10387.58	9699.46	9389.34	9242.00	9170.25	9134.89
800 000	13066.96	12421.32	10653.93	9948.17	9630.09	9478.97	9405.39	9369.12
820 000	13393.63	12731.85	10920.28	10196.87	9870.84	9715.95	9640.52	9603.35
840 000	13720.31	13042.38	11186.63	10445.57	10111.59	9952.92	9875.66	9837.58
860 000	14046.98	13352.91	11452.98	10694.28	10352.34	10189.90	10110.79	10071.80
880 000	14373.66	13663.45	11719.32	10942.98	10593.10	10426.87	10345.93	10306.03
900 000	14700.33	13973.98	11985.67	11191.69	10833.85	10663.85	10581.06	10540.26
920 000	15027.00	14284.51	12252.02	11440.39	11074.60	10900.82	10816.19	10774.49
940 000	15353.68	14595.05	12518.37	11689.10	11315.35	11137.79	11051.33	11008.72
960 000	15680.35	14905.58	12784.72	11937.80	11556.11	11374.77	11286.46	11242.94
980 000	16007.03	15216.11	13051.07	12186.50	11796.86	11611.74	11521.60	11477.17
1000 000	16333.70	15526.64	13317.41	12435.21	12037.61	11848.72	11756.73	11711.40
Coefficient	.016333701	.015526644	.013317414	.012435208	.012037610	.011848721	.011756733	.011711401

75

MONTHLY AMORTIZING PAYMENTS

AMOUNT	1 YEAR	2 YEARS	3 YEARS	4 YEARS	5 YEARS	6 YEARS	7 YEARS	8 YEARS
10 000	899.05	481.31	342.99	274.52	233.98	207.40	188.78	175.14
20 000	1798.10	962.62	685.98	549.04	467.96	414.80	377.57	350.28
30 000	2697.14	1443.93	1028.98	823.56	701.94	622.20	566.35	525.42
40 000	3596.19	1925.24	1371.97	1098.08	935.92	829.59	755.14	700.56
50 000	4495.24	2406.55	1714.96	1372.60	1169.90	1036.99	943.92	875.70
60 000	5394.29	2887.86	2057.95	1647.12	1403.88	1244.39	1132.70	1050.84
70 000	6293.34	3369.17	2400.94	1921.64	1637.86	1451.79	1321.49	1225.99
80 000	7192.38	3850.49	2743.93	2196.16	1871.85	1659.19	1510.27	1401.13
90 000	8091.43	4331.80	3086.93	2470.68	2105.83	1866.59	1699.05	1576.27
100 000	8990.48	4813.11	3429.92	2745.20	2339.81	2073.98	1887.84	1751.41
110 000	9889.53	5294.42	3772.91	3019.73	2573.79	2281.38	2076.62	1926.55
120 000	10788.58	5775.73	4115.90	3294.25	2807.77	2488.78	2265.41	2101.69
130 000	11687.62	6257.04	4458.89	3568.77	3041.75	2696.18	2454.19	2276.83
140 000	12586.67	6738.35	4801.89	3843.29	3275.73	2903.58	2642.97	2451.97
150 000	13485.72	7219.66	5144.88	4117.81	3509.71	3110.98	2831.76	2627.11
160 000	14384.77	7700.97	5487.87	4392.33	3743.69	3318.38	3020.54	2802.25
170 000	15283.82	8182.28	5830.86	4666.85	3977.67	3525.77	3209.33	2977.39
180 000	16182.86	8663.59	6173.85	4941.37	4211.65	3733.17	3398.11	3152.53
190 000	17081.91	9144.90	6516.84	5215.89	4445.63	3940.57	3586.89	3327.68
200 000	17980.96	9626.21	6859.84	5490.41	4679.61	4147.97	3775.68	3502.82
210 000	18880.01	10107.52	7202.83	5764.93	4913.59	4355.37	3964.46	3677.96
220 000	19779.06	10588.83	7545.82	6039.45	5147.57	4562.77	4153.25	3853.10
230 000	20678.10	11070.15	7888.81	6313.97	5381.55	4770.16	4342.03	4028.24
240 000	21577.15	11551.46	8231.80	6588.49	5615.54	4977.56	4530.81	4203.38
250 000	22476.20	12032.77	8574.79	6863.01	5849.52	5184.96	4719.60	4378.52
260 000	23375.25	12514.08	8917.79	7137.53	6083.50	5392.36	4908.38	4553.66
270 000	24274.30	12995.39	9260.78	7412.05	6317.48	5599.76	5097.16	4728.80
280 000	25173.34	13476.70	9603.77	7686.57	6551.46	5807.16	5285.95	4903.94
290 000	26072.39	13958.01	9946.76	7961.09	6785.44	6014.55	5474.73	5079.08
300 000	26971.44	14439.32	10289.75	8235.61	7019.42	6221.95	5663.52	5254.22
320 000	28769.54	15401.94	10975.74	8784.66	7487.38	6636.75	6041.08	5604.51
340 000	30567.63	16364.56	11661.72	9333.70	7955.34	7051.55	6418.65	5954.79
360 000	32365.73	17327.18	12347.70	9882.74	8423.30	7466.34	6796.22	6305.07
380 000	34163.82	18289.81	13033.69	10431.78	8891.26	7881.14	7173.79	6655.35
400 000	35961.92	19252.43	13719.67	10980.82	9359.23	8295.94	7551.35	7005.63
420 000	37760.01	20215.05	14405.66	11529.86	9827.19	8710.73	7928.92	7355.91
440 000	39558.11	21177.67	15091.64	12078.90	10295.15	9125.53	8306.49	7706.19
460 000	41356.21	22140.29	15777.62	12627.94	10763.11	9540.33	8684.06	8056.48
480 000	43154.30	23102.91	16463.61	13176.98	11231.07	9955.13	9061.63	8406.76
500 000	44952.40	24065.53	17149.59	13726.02	11699.03	10369.92	9439.19	8757.04
520 000	46750.49	25028.16	17835.57	14275.07	12166.99	10784.72	9816.76	9107.32
540 000	48548.59	25990.78	18521.56	14824.11	12634.95	11199.52	10194.33	9457.60
560 000	50346.69	26953.40	19207.54	15373.15	13102.92	11614.31	10571.90	9807.88
580 000	52144.78	27916.02	19893.52	15922.19	13570.88	12029.11	10949.46	10158.17
600 000	53942.88	28878.64	20579.51	16471.23	14038.84	12443.91	11327.03	10508.45
620 000	55740.97	29841.26	21265.49	17020.27	14506.80	12858.70	11704.60	10858.73
640 000	57539.07	30803.88	21951.47	17569.31	14974.76	13273.50	12082.17	11209.01
660 000	59337.17	31766.50	22637.46	18118.35	15442.72	13688.30	12459.74	11559.29
680 000	61135.26	32729.13	23323.44	18667.39	15910.68	14103.09	12837.30	11909.57
700 000	62933.36	33691.75	24009.43	19216.43	16378.64	14517.89	13214.87	12259.86
720 000	64731.45	34654.37	24695.41	19765.48	16846.61	14932.69	13592.44	12610.14
740 000	66529.55	35616.99	25381.39	20314.52	17314.57	15347.48	13970.01	12960.42
760 000	68327.65	36579.61	26067.38	20863.56	17782.53	15762.28	14347.57	13310.70
780 000	70125.74	37542.23	26753.36	21412.60	18250.49	16177.08	14725.14	13660.98
800 000	71923.84	38504.85	27439.34	21961.64	18718.45	16591.88	15102.71	14011.26
820 000	73721.93	39467.48	28125.33	22510.68	19186.41	17006.67	15480.28	14361.54
840 000	75520.03	40430.10	28811.31	23059.72	19654.37	17421.47	15857.85	14711.83
860 000	77318.13	41392.72	29497.29	23608.76	20122.33	17836.27	16235.41	15062.11
880 000	79116.22	42355.34	30183.28	24157.80	20590.30	18251.06	16612.98	15412.39
900 000	80914.32	43317.96	30869.26	24706.84	21058.26	18665.86	16990.55	15762.67
920 000	82712.41	44280.58	31555.24	25255.89	21526.22	19080.66	17368.12	16112.95
940 000	84510.51	45243.20	32241.23	25804.93	21994.18	19495.45	17745.68	16463.23
960 000	86308.61	46205.83	32927.21	26353.97	22462.14	19910.25	18123.25	16813.52
980 000	88106.70	47168.45	33613.20	26903.01	22930.10	20325.05	18500.82	17163.80
1000 000	89904.80	48131.07	34299.18	27452.05	23398.06	20739.84	18878.39	17514.08
Coefficient	.089904797	.048131068	.034299179	.027452049	.023398063	.020739844	.018878387	.017514079

MONTHLY AMORTIZING PAYMENTS — 14.25%

AMOUNT	9 YEARS	10 YEARS	15 YEARS	20 YEARS	25 YEARS	30 YEARS	35 YEARS	40 YEARS
10 000	164.80	156.77	134.86	126.17	122.29	120.47	119.59	119.16
20 000	329.61	313.55	269.72	252.34	244.59	240.94	239.18	238.32
30 000	494.41	470.32	404.57	378.52	366.88	361.41	358.77	357.49
40 000	659.22	627.09	539.43	504.69	489.17	481.87	478.36	476.65
50 000	824.02	783.87	674.29	630.86	611.46	602.34	597.95	595.81
60 000	988.82	940.64	809.15	757.03	733.76	722.81	717.54	714.97
70 000	1153.63	1097.41	944.01	883.20	856.05	843.28	837.13	834.14
80 000	1318.43	1254.18	1078.86	1009.38	978.34	963.75	956.72	953.30
90 000	1483.23	1410.96	1213.72	1135.55	1100.63	1084.22	1076.31	1072.46
100 000	1648.04	1567.73	1348.58	1261.72	1222.93	1204.69	1195.90	1191.62
110 000	1812.84	1724.50	1483.44	1387.89	1345.22	1325.16	1315.49	1310.79
120 000	1977.65	1881.28	1618.30	1514.06	1467.51	1445.62	1435.08	1429.95
130 000	2142.45	2038.05	1753.15	1640.23	1589.81	1566.09	1554.67	1549.11
140 000	2307.25	2194.82	1888.01	1766.41	1712.10	1686.56	1674.26	1668.27
150 000	2472.06	2351.60	2022.87	1892.58	1834.39	1807.03	1793.85	1787.43
160 000	2636.86	2508.37	2157.73	2018.75	1956.68	1927.50	1913.44	1906.60
170 000	2801.67	2665.14	2292.59	2144.92	2078.98	2047.97	2033.03	2025.76
180 000	2966.47	2821.92	2427.44	2271.09	2201.27	2168.44	2152.62	2144.92
190 000	3131.27	2978.69	2562.30	2397.27	2323.56	2288.91	2272.21	2264.08
200 000	3296.08	3135.46	2697.16	2523.44	2445.86	2409.37	2391.81	2383.25
210 000	3460.88	3292.24	2832.02	2649.61	2568.15	2529.84	2511.40	2502.41
220 000	3625.68	3449.01	2966.88	2775.78	2690.44	2650.31	2630.99	2621.57
230 000	3790.49	3605.78	3101.73	2901.95	2812.73	2770.78	2750.58	2740.73
240 000	3955.29	3762.55	3236.59	3028.13	2935.03	2891.25	2870.17	2859.90
250 000	4120.10	3919.33	3371.45	3154.30	3057.32	3011.72	2989.76	2979.06
260 000	4284.90	4076.10	3506.31	3280.47	3179.61	3132.19	3109.35	3098.22
270 000	4449.70	4232.87	3641.17	3406.64	3301.90	3252.66	3228.94	3217.38
280 000	4614.51	4389.65	3776.02	3532.81	3424.20	3373.12	3348.53	3336.55
290 000	4779.31	4546.42	3910.88	3658.98	3546.49	3493.59	3468.12	3455.71
300 000	4944.11	4703.19	4045.74	3785.16	3668.78	3614.06	3587.71	3574.87
320 000	5273.72	5016.74	4315.46	4037.50	3913.37	3855.00	3826.89	3813.19
340 000	5603.33	5330.29	4585.17	4289.84	4157.95	4095.94	4066.07	4051.52
360 000	5932.94	5643.83	4854.89	4542.19	4402.54	4336.87	4305.25	4289.84
380 000	6262.55	5957.38	5124.60	4794.53	4647.12	4577.81	4544.43	4528.17
400 000	6592.15	6270.92	5394.32	5046.88	4891.71	4818.75	4783.61	4766.49
420 000	6921.76	6584.47	5664.03	5299.22	5136.30	5059.69	5022.79	5004.82
440 000	7251.37	6898.02	5933.75	5551.56	5380.88	5300.62	5261.97	5243.14
460 000	7580.98	7211.56	6203.47	5803.91	5625.47	5541.56	5501.15	5481.47
480 000	7910.58	7525.11	6473.18	6056.25	5870.05	5782.50	5740.33	5719.79
500 000	8240.19	7838.66	6742.90	6308.59	6114.64	6023.44	5979.51	5958.12
520 000	8569.80	8152.20	7012.61	6560.94	6359.22	6264.37	6218.69	6196.44
540 000	8899.41	8465.75	7282.33	6813.28	6603.81	6505.31	6457.87	6434.77
560 000	9229.01	8779.29	7552.05	7065.63	6848.39	6746.25	6697.05	6673.09
580 000	9558.62	9092.84	7821.76	7317.97	7092.98	6987.19	6936.24	6911.42
600 000	9888.23	9406.39	8091.48	7570.31	7337.57	7228.12	7175.42	7149.74
620 000	10217.84	9719.93	8361.19	7822.66	7582.15	7469.06	7414.60	7388.06
640 000	10547.45	10033.48	8630.91	8075.00	7826.74	7710.00	7653.78	7626.39
660 000	10877.05	10347.03	8900.63	8327.34	8071.32	7950.93	7892.96	7864.71
680 000	11206.66	10660.57	9170.34	8579.69	8315.91	8191.87	8132.14	8103.04
700 000	11536.27	10974.12	9440.06	8832.03	8560.49	8432.81	8371.32	8341.36
720 000	11865.88	11287.66	9709.77	9084.38	8805.08	8673.75	8610.50	8579.69
740 000	12195.48	11601.21	9979.49	9336.72	9049.66	8914.68	8849.68	8818.01
760 000	12525.09	11914.76	10249.21	9589.06	9294.25	9155.62	9088.86	9056.34
780 000	12854.70	12228.30	10518.92	9841.41	9538.83	9396.56	9328.04	9294.66
800 000	13184.31	12541.85	10788.64	10093.75	9783.42	9637.50	9567.22	9532.99
820 000	13513.91	12855.40	11058.35	10346.09	10028.01	9878.43	9806.40	9771.31
840 000	13843.52	13168.94	11328.07	10598.44	10272.59	10119.37	10045.58	10009.64
860 000	14173.13	13482.49	11597.79	10850.78	10517.18	10360.31	10284.76	10247.96
880 000	14502.74	13796.03	11867.50	11103.13	10761.76	10601.25	10523.94	10486.29
900 000	14832.34	14109.58	12137.22	11355.47	11006.35	10842.18	10763.12	10724.61
920 000	15161.95	14423.13	12406.93	11607.81	11250.93	11083.12	11002.30	10962.93
940 000	15491.56	14736.67	12676.65	11860.16	11495.52	11324.06	11241.48	11201.26
960 000	15821.17	15050.22	12946.37	12112.50	11740.10	11565.00	11480.66	11439.58
980 000	16150.78	15363.76	13216.08	12364.85	11984.69	11805.93	11719.85	11677.91
1000 000	16480.38	15677.31	13485.80	12617.19	12229.28	12046.87	11959.03	11916.23
Coefficient	.016480383	.015677311	.013485797	.012617189	.012229275	.012046871	.011959026	.011916233

AMOUNT	1 YEAR	2 YEARS	3 YEARS	4 YEARS	5 YEARS	6 YEARS	7 YEARS	8 YEARS
10 000	900.23	482.49	344.21	275.78	235.28	208.74	190.17	176.57
20 000	1800.45	964.99	688.42	551.56	470.57	417.49	380.35	353.15
30 000	2700.68	1447.48	1032.63	827.34	705.85	626.23	570.52	529.72
40 000	3600.90	1929.98	1376.84	1103.12	941.13	834.98	760.69	706.29
50 000	4501.13	2412.47	1721.05	1378.90	1176.41	1043.72	950.87	882.86
60 000	5401.35	2894.97	2065.26	1654.68	1411.70	1252.47	1141.04	1059.44
70 000	6301.58	3377.46	2409.47	1930.46	1646.98	1461.21	1331.21	1236.01
80 000	7201.80	3859.95	2753.68	2206.24	1882.26	1669.95	1521.38	1412.58
90 000	8102.03	4342.45	3097.89	2482.02	2117.55	1878.70	1711.56	1589.15
100 000	9002.25	4824.94	3442.10	2757.80	2352.83	2087.44	1901.73	1765.73
110 000	9902.48	5307.44	3786.31	3033.57	2588.11	2296.19	2091.90	1942.30
120 000	10802.71	5789.93	4130.52	3309.35	2823.39	2504.93	2282.08	2118.87
130 000	11702.93	6272.43	4474.73	3585.13	3058.68	2713.68	2472.25	2295.44
140 000	12603.16	6754.92	4818.94	3860.91	3293.96	2922.42	2662.42	2472.02
150 000	13503.38	7237.41	5163.15	4136.69	3529.24	3131.16	2852.60	2648.59
160 000	14403.61	7719.91	5507.36	4412.47	3764.52	3339.91	3042.77	2825.16
170 000	15303.83	8202.40	5851.57	4688.25	3999.81	3548.65	3232.94	3001.73
180 000	16204.06	8684.90	6195.78	4964.03	4235.09	3757.40	3423.11	3178.31
190 000	17104.28	9167.39	6539.99	5239.81	4470.37	3966.14	3613.29	3354.88
200 000	18004.51	9649.89	6884.20	5515.59	4705.66	4174.89	3803.46	3531.45
210 000	18904.74	10132.38	7228.40	5791.37	4940.94	4383.63	3993.63	3708.02
220 000	19804.96	10614.87	7572.61	6067.15	5176.22	4592.37	4183.81	3884.60
230 000	20705.19	11097.37	7916.82	6342.93	5411.50	4801.12	4373.98	4061.17
240 000	21605.41	11579.86	8261.03	6618.71	5646.79	5009.86	4564.15	4237.74
250 000	22505.64	12062.36	8605.24	6894.49	5882.07	5218.61	4754.33	4414.31
260 000	23405.86	12544.85	8949.45	7170.27	6117.35	5427.35	4944.50	4590.89
270 000	24306.09	13027.35	9293.66	7446.05	6352.64	5636.10	5134.67	4767.46
280 000	25206.31	13509.84	9637.87	7721.83	6587.92	5844.84	5324.85	4944.03
290 000	26106.54	13992.33	9982.08	7997.61	6823.20	6053.58	5515.02	5120.60
300 000	27006.76	14474.83	10326.29	8273.39	7058.48	6262.33	5705.19	5297.18
320 000	28807.22	15439.82	11014.71	8824.94	7529.05	6679.82	6085.54	5650.32
340 000	30607.67	16404.81	11703.13	9376.50	7999.62	7097.30	6465.88	6003.47
360 000	32408.12	17369.79	12391.55	9928.06	8470.18	7514.79	6846.23	6356.61
380 000	34208.57	18334.78	13079.97	10479.62	8940.75	7932.28	7226.58	6709.76
400 000	36009.02	19299.77	13768.39	11031.18	9411.31	8349.77	7606.92	7062.90
420 000	37809.47	20264.76	14456.81	11582.74	9881.88	8767.26	7987.27	7416.05
440 000	39609.92	21229.75	15145.23	12134.30	10352.44	9184.75	8367.61	7769.19
460 000	41410.37	22194.74	15833.65	12685.86	10823.01	9602.24	8747.96	8122.34
480 000	43210.82	23159.73	16522.07	13237.42	11293.57	10019.72	9128.31	8475.48
500 000	45011.27	24124.71	17210.49	13788.98	11764.14	10437.21	9508.65	8828.63
520 000	46811.72	25089.70	17898.91	14340.53	12234.71	10854.70	9889.00	9181.77
540 000	48612.18	26054.69	18587.33	14892.09	12705.27	11272.19	10269.34	9534.92
560 000	50412.63	27019.68	19275.75	15443.65	13175.84	11689.68	10649.69	9888.06
580 000	52213.08	27984.67	19964.17	15995.21	13646.40	12107.17	11030.04	10241.21
600 000	54013.53	28949.66	20652.59	16546.77	14116.97	12524.66	11410.38	10594.35
620 000	55813.98	29914.65	21341.01	17098.33	14587.53	12942.14	11790.73	10947.50
640 000	57614.43	30879.63	22029.42	17649.89	15058.10	13359.63	12171.07	11300.64
660 000	59414.88	31844.62	22717.84	18201.45	15528.67	13777.12	12551.42	11653.79
680 000	61215.33	32809.61	23406.26	18753.01	15999.23	14194.61	12931.77	12006.93
700 000	63015.78	33774.60	24094.68	19304.57	16469.80	14612.10	13312.11	12360.08
720 000	64816.23	34739.59	24783.10	19856.12	16940.36	15029.59	13692.46	12713.23
740 000	66616.69	35704.58	25471.52	20407.68	17410.93	15447.08	14072.80	13066.37
760 000	68417.14	36669.57	26159.94	20959.24	17881.49	15864.56	14453.15	13419.52
780 000	70217.59	37634.55	26848.36	21510.80	18352.06	16282.05	14833.50	13772.66
800 000	72018.04	38599.54	27536.78	22062.36	18822.62	16699.54	15213.84	14125.81
820 000	73818.49	39564.53	28225.20	22613.92	19293.19	17117.03	15594.19	14478.95
840 000	75618.94	40529.52	28913.62	23165.48	19763.76	17534.52	15974.54	14832.10
860 000	77419.39	41494.51	29602.04	23717.04	20234.32	17952.01	16354.88	15185.24
880 000	79219.84	42459.50	30290.46	24268.60	20704.89	18369.49	16735.23	15538.39
900 000	81020.29	43424.49	30978.88	24820.16	21175.45	18786.98	17115.57	15891.53
920 000	82820.74	44389.47	31667.30	25371.71	21646.02	19204.47	17495.92	16244.68
940 000	84621.20	45354.46	32355.72	25923.27	22116.58	19621.96	17876.27	16597.82
960 000	86421.65	46319.45	33044.14	26474.83	22587.15	20039.45	18256.61	16950.97
980 000	88222.10	47284.44	33732.56	27026.39	23057.72	20456.94	18636.96	17304.11
1000 000	90022.55	48249.43	34420.98	27577.95	23528.28	20874.43	19017.30	17657.26
Coefficient	.090022548	.048249429	.034420976	.027577951	.023528281	.020874426	.019017304	.017657257

MONTHLY AMORTIZING PAYMENTS 14.50%

AMOUNT	9 YEARS	10 YEARS	15 YEARS	20 YEARS	25 YEARS	30 YEARS	35 YEARS	40 YEARS
10 000	166.28	158.29	136.55	128.00	124.22	122.46	121.62	121.21
20 000	332.55	316.57	273.10	256.00	248.43	244.91	243.23	242.43
30 000	498.83	474.86	409.65	384.00	372.65	367.37	364.85	363.64
40 000	665.11	633.15	546.20	512.00	496.87	489.82	486.47	484.85
50 000	831.39	791.43	682.75	640.00	621.08	612.28	608.09	606.07
60 000	997.66	949.72	819.30	768.00	745.30	734.73	729.70	727.28
70 000	1163.94	1108.01	955.85	896.00	869.51	857.19	851.32	848.49
80 000	1330.22	1266.29	1092.40	1024.00	993.73	979.64	972.94	969.71
90 000	1496.49	1424.58	1228.95	1152.00	1117.95	1102.10	1094.55	1090.92
100 000	1662.77	1582.87	1365.50	1280.00	1242.16	1224.56	1216.17	1212.13
110 000	1829.05	1741.15	1502.05	1408.00	1366.38	1347.01	1337.79	1333.35
120 000	1995.33	1899.44	1638.60	1536.00	1490.60	1469.47	1459.40	1454.56
130 000	2161.60	2057.73	1775.15	1664.00	1614.81	1591.92	1581.02	1575.77
140 000	2327.88	2216.02	1911.70	1792.00	1739.03	1714.38	1702.64	1696.99
150 000	2494.16	2374.30	2048.25	1920.00	1863.24	1836.83	1824.26	1818.20
160 000	2660.43	2532.59	2184.80	2048.00	1987.46	1959.29	1945.87	1939.41
170 000	2826.71	2690.88	2321.35	2176.00	2111.68	2081.75	2067.49	2060.63
180 000	2992.99	2849.16	2457.90	2304.00	2235.89	2204.20	2189.11	2181.84
190 000	3159.27	3007.45	2594.45	2432.00	2360.11	2326.66	2310.72	2303.05
200 000	3325.54	3165.74	2731.00	2560.00	2484.33	2449.11	2432.34	2424.27
210 000	3491.82	3324.02	2867.55	2688.00	2608.54	2571.57	2553.96	2545.48
220 000	3658.10	3482.31	3004.10	2816.00	2732.76	2694.02	2675.58	2666.69
230 000	3824.38	3640.60	3140.65	2943.99	2856.97	2816.48	2797.19	2787.91
240 000	3990.65	3798.88	3277.20	3071.99	2981.19	2938.93	2918.81	2909.12
250 000	4156.93	3957.17	3413.75	3199.99	3105.41	3061.39	3040.43	3030.33
260 000	4323.21	4115.46	3550.30	3327.99	3229.62	3183.85	3162.04	3151.55
270 000	4489.48	4273.74	3686.85	3455.99	3353.84	3306.30	3283.66	3272.76
280 000	4655.76	4432.03	3823.40	3583.99	3478.06	3428.76	3405.28	3393.97
290 000	4822.04	4590.32	3959.95	3711.99	3602.27	3551.21	3526.89	3515.19
300 000	4988.32	4748.60	4096.50	3839.99	3726.49	3673.67	3648.51	3636.40
320 000	5320.87	5065.18	4369.60	4095.99	3974.92	3918.58	3891.75	3878.83
340 000	5653.42	5381.75	4642.70	4351.99	4223.35	4163.49	4134.98	4121.25
360 000	5985.98	5698.32	4915.80	4607.99	4471.79	4408.40	4378.21	4363.68
380 000	6318.53	6014.90	5188.90	4863.99	4720.22	4653.31	4621.45	4606.11
400 000	6651.09	6331.47	5462.00	5119.99	4968.65	4898.22	4864.68	4848.53
420 000	6983.64	6648.05	5735.10	5375.99	5217.08	5143.13	5107.92	5090.96
440 000	7316.20	6964.62	6008.20	5631.99	5465.52	5388.05	5351.15	5333.38
460 000	7648.75	7281.19	6281.30	5887.99	5713.95	5632.96	5594.38	5575.81
480 000	7981.31	7597.77	6554.40	6143.99	5962.38	5877.87	5837.62	5818.24
500 000	8313.86	7914.34	6827.50	6399.99	6210.81	6122.78	6080.85	6060.66
520 000	8646.41	8230.91	7100.60	6655.99	6459.25	6367.69	6324.09	6303.09
540 000	8978.97	8547.49	7373.70	6911.99	6707.68	6612.60	6567.32	6545.52
560 000	9311.52	8864.06	7646.81	7167.99	6956.11	6857.51	6810.55	6787.94
580 000	9644.08	9180.63	7919.91	7423.99	7204.54	7102.42	7053.79	7030.37
600 000	9976.63	9497.21	8193.01	7679.99	7452.98	7347.34	7297.02	7272.80
620 000	10309.19	9813.78	8466.11	7935.99	7701.41	7592.25	7540.26	7515.22
640 000	10641.74	10130.35	8739.21	8191.99	7949.84	7837.16	7783.49	7757.65
660 000	10974.29	10446.93	9012.31	8447.99	8198.28	8082.07	8026.73	8000.08
680 000	11306.85	10763.50	9285.41	8703.99	8446.71	8326.98	8269.96	8242.50
700 000	11639.40	11080.08	9558.51	8959.98	8695.14	8571.89	8513.19	8484.93
720 000	11971.96	11396.65	9831.61	9215.98	8943.57	8816.80	8756.43	8727.36
740 000	12304.51	11713.22	10104.71	9471.98	9192.01	9061.71	8999.66	8969.78
760 000	12637.07	12029.80	10377.81	9727.98	9440.44	9306.62	9242.90	9212.21
780 000	12969.62	12346.37	10650.91	9983.98	9688.87	9551.54	9486.13	9454.64
800 000	13302.18	12662.94	10924.01	10239.98	9937.30	9796.45	9729.36	9697.06
820 000	13634.73	12979.52	11197.11	10495.98	10185.74	10041.36	9972.60	9939.49
840 000	13967.28	13296.09	11470.21	10751.98	10434.17	10286.27	10215.83	10181.92
860 000	14299.84	13612.66	11743.31	11007.98	10682.60	10531.18	10459.07	10424.34
880 000	14632.39	13929.24	12016.41	11263.98	10931.03	10776.09	10702.30	10666.77
900 000	14964.95	14245.81	12289.51	11519.98	11179.47	11021.00	10945.53	10909.20
920 000	15297.50	14562.38	12562.61	11775.98	11427.90	11265.91	11188.77	11151.63
940 000	15630.06	14878.96	12835.71	12031.98	11676.33	11510.83	11432.00	11394.05
960 000	15962.61	15195.53	13108.81	12287.98	11924.76	11755.74	11675.24	11636.48
980 000	16295.16	15512.11	13381.91	12543.98	12173.20	12000.65	11918.47	11878.90
1000 000	16627.72	15828.68	13655.01	12799.98	12421.63	12245.56	12161.71	12121.33
Coefficient	.016627719	.015828679	.013655009	.012799978	.012421629	.012245559	.012161705	.012121329

79

MONTHLY AMORTIZING PAYMENTS

AMOUNT	1 YEAR	2 YEARS	3 YEARS	4 YEARS	5 YEARS	6 YEARS	7 YEARS	8 YEARS
10 000	901.40	483.68	345.43	277.04	236.59	210.09	191.57	178.01
20 000	1802.81	967.36	690.86	554.08	473.18	420.19	383.14	356.02
30 000	2704.21	1451.04	1036.29	831.13	709.77	630.28	574.70	534.03
40 000	3605.62	1934.72	1381.72	1108.17	946.36	840.38	766.27	712.04
50 000	4507.02	2418.40	1727.15	1385.21	1182.95	1050.47	957.84	890.05
60 000	5408.42	2902.08	2072.58	1662.25	1419.53	1260.57	1149.41	1068.06
70 000	6309.83	3385.76	2418.01	1939.29	1656.12	1470.66	1340.97	1246.07
80 000	7211.23	3869.44	2763.44	2216.33	1892.71	1680.76	1532.54	1424.08
90 000	8112.64	4353.12	3108.87	2493.38	2129.30	1890.85	1724.11	1602.09
100 000	9014.04	4836.80	3454.30	2770.42	2365.89	2100.95	1915.68	1780.10
110 000	9915.44	5320.47	3799.73	3047.46	2602.48	2311.04	2107.24	1958.11
120 000	10816.85	5804.15	4145.16	3324.50	2839.07	2521.14	2298.81	2136.12
130 000	11718.25	6287.83	4490.59	3601.54	3075.66	2731.23	2490.38	2314.13
140 000	12619.65	6771.51	4836.03	3878.59	3312.25	2941.33	2681.95	2492.14
150 000	13521.06	7255.19	5181.45	4155.63	3548.84	3151.42	2873.51	2670.16
160 000	14422.46	7738.87	5526.88	4432.67	3785.42	3361.52	3065.08	2848.17
170 000	15323.87	8222.55	5872.31	4709.71	4022.01	3571.61	3256.65	3026.18
180 000	16225.27	8706.23	6217.74	4986.75	4258.60	3781.71	3448.22	3204.19
190 000	17126.67	9189.91	6563.17	5263.80	4495.19	3991.80	3639.78	3382.20
200 000	18028.08	9673.59	6908.61	5540.84	4731.78	4201.90	3831.35	3560.21
210 000	18929.48	10157.27	7254.04	5817.88	4968.37	4411.99	4022.92	3738.22
220 000	19830.89	10640.95	7599.47	6094.92	5204.96	4622.09	4214.49	3916.23
230 000	20732.29	11124.63	7944.90	6371.96	5441.55	4832.18	4406.06	4094.24
240 000	21633.69	11608.31	8290.33	6649.00	5678.14	5042.28	4597.62	4272.25
250 000	22535.10	12091.99	8635.76	6926.05	5914.73	5252.37	4789.19	4450.26
260 000	23436.50	12575.67	8981.19	7203.09	6151.31	5462.47	4980.76	4628.27
270 000	24337.91	13059.35	9326.62	7480.13	6387.90	5672.56	5172.33	4806.28
280 000	25239.31	13543.03	9672.05	7757.17	6624.49	5882.65	5363.89	4984.29
290 000	26140.71	14026.71	10017.48	8034.21	6861.08	6092.75	5555.46	5162.30
300 000	27042.12	14510.39	10362.91	8311.26	7097.67	6302.84	5747.03	5340.31
320 000	28844.92	15477.74	11053.77	8865.34	7570.85	6723.03	6130.16	5696.33
340 000	30647.73	16445.10	11744.63	9419.42	8044.03	7143.22	6513.30	6052.35
360 000	32450.54	17412.46	12435.49	9973.51	8517.21	7563.41	6896.43	6408.37
380 000	34253.35	18379.82	13126.35	10527.59	8990.38	7983.60	7279.57	6764.39
400 000	36056.16	19347.18	13817.21	11081.67	9463.56	8403.79	7662.70	7120.41
420 000	37858.96	20314.54	14508.07	11635.76	9936.74	8823.98	8045.84	7476.43
440 000	39661.77	21281.90	15198.93	12189.84	10409.92	9244.17	8428.97	7832.45
460 000	41464.58	22249.26	15889.79	12743.93	10883.10	9664.36	8812.11	8188.48
480 000	43267.39	23216.62	16580.65	13298.01	11356.27	10084.55	9195.25	8544.50
500 000	45070.19	24183.98	17271.51	13852.09	11829.45	10504.74	9578.38	8900.52
520 000	46873.00	25151.33	17962.37	14406.18	12302.63	10924.93	9961.52	9256.54
540 000	48675.81	26118.69	18653.23	14960.26	12775.81	11345.12	10344.65	9612.56
560 000	50478.62	27086.05	19344.09	15514.34	13248.99	11765.31	10727.79	9968.58
580 000	52281.43	28053.41	20034.96	16068.43	13722.16	12185.50	11110.92	10324.60
600 000	54084.23	29020.77	20725.82	16622.51	14195.34	12605.69	11494.06	10680.62
620 000	55887.04	29988.13	21416.68	17176.59	14668.52	13025.88	11877.19	11036.64
640 000	57689.85	30955.49	22107.54	17730.68	15141.70	13446.07	12260.33	11392.66
660 000	59492.66	31922.85	22798.40	18284.76	15614.88	13866.26	12643.46	11748.68
680 000	61295.46	32890.21	23489.26	18838.85	16088.05	14286.45	13026.60	12104.70
700 000	63098.27	33857.57	24180.12	19392.93	16561.23	14706.64	13409.73	12460.72
720 000	64901.08	34824.92	24870.98	19947.01	17034.41	15126.83	13792.87	12816.74
740 000	66703.89	35792.28	25561.84	20501.10	17507.59	15547.02	14176.00	13172.77
760 000	68506.70	36759.64	26252.70	21055.18	17980.77	15967.21	14559.14	13528.79
780 000	70309.50	37727.00	26943.56	21609.26	18453.94	16387.40	14942.27	13884.81
800 000	72112.31	38694.36	27634.42	22163.35	18927.12	16807.59	15325.41	14240.83
820 000	73915.12	39661.72	28325.28	22717.43	19400.30	17227.78	15708.54	14596.85
840 000	75717.93	40629.08	29016.14	23271.52	19873.48	17647.96	16091.68	14952.87
860 000	77520.73	41596.44	29707.00	23825.60	20346.66	18068.15	16474.81	15308.89
880 000	79323.54	42563.80	30397.86	24379.68	20819.83	18488.34	16857.95	15664.91
900 000	81126.35	43531.16	31088.72	24933.77	21293.01	18908.53	17241.08	16020.93
920 000	82929.16	44498.51	31779.58	25487.85	21766.19	19328.72	17624.22	16376.95
940 000	84731.97	45465.87	32470.44	26041.93	22239.37	19748.91	18007.36	16732.97
960 000	86534.77	46433.23	33161.30	26596.02	22712.55	20169.10	18390.49	17088.99
980 000	88337.58	47400.59	33852.17	27150.10	23185.72	20589.29	18773.63	17445.01
1000 000	90140.39	48367.95	34543.03	27704.19	23658.90	21009.48	19156.76	17801.03
Coefficient	.090140389	.048367950	.034543026	.027704185	.023658903	.021009482	.019156761	.017801034

MONTHLY AMORTIZING PAYMENTS — 14.75%

AMOUNT	9 YEARS	10 YEARS	15 YEARS	20 YEARS	25 YEARS	30 YEARS	35 YEARS	40 YEARS
10 000	167.76	159.81	138.25	129.84	126.15	124.45	123.65	123.27
20 000	335.51	319.61	276.50	259.67	252.29	248.90	247.29	246.53
30 000	503.27	479.42	414.75	389.51	378.44	373.34	370.94	369.80
40 000	671.03	639.23	553.00	519.34	504.59	497.79	494.59	493.07
50 000	838.79	799.04	691.25	649.18	630.73	622.24	618.24	616.33
60 000	1006.54	958.84	829.50	779.01	756.88	746.69	741.88	739.60
70 000	1174.30	1118.65	967.75	908.85	883.03	871.13	865.53	862.87
80 000	1342.06	1278.46	1106.00	1038.68	1009.17	995.58	989.18	986.13
90 000	1509.81	1438.27	1244.25	1168.52	1135.32	1120.03	1112.83	1109.40
100 000	1677.57	1598.07	1382.50	1298.36	1261.46	1244.48	1236.47	1232.67
110 000	1845.33	1757.88	1520.75	1428.19	1387.61	1368.92	1360.12	1355.93
120 000	2013.08	1917.69	1659.00	1558.03	1513.76	1493.37	1483.77	1479.20
130 000	2180.84	2077.50	1797.25	1687.86	1639.90	1617.82	1607.42	1602.47
140 000	2348.60	2237.30	1935.51	1817.70	1766.05	1742.27	1731.06	1725.73
150 000	2516.36	2397.11	2073.76	1947.53	1892.20	1866.71	1854.71	1849.00
160 000	2684.11	2556.92	2212.01	2077.37	2018.34	1991.16	1978.36	1972.27
170 000	2851.87	2716.73	2350.26	2207.20	2144.49	2115.61	2102.01	2095.53
180 000	3019.63	2876.53	2488.51	2337.04	2270.64	2240.06	2225.65	2218.80
190 000	3187.38	3036.34	2626.76	2466.88	2396.78	2364.50	2349.30	2342.07
200 000	3355.14	3196.15	2765.01	2596.71	2522.93	2488.95	2472.95	2465.33
210 000	3522.90	3355.96	2903.26	2726.55	2649.08	2613.40	2596.60	2588.60
220 000	3690.66	3515.76	3041.51	2856.38	2775.22	2737.85	2720.24	2711.87
230 000	3858.41	3675.57	3179.76	2986.22	2901.37	2862.29	2843.89	2835.13
240 000	4026.17	3835.38	3318.01	3116.05	3027.52	2986.74	2967.54	2958.40
250 000	4193.93	3995.19	3456.26	3245.89	3153.66	3111.19	3091.19	3081.67
260 000	4361.68	4154.99	3594.51	3375.72	3279.81	3235.64	3214.83	3204.93
270 000	4529.44	4314.80	3732.76	3505.56	3405.95	3360.08	3338.48	3328.20
280 000	4697.20	4474.61	3871.01	3635.39	3532.10	3484.53	3462.13	3451.47
290 000	4864.95	4634.42	4009.26	3765.23	3658.25	3608.98	3585.78	3574.73
300 000	5032.71	4794.22	4147.51	3895.07	3784.39	3733.43	3709.42	3698.00
320 000	5368.23	5113.84	4424.01	4154.74	4036.69	3982.32	3956.72	3944.54
340 000	5703.74	5433.45	4700.51	4414.41	4288.98	4231.22	4204.01	4191.07
360 000	6039.25	5753.07	4977.01	4674.08	4541.27	4480.11	4451.31	4437.60
380 000	6374.77	6072.68	5253.51	4933.75	4793.57	4729.01	4698.60	4684.14
400 000	6710.28	6392.30	5530.02	5193.42	5045.86	4977.90	4945.90	4930.67
420 000	7045.80	6711.91	5806.52	5453.09	5298.15	5226.80	5193.19	5177.20
440 000	7381.31	7031.53	6083.02	5712.76	5550.44	5475.69	5440.49	5423.74
460 000	7716.82	7351.14	6359.52	5972.43	5802.74	5724.59	5687.78	5670.27
480 000	8052.34	7670.76	6636.02	6232.11	6055.03	5973.48	5935.08	5916.80
500 000	8387.85	7990.37	6912.52	6491.78	6307.32	6222.38	6182.37	6163.34
520 000	8723.37	8309.99	7189.02	6751.45	6559.62	6471.27	6429.67	6409.87
540 000	9058.88	8629.60	7465.52	7011.12	6811.91	6720.17	6676.96	6656.40
560 000	9394.39	8949.22	7742.02	7270.79	7064.20	6969.06	6924.26	6902.94
580 000	9729.91	9268.83	8018.52	7530.46	7316.50	7217.96	7171.55	7149.47
600 000	10065.42	9588.45	8295.02	7790.13	7568.79	7466.85	7418.85	7396.00
620 000	10400.94	9908.06	8571.52	8049.80	7821.08	7715.75	7666.14	7642.54
640 000	10736.45	10227.67	8848.02	8309.47	8073.37	7964.64	7913.44	7889.07
660 000	11071.97	10547.29	9124.53	8569.14	8325.67	8213.54	8160.73	8135.60
680 000	11407.48	10866.90	9401.03	8828.82	8577.96	8462.43	8408.03	8382.14
700 000	11742.99	11186.52	9677.53	9088.49	8830.25	8711.33	8655.32	8628.67
720 000	12078.51	11506.13	9954.03	9348.16	9082.55	8960.23	8902.62	8875.20
740 000	12414.02	11825.75	10230.53	9607.83	9334.84	9209.12	9149.91	9121.74
760 000	12749.54	12145.36	10507.03	9867.50	9587.13	9458.02	9397.21	9368.27
780 000	13085.05	12464.98	10783.53	10127.17	9839.43	9706.91	9644.50	9614.80
800 000	13420.56	12784.59	11060.03	10386.84	10091.72	9955.81	9891.80	9861.34
820 000	13756.08	13104.21	11336.53	10646.51	10344.01	10204.70	10139.09	10107.87
840 000	14091.59	13423.82	11613.03	10906.18	10596.30	10453.60	10386.39	10354.40
860 000	14427.11	13743.44	11889.53	11165.86	10848.60	10702.49	10633.68	10600.94
880 000	14762.62	14063.05	12166.03	11425.53	11100.89	10951.39	10880.98	10847.47
900 000	15098.13	14382.67	12442.53	11685.20	11353.18	11200.28	11128.27	11094.00
920 000	15433.65	14702.28	12719.03	11944.87	11605.48	11449.18	11375.57	11340.54
940 000	15769.16	15021.90	12995.54	12204.54	11857.77	11698.07	11622.86	11587.07
960 000	16104.68	15341.51	13272.04	12464.21	12110.06	11946.97	11870.16	11833.61
980 000	16440.19	15661.13	13548.54	12723.88	12362.35	12195.86	12117.45	12080.14
1000 000	16775.70	15980.74	13825.04	12983.55	12614.65	12444.76	12364.75	12326.67
Coefficient	.016775705	.015980742	.013825038	.012983553	.012614647	.012444757	.012364748	.012326672

81

AMOUNT	1 YEAR	2 YEARS	3 YEARS	4 YEARS	5 YEARS	6 YEARS	7 YEARS	8 YEARS
10 000	902.58	484.87	346.65	278.31	237.90	211.45	192.97	179.45
20 000	1805.17	969.73	693.31	556.61	475.80	422.90	385.94	358.91
30 000	2707.75	1454.60	1039.96	834.92	713.70	634.35	578.90	538.36
40 000	3610.33	1939.47	1386.61	1113.23	951.60	845.80	771.87	717.82
50 000	4512.92	2424.33	1733.27	1391.54	1189.50	1057.25	964.84	897.27
60 000	5415.50	2909.20	2079.92	1669.84	1427.40	1268.70	1157.81	1076.72
70 000	6318.08	3394.07	2426.57	1948.15	1665.30	1480.15	1350.77	1256.18
80 000	7220.67	3878.93	2773.23	2226.46	1903.19	1691.60	1543.74	1435.63
90 000	8123.25	4363.80	3119.88	2504.77	2141.09	1903.05	1736.71	1615.09
100 000	9025.83	4848.67	3466.53	2783.07	2378.99	2114.50	1929.68	1794.54
110 000	9928.42	5333.53	3813.19	3061.38	2616.89	2325.95	2122.64	1973.99
120 000	10831.00	5818.40	4159.84	3339.69	2854.79	2537.40	2315.61	2153.45
130 000	11733.58	6303.26	4506.49	3618.00	3092.69	2748.85	2508.58	2332.90
140 000	12636.16	6788.13	4853.15	3896.30	3330.59	2960.30	2701.55	2512.36
150 000	13538.75	7273.00	5199.80	4174.61	3568.49	3171.75	2894.51	2691.81
160 000	14441.33	7757.86	5546.45	4452.92	3806.39	3383.20	3087.48	2871.26
170 000	15343.91	8242.73	5893.11	4731.23	4044.29	3594.65	3280.45	3050.72
180 000	16246.50	8727.60	6239.76	5009.53	4282.19	3806.10	3473.42	3230.17
190 000	17149.08	9212.46	6586.41	5287.84	4520.09	4017.55	3666.38	3409.63
200 000	18051.66	9697.33	6933.07	5566.15	4757.99	4229.00	3859.35	3589.08
210 000	18954.25	10182.20	7279.72	5844.46	4995.89	4440.45	4052.32	3768.54
220 000	19856.83	10667.06	7626.37	6122.76	5233.78	4651.90	4245.29	3947.99
230 000	20759.41	11151.93	7973.03	6401.07	5471.68	4863.35	4438.25	4127.44
240 000	21662.00	11636.80	8319.68	6679.38	5709.58	5074.80	4631.22	4306.90
250 000	22564.58	12121.66	8666.33	6957.69	5947.48	5286.25	4824.19	4486.35
260 000	23467.16	12606.53	9012.99	7235.99	6185.38	5497.70	5017.16	4665.81
270 000	24369.75	13091.40	9359.64	7514.30	6423.28	5709.15	5210.12	4845.26
280 000	25272.33	13576.26	9706.29	7792.61	6661.18	5920.60	5403.09	5024.71
290 000	26174.91	14061.13	10052.95	8070.92	6899.08	6132.05	5596.06	5204.17
300 000	27077.50	14546.00	10399.60	8349.22	7136.98	6343.50	5789.03	5383.62
320 000	28882.66	15515.73	11092.91	8905.84	7612.78	6766.40	6174.96	5742.53
340 000	30687.83	16485.46	11786.21	9462.45	8088.58	7189.30	6560.90	6101.44
360 000	32493.00	17455.19	12479.52	10019.07	8564.37	7612.20	6946.83	6460.35
380 000	34298.16	18424.93	13172.83	10575.68	9040.17	8035.10	7332.77	6819.25
400 000	36103.33	19394.66	13866.13	11132.30	9515.97	8458.01	7718.70	7178.16
420 000	37908.49	20364.39	14559.44	11688.91	9991.77	8880.91	8104.64	7537.07
440 000	39713.66	21334.13	15252.75	12245.53	10467.57	9303.81	8490.57	7895.98
460 000	41518.83	22303.86	15946.05	12802.14	10943.37	9726.71	8876.51	8254.89
480 000	43323.99	23273.59	16639.36	13358.76	11419.17	10149.61	9262.44	8613.79
500 000	45129.16	24243.33	17332.67	13915.37	11894.96	10572.51	9648.38	8972.70
520 000	46934.33	25213.06	18025.97	14471.99	12370.76	10995.41	10034.31	9331.61
540 000	48739.49	26182.79	18719.28	15028.60	12846.56	11418.31	10420.25	9690.52
560 000	50544.66	27152.52	19412.58	15585.22	13322.36	11841.21	10806.18	10049.43
580 000	52349.83	28122.26	20105.89	16141.83	13798.16	12264.11	11192.12	10408.33
600 000	54154.99	29091.99	20799.20	16698.45	14273.96	12687.01	11578.05	10767.24
620 000	55960.16	30061.72	21492.50	17255.06	14749.76	13109.91	11963.99	11126.15
640 000	57765.32	31031.46	22185.81	17811.68	15225.56	13532.81	12349.92	11485.06
660 000	59570.49	32001.19	22879.12	18368.29	15701.35	13955.71	12735.86	11843.97
680 000	61375.66	32970.92	23572.42	18924.91	16177.15	14378.61	13121.79	12202.88
700 000	63180.82	33940.66	24265.73	19481.52	16652.95	14801.51	13507.73	12561.78
720 000	64985.99	34910.39	24959.04	20038.14	17128.75	15224.41	13893.66	12920.69
740 000	66791.16	35880.12	25652.34	20594.75	17604.55	15647.31	14279.60	13279.60
760 000	68596.32	36849.85	26345.65	21151.37	18080.35	16070.21	14665.53	13638.51
780 000	70401.49	37819.59	27038.96	21707.98	18556.15	16493.11	15051.47	13997.42
800 000	72206.66	38789.32	27732.26	22264.60	19031.94	16916.01	15437.40	14356.32
820 000	74011.82	39759.05	28425.57	22821.21	19507.74	17338.91	15823.34	14715.23
840 000	75816.99	40728.79	29118.88	23377.83	19983.54	17761.81	16209.27	15074.14
860 000	77622.16	41698.52	29812.18	23934.44	20459.34	18184.71	16595.21	15433.05
880 000	79427.32	42668.25	30505.49	24491.06	20935.14	18607.61	16981.14	15791.96
900 000	81232.49	43637.99	31198.80	25047.67	21410.94	19030.51	17367.08	16150.86
920 000	83037.65	44607.72	31892.10	25604.29	21886.74	19453.41	17753.01	16509.77
940 000	84842.82	45577.45	32585.41	26160.90	22362.53	19876.31	18138.95	16868.68
960 000	86647.99	46547.18	33278.72	26717.52	22838.33	20299.21	18524.88	17227.59
980 000	88453.15	47516.92	33972.02	27274.13	23314.13	20722.11	18910.82	17586.50
1000 000	90258.32	48486.65	34665.33	27830.75	23789.93	21145.01	19296.75	17945.41
Coefficient	.090258320	.048486650	.034665330	.027830747	.023789930	.021145013	.019296754	.017945405

MONTHLY AMORTIZING PAYMENTS 15.00%

AMOUNT	9 YEARS	10 YEARS	15 YEARS	20 YEARS	25 YEARS	30 YEARS	35 YEARS	40 YEARS
10 000	169.24	161.33	139.96	131.68	128.08	126.44	125.68	125.32
20 000	338.49	322.67	279.92	263.36	256.17	252.89	251.36	250.64
30 000	507.73	484.00	419.88	395.04	384.25	379.33	377.04	375.97
40 000	676.97	645.34	559.83	526.72	512.33	505.78	502.73	501.29
50 000	846.22	806.67	699.79	658.39	640.42	632.22	628.41	626.61
60 000	1015.46	968.01	839.75	790.07	768.50	758.67	754.09	751.93
70 000	1184.70	1129.34	979.71	921.75	896.58	885.11	879.77	877.26
80 000	1353.95	1290.68	1119.67	1053.43	1024.66	1011.56	1005.45	1002.58
90 000	1523.19	1452.01	1259.63	1185.11	1152.75	1138.00	1131.13	1127.90
100 000	1692.43	1613.35	1399.59	1316.79	1280.83	1264.44	1256.81	1253.22
110 000	1861.68	1774.68	1539.55	1448.47	1408.91	1390.89	1382.49	1378.55
120 000	2030.92	1936.02	1679.50	1580.15	1537.00	1517.33	1508.18	1503.87
130 000	2200.16	2097.35	1819.46	1711.83	1665.08	1643.78	1633.86	1629.19
140 000	2369.41	2258.69	1959.42	1843.51	1793.16	1770.22	1759.54	1754.51
150 000	2538.65	2420.02	2099.38	1975.18	1921.25	1896.67	1885.22	1879.84
160 000	2707.89	2581.36	2239.34	2106.86	2049.33	2023.11	2010.90	2005.16
170 000	2877.14	2742.69	2379.30	2238.54	2177.41	2149.55	2136.58	2130.48
180 000	3046.38	2904.03	2519.26	2370.22	2305.50	2276.00	2262.26	2255.80
190 000	3215.62	3065.36	2659.22	2501.90	2433.58	2402.44	2387.95	2381.13
200 000	3384.87	3226.70	2799.17	2633.58	2561.66	2528.89	2513.63	2506.45
210 000	3554.11	3388.03	2939.13	2765.26	2689.74	2655.33	2639.31	2631.77
220 000	3723.35	3549.37	3079.09	2896.94	2817.83	2781.78	2764.99	2757.09
230 000	3892.60	3710.70	3219.05	3028.62	2945.91	2908.22	2890.67	2882.42
240 000	4061.84	3872.04	3359.01	3160.30	3073.99	3034.67	3016.35	3007.74
250 000	4231.08	4033.37	3498.97	3291.97	3202.08	3161.11	3142.03	3133.06
260 000	4400.33	4194.71	3638.93	3423.65	3330.16	3287.55	3267.71	3258.38
270 000	4569.57	4356.04	3778.89	3555.33	3458.24	3414.00	3393.40	3383.71
280 000	4738.81	4517.38	3918.84	3687.01	3586.33	3540.44	3519.08	3509.03
290 000	4908.06	4678.71	4058.80	3818.69	3714.41	3666.89	3644.76	3634.35
300 000	5077.30	4840.05	4198.76	3950.37	3842.49	3793.33	3770.44	3759.67
320 000	5415.79	5162.72	4478.68	4213.73	4098.66	4046.22	4021.80	4010.32
340 000	5754.27	5485.39	4758.60	4477.08	4354.82	4299.11	4273.17	4260.96
360 000	6092.76	5808.06	5038.51	4740.44	4610.99	4552.00	4524.53	4511.61
380 000	6431.25	6130.73	5318.43	5003.80	4867.16	4804.89	4775.89	4762.25
400 000	6769.73	6453.40	5598.35	5267.16	5123.32	5057.78	5027.25	5012.90
420 000	7108.22	6776.07	5878.27	5530.52	5379.49	5310.66	5278.62	5263.54
440 000	7446.71	7098.74	6158.18	5793.87	5635.65	5563.55	5529.98	5514.19
460 000	7785.20	7421.41	6438.10	6057.23	5891.82	5816.44	5781.34	5764.83
480 000	8123.68	7744.08	6718.02	6320.59	6147.99	6069.33	6032.70	6015.48
500 000	8462.17	8066.75	6997.94	6583.95	6404.15	6322.22	6284.07	6266.12
520 000	8800.66	8389.42	7277.85	6847.31	6660.32	6575.11	6535.43	6516.77
540 000	9139.14	8712.09	7557.77	7110.66	6916.49	6828.00	6786.79	6767.41
560 000	9477.63	9034.76	7837.69	7374.02	7172.65	7080.89	7038.15	7018.05
580 000	9816.12	9357.43	8117.61	7637.38	7428.82	7333.78	7289.52	7268.70
600 000	10154.60	9680.10	8397.52	7900.74	7684.98	7586.66	7540.88	7519.34
620 000	10493.09	10002.77	8677.44	8164.10	7941.15	7839.55	7792.24	7769.99
640 000	10831.58	10325.44	8957.36	8427.45	8197.32	8092.44	8043.61	8020.63
660 000	11170.06	10648.11	9237.27	8690.81	8453.48	8345.33	8294.97	8271.28
680 000	11508.55	10970.78	9517.19	8954.17	8709.65	8598.22	8546.33	8521.92
700 000	11847.04	11293.45	9797.11	9217.53	8965.81	8851.11	8797.69	8772.57
720 000	12185.52	11616.12	10077.03	9480.89	9221.98	9104.00	9049.06	9023.21
740 000	12524.01	11938.79	10356.94	9744.24	9478.15	9356.89	9300.42	9273.86
760 000	12862.50	12261.46	10636.86	10007.60	9734.31	9609.77	9551.78	9524.50
780 000	13200.98	12584.13	10916.78	10270.96	9990.48	9862.66	9803.14	9775.15
800 000	13539.47	12906.80	11196.70	10534.32	10246.64	10115.55	10054.51	10025.79
820 000	13877.96	13229.47	11476.61	10797.67	10502.81	10368.44	10305.87	10276.44
840 000	14216.44	13552.14	11756.53	11061.03	10758.98	10621.33	10557.23	10527.08
860 000	14554.93	13874.81	12036.45	11324.39	11015.14	10874.22	10808.59	10777.73
880 000	14893.42	14197.48	12316.37	11587.75	11271.31	11127.11	11059.96	11028.37
900 000	15231.90	14520.15	12596.28	11851.11	11527.48	11380.00	11311.32	11279.02
920 000	15570.39	14842.82	12876.20	12114.46	11783.64	11632.88	11562.68	11529.66
940 000	15908.88	15165.49	13156.12	12377.82	12039.81	11885.77	11814.05	11780.31
960 000	16247.36	15488.16	13436.04	12641.18	12295.97	12138.66	12065.41	12030.95
980 000	16585.85	15810.83	13715.95	12904.54	12552.14	12391.55	12316.77	12281.60
1000 000	16924.34	16133.50	13995.87	13167.90	12808.31	12644.44	12568.13	12532.24
Coefficient	.016924337	.016133496	.013995871	.013167896	.012808306	.012644440	.012568133	.012532241

MONTHLY AMORTIZING PAYMENTS

AMOUNT	1 YEAR	2 YEARS	3 YEARS	4 YEARS	5 YEARS	6 YEARS	7 YEARS	8 YEARS
10 000	903.76	486.06	347.88	279.58	239.21	212.81	194.37	180.90
20 000	1807.53	972.11	695.76	559.15	478.43	425.62	388.75	361.81
30 000	2711.29	1458.17	1043.64	838.73	717.64	638.43	583.12	542.71
40 000	3615.05	1944.22	1391.52	1118.31	956.85	851.24	777.49	723.61
50 000	4518.82	2430.28	1739.39	1397.88	1196.07	1064.05	971.86	904.52
60 000	5422.58	2916.33	2087.27	1677.46	1435.28	1276.86	1166.24	1085.42
70 000	6326.34	3402.39	2435.15	1957.03	1674.50	1489.67	1360.61	1266.33
80 000	7230.11	3888.44	2783.03	2236.61	1913.71	1702.48	1554.98	1447.23
90 000	8133.87	4374.50	3130.91	2516.19	2152.92	1915.29	1749.36	1628.13
100 000	9037.63	4860.55	3478.79	2795.76	2392.14	2128.10	1943.73	1809.04
110 000	9941.40	5346.61	3826.67	3075.34	2631.35	2340.91	2138.10	1989.94
120 000	10845.16	5832.66	4174.55	3354.92	2870.56	2553.72	2332.47	2170.84
130 000	11748.92	6318.72	4522.42	3634.49	3109.78	2766.53	2526.85	2351.75
140 000	12652.68	6804.77	4870.30	3914.07	3348.99	2979.34	2721.22	2532.65
150 000	13556.45	7290.83	5218.18	4193.65	3588.20	3192.15	2915.59	2713.56
160 000	14460.21	7776.88	5566.06	4473.22	3827.42	3404.96	3109.97	2894.46
170 000	15363.97	8262.94	5913.94	4752.80	4066.63	3617.77	3304.34	3075.36
180 000	16267.74	8748.99	6261.82	5032.38	4305.84	3830.58	3498.71	3256.27
190 000	17171.50	9235.05	6609.70	5311.95	4545.06	4043.39	3693.08	3437.17
200 000	18075.26	9721.10	6957.58	5591.53	4784.27	4256.20	3887.46	3618.07
210 000	18979.03	10207.16	7305.45	5871.10	5023.49	4469.01	4081.83	3798.98
220 000	19882.79	10693.21	7653.33	6150.68	5262.70	4681.82	4276.20	3979.88
230 000	20786.55	11179.27	8001.21	6430.26	5501.91	4894.63	4470.58	4160.78
240 000	21690.32	11665.32	8349.09	6709.83	5741.13	5107.44	4664.95	4341.69
250 000	22594.08	12151.38	8696.97	6989.41	5980.34	5320.25	4859.32	4522.59
260 000	23497.84	12637.43	9044.85	7268.99	6219.55	5533.06	5053.69	4703.50
270 000	24401.61	13123.49	9392.73	7548.56	6458.77	5745.87	5248.07	4884.40
280 000	25305.37	13609.54	9740.61	7828.14	6697.98	5958.68	5442.44	5065.30
290 000	26209.13	14095.60	10088.48	8107.72	6937.19	6171.49	5636.81	5246.21
300 000	27112.90	14581.65	10436.36	8387.29	7176.41	6384.30	5831.19	5427.11
320 000	28920.42	15553.76	11132.12	8946.44	7654.83	6809.93	6219.93	5788.92
340 000	30727.95	16525.87	11827.88	9505.60	8133.26	7235.55	6608.68	6150.73
360 000	32535.48	17497.98	12523.64	10064.75	8611.69	7661.17	6997.42	6512.53
380 000	34343.00	18470.09	13219.39	10623.90	9090.12	8086.79	7386.17	6874.34
400 000	36150.53	19442.20	13915.15	11183.06	9568.54	8512.41	7774.91	7236.15
420 000	37958.05	20414.31	14610.91	11742.21	10046.97	8938.03	8163.66	7597.95
440 000	39765.58	21386.42	15306.67	12301.36	10525.40	9363.65	8552.40	7959.76
460 000	41573.11	22358.54	16002.42	12860.51	11003.83	9789.27	8941.15	8321.57
480 000	43380.63	23330.65	16698.18	13419.67	11482.25	10214.89	9329.90	8683.38
500 000	45188.16	24302.76	17393.94	13978.82	11960.68	10640.51	9718.64	9045.18
520 000	46995.69	25274.87	18089.70	14537.97	12439.11	11066.13	10107.39	9406.99
540 000	48803.21	26246.98	18785.45	15097.13	12917.53	11491.75	10496.13	9768.80
560 000	50610.74	27219.09	19481.21	15656.28	13395.96	11917.37	10884.88	10130.61
580 000	52418.27	28191.20	20176.97	16215.43	13874.39	12342.99	11273.62	10492.41
600 000	54225.79	29163.31	20872.73	16774.58	14352.82	12768.61	11662.37	10854.22
620 000	56033.32	30135.42	21568.48	17333.74	14831.24	13194.23	12051.12	11216.03
640 000	57840.85	31107.53	22264.24	17892.89	15309.67	13619.85	12439.86	11577.84
660 000	59648.37	32079.64	22960.00	18452.04	15788.10	14045.47	12828.61	11939.64
680 000	61455.90	33051.75	23655.76	19011.20	16266.52	14471.09	13217.35	12301.45
700 000	63263.42	34023.86	24351.51	19570.35	16744.95	14896.71	13606.10	12663.26
720 000	65070.95	34995.97	25047.27	20129.50	17223.38	15322.33	13994.84	13025.07
740 000	66878.48	35968.08	25743.03	20688.65	17701.81	15747.95	14383.59	13386.87
760 000	68686.00	36940.19	26438.79	21247.81	18180.23	16173.57	14772.34	13748.68
780 000	70493.53	37912.30	27134.54	21806.96	18658.66	16599.19	15161.08	14110.49
800 000	72301.06	38884.41	27830.30	22366.11	19137.09	17024.81	15549.83	14472.30
820 000	74108.58	39856.52	28526.06	22925.26	19615.51	17450.43	15938.57	14834.10
840 000	75916.11	40828.63	29221.82	23484.42	20093.94	17876.05	16327.32	15195.91
860 000	77723.64	41800.74	29917.58	24043.57	20572.37	18301.67	16716.06	15557.72
880 000	79531.16	42772.85	30613.33	24602.72	21050.80	18727.29	17104.81	15919.52
900 000	81338.69	43744.96	31309.09	25161.88	21529.22	19152.91	17493.56	16281.33
920 000	83146.22	44717.07	32004.85	25721.03	22007.65	19578.53	17882.30	16643.14
940 000	84953.74	45689.18	32700.61	26280.18	22486.08	20004.16	18271.05	17004.95
960 000	86761.27	46661.29	33396.36	26839.33	22964.50	20429.78	18659.79	17366.75
980 000	88568.79	47633.40	34092.12	27398.49	23442.93	20855.40	19048.54	17728.56
1000 000	90376.32	48605.51	34787.88	27957.64	23921.36	21281.02	19437.28	18090.37
Coefficient	.090376321	.048605511	.034787878	.027957640	.023921359	.021281016	.019437284	.018090369

AMOUNT	9 YEARS	10 YEARS	15 YEARS	20 YEARS	25 YEARS	30 YEARS	35 YEARS	40 YEARS
10 000	170.74	162.87	141.67	133.53	130.03	128.45	127.72	127.38
20 000	341.47	325.74	283.35	267.06	260.05	256.89	255.44	254.76
30 000	512.21	488.61	425.02	400.59	390.08	385.34	383.16	382.14
40 000	682.94	651.48	566.70	534.12	520.10	513.78	510.87	509.52
50 000	853.68	814.35	708.37	667.65	650.13	642.23	638.59	636.90
60 000	1024.42	977.22	850.05	801.18	780.15	770.68	766.31	764.28
70 000	1195.15	1140.09	991.72	934.71	910.18	899.12	894.03	891.66
80 000	1365.89	1302.95	1133.40	1068.24	1040.21	1027.57	1021.75	1019.04
90 000	1536.63	1465.82	1275.07	1201.77	1170.23	1156.01	1149.47	1146.42
100 000	1707.36	1628.69	1416.75	1335.30	1300.26	1284.46	1277.18	1273.80
110 000	1878.10	1791.56	1558.42	1468.83	1430.28	1412.90	1404.90	1401.18
120 000	2048.83	1954.43	1700.10	1602.36	1560.31	1541.35	1532.62	1528.56
130 000	2219.57	2117.30	1841.77	1735.89	1690.34	1669.80	1660.34	1655.94
140 000	2390.31	2280.17	1983.45	1869.42	1820.36	1798.24	1788.06	1783.32
150 000	2561.04	2443.04	2125.12	2002.95	1950.39	1926.69	1915.78	1910.70
160 000	2731.78	2605.91	2266.80	2136.48	2080.41	2055.13	2043.49	2038.08
170 000	2902.51	2768.78	2408.47	2270.01	2210.44	2183.58	2171.21	2165.46
180 000	3073.25	2931.65	2550.15	2403.54	2340.46	2312.03	2298.93	2292.84
190 000	3243.99	3094.52	2691.82	2537.07	2470.49	2440.47	2426.65	2420.22
200 000	3414.72	3257.39	2833.50	2670.60	2600.52	2568.92	2554.37	2547.60
210 000	3585.46	3420.26	2975.17	2804.13	2730.54	2697.36	2682.09	2674.98
220 000	3756.19	3583.13	3116.85	2937.66	2860.57	2825.81	2809.80	2802.36
230 000	3926.93	3746.00	3258.52	3071.19	2990.59	2954.25	2937.52	2929.75
240 000	4097.67	3908.86	3400.20	3204.72	3120.62	3082.70	3065.24	3057.13
250 000	4268.40	4071.73	3541.87	3338.25	3250.65	3211.15	3192.96	3184.51
260 000	4439.14	4234.60	3683.55	3471.78	3380.67	3339.59	3320.68	3311.89
270 000	4609.88	4397.47	3825.22	3605.31	3510.70	3468.04	3448.40	3439.27
280 000	4780.61	4560.34	3966.90	3738.84	3640.72	3596.48	3576.11	3566.65
290 000	4951.35	4723.21	4108.57	3872.37	3770.75	3724.93	3703.83	3694.03
300 000	5122.08	4886.08	4250.25	4005.90	3900.77	3853.38	3831.55	3821.41
320 000	5463.56	5211.82	4533.60	4272.96	4160.83	4110.27	4086.99	4076.17
340 000	5805.03	5537.56	4816.95	4540.02	4420.88	4367.16	4342.43	4330.93
360 000	6146.50	5863.30	5100.30	4807.08	4680.93	4624.05	4597.86	4585.69
380 000	6487.97	6189.04	5383.65	5074.14	4940.98	4880.94	4853.30	4840.45
400 000	6829.44	6514.77	5667.00	5341.19	5201.03	5137.83	5108.74	5095.21
420 000	7170.92	6840.51	5950.35	5608.25	5461.08	5394.73	5364.17	5349.97
440 000	7512.39	7166.25	6233.70	5875.31	5721.14	5651.62	5619.61	5604.73
460 000	7853.86	7491.99	6517.05	6142.37	5981.19	5908.51	5875.05	5859.49
480 000	8195.33	7817.73	6800.40	6409.43	6241.24	6165.40	6130.48	6114.25
500 000	8536.81	8143.47	7083.75	6676.49	6501.29	6422.29	6385.92	6369.01
520 000	8878.28	8469.21	7367.10	6943.55	6761.34	6679.18	6641.36	6623.77
540 000	9219.75	8794.94	7650.45	7210.61	7021.39	6936.08	6896.79	6878.53
560 000	9561.22	9120.68	7933.80	7477.67	7281.45	7192.97	7152.23	7133.29
580 000	9902.69	9446.42	8217.15	7744.73	7541.50	7449.86	7407.67	7388.05
600 000	10244.17	9772.16	8500.50	8011.79	7801.55	7706.75	7663.10	7642.81
620 000	10585.64	10097.90	8783.85	8278.85	8061.60	7963.64	7918.54	7897.57
640 000	10927.11	10423.64	9067.20	8545.91	8321.65	8220.53	8173.98	8152.33
660 000	11268.58	10749.38	9350.55	8812.97	8581.70	8477.43	8429.41	8407.09
680 000	11610.06	11075.12	9633.90	9080.03	8841.76	8734.32	8684.85	8661.85
700 000	11951.53	11400.85	9917.25	9347.09	9101.81	8991.21	8940.29	8916.62
720 000	12293.00	11726.59	10200.60	9614.15	9361.86	9248.10	9195.72	9171.38
740 000	12634.47	12052.33	10483.95	9881.21	9621.91	9504.99	9451.16	9426.14
760 000	12975.95	12378.07	10767.30	10148.27	9881.96	9761.88	9706.60	9680.90
780 000	13317.42	12703.81	11050.65	10415.33	10142.01	10018.78	9962.03	9935.66
800 000	13658.89	13029.55	11334.00	10682.39	10402.07	10275.67	10217.47	10190.42
820 000	14000.36	13355.29	11617.35	10949.45	10662.12	10532.56	10472.91	10445.18
840 000	14341.83	13681.03	11900.70	11216.51	10922.17	10789.45	10728.34	10699.94
860 000	14683.31	14006.76	12184.05	11483.57	11182.22	11046.34	10983.78	10954.70
880 000	15024.78	14332.50	12467.40	11750.63	11442.27	11303.23	11239.22	11209.46
900 000	15366.25	14658.24	12750.75	12017.69	11702.32	11560.13	11494.66	11464.22
920 000	15707.72	14983.98	13034.10	12284.75	11962.38	11817.02	11750.09	11718.98
940 000	16049.20	15309.72	13317.45	12551.81	12222.43	12073.91	12005.53	11973.74
960 000	16390.67	15635.46	13600.80	12818.87	12482.48	12330.80	12260.97	12228.50
980 000	16732.14	15961.20	13884.15	13085.93	12742.53	12587.69	12516.40	12483.26
1000 000	17073.61	16286.94	14167.50	13352.99	13002.58	12844.59	12771.84	12738.02
Coefficient	.017073612	.016286935	.014167497	.013352987	.013002582	.012844585	.012771839	.012738022

15.50% MONTHLY AMORTIZING PAYMENTS

AMOUNT	1 YEAR	2 YEARS	3 YEARS	4 YEARS	5 YEARS	6 YEARS	7 YEARS	8 YEARS
10 000	904.94	487.25	349.11	280.85	240.53	214.17	195.78	182.36
20 000	1809.89	974.49	698.21	561.70	481.06	428.35	391.57	364.72
30 000	2714.83	1461.74	1047.32	842.55	721.60	642.52	587.35	547.08
40 000	3619.78	1948.98	1396.43	1123.39	962.13	856.70	783.13	729.44
50 000	4524.72	2436.23	1745.53	1404.24	1202.66	1070.87	978.92	911.80
60 000	5429.67	2923.47	2094.64	1685.09	1443.19	1285.05	1174.70	1094.16
70 000	6334.61	3410.72	2443.75	1965.94	1683.72	1499.22	1370.48	1276.51
80 000	7239.55	3897.96	2792.85	2246.79	1924.26	1713.40	1566.27	1458.87
90 000	8144.50	4385.21	3141.96	2527.64	2164.79	1927.57	1762.05	1641.23
100 000	9049.44	4872.45	3491.07	2808.49	2405.32	2141.75	1957.83	1823.59
110 000	9954.39	5359.70	3840.17	3089.33	2645.85	2355.92	2153.62	2005.95
120 000	10859.33	5846.94	4189.28	3370.18	2886.38	2570.10	2349.40	2188.31
130 000	11764.27	6334.19	4538.39	3651.03	3126.91	2784.27	2545.19	2370.67
140 000	12669.22	6821.44	4887.50	3931.88	3367.45	2998.45	2740.97	2553.03
150 000	13574.16	7308.68	5236.60	4212.73	3607.98	3212.62	2936.75	2735.39
160 000	14479.11	7795.93	5585.71	4493.58	3848.51	3426.80	3132.54	2917.75
170 000	15384.05	8283.17	5934.82	4774.43	4089.04	3640.97	3328.32	3100.11
180 000	16289.00	8770.42	6283.92	5055.27	4329.57	3855.15	3524.10	3282.47
190 000	17193.94	9257.66	6633.03	5336.12	4570.11	4069.32	3719.89	3464.83
200 000	18098.88	9744.91	6982.14	5616.97	4810.64	4283.50	3915.67	3647.18
210 000	19003.83	10232.15	7331.24	5897.82	5051.17	4497.67	4111.45	3829.54
220 000	19908.77	10719.40	7680.35	6178.67	5291.70	4711.85	4307.24	4011.90
230 000	20813.72	11206.64	8029.46	6459.52	5532.23	4926.02	4503.02	4194.26
240 000	21718.66	11693.89	8378.56	6740.37	5772.77	5140.20	4698.80	4376.62
250 000	22623.61	12181.14	8727.67	7021.21	6013.30	5354.37	4894.59	4558.98
260 000	23528.55	12668.38	9076.78	7302.06	6253.83	5568.55	5090.37	4741.34
270 000	24433.49	13155.63	9425.88	7582.91	6494.36	5782.72	5286.15	4923.70
280 000	25338.44	13642.87	9774.99	7863.76	6734.89	5996.90	5481.94	5106.06
290 000	26243.38	14130.12	10124.10	8144.61	6975.43	6211.07	5677.72	5288.42
300 000	27148.33	14617.36	10473.20	8425.46	7215.96	6425.25	5873.50	5470.78
320 000	28958.22	15591.85	11171.42	8987.15	7697.02	6853.60	6265.07	5835.50
340 000	30768.10	16566.34	11869.63	9548.85	8178.08	7281.95	6656.64	6200.21
360 000	32577.99	17540.83	12567.84	10110.55	8659.15	7710.30	7048.20	6564.93
380 000	34387.88	18515.33	13266.06	10672.25	9140.21	8138.65	7439.77	6929.65
400 000	36197.77	19489.82	13964.27	11233.94	9621.28	8567.00	7831.34	7294.37
420 000	38007.66	20464.31	14662.49	11795.64	10102.34	8995.34	8222.91	7659.09
440 000	39817.55	21438.80	15360.70	12357.34	10583.40	9423.69	8614.47	8023.81
460 000	41627.43	22413.29	16058.91	12919.03	11064.47	9852.04	9006.04	8388.52
480 000	43437.32	23387.78	16757.13	13480.73	11545.53	10280.39	9397.61	8753.24
500 000	45247.21	24362.27	17455.34	14042.43	12026.60	10708.74	9789.17	9117.96
520 000	47057.10	25336.76	18153.55	14604.13	12507.66	11137.09	10180.74	9482.68
540 000	48866.99	26311.25	18851.77	15165.82	12988.72	11565.44	10572.31	9847.40
560 000	50676.88	27285.74	19549.98	15727.52	13469.79	11993.79	10963.87	10212.12
580 000	52486.76	28260.23	20248.19	16289.22	13950.85	12422.14	11355.44	10576.83
600 000	54296.65	29234.72	20946.41	16850.91	14431.91	12850.49	11747.01	10941.55
620 000	56106.54	30209.22	21644.62	17412.61	14912.98	13278.84	12138.58	11306.27
640 000	57916.43	31183.71	22342.83	17974.31	15394.04	13707.19	12530.14	11670.99
660 000	59726.32	32158.20	23041.05	18536.01	15875.11	14135.54	12921.71	12035.71
680 000	61536.21	33132.69	23739.26	19097.70	16356.17	14563.89	13313.28	12400.43
700 000	63346.10	34107.18	24437.48	19659.40	16837.23	14992.24	13704.84	12765.15
720 000	65155.98	35081.67	25135.69	20221.10	17318.30	15420.59	14096.41	13129.86
740 000	66965.87	36056.16	25833.90	20782.79	17799.36	15848.94	14487.98	13494.58
760 000	68775.76	37030.65	26532.12	21344.49	18280.42	16277.29	14879.54	13859.30
780 000	70585.65	38005.14	27230.33	21906.19	18761.49	16705.64	15271.11	14224.02
800 000	72395.54	38979.63	27928.54	22467.89	19242.55	17133.99	15662.68	14588.74
820 000	74205.43	39954.12	28626.76	23029.58	19723.62	17562.34	16054.24	14953.46
840 000	76015.31	40928.61	29324.97	23591.28	20204.68	17990.69	16445.81	15318.17
860 000	77825.20	41903.11	30023.18	24152.98	20685.74	18419.04	16837.38	15682.89
880 000	79635.09	42877.60	30721.40	24714.68	21166.81	18847.39	17228.95	16047.61
900 000	81444.98	43852.09	31419.61	25276.37	21647.87	19275.74	17620.51	16412.33
920 000	83254.87	44826.58	32117.82	25838.07	22128.93	19704.09	18012.08	16777.05
940 000	85064.76	45801.07	32816.04	26399.77	22610.00	20132.44	18403.65	17141.77
960 000	86874.65	46775.56	33514.25	26961.46	23091.06	20560.79	18795.21	17506.49
980 000	88684.53	47750.05	34212.47	27523.16	23572.13	20989.14	19186.78	17871.20
1000 000	90494.42	48724.54	34910.68	28084.86	24053.19	21417.49	19578.35	18235.92
Coefficient	.090494422	.048724541	.034910679	.028084858	.024053190	.021417488	.019578347	.018235922

86

AMOUNT	9 YEARS	10 YEARS	15 YEARS	20 YEARS	25 YEARS	30 YEARS	35 YEARS	40 YEARS
10 000	172.24	164.41	143.40	135.39	131.97	130.45	129.76	129.44
20 000	344.47	328.82	286.80	270.78	263.95	260.90	259.52	258.88
30 000	516.71	493.23	430.20	406.16	395.92	391.36	389.28	388.32
40 000	688.94	657.64	573.60	541.55	527.90	521.81	519.03	517.76
50 000	861.18	822.05	717.00	676.94	659.87	652.26	648.79	647.20
60 000	1033.41	986.46	860.39	812.33	791.85	782.71	778.55	776.64
70 000	1205.65	1150.87	1003.79	947.72	923.82	913.16	908.31	906.08
80 000	1377.88	1315.28	1147.19	1083.10	1055.80	1043.61	1038.07	1035.52
90 000	1550.12	1479.69	1290.59	1218.49	1187.77	1174.07	1167.83	1164.96
100 000	1722.35	1644.11	1433.99	1353.88	1319.75	1304.52	1297.58	1294.40
110 000	1894.59	1808.52	1577.39	1489.27	1451.72	1434.97	1427.34	1423.84
120 000	2066.82	1972.93	1720.79	1624.66	1583.69	1565.42	1557.10	1553.28
130 000	2239.06	2137.34	1864.19	1760.04	1715.67	1695.87	1686.86	1682.72
140 000	2411.29	2301.75	2007.59	1895.43	1847.64	1826.32	1816.62	1812.16
150 000	2583.53	2466.16	2150.99	2030.82	1979.62	1956.78	1946.38	1941.60
160 000	2755.76	2630.57	2294.38	2166.21	2111.59	2087.23	2076.14	2071.04
170 000	2928.00	2794.98	2437.78	2301.60	2243.57	2217.68	2205.89	2200.48
180 000	3100.23	2959.39	2581.18	2436.99	2375.54	2348.13	2335.65	2329.92
190 000	3272.47	3123.80	2724.58	2572.37	2507.52	2478.58	2465.41	2459.36
200 000	3444.71	3288.21	2867.98	2707.76	2639.49	2609.03	2595.17	2588.80
210 000	3616.94	3452.62	3011.38	2843.15	2771.46	2739.49	2724.93	2718.24
220 000	3789.18	3617.03	3154.78	2978.54	2903.44	2869.94	2854.69	2847.68
230 000	3961.41	3781.44	3298.18	3113.93	3035.41	3000.39	2984.44	2977.12
240 000	4133.65	3945.85	3441.58	3249.31	3167.39	3130.84	3114.20	3106.56
250 000	4305.88	4110.26	3584.98	3384.70	3299.36	3261.29	3243.96	3236.00
260 000	4478.12	4274.67	3728.38	3520.09	3431.34	3391.74	3373.72	3365.44
270 000	4650.35	4439.08	3871.77	3655.48	3563.31	3522.20	3503.48	3494.88
280 000	4822.59	4603.50	4015.17	3790.87	3695.29	3652.65	3633.24	3624.32
290 000	4994.82	4767.91	4158.57	3926.25	3827.26	3783.10	3763.00	3753.76
300 000	5167.06	4932.32	4301.97	4061.64	3959.24	3913.55	3892.75	3883.20
320 000	5511.53	5261.14	4588.77	4332.42	4223.18	4174.45	4152.27	4142.08
340 000	5856.00	5589.96	4875.57	4603.19	4487.13	4435.36	4411.79	4400.96
360 000	6200.47	5918.78	5162.37	4873.97	4751.08	4696.26	4671.30	4659.84
380 000	6544.94	6247.60	5449.16	5144.75	5015.03	4957.16	4930.82	4918.72
400 000	6889.41	6576.42	5735.96	5415.52	5278.98	5218.07	5190.34	5177.60
420 000	7233.88	6905.24	6022.76	5686.30	5542.93	5478.97	5449.86	5436.48
440 000	7578.35	7234.06	6309.56	5957.08	5806.88	5739.87	5709.37	5695.36
460 000	7922.82	7562.88	6596.36	6227.85	6070.83	6000.78	5968.89	5954.24
480 000	8267.29	7891.71	6883.15	6498.63	6334.78	6261.68	6228.41	6213.12
500 000	8611.76	8220.53	7169.95	6769.40	6598.73	6522.58	6487.92	6472.00
520 000	8956.23	8549.35	7456.75	7040.18	6862.68	6783.49	6747.44	6730.88
540 000	9300.70	8878.17	7743.55	7310.96	7126.62	7044.39	7006.96	6989.76
560 000	9645.17	9206.99	8030.35	7581.73	7390.57	7305.29	7266.47	7248.64
580 000	9989.64	9535.81	8317.14	7852.51	7654.52	7566.20	7525.99	7507.52
600 000	10334.12	9864.63	8603.94	8123.28	7918.47	7827.10	7785.51	7766.40
620 000	10678.59	10193.45	8890.74	8394.06	8182.42	8088.00	8045.03	8025.28
640 000	11023.06	10522.27	9177.54	8664.84	8446.37	8348.91	8304.54	8284.16
660 000	11367.53	10851.10	9464.34	8935.61	8710.32	8609.81	8564.06	8543.04
680 000	11712.00	11179.92	9751.13	9206.39	8974.27	8870.71	8823.58	8801.92
700 000	12056.47	11508.74	10037.93	9477.16	9238.22	9131.62	9083.09	9060.80
720 000	12400.94	11837.56	10324.73	9747.94	9502.17	9392.52	9342.61	9319.68
740 000	12745.41	12166.38	10611.53	10018.72	9766.11	9653.43	9602.13	9578.56
760 000	13089.88	12495.20	10898.33	10289.49	10030.06	9914.33	9861.64	9837.44
780 000	13434.35	12824.02	11185.13	10560.27	10294.01	10175.23	10121.16	10096.32
800 000	13778.82	13152.84	11471.92	10831.05	10557.96	10436.14	10380.68	10355.20
820 000	14123.29	13481.66	11758.72	11101.82	10821.91	10697.04	10640.19	10614.08
840 000	14467.76	13810.49	12045.52	11372.60	11085.86	10957.94	10899.71	10872.96
860 000	14812.23	14139.31	12332.32	11643.37	11349.81	11218.85	11159.23	11131.84
880 000	15156.70	14468.13	12619.12	11914.15	11613.76	11479.75	11418.75	11390.72
900 000	15501.17	14796.95	12905.91	12184.93	11877.71	11740.65	11678.26	11649.60
920 000	15845.64	15125.77	13192.71	12455.70	12141.66	12001.56	11937.78	11908.48
940 000	16190.11	15454.59	13479.51	12726.48	12405.60	12262.46	12197.30	12167.36
960 000	16534.58	15783.41	13766.31	12997.25	12669.55	12523.36	12456.81	12426.24
980 000	16879.05	16112.23	14053.11	13268.03	12933.50	12784.27	12716.33	12685.12
1000 000	17223.53	16441.05	14339.90	13538.81	13197.45	13045.17	12975.85	12944.00
Coefficient	.017223525	.016441054	.014339904	.013538807	.013197452	.013045169	.012975847	.012943999

MONTHLY AMORTIZING PAYMENTS

AMOUNT	1 YEAR	2 YEARS	3 YEARS	4 YEARS	5 YEARS	6 YEARS	7 YEARS	8 YEARS
10 000	906.13	488.44	350.34	282.12	241.85	215.54	197.20	183.82
20 000	1812.25	976.87	700.67	564.25	483.71	431.09	394.40	367.64
30 000	2718.38	1465.31	1051.01	846.37	725.56	646.63	591.60	551.46
40 000	3624.50	1953.75	1401.35	1128.50	967.42	862.18	788.80	735.28
50 000	4530.63	2442.19	1751.69	1410.62	1209.27	1077.72	986.00	919.10
60 000	5436.76	2930.62	2102.02	1692.74	1451.13	1293.27	1183.20	1102.92
70 000	6342.88	3419.06	2452.36	1974.87	1692.98	1508.81	1380.40	1286.74
80 000	7249.01	3907.50	2802.70	2256.99	1934.83	1724.35	1577.60	1470.56
90 000	8155.13	4395.94	3153.04	2539.12	2176.69	1939.90	1774.79	1654.39
100 000	9061.26	4884.37	3503.37	2821.24	2418.54	2155.44	1971.99	1838.21
110 000	9967.39	5372.81	3853.71	3103.36	2660.40	2370.99	2169.19	2022.03
120 000	10873.51	5861.25	4204.05	3385.49	2902.25	2586.53	2366.39	2205.85
130 000	11779.64	6349.69	4554.39	3667.61	3144.11	2802.08	2563.59	2389.67
140 000	12685.76	6838.12	4904.72	3949.74	3385.96	3017.62	2760.79	2573.49
150 000	13591.89	7326.56	5255.06	4231.86	3627.81	3233.16	2957.99	2757.31
160 000	14498.01	7815.00	5605.40	4513.98	3869.67	3448.71	3155.19	2941.13
170 000	15404.14	8303.44	5955.73	4796.11	4111.52	3664.25	3352.39	3124.95
180 000	16310.27	8791.87	6306.07	5078.23	4353.38	3879.80	3549.59	3308.77
190 000	17216.39	9280.31	6656.41	5360.36	4595.23	4095.34	3746.79	3492.59
200 000	18122.52	9768.75	7006.75	5642.48	4837.08	4310.89	3943.99	3676.41
210 000	19028.64	10257.19	7357.08	5924.61	5078.94	4526.43	4141.19	3860.23
220 000	19934.77	10745.62	7707.42	6206.73	5320.79	4741.97	4338.39	4044.05
230 000	20840.90	11234.06	8057.76	6488.85	5562.65	4957.52	4535.59	4227.87
240 000	21747.02	11722.50	8408.10	6770.98	5804.50	5173.06	4732.79	4411.69
250 000	22653.15	12210.94	8758.43	7053.10	6046.36	5388.61	4929.99	4595.52
260 000	23559.27	12699.37	9108.77	7335.23	6288.21	5604.15	5127.18	4779.34
270 000	24465.40	13187.81	9459.11	7617.35	6530.06	5819.70	5324.38	4963.16
280 000	25371.53	13676.25	9809.44	7899.47	6771.92	6035.24	5521.58	5146.98
290 000	26277.65	14164.69	10159.78	8181.60	7013.77	6250.78	5718.78	5330.80
300 000	27183.78	14653.12	10510.12	8463.72	7255.63	6466.33	5915.98	5514.62
320 000	28996.03	15630.00	11210.79	9027.97	7739.34	6897.42	6310.38	5882.26
340 000	30808.28	16606.87	11911.47	9592.22	8223.04	7328.51	6704.78	6249.90
360 000	32620.53	17583.75	12612.14	10156.47	8706.75	7759.60	7099.18	6617.54
380 000	34432.79	18560.62	13312.82	10720.71	9190.46	8190.68	7493.58	6985.18
400 000	36245.04	19537.50	14013.49	11284.96	9674.17	8621.77	7887.98	7352.82
420 000	38057.29	20514.37	14714.17	11849.21	10157.88	9052.86	8282.38	7720.47
440 000	39869.54	21491.25	15414.84	12413.46	10641.59	9483.95	8676.77	8088.11
460 000	41681.79	22468.12	16115.52	12977.71	11125.30	9915.04	9071.17	8455.75
480 000	43494.04	23445.00	16816.19	13541.95	11609.00	10346.13	9465.57	8823.39
500 000	45306.30	24421.87	17516.87	14106.20	12092.71	10777.22	9859.97	9191.03
520 000	47118.55	25398.75	18217.54	14670.45	12576.42	11208.30	10254.37	9558.67
540 000	48930.80	26375.62	18918.21	15234.70	13060.13	11639.39	10648.77	9926.31
560 000	50743.05	27352.50	19618.89	15798.95	13543.84	12070.48	11043.17	10293.95
580 000	52555.30	28329.37	20319.56	16363.19	14027.55	12501.57	11437.57	10661.60
600 000	54367.56	29306.25	21020.24	16927.44	14511.25	12932.66	11831.96	11029.24
620 000	56179.81	30283.12	21720.91	17491.69	14994.96	13363.75	12226.36	11396.88
640 000	57992.06	31259.99	22421.59	18055.94	15478.67	13794.84	12620.76	11764.52
660 000	59804.31	32236.87	23122.26	18620.19	15962.38	14225.92	13015.16	12132.16
680 000	61616.56	33213.74	23822.94	19184.44	16446.09	14657.01	13409.56	12499.80
700 000	63428.82	34190.62	24523.61	19748.68	16929.80	15088.10	13803.96	12867.44
720 000	65241.07	35167.49	25224.29	20312.93	17413.51	15519.19	14198.36	13235.08
740 000	67053.32	36144.37	25924.96	20877.18	17897.21	15950.28	14592.76	13602.73
760 000	68865.57	37121.24	26625.64	21441.43	18380.92	16381.37	14987.16	13970.37
780 000	70677.82	38098.12	27326.31	22005.68	18864.63	16812.46	15381.55	14338.01
800 000	72490.07	39074.99	28026.98	22569.92	19348.34	17243.54	15775.95	14705.65
820 000	74302.33	40051.87	28727.66	23134.17	19832.05	17674.63	16170.35	15073.29
840 000	76114.58	41028.74	29428.33	23698.42	20315.76	18105.72	16564.75	15440.93
860 000	77926.83	42005.62	30129.01	24262.67	20799.46	18536.81	16959.15	15808.57
880 000	79739.08	42982.49	30829.68	24826.92	21283.17	18967.90	17353.55	16176.21
900 000	81551.33	43959.37	31530.36	25391.16	21766.88	19398.99	17747.95	16543.86
920 000	83363.59	44936.24	32231.03	25955.41	22250.59	19830.08	18142.35	16911.50
940 000	85175.84	45913.12	32931.71	26519.66	22734.30	20261.17	18536.74	17279.14
960 000	86988.09	46889.99	33632.38	27083.91	23218.01	20692.25	18931.14	17646.78
980 000	88800.34	47866.87	34333.06	27648.16	23701.72	21123.34	19325.54	18014.42
1000 000	90612.59	48843.74	35033.73	28212.41	24185.42	21554.43	19719.94	18382.06
Coefficient	.090612593	.048843742	.035033731	.028212405	.024185424	.021554431	.019719941	.018382062

MONTHLY AMORTIZING PAYMENTS 15.75%

AMOUNT	9 YEARS	10 YEARS	15 YEARS	20 YEARS	25 YEARS	30 YEARS	35 YEARS	40 YEARS
10 000	173.74	165.96	145.13	137.25	133.93	132.46	131.80	131.50
20 000	347.48	331.92	290.26	274.51	267.86	264.92	263.60	263.00
30 000	521.22	497.88	435.39	411.76	401.79	397.39	395.40	394.50
40 000	694.96	663.83	580.52	549.01	535.72	529.85	527.21	526.01
50 000	868.70	829.79	725.65	686.27	669.64	662.31	659.01	657.51
60 000	1042.44	995.75	870.78	823.52	803.57	794.77	790.81	789.01
70 000	1216.19	1161.71	1015.92	960.77	937.50	927.23	922.61	920.51
80 000	1389.93	1327.67	1161.05	1098.03	1071.43	1059.69	1054.41	1052.01
90 000	1563.67	1493.63	1306.18	1235.28	1205.36	1192.16	1186.21	1183.51
100 000	1737.41	1659.58	1451.31	1372.53	1339.29	1324.62	1318.01	1315.02
110 000	1911.15	1825.54	1596.44	1509.79	1473.22	1457.08	1449.82	1446.52
120 000	2084.89	1991.50	1741.57	1647.04	1607.15	1589.54	1581.62	1578.02
130 000	2258.63	2157.46	1886.70	1784.29	1741.08	1722.00	1713.42	1709.52
140 000	2432.37	2323.42	2031.83	1921.55	1875.01	1854.46	1845.22	1841.02
150 000	2606.11	2489.38	2176.96	2058.80	2008.93	1986.93	1977.02	1972.52
160 000	2779.85	2655.34	2322.09	2196.05	2142.86	2119.39	2108.82	2104.03
170 000	2953.59	2821.29	2467.22	2333.31	2276.79	2251.85	2240.62	2235.53
180 000	3127.33	2987.25	2612.35	2470.56	2410.72	2384.31	2372.42	2367.03
190 000	3301.07	3153.21	2757.48	2607.81	2544.65	2516.77	2504.23	2498.53
200 000	3474.81	3319.17	2902.62	2745.07	2678.58	2649.23	2636.03	2630.03
210 000	3648.56	3485.13	3047.75	2882.32	2812.51	2781.70	2767.83	2761.53
220 000	3822.30	3651.09	3192.88	3019.57	2946.44	2914.16	2899.63	2893.03
230 000	3996.04	3817.05	3338.01	3156.83	3080.37	3046.62	3031.43	3024.54
240 000	4169.78	3983.00	3483.14	3294.08	3214.29	3179.08	3163.23	3156.04
250 000	4343.52	4148.96	3628.27	3431.33	3348.22	3311.54	3295.03	3287.54
260 000	4517.26	4314.92	3773.40	3568.59	3482.15	3444.00	3426.84	3419.04
270 000	4691.00	4480.88	3918.53	3705.84	3616.08	3576.47	3558.64	3550.54
280 000	4864.74	4646.84	4063.66	3843.09	3750.01	3708.93	3690.44	3682.04
290 000	5038.48	4812.80	4208.79	3980.35	3883.94	3841.39	3822.24	3813.55
300 000	5212.22	4978.75	4353.92	4117.60	4017.87	3973.85	3954.04	3945.05
320 000	5559.70	5310.67	4644.18	4392.11	4285.73	4238.77	4217.64	4208.05
340 000	5907.18	5642.59	4934.45	4666.61	4553.58	4503.70	4481.25	4471.05
360 000	6254.67	5974.51	5224.71	4941.12	4821.44	4768.62	4744.85	4734.06
380 000	6602.15	6306.42	5514.97	5215.63	5089.30	5033.54	5008.45	4997.06
400 000	6949.63	6638.34	5805.23	5490.13	5357.16	5298.47	5272.05	5260.06
420 000	7297.11	6970.26	6095.49	5764.64	5625.02	5563.39	5535.66	5523.07
440 000	7644.59	7302.17	6385.75	6039.15	5892.87	5828.32	5799.26	5786.07
460 000	7992.07	7634.09	6676.02	6313.66	6160.73	6093.24	6062.86	6049.07
480 000	8339.56	7966.01	6966.28	6588.16	6428.59	6358.16	6326.47	6312.08
500 000	8687.04	8297.92	7256.54	6862.67	6696.45	6623.09	6590.07	6575.08
520 000	9034.52	8629.84	7546.80	7137.18	6964.31	6888.01	6853.67	6838.08
540 000	9382.00	8961.76	7837.06	7411.68	7232.16	7152.93	7117.27	7101.09
560 000	9729.48	9293.67	8127.32	7686.19	7500.02	7417.86	7380.88	7364.09
580 000	10076.96	9625.59	8417.59	7960.70	7767.88	7682.78	7644.48	7627.09
600 000	10424.44	9957.51	8707.85	8235.20	8035.74	7947.70	7908.08	7890.09
620 000	10771.93	10289.43	8998.11	8509.71	8303.59	8212.63	8171.68	8153.10
640 000	11119.41	10621.34	9288.37	8784.22	8571.45	8477.55	8435.29	8416.10
660 000	11466.89	10953.26	9578.63	9058.72	8839.31	8742.47	8698.89	8679.10
680 000	11814.37	11285.18	9868.89	9333.23	9107.17	9007.40	8962.49	8942.11
700 000	12161.85	11617.09	10159.15	9607.74	9375.03	9272.32	9226.10	9205.11
720 000	12509.33	11949.01	10449.42	9882.24	9642.88	9537.24	9489.70	9468.11
740 000	12856.81	12280.93	10739.68	10156.75	9910.74	9802.17	9753.30	9731.12
760 000	13204.30	12612.84	11029.94	10431.26	10178.60	10067.09	10016.90	9994.12
780 000	13551.78	12944.76	11320.20	10705.76	10446.46	10332.01	10280.51	10257.12
800 000	13899.26	13276.68	11610.46	10980.27	10714.32	10596.94	10544.11	10520.13
820 000	14246.74	13608.60	11900.72	11254.78	10982.17	10861.86	10807.71	10783.13
840 000	14594.22	13940.51	12190.99	11529.28	11250.03	11126.78	11071.32	11046.13
860 000	14941.70	14272.43	12481.25	11803.79	11517.89	11391.71	11334.92	11309.14
880 000	15289.18	14604.35	12771.51	12078.30	11785.75	11656.63	11598.52	11572.14
900 000	15636.67	14936.26	13061.77	12352.80	12053.61	11921.55	11862.12	11835.14
920 000	15984.15	15268.18	13352.03	12627.31	12321.46	12186.48	12125.73	12098.15
940 000	16331.63	15600.10	13642.29	12901.82	12589.32	12451.40	12389.33	12361.15
960 000	16679.11	15932.01	13932.55	13176.32	12857.18	12716.32	12652.93	12624.15
980 000	17026.59	16263.93	14222.82	13450.83	13125.04	12981.25	12916.53	12887.15
1000 000	17374.07	16595.85	14513.08	13725.34	13392.90	13246.17	13180.14	13150.16
Coefficient	.017374073	.016595848	.014513078	.013725337	.013392895	.013246171	.013180137	.013150158

16.00% MONTHLY AMORTIZING PAYMENTS

AMOUNT	1 YEAR	2 YEARS	3 YEARS	4 YEARS	5 YEARS	6 YEARS	7 YEARS	8 YEARS
10 000	907.31	489.63	351.57	283.40	243.18	216.92	198.62	185.29
20 000	1814.62	979.26	703.14	566.81	486.36	433.84	397.24	370.58
30 000	2721.93	1468.89	1054.71	850.21	729.54	650.76	595.86	555.86
40 000	3629.23	1958.52	1406.28	1133.61	972.72	867.67	794.48	741.15
50 000	4536.54	2448.16	1757.85	1417.01	1215.90	1084.59	993.10	926.44
60 000	5443.85	2937.79	2109.42	1700.42	1459.08	1301.51	1191.72	1111.73
70 000	6351.16	3427.42	2460.99	1983.82	1702.26	1518.43	1390.34	1297.02
80 000	7258.47	3917.05	2812.56	2267.22	1945.44	1735.35	1588.97	1482.30
90 000	8165.78	4406.68	3164.13	2550.63	2188.63	1952.27	1787.59	1667.59
100 000	9073.09	4896.31	3515.70	2834.03	2431.81	2169.18	1986.21	1852.88
110 000	9980.40	5385.94	3867.27	3117.43	2674.99	2386.10	2184.83	2038.17
120 000	10887.70	5875.57	4218.84	3400.83	2918.17	2603.02	2383.45	2223.45
130 000	11795.01	6365.20	4570.41	3684.24	3161.35	2819.94	2582.07	2408.74
140 000	12702.32	6854.84	4921.98	3967.64	3404.53	3036.86	2780.69	2594.03
150 000	13609.63	7344.47	5273.55	4251.04	3647.71	3253.78	2979.31	2779.32
160 000	14516.94	7834.10	5625.12	4534.44	3890.89	3470.69	3177.93	2964.61
170 000	15424.25	8323.73	5976.70	4817.85	4134.07	3687.61	3376.55	3149.89
180 000	16331.56	8813.36	6328.27	5101.25	4377.25	3904.53	3575.17	3335.18
190 000	17238.86	9302.99	6679.84	5384.65	4620.43	4121.45	3773.80	3520.47
200 000	18146.17	9792.62	7031.41	5668.06	4863.61	4338.37	3972.41	3705.76
210 000	19053.48	10282.25	7382.98	5951.46	5106.79	4555.29	4171.03	3891.05
220 000	19960.79	10771.88	7734.55	6234.86	5349.97	4772.20	4369.65	4076.33
230 000	20868.10	11261.52	8086.12	6518.26	5593.15	4989.12	4568.27	4261.62
240 000	21775.41	11751.15	8437.69	6801.67	5836.33	5206.04	4766.90	4446.91
250 000	22682.72	12240.78	8789.26	7085.07	6079.51	5422.96	4965.52	4632.20
260 000	23590.02	12730.41	9140.83	7368.47	6322.69	5639.88	5164.14	4817.48
270 000	24497.33	13220.04	9492.40	7651.88	6565.88	5856.80	5362.76	5002.77
280 000	25404.64	13709.67	9843.97	7935.28	6809.06	6073.72	5561.38	5188.06
290 000	26311.95	14199.30	10195.54	8218.68	7052.24	6290.63	5760.00	5373.35
300 000	27219.26	14688.93	10547.11	8502.08	7295.42	6507.55	5958.62	5558.64
320 000	29033.88	15668.20	11250.25	9068.89	7781.78	6941.39	6355.86	5929.21
340 000	30848.49	16647.46	11953.39	9635.70	8268.14	7375.23	6753.10	6299.79
360 000	32663.11	17626.72	12656.53	10202.50	8754.50	7809.06	7150.34	6670.36
380 000	34477.73	18605.98	13359.67	10769.31	9240.86	8242.90	7547.58	7040.94
400 000	36292.35	19585.24	14062.81	11336.11	9727.22	8676.74	7944.83	7411.51
420 000	38106.96	20564.51	14765.95	11902.92	10213.58	9110.57	8342.07	7782.09
440 000	39921.58	21543.77	15469.09	12469.72	10699.95	9544.41	8739.31	8152.67
460 000	41736.20	22523.03	16172.23	13036.53	11186.31	9978.25	9136.55	8523.24
480 000	43550.81	23502.29	16875.37	13603.33	11672.67	10412.08	9533.79	8893.82
500 000	45365.43	24481.56	17578.52	14170.14	12159.03	10845.92	9931.03	9264.39
520 000	47180.05	25460.82	18281.66	14736.95	12645.39	11279.76	10328.27	9634.97
540 000	48994.67	26440.08	18984.80	15303.75	13131.75	11713.59	10725.51	10005.54
560 000	50809.28	27419.34	19687.94	15870.56	13618.11	12147.43	11122.76	10376.12
580 000	52623.90	28398.60	20391.08	16437.36	14104.47	12581.27	11520.00	10746.70
600 000	54438.52	29377.87	21094.22	17004.17	14590.83	13015.10	11917.24	11117.27
620 000	56253.14	30357.13	21797.36	17570.97	15077.20	13448.94	12314.48	11487.85
640 000	58067.75	31336.39	22500.50	18137.78	15563.56	13882.78	12711.72	11858.42
660 000	59882.37	32315.65	23203.64	18704.59	16049.92	14316.61	13108.96	12229.00
680 000	61696.99	33294.92	23906.78	19271.39	16536.28	14750.45	13506.20	12599.57
700 000	63511.60	34274.18	24609.92	19838.20	17022.64	15184.29	13903.44	12970.15
720 000	65326.22	35253.44	25313.06	20405.00	17509.00	15618.12	14300.69	13340.73
740 000	67140.84	36232.70	26016.20	20971.81	17995.36	16051.96	14697.93	13711.30
760 000	68955.46	37211.97	26719.34	21538.61	18481.72	16485.80	15095.17	14081.88
780 000	70770.07	38191.23	27422.48	22105.42	18968.08	16919.64	15492.41	14452.45
800 000	72584.69	39170.49	28125.62	22672.22	19454.45	17353.47	15889.65	14823.03
820 000	74399.31	40149.75	28828.77	23239.03	19940.81	17787.31	16286.89	15193.60
840 000	76213.93	41129.01	29531.91	23805.84	20427.17	18221.15	16684.13	15564.18
860 000	78028.54	42108.28	30235.05	24372.64	20913.53	18654.98	17081.38	15934.76
880 000	79843.16	43087.54	30938.19	24939.45	21399.89	19088.82	17478.62	16305.33
900 000	81657.78	44066.80	31641.33	25506.25	21886.25	19522.66	17875.86	16675.91
920 000	83472.39	45046.06	32344.47	26073.06	22372.61	19956.49	18273.10	17046.48
940 000	85287.01	46025.33	33047.61	26639.86	22858.97	20390.33	18670.34	17417.06
960 000	87101.63	47004.59	33750.75	27206.67	23345.33	20824.17	19067.58	17787.63
980 000	88916.25	47983.85	34453.89	27773.48	23831.70	21258.00	19464.82	18158.21
1000 000	90730.86	48963.11	35157.03	28340.28	24318.06	21691.84	19862.06	18528.79
Coefficient	.090730864	.048963112	.035157031	.028340281	.024318057	.021691840	.019862064	.018528786

90

MONTHLY AMORTIZING PAYMENTS 16.00%

AMOUNT	9 YEARS	10 YEARS	15 YEARS	20 YEARS	25 YEARS	30 YEARS	35 YEARS	40 YEARS
10 000	175.25	167.51	146.87	139.13	135.89	134.48	133.85	133.56
20 000	350.51	335.03	293.74	278.25	271.78	268.95	267.69	267.13
30 000	525.76	502.54	440.61	417.38	407.67	403.43	401.54	400.69
40 000	701.01	670.05	587.48	556.50	543.56	537.90	535.39	534.26
50 000	876.26	837.57	734.35	695.63	679.44	672.38	669.23	667.82
60 000	1051.52	1005.08	881.22	834.75	815.33	806.85	803.08	801.39
70 000	1226.77	1172.59	1028.09	973.88	951.22	941.33	936.93	934.95
80 000	1402.02	1340.10	1174.96	1113.00	1087.11	1075.81	1070.78	1068.52
90 000	1577.27	1507.62	1321.83	1252.13	1223.00	1210.28	1204.62	1202.08
100 000	1752.53	1675.13	1468.70	1391.26	1358.89	1344.76	1338.47	1335.65
110 000	1927.78	1842.64	1615.57	1530.38	1494.78	1479.23	1472.32	1469.21
120 000	2103.03	2010.16	1762.44	1669.51	1630.67	1613.71	1606.16	1602.78
130 000	2278.28	2177.67	1909.31	1808.63	1766.56	1748.18	1740.01	1736.34
140 000	2453.54	2345.18	2056.18	1947.76	1902.44	1882.66	1873.86	1869.91
150 000	2628.79	2512.70	2203.05	2086.88	2038.33	2017.14	2007.70	2003.47
160 000	2804.04	2680.21	2349.92	2226.01	2174.22	2151.61	2141.55	2137.04
170 000	2979.29	2847.72	2496.79	2365.14	2310.11	2286.09	2275.40	2270.60
180 000	3154.55	3015.24	2643.66	2504.26	2446.00	2420.56	2409.24	2404.17
190 000	3329.80	3182.75	2790.53	2643.39	2581.89	2555.04	2543.09	2537.73
200 000	3505.05	3350.26	2937.40	2782.51	2717.78	2689.51	2676.94	2671.30
210 000	3680.30	3517.78	3084.27	2921.64	2853.67	2823.99	2810.79	2804.86
220 000	3855.56	3685.29	3231.14	3060.76	2989.56	2958.47	2944.63	2938.43
230 000	4030.81	3852.80	3378.01	3199.89	3125.44	3092.94	3078.48	3071.99
240 000	4206.06	4020.31	3524.88	3339.01	3261.33	3227.42	3212.33	3205.56
250 000	4381.31	4187.83	3671.75	3478.14	3397.22	3361.89	3346.17	3339.12
260 000	4556.57	4355.34	3818.62	3617.27	3533.11	3496.37	3480.02	3472.69
270 000	4731.82	4522.85	3965.49	3756.39	3669.00	3630.84	3613.87	3606.25
280 000	4907.07	4690.37	4112.36	3895.52	3804.89	3765.32	3747.71	3739.82
290 000	5082.32	4857.88	4259.23	4034.64	3940.78	3899.80	3881.56	3873.38
300 000	5257.58	5025.39	4406.10	4173.77	4076.67	4034.27	4015.41	4006.95
320 000	5608.08	5360.42	4699.84	4452.02	4348.44	4303.22	4283.10	4274.08
340 000	5958.59	5695.45	4993.58	4730.27	4620.22	4572.17	4550.80	4541.20
360 000	6309.09	6030.47	5287.32	5008.52	4892.00	4841.13	4818.49	4808.33
380 000	6659.60	6365.50	5581.06	5286.77	5163.78	5110.08	5086.18	5075.46
400 000	7010.10	6700.52	5874.80	5565.02	5435.56	5379.03	5353.88	5342.59
420 000	7360.61	7035.55	6168.54	5843.27	5707.33	5647.98	5621.57	5609.72
440 000	7711.11	7370.58	6462.28	6121.53	5979.11	5916.93	5889.27	5876.85
460 000	8061.62	7705.60	6756.02	6399.78	6250.89	6185.88	6156.96	6143.98
480 000	8412.12	8040.63	7049.76	6678.03	6522.67	6454.83	6424.65	6411.11
500 000	8762.63	8375.66	7343.50	6956.28	6794.44	6723.79	6692.35	6678.24
520 000	9113.13	8710.68	7637.24	7234.53	7066.22	6992.74	6960.04	6945.37
540 000	9463.64	9045.71	7930.98	7512.78	7338.00	7261.69	7227.73	7212.50
560 000	9814.14	9380.73	8224.72	7791.03	7609.78	7530.64	7495.43	7479.63
580 000	10164.65	9715.76	8518.46	8069.28	7881.56	7799.59	7763.12	7746.76
600 000	10515.15	10050.79	8812.20	8347.54	8153.33	8068.54	8030.82	8013.89
620 000	10865.66	10385.81	9105.94	8625.79	8425.11	8337.49	8298.51	8281.02
640 000	11216.16	10720.84	9399.69	8904.04	8696.89	8606.44	8566.20	8548.15
660 000	11566.67	11055.87	9693.43	9182.29	8968.67	8875.40	8833.90	8815.28
680 000	11917.17	11390.89	9987.17	9460.54	9240.44	9144.35	9101.59	9082.41
700 000	12267.68	11725.92	10280.91	9738.79	9512.22	9413.30	9369.29	9349.54
720 000	12618.18	12060.94	10574.65	10017.04	9784.00	9682.25	9636.98	9616.67
740 000	12968.69	12395.97	10868.39	10295.29	10055.78	9951.20	9904.67	9883.80
760 000	13319.19	12731.00	11162.13	10573.54	10327.56	10220.15	10172.37	10150.93
780 000	13669.70	13066.02	11455.87	10851.80	10599.33	10489.10	10440.06	10418.06
800 000	14020.20	13401.05	11749.61	11130.05	10871.11	10758.06	10707.76	10685.19
820 000	14370.71	13736.08	12043.35	11408.30	11142.89	11027.01	10975.45	10952.32
840 000	14721.21	14071.10	12337.09	11686.55	11414.67	11295.96	11243.14	11219.45
860 000	15071.72	14406.13	12630.83	11964.80	11686.44	11564.91	11510.84	11486.58
880 000	15422.02	14741.15	12924.57	12243.05	11958.22	11833.86	11778.53	11753.71
900 000	15772.73	15076.18	13218.31	12521.30	12230.00	12102.81	12046.22	12020.84
920 000	16123.23	15411.21	13512.05	12799.55	12501.78	12371.76	12313.92	12287.97
940 000	16473.74	15746.23	13805.79	13077.81	12773.56	12640.72	12581.61	12555.10
960 000	16824.24	16081.26	14099.53	13356.06	13045.33	12909.67	12849.31	12822.23
980 000	17174.75	16416.29	14393.27	13634.31	13317.11	13178.62	13117.00	13089.36
1000 000	17525.25	16751.31	14687.01	13912.56	13588.89	13447.57	13384.69	13356.49
Coefficient	.017525251	.016751312	.014687008	.013912559	.013588889	.013447570	.013384694	.013356485

91

16.25% MONTHLY AMORTIZING PAYMENTS

AMOUNT	1 YEAR	2 YEARS	3 YEARS	4 YEARS	5 YEARS	6 YEARS	7 YEARS	8 YEARS
10 000	908.49	490.83	352.81	284.68	244.51	218.30	200.05	186.76
20 000	1816.98	981.65	705.61	569.37	489.02	436.59	400.09	373.52
30 000	2725.48	1472.48	1058.42	854.05	733.53	654.89	600.14	560.28
40 000	3633.97	1963.31	1411.22	1138.74	978.04	873.19	800.19	747.04
50 000	4542.46	2454.13	1764.03	1423.42	1222.55	1091.49	1000.24	933.80
60 000	5450.95	2944.96	2116.84	1708.11	1467.07	1309.78	1200.28	1120.57
70 000	6359.44	3435.79	2469.64	1992.79	1711.58	1528.08	1400.33	1307.33
80 000	7267.94	3926.61	2822.45	2277.48	1956.09	1746.38	1600.38	1494.09
90 000	8176.43	4417.44	3175.25	2562.16	2200.60	1964.67	1800.42	1680.85
100 000	9084.92	4908.26	3528.06	2846.85	2445.11	2182.97	2000.47	1867.61
110 000	9993.41	5399.09	3880.86	3131.53	2689.62	2401.27	2200.52	2054.37
120 000	10901.90	5889.92	4233.67	3416.22	2934.13	2619.57	2400.57	2241.13
130 000	11810.40	6380.74	4586.48	3700.90	3178.64	2837.86	2600.61	2427.89
140 000	12718.89	6871.57	4939.28	3985.59	3423.15	3056.16	2800.66	2614.65
150 000	13627.38	7362.40	5292.09	4270.27	3667.66	3274.46	3000.71	2801.41
160 000	14535.87	7853.22	5644.89	4554.96	3912.17	3492.75	3200.75	2988.17
170 000	15444.37	8344.05	5997.70	4839.64	4156.69	3711.05	3400.80	3174.94
180 000	16352.86	8834.88	6350.51	5124.33	4401.20	3929.35	3600.85	3361.70
190 000	17261.35	9325.70	6703.31	5409.01	4645.71	4147.65	3800.90	3548.46
200 000	18169.84	9816.53	7056.12	5693.70	4890.22	4365.94	4000.94	3735.22
210 000	19078.33	10307.36	7408.92	5978.38	5134.73	4584.24	4200.99	3921.98
220 000	19986.83	10798.18	7761.73	6263.07	5379.24	4802.54	4401.04	4108.74
230 000	20895.32	11289.01	8114.53	6547.75	5623.75	5020.84	4601.08	4295.50
240 000	21803.81	11779.83	8467.34	6832.44	5868.26	5239.13	4801.13	4482.26
250 000	22712.30	12270.66	8820.15	7117.12	6112.77	5457.43	5001.18	4669.02
260 000	23620.79	12761.49	9172.95	7401.81	6357.28	5675.73	5201.23	4855.78
270 000	24529.29	13252.31	9525.76	7686.49	6601.79	5894.02	5401.27	5042.54
280 000	25437.78	13743.14	9878.56	7971.17	6846.30	6112.32	5601.32	5229.31
290 000	26346.27	14233.97	10231.37	8255.86	7090.82	6330.62	5801.37	5416.07
300 000	27254.76	14724.79	10584.18	8540.54	7335.33	6548.92	6001.41	5602.83
320 000	29071.75	15706.45	11289.79	9109.91	7824.35	6985.51	6401.51	5976.35
340 000	30888.73	16688.10	11995.40	9679.28	8313.37	7422.10	6801.60	6349.87
360 000	32705.71	17669.75	12701.01	10248.65	8802.39	7858.70	7201.70	6723.39
380 000	34522.70	18651.40	13406.62	10818.02	9291.41	8295.29	7601.79	7096.91
400 000	36339.68	19633.06	14112.23	11387.39	9780.44	8731.89	8001.89	7470.44
420 000	38156.67	20614.71	14817.85	11956.76	10269.46	9168.48	8401.98	7843.96
440 000	39973.65	21596.36	15523.46	12526.13	10758.48	9605.08	8802.07	8217.48
460 000	41790.63	22578.02	16229.07	13095.50	11247.50	10041.67	9202.17	8591.00
480 000	43607.62	23559.67	16934.68	13664.87	11736.52	10478.26	9602.26	8964.52
500 000	45424.60	24541.32	17640.29	14234.24	12225.54	10914.86	10002.36	9338.05
520 000	47241.59	25522.97	18345.90	14803.61	12714.57	11351.45	10402.45	9711.57
540 000	49058.57	26504.63	19051.52	15372.98	13203.59	11788.05	10802.55	10085.09
560 000	50875.56	27486.28	19757.13	15942.35	13692.61	12224.64	11202.64	10458.61
580 000	52692.54	28467.93	20462.74	16511.72	14181.63	12661.24	11602.73	10832.13
600 000	54509.52	29449.59	21168.35	17081.09	14670.65	13097.83	12002.83	11205.65
620 000	56326.51	30431.24	21873.96	17650.46	15159.68	13534.43	12402.92	11579.18
640 000	58143.49	31412.89	22579.57	18219.83	15648.70	13971.02	12803.02	11952.70
660 000	59960.48	32394.55	23285.19	18789.20	16137.72	14407.61	13203.11	12326.22
680 000	61777.46	33376.20	23990.80	19358.57	16626.74	14844.21	13603.21	12699.74
700 000	63594.44	34357.85	24696.41	19927.94	17115.76	15280.80	14003.30	13073.26
720 000	65411.43	35339.50	25402.02	20497.31	17604.78	15717.40	14403.39	13446.78
740 000	67228.41	36321.16	26107.63	21066.68	18093.81	16153.99	14803.49	13820.31
760 000	69045.40	37302.81	26813.24	21636.05	18582.83	16590.59	15203.58	14193.83
780 000	70862.38	38284.46	27518.86	22205.42	19071.85	17027.18	15603.68	14567.35
800 000	72679.36	39266.12	28224.47	22774.78	19560.87	17463.77	16003.77	14940.87
820 000	74496.35	40247.77	28930.08	23344.15	20049.89	17900.37	16403.87	15314.39
840 000	76313.33	41229.42	29635.69	23913.52	20538.91	18336.96	16803.96	15687.92
860 000	78130.32	42211.07	30341.30	24482.89	21027.94	18773.56	17204.05	16061.44
880 000	79947.30	43192.73	31046.91	25052.26	21516.96	19210.15	17604.15	16434.96
900 000	81764.29	44174.38	31752.53	25621.63	22005.98	19646.75	18004.24	16808.48
920 000	83581.27	45156.03	32458.14	26191.00	22495.00	20083.34	18404.34	17182.00
940 000	85398.25	46137.69	33163.75	26760.37	22984.02	20519.93	18804.43	17555.52
960 000	87215.24	47119.34	33869.36	27329.74	23473.05	20956.53	19204.53	17929.05
980 000	89032.22	48100.99	34574.97	27899.11	23962.07	21393.12	19604.62	18302.57
1000 000	90849.21	49082.64	35280.59	28468.48	24451.09	21829.71	20004.71	18676.09
Coefficient	.090849206	.049082644	.035280585	.028468481	.024451089	.021829718	.020004714	.018676090

92

AMOUNT	9 YEARS	10 YEARS	15 YEARS	20 YEARS	25 YEARS	30 YEARS	35 YEARS	40 YEARS
10 000	176.77	169.07	148.62	141.00	137.85	136.49	135.89	135.63
20 000	353.54	338.15	297.23	282.01	275.71	272.99	271.79	271.26
30 000	530.31	507.22	445.85	423.01	413.56	409.48	407.69	406.89
40 000	707.08	676.30	594.47	564.02	551.42	545.97	543.58	542.52
50 000	883.85	845.37	743.08	705.02	689.27	682.47	679.47	678.15
60 000	1060.62	1014.45	891.70	846.03	827.12	818.96	815.37	813.78
70 000	1237.39	1183.52	1040.32	987.03	964.98	955.45	951.27	949.41
80 000	1414.16	1352.60	1188.93	1128.04	1102.83	1091.95	1087.16	1085.04
90 000	1590.93	1521.67	1337.55	1269.04	1240.69	1228.44	1223.05	1220.67
100 000	1767.71	1690.74	1486.17	1410.05	1378.54	1364.93	1358.95	1356.30
110 000	1944.48	1859.82	1634.78	1551.05	1516.40	1501.43	1494.84	1491.93
120 000	2121.25	2028.89	1783.40	1692.05	1654.25	1637.92	1630.74	1627.56
130 000	2298.02	2197.97	1932.02	1833.06	1792.10	1774.41	1766.64	1763.19
140 000	2474.79	2367.04	2080.64	1974.06	1929.96	1910.91	1902.53	1898.82
150 000	2651.56	2536.12	2229.25	2115.07	2067.81	2047.40	2038.43	2034.45
160 000	2828.33	2705.19	2377.87	2256.07	2205.67	2183.90	2174.32	2170.07
170 000	3005.10	2874.26	2526.49	2397.08	2343.52	2320.39	2310.21	2305.70
180 000	3181.87	3043.34	2675.10	2538.08	2481.37	2456.88	2446.11	2441.33
190 000	3358.64	3212.41	2823.72	2679.09	2619.23	2593.38	2582.00	2576.96
200 000	3535.41	3381.49	2972.34	2820.09	2757.08	2729.87	2717.90	2712.59
210 000	3712.18	3550.56	3120.95	2961.10	2894.94	2866.36	2853.79	2848.22
220 000	3888.95	3719.64	3269.57	3102.10	3032.79	3002.86	2989.69	2983.85
230 000	4065.72	3888.71	3418.19	3243.10	3170.64	3139.35	3125.58	3119.48
240 000	4242.49	4057.79	3566.80	3384.11	3308.50	3275.84	3261.48	3255.11
250 000	4419.26	4226.86	3715.42	3525.11	3446.35	3412.34	3397.38	3390.74
260 000	4596.03	4395.93	3864.04	3666.12	3584.21	3548.83	3533.27	3526.37
270 000	4772.80	4565.01	4012.65	3807.12	3722.06	3685.32	3669.17	3662.00
280 000	4949.58	4734.08	4161.27	3948.13	3859.92	3821.82	3805.06	3797.63
290 000	5126.35	4903.16	4309.89	4089.13	3997.77	3958.31	3940.96	3933.26
300 000	5303.12	5072.23	4458.50	4230.14	4135.62	4094.80	4076.85	4068.89
320 000	5656.66	5410.38	4755.74	4512.15	4411.33	4367.79	4348.64	4340.15
340 000	6010.20	5748.53	5052.97	4794.15	4687.04	4640.78	4620.43	4611.41
360 000	6363.74	6086.68	5350.21	5076.16	4962.75	4913.76	4892.22	4882.67
380 000	6717.28	6424.83	5647.44	5358.17	5238.46	5186.75	5164.01	5153.93
400 000	7070.82	6762.98	5944.67	5640.18	5514.17	5459.74	5435.80	5425.19
420 000	7424.36	7101.13	6241.91	5922.19	5789.87	5732.73	5707.59	5696.45
440 000	7777.90	7439.27	6539.14	6204.20	6065.58	6005.71	5979.38	5967.71
460 000	8131.45	7777.42	6836.37	6486.21	6341.29	6278.70	6251.17	6238.96
480 000	8484.99	8115.57	7133.61	6768.22	6617.00	6551.69	6522.96	6510.22
500 000	8838.53	8453.72	7430.84	7050.23	6892.71	6824.67	6794.75	6781.48
520 000	9192.07	8791.87	7728.07	7332.24	7168.41	7097.66	7066.54	7052.74
540 000	9545.61	9130.02	8025.31	7614.25	7444.12	7370.65	7338.33	7324.00
560 000	9899.15	9468.17	8322.54	7896.25	7719.83	7643.63	7610.12	7595.26
580 000	10252.69	9806.32	8619.77	8178.26	7995.54	7916.62	7881.91	7866.52
600 000	10606.23	10144.46	8917.01	8460.27	8271.25	8189.61	8153.70	8137.78
620 000	10959.77	10482.61	9214.24	8742.28	8546.96	8462.59	8425.49	8409.04
640 000	11313.32	10820.76	9511.48	9024.29	8822.66	8735.58	8697.28	8680.30
660 000	11666.86	11158.91	9808.71	9306.30	9098.37	9008.57	8969.07	8951.56
680 000	12020.40	11497.06	10105.94	9588.31	9374.08	9281.56	9240.86	9222.82
700 000	12373.94	11835.21	10403.18	9870.32	9649.79	9554.54	9512.65	9494.08
720 000	12727.48	12173.36	10700.41	10152.33	9925.50	9827.53	9784.44	9765.34
740 000	13081.02	12511.51	10997.64	10434.34	10201.21	10100.52	10056.23	10036.60
760 000	13434.56	12849.66	11294.88	10716.35	10476.91	10373.50	10328.02	10307.85
780 000	13788.10	13187.80	11592.11	10998.35	10752.62	10646.49	10599.81	10579.11
800 000	14141.64	13525.95	11889.34	11280.36	11028.33	10919.48	10871.60	10850.37
820 000	14495.19	13864.10	12186.58	11562.37	11304.04	11192.46	11143.39	11121.63
840 000	14848.73	14202.25	12483.81	11844.38	11579.75	11465.45	11415.18	11392.89
860 000	15202.27	14540.40	12781.05	12126.39	11855.46	11738.44	11686.97	11664.15
880 000	15555.81	14878.55	13078.28	12408.40	12131.16	12011.42	11958.76	11935.41
900 000	15909.35	15216.70	13375.51	12690.41	12406.87	12284.41	12230.55	12206.67
920 000	16262.89	15554.85	13672.75	12972.42	12682.58	12557.40	12502.34	12477.93
940 000	16616.43	15892.99	13969.98	13254.43	12958.29	12830.39	12774.13	12749.19
960 000	16969.97	16231.14	14267.21	13536.44	13234.00	13103.37	13045.92	13020.45
980 000	17323.51	16569.29	14564.45	13818.45	13509.70	13376.36	13317.71	13291.71
1000 000	17677.06	16907.44	14861.68	14100.45	13785.41	13649.35	13589.50	13562.97
Coefficient	.017677055	.016907441	.014861681	.014100455	.013785413	.013649346	.013589500	.013562967

AMOUNT	1 YEAR	2 YEARS	3 YEARS	4 YEARS	5 YEARS	6 YEARS	7 YEARS	8 YEARS
10 000	909.68	492.02	354.04	285.97	245.85	219.68	201.48	188.24
20 000	1819.35	984.05	708.09	571.94	491.69	439.36	402.96	376.48
30 000	2729.03	1476.07	1062.13	857.91	737.54	659.04	604.44	564.72
40 000	3638.71	1968.09	1416.18	1143.88	983.38	878.72	805.92	752.96
50 000	4548.38	2460.12	1770.22	1429.85	1229.23	1098.40	1007.39	941.20
60 000	5458.06	2952.14	2124.26	1715.82	1475.07	1318.08	1208.87	1129.44
70 000	6367.73	3444.16	2478.31	2001.79	1720.92	1537.76	1410.35	1317.68
80 000	7277.41	3936.19	2832.35	2287.76	1966.76	1757.44	1611.83	1505.92
90 000	8187.09	4428.21	3186.39	2573.73	2212.61	1977.13	1813.31	1694.16
100 000	9096.76	4920.24	3540.44	2859.70	2458.45	2196.81	2014.79	1882.40
110 000	10006.44	5412.26	3894.48	3145.67	2704.30	2416.49	2216.27	2070.64
120 000	10916.12	5904.28	4248.53	3431.64	2950.14	2636.17	2417.75	2258.88
130 000	11825.79	6396.31	4602.57	3717.61	3195.99	2855.85	2619.23	2447.12
140 000	12735.47	6888.33	4956.61	4003.58	3441.83	3075.53	2820.70	2635.36
150 000	13645.15	7380.35	5310.66	4289.55	3687.68	3295.21	3022.18	2823.60
160 000	14554.82	7872.38	5664.70	4575.52	3933.52	3514.89	3223.66	3011.84
170 000	15464.50	8364.40	6018.74	4861.49	4179.37	3734.57	3425.14	3200.08
180 000	16374.17	8856.42	6372.79	5147.46	4425.21	3954.25	3626.62	3388.31
190 000	17283.85	9348.45	6726.83	5433.43	4671.06	4173.93	3828.10	3576.55
200 000	18193.53	9840.47	7080.88	5719.40	4916.90	4393.61	4029.58	3764.79
210 000	19103.20	10332.49	7434.92	6005.37	5162.75	4613.29	4231.06	3953.03
220 000	20012.88	10824.52	7788.96	6291.34	5408.59	4832.97	4432.54	4141.27
230 000	20922.56	11316.54	8143.01	6577.31	5654.44	5052.65	4634.01	4329.51
240 000	21832.23	11808.56	8497.05	6863.28	5900.28	5272.33	4835.49	4517.75
250 000	22741.91	12300.59	8851.10	7149.25	6146.13	5492.01	5036.97	4705.99
260 000	23651.59	12792.61	9205.14	7435.22	6391.98	5711.70	5238.45	4894.23
270 000	24561.26	13284.64	9559.18	7721.19	6637.82	5931.38	5439.93	5082.47
280 000	25470.94	13776.66	9913.23	8007.16	6883.67	6151.06	5641.41	5270.71
290 000	26380.61	14268.68	10267.27	8293.13	7129.51	6370.74	5842.89	5458.95
300 000	27290.29	14760.71	10621.31	8579.10	7375.36	6590.42	6044.37	5647.19
320 000	29109.64	15744.75	11329.40	9151.04	7867.05	7029.78	6447.32	6023.67
340 000	30929.00	16728.80	12037.49	9722.98	8358.74	7469.14	6850.28	6400.15
360 000	32748.35	17712.85	12745.58	10294.92	8850.43	7908.50	7253.24	6776.63
380 000	34567.70	18696.89	13453.67	10866.86	9342.12	8347.86	7656.20	7153.11
400 000	36387.05	19680.94	14161.75	11438.80	9833.81	8787.22	8059.16	7529.59
420 000	38206.41	20664.99	14869.84	12010.74	10325.50	9226.58	8462.11	7906.07
440 000	40025.76	21649.04	15577.93	12582.68	10817.19	9665.95	8865.07	8282.55
460 000	41845.11	22633.08	16286.02	13154.62	11308.88	10105.31	9268.03	8659.03
480 000	43664.47	23617.13	16994.10	13726.56	11800.57	10544.67	9670.99	9035.51
500 000	45483.82	24601.18	17702.19	14298.50	12292.26	10984.03	10073.94	9411.99
520 000	47303.17	25585.22	18410.28	14870.44	12783.95	11423.39	10476.90	9788.46
540 000	49122.52	26569.27	19118.37	15442.38	13275.64	11862.75	10879.86	10164.94
560 000	50941.88	27553.32	19826.45	16014.33	13767.33	12302.11	11282.82	10541.42
580 000	52761.23	28537.36	20534.54	16586.27	14259.02	12741.47	11685.78	10917.90
600 000	54580.58	29521.41	21242.63	17158.21	14750.71	13180.83	12088.73	11294.38
620 000	56399.93	30505.46	21950.72	17730.15	15242.40	13620.20	12491.69	11670.86
640 000	58219.29	31489.51	22658.80	18302.09	15734.09	14059.56	12894.65	12047.34
660 000	60038.64	32473.55	23366.89	18874.03	16225.78	14498.92	13297.61	12423.82
680 000	61857.99	33457.60	24074.98	19445.97	16717.47	14938.28	13700.56	12800.30
700 000	63677.35	34441.65	24783.07	20017.91	17209.16	15377.64	14103.52	13176.78
720 000	65496.70	35425.69	25491.16	20589.85	17700.85	15817.00	14506.48	13553.26
740 000	67316.05	36409.74	26199.24	21161.79	18192.54	16256.36	14909.44	13929.74
760 000	69135.40	37393.79	26907.33	21733.73	18684.24	16695.72	15312.40	14306.22
780 000	70954.76	38377.84	27615.42	22305.67	19175.93	17135.09	15715.35	14682.70
800 000	72774.11	39361.88	28323.51	22877.61	19667.62	17574.45	16118.31	15059.18
820 000	74593.46	40345.93	29031.59	23449.55	20159.31	18013.81	16521.27	15435.66
840 000	76412.82	41329.98	29739.68	24021.49	20651.00	18453.17	16924.23	15812.14
860 000	78232.17	42314.02	30447.77	24593.43	21142.69	18892.53	17327.18	16188.62
880 000	80051.52	43298.07	31155.86	25165.37	21634.38	19331.89	17730.14	16565.09
900 000	81870.87	44282.12	31863.94	25737.31	22126.07	19771.25	18133.10	16941.57
920 000	83690.23	45266.16	32572.03	26309.25	22617.76	20210.61	18536.06	17318.05
940 000	85509.58	46250.21	33280.12	26881.19	23109.45	20649.97	18939.02	17694.53
960 000	87328.93	47234.26	33988.21	27453.13	23601.14	21089.34	19341.97	18071.01
980 000	89148.28	48218.31	34696.29	28025.07	24092.83	21528.70	19744.93	18447.49
1000 000	90967.64	49202.35	35404.38	28597.01	24584.52	21968.06	20147.89	18823.97
Coefficient	.090967637	.049202353	.035404382	.028597009	.024584520	.021968058	.020147889	.018823971

MONTHLY AMORTIZING PAYMENTS 16.50%

AMOUNT	9 YEARS	10 YEARS	15 YEARS	20 YEARS	25 YEARS	30 YEARS	35 YEARS	40 YEARS
10 000	178.29	170.64	150.37	142.89	139.82	138.51	137.95	137.70
20 000	356.59	341.28	300.74	285.78	279.65	277.03	275.89	275.39
30 000	534.88	511.93	451.11	428.67	419.47	415.54	413.84	413.09
40 000	713.18	682.57	601.48	571.56	559.30	554.06	551.78	550.78
50 000	891.47	853.21	751.85	714.45	699.12	692.57	689.73	688.48
60 000	1069.77	1023.85	902.23	857.34	838.95	831.09	827.67	826.18
70 000	1248.06	1194.50	1052.60	1000.23	978.77	969.60	965.62	963.87
80 000	1426.36	1365.14	1202.97	1143.12	1118.60	1108.12	1103.56	1101.57
90 000	1604.65	1535.78	1353.34	1286.01	1258.42	1246.63	1241.51	1239.26
100 000	1782.95	1706.42	1503.71	1428.90	1398.24	1385.15	1379.45	1376.96
110 000	1961.24	1877.07	1654.08	1571.79	1538.07	1523.66	1517.40	1514.66
120 000	2139.54	2047.71	1804.45	1714.68	1677.89	1662.18	1655.34	1652.35
130 000	2317.83	2218.35	1954.82	1857.57	1817.72	1800.69	1793.29	1790.05
140 000	2496.13	2388.99	2105.19	2000.46	1957.54	1939.21	1931.24	1927.74
150 000	2674.42	2559.63	2255.56	2143.35	2097.37	2077.72	2069.18	2065.44
160 000	2852.72	2730.28	2405.93	2286.24	2237.19	2216.24	2207.13	2203.13
170 000	3031.01	2900.92	2556.30	2429.13	2377.02	2354.75	2345.07	2340.83
180 000	3209.31	3071.56	2706.68	2572.02	2516.84	2493.27	2483.02	2478.53
190 000	3387.60	3242.20	2857.05	2714.91	2656.66	2631.78	2620.96	2616.22
200 000	3565.90	3412.85	3007.42	2857.80	2796.49	2770.30	2758.91	2753.92
210 000	3744.19	3583.49	3157.79	3000.69	2936.31	2908.81	2896.85	2891.61
220 000	3922.49	3754.13	3308.16	3143.58	3076.14	3047.33	3034.80	3029.31
230 000	4100.78	3924.77	3458.53	3286.47	3215.96	3185.84	3172.74	3167.01
240 000	4279.08	4095.42	3608.90	3429.36	3355.79	3324.36	3310.69	3304.70
250 000	4457.37	4266.06	3759.27	3572.25	3495.61	3462.87	3448.63	3442.40
260 000	4635.67	4436.70	3909.64	3715.14	3635.44	3601.39	3586.58	3580.09
270 000	4813.96	4607.34	4060.01	3858.03	3775.26	3739.90	3724.53	3717.79
280 000	4992.26	4777.98	4210.38	4000.92	3915.08	3878.41	3862.47	3855.49
290 000	5170.55	4948.63	4360.75	4143.81	4054.91	4016.93	4000.42	3993.18
300 000	5348.84	5119.27	4511.13	4286.70	4194.73	4155.44	4138.36	4130.88
320 000	5705.43	5460.55	4811.87	4572.48	4474.38	4432.47	4414.25	4406.27
340 000	6062.02	5801.84	5112.61	4858.26	4754.03	4709.50	4690.14	4681.66
360 000	6418.61	6143.12	5413.35	5144.04	5033.68	4986.53	4966.03	4957.05
380 000	6775.20	6484.41	5714.09	5429.82	5313.33	5263.56	5241.92	5232.45
400 000	7131.79	6825.69	6014.83	5715.60	5592.98	5540.59	5517.82	5507.84
420 000	7488.38	7166.98	6315.58	6001.38	5872.63	5817.62	5793.71	5783.23
440 000	7844.97	7508.26	6616.32	6287.16	6152.28	6094.65	6069.60	6058.62
460 000	8201.56	7849.55	6917.06	6572.94	6431.93	6371.68	6345.49	6334.01
480 000	8558.15	8190.83	7217.80	6858.72	6711.57	6648.71	6621.38	6609.40
500 000	8914.74	8532.12	7518.54	7144.50	6991.22	6925.74	6897.27	6884.80
520 000	9271.33	8873.40	7819.28	7430.28	7270.87	7202.77	7173.16	7160.19
540 000	9627.92	9214.68	8120.03	7716.06	7550.52	7479.80	7449.05	7435.58
560 000	9984.51	9555.97	8420.77	8001.84	7830.17	7756.83	7724.94	7710.97
580 000	10341.10	9897.25	8721.51	8287.62	8109.82	8033.86	8000.83	7986.36
600 000	10697.69	10238.54	9022.25	8573.40	8389.47	8310.89	8276.72	8261.76
620 000	11054.28	10579.82	9322.99	8859.18	8669.12	8587.92	8552.61	8537.15
640 000	11410.87	10921.11	9623.74	9144.96	8948.77	8864.95	8828.50	8812.54
660 000	11767.46	11262.39	9924.48	9430.74	9228.41	9141.98	9104.40	9087.93
680 000	12124.05	11603.68	10225.22	9716.52	9508.06	9419.01	9380.29	9363.32
700 000	12480.64	11944.96	10525.96	10002.30	9787.71	9696.04	9656.18	9638.72
720 000	12837.23	12286.25	10826.70	10288.08	10067.36	9973.07	9932.07	9914.11
740 000	13193.82	12627.53	11127.44	10573.86	10347.01	10250.10	10207.96	10189.50
760 000	13550.41	12968.81	11428.19	10859.64	10626.66	10527.13	10483.85	10464.89
780 000	13907.00	13310.10	11728.93	11145.42	10906.31	10804.16	10759.74	10740.28
800 000	14263.59	13651.38	12029.67	11431.20	11185.96	11081.18	11035.63	11015.67
820 000	14620.18	13992.67	12330.41	11716.98	11465.61	11358.21	11311.52	11291.07
840 000	14976.77	14333.95	12631.15	12002.77	11745.25	11635.24	11587.41	11566.46
860 000	15333.36	14675.24	12931.89	12288.55	12024.90	11912.27	11863.30	11841.85
880 000	15689.95	15016.52	13232.64	12574.33	12304.55	12189.30	12139.19	12117.24
900 000	16046.53	15357.81	13533.38	12860.11	12584.20	12466.33	12415.09	12392.63
920 000	16403.12	15699.09	13834.12	13145.89	12863.85	12743.36	12690.98	12668.03
940 000	16759.71	16040.38	14134.86	13431.67	13143.50	13020.39	12966.87	12943.42
960 000	17116.30	16381.66	14435.60	13717.45	13423.15	13297.42	13242.76	13218.81
980 000	17472.89	16722.95	14736.34	14003.23	13702.80	13574.45	13518.65	13494.20
1000 000	17829.48	17064.23	15037.09	14289.01	13982.45	13851.48	13794.54	13769.59
Coefficient	.017829483	.017064230	.015037086	.014289006	.013982446	.013851481	.013794539	.013769593

95

MONTHLY AMORTIZING PAYMENTS

AMOUNT	1 YEAR	2 YEARS	3 YEARS	4 YEARS	5 YEARS	6 YEARS	7 YEARS	8 YEARS
10 000	910.86	493.22	355.28	287.26	247.18	221.07	202.92	189.72
20 000	1821.72	986.44	710.57	574.52	494.37	442.14	405.83	379.45
30 000	2732.58	1479.67	1065.85	861.78	741.55	663.21	608.75	569.17
40 000	3643.45	1972.89	1421.14	1149.03	988.73	884.27	811.66	758.90
50 000	4554.31	2466.11	1776.42	1436.29	1235.92	1105.34	1014.58	948.62
60 000	5465.17	2959.33	2131.71	1723.55	1483.10	1326.41	1217.50	1138.35
70 000	6376.03	3452.56	2486.99	2010.81	1730.28	1547.48	1420.41	1328.07
80 000	7286.89	3945.78	2842.27	2298.07	1977.47	1768.55	1623.33	1517.79
90 000	8197.75	4439.00	3197.56	2585.33	2224.65	1989.62	1826.24	1707.52
100 000	9108.62	4932.22	3552.84	2872.59	2471.84	2210.69	2029.16	1897.24
110 000	10019.48	5425.44	3908.13	3159.84	2719.02	2431.76	2232.07	2086.97
120 000	10930.34	5918.67	4263.41	3447.10	2966.20	2652.82	2434.99	2276.69
130 000	11841.20	6411.89	4618.70	3734.36	3213.39	2873.89	2637.91	2466.42
140 000	12752.06	6905.11	4973.98	4021.62	3460.57	3094.96	2840.82	2656.14
150 000	13662.92	7398.33	5329.26	4308.88	3707.75	3316.03	3043.74	2845.86
160 000	14573.79	7891.56	5684.55	4596.14	3954.94	3537.10	3246.65	3035.59
170 000	15484.65	8384.78	6039.83	4883.40	4202.12	3758.17	3449.57	3225.31
180 000	16395.51	8878.00	6395.12	5170.66	4449.30	3979.24	3652.49	3415.04
190 000	17306.37	9371.22	6750.40	5457.91	4696.49	4200.30	3855.40	3604.76
200 000	18217.23	9864.44	7105.69	5745.17	4943.67	4421.37	4058.32	3794.49
210 000	19128.09	10357.67	7460.97	6032.43	5190.85	4642.44	4261.23	3984.21
220 000	20038.95	10850.89	7816.25	6319.69	5438.04	4863.51	4464.15	4173.93
230 000	20949.82	11344.11	8171.54	6606.95	5685.22	5084.58	4667.07	4363.66
240 000	21860.68	11837.33	8526.82	6894.21	5932.40	5305.65	4869.98	4553.38
250 000	22771.54	12330.56	8882.11	7181.47	6179.59	5526.72	5072.90	4743.11
260 000	23682.40	12823.78	9237.39	7468.72	6426.77	5747.78	5275.81	4932.83
270 000	24593.26	13317.00	9592.68	7755.98	6673.95	5968.85	5478.73	5122.56
280 000	25504.12	13810.22	9947.96	8043.24	6921.14	6189.92	5681.64	5312.28
290 000	26414.99	14303.44	10303.24	8330.50	7168.32	6410.99	5884.56	5502.00
300 000	27325.85	14796.67	10658.53	8617.76	7415.51	6632.06	6087.48	5691.73
320 000	29147.57	15783.11	11369.10	9192.28	7909.87	7074.20	6493.31	6071.18
340 000	30969.29	16769.56	12079.67	9766.79	8404.24	7516.33	6899.14	6450.63
360 000	32791.02	17756.00	12790.23	10341.31	8898.61	7958.47	7304.97	6830.07
380 000	34612.74	18742.45	13500.80	10915.83	9392.97	8400.61	7710.80	7209.52
400 000	36434.46	19728.89	14211.37	11490.35	9887.34	8842.75	8116.63	7588.97
420 000	38256.19	20715.33	14921.94	12064.86	10381.71	9284.88	8522.47	7968.42
440 000	40077.91	21701.78	15632.51	12639.38	10876.07	9727.02	8928.30	8347.87
460 000	41899.63	22688.22	16343.08	13213.90	11370.44	10169.16	9334.13	8727.32
480 000	43721.36	23674.67	17053.65	13788.41	11864.81	10611.30	9739.96	9106.76
500 000	45543.08	24661.11	17764.21	14362.93	12359.18	11053.43	10145.79	9486.21
520 000	47364.80	25647.56	18474.78	14937.45	12853.54	11495.57	10551.63	9865.66
540 000	49186.53	26634.00	19185.35	15511.97	13347.91	11937.71	10957.46	10245.11
560 000	51008.25	27620.45	19895.92	16086.48	13842.28	12379.84	11363.29	10624.56
580 000	52829.97	28606.89	20606.49	16661.00	14336.64	12821.98	11769.12	11004.01
600 000	54651.69	29593.33	21317.06	17235.52	14831.01	13264.12	12174.95	11383.46
620 000	56473.42	30579.78	22027.63	17810.04	15325.38	13706.26	12580.78	11762.90
640 000	58295.14	31566.22	22738.19	18384.55	15819.74	14148.39	12986.62	12142.35
660 000	60116.86	32552.67	23448.76	18959.07	16314.11	14590.53	13392.45	12521.80
680 000	61938.59	33539.11	24159.33	19533.59	16808.48	15032.67	13798.28	12901.25
700 000	63760.31	34525.56	24869.90	20108.10	17302.85	15474.81	14204.11	13280.70
720 000	65582.03	35512.00	25580.47	20682.62	17797.21	15916.94	14609.94	13660.15
740 000	67403.76	36498.45	26291.04	21257.14	18291.58	16359.08	15015.77	14039.60
760 000	69225.48	37484.89	27001.61	21831.66	18785.95	16801.22	15421.61	14419.04
780 000	71047.20	38471.33	27712.17	22406.17	19280.31	17243.35	15827.44	14798.49
800 000	72868.93	39457.78	28422.74	22980.69	19774.68	17685.49	16233.27	15177.94
820 000	74690.65	40444.22	29133.31	23555.21	20269.05	18127.63	16639.10	15557.39
840 000	76512.37	41430.67	29843.88	24129.72	20763.41	18569.77	17044.93	15936.84
860 000	78334.10	42417.11	30554.45	24704.24	21257.78	19011.90	17450.76	16316.29
880 000	80155.82	43403.56	31265.02	25278.76	21752.15	19454.04	17856.60	16695.74
900 000	81977.54	44390.00	31975.59	25853.28	22246.52	19896.18	18262.43	17075.18
920 000	83799.27	45376.45	32686.15	26427.79	22740.88	20338.32	18668.26	17454.63
940 000	85620.99	46362.89	33396.72	27002.31	23235.25	20780.45	19074.09	17834.08
960 000	87442.71	47349.34	34107.29	27576.83	23729.62	21222.59	19479.92	18213.53
980 000	89264.43	48335.78	34817.86	28151.35	24223.98	21664.73	19885.75	18592.98
1000 000	91086.16	49322.22	35528.43	28725.86	24718.35	22106.87	20291.59	18972.43
Coefficient	.091086158	.049322224	.035528429	.028725863	.024718350	.022106865	.020291587	.018972427

MONTHLY AMORTIZING PAYMENTS 16.75%

AMOUNT	9 YEARS	10 YEARS	15 YEARS	20 YEARS	25 YEARS	30 YEARS	35 YEARS	40 YEARS
10 000	179.83	172.22	152.13	144.78	141.80	140.54	140.00	139.76
20 000	359.65	344.43	304.26	289.56	283.60	281.08	280.00	279.53
30 000	539.48	516.65	456.40	434.35	425.40	421.62	419.99	419.29
40 000	719.30	688.87	608.53	579.13	567.20	562.16	559.99	559.05
50 000	899.13	861.08	760.66	723.91	709.00	702.70	699.99	698.82
60 000	1078.95	1033.30	912.79	868.69	850.80	843.24	839.99	838.58
70 000	1258.78	1205.52	1064.92	1013.47	992.60	983.78	979.99	978.34
80 000	1438.60	1377.73	1217.06	1158.26	1134.40	1124.32	1119.98	1118.11
90 000	1618.43	1549.95	1369.19	1303.04	1276.20	1264.86	1259.98	1257.87
100 000	1798.25	1722.17	1521.32	1447.82	1418.00	1405.40	1399.98	1397.64
110 000	1978.08	1894.38	1673.45	1592.60	1559.80	1545.94	1539.98	1537.40
120 000	2157.90	2066.60	1825.59	1737.38	1701.60	1686.47	1679.98	1677.16
130 000	2337.73	2238.82	1977.72	1882.17	1843.40	1827.01	1819.97	1816.93
140 000	2517.55	2411.03	2129.85	2026.95	1985.20	1967.55	1959.97	1956.69
150 000	2697.38	2583.25	2281.98	2171.73	2127.00	2108.09	2099.97	2096.45
160 000	2877.20	2755.47	2434.11	2316.51	2268.80	2248.63	2239.97	2236.22
170 000	3057.03	2927.68	2586.25	2461.29	2410.60	2389.17	2379.97	2375.98
180 000	3236.86	3099.90	2738.38	2606.08	2552.39	2529.71	2519.96	2515.74
190 000	3416.68	3272.12	2890.51	2750.86	2694.19	2670.25	2659.96	2655.51
200 000	3596.51	3444.33	3042.64	2895.64	2835.99	2810.79	2799.96	2795.27
210 000	3776.33	3616.55	3194.77	3040.42	2977.79	2951.33	2939.96	2935.03
220 000	3956.16	3788.77	3346.91	3185.20	3119.59	3091.87	3079.96	3074.80
230 000	4135.98	3960.98	3499.04	3329.99	3261.39	3232.41	3219.95	3214.56
240 000	4315.81	4133.20	3651.17	3474.77	3403.19	3372.95	3359.95	3354.32
250 000	4495.63	4305.42	3803.30	3619.55	3544.99	3513.49	3499.95	3494.09
260 000	4675.46	4477.63	3955.43	3764.33	3686.79	3654.03	3639.95	3633.85
270 000	4855.28	4649.85	4107.57	3909.11	3828.59	3794.57	3779.95	3773.62
280 000	5035.11	4822.07	4259.70	4053.89	3970.39	3935.11	3919.94	3913.38
290 000	5214.93	4994.29	4411.83	4198.68	4112.19	4075.65	4059.94	4053.14
300 000	5394.76	5166.50	4563.96	4343.46	4253.99	4216.19	4199.94	4192.91
320 000	5754.41	5510.94	4868.23	4633.02	4537.59	4497.27	4479.94	4472.43
340 000	6114.06	5855.37	5172.49	4922.59	4821.19	4778.35	4759.93	4751.96
360 000	6473.71	6199.80	5476.76	5212.15	5104.79	5059.42	5039.93	5031.49
380 000	6833.36	6544.24	5781.02	5501.71	5388.39	5340.50	5319.92	5311.01
400 000	7193.01	6888.67	6085.28	5791.28	5671.99	5621.58	5599.92	5590.54
420 000	7552.66	7233.10	6389.55	6080.84	5955.59	5902.66	5879.92	5870.07
440 000	7912.31	7577.54	6693.81	6370.41	6239.19	6183.74	6159.91	6149.60
460 000	8271.96	7921.97	6998.08	6659.97	6522.79	6464.82	6439.91	6429.12
480 000	8631.61	8266.40	7302.34	6949.53	6806.39	6745.90	6719.90	6708.65
500 000	8991.26	8610.84	7606.61	7239.10	7089.99	7026.98	6999.90	6988.18
520 000	9350.91	8955.27	7910.87	7528.66	7373.58	7308.05	7279.89	7267.70
540 000	9710.57	9299.70	8215.13	7818.23	7657.18	7589.14	7559.89	7547.23
560 000	10070.22	9644.14	8519.40	8107.79	7940.78	7870.22	7839.89	7826.76
580 000	10429.87	9988.57	8823.66	8397.35	8224.38	8151.29	8119.88	8106.28
600 000	10789.52	10333.00	9127.93	8686.92	8507.98	8432.37	8399.88	8385.81
620 000	11149.17	10677.44	9432.19	8976.48	8791.58	8713.45	8679.87	8665.34
640 000	11508.82	11021.87	9736.46	9266.05	9075.18	8994.53	8959.87	8944.87
660 000	11868.47	11366.30	10040.72	9555.61	9358.78	9275.61	9239.87	9224.39
680 000	12228.12	11710.74	10344.98	9845.17	9642.38	9556.69	9519.86	9503.92
700 000	12587.77	12055.17	10649.25	10134.74	9925.98	9837.77	9799.86	9783.45
720 000	12947.42	12399.60	10953.51	10424.30	10209.58	10118.85	10079.86	10062.97
740 000	13307.07	12744.04	11257.78	10713.87	10493.18	10399.93	10359.85	10342.50
760 000	13666.72	13088.47	11562.04	11003.43	10776.78	10681.01	10639.85	10622.03
780 000	14026.37	13432.90	11866.30	11292.99	11060.38	10962.09	10919.84	10901.56
800 000	14386.02	13777.34	12170.57	11582.56	11343.98	11243.16	11199.84	11181.08
820 000	14745.67	14121.77	12474.83	11872.12	11627.58	11524.24	11479.83	11460.61
840 000	15105.32	14466.21	12779.10	12161.68	11911.18	11805.32	11759.83	11740.14
860 000	15464.97	14810.64	13083.36	12451.25	12194.78	12086.40	12039.83	12019.66
880 000	15824.62	15155.07	13387.63	12740.81	12478.37	12367.48	12319.82	12299.19
900 000	16184.28	15499.51	13691.89	13030.38	12761.97	12648.56	12599.82	12578.72
920 000	16543.93	15843.94	13996.15	13319.94	13045.57	12929.64	12879.81	12858.24
940 000	16903.58	16188.37	14300.42	13609.50	13329.17	13210.72	13159.81	13137.77
960 000	17263.23	16532.81	14604.68	13899.07	13612.77	13491.80	13439.81	13417.30
980 000	17622.88	16877.24	14908.95	14188.63	13896.37	13772.88	13719.80	13696.83
1000 000	17982.53	17221.67	15213.21	14478.20	14179.97	14053.96	13999.80	13976.35
Coefficient	.017982528	.017221673	.015213211	.014478196	.014179971	.014053956	.013999798	.013976353

97

AMOUNT	1 YEAR	2 YEARS	3 YEARS	4 YEARS	5 YEARS	6 YEARS	7 YEARS	8 YEARS
10 000	912.05	494.42	356.53	288.55	248.53	222.46	204.36	191.21
20 000	1824.10	988.85	713.05	577.10	497.05	444.92	408.72	382.43
30 000	2736.14	1483.27	1069.58	865.65	745.58	667.38	613.07	573.64
40 000	3648.19	1977.69	1426.11	1154.20	994.10	889.85	817.43	764.86
50 000	4560.24	2472.11	1782.64	1442.75	1242.63	1112.31	1021.79	956.07
60 000	5472.29	2966.54	2139.16	1731.30	1491.15	1334.77	1226.15	1147.29
70 000	6384.33	3460.96	2495.69	2019.85	1739.68	1557.23	1430.51	1338.50
80 000	7296.38	3955.38	2852.22	2308.40	1988.21	1779.69	1634.86	1529.72
90 000	8208.43	4449.80	3208.75	2596.95	2236.73	2002.15	1839.22	1720.93
100 000	9120.48	4944.23	3565.27	2885.50	2485.26	2224.61	2043.58	1912.15
110 000	10032.52	5438.65	3921.80	3174.05	2733.78	2447.07	2247.94	2103.36
120 000	10944.57	5933.07	4278.33	3462.61	2982.31	2669.54	2452.30	2294.57
130 000	11856.62	6427.49	4634.85	3751.16	3230.83	2892.00	2656.65	2485.79
140 000	12768.67	6921.92	4991.38	4039.71	3479.36	3114.46	2861.01	2677.00
150 000	13680.71	7416.34	5347.91	4328.26	3727.89	3336.92	3065.37	2868.22
160 000	14592.76	7910.76	5704.44	4616.81	3976.41	3559.38	3269.73	3059.43
170 000	15504.81	8405.18	6060.96	4905.36	4224.94	3781.84	3474.09	3250.65
180 000	16416.86	8899.61	6417.49	5193.91	4473.46	4004.30	3678.44	3441.86
190 000	17328.90	9394.03	6774.02	5482.46	4721.99	4226.76	3882.80	3633.08
200 000	18240.95	9888.45	7130.55	5771.01	4970.51	4449.23	4087.16	3824.29
210 000	19153.00	10382.88	7487.07	6059.56	5219.04	4671.69	4291.52	4015.51
220 000	20065.05	10877.30	7843.60	6348.11	5467.57	4894.15	4495.88	4206.72
230 000	20977.09	11371.72	8200.13	6636.66	5716.09	5116.61	4700.24	4397.93
240 000	21889.14	11866.14	8556.65	6925.21	5964.62	5339.07	4904.59	4589.15
250 000	22801.19	12360.57	8913.18	7213.76	6213.14	5561.53	5108.95	4780.36
260 000	23713.24	12854.99	9269.71	7502.31	6461.67	5783.99	5313.31	4971.58
270 000	24625.28	13349.41	9626.24	7790.86	6710.20	6006.46	5517.67	5162.79
280 000	25537.33	13843.83	9982.76	8079.41	6958.72	6228.92	5722.03	5354.01
290 000	26449.38	14338.26	10339.29	8367.96	7207.25	6451.38	5926.38	5545.22
300 000	27361.43	14832.68	10695.82	8656.51	7455.77	6673.84	6130.74	5736.44
320 000	29185.52	15821.52	11408.87	9233.61	7952.82	7118.76	6539.46	6118.87
340 000	31009.62	16810.37	12121.93	9810.71	8449.88	7563.68	6948.17	6501.29
360 000	32833.71	17799.22	12834.98	10387.92	8946.93	8008.61	7356.89	6883.72
380 000	34657.81	18788.06	13548.04	10964.92	9443.98	8453.53	7765.61	7266.15
400 000	36481.90	19776.91	14261.09	11542.02	9941.03	8898.45	8174.32	7648.58
420 000	38306.00	20765.75	14974.14	12119.12	10438.08	9343.38	8583.04	8031.01
440 000	40130.09	21754.60	15687.20	12696.22	10935.13	9788.30	8991.75	8413.44
460 000	41954.19	22743.44	16400.25	13273.32	11432.18	10233.22	9400.47	8795.87
480 000	43778.28	23732.29	17113.31	13850.42	11929.24	10678.14	9809.19	9178.30
500 000	45602.38	24721.13	17826.36	14427.52	12426.29	11123.07	10217.90	9560.73
520 000	47426.47	25709.98	18539.42	15004.62	12923.34	11567.99	10626.62	9943.16
540 000	49250.57	26698.82	19252.47	15581.72	13420.39	12012.91	11035.33	10325.59
560 000	51074.67	27687.67	19965.53	16158.83	13917.44	12457.83	11444.05	10708.01
580 000	52898.76	28676.51	20678.58	16735.93	14414.49	12902.76	11852.77	11090.44
600 000	54722.86	29665.36	21391.64	17313.03	14911.54	13347.68	12261.48	11472.87
620 000	56546.95	30654.20	22104.69	17890.13	15408.60	13792.60	12670.20	11855.30
640 000	58371.05	31643.05	22817.74	18467.23	15905.65	14237.52	13078.92	12237.73
660 000	60195.14	32631.89	23530.80	19044.33	16402.70	14682.45	13487.63	12620.16
680 000	62019.24	33620.74	24243.85	19621.43	16899.75	15127.37	13896.35	13002.59
700 000	63843.33	34609.58	24956.91	20198.53	17396.80	15572.29	14305.06	13385.02
720 000	65667.43	35598.43	25669.96	20775.63	17893.85	16017.21	14713.78	13767.45
740 000	67491.52	36587.28	26383.02	21352.73	18390.91	16462.14	15122.50	14149.88
760 000	69315.62	37576.12	27096.07	21929.83	18887.96	16907.06	15531.21	14532.31
780 000	71139.71	38564.97	27809.13	22506.93	19385.01	17351.98	15939.93	14914.73
800 000	72963.81	39553.81	28522.18	23084.03	19882.06	17796.90	16348.64	15297.16
820 000	74787.90	40542.66	29235.24	23661.13	20379.11	18241.83	16757.36	15679.59
840 000	76612.00	41531.50	29948.29	24238.24	20876.16	18686.75	17166.08	16062.02
860 000	78436.09	42520.35	30661.34	24815.34	21373.21	19131.67	17574.79	16444.45
880 000	80260.19	43509.19	31374.40	25392.44	21870.27	19576.60	17983.51	16826.88
900 000	82084.28	44498.04	32087.45	25969.54	22367.32	20021.52	18392.22	17209.31
920 000	83908.38	45486.88	32800.51	26546.64	22864.37	20466.44	18800.94	17591.74
940 000	85732.47	46475.73	33513.56	27123.74	23361.42	20911.36	19209.66	17974.17
960 000	87556.57	47464.57	34226.62	27700.84	23858.47	21356.29	19618.37	18356.60
980 000	89380.66	48453.42	34939.67	28277.94	24355.52	21801.21	20027.09	18739.02
1000 000	91204.76	49442.26	35652.73	28855.04	24852.57	22246.13	20435.80	19121.45
Coefficient	.091204759	.049442264	.035652726	.028855042	.024852575	.022246131	.020435805	.019121454

AMOUNT	9 YEARS	10 YEARS	15 YEARS	20 YEARS	25 YEARS	30 YEARS	35 YEARS	40 YEARS
10 000	181.36	173.80	153.90	146.68	143.78	142.57	142.05	141.83
20 000	362.72	347.60	307.80	293.36	287.56	285.14	284.11	283.66
30 000	544.09	521.39	461.70	440.04	431.34	427.70	426.16	425.50
40 000	725.45	695.19	615.60	586.72	575.12	570.27	568.21	567.33
50 000	906.81	868.99	769.50	733.40	718.90	712.84	710.26	709.16
60 000	1088.17	1042.79	923.40	880.08	862.68	855.41	852.32	850.99
70 000	1269.53	1216.58	1077.30	1026.76	1006.46	997.97	994.37	992.83
80 000	1450.90	1390.38	1231.20	1173.44	1150.24	1140.54	1136.42	1134.66
90 000	1632.26	1564.18	1385.10	1320.12	1294.02	1283.11	1278.47	1276.49
100 000	1813.62	1737.98	1539.00	1466.80	1437.80	1425.68	1420.53	1418.32
110 000	1994.98	1911.77	1692.90	1613.48	1581.58	1568.24	1562.58	1560.16
120 000	2176.34	2085.57	1846.81	1760.16	1725.36	1710.81	1704.63	1701.99
130 000	2357.70	2259.37	2000.71	1906.84	1869.14	1853.38	1846.68	1843.82
140 000	2539.07	2433.17	2154.61	2053.52	2012.92	1995.95	1988.74	1985.65
150 000	2720.43	2606.96	2308.51	2200.20	2156.69	2138.51	2130.79	2127.49
160 000	2901.79	2780.76	2462.41	2346.88	2300.47	2281.08	2272.84	2269.32
170 000	3083.15	2954.56	2616.31	2493.56	2444.25	2423.65	2414.89	2411.15
180 000	3264.51	3128.36	2770.21	2640.24	2588.03	2566.22	2556.95	2552.98
190 000	3445.88	3302.16	2924.11	2786.92	2731.81	2708.78	2699.00	2694.81
200 000	3627.24	3475.95	3078.01	2933.60	2875.59	2851.35	2841.05	2836.65
210 000	3808.60	3649.75	3231.91	3080.28	3019.37	2993.92	2983.11	2978.48
220 000	3989.96	3823.55	3385.81	3226.96	3163.15	3136.49	3125.16	3120.31
230 000	4171.32	3997.35	3539.71	3373.64	3306.93	3279.05	3267.21	3262.14
240 000	4352.69	4171.14	3693.61	3520.32	3450.71	3421.62	3409.26	3403.98
250 000	4534.05	4344.94	3847.51	3667.00	3594.49	3564.19	3551.32	3545.81
260 000	4715.41	4518.74	4001.41	3813.68	3738.27	3706.76	3693.37	3687.64
270 000	4896.77	4692.54	4155.31	3960.36	3882.05	3849.32	3835.42	3829.47
280 000	5078.13	4866.33	4309.21	4107.04	4025.83	3991.89	3977.47	3971.31
290 000	5259.49	5040.13	4463.11	4253.72	4169.61	4134.46	4119.53	4113.14
300 000	5440.86	5213.93	4617.01	4400.40	4313.39	4277.03	4261.58	4254.97
320 000	5803.58	5561.52	4924.81	4693.76	4600.95	4562.16	4545.68	4538.64
340 000	6166.30	5909.12	5232.61	4987.12	4888.51	4847.30	4829.79	4822.30
360 000	6529.03	6256.72	5540.42	5280.48	5176.07	5132.43	5113.89	5105.96
380 000	6891.75	6604.31	5848.22	5573.84	5463.63	5417.57	5398.00	5389.63
400 000	7254.48	6951.91	6156.02	5867.20	5751.19	5702.70	5682.10	5673.29
420 000	7617.20	7299.50	6463.82	6160.56	6038.75	5987.84	5966.21	5956.96
440 000	7979.92	7647.10	6771.62	6453.92	6326.31	6272.97	6250.32	6240.62
460 000	8342.65	7994.69	7079.42	6747.28	6613.86	6558.11	6534.42	6524.29
480 000	8705.37	8342.29	7387.22	7040.64	6901.42	6843.24	6818.53	6807.95
500 000	9068.09	8689.88	7695.02	7334.00	7188.98	7128.38	7102.63	7091.62
520 000	9430.82	9037.48	8002.82	7627.36	7476.54	7413.51	7386.74	7375.28
540 000	9793.54	9385.07	8310.62	7920.72	7764.10	7698.65	7670.84	7658.95
560 000	10156.27	9732.67	8618.42	8214.08	8051.66	7983.78	7954.95	7942.61
580 000	10518.99	10080.26	8926.22	8507.44	8339.22	8268.92	8239.05	8226.28
600 000	10881.71	10427.86	9234.03	8800.80	8626.78	8554.05	8523.16	8509.94
620 000	11244.44	10775.45	9541.83	9094.16	8914.34	8839.19	8807.26	8793.61
640 000	11607.16	11123.05	9849.63	9387.52	9201.90	9124.32	9091.37	9077.27
660 000	11969.88	11470.64	10157.43	9680.88	9489.46	9409.46	9375.47	9360.94
680 000	12332.61	11818.24	10465.23	9974.24	9777.02	9694.59	9659.58	9644.60
700 000	12695.33	12165.84	10773.03	10267.60	10064.58	9979.73	9943.68	9928.27
720 000	13058.06	12513.43	11080.83	10560.96	10352.14	10264.86	10227.79	10211.93
740 000	13420.78	12861.03	11388.63	10854.32	10639.69	10550.00	10511.89	10495.59
760 000	13783.50	13208.62	11696.43	11147.68	10927.25	10835.13	10796.00	10779.26
780 000	14146.23	13556.22	12004.23	11441.04	11214.81	11120.27	11080.10	11062.92
800 000	14508.95	13903.81	12312.03	11734.40	11502.37	11405.40	11364.21	11346.59
820 000	14871.67	14251.41	12619.84	12027.76	11789.93	11690.54	11648.31	11630.25
840 000	15234.40	14599.00	12927.64	12321.12	12077.49	11975.67	11932.42	11913.92
860 000	15597.12	14946.60	13235.44	12614.48	12365.05	12260.81	12216.53	12197.58
880 000	15959.85	15294.19	13543.24	12907.84	12652.61	12545.94	12500.63	12481.25
900 000	16322.57	15641.79	13851.04	13201.20	12940.17	12831.08	12784.74	12764.91
920 000	16685.29	15989.38	14158.84	13494.56	13227.73	13116.21	13068.84	13048.58
940 000	17048.02	16336.98	14466.64	13787.92	13515.29	13401.35	13352.95	13332.24
960 000	17410.74	16684.57	14774.44	14081.28	13802.85	13686.48	13637.05	13615.91
980 000	17773.46	17032.17	15082.24	14374.64	14090.41	13971.62	13921.16	13899.57
1000 000	18136.19	17379.77	15390.04	14668.01	14377.97	14256.75	14205.26	14183.24
Coefficient	.018136188	.017379765	.015390043	.014668005	.014377966	.014256753	.014205262	.014183236

AMOUNT	1 YEAR	2 YEARS	3 YEARS	4 YEARS	5 YEARS	6 YEARS	7 YEARS	8 YEARS
10 000	913.23	495.62	357.77	289.85	249.87	223.86	205.81	192.71
20 000	1826.47	991.25	715.55	579.69	499.74	447.72	411.61	385.42
30 000	2739.70	1486.87	1073.32	869.54	749.62	671.58	617.42	578.13
40 000	3652.94	1982.50	1431.09	1159.38	999.49	895.43	823.22	770.84
50 000	4566.17	2478.12	1788.86	1449.23	1249.36	1119.29	1029.03	963.55
60 000	5479.41	2973.75	2146.64	1739.07	1499.23	1343.15	1234.83	1156.26
70 000	6392.64	3469.37	2504.41	2028.92	1749.10	1567.01	1440.64	1348.97
80 000	7305.88	3965.00	2862.18	2318.76	1998.98	1790.87	1646.44	1541.68
90 000	8219.11	4460.62	3219.95	2608.61	2248.85	2014.73	1852.25	1734.39
100 000	9132.34	4956.25	3577.73	2898.45	2498.72	2238.59	2058.05	1927.10
110 000	10045.58	5451.87	3935.50	3188.30	2748.59	2462.44	2263.86	2119.82
120 000	10958.81	5947.50	4293.27	3478.15	2998.46	2686.30	2469.66	2312.53
130 000	11872.05	6443.12	4651.05	3767.99	3248.34	2910.16	2675.47	2505.24
140 000	12785.28	6938.75	5008.82	4057.84	3498.21	3134.02	2881.28	2697.95
150 000	13698.52	7434.37	5366.59	4347.68	3748.08	3357.88	3087.08	2890.66
160 000	14611.75	7930.00	5724.36	4637.53	3997.95	3581.74	3292.89	3083.37
170 000	15524.98	8425.62	6082.14	4927.37	4247.82	3805.60	3498.69	3276.08
180 000	16438.22	8921.25	6439.91	5217.22	4497.70	4029.45	3704.50	3468.79
190 000	17351.45	9416.87	6797.68	5507.06	4747.57	4253.31	3910.30	3661.50
200 000	18264.69	9912.50	7155.45	5796.91	4997.44	4477.17	4116.11	3854.21
210 000	19177.92	10408.12	7513.23	6086.75	5247.31	4701.03	4321.91	4046.92
220 000	20091.16	10903.74	7871.00	6376.60	5497.18	4924.89	4527.72	4239.63
230 000	21004.39	11399.37	8228.77	6666.45	5747.06	5148.75	4733.52	4432.34
240 000	21917.63	11894.99	8586.55	6956.29	5996.93	5372.61	4939.33	4625.05
250 000	22830.86	12390.62	8944.32	7246.14	6246.80	5596.46	5145.14	4817.76
260 000	23744.09	12886.24	9302.09	7535.98	6496.67	5820.32	5350.94	5010.47
270 000	24657.33	13381.87	9659.86	7825.83	6746.54	6044.18	5556.75	5203.18
280 000	25570.56	13877.49	10017.64	8115.67	6996.42	6268.04	5762.55	5395.89
290 000	26483.80	14373.12	10375.41	8405.52	7246.29	6491.90	5968.36	5588.60
300 000	27397.03	14868.74	10733.18	8695.36	7496.16	6715.76	6174.16	5781.31
320 000	29223.50	15859.99	11448.73	9275.05	7995.90	7163.47	6585.77	6166.74
340 000	31049.97	16851.24	12164.27	9854.75	8495.65	7611.19	6997.38	6552.16
360 000	32876.44	17842.49	12879.82	10434.44	8995.39	8058.91	7408.99	6937.58
380 000	34702.91	18833.74	13595.36	11014.13	9495.13	8506.63	7820.61	7323.00
400 000	36529.38	19824.99	14310.91	11593.82	9994.88	8954.34	8232.22	7708.42
420 000	38355.84	20816.24	15026.45	12173.51	10494.62	9402.06	8643.83	8093.84
440 000	40182.31	21807.49	15742.00	12753.20	10994.37	9849.78	9055.44	8479.26
460 000	42008.78	22798.74	16457.55	13332.89	11494.11	10297.50	9467.05	8864.68
480 000	43835.25	23789.99	17173.09	13912.58	11993.85	10745.21	9878.66	9250.10
500 000	45661.72	24781.24	17888.64	14492.27	12493.60	11192.93	10290.27	9635.52
520 000	47488.19	25772.49	18604.18	15071.96	12993.34	11640.65	10701.88	10020.95
540 000	49314.66	26763.74	19319.73	15651.65	13493.09	12088.36	11113.49	10406.37
560 000	51141.13	27754.99	20035.27	16231.35	13992.83	12536.08	11525.10	10791.79
580 000	52967.60	28746.24	20750.82	16811.04	14492.57	12983.80	11936.71	11177.21
600 000	54794.06	29737.49	21466.36	17390.73	14992.32	13431.52	12348.32	11562.63
620 000	56620.53	30728.73	22181.91	17970.42	15492.06	13879.23	12759.94	11948.05
640 000	58447.00	31719.98	22897.45	18550.11	15991.81	14326.95	13171.55	12333.47
660 000	60273.47	32711.23	23613.00	19129.80	16491.55	14774.67	13583.16	12718.89
680 000	62099.94	33702.48	24328.55	19709.49	16991.29	15222.38	13994.77	13104.31
700 000	63926.41	34693.73	25044.09	20289.18	17491.04	15670.10	14406.38	13489.73
720 000	65752.88	35684.98	25759.64	20868.87	17990.78	16117.82	14817.99	13875.16
740 000	67579.35	36676.23	26475.18	21448.56	18490.53	16565.54	15229.60	14260.58
760 000	69405.81	37667.48	27190.73	22028.25	18990.27	17013.25	15641.21	14646.00
780 000	71232.28	38658.73	27906.27	22607.95	19490.01	17460.97	16052.82	15031.42
800 000	73058.75	39649.98	28621.82	23187.64	19989.76	17908.69	16464.43	15416.84
820 000	74885.22	40641.23	29337.36	23767.33	20489.50	18356.40	16876.04	15802.26
840 000	76711.69	41632.48	30052.91	24347.02	20989.25	18804.12	17287.65	16187.68
860 000	78538.16	42623.73	30768.45	24926.71	21488.99	19251.84	17699.27	16573.10
880 000	80364.63	43614.98	31484.00	25506.40	21988.73	19699.56	18110.88	16958.52
900 000	82191.10	44606.23	32199.55	26086.09	22488.48	20147.27	18522.49	17343.94
920 000	84017.56	45597.48	32915.09	26665.78	22988.22	20594.99	18934.10	17729.37
940 000	85844.03	46588.73	33630.64	27245.47	23487.97	21042.71	19345.71	18114.79
960 000	87670.50	47579.98	34346.18	27825.16	23987.71	21490.42	19757.32	18500.21
980 000	89496.97	48571.23	35061.73	28404.85	24487.45	21938.14	20168.93	18885.63
1000 000	91323.44	49562.48	35777.27	28984.55	24987.20	22385.86	20580.54	19271.05
Coefficient	.091323440	.049562475	.035777273	.028984545	.024987197	.022385859	.020580541	.019271049

AMOUNT	9 YEARS	10 YEARS	15 YEARS	20 YEARS	25 YEARS	30 YEARS	35 YEARS	40 YEARS
10 000	182.90	175.39	155.68	148.58	145.76	144.60	144.11	143.90
20 000	365.81	350.77	311.35	297.17	291.53	289.20	288.22	287.80
30 000	548.71	526.16	467.03	445.75	437.29	433.80	432.33	431.71
40 000	731.62	701.54	622.70	594.34	583.06	578.39	576.44	575.61
50 000	914.52	876.93	778.38	742.92	728.82	722.99	720.55	719.51
60 000	1097.43	1052.31	934.05	891.51	874.58	867.59	864.66	863.41
70 000	1280.33	1227.70	1089.73	1040.09	1020.35	1012.19	1008.76	1007.32
80 000	1463.24	1403.08	1245.41	1188.67	1166.11	1156.79	1152.87	1151.22
90 000	1646.14	1578.47	1401.08	1337.26	1311.88	1301.39	1296.98	1295.12
100 000	1829.05	1753.85	1556.76	1485.84	1457.64	1445.99	1441.09	1439.02
110 000	2011.95	1929.24	1712.43	1634.43	1603.41	1590.58	1585.20	1582.93
120 000	2194.85	2104.62	1868.11	1783.01	1749.17	1735.18	1729.31	1726.83
130 000	2377.76	2280.01	2023.78	1931.59	1894.93	1879.78	1873.42	1870.73
140 000	2560.66	2455.39	2179.46	2080.18	2040.70	2024.38	2017.53	2014.63
150 000	2743.57	2630.78	2335.14	2228.76	2186.46	2168.98	2161.64	2158.53
160 000	2926.47	2806.16	2490.81	2377.35	2332.23	2313.58	2305.75	2302.44
170 000	3109.38	2981.55	2646.49	2525.93	2477.99	2458.18	2449.86	2446.34
180 000	3292.28	3156.93	2802.16	2674.52	2623.75	2602.77	2593.97	2590.24
190 000	3475.19	3332.32	2957.84	2823.10	2769.52	2747.37	2738.07	2734.14
200 000	3658.09	3507.70	3113.51	2971.68	2915.28	2891.97	2882.18	2878.05
210 000	3841.00	3683.09	3269.19	3120.27	3061.05	3036.57	3026.29	3021.95
220 000	4023.90	3858.47	3424.87	3268.85	3206.81	3181.17	3170.40	3165.85
230 000	4206.81	4033.86	3580.54	3417.44	3352.58	3325.77	3314.51	3309.75
240 000	4389.71	4209.24	3736.22	3566.02	3498.34	3470.37	3458.62	3453.66
250 000	4572.61	4384.63	3891.89	3714.60	3644.10	3614.96	3602.73	3597.56
260 000	4755.52	4560.01	4047.57	3863.19	3789.87	3759.56	3746.84	3741.46
270 000	4938.42	4735.40	4203.24	4011.77	3935.63	3904.16	3890.95	3885.36
280 000	5121.33	4910.78	4358.92	4160.36	4081.40	4048.76	4035.06	4029.26
290 000	5304.23	5086.17	4514.60	4308.94	4227.16	4193.36	4179.17	4173.17
300 000	5487.14	5261.55	4670.27	4457.53	4372.92	4337.96	4323.28	4317.07
320 000	5852.95	5612.32	4981.62	4754.69	4664.45	4627.15	4611.49	4604.87
340 000	6218.76	5963.09	5292.97	5051.86	4955.98	4916.35	4899.71	4892.68
360 000	6584.56	6313.86	5604.33	5349.03	5247.51	5205.55	5187.93	5180.48
380 000	6950.37	6664.63	5915.68	5646.20	5539.04	5494.75	5476.15	5468.29
400 000	7316.18	7015.40	6227.03	5943.37	5830.57	5783.94	5764.37	5756.09
420 000	7681.99	7366.17	6538.38	6240.54	6122.09	6073.14	6052.59	6043.90
440 000	8047.80	7716.94	6849.73	6537.70	6413.62	6362.34	6340.80	6331.70
460 000	8413.61	8067.71	7161.08	6834.87	6705.15	6651.53	6629.02	6619.51
480 000	8779.42	8418.48	7472.43	7132.04	6996.68	6940.73	6917.24	6907.31
500 000	9145.23	8769.25	7783.79	7429.21	7288.21	7229.93	7205.46	7195.12
520 000	9511.04	9120.02	8095.14	7726.38	7579.74	7519.13	7493.68	7482.92
540 000	9876.85	9470.79	8406.49	8023.55	7871.26	7808.32	7781.90	7770.73
560 000	10242.66	9821.56	8717.84	8320.71	8162.79	8097.52	8070.11	8058.53
580 000	10608.47	10172.33	9029.19	8617.88	8454.32	8386.72	8358.33	8346.33
600 000	10974.27	10523.10	9340.54	8915.05	8745.85	8675.91	8646.55	8634.14
620 000	11340.08	10873.87	9651.89	9212.22	9037.38	8965.11	8934.77	8921.94
640 000	11705.89	11224.64	9963.25	9509.39	9328.90	9254.31	9222.99	9209.75
660 000	12071.70	11575.41	10274.60	9806.56	9620.43	9543.51	9511.21	9497.55
680 000	12437.51	11926.18	10585.95	10103.72	9911.96	9832.70	9799.42	9785.36
700 000	12803.32	12276.95	10897.30	10400.89	10203.49	10121.90	10087.64	10073.16
720 000	13169.13	12627.72	11208.65	10698.06	10495.02	10411.10	10375.86	10360.97
740 000	13534.94	12978.49	11520.00	10995.23	10786.55	10700.29	10664.08	10648.77
760 000	13900.75	13329.26	11831.35	11292.40	11078.07	10989.49	10952.30	10936.58
780 000	14266.56	13680.03	12142.71	11589.57	11369.60	11278.69	11240.52	11224.38
800 000	14632.37	14030.80	12454.06	11886.74	11661.13	11567.89	11528.73	11512.19
820 000	14998.18	14381.57	12765.41	12183.90	11952.66	11857.08	11816.95	11799.99
840 000	15363.98	14732.34	13076.76	12481.07	12244.19	12146.28	12105.17	12087.79
860 000	15729.79	15083.11	13388.11	12778.24	12535.72	12435.48	12393.39	12375.60
880 000	16095.60	15433.88	13699.46	13075.41	12827.24	12724.68	12681.61	12663.40
900 000	16461.41	15784.65	14010.81	13372.58	13118.77	13013.87	12969.83	12951.21
920 000	16827.22	16135.42	14322.17	13669.75	13410.30	13303.07	13258.04	13239.01
940 000	17193.03	16486.19	14633.52	13966.91	13701.83	13592.27	13546.26	13526.82
960 000	17558.84	16836.96	14944.87	14264.08	13993.36	13881.46	13834.48	13814.62
980 000	17924.65	17187.73	15256.22	14561.25	14284.89	14170.66	14122.70	14102.43
1000 000	18290.46	17538.50	15567.57	14858.42	14576.41	14459.86	14410.92	14390.23
Coefficient	.018290458	.017538501	.015567571	.014858419	.014576414	.014459858	.014410917	.014390232

AMOUNT	1 YEAR	2 YEARS	3 YEARS	4 YEARS	5 YEARS	6 YEARS	7 YEARS	8 YEARS
10 000	914.42	496.83	359.02	291.14	251.22	225.26	207.26	194.21
20 000	1828.84	993.66	718.04	582.29	502.44	450.52	414.52	388.42
30 000	2743.27	1490.49	1077.06	873.43	753.67	675.78	621.77	582.64
40 000	3657.69	1987.31	1436.08	1164.57	1004.89	901.04	829.03	776.85
50 000	4572.11	2484.14	1795.10	1455.72	1256.11	1126.30	1036.29	971.06
60 000	5486.53	2980.97	2154.12	1746.86	1507.33	1351.56	1243.55	1165.27
70 000	6400.95	3477.80	2513.14	2038.01	1758.55	1576.82	1450.81	1359.48
80 000	7315.38	3974.63	2872.17	2329.15	2009.78	1802.08	1658.06	1553.70
90 000	8229.80	4471.46	3231.19	2620.29	2261.00	2027.34	1865.32	1747.91
100 000	9144.22	4968.28	3590.21	2911.44	2512.22	2252.60	2072.58	1942.12
110 000	10058.64	5465.11	3949.23	3202.58	2763.44	2477.86	2279.84	2136.33
120 000	10973.07	5961.94	4308.25	3493.72	3014.67	2703.13	2487.10	2330.55
130 000	11887.49	6458.77	4667.27	3784.87	3265.89	2928.39	2694.35	2524.76
140 000	12801.91	6955.60	5026.29	4076.01	3517.11	3153.65	2901.61	2718.97
150 000	13716.33	7452.43	5385.31	4367.16	3768.33	3378.91	3108.87	2913.18
160 000	14630.75	7949.26	5744.33	4658.30	4019.55	3604.17	3316.13	3107.39
170 000	15545.18	8446.08	6103.35	4949.44	4270.78	3829.43	3523.38	3301.61
180 000	16459.60	8942.91	6462.37	5240.59	4522.00	4054.69	3730.64	3495.82
190 000	17374.02	9439.74	6821.39	5531.73	4773.22	4279.95	3937.90	3690.03
200 000	18288.44	9936.57	7180.41	5822.87	5024.44	4505.21	4145.16	3884.24
210 000	19202.86	10433.40	7539.43	6114.02	5275.66	4730.47	4352.42	4078.45
220 000	20117.29	10930.23	7898.45	6405.16	5526.89	4955.73	4559.67	4272.67
230 000	21031.71	11427.05	8257.47	6696.31	5778.11	5180.99	4766.93	4466.88
240 000	21946.13	11923.88	8616.50	6987.45	6029.33	5406.25	4974.19	4661.09
250 000	22860.55	12420.71	8975.52	7278.59	6280.55	5631.51	5181.45	4855.30
260 000	23774.97	12917.54	9334.54	7569.74	6531.78	5856.77	5388.71	5049.51
270 000	24689.40	13414.37	9693.56	7860.88	6783.00	6082.03	5595.96	5243.73
280 000	25603.82	13911.20	10052.58	8152.02	7034.22	6307.29	5803.22	5437.94
290 000	26518.24	14408.03	10411.60	8443.17	7285.44	6532.55	6010.48	5632.15
300 000	27432.66	14904.85	10770.62	8734.31	7536.66	6757.81	6217.74	5826.36
320 000	29261.51	15898.51	11488.66	9316.60	8039.11	7208.33	6632.25	6214.79
340 000	31090.35	16892.17	12206.70	9898.89	8541.55	7658.86	7046.77	6603.21
360 000	32919.20	17885.82	12924.74	10481.17	9044.00	8109.38	7461.29	6991.64
380 000	34748.04	18879.48	13642.78	11063.46	9546.44	8559.90	7875.80	7380.06
400 000	36576.88	19873.14	14360.83	11645.75	10048.89	9010.42	8290.32	7768.48
420 000	38405.73	20866.80	15078.87	12228.04	10551.33	9460.94	8704.83	8156.91
440 000	40234.57	21860.45	15796.91	12810.32	11053.77	9911.46	9119.35	8545.33
460 000	42063.42	22854.11	16514.95	13392.61	11556.22	10361.98	9533.87	8933.76
480 000	43892.26	23847.77	17232.99	13974.90	12058.66	10812.50	9948.38	9322.18
500 000	45721.11	24841.42	17951.03	14557.19	12561.11	11263.02	10362.90	9710.61
520 000	47549.95	25835.08	18669.07	15139.47	13063.55	11713.54	10777.41	10099.03
540 000	49378.79	26828.74	19387.11	15721.76	13566.00	12164.06	11191.93	10487.45
560 000	51207.64	27822.39	20105.16	16304.05	14068.44	12614.59	11606.44	10875.88
580 000	53036.48	28816.05	20823.20	16886.34	14570.88	13065.11	12020.96	11264.30
600 000	54865.33	29809.71	21541.24	17468.62	15073.33	13515.63	12435.48	11652.73
620 000	56694.17	30803.36	22259.28	18050.91	15575.77	13966.15	12849.99	12041.15
640 000	58523.02	31797.02	22977.32	18633.20	16078.22	14416.67	13264.51	12429.57
660 000	60351.86	32790.68	23695.36	19215.49	16580.66	14867.19	13679.02	12818.00
680 000	62180.70	33784.34	24413.40	19797.77	17083.10	15317.71	14093.54	13206.42
700 000	64009.55	34777.99	25131.44	20380.06	17585.55	15768.23	14508.06	13594.85
720 000	65838.39	35771.65	25849.49	20962.35	18087.99	16218.75	14922.57	13983.27
740 000	67667.24	36765.31	26567.53	21544.64	18590.44	16669.27	15337.09	14371.70
760 000	69496.08	37758.96	27285.57	22126.92	19092.88	17119.79	15751.60	14760.12
780 000	71324.92	38752.62	28003.61	22709.21	19595.33	17570.32	16166.12	15148.54
800 000	73153.77	39746.28	28721.65	23291.50	20097.77	18020.84	16580.64	15536.97
820 000	74982.61	40739.93	29439.69	23873.79	20600.21	18471.36	16995.15	15925.39
840 000	76811.46	41733.59	30157.73	24456.07	21102.66	18921.88	17409.67	16313.82
860 000	78640.30	42727.25	30875.78	25038.36	21605.10	19372.40	17824.18	16702.24
880 000	80469.15	43720.90	31593.82	25620.65	22107.55	19822.92	18238.70	17090.66
900 000	82297.99	44714.56	32311.86	26202.94	22609.99	20273.44	18653.21	17479.09
920 000	84126.83	45708.22	33029.90	26785.22	23112.44	20723.96	19067.73	17867.51
940 000	85955.68	46701.88	33747.94	27367.51	23614.88	21174.48	19482.25	18255.94
960 000	87784.52	47695.53	34465.98	27949.80	24117.32	21625.00	19896.76	18644.36
980 000	89613.37	48689.19	35184.02	28532.09	24619.77	22075.52	20311.28	19032.79
1000 000	91442.21	49682.85	35902.06	29114.37	25122.21	22526.05	20725.79	19421.21
Coefficient	.091442211	.049682846	.035902064	.029114373	.025122213	.022526045	.020725794	.019421210

AMOUNT	9 YEARS	10 YEARS	15 YEARS	20 YEARS	25 YEARS	30 YEARS	35 YEARS	40 YEARS
10 000	184.45	176.98	157.46	150.49	147.75	146.63	146.17	145.97
20 000	368.91	353.96	314.92	300.99	295.51	293.27	292.34	291.95
30 000	553.36	530.94	472.37	451.48	443.26	439.90	438.50	437.92
40 000	737.81	707.92	629.83	601.98	591.01	586.53	584.67	583.89
50 000	922.27	884.89	787.29	752.47	738.76	733.16	730.84	729.87
60 000	1106.72	1061.87	944.75	902.97	886.52	879.80	877.01	875.84
70 000	1291.17	1238.85	1102.20	1053.46	1034.27	1026.43	1023.17	1021.81
80 000	1475.63	1415.83	1259.66	1203.95	1182.02	1173.06	1169.34	1167.79
90 000	1660.08	1592.81	1417.12	1354.45	1329.78	1319.69	1315.51	1313.76
100 000	1844.53	1769.79	1574.58	1504.94	1477.53	1466.33	1461.68	1459.73
110 000	2028.99	1946.77	1732.04	1655.44	1625.28	1612.96	1607.84	1605.71
120 000	2213.44	2123.75	1889.49	1805.93	1773.04	1759.59	1754.01	1751.68
130 000	2397.89	2300.72	2046.95	1956.42	1920.79	1906.22	1900.18	1897.65
140 000	2582.35	2477.70	2204.41	2106.92	2068.54	2052.86	2046.35	2043.63
150 000	2766.80	2654.68	2361.87	2257.41	2216.29	2199.49	2192.51	2189.60
160 000	2951.25	2831.66	2519.33	2407.91	2364.05	2346.12	2338.68	2335.57
170 000	3135.71	3008.64	2676.78	2558.40	2511.80	2492.75	2484.85	2481.55
180 000	3320.16	3185.62	2834.24	2708.90	2659.55	2639.39	2631.02	2627.52
190 000	3504.61	3362.60	2991.70	2859.39	2807.31	2786.02	2777.18	2773.49
200 000	3689.07	3539.58	3149.16	3009.88	2955.06	2932.65	2923.35	2919.47
210 000	3873.52	3716.55	3306.61	3160.38	3102.81	3079.28	3069.52	3065.44
220 000	4057.97	3893.53	3464.07	3310.87	3250.57	3225.92	3215.69	3211.41
230 000	4242.43	4070.51	3621.53	3461.37	3398.32	3372.55	3361.85	3357.39
240 000	4426.88	4247.49	3778.99	3611.86	3546.07	3519.18	3508.02	3503.36
250 000	4611.33	4424.47	3936.45	3762.35	3693.82	3665.81	3654.19	3649.33
260 000	4795.79	4601.45	4093.90	3912.85	3841.58	3812.45	3800.36	3795.31
270 000	4980.24	4778.43	4251.36	4063.34	3989.33	3959.08	3946.52	3941.28
280 000	5164.69	4955.41	4408.82	4213.84	4137.08	4105.71	4092.69	4087.25
290 000	5349.15	5132.38	4566.28	4364.33	4284.84	4252.34	4238.86	4233.23
300 000	5533.60	5309.36	4723.73	4514.83	4432.59	4398.98	4385.03	4379.20
320 000	5902.51	5663.32	5038.65	4815.81	4728.10	4692.24	4677.36	4671.15
340 000	6271.41	6017.28	5353.57	5116.80	5023.60	4985.51	4969.70	4963.09
360 000	6640.32	6371.24	5668.48	5417.79	5319.11	5278.77	5262.03	5255.04
380 000	7009.23	6725.19	5983.40	5718.78	5614.61	5572.04	5554.37	5546.99
400 000	7378.13	7079.15	6298.31	6019.77	5910.12	5865.30	5846.70	5838.93
420 000	7747.04	7433.11	6613.23	6320.76	6205.62	6158.57	6139.04	6130.88
440 000	8115.95	7787.07	6928.14	6621.74	6501.13	6451.83	6431.37	6422.83
460 000	8484.85	8141.02	7243.06	6922.73	6796.64	6745.10	6723.71	6714.77
480 000	8853.76	8494.98	7557.98	7223.72	7092.14	7038.36	7016.04	7006.72
500 000	9222.67	8848.94	7872.89	7524.71	7387.65	7331.63	7308.38	7298.67
520 000	9591.57	9202.90	8187.81	7825.70	7683.15	7624.89	7600.71	7590.61
540 000	9960.48	9556.85	8502.72	8126.69	7978.66	7918.16	7893.05	7882.56
560 000	10329.39	9910.81	8817.64	8427.67	8274.17	8211.42	8185.38	8174.51
580 000	10698.29	10264.77	9132.55	8728.66	8569.67	8504.69	8477.72	8466.45
600 000	11067.20	10618.73	9447.47	9029.65	8865.18	8797.95	8770.05	8758.40
620 000	11436.11	10972.68	9762.39	9330.64	9160.68	9091.22	9062.39	9050.35
640 000	11805.01	11326.64	10077.30	9631.63	9456.19	9384.48	9354.72	9342.29
660 000	12173.92	11680.60	10392.22	9932.62	9751.70	9677.75	9647.06	9634.24
680 000	12542.83	12034.56	10707.13	10233.60	10047.20	9971.01	9939.39	9926.19
700 000	12911.73	12388.51	11022.05	10534.59	10342.71	10264.28	10231.73	10218.13
720 000	13280.64	12742.47	11336.96	10835.58	10638.21	10557.54	10524.06	10510.08
740 000	13649.55	13096.43	11651.88	11136.57	10933.72	10850.81	10816.40	10802.03
760 000	14018.45	13450.39	11966.80	11437.56	11229.23	11144.07	11108.73	11093.97
780 000	14387.36	13804.34	12281.71	11738.55	11524.73	11437.34	11401.07	11385.92
800 000	14756.27	14158.30	12596.63	12039.54	11820.24	11730.60	11693.40	11677.87
820 000	15125.17	14512.26	12911.54	12340.52	12115.74	12023.87	11985.74	11969.81
840 000	15494.08	14866.22	13226.46	12641.51	12411.25	12317.13	12278.07	12261.76
860 000	15862.99	15220.17	13541.37	12942.50	12706.76	12610.40	12570.41	12553.71
880 000	16231.89	15574.13	13856.29	13243.49	13002.26	12903.66	12862.74	12845.65
900 000	16600.80	15928.09	14171.20	13544.48	13297.77	13196.93	13155.08	13137.60
920 000	16969.71	16282.05	14486.12	13845.47	13593.27	13490.19	13447.41	13429.55
940 000	17338.61	16636.00	14801.04	14146.45	13888.78	13783.46	13739.75	13721.49
960 000	17707.52	16989.96	15115.95	14447.44	14184.29	14076.72	14032.08	14013.44
980 000	18076.43	17343.92	15430.87	14748.43	14479.79	14369.99	14324.42	14305.39
1000 000	18445.33	17697.88	15745.78	15049.42	14775.30	14663.25	14616.75	14597.34
Coefficient	.018445334	.017697876	.015745783	.015049419	.014775297	.014663252	.014616753	.014597335

17.75% MONTHLY AMORTIZING PAYMENTS

AMOUNT	1 YEAR	2 YEARS	3 YEARS	4 YEARS	5 YEARS	6 YEARS	7 YEARS	8 YEARS
10 000	915.61	498.03	360.27	292.45	252.58	226.67	208.72	195.72
20 000	1831.22	996.07	720.54	584.89	505.15	453.33	417.43	391.44
30 000	2746.83	1494.10	1080.81	877.34	757.73	680.00	626.15	587.16
40 000	3662.44	1992.14	1441.08	1169.78	1010.30	906.67	834.86	782.88
50 000	4578.05	2490.17	1801.36	1462.23	1262.88	1133.33	1043.58	978.60
60 000	5493.66	2988.20	2161.63	1754.67	1515.46	1360.00	1252.29	1174.32
70 000	6409.27	3486.24	2521.90	2047.12	1768.03	1586.67	1461.01	1370.04
80 000	7324.88	3984.27	2882.17	2339.56	2020.61	1813.34	1669.72	1565.75
90 000	8240.50	4482.30	3242.44	2632.01	2273.19	2040.00	1878.44	1761.47
100 000	9156.11	4980.34	3602.71	2924.45	2525.76	2266.67	2087.16	1957.19
110 000	10071.72	5478.37	3962.98	3216.90	2778.34	2493.34	2295.87	2152.91
120 000	10987.33	5976.41	4323.25	3509.34	3030.91	2720.00	2504.59	2348.63
130 000	11902.94	6474.44	4683.52	3801.79	3283.49	2946.67	2713.30	2544.35
140 000	12818.55	6972.47	5043.79	4094.23	3536.07	3173.34	2922.02	2740.07
150 000	13734.16	7470.51	5404.07	4386.68	3788.64	3400.00	3130.73	2935.79
160 000	14649.77	7968.54	5764.34	4679.12	4041.22	3626.67	3339.45	3131.51
170 000	15565.38	8466.58	6124.61	4971.57	4293.80	3853.34	3548.17	3327.23
180 000	16480.99	8964.61	6484.88	5264.01	4546.37	4080.00	3756.88	3522.95
190 000	17396.60	9462.64	6845.15	5556.46	4798.95	4306.67	3965.60	3718.67
200 000	18312.21	9960.68	7205.42	5848.90	5051.52	4533.34	4174.31	3914.39
210 000	19227.82	10458.71	7565.69	6141.35	5304.10	4760.00	4383.03	4110.11
220 000	20143.43	10956.75	7925.96	6433.80	5556.68	4986.67	4591.74	4305.83
230 000	21059.04	11454.78	8286.23	6726.24	5809.25	5213.34	4800.46	4501.54
240 000	21974.65	11952.81	8646.51	7018.69	6061.83	5440.00	5009.17	4697.26
250 000	22890.27	12450.85	9006.78	7311.13	6314.41	5666.67	5217.89	4892.98
260 000	23805.88	12948.88	9367.05	7603.58	6566.98	5893.34	5426.61	5088.70
270 000	24721.49	13446.91	9727.32	7896.02	6819.56	6120.01	5635.32	5284.42
280 000	25637.10	13944.95	10087.59	8188.47	7072.13	6346.67	5844.04	5480.14
290 000	26552.71	14442.98	10447.86	8480.91	7324.71	6573.34	6052.75	5675.86
300 000	27468.32	14941.02	10808.13	8773.36	7577.29	6800.01	6261.47	5871.58
320 000	29299.54	15937.08	11528.67	9358.25	8082.44	7253.34	6678.90	6263.02
340 000	31130.76	16933.15	12249.22	9943.14	8587.59	7706.67	7096.33	6654.46
360 000	32961.98	17929.22	12969.76	10528.03	9092.74	8160.01	7513.76	7045.90
380 000	34793.20	18925.29	13690.30	11112.92	9597.90	8613.34	7931.19	7437.33
400 000	36624.42	19921.36	14410.84	11697.81	10103.05	9066.68	8348.62	7828.77
420 000	38455.65	20917.42	15131.38	12282.70	10608.20	9520.01	8766.06	8220.21
440 000	40286.87	21913.49	15851.93	12867.59	11113.35	9973.34	9183.49	8611.65
460 000	42118.09	22909.56	16572.47	13452.48	11618.51	10426.68	9600.92	9003.09
480 000	43949.31	23905.63	17293.01	14037.37	12123.66	10880.01	10018.35	9394.53
500 000	45780.53	24901.69	18013.55	14622.26	12628.81	11333.35	10435.78	9785.97
520 000	47611.75	25897.76	18734.10	15207.15	13133.96	11786.68	10853.21	10177.41
540 000	49442.97	26893.83	19454.64	15792.04	13639.12	12240.01	11270.64	10568.84
560 000	51274.19	27889.90	20175.18	16376.93	14144.27	12693.35	11688.07	10960.28
580 000	53105.42	28885.97	20895.72	16961.82	14649.42	13146.68	12105.50	11351.72
600 000	54936.64	29882.03	21616.26	17546.71	15154.57	13600.01	12522.94	11743.16
620 000	56767.86	30878.10	22336.81	18131.60	15659.73	14053.35	12940.37	12134.60
640 000	58599.08	31874.17	23057.35	18716.50	16164.88	14506.68	13357.80	12526.04
660 000	60430.30	32870.24	23777.89	19301.39	16670.03	14960.02	13775.23	12917.48
680 000	62261.52	33866.30	24498.43	19886.28	17175.18	15413.35	14192.66	13308.91
700 000	64092.74	34862.37	25218.97	20471.17	17680.34	15866.68	14610.09	13700.35
720 000	65923.96	35858.44	25939.52	21056.06	18185.49	16320.02	15027.52	14091.79
740 000	67755.19	36854.51	26660.06	21640.95	18690.64	16773.35	15444.95	14483.23
760 000	69586.41	37850.57	27380.60	22225.84	19195.79	17226.68	15862.39	14874.67
780 000	71417.63	38846.64	28101.14	22810.73	19700.95	17680.02	16279.82	15266.11
800 000	73248.85	39842.71	28821.69	23395.62	20206.10	18133.35	16697.25	15657.55
820 000	75080.07	40838.78	29542.23	23980.51	20711.25	18586.69	17114.68	16048.99
840 000	76911.29	41834.85	30262.77	24565.40	21216.40	19040.02	17532.11	16440.42
860 000	78742.51	42830.91	30983.31	25150.29	21721.56	19493.35	17949.54	16831.86
880 000	80573.73	43826.98	31703.85	25735.18	22226.71	19946.69	18366.97	17223.30
900 000	82404.96	44823.05	32424.40	26320.07	22731.86	20400.02	18784.40	17614.74
920 000	84236.18	45819.12	33144.94	26904.96	23237.01	20853.35	19201.84	18006.18
940 000	86067.40	46815.18	33865.48	27489.85	23742.17	21306.69	19619.27	18397.62
960 000	87898.62	47811.25	34586.02	28074.74	24247.32	21760.02	20036.70	18789.06
980 000	89729.84	48807.32	35306.56	28659.63	24752.47	22213.36	20454.13	19180.49
1000 000	91561.06	49803.39	36027.11	29244.52	25257.62	22666.69	20871.56	19571.93
Coefficient	.091561062	.049803388	.036027107	.029244524	.025257624	.022666690	.020871560	.019571933

104

MONTHLY AMORTIZING PAYMENTS 17.75%

AMOUNT	9 YEARS	10 YEARS	15 YEARS	20 YEARS	25 YEARS	30 YEARS	35 YEARS	40 YEARS
10 000	186.01	178.58	159.25	152.41	149.75	148.67	148.23	148.05
20 000	372.02	357.16	318.49	304.82	299.49	297.34	296.46	296.09
30 000	558.02	535.74	477.74	457.23	449.24	446.01	444.68	444.14
40 000	744.03	714.32	636.99	609.64	598.98	594.68	592.91	592.18
50 000	930.04	892.89	796.23	762.05	748.73	743.35	741.14	740.23
60 000	1116.05	1071.47	955.48	914.46	898.48	892.02	889.37	888.27
70 000	1302.06	1250.05	1114.73	1066.87	1048.22	1040.68	1037.59	1036.32
80 000	1488.06	1428.63	1273.97	1219.28	1197.97	1189.35	1185.82	1184.36
90 000	1674.07	1607.21	1433.22	1371.69	1347.71	1338.02	1334.05	1332.41
100 000	1860.08	1785.79	1592.47	1524.10	1497.46	1486.69	1482.28	1480.45
110 000	2046.09	1964.37	1751.71	1676.51	1647.21	1635.36	1630.50	1628.50
120 000	2232.10	2142.95	1910.96	1828.92	1796.95	1784.03	1778.73	1776.54
130 000	2418.11	2321.52	2070.21	1981.33	1946.70	1932.70	1926.96	1924.59
140 000	2604.11	2500.10	2229.45	2133.74	2096.44	2081.37	2075.19	2072.63
150 000	2790.12	2678.68	2388.70	2286.15	2246.19	2230.04	2223.41	2220.68
160 000	2976.13	2857.26	2547.95	2438.56	2395.94	2378.71	2371.64	2368.73
170 000	3162.14	3035.84	2707.19	2590.97	2545.68	2527.38	2519.87	2516.77
180 000	3348.15	3214.42	2866.44	2743.38	2695.43	2676.05	2668.10	2664.82
190 000	3534.15	3393.00	3025.69	2895.79	2845.17	2824.72	2816.32	2812.86
200 000	3720.16	3571.58	3184.93	3048.20	2994.92	2973.38	2964.55	2960.91
210 000	3906.17	3750.16	3344.18	3200.61	3144.67	3122.05	3112.78	3108.95
220 000	4092.18	3928.73	3503.43	3353.02	3294.41	3270.72	3261.01	3257.00
230 000	4278.19	4107.31	3662.67	3505.43	3444.16	3419.39	3409.23	3405.04
240 000	4464.19	4285.89	3821.92	3657.84	3593.90	3568.06	3557.46	3553.09
250 000	4650.20	4464.47	3981.17	3810.25	3743.65	3716.73	3705.69	3701.13
260 000	4836.21	4643.05	4140.41	3962.66	3893.40	3865.40	3853.92	3849.18
270 000	5022.22	4821.63	4299.66	4115.07	4043.14	4014.07	4002.14	3997.22
280 000	5208.23	5000.21	4458.91	4267.48	4192.89	4162.74	4150.37	4145.27
290 000	5394.24	5178.79	4618.15	4419.89	4342.63	4311.41	4298.60	4293.31
300 000	5580.24	5357.37	4777.40	4572.30	4492.38	4460.08	4446.83	4441.36
320 000	5952.26	5714.52	5095.89	4877.12	4791.87	4757.42	4743.28	4737.45
340 000	6324.28	6071.68	5414.39	5181.94	5091.36	5054.75	5039.74	5033.54
360 000	6696.29	6428.84	5732.88	5486.76	5390.86	5352.09	5336.19	5329.63
380 000	7068.31	6786.00	6051.37	5791.58	5690.35	5649.43	5632.65	5625.72
400 000	7440.32	7143.15	6369.87	6096.40	5989.84	5946.77	5929.10	5921.81
420 000	7812.34	7500.31	6688.36	6401.22	6289.33	6244.11	6225.56	6217.90
440 000	8184.36	7857.47	7006.85	6706.04	6588.82	6541.45	6522.01	6513.99
460 000	8556.37	8214.63	7325.35	7010.86	6888.32	6838.78	6818.47	6810.09
480 000	8928.39	8571.78	7643.84	7315.68	7187.81	7136.12	7114.92	7106.18
500 000	9300.41	8928.94	7962.33	7620.50	7487.30	7433.46	7411.38	7402.27
520 000	9672.42	9286.10	8280.83	7925.31	7786.79	7730.80	7707.83	7698.36
540 000	10044.44	9643.26	8599.32	8230.13	8086.28	8028.14	8004.29	7994.45
560 000	10416.45	10000.42	8917.81	8534.95	8385.77	8325.48	8300.74	8290.54
580 000	10788.47	10357.57	9236.31	8839.77	8685.27	8622.81	8597.20	8586.63
600 000	11160.49	10714.73	9554.80	9144.59	8984.76	8920.15	8893.65	8882.72
620 000	11532.50	11071.89	9873.29	9449.41	9284.25	9217.49	9190.11	9178.81
640 000	11904.52	11429.05	10191.79	9754.23	9583.74	9514.83	9486.57	9474.90
660 000	12276.54	11786.20	10510.28	10059.05	9883.23	9812.17	9783.02	9770.99
680 000	12648.55	12143.36	10828.77	10363.87	10182.73	10109.51	10079.48	10067.08
700 000	13020.57	12500.52	11147.27	10668.69	10482.22	10406.85	10375.93	10363.17
720 000	13392.58	12857.68	11465.76	10973.51	10781.71	10704.18	10672.39	10659.26
740 000	13764.60	13214.83	11784.25	11278.33	11081.20	11001.52	10968.84	10955.36
760 000	14136.62	13571.99	12102.75	11583.15	11380.69	11298.86	11265.30	11251.45
780 000	14508.63	13929.15	12421.24	11887.97	11680.19	11596.20	11561.75	11547.54
800 000	14880.65	14286.31	12739.73	12192.79	11979.68	11893.54	11858.21	11843.63
820 000	15252.67	14643.46	13058.23	12497.61	12279.17	12190.88	12154.66	12139.72
840 000	15624.68	15000.62	13376.72	12802.43	12578.66	12488.21	12451.12	12435.81
860 000	15996.70	15357.78	13695.21	13107.25	12878.15	12785.55	12747.57	12731.90
880 000	16368.71	15714.94	14013.71	13412.07	13177.65	13082.89	13044.03	13027.99
900 000	16740.73	16072.10	14332.20	13716.89	13477.14	13380.23	13340.48	13324.08
920 000	17112.75	16429.25	14650.69	14021.71	13776.63	13677.57	13636.94	13620.17
940 000	17484.76	16786.41	14969.19	14326.53	14076.12	13974.91	13933.39	13916.26
960 000	17856.78	17143.57	15287.68	14631.35	14375.61	14272.25	14229.85	14212.35
980 000	18228.80	17500.73	15606.17	14936.17	14675.11	14569.58	14526.30	14508.44
1000 000	18600.81	17857.88	15924.67	15240.99	14974.60	14866.92	14822.76	14804.53
Coefficient	.018600812	.017857884	.015924666	.015240990	.014974598	.014866922	.014822758	.014804534

AMOUNT	1 YEAR	2 YEARS	3 YEARS	4 YEARS	5 YEARS	6 YEARS	7 YEARS	8 YEARS
10 000	916.80	499.24	361.52	293.75	253.93	228.08	210.18	197.23
20 000	1833.60	998.48	723.05	587.50	507.87	456.16	420.36	394.46
30 000	2750.40	1497.72	1084.57	881.25	761.80	684.23	630.54	591.70
40 000	3667.20	1996.96	1446.10	1175.00	1015.74	912.31	840.71	788.93
50 000	4584.00	2496.20	1807.62	1468.75	1269.67	1140.39	1050.89	986.16
60 000	5500.80	2995.45	2169.14	1762.50	1523.61	1368.47	1261.07	1183.39
70 000	6417.60	3494.69	2530.67	2056.25	1777.54	1596.55	1471.25	1380.62
80 000	7334.40	3993.93	2892.19	2350.00	2031.47	1824.62	1681.43	1577.86
90 000	8251.20	4493.17	3253.72	2643.75	2285.41	2052.70	1891.61	1775.09
100 000	9168.00	4992.41	3615.24	2937.50	2539.34	2280.78	2101.78	1972.32
110 000	10084.80	5491.65	3976.76	3231.25	2793.28	2508.86	2311.96	2169.55
120 000	11001.60	5990.89	4338.29	3525.00	3047.21	2736.93	2522.14	2366.79
130 000	11918.40	6490.13	4699.81	3818.75	3301.15	2965.01	2732.32	2564.02
140 000	12835.20	6989.37	5061.34	4112.50	3555.08	3193.09	2942.50	2761.25
150 000	13752.00	7488.61	5422.86	4406.25	3809.01	3421.17	3152.68	2958.48
160 000	14668.80	7987.86	5784.38	4700.00	4062.95	3649.25	3362.85	3155.71
170 000	15585.60	8487.10	6145.91	4993.75	4316.88	3877.32	3573.03	3352.95
180 000	16502.40	8986.34	6507.43	5287.50	4570.82	4105.40	3783.21	3550.18
190 000	17419.20	9485.58	6868.95	5581.25	4824.75	4333.48	3993.39	3747.41
200 000	18336.00	9984.82	7230.48	5875.00	5078.69	4561.56	4203.57	3944.64
210 000	19252.80	10484.06	7592.00	6168.75	5332.62	4789.64	4413.75	4141.87
220 000	20169.60	10983.30	7953.53	6462.50	5586.55	5017.71	4623.92	4339.11
230 000	21086.40	11482.54	8315.05	6756.25	5840.49	5245.79	4834.10	4536.34
240 000	22003.20	11981.78	8676.57	7050.00	6094.42	5473.87	5044.28	4733.57
250 000	22920.00	12481.02	9038.10	7343.75	6348.36	5701.95	5254.46	4930.80
260 000	23836.80	12980.27	9399.62	7637.50	6602.29	5930.03	5464.64	5128.04
270 000	24753.60	13479.51	9761.15	7931.25	6856.23	6158.10	5674.82	5325.27
280 000	25670.40	13978.75	10122.67	8225.00	7110.16	6386.18	5884.99	5522.50
290 000	26587.20	14477.99	10484.19	8518.75	7364.09	6614.26	6095.17	5719.73
300 000	27504.00	14977.23	10845.72	8812.50	7618.03	6842.34	6305.35	5916.96
320 000	29337.60	15975.71	11568.77	9400.00	8125.90	7298.49	6725.71	6311.43
340 000	31171.20	16974.19	12291.81	9987.50	8633.77	7754.65	7146.06	6705.89
360 000	33004.80	17972.68	13014.86	10575.00	9141.63	8210.80	7566.42	7100.36
380 000	34838.40	18971.16	13737.91	11162.50	9649.50	8666.96	7986.78	7494.82
400 000	36672.00	19969.64	14460.96	11750.00	10157.37	9123.12	8407.14	7889.29
420 000	38505.60	20968.12	15184.01	12337.50	10665.24	9579.27	8827.49	8283.75
440 000	40339.20	21966.60	15907.05	12925.00	11173.11	10035.43	9247.85	8678.21
460 000	42172.80	22965.09	16630.10	13512.50	11680.98	10491.58	9668.21	9072.68
480 000	44006.40	23963.57	17353.15	14100.00	12188.84	10947.74	10088.56	9467.14
500 000	45840.00	24962.05	18076.20	14687.50	12696.71	11403.90	10508.92	9861.61
520 000	47673.60	25960.53	18799.24	15275.00	13204.58	11860.05	10929.28	10256.07
540 000	49507.20	26959.01	19522.29	15862.50	13712.45	12316.21	11349.63	10650.54
560 000	51340.80	27957.50	20245.34	16450.00	14220.32	12772.36	11769.99	11045.00
580 000	53174.40	28955.98	20968.39	17037.50	14728.19	13228.52	12190.35	11439.46
600 000	55008.00	29954.46	21691.44	17625.00	15236.06	13684.67	12610.70	11833.93
620 000	56841.60	30952.94	22414.48	18212.50	15743.92	14140.83	13031.06	12228.39
640 000	58675.20	31951.42	23137.53	18800.00	16251.79	14596.99	13451.42	12622.86
660 000	60508.80	32949.91	23860.58	19387.50	16759.66	15053.14	13871.77	13017.32
680 000	62342.40	33948.39	24583.63	19975.00	17267.53	15509.30	14292.13	13411.79
700 000	64176.00	34946.87	25306.68	20562.50	17775.40	15965.45	14712.49	13806.25
720 000	66009.59	35945.35	26029.72	21150.00	18283.27	16421.61	15132.84	14200.71
740 000	67843.19	36943.83	26752.77	21737.50	18791.14	16877.77	15553.20	14595.18
760 000	69676.79	37942.32	27475.82	22325.00	19299.00	17333.92	15973.56	14989.64
780 000	71510.39	38940.80	28198.87	22912.50	19806.87	17790.08	16393.91	15384.11
800 000	73343.99	39939.28	28921.92	23500.00	20314.74	18246.23	16814.27	15778.57
820 000	75177.59	40937.76	29644.96	24087.50	20822.61	18702.39	17234.63	16173.04
840 000	77011.19	41936.24	30368.01	24675.00	21330.48	19158.54	17654.98	16567.50
860 000	78844.79	42934.73	31091.06	25262.50	21838.35	19614.70	18075.34	16961.96
880 000	80678.39	43933.21	31814.11	25850.00	22346.22	20070.86	18495.70	17356.43
900 000	82511.99	44931.69	32537.15	26437.50	22854.08	20527.01	18916.05	17750.89
920 000	84345.59	45930.17	33260.20	27025.00	23361.95	20983.17	19336.41	18145.36
940 000	86179.19	46928.65	33983.25	27612.50	23869.82	21439.32	19756.77	18539.82
960 000	88012.79	47927.14	34706.30	28200.00	24377.69	21895.48	20177.12	18934.29
980 000	89846.39	48925.62	35429.35	28787.50	24885.56	22351.64	20597.48	19328.75
1000 000	91679.99	49924.10	36152.39	29375.00	25393.43	22807.79	21017.84	19723.21
Coefficient	.091679993	.049924099	.036152394	.029374998	.025393427	.022807791	.021017838	.019723214

MONTHLY AMORTIZING PAYMENTS — 18.00%

AMOUNT	9 YEARS	10 YEARS	15 YEARS	20 YEARS	25 YEARS	30 YEARS	35 YEARS	40 YEARS
10 000	187.57	180.19	161.04	154.33	151.74	150.71	150.29	150.12
20 000	375.14	360.37	322.08	308.66	303.49	301.42	300.58	300.24
30 000	562.71	540.56	483.13	462.99	455.23	452.13	450.87	450.35
40 000	750.28	720.74	644.17	617.32	606.97	602.83	601.16	600.47
50 000	937.84	900.93	805.21	771.66	758.71	753.54	751.45	750.59
60 000	1125.41	1081.11	966.25	925.99	910.46	904.25	901.74	900.71
70 000	1312.98	1261.30	1127.29	1080.32	1062.20	1054.96	1052.02	1050.83
80 000	1500.55	1441.48	1288.34	1234.65	1213.94	1205.67	1202.31	1200.95
90 000	1688.12	1621.67	1449.38	1388.98	1365.69	1356.38	1352.60	1351.06
100 000	1875.69	1801.85	1610.42	1543.31	1517.43	1507.09	1502.89	1501.18
110 000	2063.26	1982.04	1771.46	1697.64	1669.17	1657.79	1653.18	1651.30
120 000	2250.83	2162.22	1932.51	1851.97	1820.92	1808.50	1803.47	1801.42
130 000	2438.40	2342.41	2093.55	2006.30	1972.66	1959.21	1953.76	1951.54
140 000	2625.96	2522.59	2254.59	2160.64	2124.40	2109.92	2104.05	2101.66
150 000	2813.53	2702.78	2415.63	2314.97	2276.14	2260.63	2254.34	2251.77
160 000	3001.10	2882.96	2576.67	2469.30	2427.89	2411.34	2404.63	2401.89
170 000	3188.67	3063.15	2737.72	2623.63	2579.63	2562.05	2554.92	2552.01
180 000	3376.24	3243.33	2898.76	2777.96	2731.37	2712.75	2705.21	2702.13
190 000	3563.81	3423.52	3059.80	2932.29	2883.12	2863.46	2855.49	2852.25
200 000	3751.38	3603.70	3220.84	3086.62	3034.86	3014.17	3005.78	3002.36
210 000	3938.95	3783.89	3381.88	3240.95	3186.60	3164.88	3156.07	3152.48
220 000	4126.52	3964.07	3542.93	3395.29	3338.35	3315.59	3306.36	3302.60
230 000	4314.08	4144.26	3703.97	3549.62	3490.09	3466.30	3456.65	3452.72
240 000	4501.65	4324.44	3865.01	3703.95	3641.83	3617.00	3606.94	3602.84
250 000	4689.22	4504.63	4026.05	3858.28	3793.57	3767.71	3757.23	3752.96
260 000	4876.79	4684.82	4187.09	4012.61	3945.32	3918.42	3907.52	3903.07
270 000	5064.36	4865.00	4348.14	4166.94	4097.06	4069.13	4057.81	4053.19
280 000	5251.93	5045.19	4509.18	4321.27	4248.80	4219.84	4208.10	4203.31
290 000	5439.50	5225.37	4670.22	4475.60	4400.55	4370.55	4358.39	4353.43
300 000	5627.07	5405.56	4831.26	4629.93	4552.29	4521.26	4508.68	4503.55
320 000	6002.20	5765.93	5153.35	4938.60	4855.78	4822.67	4809.25	4803.78
340 000	6377.34	6126.30	5475.43	5247.26	5159.26	5124.09	5109.83	5104.02
360 000	6752.48	6486.67	5797.52	5555.92	5462.75	5425.51	5410.41	5404.26
380 000	7127.62	6847.04	6119.60	5864.58	5766.23	5726.92	5710.99	5704.49
400 000	7502.76	7207.41	6441.68	6173.25	6069.72	6028.34	6011.57	6004.73
420 000	7877.89	7567.78	6763.77	6481.91	6373.21	6329.76	6312.15	6304.97
440 000	8253.03	7928.15	7085.85	6790.57	6676.69	6631.18	6612.72	6605.20
460 000	8628.17	8288.52	7407.94	7099.23	6980.18	6932.59	6913.30	6905.44
480 000	9003.31	8648.89	7730.02	7407.90	7283.66	7234.01	7213.88	7205.68
500 000	9378.44	9009.26	8052.11	7716.56	7587.15	7535.43	7514.46	7505.91
520 000	9753.58	9369.63	8374.19	8025.22	7890.64	7836.84	7815.04	7806.15
540 000	10128.72	9730.00	8696.27	8333.88	8194.12	8138.26	8115.62	8106.38
560 000	10503.86	10090.37	9018.36	8642.54	8497.61	8439.68	8416.19	8406.62
580 000	10879.00	10450.74	9340.44	8951.21	8801.09	8741.10	8716.77	8706.86
600 000	11254.13	10811.11	9662.53	9259.87	9104.58	9042.51	9017.35	9007.09
620 000	11629.27	11171.48	9984.61	9568.53	9408.07	9343.93	9317.93	9307.33
640 000	12004.41	11531.85	10306.69	9877.19	9711.55	9645.35	9618.51	9607.57
660 000	12379.55	11892.22	10628.78	10185.86	10015.04	9946.76	9919.09	9907.80
680 000	12754.68	12252.59	10950.86	10494.52	10318.52	10248.18	10219.66	10208.04
700 000	13129.82	12612.96	11272.95	10803.18	10622.01	10549.60	10520.24	10508.28
720 000	13504.96	12973.33	11595.03	11111.84	10925.50	10851.01	10820.82	10808.51
740 000	13880.10	13333.70	11917.12	11420.51	11228.98	11152.43	11121.40	11108.75
760 000	14255.23	13694.08	12239.20	11729.17	11532.47	11453.85	11421.98	11408.99
780 000	14630.37	14054.45	12561.28	12037.83	11835.95	11755.27	11722.56	11709.22
800 000	15005.51	14414.82	12883.37	12346.49	12139.44	12056.68	12023.14	12009.46
820 000	15380.65	14775.19	13205.45	12655.15	12442.93	12358.10	12323.71	12309.69
840 000	15755.79	15135.56	13527.54	12963.82	12746.41	12659.52	12624.29	12609.93
860 000	16130.92	15495.93	13849.62	13272.48	13049.90	12960.93	12924.87	12910.17
880 000	16506.06	15856.30	14171.70	13581.14	13353.38	13262.35	13225.45	13210.41
900 000	16881.20	16216.67	14493.79	13889.80	13656.87	13563.77	13526.03	13510.64
920 000	17256.34	16577.04	14815.87	14198.47	13960.36	13865.19	13826.61	13810.88
940 000	17631.47	16937.41	15137.96	14507.13	14263.84	14166.60	14127.18	14111.11
960 000	18006.61	17297.78	15460.04	14815.79	14567.33	14468.02	14427.76	14411.35
980 000	18381.75	17658.15	15782.13	15124.45	14870.81	14769.44	14728.34	14711.59
1000 000	18756.89	18018.52	16104.21	15433.12	15174.30	15070.85	15028.92	15011.82
Coefficient	.018756888	.018018520	.016104210	.015433115	.015174299	.015070854	.015028919	.015011823

MONTHLY AMORTIZING PAYMENTS

AMOUNT	1 YEAR	2 YEARS	3 YEARS	4 YEARS	5 YEARS	6 YEARS	7 YEARS	8 YEARS
10 000	917.99	500.45	362.78	295.06	255.30	229.49	211.65	198.75
20 000	1835.98	1000.90	725.56	590.12	510.59	458.99	423.29	397.50
30 000	2753.97	1501.35	1088.34	885.17	765.89	688.48	634.94	596.25
40 000	3671.96	2001.80	1451.12	1180.23	1021.18	917.97	846.58	795.00
50 000	4589.95	2502.25	1813.90	1475.29	1276.48	1147.47	1058.23	993.75
60 000	5507.94	3002.70	2176.68	1770.35	1531.78	1376.96	1269.88	1192.50
70 000	6425.93	3503.15	2539.46	2065.41	1787.07	1606.45	1481.52	1391.25
80 000	7343.92	4003.60	2902.23	2360.46	2042.37	1835.95	1693.17	1590.00
90 000	8261.91	4504.05	3265.01	2655.52	2297.67	2065.44	1904.82	1788.75
100 000	9179.90	5004.50	3627.79	2950.58	2552.96	2294.93	2116.46	1987.51
110 000	10097.89	5504.95	3990.57	3245.64	2808.26	2524.43	2328.11	2186.26
120 000	11015.88	6005.40	4353.35	3540.70	3063.55	2753.92	2539.76	2385.01
130 000	11933.87	6505.85	4716.13	3835.75	3318.85	2983.41	2751.40	2583.76
140 000	12851.86	7006.30	5078.91	4130.81	3574.15	3212.91	2963.05	2782.51
150 000	13769.85	7506.75	5441.69	4425.87	3829.44	3442.40	3174.69	2981.26
160 000	14687.84	8007.20	5804.47	4720.93	4084.74	3671.90	3386.34	3180.01
170 000	15605.83	8507.65	6167.25	5015.99	4340.04	3901.39	3597.99	3378.76
180 000	16523.82	9008.10	6530.03	5311.04	4595.33	4130.88	3809.63	3577.51
190 000	17441.81	9508.55	6892.81	5606.10	4850.63	4360.38	4021.28	3776.26
200 000	18359.80	10009.00	7255.59	5901.16	5105.92	4589.87	4232.93	3975.01
210 000	19277.79	10509.45	7618.37	6196.22	5361.22	4819.36	4444.57	4173.76
220 000	20195.78	11009.89	7981.14	6491.28	5616.52	5048.86	4656.22	4372.51
230 000	21113.77	11510.34	8343.92	6786.33	5871.81	5278.35	4867.86	4571.26
240 000	22031.76	12010.79	8706.70	7081.39	6127.11	5507.84	5079.51	4770.01
250 000	22949.75	12511.24	9069.48	7376.45	6382.41	5737.34	5291.16	4968.76
260 000	23867.74	13011.69	9432.26	7671.51	6637.70	5966.83	5502.80	5167.51
270 000	24785.73	13512.14	9795.04	7966.56	6893.00	6196.32	5714.45	5366.26
280 000	25703.72	14012.59	10157.82	8261.62	7148.29	6425.82	5926.10	5565.01
290 000	26621.71	14513.04	10520.60	8556.68	7403.59	6655.31	6137.74	5763.77
300 000	27539.70	15013.49	10883.38	8851.74	7658.89	6884.80	6349.39	5962.52
320 000	29375.68	16014.39	11608.94	9441.85	8169.48	7343.79	6772.68	6360.02
340 000	31211.66	17015.29	12334.50	10031.97	8680.07	7802.78	7195.99	6757.52
360 000	33047.65	18016.19	13060.06	10622.09	9190.66	8261.76	7619.27	7155.02
380 000	34883.63	19017.09	13785.61	11212.20	9701.26	8720.75	8042.56	7552.52
400 000	36719.61	20017.99	14511.17	11802.32	10211.85	9179.74	8465.85	7950.02
420 000	38555.59	21018.89	15236.73	12392.43	10722.44	9638.73	8889.14	8347.52
440 000	40391.57	22019.79	15962.29	12982.55	11233.03	10097.71	9312.44	8745.02
460 000	42227.55	23020.69	16687.85	13572.67	11743.63	10556.70	9735.73	9142.52
480 000	44063.53	24021.59	17413.41	14162.78	12254.22	11015.69	10159.02	9540.02
500 000	45899.51	25022.49	18138.97	14752.90	12764.81	11474.67	10582.31	9937.53
520 000	47735.49	26023.39	18864.52	15343.01	13275.40	11933.66	11005.60	10335.03
540 000	49571.47	27024.29	19590.08	15933.13	13786.00	12392.65	11428.90	10732.53
560 000	51407.45	28025.19	20315.64	16523.25	14296.59	12851.63	11852.19	11130.03
580 000	53243.43	29026.09	21041.20	17113.36	14807.18	13310.62	12275.48	11527.53
600 000	55079.41	30026.99	21766.76	17703.48	15317.77	13769.61	12698.78	11925.03
620 000	56915.39	31027.89	22492.32	18293.59	15828.37	14228.59	13122.07	12322.53
640 000	58751.37	32028.79	23217.88	18883.71	16338.96	14687.58	13545.36	12720.03
660 000	60587.35	33029.68	23943.43	19473.83	16849.55	15146.57	13968.65	13117.53
680 000	62423.33	34030.58	24668.99	20063.94	17360.14	15605.56	14391.95	13515.04
700 000	64259.31	35031.48	25394.55	20654.06	17870.74	16064.54	14815.24	13912.54
720 000	66095.29	36032.38	26120.11	21244.17	18381.33	16523.53	15238.53	14310.04
740 000	67931.27	37033.28	26845.67	21834.29	18891.92	16982.52	15661.82	14707.54
760 000	69767.25	38034.18	27571.23	22424.40	19402.51	17441.50	16085.12	15105.04
780 000	71603.23	39035.08	28296.79	23014.52	19913.11	17900.49	16508.41	15502.54
800 000	73439.21	40035.98	29022.34	23604.64	20423.70	18359.48	16931.70	15900.04
820 000	75275.19	41036.88	29747.90	24194.75	20934.29	18818.46	17354.99	16297.54
840 000	77111.17	42037.78	30473.46	24784.87	21444.88	19277.45	17778.29	16695.04
860 000	78947.15	43038.68	31199.02	25374.98	21955.47	19736.44	18201.58	17092.54
880 000	80783.13	44039.58	31924.58	25965.10	22466.07	20195.42	18624.87	17490.05
900 000	82619.11	45040.48	32650.14	26555.22	22976.66	20654.41	19048.16	17887.55
920 000	84455.09	46041.38	33375.70	27145.33	23487.25	21113.40	19471.45	18285.05
940 000	86291.07	47042.28	34101.26	27735.45	23997.84	21572.39	19894.75	18682.55
960 000	88127.05	48043.18	34826.81	28325.56	24508.44	22031.37	20318.04	19080.05
980 000	89963.03	49044.08	35552.37	28915.68	25019.03	22490.36	20741.33	19477.55
1000 000	91799.01	50044.98	36277.93	29505.80	25529.62	22949.35	21164.63	19875.05
Coefficient	.091799014	.050044977	.036277931	.029505796	.025529622	.022949346	.021164625	.019875052

MONTHLY AMORTIZING PAYMENTS 18.25%

AMOUNT	9 YEARS	10 YEARS	15 YEARS	20 YEARS	25 YEARS	30 YEARS	35 YEARS	40 YEARS
10 000	189.14	181.80	162.84	156.26	153.74	152.75	152.35	152.19
20 000	378.27	363.60	325.69	312.52	307.49	305.50	304.70	304.38
30 000	567.41	545.39	488.53	468.77	461.23	458.25	457.06	456.58
40 000	756.54	727.19	651.38	625.03	614.98	611.00	609.41	608.77
50 000	945.68	908.99	814.22	781.29	768.72	763.75	761.76	760.96
60 000	1134.81	1090.79	977.06	937.55	922.46	916.50	914.11	913.15
70 000	1323.95	1272.58	1139.91	1093.80	1076.21	1069.25	1066.47	1065.34
80 000	1513.08	1454.38	1302.75	1250.06	1229.95	1222.00	1218.82	1217.54
90 000	1702.22	1636.18	1465.60	1406.32	1383.69	1374.75	1371.17	1369.73
100 000	1891.36	1817.98	1628.44	1562.58	1537.44	1527.50	1523.52	1521.92
110 000	2080.49	1999.78	1791.28	1718.84	1691.18	1680.25	1675.88	1674.11
120 000	2269.63	2181.57	1954.13	1875.09	1844.93	1833.00	1828.23	1826.30
130 000	2458.76	2363.37	2116.97	2031.35	1998.67	1985.75	1980.58	1978.50
140 000	2647.90	2545.17	2279.82	2187.61	2152.41	2138.50	2132.93	2130.69
150 000	2837.03	2726.97	2442.66	2343.87	2306.16	2291.25	2285.28	2282.88
160 000	3026.17	2908.76	2605.50	2500.12	2459.90	2444.01	2437.64	2435.07
170 000	3215.30	3090.56	2768.35	2656.38	2613.65	2596.76	2589.99	2587.26
180 000	3404.44	3272.36	2931.19	2812.64	2767.39	2749.51	2742.34	2739.46
190 000	3593.58	3454.16	3094.04	2968.90	2921.13	2902.26	2894.69	2891.65
200 000	3782.71	3635.96	3256.88	3125.16	3074.88	3055.01	3047.05	3043.84
210 000	3971.85	3817.75	3419.72	3281.41	3228.62	3207.76	3199.40	3196.03
220 000	4160.98	3999.55	3582.57	3437.67	3382.36	3360.51	3351.75	3348.22
230 000	4350.12	4181.35	3745.41	3593.93	3536.11	3513.26	3504.10	3500.41
240 000	4539.25	4363.15	3908.26	3750.19	3689.85	3666.01	3656.45	3652.61
250 000	4728.39	4544.94	4071.10	3906.44	3843.60	3818.76	3808.81	3804.80
260 000	4917.52	4726.74	4233.94	4062.70	3997.34	3971.51	3961.16	3956.99
270 000	5106.66	4908.54	4396.79	4218.96	4151.08	4124.26	4113.51	4109.18
280 000	5295.80	5090.34	4559.63	4375.22	4304.83	4277.01	4265.86	4261.37
290 000	5484.93	5272.14	4722.48	4531.48	4458.57	4429.76	4418.22	4413.57
300 000	5674.07	5453.93	4885.32	4687.73	4612.32	4582.51	4570.57	4565.76
320 000	6052.34	5817.53	5211.01	5000.25	4919.80	4888.01	4875.27	4870.14
340 000	6430.61	6181.12	5536.70	5312.76	5227.29	5193.51	5179.98	5174.53
360 000	6808.88	6544.72	5862.39	5625.28	5534.78	5499.01	5484.68	5478.91
380 000	7187.15	6908.32	6188.07	5937.80	5842.27	5804.51	5789.39	5783.29
400 000	7565.42	7271.91	6513.76	6250.31	6149.75	6110.01	6094.09	6087.68
420 000	7943.69	7635.51	6839.45	6562.83	6457.24	6415.52	6398.80	6392.06
440 000	8321.97	7999.10	7165.14	6875.34	6764.73	6721.02	6703.50	6696.45
460 000	8700.24	8362.70	7490.83	7187.86	7072.22	7026.52	7008.21	7000.83
480 000	9078.51	8726.29	7816.51	7500.37	7379.71	7332.02	7312.91	7305.21
500 000	9456.78	9089.89	8142.20	7812.89	7687.19	7637.52	7617.61	7609.60
520 000	9835.05	9453.48	8467.89	8125.41	7994.68	7943.02	7922.32	7913.98
540 000	10213.32	9817.08	8793.58	8437.92	8302.17	8248.52	8227.02	8218.37
560 000	10591.59	10180.68	9119.27	8750.44	8609.66	8554.02	8531.73	8522.75
580 000	10969.86	10544.27	9444.95	9062.95	8917.14	8859.52	8836.43	8827.13
600 000	11348.13	10907.87	9770.64	9375.47	9224.63	9165.02	9141.14	9131.52
620 000	11726.41	11271.46	10096.33	9687.99	9532.12	9470.52	9445.84	9435.90
640 000	12104.68	11635.06	10422.02	10000.50	9839.61	9776.02	9750.55	9740.28
660 000	12482.95	11998.65	10747.71	10313.01	10147.09	10081.52	10055.25	10044.67
680 000	12861.22	12362.25	11073.39	10625.53	10454.58	10387.02	10359.96	10349.05
700 000	13239.49	12725.84	11399.08	10938.05	10762.07	10692.52	10664.66	10653.44
720 000	13617.76	13089.44	11724.77	11250.56	11069.56	10998.02	10969.36	10957.82
740 000	13996.03	13453.04	12050.46	11563.08	11377.05	11303.52	11274.07	11262.00
760 000	14374.30	13816.63	12376.15	11875.59	11684.53	11609.02	11578.77	11566.59
780 000	14752.57	14180.23	12701.83	12188.11	11992.02	11914.52	11883.48	11870.97
800 000	15130.85	14543.82	13027.52	12500.62	12299.51	12220.03	12188.18	12175.36
820 000	15509.12	14907.42	13353.21	12813.14	12607.00	12525.53	12492.89	12479.74
840 000	15887.39	15271.01	13678.90	13125.65	12914.48	12831.03	12797.59	12784.12
860 000	16265.66	15634.61	14004.59	13438.17	13221.97	13136.53	13102.30	13088.51
880 000	16643.93	15998.20	14330.27	13750.69	13529.46	13442.03	13407.00	13392.89
900 000	17022.20	16361.80	14655.96	14063.20	13836.95	13747.53	13711.71	13697.28
920 000	17400.47	16725.40	14981.65	14375.72	14144.44	14053.03	14016.41	14001.66
940 000	17778.74	17088.99	15307.34	14688.23	14451.92	14358.53	14321.12	14306.04
960 000	18157.01	17452.59	15633.03	15000.75	14759.41	14664.03	14625.82	14610.43
980 000	18535.29	17816.18	15958.71	15313.26	15066.90	14969.53	14930.52	14914.81
1000 000	18913.56	18179.78	16284.40	15625.78	15374.39	15275.03	15235.23	15219.20
Coefficient	.018913557	.018179778	.016284403	.015625779	.015374386	.015275032	.015235229	.015219195

109

MONTHLY AMORTIZING PAYMENTS

AMOUNT	1 YEAR	2 YEARS	3 YEARS	4 YEARS	5 YEARS	6 YEARS	7 YEARS	8 YEARS
10 000	919.18	501.66	364.04	296.37	256.66	230.91	213.12	200.27
20 000	1838.36	1003.32	728.07	592.74	513.32	461.83	426.24	400.55
30 000	2757.54	1504.98	1092.11	889.11	769.99	692.74	639.36	600.82
40 000	3676.72	2006.64	1456.15	1185.48	1026.65	923.65	852.48	801.10
50 000	4595.91	2508.30	1820.19	1481.85	1283.31	1154.57	1065.60	1001.37
60 000	5515.09	3009.96	2184.22	1778.21	1539.97	1385.48	1278.72	1201.65
70 000	6434.27	3511.62	2548.26	2074.58	1796.63	1616.39	1491.83	1401.92
80 000	7353.45	4013.28	2912.30	2370.95	2053.30	1847.31	1704.95	1602.20
90 000	8272.63	4514.94	3276.33	2667.32	2309.96	2078.22	1918.07	1802.47
100 000	9191.81	5016.60	3640.37	2963.69	2566.62	2309.14	2131.19	2002.74
110 000	10110.99	5518.26	4004.41	3260.06	2823.28	2540.05	2344.31	2203.02
120 000	11030.17	6019.92	4368.45	3556.43	3079.95	2770.96	2557.43	2403.29
130 000	11949.36	6521.58	4732.48	3852.80	3336.61	3001.88	2770.55	2603.57
140 000	12868.54	7023.24	5096.52	4149.17	3593.27	3232.79	2983.67	2803.84
150 000	13787.72	7524.90	5460.56	4445.54	3849.93	3463.70	3196.79	3004.12
160 000	14706.90	8026.56	5824.59	4741.91	4106.59	3694.62	3409.91	3204.39
170 000	15626.08	8528.22	6188.63	5038.28	4363.26	3925.53	3623.03	3404.66
180 000	16545.26	9029.89	6552.67	5334.64	4619.92	4156.44	3836.15	3604.94
190 000	17464.44	9531.55	6916.71	5631.01	4876.58	4387.36	4049.26	3805.21
200 000	18383.62	10033.21	7280.74	5927.38	5133.24	4618.27	4262.38	4005.49
210 000	19302.80	10534.87	7644.78	6223.75	5389.90	4849.18	4475.50	4205.76
220 000	20221.99	11036.53	8008.82	6520.12	5646.57	5080.10	4688.62	4406.04
230 000	21141.17	11538.19	8372.85	6816.49	5903.23	5311.01	4901.74	4606.31
240 000	22060.35	12039.85	8736.89	7112.86	6159.89	5541.92	5114.86	4806.59
250 000	22979.53	12541.51	9100.93	7409.23	6416.55	5772.84	5327.98	5006.86
260 000	23898.71	13043.17	9464.97	7705.60	6673.21	6003.75	5541.10	5207.13
270 000	24817.89	13544.83	9829.00	8001.97	6929.88	6234.67	5754.22	5407.41
280 000	25737.07	14046.49	10193.04	8298.34	7186.54	6465.58	5967.34	5607.68
290 000	26656.25	14548.15	10557.08	8594.71	7443.20	6696.49	6180.46	5807.96
300 000	27575.43	15049.81	10921.11	8891.07	7699.86	6927.41	6393.58	6008.23
320 000	29413.80	16053.13	11649.19	9483.81	8213.19	7389.23	6819.81	6408.78
340 000	31252.16	17056.45	12377.26	10076.55	8726.51	7851.06	7246.05	6809.33
360 000	33090.52	18059.77	13105.34	10669.29	9239.84	8312.89	7672.29	7209.88
380 000	34928.88	19063.09	13833.41	11262.03	9753.16	8774.71	8098.53	7610.43
400 000	36767.25	20066.41	14561.49	11854.77	10266.48	9236.54	8524.77	8010.98
420 000	38605.61	21069.73	15289.56	12447.50	10779.81	9698.37	8951.00	8411.53
440 000	40443.97	22073.05	16017.63	13040.24	11293.13	10160.20	9377.24	8812.07
460 000	42282.33	23076.37	16745.71	13632.98	11806.46	10622.02	9803.48	9212.62
480 000	44120.70	24079.69	17473.78	14225.72	12319.78	11083.85	10229.72	9613.17
500 000	45959.06	25083.01	18201.86	14818.46	12833.10	11545.68	10655.96	10013.72
520 000	47797.42	26086.33	18929.93	15411.20	13346.43	12007.50	11082.20	10414.27
540 000	49635.78	27089.66	19658.01	16003.93	13859.75	12469.33	11508.44	10814.82
560 000	51474.14	28092.98	20386.08	16596.67	14373.08	12931.16	11934.67	11215.37
580 000	53312.51	29096.30	21114.15	17189.41	14886.40	13392.99	12360.91	11615.92
600 000	55150.87	30099.62	21842.23	17782.15	15399.73	13854.81	12787.15	12016.46
620 000	56989.23	31102.94	22570.30	18374.89	15913.05	14316.64	13213.39	12417.01
640 000	58827.59	32106.26	23298.38	18967.63	16426.37	14778.47	13639.63	12817.56
660 000	60665.96	33109.58	24026.45	19560.36	16939.70	15240.29	14065.87	13218.11
680 000	62504.32	34112.90	24754.52	20153.10	17453.02	15702.12	14492.10	13618.66
700 000	64342.68	35116.22	25482.60	20745.84	17966.35	16163.95	14918.34	14019.21
720 000	66181.04	36119.54	26210.67	21338.58	18479.67	16625.77	15344.58	14419.76
740 000	68019.41	37122.86	26938.75	21931.32	18992.99	17087.60	15770.82	14820.31
760 000	69857.77	38126.18	27666.82	22524.06	19506.32	17549.43	16197.06	15220.86
780 000	71696.13	39129.50	28394.90	23116.79	20019.64	18011.26	16623.30	15621.40
800 000	73534.49	40132.82	29122.97	23709.53	20532.97	18473.08	17049.54	16021.95
820 000	75372.86	41136.14	29851.04	24302.27	21046.29	18934.91	17475.77	16422.50
840 000	77211.22	42139.46	30579.12	24895.01	21559.62	19396.74	17902.01	16823.05
860 000	79049.58	43142.78	31307.19	25487.75	22072.94	19858.56	18328.25	17223.60
880 000	80887.94	44146.10	32035.27	26080.49	22586.26	20320.39	18754.49	17624.15
900 000	82726.30	45149.43	32763.34	26673.22	23099.59	20782.22	19180.73	18024.70
920 000	84564.67	46152.75	33491.42	27265.96	23612.91	21244.05	19606.97	18425.25
940 000	86403.03	47156.07	34219.49	27858.70	24126.24	21705.87	20033.20	18825.79
960 000	88241.39	48159.39	34947.56	28451.44	24639.56	22167.70	20459.44	19226.34
980 000	90079.75	49162.71	35675.64	29044.18	25152.88	22629.53	20885.68	19626.89
1 000 000	91918.12	50166.03	36403.71	29636.92	25666.21	23091.35	21311.92	20027.44
Coefficient	.091918116	.050166028	.036403713	.029636915	.025666209	.023091354	.021311919	.020027441

MONTHLY AMORTIZING PAYMENTS 18.50%

AMOUNT	9 YEARS	10 YEARS	15 YEARS	20 YEARS	25 YEARS	30 YEARS	35 YEARS	40 YEARS
10 000	190.71	183.42	164.65	158.19	155.75	154.79	154.42	154.27
20 000	381.42	366.83	329.30	316.38	311.50	309.59	308.83	308.53
30 000	572.12	550.25	493.96	474.57	467.25	464.38	463.25	462.80
40 000	762.83	733.67	658.61	632.76	622.99	619.18	617.67	617.07
50 000	953.54	917.08	823.26	790.95	778.74	773.97	772.08	771.33
60 000	1144.25	1100.50	987.91	949.14	934.49	928.77	926.50	925.60
70 000	1334.96	1283.92	1152.57	1107.33	1090.24	1083.56	1080.92	1079.87
80 000	1525.67	1467.33	1317.22	1265.52	1245.99	1238.36	1235.33	1234.13
90 000	1716.37	1650.75	1481.87	1423.71	1401.74	1393.15	1389.75	1388.40
100 000	1907.08	1834.17	1646.52	1581.90	1557.48	1547.94	1544.17	1542.66
110 000	2097.79	2017.58	1811.18	1740.09	1713.23	1702.74	1698.58	1696.93
120 000	2288.50	2201.00	1975.83	1898.28	1868.98	1857.53	1853.00	1851.20
130 000	2479.21	2384.42	2140.48	2056.47	2024.73	2012.33	2007.42	2005.46
140 000	2669.91	2567.83	2305.13	2214.66	2180.48	2167.12	2161.83	2159.73
150 000	2860.62	2751.25	2469.79	2372.84	2336.23	2321.92	2316.25	2314.00
160 000	3051.33	2934.66	2634.44	2531.03	2491.97	2476.71	2470.67	2468.26
170 000	3242.04	3118.08	2799.09	2689.22	2647.72	2631.51	2625.08	2622.53
180 000	3432.75	3301.50	2963.74	2847.41	2803.47	2786.30	2779.50	2776.80
190 000	3623.45	3484.91	3128.39	3005.60	2959.22	2941.09	2933.92	2931.06
200 000	3814.16	3668.33	3293.05	3163.79	3114.97	3095.89	3088.34	3085.33
210 000	4004.87	3851.75	3457.70	3321.98	3270.72	3250.68	3242.75	3239.60
220 000	4195.58	4035.16	3622.35	3480.17	3426.47	3405.48	3397.17	3393.86
230 000	4386.29	4218.58	3787.00	3638.36	3582.21	3560.27	3551.59	3548.13
240 000	4577.00	4402.00	3951.66	3796.55	3737.96	3715.07	3706.00	3702.39
250 000	4767.70	4585.41	4116.31	3954.74	3893.71	3869.86	3860.42	3856.66
260 000	4958.41	4768.83	4280.96	4112.93	4049.46	4024.66	4014.84	4010.93
270 000	5149.12	4952.25	4445.61	4271.12	4205.21	4179.45	4169.25	4165.19
280 000	5339.83	5135.66	4610.27	4429.31	4360.96	4334.24	4323.67	4319.46
290 000	5530.54	5319.08	4774.92	4587.50	4516.70	4489.04	4478.09	4473.73
300 000	5721.24	5502.50	4939.57	4745.69	4672.45	4643.83	4632.50	4627.99
320 000	6102.66	5869.33	5268.87	5062.07	4983.95	4953.42	4941.34	4936.53
340 000	6484.08	6236.16	5598.18	5378.45	5295.45	5263.01	5250.17	5245.06
360 000	6865.49	6603.00	5927.48	5694.83	5606.94	5572.60	5559.00	5553.59
380 000	7246.91	6969.83	6256.79	6011.21	5918.44	5882.19	5867.84	5862.12
400 000	7628.33	7336.66	6586.09	6327.59	6229.94	6191.78	6176.67	6170.66
420 000	8009.74	7703.49	6915.40	6643.97	6541.43	6501.37	6485.50	6479.19
440 000	8391.16	8070.33	7244.70	6960.35	6852.93	6810.96	6794.34	6787.72
460 000	8772.57	8437.16	7574.01	7276.72	7164.43	7120.54	7103.17	7096.26
480 000	9153.99	8803.99	7903.31	7593.10	7475.92	7430.13	7412.00	7404.79
500 000	9535.41	9170.83	8232.62	7909.48	7787.42	7739.72	7720.84	7713.32
520 000	9916.82	9537.66	8561.92	8225.86	8098.92	8049.31	8029.67	8021.85
540 000	10298.24	9904.49	8891.23	8542.24	8410.41	8358.90	8338.51	8330.39
560 000	10679.66	10271.33	9220.53	8858.62	8721.91	8668.49	8647.34	8638.92
580 000	11061.07	10638.16	9549.84	9175.00	9033.41	8978.08	8956.17	8947.45
600 000	11442.49	11004.99	9879.14	9491.38	9344.90	9287.67	9265.01	9255.99
620 000	11823.91	11371.83	10208.45	9807.76	9656.40	9597.26	9573.84	9564.52
640 000	12205.32	11738.66	10537.75	10124.14	9967.90	9906.84	9882.67	9873.05
660 000	12586.74	12105.49	10867.05	10440.52	10279.40	10216.43	10191.51	10181.59
680 000	12968.15	12472.32	11196.36	10756.90	10590.89	10526.02	10500.34	10490.12
700 000	13349.57	12839.16	11525.66	11073.28	10902.39	10835.61	10809.17	10798.65
720 000	13730.99	13205.99	11854.97	11389.66	11213.89	11145.20	11118.01	11107.18
740 000	14112.40	13572.82	12184.27	11706.03	11525.38	11454.79	11426.84	11415.72
760 000	14493.82	13939.66	12513.58	12022.41	11836.88	11764.38	11735.67	11724.25
780 000	14875.24	14306.49	12842.88	12338.79	12148.38	12073.97	12044.51	12032.78
800 000	15256.65	14673.32	13172.19	12655.17	12459.87	12383.56	12353.34	12341.32
820 000	15638.07	15040.16	13501.49	12971.55	12771.37	12693.14	12662.17	12649.85
840 000	16019.48	15406.99	13830.80	13287.93	13082.87	13002.73	12971.01	12958.38
860 000	16400.90	15773.82	14160.10	13604.31	13394.36	13312.32	13279.84	13266.91
880 000	16782.32	16140.66	14489.41	13920.69	13705.86	13621.91	13588.67	13575.45
900 000	17163.73	16507.49	14818.71	14237.07	14017.36	13931.50	13897.51	13883.98
920 000	17545.15	16874.32	15148.02	14553.45	14328.85	14241.09	14206.34	14192.51
940 000	17926.57	17241.15	15477.32	14869.83	14640.35	14550.68	14515.18	14501.05
960 000	18307.98	17607.99	15806.62	15186.21	14951.85	14860.27	14824.01	14809.58
980 000	18689.40	17974.82	16135.93	15502.59	15263.34	15169.86	15132.84	15118.11
1000 000	19070.81	18341.65	16465.23	15818.97	15574.84	15479.45	15441.68	15426.64
Coefficient	.019070815	.018341654	.016465234	.015818966	.015574841	.015479445	.015441676	.015426644

111

18.75% MONTHLY AMORTIZING PAYMENTS

AMOUNT	1 YEAR	2 YEARS	3 YEARS	4 YEARS	5 YEARS	6 YEARS	7 YEARS	8 YEARS
10 000	920.37	502.87	365.30	297.58	258.03	232.34	214.60	201.80
20 000	1840.75	1005.74	730.59	595.37	516.06	464.68	429.19	403.61
30 000	2761.12	1508.62	1095.89	893.05	774.10	697.01	643.79	605.41
40 000	3681.49	2011.49	1461.19	1190.73	1032.13	929.35	858.39	807.22
50 000	4601.87	2514.36	1826.49	1488.42	1290.16	1161.69	1072.99	1009.02
60 000	5522.24	3017.23	2191.78	1786.10	1548.19	1394.03	1287.58	1210.82
70 000	6442.61	3520.11	2557.08	2083.78	1806.22	1626.37	1502.18	1412.63
80 000	7362.98	4022.98	2922.38	2381.47	2064.25	1858.71	1716.78	1614.43
90 000	8283.36	4525.85	3287.68	2679.15	2322.29	2091.04	1931.37	1816.23
100 000	9203.73	5028.72	3652.97	2976.84	2580.32	2323.38	2145.97	2018.04
110 000	10124.10	5531.60	4018.27	3274.52	2838.35	2555.72	2360.57	2219.84
120 000	11044.48	6034.47	4383.57	3572.20	3096.38	2788.06	2575.17	2421.65
130 000	11964.85	6537.34	4748.87	3869.89	3354.41	3020.40	2789.76	2623.45
140 000	12885.22	7040.21	5114.16	4167.57	3612.45	3252.73	3004.36	2825.25
150 000	13805.60	7543.09	5479.46	4465.25	3870.48	3485.07	3218.96	3027.06
160 000	14725.97	8045.96	5844.76	4762.94	4128.51	3717.41	3433.55	3228.86
170 000	15646.34	8548.83	6210.06	5060.62	4386.54	3949.75	3648.15	3430.66
180 000	16566.72	9051.70	6575.35	5358.30	4644.57	4182.09	3862.75	3632.47
190 000	17487.09	9554.58	6940.65	5655.99	4902.61	4414.42	4077.35	3834.27
200 000	18407.46	10057.45	7305.95	5953.67	5160.64	4646.76	4291.94	4036.08
210 000	19327.83	10560.32	7671.25	6251.35	5418.67	4879.10	4506.54	4237.88
220 000	20248.21	11063.19	8036.54	6549.04	5676.70	5111.44	4721.14	4439.68
230 000	21168.58	11566.06	8401.84	6846.72	5934.73	5343.78	4935.74	4641.49
240 000	22088.95	12068.94	8767.14	7144.41	6192.76	5576.12	5150.33	4843.29
250 000	23009.33	12571.81	9132.44	7442.09	6450.80	5808.45	5364.93	5045.09
260 000	23929.70	13074.68	9497.73	7739.77	6708.83	6040.79	5579.53	5246.90
270 000	24850.07	13577.55	9863.03	8037.46	6966.86	6273.13	5794.12	5448.70
280 000	25770.45	14080.43	10228.33	8335.14	7224.89	6505.47	6008.72	5650.51
290 000	26690.82	14583.30	10593.63	8632.82	7482.92	6737.81	6223.32	5852.31
300 000	27611.19	15086.17	10958.92	8930.51	7740.96	6970.14	6437.92	6054.11
320 000	29451.94	16091.92	11689.52	9525.87	8257.02	7434.82	6867.11	6457.72
340 000	31292.68	17097.66	12420.11	10121.24	8773.08	7899.50	7296.30	6861.33
360 000	33133.43	18103.41	13150.71	10716.61	9289.15	8364.17	7725.50	7264.94
380 000	34974.18	19109.15	13881.30	11311.98	9805.21	8828.85	8154.69	7668.54
400 000	36814.92	20114.90	14611.90	11907.34	10321.27	9293.53	8583.89	8072.15
420 000	38655.67	21120.64	15342.49	12502.71	10837.34	9758.20	9013.08	8475.76
440 000	40496.42	22126.38	16073.09	13098.08	11353.40	10222.88	9442.28	8879.37
460 000	42337.16	23132.13	16803.68	13693.44	11869.47	10687.55	9871.47	9282.97
480 000	44177.91	24137.87	17534.28	14288.81	12385.53	11152.23	10300.66	9686.58
500 000	46018.65	25143.62	18264.87	14884.18	12901.59	11616.91	10729.86	10090.19
520 000	47859.40	26149.36	18995.47	15479.55	13417.66	12081.58	11159.05	10493.80
540 000	49700.15	27155.11	19726.06	16074.91	13933.72	12546.26	11588.25	10897.41
560 000	51540.89	28160.85	20456.66	16670.28	14449.78	13010.94	12017.44	11301.01
580 000	53381.64	29166.60	21187.25	17265.65	14965.85	13475.61	12446.64	11704.62
600 000	55222.38	30172.34	21917.85	17861.01	15481.91	13940.29	12875.83	12108.23
620 000	57063.13	31178.09	22648.44	18456.38	15997.97	14404.96	13305.03	12511.84
640 000	58903.88	32183.83	23379.04	19051.75	16514.04	14869.64	13734.22	12915.44
660 000	60744.62	33189.58	24109.63	19647.11	17030.10	15334.32	14163.41	13319.05
680 000	62585.37	34195.32	24840.23	20242.48	17546.17	15798.99	14592.61	13722.66
700 000	64426.11	35201.07	25570.82	20837.85	18062.23	16263.67	15021.80	14126.27
720 000	66266.86	36206.81	26301.42	21433.22	18578.29	16728.35	15451.00	14529.87
740 000	68107.61	37212.56	27032.01	22028.58	19094.36	17193.02	15880.19	14933.48
760 000	69948.35	38218.30	27762.61	22623.95	19610.42	17657.70	16309.39	15337.09
780 000	71789.10	39224.05	28493.20	23219.32	20126.48	18122.37	16738.58	15740.70
800 000	73629.85	40229.79	29223.80	23814.68	20642.55	18587.05	17167.77	16144.30
820 000	75470.59	41235.54	29954.39	24410.05	21158.61	19051.73	17596.97	16547.91
840 000	77311.34	42241.28	30684.99	25005.42	21674.68	19516.40	18026.16	16951.52
860 000	79152.08	43247.02	31415.58	25600.79	22190.74	19981.08	18455.36	17355.13
880 000	80992.83	44252.77	32146.18	26196.15	22706.80	20445.76	18884.55	17758.73
900 000	82833.58	45258.51	32876.77	26791.52	23222.87	20910.43	19313.75	18162.34
920 000	84674.32	46264.26	33607.37	27386.89	23738.93	21375.11	19742.94	18565.95
940 000	86515.07	47270.00	34337.96	27982.25	24254.99	21839.79	20172.13	18969.56
960 000	88355.81	48275.75	35068.56	28577.62	24771.06	22304.46	20601.33	19373.16
980 000	90196.56	49281.49	35799.15	29172.99	25287.12	22769.14	21030.52	19776.77
1000 000	92037.31	50287.24	36529.75	29768.36	25803.19	23233.81	21459.72	20180.38
Coefficient	.092037307	.050287238	.036529746	.029768356	.025803185	.023233814	.021459718	.020180380

112

MONTHLY AMORTIZING PAYMENTS 18.75%

AMOUNT	9 YEARS	10 YEARS	15 YEARS	20 YEARS	25 YEARS	30 YEARS	35 YEARS	40 YEARS
10 000	192.29	185.04	166.47	160.13	157.76	156.84	156.48	156.34
20 000	384.57	370.08	332.93	320.25	315.51	313.68	312.97	312.68
30 000	576.86	555.12	499.40	480.38	473.27	470.52	469.45	469.02
40 000	769.15	740.17	665.87	640.51	631.03	627.36	625.93	625.37
50 000	961.43	925.21	832.33	800.63	788.78	784.20	782.41	781.71
60 000	1153.72	1110.25	998.80	960.76	946.54	941.04	938.90	938.05
70 000	1346.01	1295.29	1165.27	1120.89	1104.30	1097.89	1095.38	1094.39
80 000	1538.29	1480.33	1331.74	1281.01	1262.05	1254.73	1251.86	1250.73
90 000	1730.58	1665.37	1498.20	1441.14	1419.81	1411.57	1408.34	1407.07
100 000	1922.87	1850.41	1664.67	1601.27	1577.57	1568.41	1564.83	1563.42
110 000	2115.15	2035.46	1831.14	1761.39	1735.32	1725.25	1721.31	1719.76
120 000	2307.44	2220.50	1997.60	1921.52	1893.08	1882.09	1877.79	1876.10
130 000	2499.73	2405.54	2164.07	2081.65	2050.83	2038.93	2034.27	2032.44
140 000	2692.01	2590.58	2330.54	2241.77	2208.59	2195.77	2190.76	2188.78
150 000	2884.30	2775.62	2497.00	2401.90	2366.35	2352.61	2347.24	2345.12
160 000	3076.59	2960.66	2663.47	2562.03	2524.10	2509.45	2503.72	2501.47
170 000	3268.87	3145.70	2829.94	2722.15	2681.86	2666.29	2660.20	2657.81
180 000	3461.16	3330.75	2996.40	2882.28	2839.62	2823.13	2816.69	2814.15
190 000	3653.45	3515.79	3162.87	3042.41	2997.37	2979.98	2973.17	2970.49
200 000	3845.73	3700.83	3329.34	3202.53	3155.13	3136.82	3129.65	3126.83
210 000	4038.02	3885.87	3495.80	3362.66	3312.89	3293.66	3286.13	3283.17
220 000	4230.30	4070.91	3662.27	3522.79	3470.64	3450.50	3442.62	3439.52
230 000	4422.59	4255.95	3828.74	3682.91	3628.40	3607.34	3599.10	3595.86
240 000	4614.88	4440.99	3995.21	3843.04	3786.16	3764.18	3755.58	3752.20
250 000	4807.16	4626.04	4161.67	4003.17	3943.91	3921.02	3912.06	3908.54
260 000	4999.45	4811.08	4328.14	4163.29	4101.67	4077.86	4068.55	4064.88
270 000	5191.74	4996.12	4494.61	4323.42	4259.43	4234.70	4225.03	4221.22
280 000	5384.02	5181.16	4661.07	4483.55	4417.18	4391.54	4381.51	4377.57
290 000	5576.31	5366.20	4827.54	4643.67	4574.94	4548.38	4537.99	4533.91
300 000	5768.60	5551.24	4994.01	4803.80	4732.70	4705.22	4694.48	4690.25
320 000	6153.17	5921.33	5326.94	5124.05	5048.21	5018.91	5007.44	5002.93
340 000	6537.74	6291.41	5659.87	5444.30	5363.72	5332.59	5320.41	5315.62
360 000	6922.32	6661.49	5992.81	5764.56	5679.23	5646.27	5633.37	5628.30
380 000	7306.89	7031.57	6325.74	6084.81	5994.75	5959.95	5946.34	5940.98
400 000	7691.46	7401.66	6658.68	6405.06	6310.26	6273.63	6259.30	6253.67
420 000	8076.04	7771.74	6991.61	6725.32	6625.77	6587.31	6572.27	6566.35
440 000	8460.61	8141.82	7324.54	7045.57	6941.29	6901.00	6885.23	6879.03
460 000	8845.18	8511.91	7657.48	7365.82	7256.80	7214.68	7198.20	7191.71
480 000	9229.76	8881.99	7990.41	7686.08	7572.31	7528.36	7511.16	7504.40
500 000	9614.33	9252.07	8323.34	8006.33	7887.83	7842.04	7824.13	7817.08
520 000	9998.90	9622.15	8656.28	8326.58	8203.34	8155.72	8137.09	8129.76
540 000	10383.48	9992.24	8989.21	8646.84	8518.85	8469.40	8450.06	8442.45
560 000	10768.05	10362.32	9322.15	8967.09	8834.36	8783.08	8763.02	8755.13
580 000	11152.62	10732.40	9655.08	9287.34	9149.88	9096.77	9075.99	9067.81
600 000	11537.20	11102.49	9988.01	9607.60	9465.39	9410.45	9388.95	9380.50
620 000	11921.77	11472.57	10320.95	9927.85	9780.90	9724.13	9701.92	9693.18
640 000	12306.34	11842.65	10653.88	10248.10	10096.42	10037.81	10014.88	10005.86
660 000	12690.91	12212.73	10986.82	10568.36	10411.93	10351.49	10327.85	10318.55
680 000	13075.49	12582.82	11319.75	10888.61	10727.44	10665.17	10640.81	10631.23
700 000	13460.06	12952.90	11652.68	11208.86	11042.96	10978.86	10953.78	10943.91
720 000	13844.63	13322.98	11985.62	11529.12	11358.47	11292.54	11266.74	11256.60
740 000	14229.21	13693.07	12318.55	11849.37	11673.98	11606.22	11579.71	11569.28
760 000	14613.78	14063.15	12651.48	12169.62	11989.49	11919.90	11892.67	11881.96
780 000	14998.35	14433.23	12984.42	12489.88	12305.01	12233.58	12205.64	12194.65
800 000	15382.93	14803.31	13317.35	12810.13	12620.52	12547.26	12518.60	12507.33
820 000	15767.50	15173.40	13650.29	13130.38	12936.03	12860.95	12831.57	12820.01
840 000	16152.07	15543.48	13983.22	13450.64	13251.55	13174.63	13144.53	13132.70
860 000	16536.65	15913.56	14316.15	13770.89	13567.06	13488.31	13457.50	13445.38
880 000	16921.22	16283.64	14649.09	14091.14	13882.57	13801.99	13770.46	13758.06
900 000	17305.79	16653.73	14982.02	14411.39	14198.09	14115.67	14083.43	14070.75
920 000	17690.37	17023.81	15314.95	14731.65	14513.60	14429.35	14396.39	14383.43
940 000	18074.94	17393.89	15647.89	15051.90	14829.11	14743.04	14709.36	14696.11
960 000	18459.51	17763.98	15980.82	15372.15	15144.62	15056.72	15022.32	15008.80
980 000	18844.09	18134.06	16313.76	15692.41	15460.14	15370.40	15335.29	15321.48
1000 000	19228.66	18504.14	16646.69	16012.66	15775.65	15684.08	15648.25	15634.16
Coefficient	.019228659	.018504142	.016646690	.016012661	.015775651	.015684080	.015648251	.015634163

113

MONTHLY AMORTIZING PAYMENTS

AMOUNT	1 YEAR	2 YEARS	3 YEARS	4 YEARS	5 YEARS	6 YEARS	7 YEARS	8 YEARS
10 000	921.57	504.09	366.56	299.00	259.41	233.77	216.08	203.34
20 000	1843.13	1008.17	733.12	598.00	518.81	467.53	432.16	406.68
30 000	2764.70	1512.26	1099.68	897.00	778.22	701.30	648.24	610.02
40 000	3686.26	2016.34	1466.24	1196.00	1037.62	935.07	864.32	813.35
50 000	4607.83	2520.43	1832.80	1495.01	1297.03	1168.84	1080.40	1016.69
60 000	5529.39	3024.52	2199.36	1794.01	1556.43	1402.60	1296.48	1220.03
70 000	6450.96	3528.60	2565.92	2093.01	1815.84	1636.37	1512.56	1423.37
80 000	7372.53	4032.69	2932.48	2392.01	2075.24	1870.14	1728.64	1626.71
90 000	8294.09	4536.78	3299.04	2691.01	2334.65	2103.90	1944.72	1830.05
100 000	9215.66	5040.86	3665.60	2990.01	2594.06	2337.67	2160.80	2033.39
110 000	10137.22	5544.95	4032.16	3289.01	2853.46	2571.44	2376.88	2236.73
120 000	11058.79	6049.03	4398.72	3588.01	3112.87	2805.21	2592.96	2440.06
130 000	11980.36	6553.12	4765.28	3887.02	3372.27	3038.97	2809.04	2643.40
140 000	12901.92	7057.21	5131.84	4186.02	3631.68	3272.74	3025.12	2846.74
150 000	13823.49	7561.29	5498.40	4485.02	3891.08	3506.51	3241.20	3050.08
160 000	14745.05	8065.38	5864.96	4784.02	4150.49	3740.28	3457.28	3253.42
170 000	15666.62	8569.47	6231.52	5083.02	4409.89	3974.04	3673.36	3456.76
180 000	16588.18	9073.55	6598.08	5382.02	4669.30	4207.81	3889.44	3660.10
190 000	17509.75	9577.64	6964.64	5681.02	4928.70	4441.58	4105.52	3863.43
200 000	18431.32	10081.72	7331.20	5980.02	5188.11	4675.34	4321.60	4066.77
210 000	19352.88	10585.81	7697.76	6279.02	5447.52	4909.11	4537.68	4270.11
220 000	20274.45	11089.90	8064.32	6578.03	5706.92	5142.88	4753.76	4473.45
230 000	21196.01	11593.98	8430.88	6877.03	5966.33	5376.65	4969.84	4676.79
240 000	22117.58	12098.07	8797.44	7176.03	6225.73	5610.41	5185.92	4880.13
250 000	23039.14	12602.15	9164.00	7475.03	6485.14	5844.18	5402.00	5083.47
260 000	23960.71	13106.24	9530.56	7774.03	6744.54	6077.95	5618.08	5286.80
270 000	24882.28	13610.33	9897.13	8073.03	7003.95	6311.71	5834.17	5490.14
280 000	25803.84	14114.41	10263.69	8372.03	7263.35	6545.48	6050.25	5693.48
290 000	26725.41	14618.50	10630.25	8671.03	7522.76	6779.25	6266.33	5896.82
300 000	27646.97	15122.59	10996.81	8970.04	7782.17	7013.02	6482.41	6100.16
320 000	29490.10	16130.76	11729.93	9568.04	8300.98	7480.55	6914.57	6506.84
340 000	31333.24	17138.93	12463.05	10166.04	8819.79	7948.09	7346.73	6913.51
360 000	33176.37	18147.10	13196.17	10764.04	9338.60	8415.62	7778.89	7320.19
380 000	35019.50	19155.28	13929.29	11362.04	9857.41	8883.15	8211.05	7726.87
400 000	36862.63	20163.45	14662.41	11960.05	10376.22	9350.69	8643.21	8133.55
420 000	38705.76	21171.62	15395.53	12558.05	10895.03	9818.22	9075.37	8540.22
440 000	40548.89	22179.79	16128.65	13156.05	11413.84	10285.76	9507.53	8946.90
460 000	42392.03	23187.96	16861.77	13754.05	11932.65	10753.29	9939.69	9353.58
480 000	44235.16	24196.14	17594.89	14352.06	12451.46	11220.83	10371.85	9760.26
500 000	46078.29	25204.31	18328.01	14950.06	12970.28	11688.36	10804.01	10166.93
520 000	47921.42	26212.48	19061.13	15548.06	13489.09	12155.90	11236.17	10573.61
540 000	49764.55	27220.65	19794.25	16146.06	14007.90	12623.43	11668.33	10980.29
560 000	51607.68	28228.83	20527.37	16744.07	14526.71	13090.96	12100.49	11386.96
580 000	53450.82	29237.00	21260.49	17342.07	15045.52	13558.50	12532.65	11793.64
600 000	55293.95	30245.17	21993.61	17940.07	15564.33	14026.03	12964.81	12200.32
620 000	57137.08	31253.34	22726.73	18538.07	16083.14	14493.57	13396.97	12607.00
640 000	58980.21	32261.52	23459.85	19136.07	16601.95	14961.10	13829.13	13013.67
660 000	60823.34	33269.69	24192.97	19734.08	17120.76	15428.64	14261.29	13420.35
680 000	62666.47	34277.86	24926.09	20332.08	17639.57	15896.17	14693.45	13827.03
700 000	64509.60	35286.03	25659.21	20930.08	18158.39	16363.71	15125.61	14233.71
720 000	66352.74	36294.21	26392.33	21528.08	18677.20	16831.24	15557.77	14640.38
740 000	68195.87	37302.38	27125.45	22126.09	19196.01	17298.77	15989.93	15047.06
760 000	70039.00	38310.55	27858.57	22724.09	19714.82	17766.31	16422.09	15453.74
780 000	71882.13	39318.72	28591.69	23322.09	20233.63	18233.84	16854.25	15860.41
800 000	73725.26	40326.90	29324.82	23920.09	20752.44	18701.38	17286.42	16267.09
820 000	75568.39	41335.07	30057.94	24518.10	21271.25	19168.91	17718.58	16673.77
840 000	77411.53	42343.24	30791.06	25116.10	21790.06	19636.45	18150.74	17080.45
860 000	79254.66	43351.41	31524.18	25714.10	22308.87	20103.98	18582.90	17487.12
880 000	81097.79	44359.58	32257.30	26312.10	22827.68	20571.52	19015.06	17893.80
900 000	82940.92	45367.76	32990.42	26910.11	23346.50	21039.05	19447.22	18300.48
920 000	84784.05	46375.93	33723.54	27508.11	23865.31	21506.58	19879.38	18707.16
940 000	86627.18	47384.10	34456.66	28106.11	24384.12	21974.12	20311.54	19113.83
960 000	88470.31	48392.27	35189.78	28704.11	24902.93	22441.65	20743.70	19520.51
980 000	90313.45	49400.45	35922.90	29302.11	25421.74	22909.19	21175.86	19927.19
1000 000	92156.58	50408.62	36656.02	29900.12	25940.55	23376.72	21608.02	20333.86
Coefficient	.092156578	.050408619	.036656019	.029900117	.025940551	.023376722	.021608019	.020333865

114

AMOUNT	9 YEARS	10 YEARS	15 YEARS	20 YEARS	25 YEARS	30 YEARS	35 YEARS	40 YEARS
10 000	193.87	186.67	168.29	162.01	159.77	158.89	158.55	158.42
20 000	387.74	373.34	336.58	324.14	319.54	317.78	317.10	316.83
30 000	581.61	560.02	504.86	486.21	479.30	476.67	475.65	475.25
40 000	775.48	746.69	673.15	648.27	639.07	635.56	634.20	633.67
50 000	969.35	933.36	841.44	810.34	798.84	794.45	792.75	792.09
60 000	1163.22	1120.03	1009.73	972.41	958.61	953.34	951.30	950.50
70 000	1357.10	1306.71	1178.01	1134.48	1118.38	1112.22	1109.85	1108.92
80 000	1550.97	1493.38	1346.30	1296.55	1278.14	1271.11	1268.40	1267.34
90 000	1744.84	1680.05	1514.59	1458.62	1437.91	1430.00	1426.95	1425.76
100 000	1938.71	1866.72	1682.88	1620.68	1597.68	1588.89	1585.49	1584.17
110 000	2132.58	2053.40	1851.16	1782.75	1757.45	1747.78	1744.04	1742.59
120 000	2326.45	2240.07	2019.45	1944.82	1917.22	1906.67	1902.59	1901.01
130 000	2520.32	2426.74	2187.74	2106.89	2076.98	2065.56	2061.14	2059.43
140 000	2714.19	2613.41	2356.03	2268.96	2236.75	2224.45	2219.69	2217.84
150 000	2908.06	2800.09	2524.31	2431.03	2396.52	2383.34	2378.24	2376.26
160 000	3101.93	2986.76	2692.60	2593.10	2556.29	2542.23	2536.79	2534.68
170 000	3295.80	3173.43	2860.89	2755.16	2716.06	2701.12	2695.34	2693.10
180 000	3489.67	3360.10	3029.18	2917.23	2875.82	2860.01	2853.89	2851.51
190 000	3683.55	3546.77	3197.46	3079.30	3035.59	3018.90	3012.44	3009.93
200 000	3877.42	3733.45	3365.75	3241.37	3195.36	3177.79	3170.99	3168.35
210 000	4071.29	3920.12	3534.04	3403.44	3355.13	3336.67	3329.54	3326.77
220 000	4265.16	4106.79	3702.33	3565.51	3514.90	3495.56	3488.09	3485.18
230 000	4459.03	4293.46	3870.61	3727.58	3674.66	3654.45	3646.64	3643.60
240 000	4652.90	4480.14	4038.90	3889.64	3834.43	3813.34	3805.19	3802.02
250 000	4846.77	4666.81	4207.19	4051.71	3994.20	3972.23	3963.74	3960.44
260 000	5040.64	4853.48	4375.48	4213.78	4153.97	4131.12	4122.29	4118.85
270 000	5234.51	5040.15	4543.77	4375.85	4313.74	4290.01	4280.84	4277.27
280 000	5428.38	5226.83	4712.05	4537.92	4473.50	4448.90	4439.39	4435.69
290 000	5622.25	5413.50	4880.34	4699.99	4633.27	4607.79	4597.93	4594.11
300 000	5816.12	5600.17	5048.63	4862.05	4793.04	4766.68	4756.48	4752.52
320 000	6203.87	5973.52	5385.20	5186.19	5112.58	5084.46	5073.58	5069.36
340 000	6591.61	6346.86	5721.78	5510.33	5432.11	5402.23	5390.68	5386.19
360 000	6979.35	6720.20	6058.35	5834.47	5751.65	5720.01	5707.78	5703.03
380 000	7367.09	7093.55	6394.93	6158.60	6071.18	6037.79	6024.88	6019.86
400 000	7754.83	7466.89	6731.50	6482.74	6390.72	6355.57	6341.98	6336.70
420 000	8142.57	7840.24	7068.08	6806.88	6710.26	6673.35	6659.08	6653.53
440 000	8530.32	8213.58	7404.65	7131.01	7029.79	6991.13	6976.18	6970.37
460 000	8918.06	8586.93	7741.23	7455.15	7349.33	7308.91	7293.28	7287.20
480 000	9305.80	8960.27	8077.80	7779.29	7668.86	7626.68	7610.37	7604.04
500 000	9693.54	9333.62	8414.38	8103.42	7988.40	7944.46	7927.47	7920.87
520 000	10081.28	9706.96	8750.96	8427.56	8307.94	8262.24	8244.57	8237.71
540 000	10469.02	10080.31	9087.53	8751.70	8627.47	8580.02	8561.67	8554.54
560 000	10856.77	10453.65	9424.11	9075.83	8947.01	8897.80	8878.77	8871.38
580 000	11244.51	10827.00	9760.68	9399.97	9266.54	9215.58	9195.87	9188.21
600 000	11632.25	11200.34	10097.26	9724.11	9586.08	9533.36	9512.97	9505.05
620 000	12019.99	11573.69	10433.83	10048.25	9905.62	9851.13	9830.07	9821.88
640 000	12407.73	11947.03	10770.41	10372.38	10225.15	10168.91	10147.17	10138.72
660 000	12795.47	12320.38	11106.98	10696.52	10544.69	10486.69	10464.27	10455.55
680 000	13183.22	12693.72	11443.56	11020.66	10864.22	10804.47	10781.36	10772.39
700 000	13570.96	13067.07	11780.13	11344.79	11183.76	11122.25	11098.46	11089.22
720 000	13958.70	13440.41	12116.71	11668.93	11503.30	11440.03	11415.56	11406.06
740 000	14346.44	13813.75	12453.28	11993.07	11822.83	11757.80	11732.66	11722.89
760 000	14734.18	14187.10	12789.86	12317.20	12142.37	12075.58	12049.76	12039.73
780 000	15121.92	14560.44	13126.43	12641.34	12461.90	12393.36	12366.86	12356.56
800 000	15509.67	14933.79	13463.01	12965.48	12781.44	12711.14	12683.96	12673.40
820 000	15897.41	15307.13	13799.58	13289.62	13100.98	13028.92	13001.06	12990.23
840 000	16285.15	15680.48	14136.16	13613.75	13420.51	13346.70	13318.16	13307.07
860 000	16672.89	16053.82	14472.73	13937.89	13740.05	13664.48	13635.25	13623.90
880 000	17060.63	16427.17	14809.31	14262.03	14059.58	13982.25	13952.35	13940.74
900 000	17448.37	16800.51	15145.88	14586.16	14379.12	14300.03	14269.45	14257.57
920 000	17836.12	17173.86	15482.46	14910.30	14698.66	14617.81	14586.55	14574.41
940 000	18223.86	17547.20	15819.03	15234.44	15018.19	14935.59	14903.65	14891.24
960 000	18611.60	17920.55	16155.61	15558.57	15337.73	15253.37	15220.75	15208.08
980 000	18999.34	18293.89	16492.18	15882.71	15657.26	15571.15	15537.85	15524.91
1000 000	19387.08	18667.24	16828.76	16206.85	15976.30	15888.93	15854.95	15841.75
Coefficient	.019387083	.018667236	.016828760	.016206848	.015976800	.015888925	.015854947	.015841748

AMOUNT	1 YEAR	2 YEARS	3 YEARS	4 YEARS	5 YEARS	6 YEARS	7 YEARS	8 YEARS
10 000	922.76	505.30	367.83	300.32	260.78	235.20	217.57	204.88
20 000	1845.52	1010.60	735.65	600.64	521.57	470.40	435.14	409.76
30 000	2768.28	1515.90	1103.48	900.97	782.35	705.60	652.70	614.64
40 000	3691.04	2021.21	1471.30	1201.29	1043.13	940.80	870.27	819.52
50 000	4613.80	2526.51	1839.13	1501.61	1303.92	1176.00	1087.84	1024.39
60 000	5536.56	3031.81	2206.95	1801.93	1564.70	1411.20	1305.41	1229.27
70 000	6459.32	3537.11	2574.78	2102.25	1825.48	1646.41	1522.98	1434.15
80 000	7382.08	4042.41	2942.60	2402.58	2086.26	1881.61	1740.55	1639.03
90 000	8304.83	4547.71	3310.43	2702.90	2347.05	2116.81	1958.11	1843.91
100 000	9227.59	5053.02	3678.25	3003.22	2607.83	2352.01	2175.68	2048.79
110 000	10150.35	5558.32	4046.08	3303.54	2868.61	2587.21	2393.25	2253.67
120 000	11073.11	6063.62	4413.90	3603.86	3129.40	2822.41	2610.82	2458.55
130 000	11995.87	6568.92	4781.73	3904.19	3390.18	3057.61	2828.39	2663.43
140 000	12918.63	7074.22	5149.56	4204.51	3650.96	3292.81	3045.95	2868.30
150 000	13841.39	7579.52	5517.38	4504.83	3911.75	3528.01	3263.52	3073.18
160 000	14764.15	8084.83	5885.21	4805.15	4172.53	3763.21	3481.09	3278.06
170 000	15686.91	8590.13	6253.03	5105.47	4433.31	3998.41	3698.66	3482.94
180 000	16609.67	9095.43	6620.86	5405.80	4694.09	4233.61	3916.23	3687.82
190 000	17532.43	9600.73	6988.68	5706.12	4954.88	4468.82	4133.80	3892.70
200 000	18455.19	10106.03	7356.51	6006.44	5215.66	4704.02	4351.36	4097.58
210 000	19377.95	10611.33	7724.33	6306.76	5476.44	4939.22	4568.93	4302.46
220 000	20300.71	11116.64	8092.16	6607.08	5737.23	5174.42	4786.50	4507.34
230 000	21223.47	11621.94	8459.98	6907.41	5998.01	5409.62	5004.07	4712.22
240 000	22146.23	12127.24	8827.81	7207.73	6258.79	5644.82	5221.64	4917.09
250 000	23068.98	12632.54	9195.64	7508.05	6519.58	5880.02	5439.21	5121.97
260 000	23991.74	13137.84	9563.46	7808.37	6780.36	6115.20	5656.77	5326.85
270 000	24914.50	13643.14	9931.29	8108.69	7041.14	6350.42	5874.34	5531.73
280 000	25837.26	14148.44	10299.11	8409.02	7301.93	6585.62	6091.91	5736.61
290 000	26760.02	14653.75	10666.94	8709.34	7562.71	6820.82	6309.48	5941.49
300 000	27682.78	15159.05	11034.76	9009.66	7823.49	7056.02	6527.05	6146.37
320 000	29528.30	16169.65	11770.41	9610.30	8345.06	7526.43	6962.18	6556.13
340 000	31373.82	17180.25	12506.06	10210.95	8866.62	7996.83	7397.32	6965.88
360 000	33219.34	18190.86	13241.71	10811.59	9388.19	8467.23	7832.46	7375.64
380 000	35064.86	19201.46	13977.37	11412.24	9909.76	8937.63	8267.59	7785.40
400 000	36910.38	20212.06	14713.02	12012.88	10431.33	9408.03	8702.73	8195.16
420 000	38755.89	21222.67	15448.67	12613.52	10952.89	9878.43	9137.86	8604.91
440 000	40601.41	22233.27	16184.32	13214.17	11474.45	10348.84	9573.00	9014.67
460 000	42446.93	23243.87	16919.97	13814.81	11996.02	10819.24	10008.14	9424.43
480 000	44292.45	24254.48	17655.62	14415.46	12517.59	11289.64	10443.27	9834.19
500 000	46137.97	25265.08	18391.27	15016.10	13039.15	11760.04	10878.41	10243.95
520 000	47983.49	26275.68	19126.92	15616.74	13560.72	12230.44	11313.55	10653.70
540 000	49829.01	27286.29	19862.57	16217.39	14082.28	12700.84	11748.68	11063.46
560 000	51674.53	28296.89	20598.22	16818.03	14603.85	13171.24	12183.82	11473.22
580 000	53520.04	29307.49	21333.87	17418.68	15125.42	13641.65	12618.96	11882.98
600 000	55365.56	30318.10	22069.52	18019.32	15646.98	14112.05	13054.09	12292.74
620 000	57211.08	31328.70	22805.18	18619.96	16168.55	14582.45	13489.23	12702.49
640 000	59056.60	32339.30	23540.83	19220.61	16690.11	15052.85	13924.36	13112.25
660 000	60902.12	33349.91	24276.48	19821.25	17211.68	15523.25	14359.50	13522.01
680 000	62747.64	34360.51	25012.13	20421.90	17733.25	15993.65	14794.64	13931.77
700 000	64593.16	35371.11	25747.78	21022.54	18254.81	16464.06	15229.77	14341.52
720 000	66438.68	36381.72	26483.43	21623.18	18776.38	16934.46	15664.91	14751.28
740 000	68284.19	37392.32	27219.08	22223.83	19297.94	17404.86	16100.05	15161.04
760 000	70129.71	38402.92	27954.73	22824.47	19819.51	17875.26	16535.18	15570.80
780 000	71975.23	39413.52	28690.38	23425.12	20341.08	18345.66	16970.32	15980.56
800 000	73820.75	40424.13	29426.03	24025.76	20862.64	18816.06	17405.46	16390.31
820 000	75666.27	41434.73	30161.68	24626.40	21384.21	19286.47	17840.59	16800.07
840 000	77511.79	42445.33	30897.33	25227.05	21905.78	19756.87	18275.73	17209.83
860 000	79357.31	43455.94	31632.99	25827.69	22427.34	20227.27	18710.87	17619.59
880 000	81202.83	44466.54	32368.64	26428.34	22948.91	20697.67	19146.00	18029.34
900 000	83048.35	45477.14	33104.29	27028.98	23470.47	21168.07	19581.14	18439.10
920 000	84893.86	46487.75	33839.94	27629.62	23992.04	21638.47	20016.27	18848.86
940 000	86739.38	47498.35	34575.59	28230.27	24513.61	22108.88	20451.41	19258.62
960 000	88584.90	48508.95	35311.24	28830.91	25035.17	22579.28	20886.55	19668.38
980 000	90430.42	49519.56	36046.89	29431.56	25556.74	23049.68	21321.68	20078.13
1000 000	92275.94	50530.16	36782.54	30032.20	26078.30	23520.08	21756.82	20487.89
Coefficient	.092275939	.050530160	.036782541	.030032200	.026078304	.023520080	.021756820	.020487892

AMOUNT	9 YEARS	10 YEARS	15 YEARS	20 YEARS	25 YEARS	30 YEARS	35 YEARS	40 YEARS
10 000	195.46	188.31	170.11	164.02	161.78	160.94	160.62	160.49
20 000	390.92	376.62	340.23	328.03	323.57	321.88	321.24	320.99
30 000	586.38	564.93	510.34	492.05	485.35	482.82	481.85	481.48
40 000	781.84	753.24	680.46	656.06	647.13	643.76	642.47	641.98
50 000	977.30	941.55	850.57	820.08	808.91	804.70	803.09	802.47
60 000	1172.77	1129.86	1020.69	984.09	970.70	965.64	963.71	962.96
70 000	1368.23	1318.17	1190.80	1148.11	1132.48	1126.58	1124.32	1123.46
80 000	1563.69	1506.47	1360.91	1312.12	1294.26	1287.52	1284.94	1283.95
90 000	1759.15	1694.78	1531.03	1476.14	1456.04	1448.46	1445.56	1444.45
100 000	1954.61	1883.09	1701.14	1640.15	1617.83	1609.40	1606.18	1604.94
110 000	2150.07	2071.40	1871.26	1804.17	1779.61	1770.34	1766.79	1765.43
120 000	2345.53	2259.71	2041.37	1968.18	1941.39	1931.28	1927.41	1925.93
130 000	2540.99	2448.02	2211.49	2132.20	2103.18	2092.22	2088.03	2086.42
140 000	2736.45	2636.33	2381.60	2296.21	2264.96	2253.16	2248.65	2246.91
150 000	2931.91	2824.64	2551.72	2460.23	2426.74	2414.10	2409.26	2407.41
160 000	3127.37	3012.95	2721.83	2624.24	2588.52	2575.03	2569.88	2567.90
170 000	3322.83	3201.26	2891.94	2788.26	2750.31	2735.97	2730.50	2728.40
180 000	3518.30	3389.57	3062.06	2952.27	2912.09	2896.91	2891.12	2888.89
190 000	3713.76	3577.88	3232.17	3116.29	3073.87	3057.85	3051.73	3049.38
200 000	3909.22	3766.19	3402.29	3280.30	3235.66	3218.79	3212.35	3209.88
210 000	4104.68	3954.50	3572.40	3444.32	3397.44	3379.73	3372.97	3370.37
220 000	4300.14	4142.80	3742.52	3608.33	3559.22	3540.67	3533.59	3530.87
230 000	4495.60	4331.11	3912.63	3772.35	3721.00	3701.61	3694.20	3691.36
240 000	4691.06	4519.42	4082.74	3936.36	3882.79	3862.55	3854.82	3851.85
250 000	4886.52	4707.73	4252.86	4100.38	4044.57	4023.49	4015.44	4012.35
260 000	5081.98	4896.04	4422.97	4264.39	4206.35	4184.43	4176.06	4172.84
270 000	5277.44	5084.35	4593.09	4428.41	4368.13	4345.37	4336.67	4333.34
280 000	5472.90	5272.66	4763.20	4592.42	4529.92	4506.31	4497.29	4493.83
290 000	5668.36	5460.97	4933.32	4756.44	4691.70	4667.25	4657.91	4654.32
300 000	5863.83	5649.28	5103.43	4920.45	4853.48	4828.19	4818.53	4814.82
320 000	6254.75	6025.90	5443.66	5248.48	5177.05	5150.07	5139.76	5135.81
340 000	6645.67	6402.52	5783.89	5576.52	5500.61	5471.95	5461.00	5456.79
360 000	7036.59	6779.14	6124.12	5904.55	5824.18	5793.83	5782.23	5777.78
380 000	7427.51	7155.75	6464.34	6232.58	6147.74	6115.71	6103.47	6098.77
400 000	7818.43	7532.37	6804.57	6560.61	6471.31	6437.59	6424.70	6419.76
420 000	8209.36	7908.99	7144.80	6888.64	6794.88	6759.47	6745.94	6740.74
440 000	8600.28	8285.61	7485.03	7216.67	7118.44	7081.35	7067.17	7061.73
460 000	8991.20	8662.23	7825.26	7544.70	7442.01	7403.23	7388.41	7382.72
480 000	9382.12	9038.85	8165.49	7872.73	7765.57	7725.10	7709.64	7703.71
500 000	9773.04	9415.47	8505.72	8200.76	8089.14	8046.98	8030.88	8024.70
520 000	10163.96	9792.08	8845.95	8528.79	8412.70	8368.86	8352.11	8345.68
540 000	10554.89	10168.70	9186.17	8856.82	8736.27	8690.74	8673.35	8666.67
560 000	10945.81	10545.32	9526.40	9184.85	9059.83	9012.62	8994.58	8987.66
580 000	11336.73	10921.94	9866.63	9512.88	9383.40	9334.50	9315.82	9308.65
600 000	11727.65	11298.56	10206.86	9840.91	9706.97	9656.38	9637.05	9629.64
620 000	12118.57	11675.18	10547.09	10168.94	10030.53	9978.26	9958.29	9950.62
640 000	12509.49	12051.80	10887.32	10496.97	10354.10	10300.14	10279.52	10271.61
660 000	12900.42	12428.41	11227.55	10825.00	10677.66	10622.02	10600.76	10592.60
680 000	13291.34	12805.03	11567.78	11153.03	11001.23	10943.90	10921.99	10913.59
700 000	13682.26	13181.65	11908.00	11481.06	11324.79	11265.78	11243.23	11234.57
720 000	14073.18	13558.27	12248.23	11809.09	11648.36	11587.66	11564.46	11555.56
740 000	14464.10	13934.89	12588.46	12137.12	11971.92	11909.54	11885.70	11876.55
760 000	14855.02	14311.51	12928.69	12465.15	12295.49	12231.42	12206.93	12197.54
780 000	15245.95	14688.13	13268.92	12793.18	12619.05	12553.30	12528.17	12518.53
800 000	15636.87	15064.74	13609.15	13121.21	12942.62	12875.17	12849.40	12839.51
820 000	16027.79	15441.36	13949.38	13449.24	13266.19	13197.05	13170.64	13160.50
840 000	16418.71	15817.98	14289.60	13777.27	13589.75	13518.93	13491.88	13481.49
860 000	16809.63	16194.60	14629.83	14105.30	13913.32	13840.81	13813.11	13802.48
880 000	17200.55	16571.22	14970.06	14433.33	14236.88	14162.69	14134.35	14123.46
900 000	17591.48	16947.84	15310.29	14761.36	14560.45	14484.57	14455.58	14444.45
920 000	17982.40	17324.46	15650.52	15089.39	14884.01	14806.45	14776.82	14765.44
940 000	18373.32	17701.08	15990.75	15417.42	15207.58	15128.33	15098.05	15086.43
960 000	18764.24	18077.69	16330.98	15745.45	15531.14	15450.21	15419.29	15407.42
980 000	19155.16	18454.31	16671.21	16073.48	15854.71	15772.09	15740.52	15728.40
1000 000	19546.08	18830.93	17011.43	16401.52	16178.28	16093.97	16061.76	16049.39
Coefficient	.019546084	.018830931	.017011434	.016401515	.016178275	.016093968	.016061756	.016049392

117

MONTHLY AMORTIZING PAYMENTS

AMOUNT	1 YEAR	2 YEARS	3 YEARS	4 YEARS	5 YEARS	6 YEARS	7 YEARS	8 YEARS
10 000	923.95	506.52	369.09	301.65	262.16	236.64	219.06	206.42
20 000	1847.91	1013.04	738.19	603.29	524.33	473.28	438.12	412.85
30 000	2771.86	1519.56	1107.28	904.94	786.49	709.92	657.18	619.27
40 000	3695.82	2026.08	1476.37	1206.58	1048.66	946.56	876.24	825.70
50 000	4619.77	2532.59	1845.47	1508.23	1310.82	1183.19	1095.31	1032.12
60 000	5543.72	3039.11	2214.56	1809.88	1572.99	1419.83	1314.37	1238.55
70 000	6467.68	3545.63	2583.65	2111.52	1835.15	1656.47	1533.43	1444.97
80 000	7391.63	4052.15	2952.74	2413.17	2097.32	1893.11	1752.49	1651.40
90 000	8315.58	4558.67	3321.84	2714.81	2359.48	2129.75	1971.55	1857.82
100 000	9239.54	5065.19	3690.93	3016.46	2621.64	2366.39	2190.61	2064.25
110 000	10163.49	5571.71	4060.02	3318.11	2883.81	2603.03	2409.67	2270.67
120 000	11087.45	6078.23	4429.12	3619.75	3145.97	2839.67	2628.73	2477.10
130 000	12011.40	6584.74	4798.21	3921.40	3408.14	3076.30	2847.80	2683.52
140 000	12935.35	7091.26	5167.30	4223.04	3670.30	3312.94	3066.86	2889.94
150 000	13859.31	7597.78	5536.40	4524.69	3932.47	3549.58	3285.92	3096.37
160 000	14783.26	8104.30	5905.49	4826.34	4194.63	3786.22	3504.98	3302.79
170 000	15707.21	8610.82	6274.58	5127.98	4456.80	4022.86	3724.04	3509.22
180 000	16631.17	9117.34	6643.68	5429.63	4718.96	4259.50	3943.10	3715.64
190 000	17555.12	9623.86	7012.77	5731.27	4981.12	4496.14	4162.16	3922.07
200 000	18479.08	10130.38	7381.86	6032.92	5243.29	4732.78	4381.22	4128.49
210 000	19403.03	10636.89	7750.95	6334.57	5505.45	4969.42	4600.28	4334.92
220 000	20326.98	11143.41	8120.05	6636.21	5767.62	5206.05	4819.35	4541.34
230 000	21250.94	11649.93	8489.14	6937.86	6029.78	5442.69	5038.41	4747.77
240 000	22174.89	12156.45	8858.23	7239.50	6291.95	5679.33	5257.47	4954.19
250 000	23098.85	12662.97	9227.33	7541.15	6554.11	5915.97	5476.53	5160.62
260 000	24022.80	13169.49	9596.42	7842.80	6816.28	6152.61	5695.59	5367.04
270 000	24946.75	13676.01	9965.51	8144.44	7078.44	6389.25	5914.65	5573.46
280 000	25870.71	14182.53	10334.61	8446.09	7340.60	6625.89	6133.71	5779.89
290 000	26794.66	14689.05	10703.70	8747.73	7602.77	6862.53	6352.77	5986.31
300 000	27718.61	15195.56	11072.79	9049.38	7864.93	7099.17	6571.84	6192.74
320 000	29566.52	16208.60	11810.98	9652.67	8389.26	7572.44	7009.96	6605.59
340 000	31414.43	17221.64	12549.17	10255.96	8913.59	8045.72	7448.08	7018.44
360 000	33262.34	18234.68	13287.35	10859.26	9437.92	8519.00	7886.20	7431.29
380 000	35110.24	19247.71	14025.54	11462.55	9962.25	8992.28	8324.32	7844.14
400 000	36958.15	20260.75	14763.72	12065.84	10486.58	9465.55	8762.45	8256.98
420 000	38806.06	21273.79	15501.91	12669.13	11010.91	9938.83	9200.57	8669.83
440 000	40653.97	22286.83	16240.10	13272.42	11535.24	10412.11	9638.69	9082.68
460 000	42501.87	23299.86	16978.28	13875.72	12059.56	10885.39	10076.81	9495.53
480 000	44349.78	24312.90	17716.47	14479.01	12583.89	11358.66	10514.94	9908.38
500 000	46197.69	25325.94	18454.65	15082.30	13108.22	11831.94	10953.06	10321.23
520 000	48045.60	26338.98	19192.84	15685.59	13632.55	12305.22	11391.18	10734.08
540 000	49893.51	27352.02	19931.03	16288.88	14156.88	12778.50	11829.30	11146.93
560 000	51741.41	28365.05	20669.21	16892.18	14681.21	13251.78	12267.43	11559.78
580 000	53589.32	29378.09	21407.40	17495.47	15205.54	13725.05	12705.55	11972.63
600 000	55437.23	30391.13	22145.59	18098.76	15729.87	14198.33	13143.67	12385.48
620 000	57285.14	31404.17	22883.77	18702.05	16254.20	14671.61	13581.79	12798.33
640 000	59133.04	32417.20	23621.96	19305.34	16778.52	15144.89	14019.92	13211.18
660 000	60980.95	33430.24	24360.14	19908.64	17302.85	15618.16	14458.04	13624.02
680 000	62828.86	34443.28	25098.33	20511.93	17827.18	16091.44	14896.16	14036.87
700 000	64676.77	35456.32	25836.52	21115.22	18351.51	16564.72	15334.28	14449.72
720 000	66524.67	36469.35	26574.70	21718.51	18875.84	17038.00	15772.40	14862.57
740 000	68372.58	37482.39	27312.89	22321.80	19400.17	17511.27	16210.53	15275.42
760 000	70220.49	38495.43	28051.07	22925.10	19924.50	17984.55	16648.65	15688.27
780 000	72068.40	39508.47	28789.26	23528.39	20448.83	18457.83	17086.77	16101.12
800 000	73916.30	40521.50	29527.45	24131.68	20973.16	18931.11	17524.89	16513.97
820 000	75764.21	41534.54	30265.63	24734.97	21497.48	19404.38	17963.02	16926.82
840 000	77612.12	42547.58	31003.82	25338.26	22021.81	19877.66	18401.14	17339.67
860 000	79460.03	43560.62	31742.01	25941.56	22546.14	20350.94	18839.26	17752.52
880 000	81307.93	44573.65	32480.19	26544.85	23070.47	20824.22	19277.38	18165.37
900 000	83155.84	45586.69	33218.38	27148.14	23594.80	21297.50	19715.51	18578.21
920 000	85003.75	46599.73	33956.56	27751.43	24119.13	21770.77	20153.63	18991.06
940 000	86851.66	47612.77	34694.75	28354.72	24643.46	22244.05	20591.75	19403.91
960 000	88699.56	48625.80	35432.94	28958.02	25167.79	22717.33	21029.87	19816.76
980 000	90547.47	49638.84	36171.12	29561.31	25692.12	23190.61	21468.00	20229.61
1000 000	92395.38	50651.88	36909.31	30164.60	26216.45	23663.88	21906.12	20642.46
Coefficient	.092395380	.050651880	.036909309	.030164601	.026216445	.023663884	.021906118	.020642461

MONTHLY AMORTIZING PAYMENTS 19.50%

AMOUNT	9 YEARS	10 YEARS	15 YEARS	20 YEARS	25 YEARS	30 YEARS	35 YEARS	40 YEARS
10 000	197.06	189.95	171.95	165.97	163.80	162.99	162.69	162.57
20 000	394.11	379.90	343.89	331.93	327.60	325.98	325.39	325.14
30 000	591.17	569.86	515.84	497.90	491.40	488.98	488.06	487.71
40 000	788.23	759.81	687.79	663.87	655.20	651.97	650.75	650.28
50 000	985.28	949.76	859.74	829.83	819.00	814.96	813.43	812.85
60 000	1182.34	1139.71	1031.68	995.80	982.80	977.95	976.12	975.43
70 000	1379.40	1329.67	1203.63	1161.77	1146.60	1140.94	1138.81	1138.00
80 000	1576.45	1519.62	1375.58	1327.73	1310.40	1303.94	1301.49	1300.57
90 000	1773.51	1709.57	1547.52	1493.70	1474.21	1466.93	1464.18	1463.14
100 000	1970.57	1899.52	1719.47	1659.66	1638.01	1629.92	1626.87	1625.71
110 000	2167.62	2089.47	1891.42	1825.63	1801.81	1792.91	1789.55	1788.28
120 000	2354.68	2279.43	2063.36	1991.60	1965.61	1955.90	1952.24	1950.85
130 000	2561.74	2469.38	2235.31	2157.56	2129.41	2118.90	2114.93	2113.42
140 000	2758.79	2659.33	2407.26	2323.53	2293.21	2281.89	2277.61	2275.99
150 000	2955.85	2849.28	2579.21	2489.50	2457.01	2444.88	2440.30	2438.56
160 000	3152.91	3039.24	2751.15	2655.46	2620.81	2607.87	2602.99	2601.13
170 000	3349.96	3229.19	2923.10	2821.43	2784.61	2770.86	2765.67	2763.71
180 000	3547.02	3419.14	3095.05	2987.40	2948.41	2933.86	2928.36	2926.28
190 000	3744.07	3609.09	3266.99	3153.36	3112.21	3096.85	3091.05	3088.85
200 000	3941.13	3799.04	3438.94	3319.33	3276.01	3259.84	3253.73	3251.42
210 000	4138.19	3989.00	3610.89	3485.30	3439.81	3422.83	3416.42	3413.99
220 000	4335.24	4178.95	3782.83	3651.26	3603.61	3585.82	3579.11	3576.56
230 000	4532.30	4368.90	3954.78	3817.23	3767.41	3748.82	3741.79	3739.13
240 000	4729.36	4558.85	4126.73	3983.20	3931.21	3911.81	3904.48	3901.70
250 000	4926.41	4748.81	4298.68	4149.16	4095.02	4074.80	4067.17	4064.27
260 000	5123.47	4938.76	4470.62	4315.13	4258.82	4237.79	4229.85	4226.84
270 000	5320.53	5128.71	4642.57	4481.09	4422.62	4400.78	4392.54	4389.41
280 000	5517.58	5318.66	4814.47	4647.06	4586.42	4563.78	4555.23	4551.99
290 000	5714.64	5508.61	4986.46	4813.03	4750.22	4726.77	4717.91	4714.56
300 000	5911.70	5698.57	5158.41	4978.99	4914.02	4889.76	4880.60	4877.13
320 000	6305.81	6078.47	5502.30	5310.93	5241.62	5215.74	5205.97	5202.27
340 000	6699.92	6458.38	5846.20	5642.86	5569.22	5541.73	5531.35	5527.41
360 000	7094.04	6838.28	6190.09	5974.79	5896.82	5867.71	5856.72	5852.55
380 000	7488.15	7218.18	6533.99	6306.73	6224.42	6193.70	6182.09	6177.69
400 000	7882.26	7598.09	6877.88	6638.66	6552.02	6519.68	6507.47	6502.84
420 000	8276.38	7977.99	7221.77	6970.59	6879.63	6845.66	6832.84	6827.98
440 000	8670.49	8357.90	7565.67	7302.52	7207.23	7171.65	7158.21	7153.12
460 000	9064.60	8737.80	7909.56	7634.46	7534.83	7497.63	7483.59	7478.26
480 000	9458.72	9117.71	8253.46	7966.39	7862.43	7823.62	7808.96	7803.40
500 000	9852.83	9497.61	8597.35	8298.32	8190.03	8149.60	8134.33	8128.55
520 000	10246.94	9877.51	8941.24	8630.26	8517.63	8475.58	8459.71	8453.69
540 000	10641.05	10257.42	9285.14	8962.19	8845.23	8801.57	8785.08	8778.83
560 000	11035.17	10637.32	9629.03	9294.12	9172.83	9127.55	9110.45	9103.97
580 000	11429.28	11017.23	9972.93	9626.05	9500.44	9453.54	9435.83	9429.11
600 000	11823.39	11397.13	10316.82	9957.99	9828.04	9779.52	9761.20	9754.26
620 000	12217.51	11777.04	10660.71	10289.92	10155.64	10105.50	10086.57	10079.40
640 000	12611.62	12156.94	11004.61	10621.85	10483.24	10431.49	10411.95	10404.54
660 000	13005.73	12536.85	11348.50	10953.79	10810.84	10757.47	10737.32	10729.68
680 000	13399.85	12916.75	11692.40	11285.72	11138.44	11083.46	11062.69	11054.82
700 000	13793.96	13296.65	12036.29	11617.65	11466.04	11409.44	11388.07	11379.96
720 000	14188.07	13676.56	12380.18	11949.59	11793.64	11735.42	11713.44	11705.11
740 000	14582.19	14056.46	12724.08	12281.52	12121.25	12061.41	12038.82	12030.25
760 000	14976.30	14436.37	13067.97	12613.45	12448.85	12387.39	12364.19	12355.39
780 000	15370.41	14816.27	13411.87	12945.38	12776.45	12713.38	12689.56	12680.53
800 000	15764.53	15196.18	13755.76	13277.32	13104.05	13039.36	13014.94	13005.67
820 000	16158.64	15576.08	14099.65	13609.25	13431.65	13365.34	13340.31	13330.82
840 000	16552.75	15955.99	14443.55	13941.18	13759.25	13691.33	13665.68	13655.96
860 000	16946.87	16335.89	14787.44	14273.12	14086.85	14017.31	13991.06	13981.10
880 000	17340.98	16715.79	15131.34	14605.05	14414.45	14343.30	14316.43	14306.24
900 000	17735.09	17095.70	15475.23	14936.98	14742.05	14669.28	14641.80	14631.38
920 000	18129.20	17475.60	15819.12	15268.91	15069.66	14995.26	14967.18	14956.52
940 000	18523.32	17855.51	16163.02	15600.85	15397.26	15321.25	15292.55	15281.67
960 000	18917.43	18235.41	16506.91	15932.78	15724.86	15647.23	15617.92	15606.81
980 000	19311.54	18615.32	16850.81	16264.71	16052.46	15973.22	15943.30	15931.95
1000 000	19705.66	18995.22	17194.70	16596.65	16380.06	16299.20	16268.67	16257.09
Coefficient	.019705657	.018995221	.017194700	.016596646	.016380061	.016299200	.016268669	.016257092

119

AMOUNT	1 YEAR	2 YEARS	3 YEARS	4 YEARS	5 YEARS	6 YEARS	7 YEARS	8 YEARS
10 000	925.15	507.74	370.36	302.97	263.55	238.08	220.56	207.98
20 000	1850.30	1015.48	740.73	605.95	527.10	476.16	441.12	415.95
30 000	2775.45	1523.21	1111.09	908.92	790.65	714.24	661.68	623.93
40 000	3700.60	2030.95	1481.45	1211.89	1054.20	952.33	882.24	831.90
50 000	4625.75	2538.69	1851.82	1514.87	1317.75	1190.41	1102.80	1039.88
60 000	5550.89	3046.43	2222.18	1817.84	1581.30	1428.49	1323.35	1247.85
70 000	6476.04	3554.16	2592.54	2120.81	1844.85	1666.57	1543.91	1455.83
80 000	7401.19	4061.90	2962.91	2423.79	2108.40	1904.65	1764.47	1663.81
90 000	8326.34	4569.64	3333.27	2726.76	2371.95	2142.73	1985.03	1871.78
100 000	9251.49	5077.38	3703.63	3029.73	2635.50	2380.81	2205.59	2079.76
110 000	10176.64	5585.11	4074.00	3332.71	2899.05	2618.89	2426.15	2287.73
120 000	11101.79	6092.85	4444.36	3635.68	3162.60	2856.98	2646.71	2495.71
130 000	12026.94	6600.59	4814.72	3938.65	3426.15	3095.06	2867.27	2703.68
140 000	12952.09	7108.33	5185.09	4241.63	3689.70	3333.14	3087.83	2911.66
150 000	13877.24	7616.06	5555.45	4544.60	3953.25	3571.22	3308.39	3119.63
160 000	14802.38	8123.80	5925.81	4847.57	4216.80	3809.30	3528.95	3327.61
170 000	15727.53	8631.54	6296.18	5150.54	4480.35	4047.38	3749.51	3535.59
180 000	16652.68	9139.28	6666.54	5453.52	4743.89	4285.46	3970.06	3743.56
190 000	17577.83	9647.01	7036.90	5756.49	5007.44	4523.55	4190.62	3951.54
200 000	18502.98	10154.75	7407.26	6059.46	5270.99	4761.63	4411.18	4159.51
210 000	19428.13	10662.49	7777.63	6362.44	5534.54	4999.71	4631.74	4367.49
220 000	20353.28	11170.23	8147.99	6665.41	5798.09	5237.79	4852.30	4575.46
230 000	21278.43	11677.96	8518.35	6968.38	6061.64	5475.87	5072.86	4783.44
240 000	22203.58	12185.70	8888.72	7271.36	6325.19	5713.95	5293.42	4991.42
250 000	23128.73	12693.44	9259.08	7574.33	6588.74	5952.03	5513.98	5199.39
260 000	24053.87	13201.18	9629.44	7877.30	6852.29	6190.11	5734.54	5407.37
270 000	24979.02	13708.91	9999.81	8180.28	7115.84	6428.20	5955.10	5615.34
280 000	25904.17	14216.65	10370.17	8483.25	7379.39	6666.28	6175.66	5823.32
290 000	26829.32	14724.39	10740.53	8786.22	7642.94	6904.36	6396.21	6031.29
300 000	27754.47	15232.13	11110.90	9089.20	7906.49	7142.44	6616.77	6239.27
320 000	29604.77	16247.60	11851.62	9695.14	8433.59	7618.60	7057.89	6655.22
340 000	31455.07	17263.08	12592.35	10301.09	8960.69	8094.77	7499.01	7071.17
360 000	33305.36	18278.55	13333.08	10907.04	9487.79	8570.93	7940.13	7487.12
380 000	35155.66	19294.03	14073.80	11512.98	10014.89	9047.09	8381.25	7903.07
400 000	37005.96	20309.50	14814.53	12118.93	10541.99	9523.25	8822.36	8319.03
420 000	38856.26	21324.98	15555.26	12724.88	11069.09	9999.42	9263.48	8734.98
440 000	40706.56	22340.45	16295.98	13330.82	11596.19	10475.58	9704.60	9150.93
460 000	42556.85	23355.93	17036.71	13936.77	12123.29	10951.74	10145.72	9566.88
480 000	44407.15	24371.40	17777.44	14542.71	12650.39	11427.90	10586.84	9982.83
500 000	46257.45	25386.88	18518.16	15148.66	13177.49	11904.07	11027.96	10398.78
520 000	48107.75	26402.35	19258.89	15754.61	13704.59	12380.23	11469.07	10814.73
540 000	49958.05	27417.83	19999.61	16360.55	14231.68	12856.39	11910.19	11230.68
560 000	51808.34	28433.30	20740.34	16966.50	14758.78	13332.56	12351.31	11646.64
580 000	53658.64	29448.78	21481.07	17572.45	15285.88	13808.72	12792.43	12062.59
600 000	55508.94	30464.25	22221.79	18178.39	15812.98	14284.88	13233.55	12478.54
620 000	57359.24	31479.73	22962.52	18784.34	16340.08	14761.04	13674.67	12894.49
640 000	59209.54	32495.20	23703.25	19390.29	16867.18	15237.21	14115.78	13310.44
660 000	61059.83	33510.68	24443.97	19996.23	17394.28	15713.37	14556.90	13726.39
680 000	62910.13	34526.15	25184.70	20602.18	17921.38	16189.53	14998.02	14142.34
700 000	64760.43	35541.63	25925.43	21208.13	18448.48	16665.69	15439.14	14558.29
720 000	66610.73	36557.10	26666.15	21814.07	18975.58	17141.86	15880.26	14974.25
740 000	68461.03	37572.58	27406.88	22420.02	19502.68	17618.02	16321.37	15390.20
760 000	70311.32	38588.05	28147.61	23025.96	20029.78	18094.18	16762.49	15806.15
780 000	72161.62	39603.53	28888.33	23631.91	20556.88	18570.34	17203.61	16222.10
800 000	74011.92	40619.00	29629.06	24237.86	21083.98	19046.51	17644.73	16638.05
820 000	75862.22	41634.48	30369.79	24843.80	21611.08	19522.67	18085.85	17054.00
840 000	77712.52	42649.95	31110.51	25449.75	22138.18	19998.83	18526.97	17469.95
860 000	79562.81	43665.43	31851.24	26055.70	22665.28	20475.00	18968.08	17885.91
880 000	81413.11	44680.90	32591.97	26661.64	23192.38	20951.16	19409.20	18301.86
900 000	83263.41	45696.38	33332.69	27267.59	23719.47	21427.32	19850.32	18717.81
920 000	85113.71	46711.85	34073.42	27873.54	24246.57	21903.48	20291.44	19133.76
940 000	86964.01	47727.33	34814.14	28479.48	24773.67	22379.65	20732.56	19549.71
960 000	88814.30	48742.80	35554.87	29085.43	25300.77	22855.81	21173.68	19965.66
980 000	90664.60	49758.28	36295.60	29691.38	25827.87	23331.97	21614.79	20381.61
1000 000	92514.90	50773.75	37036.32	30297.32	26354.97	23808.13	22055.91	20797.56
Coefficient	.092514901	.050773754	.037036324	.030297322	.026354972	.023808134	.022055912	.020797564

MONTHLY AMORTIZING PAYMENTS

19.75%

AMOUNT	9 YEARS	10 YEARS	15 YEARS	20 YEARS	25 YEARS	30 YEARS	35 YEARS	40 YEARS
10 000	198.66	191.60	173.79	167.92	165.82	165.05	164.76	164.65
20 000	397.32	383.20	347.57	335.84	331.64	330.09	329.51	329.30
30 000	595.97	574.80	521.36	503.77	497.46	495.14	494.27	493.95
40 000	794.63	766.40	695.14	671.69	663.29	660.18	659.03	658.59
50 000	993.29	958.01	868.93	839.61	829.11	825.23	823.78	823.24
60 000	1191.95	1149.61	1042.71	1007.53	994.93	990.28	988.54	987.89
70 000	1390.61	1341.21	1216.50	1175.46	1160.75	1155.32	1153.30	1152.54
80 000	1589.26	1532.81	1390.28	1343.38	1326.57	1320.37	1318.05	1317.19
90 000	1787.92	1724.41	1564.07	1511.30	1492.39	1485.41	1482.81	1481.84
100 000	1986.58	1916.01	1737.85	1679.22	1658.21	1650.46	1647.57	1646.48
110 000	2185.24	2107.61	1911.64	1847.15	1824.04	1815.51	1812.32	1811.13
120 000	2383.90	2299.21	2085.43	2015.07	1989.86	1980.55	1977.08	1975.78
130 000	2582.55	2490.81	2259.21	2182.99	2155.68	2145.60	2141.84	2140.43
140 000	2781.21	2682.41	2433.00	2350.91	2321.50	2310.65	2306.60	2305.08
150 000	2979.87	2874.02	2606.78	2518.83	2487.32	2475.69	2471.35	2469.73
160 000	3178.53	3065.62	2780.57	2686.76	2653.14	2640.74	2636.11	2634.37
170 000	3377.19	3257.22	2954.35	2854.68	2818.96	2805.78	2800.87	2799.02
180 000	3575.84	3448.82	3128.14	3022.60	2984.79	2970.83	2965.62	2963.67
190 000	3774.50	3640.42	3301.92	3190.52	3150.61	3135.88	3130.38	3128.32
200 000	3973.16	3832.02	3475.71	3358.45	3316.43	3300.92	3295.14	3292.97
210 000	4171.82	4023.62	3649.50	3526.37	3482.25	3465.97	3459.89	3457.62
220 000	4370.48	4215.22	3823.28	3694.29	3648.07	3631.01	3624.65	3622.27
230 000	4569.13	4406.82	3997.07	3862.21	3813.89	3796.06	3789.41	3786.91
240 000	4767.79	4598.42	4170.85	4030.13	3979.72	3961.11	3954.16	3951.56
250 000	4966.45	4790.03	4344.64	4198.06	4145.54	4126.15	4118.92	4116.21
260 000	5165.11	4981.63	4518.42	4365.98	4311.36	4291.20	4283.68	4280.86
270 000	5363.77	5173.23	4692.21	4533.90	4477.18	4456.24	4448.43	4445.51
280 000	5562.42	5364.83	4865.99	4701.82	4643.00	4621.29	4613.19	4610.16
290 000	5761.08	5556.43	5039.78	4869.75	4808.82	4786.34	4777.95	4774.80
300 000	5959.74	5748.03	5213.56	5037.67	4974.64	4951.38	4942.70	4939.45
320 000	6357.06	6131.23	5561.14	5373.51	5306.29	5281.47	5272.22	5268.75
340 000	6754.37	6514.43	5908.71	5709.36	5637.93	5611.57	5601.73	5598.05
360 000	7151.69	6897.64	6256.28	6045.20	5969.57	5941.66	5931.24	5927.34
380 000	7549.00	7280.84	6603.85	6381.05	6301.22	6271.75	6260.76	6256.64
400 000	7946.32	7664.04	6951.42	6716.89	6632.86	6601.84	6590.27	6585.94
420 000	8343.63	8047.24	7298.99	7052.74	6964.50	6931.94	6919.79	6915.23
440 000	8740.95	8430.44	7646.56	7388.58	7296.14	7262.03	7249.30	7244.53
460 000	9138.27	8813.65	7994.13	7724.42	7627.79	7592.12	7578.81	7573.83
480 000	9535.58	9196.85	8341.70	8060.27	7959.43	7922.21	7908.33	7903.12
500 000	9932.90	9580.05	8689.27	8396.11	8291.07	8252.30	8237.84	8232.42
520 000	10330.21	9963.25	9036.84	8731.96	8622.72	8582.40	8567.35	8561.72
540 000	10727.53	10346.46	9384.42	9067.80	8954.36	8912.49	8896.87	8891.02
560 000	11124.85	10729.66	9731.99	9403.65	9286.00	9242.58	9226.38	9220.31
580 000	11522.16	11112.86	10079.56	9739.49	9617.64	9572.67	9555.89	9549.61
600 000	11919.48	11496.06	10427.13	10075.34	9949.29	9902.77	9885.41	9878.91
620 000	12316.79	11879.26	10774.70	10411.18	10280.93	10232.86	10214.92	10208.20
640 000	12714.11	12262.47	11122.27	10747.03	10612.57	10562.95	10544.44	10537.50
660 000	13111.43	12645.67	11469.84	11082.87	10944.22	10893.04	10873.95	10866.80
680 000	13508.74	13028.87	11817.41	11418.72	11275.86	11223.13	11203.46	11196.09
700 000	13906.06	13412.07	12164.98	11754.56	11607.50	11553.23	11532.98	11525.39
720 000	14303.37	13795.27	12512.55	12090.40	11939.15	11883.32	11862.49	11854.69
740 000	14700.69	14178.48	12860.13	12426.25	12270.79	12213.41	12192.00	12183.98
760 000	15098.01	14561.68	13207.70	12762.09	12602.43	12543.50	12521.52	12513.28
780 000	15495.32	14944.88	13555.27	13097.94	12934.07	12873.60	12851.03	12842.58
800 000	15892.64	15328.08	13902.84	13433.78	13265.72	13203.69	13180.54	13171.87
820 000	16289.95	15711.28	14250.41	13769.63	13597.36	13533.78	13510.06	13501.17
840 000	16687.27	16094.49	14597.98	14105.47	13929.00	13863.87	13839.57	13830.47
860 000	17084.59	16477.69	14945.55	14441.32	14260.65	14193.96	14169.08	14159.76
880 000	17481.90	16860.89	15293.12	14777.16	14592.29	14524.06	14498.60	14489.06
900 000	17879.22	17244.09	15640.69	15113.01	14923.93	14854.15	14828.11	14818.36
920 000	18276.53	17627.29	15988.26	15448.85	15255.57	15184.24	15157.63	15147.66
940 000	18673.85	18010.50	16335.84	15784.69	15587.22	15514.33	15487.14	15476.95
960 000	19071.17	18393.70	16683.41	16120.54	15918.86	15844.42	15816.65	15806.25
980 000	19468.48	18776.90	17030.98	16456.38	16250.50	16174.52	16146.17	16135.55
1000 000	19865.80	19160.10	17378.55	16792.23	16582.15	16504.61	16475.68	16464.84
Coefficient	.019865797	.019160102	.017378548	.016792228	.016582146	.016504609	.016475680	.016464843

121

MONTHLY AMORTIZING PAYMENTS

AMOUNT	1 YEAR	2 YEARS	3 YEARS	4 YEARS	5 YEARS	6 YEARS	7 YEARS	8 YEARS
10 000	926.35	508.96	371.64	304.30	264.94	239.53	222.06	209.53
20 000	1852.69	1017.92	743.27	608.61	529.88	479.06	444.12	419.06
30 000	2779.04	1526.87	1114.91	912.91	794.82	718.58	666.19	628.60
40 000	3705.38	2035.83	1486.54	1217.21	1059.76	958.11	888.25	838.13
50 000	4631.73	2544.79	1858.18	1521.52	1324.69	1197.64	1110.31	1047.66
60 000	5558.07	3053.75	2229.81	1825.82	1589.63	1437.17	1332.37	1257.19
70 000	6484.42	3562.71	2601.45	2130.13	1854.57	1676.70	1554.43	1466.72
80 000	7410.76	4071.66	2973.09	2434.43	2119.51	1916.23	1776.50	1676.26
90 000	8337.11	4580.62	3344.72	2738.73	2384.45	2155.75	1998.56	1885.79
100 000	9263.45	5089.58	3716.36	3043.04	2649.39	2395.28	2220.62	2095.32
110 000	10189.80	5598.54	4087.99	3347.34	2914.33	2634.81	2442.68	2304.85
120 000	11116.14	6107.50	4459.63	3651.64	3179.27	2874.34	2664.74	2514.38
130 000	12042.49	6616.45	4831.27	3955.95	3444.20	3113.87	2886.81	2723.92
140 000	12968.83	7125.41	5202.90	4260.25	3709.14	3353.40	3108.87	2933.45
150 000	13895.18	7634.37	5574.54	4564.55	3974.08	3592.92	3330.93	3142.98
160 000	14821.52	8143.33	5946.17	4868.86	4239.02	3832.45	3552.99	3352.51
170 000	15747.87	8652.29	6317.81	5173.16	4503.96	4071.98	3775.05	3562.04
180 000	16674.21	9161.24	6689.44	5477.47	4768.90	4311.51	3997.12	3771.58
190 000	17600.56	9670.20	7061.08	5781.77	5033.84	4551.04	4219.18	3981.11
200 000	18526.90	10179.16	7432.72	6086.07	5298.78	4790.57	4441.24	4190.64
210 000	19453.25	10688.12	7804.35	6390.38	5563.72	5030.09	4663.30	4400.17
220 000	20379.59	11197.08	8175.99	6694.68	5828.65	5269.62	4885.36	4609.70
230 000	21305.94	11706.03	8547.62	6998.98	6093.59	5509.15	5107.43	4819.24
240 000	22232.28	12214.99	8919.26	7303.29	6358.53	5748.68	5329.49	5028.77
250 000	23158.63	12723.95	9290.90	7607.59	6623.47	5988.21	5551.55	5238.30
260 000	24084.97	13232.91	9662.53	7911.89	6888.41	6227.73	5773.61	5447.83
270 000	25011.32	13741.87	10034.17	8216.20	7153.35	6467.26	5995.67	5657.36
280 000	25937.66	14250.82	10405.80	8520.50	7418.29	6706.79	6217.74	5866.90
290 000	26864.01	14759.78	10777.44	8824.80	7683.23	6946.32	6439.80	6076.43
300 000	27790.35	15268.74	11149.07	9129.11	7948.17	7185.85	6661.86	6285.96
320 000	29643.04	16286.66	11892.35	9737.72	8478.04	7664.90	7105.98	6705.02
340 000	31495.73	17304.57	12635.62	10346.32	9007.92	8143.96	7550.11	7124.09
360 000	33348.42	18322.49	13378.89	10954.93	9537.80	8623.02	7994.23	7543.15
380 000	35201.11	19340.40	14122.16	11563.54	10067.68	9102.07	8438.36	7962.22
400 000	37053.80	20358.32	14865.43	12172.14	10597.55	9581.13	8882.48	8381.28
420 000	38906.50	21376.24	15608.70	12780.75	11127.43	10060.19	9326.60	8800.34
440 000	40759.19	22394.15	16351.98	13389.36	11657.31	10539.24	9770.73	9219.41
460 000	42611.88	23412.07	17095.25	13997.97	12187.19	11018.30	10214.85	9638.47
480 000	44464.57	24429.98	17838.52	14606.57	12717.06	11497.36	10658.98	10057.54
500 000	46317.26	25447.90	18581.79	15215.18	13246.94	11976.41	11103.10	10476.60
520 000	48169.95	26465.82	19325.06	15823.79	13776.82	12455.47	11547.22	10895.66
540 000	50022.64	27483.73	20068.33	16432.40	14306.70	12934.53	11991.35	11314.73
560 000	51875.33	28501.65	20811.61	17041.00	14836.58	13413.58	12435.47	11733.79
580 000	53728.02	29519.56	21554.88	17649.61	15366.45	13892.64	12879.60	12152.86
600 000	55580.71	30537.48	22298.15	18258.22	15896.33	14371.70	13323.72	12571.92
620 000	57433.40	31555.40	23041.42	18866.82	16426.21	14850.75	13767.84	12990.98
640 000	59286.09	32573.31	23784.69	19475.43	16956.09	15329.81	14211.97	13410.05
660 000	61138.78	33591.23	24527.96	20084.04	17485.96	15808.86	14656.09	13829.11
680 000	62991.47	34609.14	25271.24	20692.65	18015.84	16287.92	15100.22	14248.18
700 000	64844.16	35627.06	26014.51	21301.25	18545.72	16766.98	15544.34	14667.24
720 000	66696.85	36644.98	26757.78	21909.86	19075.60	17246.03	15988.46	15086.30
740 000	68549.54	37662.89	27501.05	22518.47	19605.47	17725.09	16432.59	15505.37
760 000	70402.23	38680.81	28244.32	23127.08	20135.35	18204.15	16876.71	15924.43
780 000	72254.92	39698.72	28987.59	23735.68	20665.23	18683.20	17320.84	16343.50
800 000	74107.61	40716.64	29730.87	24344.29	21195.11	19162.26	17764.96	16762.56
820 000	75960.30	41734.56	30474.14	24952.90	21724.98	19641.32	18209.08	17181.62
840 000	77812.99	42752.47	31217.41	25561.50	22254.86	20120.37	18653.21	17600.69
860 000	79665.68	43770.39	31960.68	26170.11	22784.74	20599.43	19097.33	18019.75
880 000	81518.37	44788.30	32703.95	26778.72	23314.62	21078.49	19541.46	18438.82
900 000	83371.06	45806.22	33447.22	27387.33	23844.50	21557.54	19985.58	18857.88
920 000	85223.75	46824.14	34190.50	27995.93	24374.37	22036.60	20429.70	19276.94
940 000	87076.44	47842.05	34933.77	28604.54	24904.25	22515.66	20873.83	19696.01
960 000	88929.13	48859.97	35677.04	29213.15	25434.13	22994.71	21317.95	20115.07
980 000	90781.82	49877.88	36420.31	29821.75	25964.01	23473.77	21762.08	20534.14
1000 000	92634.51	50895.80	37163.58	30430.36	26493.88	23952.83	22206.20	20953.20
Coefficient	.092634512	.050895801	.037163582	.030430362	.026493884	.023952825	.022206200	.020953201

122

MONTHLY AMORTIZING PAYMENTS 20.00%

AMOUNT	9 YEARS	10 YEARS	15 YEARS	20 YEARS	25 YEARS	30 YEARS	35 YEARS	40 YEARS
10 000	200.27	193.26	175.63	169.88	167.85	167.10	166.83	166.73
20 000	400.53	386.51	351.26	339.76	335.69	334.20	333.66	333.45
30 000	600.80	579.77	526.89	509.65	503.54	501.31	500.48	500.18
40 000	801.06	773.02	702.52	679.53	671.38	668.41	667.31	666.91
50 000	1001.33	966.28	878.15	849.41	839.23	835.51	834.14	833.63
60 000	1201.59	1159.53	1053.78	1019.29	1007.07	1002.61	1000.97	1000.36
70 000	1401.86	1352.79	1229.41	1189.18	1174.92	1169.71	1167.79	1167.08
80 000	1602.12	1546.05	1405.04	1359.06	1342.76	1336.81	1334.62	1333.81
90 000	1802.39	1739.30	1580.67	1528.94	1510.61	1503.92	1501.45	1500.54
100 000	2002.65	1932.56	1756.30	1698.82	1678.45	1671.02	1668.28	1667.26
110 000	2202.92	2125.81	1931.93	1868.71	1846.30	1838.12	1835.11	1833.99
120 000	2403.18	2319.07	2107.56	2038.59	2014.14	2005.22	2001.93	2000.72
130 000	2603.45	2512.32	2283.19	2208.47	2181.99	2172.32	2168.76	2167.44
140 000	2803.71	2705.58	2458.82	2378.35	2349.83	2339.43	2335.59	2334.17
150 000	3003.98	2898.84	2634.44	2548.24	2517.68	2506.53	2502.42	2500.90
160 000	3204.24	3092.09	2810.07	2718.12	2685.52	2673.63	2669.25	2667.62
170 000	3404.51	3285.35	2985.70	2888.00	2853.37	2840.73	2836.07	2834.35
180 000	3604.77	3478.60	3161.33	3057.88	3021.21	3007.83	3002.90	3001.08
190 000	3805.04	3671.86	3336.96	3227.77	3189.06	3174.94	3169.73	3167.80
200 000	4005.30	3865.11	3512.59	3397.65	3356.90	3342.04	3336.56	3334.53
210 000	4205.57	4058.37	3688.22	3567.53	3524.75	3509.14	3503.38	3501.25
220 000	4405.83	4251.62	3863.85	3737.41	3692.59	3676.24	3670.21	3667.98
230 000	4606.10	4444.88	4039.48	3907.30	3860.44	3843.34	3837.04	3834.71
240 000	4806.36	4638.14	4215.11	4077.18	4028.28	4010.44	4003.87	4001.43
250 000	5006.63	4831.39	4390.74	4247.06	4196.13	4177.55	4170.70	4168.16
260 000	5206.89	5024.65	4566.37	4416.94	4363.97	4344.65	4337.52	4334.89
270 000	5407.16	5217.90	4742.00	4586.83	4531.82	4511.75	4504.35	4501.61
280 000	5607.42	5411.16	4917.63	4756.71	4699.67	4678.85	4671.18	4668.34
290 000	5807.69	5604.41	5093.26	4926.59	4867.51	4845.95	4838.01	4835.07
300 000	6007.95	5797.67	5268.89	5096.47	5035.36	5013.06	5004.83	5001.79
320 000	6408.48	6184.18	5620.15	5436.24	5371.05	5347.26	5338.49	5335.25
340 000	6809.01	6570.69	5971.41	5776.00	5706.74	5681.46	5672.15	5668.70
360 000	7209.54	6957.20	6322.67	6115.77	6042.43	6015.67	6005.80	6002.15
380 000	7610.07	7343.72	6673.93	6455.53	6378.12	6349.87	6339.46	6335.60
400 000	8010.60	7730.23	7025.19	6795.30	6713.81	6684.07	6673.11	6669.06
420 000	8411.13	8116.74	7376.45	7135.06	7049.50	7018.28	7006.77	7002.51
440 000	8811.66	8503.25	7727.70	7474.83	7385.19	7352.48	7340.42	7335.96
460 000	9212.19	8889.76	8078.96	7814.59	7720.88	7686.69	7674.08	7669.41
480 000	9612.72	9276.27	8430.22	8154.36	8056.57	8020.89	8007.74	8002.87
500 000	10013.25	9662.78	8781.48	8494.12	8392.26	8355.09	8341.39	8336.32
520 000	10413.78	10049.29	9132.74	8833.89	8727.95	8689.30	8675.05	8669.77
540 000	10814.31	10435.81	9484.00	9173.65	9063.64	9023.50	9008.70	9003.23
560 000	11214.84	10822.32	9835.26	9513.42	9399.33	9357.70	9342.36	9336.68
580 000	11615.37	11208.83	10186.52	9853.18	9735.02	9691.91	9676.01	9670.13
600 000	12015.90	11595.34	10537.78	10192.95	10070.71	10026.11	10009.67	10003.58
620 000	12416.43	11981.85	10889.04	10532.71	10406.40	10360.32	10343.33	10337.04
640 000	12816.96	12368.36	11240.30	10872.48	10742.09	10694.52	10676.98	10670.49
660 000	13217.49	12754.87	11591.56	11212.24	11077.78	11028.72	11010.64	11003.94
680 000	13618.02	13141.39	11942.82	11552.01	11413.47	11362.93	11344.29	11337.40
700 000	14018.55	13527.90	12294.08	11891.77	11749.16	11697.13	11677.95	11670.85
720 000	14419.08	13914.41	12645.33	12231.54	12084.85	12031.33	12011.60	12004.30
740 000	14819.61	14300.92	12996.59	12571.30	12420.54	12365.54	12345.26	12337.75
760 000	15220.14	14687.43	13347.85	12911.07	12756.23	12699.74	12678.92	12671.21
780 000	15620.67	15073.94	13699.11	13250.83	13091.92	13033.95	13012.57	13004.66
800 000	16021.20	15460.45	14050.37	13590.60	13427.61	13368.15	13346.23	13338.11
820 000	16421.73	15846.96	14401.63	13930.36	13763.30	13702.35	13679.88	13671.57
840 000	16822.26	16233.48	14752.89	14270.13	14099.00	14036.56	14013.54	14005.02
860 000	17222.79	16619.99	15104.15	14609.89	14434.69	14370.76	14347.19	14338.47
880 000	17623.32	17006.50	15455.41	14949.66	14770.38	14704.96	14680.85	14671.92
900 000	18023.85	17393.01	15806.67	15289.42	15106.07	15039.17	15014.50	15005.38
920 000	18424.38	17779.52	16157.93	15629.19	15441.76	15373.37	15348.16	15338.83
940 000	18824.91	18166.03	16509.19	15968.95	15777.45	15707.58	15681.82	15672.28
960 000	19225.44	18552.54	16860.45	16308.72	16113.14	16041.78	16015.47	16005.74
980 000	19625.97	18939.06	17211.71	16648.48	16448.83	16375.98	16349.13	16339.19
1000 000	20026.50	19325.57	17562.97	16988.25	16784.52	16710.19	16682.78	16672.64
Coefficient	.020026502	.019325567	.017562965	.016988246	.016784518	.016710187	.016682783	.016672641

123

MONTHLY AMORTIZING PAYMENTS

AMOUNT	1 YEAR	2 YEARS	3 YEARS	4 YEARS	5 YEARS	6 YEARS	7 YEARS	8 YEARS
10 000	927.54	510.18	372.91	305.64	266.33	240.98	223.57	211.09
20 000	1855.08	1020.36	745.82	611.27	532.66	481.96	447.14	422.19
30 000	2782.63	1530.54	1118.73	916.91	799.00	722.94	670.71	633.28
40 000	3710.17	2040.72	1491.64	1222.55	1065.33	963.92	894.28	844.37
50 000	4637.71	2550.90	1864.55	1528.19	1331.66	1204.90	1117.85	1055.47
60 000	5565.25	3061.08	2237.47	1833.82	1597.99	1445.88	1341.42	1266.56
70 000	6492.79	3571.26	2610.38	2139.46	1864.32	1686.86	1564.99	1477.66
80 000	7420.34	4081.44	2983.29	2445.10	2130.65	1927.84	1788.56	1688.75
90 000	8347.88	4591.62	3356.20	2750.73	2396.99	2168.82	2012.13	1899.84
100 000	9275.42	5101.80	3729.11	3056.37	2663.32	2409.80	2235.70	2110.94
110 000	10202.96	5611.98	4102.02	3362.01	2929.65	2650.78	2459.27	2322.03
120 000	11130.50	6122.16	4474.93	3667.65	3195.98	2891.76	2682.84	2533.12
130 000	12058.05	6632.34	4847.84	3973.28	3462.31	3132.73	2906.41	2744.22
140 000	12985.59	7142.52	5220.75	4278.92	3728.65	3373.71	3129.98	2955.31
150 000	13913.13	7652.70	5593.66	4584.56	3994.98	3614.69	3353.55	3166.41
160 000	14840.67	8162.88	5966.57	4890.20	4261.31	3855.67	3577.12	3377.50
170 000	15768.21	8673.06	6339.48	5195.83	4527.64	4096.65	3800.69	3588.59
180 000	16695.76	9183.24	6712.40	5501.47	4793.97	4337.63	4024.26	3799.69
190 000	17623.30	9693.42	7085.31	5807.11	5060.30	4578.61	4247.83	4010.78
200 000	18550.84	10203.60	7458.22	6112.74	5326.64	4819.59	4471.40	4221.87
210 000	19478.38	10713.78	7831.13	6418.38	5592.97	5060.57	4694.97	4432.97
220 000	20405.92	11223.96	8204.04	6724.02	5859.30	5301.55	4918.53	4644.06
230 000	21333.47	11734.14	8576.95	7029.66	6125.63	5542.53	5142.10	4855.15
240 000	22261.01	12244.32	8949.86	7335.29	6391.96	5783.51	5365.67	5066.25
250 000	23188.55	12754.50	9322.77	7640.93	6658.29	6024.49	5589.24	5277.34
260 000	24116.09	13264.68	9695.68	7946.57	6924.63	6265.47	5812.81	5488.44
270 000	25043.63	13774.86	10068.59	8252.20	7190.96	6506.45	6036.38	5699.53
280 000	25971.18	14285.04	10441.50	8557.84	7457.29	6747.43	6259.95	5910.62
290 000	26898.72	14795.22	10814.42	8863.48	7723.62	6988.41	6483.52	6121.72
300 000	27826.26	15305.40	11187.33	9169.12	7989.95	7229.39	6707.09	6332.81
320 000	29681.34	16325.76	11933.15	9780.39	8522.62	7711.35	7154.23	6755.00
340 000	31536.43	17346.12	12678.97	10391.66	9055.28	8193.31	7601.37	7177.18
360 000	33391.51	18366.48	13424.79	11002.94	9587.94	8675.27	8048.51	7599.37
380 000	35246.60	19386.84	14170.61	11614.21	10120.61	9157.22	8495.65	8021.56
400 000	37101.68	20407.21	14916.44	12225.49	10653.27	9639.18	8942.79	8443.75
420 000	38956.77	21427.57	15662.26	12836.76	11185.94	10121.14	9389.93	8865.93
440 000	40811.85	22447.93	16408.08	13448.04	11718.60	10603.10	9837.07	9288.12
460 000	42666.93	23468.29	17153.90	14059.31	12251.26	11085.06	10284.21	9710.31
480 000	44522.02	24488.65	17899.72	14670.59	12783.93	11567.02	10731.35	10132.50
500 000	46377.10	25509.01	18645.54	15281.86	13316.59	12048.98	11178.49	10554.68
520 000	48232.19	26529.37	19391.37	15893.13	13849.25	12530.94	11625.63	10976.87
540 000	50087.27	27549.73	20137.19	16504.41	14381.92	13012.90	12072.77	11399.06
560 000	51942.35	28570.09	20883.01	17115.68	14914.58	13494.86	12519.91	11821.25
580 000	53797.44	29590.45	21628.83	17726.96	15447.24	13976.82	12967.05	12243.43
600 000	55652.52	30610.81	22374.65	18338.23	15979.91	14458.78	13414.19	12665.62
620 000	57507.61	31631.17	23120.47	18949.51	16512.57	14940.74	13861.33	13087.81
640 000	59362.69	32651.53	23866.30	19560.78	17045.23	15422.69	14308.47	13509.99
660 000	61217.77	33671.89	24612.12	20172.05	17577.90	15904.65	14755.60	13932.18
680 000	63072.86	34692.25	25357.94	20783.33	18110.56	16386.61	15202.74	14354.37
700 000	64927.94	35712.61	26103.76	21394.60	18643.23	16868.57	15649.88	14776.56
720 000	66783.03	36732.97	26849.58	22005.88	19175.89	17350.53	16097.02	15198.74
740 000	68638.11	37753.33	27595.41	22617.15	19708.55	17832.49	16544.16	15620.93
760 000	70493.19	38773.69	28341.23	23228.43	20241.22	18314.45	16991.30	16043.12
780 000	72348.28	39794.05	29087.05	23839.70	20773.88	18796.41	17438.44	16465.31
800 000	74203.36	40814.41	29832.87	24450.98	21306.54	19278.37	17885.58	16887.49
820 000	76058.45	41834.77	30578.69	25062.25	21839.21	19760.33	18332.72	17309.68
840 000	77913.53	42855.13	31324.51	25673.52	22371.87	20242.29	18779.86	17731.87
860 000	79768.61	43875.49	32070.34	26284.80	22904.53	20724.25	19227.00	18154.06
880 000	81623.70	44895.85	32816.16	26896.07	23437.20	21206.20	19674.14	18576.24
900 000	83478.78	45916.21	33561.98	27507.35	23969.86	21688.16	20121.28	18998.43
920 000	85333.87	46936.57	34307.80	28118.62	24502.52	22170.12	20568.42	19420.62
940 000	87188.95	47956.93	35053.62	28729.90	25035.19	22652.08	21015.56	19842.80
960 000	89044.03	48977.29	35799.44	29341.17	25567.85	23134.04	21462.70	20264.99
980 000	90899.12	49997.65	36545.27	29952.44	26100.52	23616.00	21909.84	20687.18
1000 000	92754.20	51018.01	37291.09	30563.72	26633.18	24097.96	22356.98	21109.37
Coefficient	.092754203	.051018013	.037291088	.030563719	.026633179	.02409796	.022356977	.021109367

AMOUNT	9 YEARS	10 YEARS	15 YEARS	20 YEARS	25 YEARS	30 YEARS	35 YEARS	40 YEARS
10 000	201.88	194.92	177.48	171.85	169.87	169.16	168.90	168.80
20 000	403.76	389.83	354.96	343.69	339.74	338.32	337.80	337.61
30 000	605.63	584.75	532.44	515.54	509.61	507.48	506.70	506.41
40 000	807.51	779.66	709.92	687.39	679.49	676.64	675.60	675.22
50 000	1009.39	974.58	887.40	859.23	849.36	845.80	844.50	844.02
60 000	1211.27	1169.50	1064.88	1031.08	1019.23	1014.96	1013.40	1012.83
70 000	1413.14	1364.41	1242.36	1202.93	1189.10	1184.11	1182.30	1181.63
80 000	1615.02	1559.33	1419.84	1374.78	1358.97	1353.27	1351.20	1350.44
90 000	1816.90	1754.25	1597.31	1546.62	1528.84	1522.43	1520.10	1519.24
100 000	2018.78	1949.16	1774.79	1718.47	1698.72	1691.59	1689.00	1688.05
110 000	2220.65	2144.08	1952.27	1890.32	1868.59	1860.75	1857.90	1856.85
120 000	2422.53	2338.99	2129.75	2062.16	2038.46	2029.91	2026.80	2025.66
130 000	2624.41	2533.91	2307.23	2234.01	2208.33	2199.07	2195.70	2194.46
140 000	2826.29	2728.83	2484.71	2405.86	2378.20	2368.23	2364.60	2363.27
150 000	3028.16	2923.74	2662.19	2577.70	2548.07	2537.39	2533.50	2532.07
160 000	3230.04	3118.66	2839.67	2749.55	2717.95	2706.55	2702.40	2700.88
170 000	3431.92	3313.57	3017.15	2921.40	2887.82	2875.71	2871.30	2869.68
180 000	3633.80	3508.49	3194.63	3093.24	3057.69	3044.87	3040.19	3038.49
190 000	3835.68	3703.41	3372.11	3265.09	3227.56	3214.03	3209.09	3207.29
200 000	4037.55	3898.32	3549.59	3436.94	3397.43	3383.18	3377.99	3376.10
210 000	4239.43	4093.24	3727.07	3608.78	3567.30	3552.34	3546.89	3544.90
220 000	4441.31	4288.15	3904.55	3780.63	3737.18	3721.50	3715.79	3713.71
230 000	4643.19	4483.07	4082.03	3952.48	3907.05	3890.66	3884.69	3882.51
240 000	4845.06	4677.99	4259.51	4124.33	4076.92	4059.82	4053.59	4051.32
250 000	5046.94	4872.90	4436.99	4296.17	4246.79	4228.98	4222.49	4220.12
260 000	5248.82	5067.82	4614.46	4468.02	4416.66	4398.14	4391.39	4388.93
270 000	5450.70	5262.74	4791.94	4639.87	4586.53	4567.30	4560.29	4557.73
280 000	5652.57	5457.65	4969.42	4811.71	4756.41	4736.46	4729.19	4726.53
290 000	5854.45	5652.57	5146.90	4983.56	4926.28	4905.62	4898.09	4895.34
300 000	6056.33	5847.48	5324.38	5155.41	5096.15	5074.78	5066.99	5064.14
320 000	6460.08	6237.32	5679.34	5499.10	5435.89	5413.10	5404.79	5401.75
340 000	6863.84	6627.15	6034.30	5842.79	5775.64	5751.41	5742.59	5739.36
360 000	7267.60	7016.98	6389.26	6186.49	6115.38	6089.73	6080.39	6076.97
380 000	7671.35	7406.81	6744.22	6530.18	6455.12	6428.05	6418.19	6414.58
400 000	8075.11	7796.64	7099.18	6873.88	6794.87	6766.37	6755.99	6752.19
420 000	8478.86	8186.48	7454.14	7217.57	7134.61	7104.69	7093.79	7089.80
440 000	8882.62	8576.31	7809.09	7561.26	7474.35	7443.01	7431.59	7427.41
460 000	9286.37	8966.14	8164.05	7904.96	7814.09	7781.32	7769.39	7765.02
480 000	9690.13	9355.97	8519.01	8248.65	8153.84	8119.64	8107.19	8102.63
500 000	10093.88	9745.81	8873.97	8592.34	8493.58	8457.96	8444.99	8440.24
520 000	10497.64	10135.64	9228.93	8936.04	8833.32	8796.28	8782.78	8777.85
540 000	10901.39	10525.47	9583.89	9279.73	9173.07	9134.60	9120.58	9115.46
560 000	11305.15	10915.30	9938.85	9623.43	9512.81	9472.92	9458.38	9453.07
580 000	11708.90	11305.13	10293.81	9967.12	9852.55	9811.24	9796.18	9790.68
600 000	12112.66	11694.97	10648.77	10310.81	10192.30	10149.55	10133.98	10128.29
620 000	12516.41	12084.80	11003.72	10654.51	10532.04	10487.87	10471.78	10465.90
640 000	12920.17	12474.63	11358.68	10998.20	10871.78	10826.19	10809.58	10803.51
660 000	13323.92	12864.46	11713.64	11341.89	11211.53	11164.51	11147.38	11141.12
680 000	13727.68	13254.30	12068.60	11685.59	11551.27	11502.83	11485.18	11478.73
700 000	14131.44	13644.13	12423.56	12029.28	11891.01	11841.15	11822.98	11816.34
720 000	14535.19	14033.96	12778.52	12372.98	12230.76	12179.46	12160.78	12153.95
740 000	14938.95	14423.79	13133.48	12716.67	12570.50	12517.78	12498.58	12491.56
760 000	15342.70	14813.63	13488.44	13060.36	12910.24	12856.10	12836.38	12829.17
780 000	15746.46	15203.46	13843.39	13404.06	13249.99	13194.42	13174.18	13166.78
800 000	16150.21	15593.29	14198.35	13747.75	13589.73	13532.74	13511.98	13504.39
820 000	16553.97	15983.12	14553.31	14091.44	13929.47	13871.06	13849.78	13842.00
840 000	16957.72	16372.95	14908.27	14435.14	14269.22	14209.38	14187.58	14179.60
860 000	17361.48	16762.79	15263.23	14778.83	14608.96	14547.69	14525.38	14517.21
880 000	17765.23	17152.62	15618.19	15122.53	14948.70	14886.01	14863.17	14854.82
900 000	18168.99	17542.45	15973.15	15466.22	15288.45	15224.33	15200.97	15192.43
920 000	18572.74	17932.28	16328.11	15809.91	15628.19	15562.65	15538.77	15530.04
940 000	18976.50	18322.12	16683.07	16153.61	15967.93	15900.97	15876.57	15867.65
960 000	19380.25	18711.95	17038.02	16497.30	16307.68	16239.29	16214.37	16205.26
980 000	19784.01	19101.78	17392.98	16840.99	16647.42	16577.60	16552.17	16542.87
1000 000	20187.77	19491.61	17747.94	17184.69	16987.16	16915.92	16889.97	16880.48
Coefficient	.020187765	.019491612	.017747942	.017184688	.016987163	.016915923	.016889971	.016880482

MONTHLY AMORTIZING PAYMENTS

AMOUNT	1 YEAR	2 YEARS	3 YEARS	4 YEARS	5 YEARS	6 YEARS	7 YEARS	8 YEARS
10 000	928.74	511.40	374.19	306.97	267.73	242.44	225.08	212.66
20 000	1857.48	1022.81	748.38	613.95	535.46	484.87	450.16	425.32
30 000	2786.22	1534.21	1122.57	920.92	803.19	727.31	675.25	637.98
40 000	3714.96	2045.62	1496.75	1227.90	1070.91	969.74	900.33	850.64
50 000	4643.70	2557.02	1870.94	1534.87	1338.64	1212.18	1125.41	1063.30
60 000	5572.44	3068.42	2245.13	1841.84	1606.37	1454.61	1350.49	1275.96
70 000	6501.18	3579.83	2619.32	2148.82	1874.10	1697.05	1575.58	1488.62
80 000	7429.92	4091.23	2993.51	2455.79	2141.83	1939.48	1800.66	1701.28
90 000	8358.66	4602.64	3367.70	2762.77	2409.56	2181.92	2025.74	1913.95
100 000	9287.40	5114.04	3741.88	3069.74	2677.29	2424.35	2250.82	2126.61
110 000	10216.14	5625.44	4116.07	3376.71	2945.01	2666.79	2475.91	2339.27
120 000	11144.88	6136.85	4490.26	3683.69	3212.74	2909.22	2700.99	2551.93
130 000	12073.62	6648.25	4864.45	3990.66	3480.47	3151.66	2926.07	2764.59
140 000	13002.36	7159.65	5238.64	4297.64	3748.20	3394.09	3151.15	2977.25
150 000	13931.10	7671.06	5612.83	4604.61	4015.93	3636.53	3376.24	3189.91
160 000	14859.84	8182.46	5987.01	4911.58	4283.66	3878.97	3601.32	3402.57
170 000	15788.58	8693.87	6361.20	5218.56	4551.39	4121.40	3826.40	3615.23
180 000	16717.32	9205.27	6735.39	5525.53	4819.11	4363.84	4051.48	3827.89
190 000	17646.06	9716.67	7109.58	5832.51	5086.84	4606.27	4276.57	4040.55
200 000	18574.79	10228.08	7483.77	6139.48	5354.57	4848.71	4501.65	4253.21
210 000	19503.53	10739.48	7857.96	6446.45	5622.30	5091.14	4726.73	4465.87
220 000	20432.27	11250.89	8232.14	6753.43	5890.03	5333.58	4951.81	4678.53
230 000	21361.01	11762.29	8606.33	7060.40	6157.76	5576.01	5176.90	4891.19
240 000	22289.75	12273.69	8980.52	7367.38	6425.49	5818.45	5401.98	5103.85
250 000	23218.49	12785.10	9354.71	7674.35	6693.21	6060.88	5627.06	5316.51
260 000	24147.23	13296.50	9728.90	7981.32	6960.94	6303.32	5852.14	5529.18
270 000	25075.97	13807.91	10103.09	8288.30	7228.67	6545.75	6077.23	5741.84
280 000	26004.71	14319.31	10477.27	8595.27	7496.40	6788.19	6302.31	5954.50
290 000	26933.45	14830.71	10851.46	8902.24	7764.13	7030.62	6527.39	6167.16
300 000	27862.19	15342.12	11225.65	9209.22	8031.86	7273.06	6752.47	6379.82
320 000	29719.67	16364.93	11974.03	9823.17	8567.31	7757.93	7202.64	6805.14
340 000	31577.15	17387.73	12722.40	10437.11	9102.77	8242.80	7652.80	7230.46
360 000	33434.63	18410.54	13470.78	11051.06	9638.23	8727.67	8102.97	7655.78
380 000	35292.11	19433.35	14219.16	11665.01	10173.69	9212.54	8553.13	8081.10
400 000	37149.59	20456.16	14967.53	12278.96	10709.14	9697.41	9003.30	8506.42
420 000	39007.07	21478.96	15715.91	12892.91	11244.60	10182.28	9453.46	8931.74
440 000	40864.55	22501.77	16464.29	13506.85	11780.06	10667.15	9903.63	9357.07
460 000	42722.03	23524.58	17212.66	14120.80	12315.52	11152.03	10353.79	9782.39
480 000	44579.51	24547.39	17961.04	14734.75	12850.97	11636.90	10803.96	10207.71
500 000	46436.99	25570.20	18709.42	15348.70	13386.43	12121.77	11254.12	10633.03
520 000	48294.47	26593.00	19457.79	15962.65	13921.89	12606.64	11704.29	11058.35
540 000	50151.95	27615.81	20206.17	16576.59	14457.34	13091.51	12154.45	11483.67
560 000	52009.43	28638.62	20954.55	17190.54	14992.80	13576.38	12604.62	11908.99
580 000	53866.90	29661.43	21702.92	17804.49	15528.26	14061.25	13054.78	12334.31
600 000	55724.38	30684.24	22451.30	18418.44	16063.72	14546.12	13504.95	12759.64
620 000	57581.86	31707.04	23199.68	19032.39	16599.17	15030.99	13955.11	13184.96
640 000	59439.34	32729.85	23948.05	19646.33	17134.63	15515.86	14405.27	13610.28
660 000	61296.82	33752.66	24696.43	20260.28	17670.09	16000.73	14855.44	14035.60
680 000	63154.30	34775.47	25444.81	20874.23	18205.54	16485.60	15305.60	14460.92
700 000	65011.78	35798.27	26193.18	21488.18	18741.00	16970.47	15755.77	14886.24
720 000	66869.26	36821.08	26941.56	22102.13	19276.46	17455.34	16205.93	15311.56
740 000	68726.74	37843.89	27689.94	22716.07	19811.92	17940.22	16656.10	15736.88
760 000	70584.22	38866.70	28438.31	23330.02	20347.37	18425.09	17106.26	16162.20
780 000	72441.70	39889.51	29186.69	23943.97	20882.83	18909.96	17556.43	16587.53
800 000	74299.18	40912.31	29935.07	24557.92	21418.29	19394.83	18006.59	17012.85
820 000	76156.66	41935.12	30683.44	25171.86	21953.74	19879.70	18456.76	17438.17
840 000	78014.14	42957.93	31431.82	25785.81	22489.20	20364.57	18906.92	17863.49
860 000	79871.62	43980.74	32180.20	26399.76	23024.66	20849.44	19357.09	18288.81
880 000	81729.10	45003.54	32928.57	27013.71	23560.12	21334.31	19807.25	18714.13
900 000	83586.58	46026.35	33676.95	27627.66	24095.57	21819.18	20257.42	19139.45
920 000	85444.06	47049.16	34425.33	28241.60	24631.03	22304.05	20707.58	19564.77
940 000	87301.54	48071.97	35173.70	28855.55	25166.49	22788.92	21157.75	19990.10
960 000	89159.02	49094.78	35922.08	29469.50	25701.94	23273.79	21607.91	20415.42
980 000	91016.49	50117.58	36670.46	30083.45	26237.40	23758.66	22058.08	20840.74
1000 000	92873.97	51140.39	37418.84	30697.40	26772.86	24243.53	22508.24	21266.06
Coefficient	.092873974	.051140392	.037418835	.030697396	.026772859	.024243534	.022508242	.021266059

AMOUNT	9 YEARS	10 YEARS	15 YEARS	20 YEARS	25 YEARS	30 YEARS	35 YEARS	40 YEARS
10 000	203.50	196.58	179.33	173.82	171.90	171.22	170.97	170.88
20 000	406.99	393.16	358.67	347.63	343.80	342.44	341.94	341.77
30 000	610.49	589.75	538.00	521.45	515.70	513.65	512.92	512.65
40 000	813.98	786.33	717.34	695.26	687.60	684.87	683.89	683.53
50 000	1017.48	902.91	896.67	869.08	859.50	856.09	854.86	854.42
60 000	1220.97	1179.49	1076.01	1042.89	1031.40	1027.31	1025.83	1025.30
70 000	1424.47	1376.08	1255.34	1216.71	1203.30	1198.53	1196.81	1196.19
80 000	1627.97	1572.66	1434.68	1390.52	1375.21	1369.74	1367.78	1367.07
90 000	1831.46	1769.24	1614.01	1564.34	1547.11	1540.96	1538.75	1537.95
100 000	2034.96	1965.83	1793.35	1738.15	1719.01	1712.18	1709.72	1708.84
110 000	2238.45	2162.41	1972.68	1911.97	1890.91	1883.40	1880.70	1879.72
120 000	2441.95	2358.99	2152.02	2085.78	2062.81	2054.62	2051.67	2050.60
130 000	2645.45	2555.57	2331.35	2259.60	2234.71	2225.84	2222.64	2221.49
140 000	2848.94	2752.15	2510.69	2433.42	2406.61	2397.05	2393.61	2392.37
150 000	3052.44	2948.73	2690.02	2607.23	2578.51	2568.27	2564.59	2563.25
160 000	3255.93	3145.32	2869.35	2781.05	2750.41	2739.49	2735.56	2734.14
170 000	3459.43	3341.90	3048.69	2954.86	2922.31	2910.71	2906.53	2905.02
180 000	3662.92	3538.48	3228.02	3128.68	3094.21	3081.93	3077.50	3075.91
190 000	3866.42	3735.06	3407.36	3302.49	3266.11	3253.14	3248.48	3246.79
200 000	4069.92	3931.65	3586.69	3476.31	3438.01	3424.36	3419.45	3417.67
210 000	4273.41	4128.23	3766.03	3650.12	3609.91	3595.58	3590.42	3588.56
220 000	4476.91	4324.81	3945.36	3823.94	3781.82	3766.80	3761.39	3759.44
230 000	4680.40	4521.39	4124.70	3997.75	3953.72	3938.02	3932.36	3930.32
240 000	4883.90	4717.98	4304.03	4171.57	4125.62	4109.23	4103.34	4101.21
250 000	5087.40	4914.56	4483.37	4345.39	4297.52	4280.45	4274.31	4272.09
260 000	5290.89	5111.14	4662.70	4519.20	4469.42	4451.67	4445.28	4442.97
270 000	5494.39	5307.72	4842.04	4693.02	4641.32	4622.89	4616.25	4613.86
280 000	5697.88	5504.30	5021.37	4866.83	4813.22	4794.11	4787.23	4784.74
290 000	5901.38	5700.89	5200.71	5040.65	4985.12	4965.32	4958.20	4955.63
300 000	6104.87	5897.47	5380.04	5214.46	5157.02	5136.54	5129.17	5126.51
320 000	6511.87	6290.63	5738.71	5562.09	5500.82	5478.98	5471.12	5468.28
340 000	6918.86	6683.80	6097.38	5909.72	5844.62	5821.42	5813.06	5810.04
360 000	7325.85	7076.96	6456.05	6257.35	6188.43	6163.85	6155.01	6151.81
380 000	7732.84	7470.13	6814.72	6604.99	6532.23	6506.29	6496.95	6493.58
400 000	8139.83	7863.29	7173.39	6952.62	6876.03	6848.72	6838.90	6835.35
420 000	8546.82	8256.46	7532.06	7300.25	7219.83	7191.16	7180.84	7177.11
440 000	8953.82	8649.62	7890.73	7647.88	7563.63	7533.60	7522.79	7518.88
460 000	9360.81	9042.79	8249.40	7995.51	7907.43	7876.03	7864.73	7860.65
480 000	9767.80	9435.95	8608.06	8343.14	8251.23	8218.47	8206.67	8202.41
500 000	10174.79	9829.12	8966.73	8690.77	8595.04	8560.91	8548.62	8544.18
520 000	10581.78	10222.28	9325.40	9038.40	8938.84	8903.34	8890.56	8885.95
540 000	10988.78	10615.44	9684.07	9386.03	9282.64	9245.78	9232.51	9227.72
560 000	11395.77	11008.61	10042.74	9733.66	9626.44	9588.21	9574.45	9569.48
580 000	11802.76	11401.77	10401.41	10081.29	9970.24	9930.65	9916.40	9911.25
600 000	12209.75	11794.94	10760.08	10428.92	10314.04	10273.09	10258.34	10253.02
620 000	12616.74	12188.10	11118.75	10776.56	10657.84	10615.52	10600.29	10594.79
640 000	13023.73	12581.27	11477.42	11124.19	11001.65	10957.96	10942.23	10936.55
660 000	13430.72	12974.43	11836.09	11471.82	11345.45	11300.39	11284.18	11278.32
680 000	13837.72	13367.60	12194.76	11819.45	11689.25	11642.83	11626.12	11620.09
700 000	14244.71	13760.76	12553.43	12167.08	12033.05	11985.27	11968.07	11961.85
720 000	14651.70	14153.93	12912.10	12514.71	12376.85	12327.70	12310.01	12303.62
740 000	15058.69	14547.09	13270.77	12862.34	12720.65	12670.14	12651.96	12645.39
760 000	15465.68	14940.25	13629.44	13209.97	13064.45	13012.58	12993.90	12987.16
780 000	15872.67	15333.42	13988.11	13557.60	13408.26	13355.01	13335.85	13328.92
800 000	16279.67	15726.58	14346.77	13905.23	13752.06	13697.45	13677.79	13670.69
820 000	16686.66	16119.75	14705.44	14252.86	14095.86	14039.88	14019.74	14012.46
840 000	17093.65	16512.91	15064.11	14600.49	14439.66	14382.32	14361.68	14354.22
860 000	17500.64	16906.08	15422.78	14948.13	14783.46	14724.76	14703.63	14695.99
880 000	17907.63	17299.24	15781.45	15295.76	15127.26	15067.19	15045.57	15037.76
900 000	18314.62	17692.41	16140.12	15643.39	15471.06	15409.63	15387.52	15379.53
920 000	18721.62	18085.57	16498.79	15991.02	15814.87	15752.07	15729.46	15721.29
940 000	19128.61	18478.74	16857.46	16338.65	16158.67	16094.50	16071.40	16063.06
960 000	19535.60	18871.90	17216.13	16686.28	16502.47	16436.94	16413.35	16404.83
980 000	19942.59	19265.07	17574.80	17033.91	16846.27	16779.37	16755.29	16746.60
1000 000	20349.58	19658.23	17933.47	17381.54	17190.07	17121.81	17097.24	17088.36
Coefficient	.020349583	.019658230	.017933468	.017381541	.017190071	.017121810	.017097239	.017088363

MONTHLY AMORTIZING PAYMENTS

AMOUNT	1 YEAR	2 YEARS	3 YEARS	4 YEARS	5 YEARS	6 YEARS	7 YEARS	8 YEARS
10 000	929.94	512.63	375.47	308.31	269.13	243.90	226.60	214.23
20 000	1859.88	1025.26	750.94	616.63	538.26	487.79	453.20	428.47
30 000	2789.82	1537.89	1126.40	924.94	807.39	731.69	679.80	642.70
40 000	3719.75	2050.52	1501.87	1233.26	1076.52	975.58	906.40	856.93
50 000	4649.69	2563.15	1877.34	1541.57	1345.65	1219.48	1133.00	1071.16
60 000	5579.63	3075.78	2252.81	1849.88	1614.78	1463.37	1359.60	1285.40
70 000	6509.57	3588.41	2628.28	2158.20	1883.90	1707.27	1586.20	1499.63
80 000	7439.51	4101.04	3003.75	2466.51	2153.03	1951.16	1812.80	1713.86
90 000	8369.45	4613.66	3379.21	2774.82	2422.16	2195.06	2039.40	1928.09
100 000	9299.38	5126.29	3754.68	3083.14	2691.29	2438.95	2266.00	2142.33
110 000	10229.32	5638.92	4130.15	3391.45	2960.42	2682.85	2492.60	2356.56
120 000	11159.26	6151.55	4505.62	3699.77	3229.55	2926.75	2719.20	2570.79
130 000	12089.20	6664.18	4881.09	4008.08	3498.68	3170.64	2945.80	2785.03
140 000	13019.14	7176.81	5256.56	4316.39	3767.81	3414.54	3172.40	2999.26
150 000	13949.08	7689.44	5632.02	4624.71	4036.94	3658.43	3399.00	3213.49
160 000	14879.01	8202.07	6007.49	4933.02	4306.07	3902.33	3625.60	3427.72
170 000	15808.95	8714.70	6382.96	5241.34	4575.20	4146.22	3852.20	3641.96
180 000	16738.89	9227.33	6758.43	5549.65	4844.33	4390.12	4078.80	3856.19
190 000	17668.83	9739.96	7133.90	5857.96	5113.45	4634.01	4305.40	4070.42
200 000	18598.77	10252.59	7509.37	6166.28	5382.58	4877.91	4532.00	4284.66
210 000	19528.71	10765.22	7884.83	6474.59	5651.71	5121.80	4758.60	4498.89
220 000	20458.64	11277.85	8260.30	6782.90	5920.84	5365.70	4985.20	4713.12
230 000	21388.58	11790.48	8635.77	7091.22	6189.97	5609.60	5211.80	4927.35
240 000	22318.52	12303.11	9011.24	7399.53	6459.10	5853.49	5438.40	5141.59
250 000	23248.46	12815.74	9386.71	7707.85	6728.23	6097.39	5665.00	5355.82
260 000	24178.40	13328.37	9762.18	8016.16	6997.36	6341.28	5891.60	5570.05
270 000	25108.34	13840.99	10137.64	8324.47	7266.49	6585.18	6118.20	5784.28
280 000	26038.27	14353.62	10513.11	8632.79	7535.62	6829.07	6344.80	5998.52
290 000	26968.21	14866.25	10888.58	8941.10	7804.75	7072.97	6571.40	6212.75
300 000	27898.15	15378.88	11264.05	9249.42	8073.88	7316.86	6798.00	6426.98
320 000	29758.03	16404.14	12014.98	9866.04	8612.13	7804.66	7251.20	6855.45
340 000	31617.90	17429.40	12765.92	10482.67	9150.39	8292.45	7704.40	7283.91
360 000	33477.78	18454.66	13516.86	11099.30	9688.65	8780.24	8157.60	7712.38
380 000	35337.66	19479.92	14267.79	11715.93	10226.91	9268.03	8610.80	8140.84
400 000	37197.53	20505.18	15018.73	12332.55	10765.17	9755.82	9064.00	8569.31
420 000	39057.41	21530.44	15769.67	12949.18	11303.43	10243.61	9517.20	8997.78
440 000	40917.29	22555.69	16520.60	13565.81	11841.68	10731.40	9970.40	9426.24
460 000	42777.16	23580.95	17271.54	14182.44	12379.94	11219.19	10423.60	9854.71
480 000	44637.04	24606.21	18022.48	14799.07	12918.20	11706.98	10876.80	10283.17
500 000	46496.92	25631.47	18773.41	15415.69	13456.46	12194.77	11330.00	10711.64
520 000	48356.79	26656.73	19524.35	16032.32	13994.72	12682.56	11783.20	11140.10
540 000	50216.67	27681.99	20275.29	16648.95	14532.98	13170.36	12236.40	11568.57
560 000	52076.55	28707.25	21026.22	17265.58	15071.23	13658.15	12689.60	11997.03
580 000	53936.42	29732.51	21777.16	17882.20	15609.49	14145.94	13142.80	12425.50
600 000	55796.30	30757.77	22528.10	18498.83	16147.75	14633.73	13596.00	12853.96
620 000	57656.18	31783.02	23279.03	19115.46	16686.01	15121.52	14049.20	13282.43
640 000	59516.06	32808.28	24029.97	19732.09	17224.27	15609.31	14502.39	13710.90
660 000	61375.93	33833.54	24780.91	20348.71	17762.53	16097.10	14955.59	14139.36
680 000	63235.81	34858.80	25531.84	20965.34	18300.78	16584.89	15408.79	14567.83
700 000	65095.69	35884.06	26282.78	21581.97	18839.04	17072.68	15861.99	14996.29
720 000	66955.56	36909.32	27033.72	22198.60	19377.30	17560.47	16315.19	15424.76
740 000	68815.44	37934.58	27784.65	22815.23	19915.56	18048.26	16768.39	15853.22
760 000	70675.32	38959.84	28535.59	23431.85	20453.82	18536.06	17221.59	16281.69
780 000	72535.19	39985.10	29286.53	24048.48	20992.08	19023.85	17674.79	16710.15
800 000	74395.07	41010.35	30037.46	24665.11	21530.33	19511.64	18127.99	17138.62
820 000	76254.95	42035.61	30788.40	25281.74	22068.59	19999.43	18581.19	17567.09
840 000	78114.82	43060.87	31539.34	25898.36	22606.85	20487.22	19034.39	17995.55
860 000	79974.70	44086.13	32290.27	26514.99	23145.11	20975.01	19487.59	18424.02
880 000	81834.58	45111.39	33041.21	27131.62	23683.37	21462.80	19940.79	18852.48
900 000	83694.45	46136.65	33792.15	27748.25	24221.63	21950.59	20393.99	19280.95
920 000	85554.33	47161.91	34543.08	28364.88	24759.88	22438.38	20847.19	19709.41
940 000	87414.21	48187.17	35294.02	28981.50	25298.14	22926.17	21300.39	20137.88
960 000	89274.08	49212.43	36044.95	29598.13	25836.40	23413.97	21753.59	20566.34
980 000	91133.96	50237.68	36795.89	30214.76	26374.66	23901.76	22206.79	20994.81
1000 000	92993.84	51262.94	37546.83	30831.39	26912.92	24389.55	22659.99	21423.28
Coefficient	.092993836	.051262943	.037546828	.030831386	.026912918	.024389547	.022659992	.021423275

MONTHLY AMORTIZING PAYMENTS 20.75%

AMOUNT	9 YEARS	10 YEARS	15 YEARS	20 YEARS	25 YEARS	30 YEARS	35 YEARS	40 YEARS
10 000	205.12	198.25	181.20	175.79	173.93	173.28	173.05	172.96
20 000	410.24	396.51	362.39	351.58	347.86	346.56	346.09	345.93
30 000	615.36	594.76	543.59	527.36	521.80	519.84	519.14	518.89
40 000	820.48	793.02	724.78	703.15	695.73	693.11	692.18	691.85
50 000	1025.60	991.27	905.98	878.94	869.66	866.39	865.23	864.81
60 000	1230.72	1189.53	1087.17	1054.73	1043.59	1039.67	1038.27	1037.78
70 000	1435.84	1387.78	1268.37	1230.52	1217.53	1212.95	1211.32	1210.74
80 000	1640.96	1586.03	1449.56	1406.30	1391.46	1386.23	1384.37	1383.70
90 000	1846.08	1784.29	1630.76	1582.09	1565.39	1559.51	1557.41	1556.67
100 000	2051.20	1982.54	1811.95	1757.88	1739.32	1732.78	1730.46	1729.63
110 000	2256.31	2180.80	1993.15	1933.67	1913.26	1906.06	1903.50	1902.59
120 000	2461.43	2379.05	2174.34	2109.46	2087.19	2079.34	2076.55	2075.55
130 000	2666.55	2577.30	2355.54	2285.24	2261.12	2252.62	2249.60	2248.52
140 000	2871.67	2775.56	2536.73	2461.03	2435.05	2425.90	2422.64	2421.48
150 000	3076.79	2973.81	2717.93	2636.82	2608.98	2599.18	2595.69	2594.44
160 000	3281.91	3172.07	2899.12	2812.61	2782.92	2772.45	2768.73	2767.40
170 000	3487.03	3370.32	3080.32	2988.39	2956.85	2945.73	2941.78	2940.37
180 000	3692.15	3568.58	3261.52	3164.18	3130.78	3119.01	3114.82	3113.33
190 000	3897.27	3766.83	3442.71	3339.97	3304.71	3292.29	3287.87	3286.29
200 000	4102.39	3965.08	3623.91	3515.76	3478.65	3465.57	3460.92	3459.26
210 000	4307.51	4163.34	3805.10	3691.55	3652.58	3638.85	3633.96	3632.22
220 000	4512.63	4361.59	3986.30	3867.33	3826.51	3812.12	3807.01	3805.18
230 000	4717.75	4559.85	4167.49	4043.12	4000.44	3985.40	3980.05	3978.14
240 000	4922.87	4758.10	4348.69	4218.91	4174.37	4158.68	4153.10	4151.11
250 000	5127.99	4956.35	4529.88	4394.70	4348.31	4331.96	4326.15	4324.07
260 000	5333.11	5154.61	4711.08	4570.49	4522.24	4505.24	4499.19	4497.03
270 000	5538.23	5352.86	4892.27	4746.27	4696.17	4678.52	4672.24	4670.00
280 000	5743.35	5551.12	5073.47	4922.06	4870.10	4851.79	4845.28	4842.96
290 000	5948.47	5749.37	5254.66	5097.85	5044.04	5025.07	5018.33	5015.92
300 000	6153.59	5947.63	5435.86	5273.64	5217.97	5198.35	5191.37	5188.88
320 000	6563.82	6344.13	5798.25	5625.21	5565.83	5544.91	5537.47	5534.81
340 000	6974.06	6740.64	6160.64	5976.79	5913.70	5891.46	5883.56	5880.74
360 000	7384.30	7137.15	6523.03	6328.37	6261.56	6238.02	6229.65	6226.66
380 000	7794.54	7533.66	6885.42	6679.94	6609.43	6584.58	6575.74	6572.59
400 000	8204.78	7930.17	7247.81	7031.52	6957.29	6931.14	6921.83	6918.51
420 000	8615.02	8326.68	7610.20	7383.09	7305.16	7277.69	7267.92	7264.44
440 000	9025.26	8723.18	7972.59	7734.67	7653.02	7624.25	7614.02	7610.36
460 000	9435.50	9119.69	8334.98	8086.24	8000.89	7970.81	7960.11	7956.29
480 000	9845.74	9516.20	8697.37	8437.82	8348.75	8317.36	8306.20	8302.21
500 000	10255.98	9912.71	9059.77	8789.40	8696.61	8663.92	8652.29	8648.14
520 000	10666.22	10309.22	9422.16	9140.97	9044.48	9010.48	8998.38	8994.07
540 000	11076.45	10705.73	9784.55	9492.55	9392.34	9357.03	9344.47	9339.99
560 000	11486.69	11102.23	10146.94	9844.12	9740.21	9703.59	9690.57	9685.92
580 000	11896.93	11498.74	10509.33	10195.70	10088.07	10050.15	10036.66	10031.84
600 000	12307.17	11895.25	10871.72	10547.28	10435.94	10396.70	10382.75	10377.77
620 000	12717.41	12291.76	11234.11	10898.85	10783.80	10743.26	10728.84	10723.69
640 000	13127.65	12688.27	11596.50	11250.43	11131.67	11089.82	11074.93	11069.62
660 000	13537.89	13084.78	11958.89	11602.00	11479.53	11436.37	11421.02	11415.55
680 000	13948.13	13481.28	12321.28	11953.58	11827.40	11782.93	11767.12	11761.47
700 000	14358.37	13877.79	12683.67	12305.15	12175.26	12129.49	12113.21	12107.40
720 000	14768.61	14274.30	13046.06	12656.73	12523.12	12476.04	12459.30	12453.32
740 000	15178.84	14670.81	13408.45	13008.31	12870.99	12822.60	12805.39	12799.25
760 000	15589.08	15067.32	13770.84	13359.88	13218.85	13169.16	13151.48	13145.17
780 000	15999.32	15463.83	14133.23	13711.46	13566.72	13515.71	13497.57	13491.10
800 000	16409.56	15860.33	14495.62	14063.03	13914.58	13862.27	13843.66	13837.02
820 000	16819.80	16256.84	14858.02	14414.61	14262.45	14208.83	14189.76	14182.95
840 000	17230.04	16653.35	15220.41	14766.19	14610.31	14555.38	14535.85	14528.88
860 000	17640.28	17049.86	15582.80	15117.76	14958.18	14901.94	14881.94	14874.80
880 000	18050.52	17446.37	15945.19	15469.34	15306.04	15248.50	15228.03	15220.73
900 000	18460.76	17842.88	16307.58	15820.91	15653.91	15595.05	15574.12	15566.65
920 000	18871.00	18239.38	16669.97	16172.49	16001.77	15941.61	15920.21	15912.58
940 000	19281.23	18635.89	17032.36	16524.06	16349.64	16288.17	16266.31	16258.50
960 000	19691.47	19032.40	17394.75	16875.64	16697.50	16634.72	16612.40	16604.43
980 000	20101.71	19428.91	17757.14	17227.22	17045.36	16981.28	16958.49	16950.36
1000 000	20511.95	19825.42	18119.53	17578.79	17393.23	17327.84	17304.58	17296.28
Coefficient	.020511952	.019825408	.018119531	.017578792	.017393229	.017327838	.017304581	.017296281

129

21.00% MONTHLY AMORTIZING PAYMENTS

AMOUNT	1 YEAR	2 YEARS	3 YEARS	4 YEARS	5 YEARS	6 YEARS	7 YEARS	8 YEARS
10 000	931.14	513.86	376.75	309.66	270.53	245.36	228.12	215.81
20 000	1862.28	1027.71	753.50	619.31	541.07	490.72	456.24	431.62
30 000	2793.41	1541.57	1130.25	928.97	811.60	736.08	684.37	647.43
40 000	3724.55	2055.43	1507.00	1238.63	1082.13	981.44	912.49	863.24
50 000	4655.69	2569.28	1883.75	1548.28	1352.67	1226.80	1140.61	1079.05
60 000	5586.83	3083.14	2260.50	1857.94	1623.20	1472.16	1368.73	1294.86
70 000	6517.96	3597.00	2637.25	2167.60	1893.74	1717.52	1596.86	1510.67
80 000	7449.10	4110.85	3014.01	2477.26	2164.27	1962.88	1824.98	1726.48
90 000	8380.24	4624.71	3390.76	2786.91	2434.80	2208.24	2053.10	1942.29
100 000	9311.38	5138.57	3767.51	3096.57	2705.34	2453.60	2281.22	2158.10
110 000	10242.51	5652.42	4144.26	3406.23	2975.87	2698.96	2509.34	2373.91
120 000	11173.65	6166.28	4521.01	3715.88	3246.40	2944.32	2737.47	2589.72
130 000	12104.79	6680.13	4897.76	4025.54	3516.94	3189.68	2965.59	2805.53
140 000	13035.93	7193.99	5274.51	4335.20	3787.47	3435.04	3193.71	3021.34
150 000	13967.06	7707.85	5651.26	4644.85	4058.00	3680.40	3421.83	3237.15
160 000	14898.20	8221.70	6028.01	4954.51	4328.54	3925.76	3649.96	3452.96
170 000	15829.34	8735.56	6404.76	5264.17	4599.07	4171.12	3878.08	3668.77
180 000	16760.48	9249.42	6781.51	5573.82	4869.60	4416.48	4106.20	3884.58
190 000	17691.62	9763.27	7158.26	5883.48	5140.14	4661.84	4334.32	4100.39
200 000	18622.75	10277.13	7535.01	6193.14	5410.67	4907.20	4562.45	4316.20
210 000	19553.89	10790.99	7911.76	6502.80	5681.21	5152.56	4790.57	4532.01
220 000	20485.03	11304.84	8288.52	6812.45	5951.74	5397.92	5018.69	4747.82
230 000	21416.17	11818.70	8665.27	7122.11	6222.27	5643.28	5246.81	4963.63
240 000	22347.30	12332.56	9042.02	7431.77	6492.81	5888.64	5474.93	5179.44
250 000	23278.44	12846.41	9418.77	7741.42	6763.34	6134.00	5703.06	5395.25
260 000	24209.58	13360.27	9795.52	8051.08	7033.87	6379.36	5931.18	5611.06
270 000	25140.72	13874.13	10172.27	8360.74	7304.41	6624.72	6159.30	5826.87
280 000	26071.85	14387.98	10549.02	8670.39	7574.94	6870.08	6387.42	6042.68
290 000	27002.99	14901.84	10925.77	8980.05	7845.47	7115.44	6615.55	6258.49
300 000	27934.13	15415.70	11302.52	9289.71	8116.01	7360.80	6843.67	6474.30
320 000	29796.41	16443.41	12056.02	9909.02	8657.07	7851.52	7299.91	6905.92
340 000	31658.68	17471.12	12809.52	10528.34	9198.14	8342.24	7756.16	7337.54
360 000	33520.96	18498.84	13563.02	11147.65	9739.21	8832.96	8212.40	7769.16
380 000	35383.23	19526.55	14316.53	11766.96	10280.28	9323.68	8668.65	8200.78
400 000	37245.51	20554.26	15070.03	12386.28	10821.34	9814.40	9124.89	8632.40
420 000	39107.78	21581.97	15823.53	13005.59	11362.41	10305.12	9581.13	9064.02
440 000	40970.06	22609.69	16577.03	13624.91	11903.48	10795.84	10037.38	9495.64
460 000	42832.33	23637.40	17330.53	14244.22	12444.55	11286.56	10493.62	9927.26
480 000	44694.61	24665.11	18084.03	14863.53	12985.61	11777.28	10949.87	10358.88
500 000	46556.88	25692.83	18837.53	15482.85	13526.68	12268.00	11406.11	10790.51
520 000	48419.16	26720.54	19591.04	16102.16	14067.75	12758.72	11862.36	11222.13
540 000	50281.43	27748.25	20344.54	16721.47	14608.81	13249.44	12318.60	11653.75
560 000	52143.71	28775.97	21098.04	17340.79	15149.88	13740.16	12774.85	12085.37
580 000	54005.98	29803.68	21851.54	17960.10	15690.95	14230.88	13231.09	12516.99
600 000	55868.26	30831.39	22605.04	18579.42	16232.02	14721.60	13687.34	12948.61
620 000	57730.54	31859.10	23358.54	19198.73	16773.08	15212.32	14143.58	13380.23
640 000	59592.81	32886.82	24112.04	19818.04	17314.15	15703.04	14599.82	13811.85
660 000	61455.09	33914.53	24865.55	20437.36	17855.22	16193.76	15056.07	14243.47
680 000	63317.36	34942.24	25619.05	21056.67	18396.28	16684.48	15512.31	14675.09
700 000	65179.64	35969.96	26372.55	21675.99	18937.35	17175.20	15968.56	15106.71
720 000	67041.91	36997.67	27126.05	22295.30	19478.42	17665.92	16424.80	15538.33
740 000	68904.19	38025.38	27879.55	22914.61	20019.49	18156.64	16881.05	15969.95
760 000	70766.46	39053.10	28633.05	23533.93	20560.55	18647.36	17337.29	16401.57
780 000	72628.74	40080.81	29386.55	24153.24	21101.62	19138.08	17793.54	16833.19
800 000	74491.01	41108.52	30140.06	24772.56	21642.69	19628.80	18249.78	17264.81
820 000	76353.29	42136.24	30893.56	25391.87	22183.75	20119.52	18706.03	17696.43
840 000	78215.56	43163.95	31647.06	26011.18	22724.82	20610.24	19162.27	18128.05
860 000	80077.84	44191.66	32400.56	26630.50	23265.89	21100.96	19618.51	18559.67
880 000	81940.11	45219.37	33154.06	27249.81	23806.96	21591.68	20074.76	18991.29
900 000	83802.39	46247.09	33907.56	27869.12	24348.02	22082.40	20531.00	19422.91
920 000	85664.67	47274.80	34661.06	28488.44	24889.09	22573.12	20987.25	19854.53
940 000	87526.94	48302.51	35414.56	29107.75	25430.16	23063.84	21443.49	20286.15
960 000	89389.22	49330.23	36168.07	29727.07	25971.22	23554.56	21899.74	20717.77
980 000	91251.49	50357.94	36921.57	30346.38	26512.29	24045.28	22355.98	21149.39
1000 000	93113.77	51385.65	37675.07	30965.69	27053.36	24536.00	22812.23	21581.01
Coefficient	.093113767	.051385653	.037675069	.030965694	.027053359	.024535996	.022812226	.021581010

130

MONTHLY AMORTIZING PAYMENTS 21.00%

AMOUNT	9 YEARS	10 YEARS	15 YEARS	20 YEARS	25 YEARS	30 YEARS	35 YEARS	40 YEARS
10 000	206.75	199.93	183.06	177.76	175.97	175.34	175.12	175.04
20 000	413.50	399.86	366.12	355.53	351.93	350.68	350.24	350.08
30 000	620.25	599.80	549.18	533.29	527.90	526.02	525.36	525.13
40 000	826.99	799.73	732.24	711.06	703.87	701.36	700.48	700.17
50 000	1033.74	999.66	915.31	888.82	879.83	876.70	875.60	875.21
60 000	1240.49	1199.59	1098.37	1066.59	1055.80	1052.04	1050.72	1050.25
70 000	1447.24	1399.52	1281.43	1244.35	1231.76	1227.38	1225.84	1225.30
80 000	1653.99	1599.45	1464.49	1422.11	1407.73	1402.72	1400.96	1400.34
90 000	1860.74	1799.39	1647.55	1599.88	1583.70	1578.06	1576.08	1575.38
100 000	2067.49	1999.32	1830.61	1777.64	1759.66	1753.40	1751.20	1750.42
110 000	2274.24	2199.25	2013.67	1955.41	1935.63	1928.74	1926.32	1925.47
120 000	2480.98	2399.18	2196.73	2133.17	2111.60	2104.08	2101.44	2100.51
130 000	2687.73	2599.11	2379.80	2310.94	2287.56	2279.42	2276.56	2275.55
140 000	2894.48	2799.04	2562.86	2488.70	2463.53	2454.76	2451.68	2450.59
150 000	3101.23	2998.98	2745.92	2666.46	2639.49	2630.10	2626.80	2625.63
160 000	3307.98	3198.91	2928.98	2844.23	2815.46	2805.44	2801.92	2800.68
170 000	3514.73	3398.84	3112.04	3021.99	2991.43	2980.78	2977.04	2975.72
180 000	3721.48	3598.77	3295.10	3199.76	3167.39	3156.12	3152.16	3150.76
190 000	3928.22	3798.70	3478.16	3377.52	3343.36	3331.46	3327.28	3325.80
200 000	4134.97	3998.63	3661.22	3555.29	3519.33	3506.80	3502.40	3500.85
210 000	4341.72	4198.57	3844.29	3733.05	3695.29	3682.14	3677.52	3675.89
220 000	4548.47	4398.50	4027.35	3910.81	3871.26	3857.48	3852.64	3850.93
230 000	4755.22	4598.43	4210.41	4088.58	4047.22	4032.82	4027.76	4025.97
240 000	4961.97	4798.36	4393.47	4266.34	4223.19	4208.16	4202.88	4201.02
250 000	5168.72	4998.29	4576.53	4444.11	4399.16	4383.50	4378.00	4376.06
260 000	5375.47	5198.22	4759.59	4621.87	4575.12	4558.84	4553.12	4551.10
270 000	5582.21	5398.16	4942.65	4799.64	4751.09	4734.18	4728.24	4726.14
280 000	5788.96	5598.09	5125.71	4977.40	4927.06	4909.52	4903.36	4901.19
290 000	5995.71	5798.02	5308.78	5155.16	5103.02	5084.86	5078.48	5076.23
300 000	6202.46	5997.95	5491.84	5332.93	5278.99	5260.20	5253.60	5251.27
320 000	6615.96	6397.81	5857.96	5688.46	5630.92	5610.88	5603.84	5601.35
340 000	7029.45	6797.68	6224.08	6043.99	5982.85	5961.56	5954.08	5951.44
360 000	7442.95	7197.54	6590.20	6399.51	6334.79	6312.24	6304.32	6301.52
380 000	7856.45	7597.40	6956.33	6755.04	6686.72	6662.92	6654.56	6651.61
400 000	8269.95	7997.27	7322.45	7110.57	7038.65	7013.60	7004.80	7001.69
420 000	8683.44	8397.13	7688.57	7466.10	7390.58	7364.28	7355.04	7351.78
440 000	9096.94	8796.99	8054.69	7821.63	7742.52	7714.96	7705.28	7701.86
460 000	9510.44	9196.86	8420.82	8177.16	8094.45	8065.64	8055.52	8051.95
480 000	9923.94	9596.72	8786.94	8532.69	8446.38	8416.32	8405.76	8402.03
500 000	10337.43	9996.58	9153.06	8888.21	8798.31	8767.00	8756.00	8752.12
520 000	10750.93	10396.45	9519.18	9243.74	9150.25	9117.68	9106.24	9102.20
540 000	11164.43	10796.31	9885.31	9599.27	9502.18	9468.36	9456.48	9452.29
560 000	11577.93	11196.17	10251.43	9954.80	9854.11	9819.04	9806.72	9802.37
580 000	11991.42	11596.04	10617.55	10310.33	10206.04	10169.72	10156.96	10152.46
600 000	12404.92	11995.90	10983.67	10665.86	10557.98	10520.40	10507.20	10502.54
620 000	12818.42	12395.76	11349.80	11021.39	10909.91	10871.08	10857.44	10852.62
640 000	13231.91	12795.63	11715.92	11376.91	11261.84	11221.76	11207.67	11202.71
660 000	13645.41	13195.49	12082.04	11732.44	11613.77	11572.44	11557.91	11552.79
680 000	14058.91	13595.35	12448.16	12087.97	11965.71	11923.12	11908.15	11902.88
700 000	14472.41	13995.22	12814.29	12443.50	12317.64	12273.80	12258.39	12252.96
720 000	14885.90	14395.08	13180.41	12799.03	12669.57	12624.48	12608.63	12603.05
740 000	15299.40	14794.94	13546.53	13154.56	13021.50	12975.16	12958.87	12953.13
760 000	15712.90	15194.81	13912.65	13510.09	13373.44	13325.84	13309.11	13303.22
780 000	16126.40	15594.67	14278.78	13865.61	13725.37	13676.52	13659.35	13653.30
800 000	16539.89	15994.53	14644.90	14221.14	14077.30	14027.20	14009.59	14003.39
820 000	16953.39	16394.40	15011.02	14576.67	14429.23	14377.88	14359.83	14353.47
840 000	17366.89	16794.26	15377.14	14932.20	14781.17	14728.56	14710.07	14703.56
860 000	17780.39	17194.12	15743.27	15287.73	15133.10	15079.24	15060.31	15053.64
880 000	18193.88	17593.99	16109.39	15643.26	15485.03	15429.92	15410.55	15403.73
900 000	18607.38	17993.85	16475.51	15998.79	15836.97	15780.60	15760.79	15753.81
920 000	19020.88	18393.71	16841.63	16354.31	16188.90	16131.28	16111.03	16103.89
940 000	19434.37	18793.58	17207.76	16709.84	16540.83	16481.96	16461.27	16453.98
960 000	19847.87	19193.44	17573.88	17065.37	16892.76	16832.64	16811.51	16804.06
980 000	20261.37	19593.30	17940.00	17420.90	17244.70	17183.32	17161.75	17154.15
1000 000	20674.87	19993.17	18306.12	17776.43	17596.63	17534.00	17511.99	17504.23
Coefficient	.020674867	.019993168	.018306123	.017776429	.017596628	.017534001	.017511992	.017504233

131

AMOUNT	1 YEAR	2 YEARS	3 YEARS	4 YEARS	5 YEARS	6 YEARS	7 YEARS	8 YEARS
10 000	932.34	515.09	378.04	311.00	271.94	246.83	229.65	217.39
20 000	1864.68	1030.17	756.07	622.01	543.88	493.66	459.30	434.79
30 000	2797.01	1545.26	1134.11	933.01	815.83	740.49	688.95	652.18
40 000	3729.35	2060.34	1512.14	1244.01	1087.77	987.32	918.60	869.57
50 000	4661.69	2575.43	1890.18	1555.02	1359.71	1234.14	1148.25	1086.96
60 000	5594.03	3090.51	2268.21	1866.02	1631.65	1480.97	1377.90	1304.36
70 000	6526.37	3605.60	2646.25	2177.02	1903.59	1727.80	1607.55	1521.75
80 000	7458.70	4120.68	3024.28	2488.03	2175.53	1974.63	1837.20	1739.14
90 000	8391.04	4635.77	3402.32	2799.03	2447.48	2221.46	2066.84	1956.53
100 000	9323.38	5150.85	3780.35	3110.03	2719.42	2468.29	2296.49	2173.93
110 000	10255.72	5665.94	4158.39	3421.03	2991.36	2715.12	2526.14	2391.32
120 000	11188.06	6181.02	4536.43	3732.04	3263.30	2961.95	2755.79	2608.71
130 000	12120.39	6696.11	4914.46	4043.04	3535.24	3208.77	2985.44	2826.10
140 000	13052.73	7211.19	5292.50	4354.04	3807.19	3455.60	3215.09	3043.50
150 000	13985.07	7726.28	5670.53	4665.05	4079.13	3702.43	3444.74	3260.89
160 000	14917.41	8241.36	6048.57	4976.05	4351.07	3949.26	3674.39	3478.28
170 000	15849.75	8756.45	6426.60	5287.05	4623.01	4196.09	3904.04	3695.67
180 000	16782.08	9271.53	6804.64	5598.06	4894.95	4442.92	4133.69	3913.07
190 000	17714.42	9786.62	7182.67	5909.06	5166.89	4689.75	4363.34	4130.46
200 000	18646.76	10301.71	7560.71	6220.06	5438.84	4936.58	4592.99	4347.85
210 000	19579.10	10816.79	7938.74	6531.07	5710.78	5183.41	4822.64	4565.24
220 000	20511.44	11331.88	8316.78	6842.07	5982.72	5430.23	5052.29	4782.64
230 000	21443.77	11846.96	8694.82	7153.07	6254.66	5677.06	5281.94	5000.03
240 000	22376.11	12362.05	9072.85	7464.08	6526.60	5923.89	5511.59	5217.42
250 000	23308.45	12877.13	9450.89	7775.08	6798.55	6170.72	5741.24	5434.82
260 000	24240.79	13392.22	9828.92	8086.08	7070.49	6417.55	5970.88	5652.21
270 000	25173.13	13907.30	10206.96	8397.09	7342.43	6664.38	6200.53	5869.60
280 000	26105.46	14422.39	10584.99	8708.09	7614.37	6911.21	6430.18	6086.99
290 000	27037.80	14937.47	10963.03	9019.09	7886.31	7158.04	6659.83	6304.39
300 000	27970.14	15452.56	11341.06	9330.10	8158.25	7404.86	6889.48	6521.78
320 000	29834.82	16482.73	12097.14	9952.10	8702.14	7898.52	7348.78	6956.56
340 000	31699.49	17512.90	12853.21	10574.11	9246.02	8392.18	7808.08	7391.35
360 000	33564.17	18543.07	13609.28	11196.11	9789.91	8885.84	8267.38	7826.13
380 000	35428.84	19573.24	14365.35	11818.12	10333.79	9379.49	8726.68	8260.92
400 000	37293.52	20603.41	15121.42	12440.13	10877.67	9873.15	9185.98	8695.70
420 000	39158.20	21633.58	15877.49	13062.13	11421.56	10366.81	9645.27	9130.49
440 000	41022.87	22663.75	16633.56	13684.14	11965.44	10860.47	10104.57	9565.27
460 000	42887.55	23693.92	17389.63	14306.15	12509.32	11354.13	10563.87	10000.06
480 000	44752.22	24724.09	18145.70	14928.15	13053.21	11847.78	11023.17	10434.85
500 000	46616.90	25754.26	18901.77	15550.16	13597.09	12341.44	11482.47	10869.63
520 000	48481.57	26784.43	19657.84	16172.17	14140.97	12835.10	11941.77	11304.42
540 000	50346.25	27814.60	20413.92	16794.17	14684.86	13328.76	12401.07	11739.20
560 000	52210.93	28844.77	21169.99	17416.18	15228.74	13822.41	12860.37	12173.99
580 000	54075.60	29874.94	21926.06	18038.18	15772.62	14316.07	13319.67	12608.77
600 000	55940.28	30905.12	22682.13	18660.19	16316.51	14809.73	13778.96	13043.56
620 000	57804.95	31935.29	23438.20	19282.20	16860.39	15303.39	14238.26	13478.34
640 000	59669.63	32965.46	24194.27	19904.20	17404.28	15797.04	14697.56	13913.13
660 000	61534.31	33995.63	24950.34	20526.21	17948.16	16290.70	15156.86	14347.91
680 000	63398.98	35025.80	25706.41	21148.22	18492.04	16784.36	15616.16	14782.70
700 000	65263.66	36055.97	26462.48	21770.22	19035.93	17278.02	16075.46	15217.48
720 000	67128.33	37086.14	27218.55	22392.23	19579.81	17771.67	16534.76	15652.27
740 000	68993.01	38116.31	27974.62	23014.24	20123.69	18265.33	16994.06	16087.05
760 000	70857.69	39146.48	28730.70	23636.24	20667.58	18758.99	17453.35	16521.84
780 000	72722.36	40176.65	29486.77	24258.25	21211.46	19252.65	17912.65	16956.62
800 000	74587.04	41206.82	30242.84	24880.25	21755.34	19746.30	18371.95	17391.41
820 000	76451.71	42236.99	30998.91	25502.26	22299.23	20239.96	18831.25	17826.19
840 000	78316.39	43267.16	31754.98	26124.27	22843.11	20733.62	19290.55	18260.98
860 000	80181.07	44297.33	32511.05	26746.27	23387.00	21227.28	19749.85	18695.76
880 000	82045.74	45327.50	33267.12	27368.28	23930.88	21720.94	20209.15	19130.55
900 000	83910.42	46357.67	34023.19	27990.29	24474.76	22214.59	20668.45	19565.33
920 000	85775.09	47387.84	34779.26	28612.29	25018.65	22708.25	21127.74	20000.12
940 000	87639.77	48418.01	35535.33	29234.30	25562.53	23201.91	21587.04	20434.91
960 000	89504.45	49448.18	36291.41	29856.31	26106.41	23695.57	22046.34	20869.69
980 000	91369.12	50478.35	37047.48	30478.31	26650.30	24189.22	22505.64	21304.48
1000 000	93233.80	51508.53	37803.55	31100.32	27194.18	24682.88	22964.94	21739.26
Coefficient	.093233798	.051508525	.037803547	.031100318	.027194181	.024682881	.022964940	.021739261

MONTHLY AMORTIZING PAYMENTS 21.25%

AMOUNT	9 YEARS	10 YEARS	15 YEARS	20 YEARS	25 YEARS	30 YEARS	35 YEARS	40 YEARS
10 000	208.38	201.61	184.93	179.74	178.00	177.40	177.19	177.12
20 000	416.77	403.23	369.86	359.49	356.01	354.81	354.39	354.24
30 000	625.15	604.84	554.80	539.23	534.01	532.21	531.58	531.37
40 000	833.53	806.46	739.73	718.98	712.01	709.61	708.78	708.49
50 000	1041.92	1008.07	924.66	898.72	890.01	887.01	885.97	885.61
60 000	1250.30	1209.69	1109.59	1078.47	1068.02	1064.42	1063.17	1062.73
70 000	1458.68	1411.30	1294.53	1258.21	1246.02	1241.82	1240.36	1239.86
80 000	1667.07	1612.92	1479.46	1437.96	1424.02	1419.22	1417.56	1416.98
90 000	1875.45	1814.53	1664.39	1617.70	1602.02	1596.63	1594.75	1594.10
100 000	2083.83	2016.15	1849.32	1797.44	1780.03	1774.03	1771.95	1771.22
110 000	2292.22	2217.76	2034.26	1977.19	1958.03	1951.43	1949.14	1948.34
120 000	2500.60	2419.38	2219.19	2156.93	2136.03	2128.83	2126.34	2125.47
130 000	2708.98	2620.99	2404.12	2336.68	2314.03	2306.24	2303.53	2302.59
140 000	2917.37	2822.61	2589.05	2516.42	2492.04	2483.64	2480.73	2479.71
150 000	3125.75	3024.22	2773.98	2696.17	2670.04	2661.04	2657.92	2656.83
160 000	3334.13	3225.84	2958.92	2875.91	2848.04	2838.45	2835.11	2833.95
170 000	3542.52	3427.45	3143.85	3055.65	3026.04	3015.85	3012.31	3011.08
180 000	3750.90	3629.07	3328.78	3235.40	3204.05	3193.25	3189.50	3188.20
190 000	3959.28	3830.68	3513.71	3415.14	3382.05	3370.66	3366.70	3365.32
200 000	4167.66	4032.30	3698.65	3594.89	3560.05	3548.06	3543.89	3542.44
210 000	4376.05	4233.91	3883.58	3774.63	3738.05	3725.46	3721.09	3719.57
220 000	4584.43	4435.52	4068.51	3954.38	3916.06	3902.86	3898.28	3896.69
230 000	4792.81	4637.14	4253.44	4134.12	4094.06	4080.27	4075.48	4073.81
240 000	5001.20	4838.75	4438.38	4313.87	4272.06	4257.67	4252.67	4250.93
250 000	5209.58	5040.37	4623.31	4493.61	4450.06	4435.07	4429.87	4428.05
260 000	5417.96	5241.98	4808.24	4673.35	4628.07	4612.48	4607.06	4605.18
270 000	5626.35	5443.60	4993.17	4853.10	4806.07	4789.88	4784.26	4782.30
280 000	5834.73	5645.21	5178.10	5032.84	4984.07	4967.28	4961.45	4959.42
290 000	6043.11	5846.83	5363.04	5212.59	5162.07	5144.68	5138.65	5136.54
300 000	6251.50	6048.44	5547.97	5392.33	5340.08	5322.09	5315.84	5313.66
320 000	6668.26	6451.67	5917.83	5751.82	5696.08	5676.89	5670.23	5667.91
340 000	7085.03	6854.90	6287.70	6111.31	6052.09	6031.70	6024.62	6022.15
360 000	7501.80	7258.13	6657.56	6470.80	6408.09	6386.50	6379.01	6376.40
380 000	7918.56	7661.36	7027.43	6830.29	6764.10	6741.31	6733.40	6730.64
400 000	8335.33	8064.59	7397.29	7189.78	7120.10	7096.12	7087.79	7084.89
420 000	8752.10	8467.82	7767.16	7549.26	7476.11	7450.92	7442.18	7439.13
440 000	9168.86	8871.05	8137.02	7908.75	7832.11	7805.73	7796.57	7793.37
460 000	9585.63	9274.28	8506.89	8268.24	8188.12	8160.53	8150.95	8147.62
480 000	10002.40	9677.51	8876.75	8627.73	8544.12	8515.34	8505.34	8501.86
500 000	10419.16	10080.74	9246.62	8987.22	8900.13	8870.14	8859.73	8856.11
520 000	10835.93	10483.97	9616.48	9346.71	9256.13	9224.95	9214.12	9210.35
540 000	11252.69	10887.20	9986.34	9706.20	9612.14	9579.76	9568.51	9564.60
560 000	11669.46	11290.43	10356.21	10065.69	9968.14	9934.56	9922.90	9918.84
580 000	12086.23	11693.66	10726.07	10425.18	10324.15	10289.37	10277.29	10273.08
600 000	12502.99	12096.89	11095.94	10784.66	10680.15	10644.17	10631.68	10627.33
620 000	12919.76	12500.11	11465.80	11144.15	11036.16	10998.98	10986.07	10981.57
640 000	13336.53	12903.34	11835.67	11503.64	11392.16	11353.79	11340.46	11335.82
660 000	13753.29	13306.57	12205.53	11863.13	11748.17	11708.59	11694.85	11690.06
680 000	14170.06	13709.80	12575.40	12222.62	12104.17	12063.40	12049.24	12044.31
700 000	14586.83	14113.03	12945.26	12582.11	12460.18	12418.20	12403.63	12398.55
720 000	15003.59	14516.26	13315.13	12941.60	12816.19	12773.01	12758.02	12752.79
740 000	15420.36	14919.49	13684.99	13301.09	13172.19	13127.81	13112.41	13107.04
760 000	15837.13	15322.72	14054.86	13660.57	13528.20	13482.62	13466.79	13461.28
780 000	16253.89	15725.95	14424.72	14020.06	13884.20	13837.43	13821.18	13815.53
800 000	16670.66	16129.18	14794.58	14379.55	14240.21	14192.23	14175.57	14169.77
820 000	17087.43	16532.41	15164.45	14739.04	14596.21	14547.04	14529.96	14524.02
840 000	17504.19	16935.64	15534.31	15098.53	14952.22	14901.84	14884.35	14878.26
860 000	17920.96	17338.87	15904.18	15458.02	15308.22	15256.65	15238.74	15232.50
880 000	18337.73	17742.10	16274.04	15817.51	15664.23	15611.46	15593.13	15586.75
900 000	18754.49	18145.33	16643.91	16177.00	16020.23	15966.26	15947.52	15940.99
920 000	19171.26	18548.56	17013.77	16536.48	16376.24	16321.07	16301.91	16295.24
940 000	19588.02	18951.79	17383.64	16895.97	16732.24	16675.87	16656.30	16649.48
960 000	20004.79	19355.02	17753.50	17255.46	17088.25	17030.68	17010.69	17003.73
980 000	20421.56	19758.25	18123.37	17614.95	17444.25	17385.48	17365.08	17357.97
1000 000	20838.32	20161.48	18493.23	17974.44	17800.26	17740.29	17719.47	17712.22
Coefficient	.020838324	.020161475	.018493231	.017974440	.017800257	.017740290	.017719467	.017712215

133

MONTHLY AMORTIZING PAYMENTS

AMOUNT	1 YEAR	2 YEARS	3 YEARS	4 YEARS	5 YEARS	6 YEARS	7 YEARS	8 YEARS
10 000	933.54	516.32	379.32	312.35	273.35	248.30	231.18	218.98
20 000	1867.08	1032.63	758.65	624.71	546.71	496.60	462.36	437.96
30 000	2800.62	1548.95	1137.97	937.06	820.06	744.91	693.54	656.94
40 000	3734.16	2065.26	1517.29	1249.41	1093.42	993.21	924.73	875.92
50 000	4667.70	2581.58	1896.61	1561.76	1366.77	1241.51	1155.91	1094.90
60 000	5601.23	3097.89	2275.94	1874.12	1640.12	1489.81	1387.09	1313.88
70 000	6534.77	3614.21	2655.26	2186.47	1913.48	1738.11	1618.27	1532.86
80 000	7468.31	4130.53	3034.58	2498.82	2186.83	1986.42	1849.45	1751.84
90 000	8401.85	4646.84	3413.90	2811.17	2460.18	2234.72	2080.63	1970.82
100 000	9335.39	5163.16	3793.23	3123.53	2733.54	2483.02	2311.81	2189.80
110 000	10268.93	5679.47	4172.55	3435.88	3006.89	2731.32	2542.99	2408.78
120 000	11202.47	6195.79	4551.87	3748.23	3280.25	2979.62	2774.18	2627.76
130 000	12136.01	6712.10	4931.20	4060.58	3553.60	3227.93	3005.36	2846.74
140 000	13069.55	7228.42	5310.52	4372.94	3826.95	3476.23	3236.54	3065.72
150 000	14003.09	7744.74	5689.84	4685.29	4100.31	3724.53	3467.72	3284.70
160 000	14936.63	8261.05	6069.16	4997.64	4373.66	3972.83	3698.90	3503.68
170 000	15870.16	8777.37	6448.49	5309.99	4647.01	4221.13	3930.08	3722.66
180 000	16803.70	9293.68	6827.81	5622.35	4920.37	4469.44	4161.26	3941.64
190 000	17737.24	9810.00	7207.13	5934.70	5193.72	4717.74	4392.45	4160.62
200 000	18670.78	10326.31	7586.45	6247.05	5467.08	4966.04	4623.63	4379.61
210 000	19604.32	10842.63	7965.78	6559.40	5740.43	5214.34	4854.81	4598.59
220 000	20537.86	11358.95	8345.10	6871.76	6013.78	5462.64	5085.99	4817.57
230 000	21471.40	11875.26	8724.42	7184.11	6287.14	5710.95	5317.17	5036.55
240 000	22404.94	12391.58	9103.75	7496.46	6560.49	5959.25	5548.35	5255.53
250 000	23338.48	12907.89	9483.07	7808.81	6833.85	6207.55	5779.53	5474.51
260 000	24272.02	13424.21	9862.39	8121.17	7107.20	6455.85	6010.71	5693.49
270 000	25205.56	13940.52	10241.71	8433.52	7380.55	6704.15	6241.90	5912.47
280 000	26139.09	14456.84	10621.04	8745.87	7653.91	6952.46	6473.08	6131.45
290 000	27072.63	14973.16	11000.36	9058.22	7927.26	7200.76	6704.26	6350.43
300 000	28006.17	15489.47	11379.68	9370.58	8200.61	7449.06	6935.44	6569.41
310 000	28973.25	16522.10	13138.33	9995.28	8747.32	7945.66	7397.80	7007.37
340 000	31740.33	17554.74	12896.97	10619.99	9294.03	8442.27	7860.17	7445.33
360 000	33607.41	18587.37	13655.62	11244.69	9840.74	8938.87	8322.53	7883.29
380 000	35474.49	19620.00	14414.26	11869.40	10387.44	9435.48	8784.89	8321.25
400 000	37341.56	20652.63	15172.91	12494.10	10934.15	9932.08	9247.25	8759.21
420 000	39208.64	21685.26	15931.55	13118.81	11480.86	10428.68	9709.62	9197.17
440 000	41075.72	22717.89	16690.20	13743.51	12027.57	10925.29	10171.98	9635.13
460 000	42942.80	23750.52	17448.85	14368.22	12574.27	11421.89	10634.34	10073.09
480 000	44809.88	24783.16	18207.49	14992.92	13120.98	11918.50	11096.70	10511.05
500 000	46676.95	25815.79	18966.14	15617.63	13667.69	12415.10	11559.07	10949.01
520 000	48544.03	26848.42	19724.78	16242.33	14214.40	12911.70	12021.43	11386.97
540 000	50411.11	27881.05	20483.43	16867.04	14761.11	13408.31	12483.79	11824.93
560 000	52278.19	28913.68	21242.07	17491.74	15307.81	13904.91	12946.16	12262.89
580 000	54145.27	29946.31	22000.72	18116.45	15854.52	14401.51	13408.52	12700.86
600 000	56012.35	30978.94	22759.36	18741.15	16401.23	14898.12	13870.88	13138.82
620 000	57879.42	32011.58	23518.01	19365.86	16947.94	15394.72	14333.24	13576.78
640 000	59746.50	33044.21	24276.65	19990.56	17494.64	15891.33	14795.61	14014.74
660 000	61613.58	34076.84	25035.30	20615.27	18041.35	16387.93	15257.97	14452.70
680 000	63480.66	35109.47	25793.95	21239.97	18588.06	16884.53	15720.33	14890.66
700 000	65347.74	36142.10	26552.59	21864.68	19134.77	17381.14	16182.69	15328.62
720 000	67214.81	37174.73	27311.24	22489.39	19681.47	17877.74	16645.06	15766.58
740 000	69081.89	38207.36	28069.88	23114.09	20228.18	18374.35	17107.42	16204.54
760 000	70948.97	39240.00	28828.53	23738.80	20774.89	18870.95	17569.78	16642.50
780 000	72816.05	40272.63	29587.17	24363.50	21321.60	19367.55	18032.14	17080.46
800 000	74683.13	41305.26	30345.82	24988.21	21868.30	19864.16	18494.51	17518.42
820 000	76550.21	42337.89	31104.46	25612.91	22415.01	20360.76	18956.87	17956.38
840 000	78417.28	43370.52	31863.11	26237.62	22961.72	20857.37	19419.23	18394.34
860 000	80284.36	44403.15	32621.75	26862.32	23508.43	21353.97	19881.60	18832.30
880 000	82151.44	45435.79	33380.40	27487.03	24055.13	21850.57	20343.96	19270.26
900 000	84018.52	46468.42	34139.05	28111.73	24601.84	22347.18	20806.32	19708.22
920 000	85885.60	47501.05	34897.69	28736.44	25148.55	22843.78	21268.68	20146.18
940 000	87752.67	48533.68	35656.34	29361.14	25695.26	23340.39	21731.05	20584.14
960 000	89619.75	49536.31	36414.98	29985.85	26241.96	23836.99	22193.41	21022.10
980 000	91486.83	50598.94	37173.63	30610.55	26788.67	24333.59	22655.77	21460.07
1000 000	93353.91	51631.57	37932.27	31235.26	27335.38	24830.20	23118.13	21898.03
Coefficient	.093353909	.051631574	.037932273	.031235257	.027335380	.024830198	.023118134	.021898026

134

MONTHLY AMORTIZING PAYMENTS 21.50%

AMOUNT	9 YEARS	10 YEARS	15 YEARS	20 YEARS	25 YEARS	30 YEARS	35 YEARS	40 YEARS
10 000	210.02	203.30	186.81	181.73	180.04	179.47	179.27	179.20
20 000	420.05	406.61	373.62	363.46	360.08	358.93	358.54	358.40
30 000	630.07	609.91	560.43	545.18	540.12	538.40	537.81	537.61
40 000	840.09	813.21	747.23	726.91	720.16	717.87	717.08	716.81
50 000	1050.12	1016.52	934.04	908.64	900.21	897.33	896.35	896.01
60 000	1260.14	1219.82	1120.85	1090.37	1080.25	1076.80	1075.62	1075.21
70 000	1470.16	1423.12	1307.66	1272.10	1260.29	1256.27	1254.89	1254.42
80 000	1680.19	1626.43	1494.47	1453.83	1440.33	1435.74	1434.16	1433.62
90 000	1890.21	1829.73	1681.28	1635.55	1620.37	1615.20	1613.43	1612.82
100 000	2100.23	2033.03	1868.08	1817.28	1800.41	1794.67	1792.70	1792.02
110 000	2310.25	2236.34	2054.89	1999.01	1980.45	1974.14	1971.97	1971.22
120 000	2520.28	2439.64	2241.70	2180.74	2160.49	2153.60	2151.24	2150.43
130 000	2730.30	2642.94	2428.51	2362.47	2340.53	2333.07	2330.51	2329.63
140 000	2940.32	2846.25	2615.32	2544.19	2520.57	2512.54	2509.78	2508.83
150 000	3150.35	3049.55	2802.13	2725.92	2700.62	2692.00	2689.05	2688.03
160 000	3360.37	3252.85	2988.94	2907.65	2880.66	2871.47	2868.32	2867.24
170 000	3570.39	3456.16	3175.74	3089.38	3060.70	3050.94	3047.59	3046.44
180 000	3780.42	3659.46	3362.55	3271.11	3240.74	3230.41	3226.86	3225.64
190 000	3990.44	3862.76	3549.36	3452.83	3420.78	3409.87	3406.13	3404.84
200 000	4200.46	4066.07	3736.17	3634.56	3600.82	3589.34	3585.40	3584.05
210 000	4410.49	4269.37	3922.98	3816.29	3780.86	3768.81	3764.67	3763.25
220 000	4620.51	4472.67	4109.79	3998.02	3960.90	3948.27	3943.94	3942.45
230 000	4830.53	4675.98	4296.59	4179.75	4140.94	4127.74	4123.21	4121.65
240 000	5040.56	4879.28	4483.40	4361.48	4320.99	4307.21	4302.48	4300.85
250 000	5250.58	5082.58	4670.21	4543.20	4501.03	4486.67	4481.75	4480.06
260 000	5460.60	5285.89	4857.02	4724.93	4681.07	4666.14	4661.02	4659.26
270 000	5670.63	5489.19	5043.83	4906.66	4861.11	4845.61	4840.29	4838.46
280 000	5880.65	5692.49	5230.64	5088.39	5041.15	5025.08	5019.56	5017.66
290 000	6090.67	5895.80	5417.45	5270.12	5221.19	5204.54	5198.83	5196.87
300 000	6300.70	6099.10	5604.25	5451.84	5401.23	5384.01	5378.10	5376.07
320 000	6720.74	6505.71	5977.87	5815.30	5761.31	5742.94	5736.64	5734.47
340 000	7140.79	6912.31	6351.49	6178.76	6121.40	6101.88	6095.18	6092.88
360 000	7560.83	7318.92	6725.10	6542.21	6481.48	6460.81	6453.72	6451.28
380 000	7980.88	7725.53	7098.72	6905.67	6841.56	6819.75	6812.26	6809.69
400 000	8400.93	8132.13	7472.34	7269.13	7201.64	7178.68	7170.80	7168.09
420 000	8820.97	8538.74	7845.96	7632.58	7561.72	7537.61	7529.34	7526.50
440 000	9241.02	8945.35	8219.57	7996.04	7921.81	7896.55	7887.88	7884.90
460 000	9661.07	9351.95	8593.19	8359.49	8281.89	8255.48	8246.42	8243.30
480 000	10081.11	9758.56	8966.81	8722.95	8641.97	8614.42	8604.96	8601.71
500 000	10501.16	10165.17	9340.42	9086.41	9002.05	8973.35	8963.50	8960.11
520 000	10921.21	10571.77	9714.04	9449.86	9362.13	9332.28	9322.04	9318.51
540 000	11341.25	10978.38	10087.66	9813.32	9722.22	9691.22	9680.58	9676.92
560 000	11761.30	11384.99	10461.27	10176.78	10082.30	10050.15	10039.12	10035.33
580 000	12181.34	11791.59	10834.89	10540.23	10442.38	10409.09	10397.66	10393.73
600 000	12601.39	12198.20	11208.51	10903.69	10802.46	10768.02	10756.20	10752.14
620 000	13021.44	12604.81	11582.13	11267.14	11162.55	11126.95	11114.74	11110.54
640 000	13441.48	13011.41	11955.74	11630.60	11522.63	11485.89	11473.28	11468.95
660 000	13861.53	13418.02	12329.36	11994.06	11882.71	11844.82	11831.82	11827.35
680 000	14281.58	13824.63	12702.98	12357.51	12242.79	12203.76	12190.36	12185.75
700 000	14701.62	14231.23	13076.59	12720.97	12602.87	12562.69	12548.90	12544.16
720 000	15121.67	14637.84	13450.21	13084.43	12962.96	12921.62	12907.44	12902.56
740 000	15541.72	15044.45	13823.83	13447.88	13323.04	13280.56	13265.98	13260.97
760 000	15961.76	15451.05	14197.44	13811.34	13683.12	13639.49	13624.52	13619.37
780 000	16381.81	15857.66	14571.06	14174.79	14043.20	13998.43	13983.06	13977.78
800 000	16801.85	16264.27	14944.68	14538.25	14403.28	14357.36	14341.60	14336.18
820 000	17221.90	16670.87	15318.29	14901.71	14763.37	14716.29	14700.14	14694.59
840 000	17641.95	17077.48	15691.91	15265.16	15123.45	15075.23	15058.68	15052.99
860 000	18061.99	17484.09	16065.53	15628.62	15483.53	15434.16	15417.22	15411.40
880 000	18482.04	17890.69	16439.15	15992.08	15843.61	15793.10	15775.76	15769.80
900 000	18902.09	18297.30	16812.76	16355.53	16203.69	16152.03	16134.30	16128.20
920 000	19322.13	18703.91	17186.38	16718.99	16563.78	16510.96	16492.84	16486.61
940 000	19742.18	19110.51	17560.00	17082.44	16923.86	16869.90	16851.38	16845.01
960 000	20162.23	19517.12	17933.61	17445.90	17283.94	17228.83	17209.92	17203.42
980 000	20582.27	19923.73	18307.23	17809.36	17644.02	17587.77	17568.46	17561.82
1000 000	21002.32	20330.34	18680.85	18172.81	18004.11	17946.70	17927.00	17920.23
Coefficient	.021002318	.020330335	.018680847	.018172813	.018004105	.017946699	.017927003	.017920227

135

MONTHLY AMORTIZING PAYMENTS

AMOUNT	1 YEAR	2 YEARS	3 YEARS	4 YEARS	5 YEARS	6 YEARS	7 YEARS	8 YEARS
10 000	934.74	517.55	380.61	313.71	274.77	249.78	232.72	220.57
20 000	1869.48	1035.10	761.22	627.41	549.54	499.56	465.44	441.15
30 000	2804.22	1552.64	1141.84	941.12	824.31	749.34	698.15	661.72
40 000	3738.96	2070.19	1522.45	1254.82	1099.08	999.12	930.87	882.29
50 000	4673.71	2587.74	1903.06	1568.53	1373.85	1248.90	1163.59	1102.87
60 000	5608.45	3105.29	2283.67	1882.23	1648.62	1498.68	1396.31	1323.44
70 000	6543.19	3622.83	2664.29	2195.94	1923.39	1748.46	1629.03	1544.01
80 000	7477.93	4140.38	3044.90	2509.64	2198.16	1998.24	1861.74	1764.58
90 000	8412.67	4657.93	3425.51	2823.35	2472.93	2248.02	2094.46	1985.16
100 000	9347.41	5175.48	3806.12	3137.05	2747.70	2497.79	2327.18	2205.73
110 000	10282.15	5693.03	4186.74	3450.76	3022.47	2747.57	2559.90	2426.30
120 000	11216.89	6210.57	4567.35	3764.46	3297.23	2997.35	2792.62	2646.88
130 000	12151.63	6728.12	4947.96	4078.17	3572.00	3247.13	3025.33	2867.45
140 000	13086.38	7245.67	5328.57	4391.87	3846.77	3496.91	3258.05	3088.02
150 000	14021.12	7763.22	5709.19	4705.58	4121.54	3746.69	3490.77	3308.60
160 000	14955.86	8280.76	6089.80	5019.28	4396.31	3996.47	3723.49	3529.17
170 000	15890.60	8798.31	6470.41	5332.99	4671.08	4246.25	3956.21	3749.74
180 000	16825.34	9315.86	6851.02	5646.69	4945.85	4496.03	4188.92	3970.31
190 000	17760.08	9833.41	7231.64	5960.40	5220.62	4745.81	4421.64	4190.89
200 000	18694.82	10350.96	7612.25	6274.10	5495.39	4995.59	4654.36	4411.46
210 000	19629.56	10868.50	7992.86	6587.81	5770.16	5245.37	4887.08	4632.03
220 000	20564.30	11386.05	8373.47	6901.51	6044.93	5495.15	5119.80	4852.61
230 000	21499.05	11903.60	8754.09	7215.22	6319.70	5744.93	5352.51	5073.18
240 000	22433.79	12421.15	9134.70	7528.92	6594.47	5994.71	5585.23	5293.75
250 000	23368.53	12938.69	9515.31	7842.63	6869.24	6244.49	5817.95	5514.33
260 000	24303.27	13456.24	9895.92	8156.33	7144.01	6494.27	6050.67	5734.90
270 000	25238.01	13973.79	10276.53	8470.04	7418.78	6744.05	6283.39	5955.47
280 000	26172.75	14491.34	10657.15	8783.74	7693.55	6993.83	6516.10	6176.04
290 000	27107.49	15008.89	11037.76	9097.45	7968.32	7243.60	6748.82	6396.62
300 000	28042.23	15526.43	11418.37	9411.15	8243.09	7493.38	6981.54	6617.19
320 000	29911.72	16561.53	12179.60	10038.56	8792.63	7992.94	7446.98	7058.34
340 000	31781.20	17596.62	12940.82	10665.97	9342.17	8492.50	7912.41	7499.48
360 000	33650.68	18631.72	13702.05	11293.38	9891.70	8992.06	8377.85	7940.63
380 000	35520.16	19666.82	14463.27	11920.79	10441.24	9491.62	8843.28	8381.77
400 000	37389.64	20701.91	15224.50	12548.20	10990.78	9991.18	9308.72	8822.92
420 000	39259.13	21737.01	15985.72	13175.61	11540.32	10490.74	9774.16	9264.07
440 000	41128.61	22772.10	16746.95	13803.02	12089.86	10990.30	10239.59	9705.21
460 000	42998.09	23807.20	17508.17	14430.43	12639.40	11489.86	10705.03	10146.36
480 000	44867.57	24842.29	18269.40	15057.84	13188.94	11989.42	11170.46	10587.50
500 000	46737.06	25877.39	19030.62	15685.26	13738.48	12488.97	11635.90	11028.65
520 000	48606.54	26912.48	19791.84	16312.67	14288.02	12988.53	12101.34	11469.80
540 000	50476.02	27947.58	20553.07	16940.08	14837.56	13488.09	12566.77	11910.94
560 000	52345.50	28982.68	21314.29	17567.49	15387.10	13987.65	13032.21	12352.09
580 000	54214.98	30017.77	22075.52	18194.90	15936.64	14487.21	13497.65	12793.23
600 000	56084.47	31052.87	22836.74	18822.31	16486.17	14986.77	13963.08	13234.38
620 000	57953.95	32087.96	23597.97	19449.72	17035.71	15486.33	14428.52	13675.53
640 000	59823.43	33123.06	24359.19	20077.13	17585.25	15985.89	14893.95	14116.67
660 000	61692.91	34158.15	25120.42	20704.54	18134.79	16485.45	15359.39	14557.82
680 000	63562.39	35193.25	25881.64	21331.95	18684.33	16985.00	15824.83	14998.96
700 000	65431.88	36228.34	26642.87	21959.36	19233.87	17484.56	16290.26	15440.11
720 000	67301.36	37263.44	27404.09	22586.77	19783.41	17984.12	16755.70	15881.26
740 000	69170.84	38298.53	28165.32	23214.18	20332.95	18483.68	17221.13	16322.40
760 000	71040.32	39333.63	28926.54	23841.59	20882.49	18983.24	17686.57	16763.55
780 000	72909.81	40368.73	29687.77	24469.00	21432.03	19482.80	18152.01	17204.69
800 000	74779.29	41403.82	30448.99	25096.41	21981.57	19982.36	18617.44	17645.84
820 000	76648.77	42438.92	31210.22	25723.82	22531.11	20481.92	19082.88	18086.99
840 000	78518.25	43474.01	31971.44	26351.23	23080.64	20981.48	19548.31	18528.13
860 000	80387.73	44509.11	32732.67	26978.64	23630.18	21481.04	20013.75	18969.28
880 000	82257.22	45544.20	33493.89	27606.05	24179.72	21980.59	20479.19	19410.42
900 000	84126.70	46579.30	34255.12	28233.46	24729.26	22480.15	20944.62	19851.57
920 000	85996.18	47614.39	35016.34	28860.87	25278.80	22979.71	21410.06	20292.72
940 000	87865.66	48649.49	35777.57	29488.28	25828.34	23479.27	21875.49	20733.86
960 000	89735.15	49684.59	36538.79	30115.69	26377.88	23978.83	22340.93	21175.01
980 000	91604.63	50719.68	37300.02	30743.10	26927.42	24478.39	22806.37	21616.15
1000 000	93474.11	51754.78	38061.24	31370.51	27476.96	24977.95	23271.80	22057.30
Coefficient	.093474110	.051754777	.038061240	.031370510	.027476958	.024977948	.023271802	.022057300

AMOUNT	9 YEARS	10 YEARS	15 YEARS	20 YEARS	25 YEARS	30 YEARS	35 YEARS	40 YEARS
10 000	211.67	205.00	188.69	183.72	182.08	181.53	181.35	181.28
20 000	423.34	409.99	377.38	367.43	364.16	363.06	362.69	362.57
30 000	635.01	614.99	566.07	551.15	546.24	544.60	544.04	543.85
40 000	846.67	819.99	754.76	734.86	728.33	726.13	725.38	725.13
50 000	1058.34	1024.99	943.45	918.58	910.41	907.66	906.73	906.41
60 000	1270.01	1229.98	1132.14	1102.29	1092.49	1089.19	1088.08	1087.70
70 000	1481.68	1434.98	1320.83	1286.01	1274.57	1270.73	1269.42	1268.98
80 000	1693.35	1639.98	1509.52	1469.72	1456.65	1452.26	1450.77	1450.26
90 000	1905.02	1844.98	1698.21	1653.44	1638.73	1633.79	1632.11	1631.54
100 000	2116.68	2049.97	1886.90	1837.15	1820.82	1815.32	1813.46	1812.83
110 000	2328.35	2254.97	2075.59	2020.87	2002.90	1996.85	1994.81	1994.11
120 000	2540.02	2459.97	2264.28	2204.58	2184.98	2178.39	2176.15	2175.39
130 000	2751.69	2664.97	2452.96	2388.30	2367.06	2359.92	2357.50	2356.67
140 000	2963.36	2869.96	2641.65	2572.02	2549.14	2541.45	2538.84	2537.96
150 000	3175.03	3074.96	2830.34	2755.73	2731.22	2722.98	2720.19	2719.24
160 000	3386.70	3279.96	3019.03	2939.45	2913.31	2904.52	2901.54	2900.52
170 000	3598.36	3484.96	3207.72	3123.16	3095.39	3086.05	3082.88	3081.81
180 000	3810.03	3689.95	3396.41	3306.88	3277.47	3267.58	3264.23	3263.09
190 000	4021.70	3894.95	3585.10	3490.59	3459.55	3449.11	3445.57	3444.37
200 000	4233.37	4099.95	3773.79	3674.31	3641.63	3630.64	3626.92	3625.65
210 000	4445.04	4304.95	3962.48	3858.02	3823.71	3812.18	3808.26	3806.94
220 000	4656.71	4509.94	4151.17	4041.74	4005.80	3993.71	3989.61	3988.22
230 000	4868.37	4714.94	4339.86	4225.45	4187.88	4175.24	4170.96	4169.50
240 000	5080.04	4919.94	4528.55	4409.17	4369.96	4356.77	4352.30	4350.78
250 000	5291.71	5124.94	4717.24	4592.88	4552.04	4538.31	4533.65	4532.07
260 000	5503.38	5329.93	4905.93	4776.60	4734.12	4719.84	4714.99	4713.35
270 000	5715.05	5534.93	5094.62	4960.31	4916.20	4901.37	4896.34	4894.63
280 000	5926.72	5739.93	5283.31	5144.03	5098.29	5082.90	5077.69	5075.91
290 000	6138.39	5944.92	5472.00	5327.75	5280.37	5264.43	5259.03	5257.20
300 000	6350.05	6149.92	5660.69	5511.46	5462.45	5445.97	5440.38	5438.48
320 000	6773.39	6559.92	6038.07	5878.89	5826.61	5809.03	5803.07	5801.04
340 000	7196.73	6969.91	6415.45	6246.32	6190.78	6172.09	6165.76	6163.61
360 000	7620.06	7379.91	6792.83	6613.75	6554.94	6535.16	6528.45	6526.18
380 000	8043.40	7789.90	7170.20	6981.18	6919.10	6898.22	6891.15	6888.74
400 000	8466.74	8199.90	7547.58	7348.61	7283.27	7261.29	7253.84	7251.31
420 000	8890.07	8609.89	7924.96	7716.05	7647.43	7624.35	7616.53	7613.87
440 000	9313.41	9019.89	8302.34	8083.48	8011.59	7987.42	7979.22	7976.44
460 000	9736.75	9429.88	8679.72	8450.91	8375.76	8350.48	8341.91	8339.00
480 000	10160.09	9839.88	9057.10	8818.34	8739.92	8713.55	8704.61	8701.57
500 000	10583.42	10249.87	9434.48	9185.77	9104.08	9076.61	9067.30	9064.13
520 000	11006.76	10659.87	9811.86	9553.20	9468.25	9439.67	9429.99	9426.70
540 000	11430.10	11069.86	10189.24	9920.63	9832.41	9802.74	9792.68	9789.26
560 000	11853.43	11479.85	10566.62	10288.06	10196.57	10165.80	10155.37	10151.83
580 000	12276.77	11889.85	10944.00	10655.49	10560.74	10528.87	10518.07	10514.39
600 000	12700.11	12299.84	11321.38	11022.92	10924.90	10891.93	10880.76	10876.96
620 000	13123.44	12709.84	11698.76	11390.35	11289.06	11255.00	11243.45	11239.52
640 000	13546.78	13119.83	12076.13	11757.78	11653.22	11618.06	11606.14	11602.09
660 000	13970.12	13529.83	12453.51	12125.21	12017.39	11981.13	11968.83	11964.65
680 000	14393.45	13939.82	12830.89	12492.64	12381.55	12344.19	12331.52	12327.22
700 000	14816.79	14349.82	13208.27	12860.08	12745.71	12707.25	12694.22	12689.79
720 000	15240.13	14759.81	13585.65	13227.51	13109.88	13070.32	13056.91	13052.35
740 000	15663.47	15169.81	13963.03	13594.94	13474.04	13433.38	13419.60	13414.92
760 000	16086.80	15579.80	14340.41	13962.37	13838.20	13796.45	13782.29	13777.48
780 000	16510.14	15989.80	14717.79	14329.80	14202.37	14159.51	14144.98	14140.05
800 000	16933.48	16399.79	15095.17	14697.23	14566.53	14522.58	14507.68	14502.61
820 000	17356.81	16809.79	15472.55	15064.66	14930.69	14885.64	14870.37	14865.18
840 000	17780.15	17219.78	15849.93	15432.09	15294.86	15248.70	15233.06	15227.74
860 000	18203.49	17629.78	16227.31	15799.52	15659.02	15611.77	15595.75	15590.31
880 000	18626.82	18039.77	16604.68	16166.95	16023.18	15974.83	15958.44	15952.87
900 000	19050.16	18449.77	16982.06	16534.38	16387.35	16337.90	16321.14	16315.44
920 000	19473.50	18859.76	17359.44	16901.81	16751.51	16700.96	16683.83	16678.00
940 000	19896.83	19269.76	17736.82	17269.24	17115.67	17064.03	17046.52	17040.57
960 000	20320.17	19679.75	18114.20	17636.67	17479.84	17427.09	17409.21	17403.13
980 000	20743.51	20089.75	18491.58	18004.11	17844.00	17790.16	17771.90	17765.70
1000 000	21166.85	20499.74	18868.96	18371.54	18208.16	18153.22	18134.60	18128.27
Coefficient	.021166845	.020499741	.018868960	.018371536	.018208164	.018153220	.018134595	.018128265

AMOUNT	1 YEAR	2 YEARS	3 YEARS	4 YEARS	5 YEARS	6 YEARS	7 YEARS	8 YEARS
10 000	935.94	518.78	381.90	315.06	276.19	251.26	234.26	222.17
20 000	1871.89	1037.56	763.81	630.12	552.38	502.52	468.52	444.34
30 000	2807.83	1556.34	1145.71	945.18	828.57	753.78	702.78	666.51
40 000	3743.78	2075.13	1527.62	1260.24	1104.76	1005.05	937.04	888.68
50 000	4679.72	2593.91	1909.52	1575.30	1380.95	1256.31	1171.30	1110.85
60 000	5615.66	3112.69	2291.43	1890.36	1657.13	1507.57	1405.56	1333.02
70 000	6551.61	3631.47	2673.33	2205.43	1933.32	1758.83	1639.82	1555.20
80 000	7487.55	4150.25	3055.24	2520.49	2209.51	2010.09	1874.08	1777.37
90 000	8423.49	4669.03	3437.14	2835.55	2485.70	2261.35	2108.33	1999.54
100 000	9359.44	5187.82	3819.05	3150.61	2761.89	2512.61	2342.59	2221.71
110 000	10295.38	5706.60	4200.95	3465.67	3038.08	2763.87	2576.85	2443.88
120 000	11231.33	6225.38	4582.85	3780.73	3314.27	3015.14	2811.11	2666.05
130 000	12167.27	6744.16	4964.76	4095.79	3590.46	3266.40	3045.37	2888.22
140 000	13103.21	7262.94	5346.66	4410.85	3866.65	3517.66	3279.63	3110.39
150 000	14039.16	7781.72	5728.57	4725.91	4142.84	3768.92	3513.89	3332.56
160 000	14975.10	8300.50	6110.47	5040.97	4419.03	4020.18	3748.15	3554.73
170 000	15911.04	8819.29	6492.38	5356.03	4695.22	4271.44	3982.41	3776.90
180 000	16846.99	9338.07	6874.28	5671.09	4971.40	4522.70	4216.67	3999.07
190 000	17782.93	9856.85	7256.19	5986.15	5247.59	4773.96	4450.93	4221.25
200 000	18718.88	10375.63	7638.09	6301.22	5523.78	5025.23	4685.19	4443.42
210 000	19654.82	10894.41	8019.99	6616.28	5799.97	5276.49	4919.45	4665.59
220 000	20590.76	11413.19	8401.90	6931.34	6076.16	5527.75	5153.71	4887.76
230 000	21526.71	11931.98	8783.80	7246.40	6352.35	5779.01	5387.97	5109.93
240 000	22462.65	12450.76	9165.71	7561.46	6628.54	6030.27	5622.23	5332.10
250 000	23398.60	12969.54	9547.61	7876.52	6904.73	6281.53	5856.49	5554.27
260 000	24334.54	13488.32	9929.52	8191.58	7180.92	6532.79	6090.75	5776.44
270 000	25270.48	14007.10	10311.42	8506.64	7457.11	6784.05	6325.00	5998.61
280 000	26206.43	14525.88	10693.33	8821.70	7733.30	7035.32	6559.26	6220.78
290 000	27142.37	15044.67	11075.23	9136.76	8009.48	7286.58	6793.52	6442.95
300 000	28078.31	15563.45	11457.14	9451.82	8285.67	7537.84	7027.78	6665.12
320 000	29950.20	16601.01	12220.94	10081.94	8838.05	8040.36	7496.30	7109.47
340 000	31822.09	17638.57	12984.75	10712.07	9390.43	8542.88	7964.82	7553.81
360 000	33693.98	18676.14	13748.56	11342.19	9942.81	9045.41	8433.34	7998.15
380 000	35565.86	19713.70	14512.37	11972.31	10495.19	9547.93	8901.86	8442.49
400 000	37437.75	20751.26	15276.18	12602.43	11047.56	10050.45	9370.38	8886.83
420 000	39309.64	21788.83	16039.99	13232.55	11599.94	10552.97	9838.90	9331.17
440 000	41181.53	22826.39	16803.80	13862.67	12152.32	11055.50	10307.42	9775.52
460 000	43053.42	23863.95	17567.61	14492.80	12704.70	11558.02	10775.93	10219.86
480 000	44925.30	24901.51	18331.42	15122.92	13257.08	12060.54	11244.45	10664.20
500 000	46797.19	25939.08	19095.23	15753.04	13809.46	12563.06	11712.97	11108.54
520 000	48669.08	26976.64	19859.04	16383.16	14361.83	13065.59	12181.49	11552.88
540 000	50540.97	28014.20	20622.84	17013.28	14914.21	13568.11	12650.01	11997.22
560 000	52412.85	29051.77	21386.65	17643.40	15466.59	14070.63	13118.53	12441.56
580 000	54284.74	30089.33	22150.46	18273.53	16018.97	14573.15	13587.05	12885.91
600 000	56156.63	31126.89	22914.27	18903.65	16571.35	15075.68	14055.57	13330.25
620 000	58028.52	32164.46	23678.08	19533.77	17123.73	15578.20	14524.09	13774.59
640 000	59900.40	33202.02	24441.89	20163.89	17676.10	16080.72	14992.60	14218.93
660 000	61772.29	34239.58	25205.70	20794.01	18228.48	16583.24	15461.12	14663.27
680 000	63644.18	35277.15	25969.51	21424.13	18780.86	17085.77	15929.64	15107.61
700 000	65516.07	36314.71	26733.32	22054.25	19333.24	17588.29	16398.16	15551.96
720 000	67387.95	37352.27	27497.13	22684.38	19885.62	18090.81	16866.68	15996.30
740 000	69259.84	38389.84	28260.93	23314.50	20437.99	18593.33	17335.20	16440.64
760 000	71131.73	39427.40	29024.74	23944.62	20990.37	19095.86	17803.72	16884.98
780 000	73003.62	40464.96	29788.55	24574.74	21542.75	19598.38	18272.24	17329.32
800 000	74875.50	41502.52	30552.36	25204.86	22095.13	20100.90	18740.76	17773.66
820 000	76747.39	42540.09	31316.17	25834.98	22647.51	20603.42	19209.27	18218.01
840 000	78619.28	43577.65	32079.98	26465.11	23199.89	21105.95	19677.79	18662.35
860 000	80491.17	44615.21	32843.79	27095.23	23752.26	21608.47	20146.31	19106.69
880 000	82363.06	45652.78	33607.60	27725.35	24304.64	22110.99	20614.83	19551.03
900 000	84234.94	46690.34	34371.41	28355.47	24857.02	22613.52	21083.35	19995.37
920 000	86106.83	47727.90	35135.22	28985.59	25409.40	23116.04	21551.87	20439.71
940 000	87978.72	48765.47	35899.02	29615.71	25961.78	23618.56	22020.39	20884.06
960 000	89850.61	49803.03	36662.83	30245.83	26514.16	24121.08	22488.91	21328.40
980 000	91722.49	50840.59	37426.64	30875.96	27066.53	24623.61	22957.43	21772.74
1000 000	93594.38	51878.16	38190.45	31506.08	27618.91	25126.13	23425.94	22217.08
Coefficient	.093594381	.051878156	.038190452	.031506078	.027618912	.025126128	.023425944	.022217080

138

AMOUNT	9 YEARS	10 YEARS	15 YEARS	20 YEARS	25 YEARS	30 YEARS	35 YEARS	40 YEARS
10 000	213.32	206.70	190.58	185.71	184.12	183.60	183.42	183.36
20 000	426.64	413.39	381.15	371.41	368.25	367.20	366.84	366.73
30 000	639.96	620.09	571.73	557.12	552.37	550.80	550.27	550.09
40 000	853.28	826.79	762.30	742.82	736.50	734.39	733.69	733.45
50 000	1066.60	1033.48	952.88	928.53	920.62	917.99	917.11	916.82
60 000	1279.91	1240.18	1143.45	1114.24	1104.75	1101.59	1100.53	1100.18
70 000	1493.23	1446.88	1334.03	1299.94	1288.87	1285.19	1283.96	1283.54
80 000	1706.55	1653.58	1524.60	1485.65	1472.99	1468.79	1467.38	1466.91
90 000	1919.87	1860.27	1715.18	1671.35	1657.12	1652.39	1650.80	1650.27
100 000	2133.19	2066.97	1905.76	1857.06	1841.24	1835.98	1834.22	1833.63
110 000	2346.51	2273.67	2096.33	2042.77	2025.37	2019.58	2017.65	2017.00
120 000	2559.83	2480.36	2286.91	2228.47	2209.49	2203.18	2201.07	2200.36
130 000	2773.15	2687.06	2477.48	2414.18	2393.62	2386.78	2384.49	2383.72
140 000	2986.47	2893.76	2668.06	2599.88	2577.74	2570.38	2567.91	2567.09
150 000	3199.79	3100.45	2858.63	2785.59	2761.86	2753.98	2751.34	2750.45
160 000	3413.10	3307.15	3049.21	2971.30	2945.99	2937.58	2934.76	2933.81
170 000	3626.42	3513.85	3239.79	3157.00	3130.11	3121.17	3118.18	3117.18
180 000	3839.74	3720.54	3430.36	3342.71	3314.24	3304.77	3301.60	3300.54
190 000	4053.06	3927.24	3620.94	3528.41	3498.36	3488.37	3485.03	3483.90
200 000	4266.38	4133.94	3811.51	3714.12	3682.48	3671.97	3668.45	3667.27
210 000	4479.70	4340.63	4002.09	3899.83	3866.61	3855.57	3851.87	3850.63
220 000	4693.02	4547.33	4192.66	4085.53	4050.73	4039.17	4035.29	4033.99
230 000	4906.34	4754.03	4383.24	4271.24	4234.86	4222.77	4218.71	4217.36
240 000	5119.66	4960.73	4573.81	4456.94	4418.98	4406.36	4402.14	4400.72
250 000	5332.98	5167.42	4764.39	4642.65	4603.11	4589.96	4585.56	4584.08
260 000	5546.29	5374.12	4954.97	4828.36	4787.23	4773.56	4768.98	4767.45
270 000	5759.61	5580.82	5145.54	5014.06	4971.35	4957.16	4952.40	4950.81
280 000	5972.93	5787.51	5336.12	5199.77	5155.48	5140.76	5135.83	5134.17
290 000	6186.25	5994.21	5526.69	5385.47	5339.60	5324.36	5319.25	5317.53
300 000	6399.57	6200.91	5717.27	5571.18	5523.73	5507.95	5502.67	5500.90
320 000	6826.21	6614.30	6098.42	5942.59	5891.98	5875.15	5869.52	5867.62
340 000	7252.85	7027.69	6479.57	6314.00	6260.22	6242.35	6236.36	6234.35
360 000	7679.48	7441.09	6860.72	6685.42	6628.47	6609.55	6603.21	6601.08
380 000	8106.12	7854.48	7241.87	7056.83	6996.72	6976.74	6970.05	6967.80
400 000	8532.76	8267.88	7623.02	7428.24	7364.97	7343.94	7336.90	7334.53
420 000	8959.40	8681.27	8004.18	7799.65	7733.22	7711.14	7703.74	7701.26
440 000	9386.04	9094.66	8385.33	8171.06	8101.47	8078.33	8070.59	8067.98
460 000	9812.67	9508.06	8766.48	8542.48	8469.72	8445.53	8437.43	8434.71
480 000	10239.31	9921.45	9147.63	8913.89	8837.96	8812.73	8804.27	8801.44
500 000	10665.95	10334.84	9528.78	9285.30	9206.21	9179.92	9171.12	9168.16
520 000	11092.59	10748.24	9909.93	9656.71	9574.46	9547.12	9537.96	9534.89
540 000	11519.23	11161.63	10291.08	10028.12	9942.71	9914.32	9904.81	9901.62
560 000	11945.86	11575.03	10672.23	10399.54	10310.96	10281.51	10271.65	10268.34
580 000	12372.50	11988.42	11053.38	10770.95	10679.21	10648.71	10638.50	10635.07
600 000	12799.14	12401.81	11434.54	11142.36	11047.45	11015.91	11005.34	11001.80
620 000	13225.78	12815.21	11815.69	11513.77	11415.70	11383.11	11372.19	11368.52
640 000	13652.42	13228.60	12196.84	11885.18	11783.95	11750.30	11739.03	11735.25
660 000	14079.05	13641.99	12577.99	12256.60	12152.20	12117.50	12105.88	12101.98
680 000	14505.69	14055.39	12959.14	12628.01	12520.45	12484.70	12472.72	12468.70
700 000	14932.33	14468.78	13340.29	12999.42	12888.70	12851.89	12839.57	12835.43
720 000	15358.97	14882.18	13721.44	13370.83	13256.95	13219.09	13206.41	13202.16
740 000	15785.61	15295.57	14102.59	13742.24	13625.19	13586.29	13573.26	13568.88
760 000	16212.24	15708.96	14483.75	14113.66	13993.44	13953.48	13940.10	13935.61
780 000	16638.88	16122.36	14864.90	14485.07	14361.69	14320.68	14306.95	14302.34
800 000	17065.52	16535.75	15246.05	14856.48	14729.94	14687.88	14673.79	14669.06
820 000	17492.16	16949.14	15627.20	15227.89	15098.19	15055.08	15040.64	15035.79
840 000	17918.80	17362.54	16008.35	15599.30	15466.44	15422.27	15407.48	15402.51
860 000	18345.43	17775.93	16389.50	15970.72	15834.68	15789.47	15774.33	15769.24
880 000	18772.07	18189.33	16770.65	16342.13	16202.93	16156.67	16141.17	16135.97
900 000	19198.71	18602.72	17151.80	16713.54	16571.18	16523.86	16508.02	16502.69
920 000	19625.35	19016.11	17532.96	17084.95	16939.43	16891.06	16874.86	16869.42
940 000	20051.99	19429.51	17914.11	17456.36	17307.68	17258.26	17241.70	17236.15
960 000	20478.62	19842.90	18295.26	17827.78	17675.93	17625.45	17608.55	17602.87
980 000	20905.26	20256.29	18676.41	18199.19	18044.18	17992.65	17975.39	17969.60
1000 000	21331.90	20669.69	19057.56	18570.60	18412.42	18359.85	18342.24	18336.33
Coefficient	.021331901	.020669688	.019057560	.018570599	.018412424	.018359848	.018342239	.018336327

MONTHLY AMORTIZING PAYMENTS

AMOUNT	1 YEAR	2 YEARS	3 YEARS	4 YEARS	5 YEARS	6 YEARS	7 YEARS	8 YEARS
10 000	937.15	520.02	383.20	316.42	277.61	252.75	235.81	223.77
20 000	1874.29	1040.03	766.40	632.84	555.22	505.49	471.61	447.55
30 000	2811.44	1560.05	1149.60	949.26	832.84	758.24	707.42	671.32
40 000	3748.59	2080.07	1532.80	1265.68	1110.45	1010.99	943.22	895.09
50 000	4685.74	2600.08	1916.00	1582.10	1388.06	1263.74	1179.03	1118.87
60 000	5622.88	3120.10	2299.19	1898.52	1665.67	1516.48	1414.83	1342.64
70 000	6560.03	3640.12	2682.39	2214.94	1943.29	1769.23	1650.64	1566.42
80 000	7497.18	4160.14	3065.59	2531.36	2220.90	2021.98	1886.44	1790.19
90 000	8434.33	4680.15	3448.79	2847.78	2498.51	2274.73	2122.25	2013.96
100 000	9371.47	5200.17	3831.99	3164.20	2776.12	2527.47	2358.06	2237.74
110 000	10308.62	5720.19	4215.19	3480.62	3053.74	2780.22	2593.86	2461.51
120 000	11245.77	6240.20	4598.39	3797.03	3331.35	3032.97	2829.67	2685.28
130 000	12182.92	6760.22	4981.59	4113.45	3608.96	3285.72	3065.47	2909.06
140 000	13120.06	7280.24	5364.79	4429.87	3886.57	3538.46	3301.28	3132.83
150 000	14057.21	7800.25	5747.99	4746.29	4164.19	3791.21	3537.08	3356.60
160 000	14994.36	8320.27	6131.18	5062.71	4441.80	4043.96	3772.89	3580.38
170 000	15931.51	8840.29	6514.38	5379.13	4719.41	4296.70	4008.69	3804.15
180 000	16868.65	9360.31	6897.58	5695.55	4997.02	4549.45	4244.50	4027.93
190 000	17805.80	9880.32	7280.78	6011.97	5274.64	4802.20	4480.31	4251.70
200 000	18742.95	10400.34	7663.98	6328.39	5552.25	5054.95	4716.11	4475.47
210 000	19680.10	10920.36	8047.18	6644.81	5829.86	5307.69	4951.92	4699.25
220 000	20617.24	11440.37	8430.38	6961.23	6107.47	5560.44	5187.72	4923.02
230 000	21554.39	11960.39	8813.58	7277.65	6385.09	5813.19	5423.53	5146.79
240 000	22491.54	12480.41	9196.78	7594.07	6662.70	6065.94	5659.33	5370.57
250 000	23428.69	13000.42	9579.98	7910.49	6940.31	6318.68	5895.14	5594.34
260 000	24365.83	13520.44	9963.18	8226.91	7217.92	6571.43	6130.94	5818.11
270 000	25302.98	14040.46	10346.37	8543.33	7495.54	6824.18	6366.75	6041.89
280 000	26240.13	14560.47	10729.57	8859.75	7773.15	7076.93	6602.56	6265.66
290 000	27177.28	15080.49	11112.77	9176.17	8050.76	7329.67	6838.36	6489.43
300 000	28114.42	15600.51	11495.97	9492.59	8328.37	7582.42	7074.17	6713.21
320 000	29988.72	16640.54	12262.37	10125.43	8883.60	8087.92	7545.78	7160.76
340 000	31863.01	17680.58	13028.77	10758.27	9438.82	8593.41	8017.39	7608.30
360 000	33737.31	18720.61	13795.17	11391.10	9994.05	9098.90	8489.00	8055.85
380 000	35611.60	19760.64	14561.56	12023.94	10549.27	9604.40	8960.61	8503.40
400 000	37485.90	20800.68	15327.96	12656.78	11104.50	10109.89	9432.22	8950.94
420 000	39360.19	21840.71	16094.36	13289.62	11659.72	10615.39	9903.83	9398.49
440 000	41234.49	22880.75	16860.76	13922.46	12214.95	11120.88	10375.44	9846.04
460 000	43108.78	23920.78	17627.16	14555.30	12770.17	11626.38	10847.06	10293.59
480 000	44983.08	24960.81	18393.55	15188.14	13325.40	12131.87	11318.67	10741.13
500 000	46857.37	26000.85	19159.95	15820.98	13880.62	12637.37	11790.28	11188.68
520 000	48731.67	27040.88	19926.35	16453.82	14435.85	13142.86	12261.89	11636.23
540 000	50605.96	28080.92	20692.75	17086.66	14991.07	13648.36	12733.50	12083.78
560 000	52480.26	29120.95	21459.15	17719.50	15546.29	14153.85	13205.11	12531.32
580 000	54354.55	30160.98	22225.55	18352.34	16101.52	14659.35	13676.72	12978.87
600 000	56228.85	31201.02	22991.94	18985.17	16656.74	15164.84	14148.33	13426.42
620 000	58103.14	32241.05	23758.34	19618.01	17211.97	15670.34	14619.94	13873.96
640 000	59977.43	33281.09	24524.74	20250.85	17767.19	16175.83	15091.56	14321.51
660 000	61851.73	34321.12	25291.14	20883.69	18322.42	16681.33	15563.17	14769.06
680 000	63726.02	35361.15	26057.54	21516.53	18877.64	17186.82	16034.78	15216.61
700 000	65600.32	36401.19	26823.93	22149.37	19432.87	17692.31	16506.39	15664.15
720 000	67474.61	37441.22	27590.33	22782.21	19988.09	18197.81	16978.00	16111.70
740 000	69348.91	38481.26	28356.73	23415.05	20543.32	18703.30	17449.61	16559.25
760 000	71223.20	39521.29	29123.13	24047.89	21098.54	19208.80	17921.22	17006.80
780 000	73097.50	40561.32	29889.53	24680.73	21653.77	19714.29	18392.83	17454.34
800 000	74971.79	41601.36	30655.92	25313.57	22208.99	20219.79	18864.44	17901.89
820 000	76846.09	42641.39	31422.32	25946.41	22764.22	20725.28	19336.06	18349.44
840 000	78720.38	43681.42	32188.72	26579.24	23319.44	21230.78	19807.67	18796.98
860 000	80594.68	44721.46	32955.12	27212.08	23874.67	21736.27	20279.28	19244.53
880 000	82468.97	45761.49	33721.52	27844.92	24429.89	22241.77	20750.89	19692.08
900 000	84343.27	46801.53	34487.92	28477.76	24985.12	22747.26	21222.50	20139.63
920 000	86217.56	47841.56	35254.31	29110.60	25540.34	23252.76	21694.11	20587.17
940 000	88091.86	48881.59	36020.71	29743.44	26095.57	23758.25	22165.72	21034.72
960 000	89966.15	49921.63	36787.11	30376.28	26650.79	24263.75	22637.33	21482.27
980 000	91840.45	50961.66	37553.51	31009.12	27206.02	24769.24	23108.94	21929.81
1 000 000	93714.74	52001.70	38319.91	31641.96	27761.24	25274.74	23580.56	22377.36
Coefficient	.093714742	.052001696	.038319906	.031641958	.027761241	.025274735	.023580556	.022377362

MONTHLY AMORTIZING PAYMENTS 22.25%

AMOUNT	9 YEARS	10 YEARS	15 YEARS	20 YEARS	25 YEARS	30 YEARS	35 YEARS	40 YEARS
10 000	214.97	208.40	192.47	187.70	186.17	185.67	185.50	185.44
20 000	429.95	416.80	384.93	375.40	372.34	371.33	371.00	370.89
30 000	644.92	625.21	577.40	563.10	558.51	557.00	556.50	556.33
40 000	859.90	833.61	769.87	750.80	744.68	742.66	742.00	741.78
50 000	1074.87	1042.01	962.33	938.50	930.84	928.33	927.50	927.22
60 000	1289.85	1250.41	1154.80	1126.20	1117.01	1113.99	1113.00	1112.66
70 000	1504.82	1458.81	1347.26	1313.90	1303.18	1299.66	1298.50	1298.11
80 000	1719.80	1667.21	1539.73	1501.60	1489.35	1485.33	1483.99	1483.55
90 000	1934.77	1875.62	1732.20	1689.30	1675.52	1670.99	1669.49	1669.00
100 000	2149.75	2084.02	1924.66	1877.00	1861.69	1856.66	1854.99	1854.44
110 000	2364.72	2292.42	2117.13	2064.70	2047.86	2042.32	2040.49	2039.89
120 000	2579.70	2500.82	2309.60	2252.40	2234.03	2227.99	2225.99	2225.33
130 000	2794.67	2709.22	2502.06	2440.10	2420.19	2413.65	2411.49	2410.77
140 000	3009.65	2917.62	2694.53	2627.80	2606.36	2599.32	2596.99	2596.22
150 000	3224.62	3126.03	2887.00	2815.50	2792.53	2784.99	2782.49	2781.66
160 000	3439.60	3334.43	3079.46	3003.20	2978.70	2970.65	2967.99	2967.11
170 000	3654.57	3542.83	3271.93	3190.90	3164.87	3156.32	3153.49	3152.55
180 000	3869.55	3751.23	3464.39	3378.60	3351.04	3341.98	3338.99	3337.99
190 000	4084.52	3959.63	3656.86	3566.30	3537.21	3527.65	3524.49	3523.44
200 000	4299.50	4168.03	3849.33	3754.00	3723.38	3713.32	3709.99	3708.88
210 000	4514.47	4376.44	4041.79	3941.70	3909.54	3898.98	3895.49	3894.33
220 000	4729.45	4584.84	4234.26	4129.40	4095.71	4084.65	4080.99	4079.77
230 000	4944.42	4793.24	4426.73	4317.10	4281.88	4270.31	4266.48	4265.21
240 000	5159.40	5001.64	4619.19	4504.80	4468.05	4455.98	4451.98	4450.66
250 000	5374.37	5210.04	4811.66	4692.50	4654.22	4641.64	4637.48	4636.10
260 000	5589.35	5418.44	5004.13	4880.20	4840.39	4827.31	4822.98	4821.55
270 000	5804.32	5626.85	5196.59	5067.90	5026.56	5012.98	5008.48	5006.99
280 000	6019.29	5835.25	5389.06	5255.60	5212.73	5198.64	5193.98	5192.44
290 000	6234.27	6043.65	5581.52	5443.30	5398.89	5384.31	5379.48	5377.88
300 000	6449.24	6252.05	5773.99	5631.00	5585.06	5569.97	5564.98	5563.32
320 000	6879.19	6668.85	6158.92	6006.40	5957.40	5941.30	5935.98	5934.21
340 000	7309.14	7085.66	6543.86	6381.80	6329.74	6312.64	6306.98	6305.10
360 000	7739.09	7502.46	6928.79	6757.20	6702.08	6683.97	6677.98	6675.99
380 000	8169.04	7919.26	7313.72	7132.60	7074.41	7055.30	7048.97	7046.88
400 000	8598.99	8336.07	7698.65	7508.00	7446.75	7426.63	7419.97	7417.76
420 000	9028.94	8752.87	8083.59	7883.40	7819.09	7797.96	7790.97	7788.65
440 000	9458.89	9169.68	8468.52	8258.80	8191.43	8169.29	8161.97	8159.54
460 000	9888.84	9586.48	8853.45	8634.20	8563.76	8540.62	8532.97	8530.43
480 000	10318.79	10003.28	9238.39	9009.60	8936.10	8911.96	8903.97	8901.32
500 000	10748.74	10420.09	9623.32	9385.00	9308.44	9283.29	9274.97	9272.21
520 000	11178.69	10836.89	10008.25	9760.40	9680.78	9654.62	9645.96	9643.09
540 000	11608.64	11253.69	10393.18	10135.80	10053.11	10025.95	10016.96	10013.98
560 000	12038.59	11670.50	10778.12	10511.19	10425.45	10397.28	10387.96	10384.87
580 000	12468.54	12087.30	11163.05	10886.59	10797.79	10768.61	10758.96	10755.76
600 000	12898.49	12504.10	11547.98	11261.99	11170.13	11139.95	11129.96	11126.65
620 000	13328.44	12920.91	11932.91	11637.39	11542.46	11511.28	11500.96	11497.53
640 000	13758.39	13337.71	12317.85	12012.79	11914.80	11882.61	11871.96	11868.42
660 000	14188.34	13754.51	12702.78	12388.19	12287.14	12253.94	12242.96	12239.31
680 000	14618.29	14171.32	13087.71	12763.59	12659.48	12625.27	12613.95	12610.20
700 000	15048.24	14588.12	13472.65	13138.99	13031.81	12996.60	12984.95	12981.09
720 000	15478.19	15004.92	13857.58	13514.39	13404.15	13367.93	13355.95	13351.98
740 000	15908.14	15421.73	14242.51	13889.79	13776.49	13739.27	13726.95	13722.86
760 000	16338.09	15838.53	14627.44	14265.19	14148.83	14110.60	14097.95	14093.75
780 000	16768.04	16255.33	15012.38	14640.59	14521.16	14481.93	14468.95	14464.64
800 000	17197.98	16672.14	15397.31	15015.99	14893.50	14853.26	14839.95	14835.53
820 000	17627.93	17088.94	15782.24	15391.39	15265.84	15224.59	15210.94	15206.42
840 000	18057.88	17505.74	16167.18	15766.79	15638.18	15595.92	15581.94	15577.31
860 000	18487.83	17922.55	16552.11	16142.19	16010.51	15967.26	15952.94	15948.19
880 000	18917.78	18339.35	16937.04	16517.59	16382.85	16338.59	16323.94	16319.08
900 000	19347.73	18756.15	17321.97	16892.99	16755.19	16709.92	16694.94	16689.97
920 000	19777.68	19172.96	17706.91	17268.39	17127.53	17081.25	17065.94	17060.86
940 000	20207.63	19589.76	18091.84	17643.79	17499.86	17452.58	17436.94	17431.75
960 000	20637.58	20006.56	18476.77	18019.19	17872.20	17823.91	17807.93	17802.63
980 000	21067.53	20423.37	18861.70	18394.59	18244.54	18195.24	18178.93	18173.52
1000 000	21497.48	20840.17	19246.64	18769.99	18616.88	18566.58	18549.93	18544.41
Coefficient	.021497481	.020840171	.019246637	.018769991	.018616875	.018566576	.018549932	.018544411

141

22.50% MONTHLY AMORTIZING PAYMENTS

AMOUNT	1 YEAR	2 YEARS	3 YEARS	4 YEARS	5 YEARS	6 YEARS	7 YEARS	8 YEARS
10 000	938.35	521.25	384.50	317.78	279.04	254.24	237.36	225.38
20 000	1876.70	1042.51	768.99	635.56	558.08	508.48	474.71	450.76
30 000	2815.06	1563.76	1153.49	953.34	837.12	762.71	712.07	676.14
40 000	3753.41	2085.02	1537.98	1271.13	1116.16	1016.95	949.43	901.53
50 000	4691.76	2606.27	1922.48	1588.91	1395.20	1271.19	1186.78	1126.91
60 000	5630.11	3127.52	2306.98	1906.69	1674.24	1525.43	1424.14	1352.29
70 000	6568.46	3648.78	2691.47	2224.47	1953.28	1779.66	1661.49	1577.67
80 000	7506.81	4170.03	3075.97	2542.25	2232.32	2033.90	1898.85	1803.05
90 000	8445.17	4691.29	3460.46	2860.03	2511.36	2288.14	2136.21	2028.43
100 000	9383.52	5212.54	3844.96	3177.81	2790.39	2542.38	2373.56	2253.81
110 000	10321.87	5733.79	4229.46	3495.60	3069.43	2796.61	2610.92	2479.20
120 000	11260.22	6255.05	4613.95	3813.38	3348.47	3050.85	2848.28	2704.58
130 000	12198.57	6776.30	4998.45	4131.16	3627.51	3305.09	3085.63	2929.96
140 000	13136.93	7297.56	5382.94	4448.94	3906.55	3559.33	3322.99	3155.34
150 000	14075.28	7818.81	5767.44	4766.72	4185.59	3813.57	3560.35	3380.72
160 000	15013.63	8340.06	6151.94	5084.50	4464.63	4067.80	3797.70	3606.10
170 000	15951.98	8861.32	6536.43	5402.29	4743.67	4322.04	4035.06	3831.48
180 000	16890.33	9382.57	6920.93	5720.07	5022.71	4576.28	4272.41	4056.87
190 000	17828.68	9903.83	7305.42	6037.85	5301.75	4830.52	4509.77	4282.25
200 000	18767.04	10425.08	7689.92	6355.63	5580.79	5084.75	4747.13	4507.63
210 000	19705.39	10946.33	8074.42	6673.41	5859.83	5338.99	4984.48	4733.01
220 000	20643.74	11467.59	8458.91	6991.19	6138.87	5593.23	5221.84	4958.39
230 000	21582.09	11988.84	8843.41	7308.97	6417.91	5847.47	5459.20	5183.77
240 000	22520.44	12510.10	9227.90	7626.76	6696.95	6101.70	5696.55	5409.15
250 000	23458.80	13031.35	9612.40	7944.54	6975.99	6355.94	5933.91	5634.54
260 000	24397.15	13552.60	9996.90	8262.32	7255.03	6610.18	6171.27	5859.92
270 000	25335.50	14073.86	10381.39	8580.10	7534.07	6864.42	6408.62	6085.30
280 000	26273.85	14595.11	10765.89	8897.88	7813.10	7118.66	6645.98	6310.68
290 000	27212.20	15116.37	11150.38	9215.66	8092.14	7372.89	6883.33	6536.06
300 000	28150.55	15637.62	11534.88	9533.45	8371.18	7627.13	7120.69	6761.44
320 000	30027.26	16680.13	12303.87	10169.01	8929.26	8135.61	7595.40	7212.21
340 000	31903.96	17722.63	13072.86	10804.57	9487.34	8644.08	8070.12	7662.97
360 000	33780.67	18765.14	13841.86	11440.13	10045.42	9152.56	8544.83	8113.73
380 000	35657.37	19807.65	14610.85	12075.70	10603.50	9661.03	9019.54	8564.49
400 000	37534.07	20850.16	15379.84	12711.26	11161.58	10169.51	9494.25	9015.26
420 000	39410.78	21892.67	16148.83	13346.82	11719.66	10677.98	9968.97	9466.02
440 000	41287.48	22935.17	16917.82	13982.39	12277.74	11186.46	10443.68	9916.78
460 000	43164.18	23977.68	17686.82	14617.95	12835.81	11694.93	10918.39	10367.55
480 000	45040.89	25020.19	18455.81	15253.51	13393.89	12203.41	11393.11	10818.31
500 000	46917.59	26062.70	19224.80	15889.08	13951.97	12711.88	11867.82	11269.07
520 000	48794.30	27105.21	19993.79	16524.64	14510.05	13220.36	12342.53	11719.83
540 000	50671.00	28147.71	20762.79	17160.20	15068.13	13728.84	12817.24	12170.60
560 000	52547.70	29190.22	21531.78	17795.76	15626.21	14237.31	13291.96	12621.36
580 000	54424.41	30232.73	22300.77	18431.33	16184.29	14745.79	13766.67	13072.12
600 000	56301.11	31275.24	23069.76	19066.89	16742.37	15254.26	14241.38	13522.89
620 000	58177.81	32317.75	23838.75	19702.45	17300.45	15762.74	14716.09	13973.65
640 000	60054.52	33360.25	24607.75	20338.02	17858.52	16271.21	15190.81	14424.41
660 000	61931.22	34402.76	25376.74	20973.58	18416.60	16779.69	15665.52	14875.18
680 000	63807.92	35445.27	26145.73	21609.14	18974.68	17288.16	16140.23	15325.94
700 000	65684.63	36487.78	26914.72	22244.71	19532.76	17796.64	16614.95	15776.70
720 000	67561.33	37530.29	27683.71	22880.27	20090.84	18305.11	17089.66	16227.46
740 000	69438.04	38572.79	28452.71	23515.83	20648.92	18813.59	17564.37	16678.23
760 000	71314.74	39615.30	29221.70	24151.39	21207.00	19322.06	18039.08	17128.99
780 000	73191.44	40657.81	29990.69	24786.96	21765.08	19830.54	18513.80	17579.75
800 000	75068.15	41700.32	30759.68	25422.52	22323.16	20339.02	18988.51	18030.52
820 000	76944.85	42742.83	31528.67	26058.08	22881.23	20847.49	19463.22	18481.28
840 000	78821.55	43785.33	32297.67	26693.65	23439.31	21355.97	19937.94	18932.04
860 000	80698.26	44827.84	33066.66	27329.21	23997.39	21864.44	20412.65	19382.80
880 000	82574.96	45870.35	33835.65	27964.77	24555.47	22372.92	20887.36	19833.57
900 000	84451.66	46912.86	34604.64	28600.34	25113.55	22881.39	21362.07	20284.33
920 000	86328.37	47955.37	35373.63	29235.90	25671.63	23389.87	21836.79	20735.09
940 000	88205.07	48997.87	36142.63	29871.46	26229.71	23898.34	22311.50	21185.86
960 000	90081.78	50040.38	36911.62	30507.02	26787.79	24406.82	22786.21	21636.62
980 000	91958.48	51082.89	37680.61	31142.59	27345.87	24915.29	23260.92	22087.38
1000 000	93835.18	52125.40	38449.60	31778.15	27903.95	25423.77	23735.64	22538.14
Coefficient	.093835183	.052125397	.038449602	.031778150	.027903945	.025423769	.023735637	.022538144

AMOUNT	9 YEARS	10 YEARS	15 YEARS	20 YEARS	25 YEARS	30 YEARS	35 YEARS	40 YEARS
10 000	216.64	210.11	194.36	189.70	188.22	187.73	187.58	187.53
20 000	433.27	420.22	388.72	379.39	376.43	375.47	375.15	375.05
30 000	649.91	630.34	583.09	569.09	564.65	563.20	562.73	562.58
40 000	866.54	840.45	777.45	758.79	752.86	750.94	750.31	750.10
50 000	1083.18	1050.56	971.81	948.49	941.08	938.67	937.88	937.63
60 000	1299.81	1260.67	1166.17	1138.18	1129.29	1126.40	1125.46	1125.15
70 000	1516.45	1470.78	1360.53	1327.88	1317.51	1314.14	1313.04	1312.68
80 000	1733.09	1680.89	1554.89	1517.58	1505.72	1501.87	1500.61	1500.20
90 000	1949.72	1891.01	1749.26	1707.27	1693.94	1689.61	1688.19	1687.73
100 000	2166.36	2101.12	1943.62	1896.97	1882.15	1877.34	1875.77	1875.25
110 000	2382.99	2311.23	2137.98	2086.67	2070.37	2065.07	2063.34	2062.78
120 000	2599.63	2521.34	2332.34	2276.36	2258.58	2252.81	2250.92	2250.30
130 000	2816.27	2731.45	2526.70	2466.06	2446.80	2440.54	2438.50	2437.83
140 000	3032.90	2941.57	2721.07	2655.76	2635.01	2628.28	2626.07	2625.35
150 000	3249.54	3151.68	2915.43	2845.46	2823.23	2816.01	2813.65	2812.88
160 000	3466.17	3361.79	3109.79	3035.15	3011.44	3003.74	3001.23	3000.40
170 000	3682.81	3571.90	3304.15	3224.85	3199.66	3191.48	3188.80	3187.93
180 000	3899.44	3782.01	3498.51	3414.55	3387.87	3379.21	3376.38	3375.45
190 000	4116.08	3992.12	3692.87	3604.24	3576.09	3566.95	3563.96	3562.98
200 000	4332.72	4202.24	3887.24	3793.94	3764.30	3754.68	3751.53	3750.50
210 000	4549.35	4412.35	4081.60	3983.64	3952.52	3942.41	3939.11	3938.03
220 000	4765.99	4622.46	4275.96	4173.33	4140.73	4130.15	4126.69	4125.55
230 000	4982.62	4832.57	4470.32	4363.03	4328.95	4317.88	4314.26	4313.08
240 000	5199.26	5042.68	4664.68	4552.73	4517.16	4505.62	4501.84	4500.60
250 000	5415.90	5252.80	4859.05	4742.43	4705.38	4693.35	4689.42	4688.13
260 000	5632.53	5462.91	5053.41	4932.12	4893.59	4881.08	4876.99	4875.65
270 000	5849.17	5673.02	5247.77	5121.82	5081.81	5068.82	5064.57	5063.18
280 000	6065.80	5883.13	5442.13	5311.52	5270.02	5256.55	5252.15	5250.70
290 000	6282.44	6093.24	5636.49	5501.21	5458.24	5444.29	5439.72	5438.23
300 000	6499.07	6303.36	5830.85	5690.91	5646.45	5632.02	5627.30	5625.75
320 000	6932.35	6723.58	6219.58	6070.30	6022.88	6007.49	6002.45	6000.80
340 000	7365.62	7143.80	6608.30	6449.70	6399.31	6382.96	6377.61	6375.86
360 000	7798.89	7564.03	6997.03	6829.09	6775.74	6758.42	6752.76	6750.91
380 000	8232.16	7984.25	7385.75	7208.49	7152.17	7133.89	7127.91	7125.96
400 000	8665.43	8404.47	7774.47	7587.88	7528.60	7509.36	7503.07	7501.01
420 000	9098.70	8824.70	8163.20	7967.27	7905.03	7884.83	7878.22	7876.06
440 000	9531.98	9244.92	8551.92	8346.67	8281.46	8260.30	8253.37	8251.11
460 000	9965.25	9665.14	8940.64	8726.06	8657.89	8635.76	8628.53	8626.16
480 000	10398.52	10085.37	9329.37	9105.46	9034.32	9011.23	9003.68	9001.21
500 000	10831.79	10505.59	9718.09	9484.85	9410.75	9386.70	9378.84	9376.26
520 000	11265.06	10925.82	10106.81	9864.24	9787.19	9762.17	9753.99	9751.31
540 000	11698.33	11346.04	10495.54	10243.64	10163.62	10137.64	10129.14	10126.36
560 000	12131.61	11766.26	10884.26	10623.03	10540.05	10513.10	10504.30	10501.41
580 000	12564.88	12186.49	11272.99	11002.43	10916.48	10888.57	10879.45	10876.46
600 000	12998.15	12606.71	11661.71	11381.82	11292.91	11264.04	11254.60	11251.51
620 000	13431.42	13026.93	12050.43	11761.21	11669.34	11639.51	11629.76	11626.56
640 000	13864.69	13447.16	12439.16	12140.61	12045.77	12014.98	12004.91	12001.61
660 000	14297.96	13867.38	12827.88	12520.00	12422.20	12390.44	12380.06	12376.66
680 000	14731.24	14287.61	13216.60	12899.40	12798.63	12765.91	12755.22	12751.71
700 000	15164.51	14707.83	13605.33	13278.79	13175.06	13141.38	13130.37	13126.76
720 000	15597.78	15128.05	13994.05	13658.18	13551.49	13516.85	13505.52	13501.81
740 000	16031.05	15548.28	14382.77	14037.58	13927.92	13892.32	13880.68	13876.86
760 000	16464.32	15968.50	14771.50	14416.97	14304.35	14267.78	14255.83	14251.91
780 000	16897.59	16388.72	15160.22	14796.37	14680.78	14643.25	14630.98	14626.96
800 000	17330.86	16808.95	15548.95	15175.76	15057.21	15018.72	15006.14	15002.01
820 000	17764.14	17229.17	15937.67	15555.15	15433.64	15394.19	15381.29	15377.06
840 000	18197.41	17649.39	16326.39	15934.55	15810.07	15769.66	15756.44	15752.11
860 000	18630.68	18069.62	16715.12	16313.94	16186.50	16145.12	16131.60	16127.16
880 000	19063.95	18489.84	17103.84	16693.34	16562.93	16520.59	16506.75	16502.21
900 000	19497.22	18910.07	17492.56	17072.73	16939.36	16896.06	16881.90	16877.26
920 000	19930.49	19330.29	17881.29	17452.12	17315.79	17271.53	17257.06	17252.31
940 000	20363.77	19750.51	18270.01	17831.52	17692.22	17647.00	17632.21	17627.36
960 000	20797.04	20170.74	18658.73	18210.91	18068.65	18022.46	18007.36	18002.41
980 000	21230.31	20590.96	19047.46	18590.31	18445.08	18397.93	18382.52	18377.46
1000 000	21663.58	21011.18	19436.18	18969.70	18821.51	18773.40	18757.67	18752.52
Coefficient	.021663581	.021011184	.019436182	.018969701	.018821510	.018773399	.018757670	.018752515

MONTHLY AMORTIZING PAYMENTS

AMOUNT	1 YEAR	2 YEARS	3 YEARS	4 YEARS	5 YEARS	6 YEARS	7 YEARS	8 YEARS
10 000	939.56	522.49	385.80	319.15	280.47	255.73	238.91	226.99
20 000	1879.11	1044.99	771.59	638.29	560.94	511.46	477.82	453.99
30 000	2818.67	1567.48	1157.39	957.44	841.41	767.20	716.74	680.98
40 000	3758.23	2089.97	1543.18	1276.59	1121.88	1022.93	955.65	907.98
50 000	4697.79	2612.46	1928.98	1595.73	1402.35	1278.66	1194.56	1134.97
60 000	5637.34	3134.96	2314.77	1914.88	1682.82	1534.39	1433.47	1361.97
70 000	6576.90	3657.45	2700.57	2234.03	1963.29	1790.13	1672.38	1588.96
80 000	7516.46	4179.94	3086.36	2553.17	2243.76	2045.86	1911.29	1815.95
90 000	8456.01	4702.43	3472.16	2872.32	2524.23	2301.59	2150.21	2042.95
100 000	9395.57	5224.93	3857.95	3191.47	2804.70	2557.32	2389.12	2269.94
110 000	10335.13	5747.42	4243.75	3510.61	3085.17	2813.05	2628.03	2496.94
120 000	11274.69	6269.91	4629.54	3829.76	3365.64	3068.79	2866.94	2723.93
130 000	12214.24	6792.40	5015.34	4148.91	3646.11	3324.52	3105.85	2950.92
140 000	13153.80	7314.90	5401.14	4468.05	3926.58	3580.25	3344.77	3177.92
150 000	14093.36	7837.39	5786.93	4787.20	4207.05	3835.98	3583.68	3404.91
160 000	15032.91	8359.88	6172.73	5106.34	4487.52	4091.72	3822.59	3631.91
170 000	15972.47	8882.38	6558.52	5425.49	4767.99	4347.45	4061.50	3858.90
180 000	16912.03	9404.87	6944.32	5744.64	5048.46	4603.18	4300.41	4085.90
190 000	17851.59	9927.36	7330.11	6063.78	5328.93	4858.91	4539.32	4312.89
200 000	18791.14	10449.85	7715.91	6382.93	5609.40	5114.65	4778.24	4539.88
210 000	19730.70	10972.35	8101.70	6702.08	5889.87	5370.38	5017.15	4766.88
220 000	20670.26	11494.84	8487.50	7021.22	6170.34	5626.11	5256.06	4993.87
230 000	21609.81	12017.33	8873.29	7340.37	6450.82	5881.84	5494.97	5220.87
240 000	22549.37	12539.82	9259.09	7659.52	6731.29	6137.57	5733.88	5447.86
250 000	23488.93	13062.32	9644.89	7978.66	7011.76	6393.31	5972.80	5674.86
260 000	24428.49	13584.81	10030.68	8297.81	7292.23	6649.04	6211.71	5901.85
270 000	25368.04	14107.30	10416.48	8616.96	7572.70	6904.77	6450.62	6128.84
280 000	26307.60	14629.79	10802.27	8936.10	7853.17	7160.50	6689.53	6355.84
290 000	27247.16	15152.29	11188.07	9255.25	8133.64	7416.24	6928.44	6582.83
300 000	28186.71	15674.78	11573.86	9574.40	8414.11	7671.97	7167.35	6809.83
320 000	30065.83	16719.77	12345.45	10212.69	8975.05	8183.43	7645.18	7263.81
340 000	31944.94	17764.75	13117.04	10850.98	9535.99	8694.90	8123.00	7717.80
360 000	33824.06	18809.74	13888.63	11489.28	10096.93	9206.36	8600.83	8171.79
380 000	35703.17	19854.72	14660.23	12127.57	10657.87	9717.83	9078.65	8625.78
400 000	37582.29	20899.71	15431.82	12765.86	11218.81	10229.29	9556.47	9079.77
420 000	39461.40	21944.69	16203.41	13404.16	11779.75	10740.76	10034.30	9533.76
440 000	41340.51	22989.68	16975.00	14042.45	12340.69	11252.22	10512.12	9987.75
460 000	43219.63	24034.66	17746.59	14680.74	12901.63	11763.68	10989.94	10441.73
480 000	45098.74	25079.65	18518.18	15319.03	13462.57	12275.15	11467.77	10895.72
500 000	46977.86	26124.63	19289.77	15957.33	14023.51	12786.61	11945.59	11349.71
520 000	48856.97	27169.62	20061.36	16595.62	14584.45	13298.08	12423.42	11803.70
540 000	50736.09	28214.60	20832.95	17233.91	15145.39	13809.54	12901.24	12257.69
560 000	52615.20	29259.59	21604.54	17872.21	15706.33	14321.01	13379.06	12711.68
580 000	54494.31	30304.57	22376.13	18510.50	16267.27	14832.47	13856.89	13165.66
600 000	56373.43	31349.56	23147.72	19148.79	16828.21	15343.94	14334.71	13619.65
620 000	58252.54	32394.55	23919.31	19787.09	17389.15	15855.40	14812.53	14073.64
640 000	60131.66	33439.53	24690.91	20425.38	17950.09	16366.87	15290.36	14527.63
660 000	62010.77	34484.52	25462.50	21063.67	18511.03	16878.33	15768.18	14981.62
680 000	63889.89	35529.50	26234.09	21701.97	19071.97	17389.79	16246.00	15435.61
700 000	65769.00	36574.49	27005.68	22340.26	19632.92	17901.26	16723.83	15889.59
720 000	67648.11	37619.47	27777.27	22978.55	20193.86	18412.72	17201.65	16343.58
740 000	69527.23	38664.46	28548.86	23616.84	20754.80	18924.19	17679.48	16797.57
760 000	71406.34	39709.44	29320.45	24255.14	21315.74	19435.65	18157.30	17251.56
780 000	73285.46	40754.43	30092.04	24893.43	21876.68	19947.12	18635.12	17705.55
800 000	75164.57	41799.41	30863.63	25531.72	22437.62	20458.58	19112.95	18159.54
820 000	77043.69	42844.40	31635.22	26170.02	22998.56	20970.05	19590.77	18613.53
840 000	78922.80	43889.38	32406.81	26808.31	23559.50	21481.51	20068.59	19067.51
860 000	80801.91	44934.37	33178.40	27446.60	24120.44	21992.98	20546.42	19521.50
880 000	82681.03	45979.35	33950.00	28084.90	24681.38	22504.44	21024.24	19975.49
900 000	84560.14	47024.34	34721.59	28723.19	25242.32	23015.90	21502.06	20429.48
920 000	86439.26	48069.33	35493.18	29361.48	25803.26	23527.37	21979.89	20883.47
940 000	88318.37	49114.31	36264.77	29999.78	26364.20	24038.83	22457.71	21337.46
960 000	90197.49	50159.30	37036.36	30638.07	26925.14	24550.30	22935.54	21791.44
980 000	92076.60	51204.28	37807.95	31276.36	27486.08	25061.76	23413.36	22245.43
1000 000	93955.71	52249.27	38579.54	31914.66	28047.02	25573.23	23891.18	22699.42
Coefficient	.093955714	.052249267	.038579540	.031914655	.028047022	.025573227	.023891183	.022699421

144

MONTHLY AMORTIZING PAYMENTS   22.75%

AMOUNT	9 YEARS	10 YEARS	15 YEARS	20 YEARS	25 YEARS	30 YEARS	35 YEARS	40 YEARS
10 000	218.30	211.83	196.26	191.70	190.26	189.80	189.65	189.61
20 000	436.60	423.65	392.52	383.39	380.53	379.61	379.31	379.21
30 000	654.91	635.48	588.79	575.09	570.79	569.41	568.96	568.82
40 000	873.21	847.31	785.05	766.79	761.05	759.21	758.62	758.43
50 000	1091.51	1059.14	981.31	958.49	951.32	949.02	948.27	948.03
60 000	1309.81	1270.96	1177.57	1150.18	1141.58	1138.82	1137.93	1137.64
70 000	1528.11	1482.79	1373.83	1341.88	1331.84	1328.62	1327.58	1327.24
80 000	1746.42	1694.62	1570.09	1533.58	1522.11	1518.42	1517.24	1516.85
90 000	1964.72	1906.44	1766.36	*725.27	1712.37	1708.23	1706.89	1706.46
100 000	2183.02	2118.27	1962.62	1916.97	1902.63	1898.03	1896.54	1896.06
110 000	2401.32	2330.10	2158.88	2108.67	2092.90	2087.83	2086.20	2085.67
120 000	2619.62	2541.93	2355.14	2300.37	2283.16	2277.64	2275.85	2275.28
130 000	2837.93	2753.75	2551.40	2492.06	2473.42	2467.44	2465.51	2464.88
140 000	3056.23	2965.58	2747.67	2683.76	2663.68	2657.24	2655.16	2654.49
150 000	3274.53	3177.41	2943.93	2875.46	2853.95	2847.05	2844.82	2844.10
160 000	3492.83	3389.24	3140.19	3067.15	3044.21	3036.85	3034.47	3033.70
170 000	3711.13	3601.06	3336.45	3258.85	3234.47	3226.65	3224.13	3223.31
180 000	3929.44	3812.89	3532.71	3450.55	3424.74	3416.46	3413.78	3412.92
190 000	4147.74	4024.72	3728.97	3642.25	3615.00	3606.26	3603.44	3602.52
200 000	4366.04	4236.54	3925.24	3833.94	3805.26	3796.06	3793.09	3792.13
210 000	4584.34	4448.37	4121.50	4025.64	3995.53	3985.87	3982.74	3981.73
220 000	4802.64	4660.20	4317.76	4217.34	4185.79	4175.67	4172.40	4171.34
230 000	5020.95	4872.03	4514.02	4409.04	4376.05	4365.47	4362.05	4360.95
240 000	5239.25	5083.85	4710.28	4600.73	4566.32	4555.27	4551.71	4550.55
250 000	5457.55	5295.68	4906.55	4792.43	4756.58	4745.08	4741.36	4740.16
260 000	5675.85	5507.51	5102.81	4984.13	4946.84	4934.88	4931.02	4929.77
270 000	5894.15	5719.33	5299.07	5175.82	5137.11	5124.68	5120.67	5119.37
280 000	6112.45	5931.16	5495.33	5367.52	5327.37	5314.49	5310.33	5308.98
290 000	6330.76	6142.99	5691.59	5559.22	5517.63	5504.29	5499.98	5498.59
300 000	6549.06	6354.82	5887.86	5750.92	5707.90	5694.09	5689.63	5688.19
320 000	6985.66	6778.47	6280.38	6134.31	6088.42	6073.70	6068.94	6067.40
340 000	7422.27	7202.13	6672.90	6517.70	6468.95	6453.31	6448.25	6446.62
360 000	7858.87	7625.78	7065.43	6901.10	6849.48	6832.91	6827.56	6825.83
380 000	8295.47	8049.43	7457.95	7284.49	7230.00	7212.52	7206.87	7205.04
400 000	8732.08	8473.09	7850.47	7667.89	7610.53	7592.12	7586.18	7584.26
420 000	9168.68	8896.74	8243.00	8051.28	7991.05	7971.73	7965.49	7963.47
440 000	9605.29	9320.40	8635.52	8434.68	8371.58	8351.34	8344.80	8342.68
460 000	10041.89	9744.05	9028.04	8818.07	8752.11	8730.94	8724.11	8721.89
480 000	10478.49	10167.71	9420.57	9201.46	9132.63	9110.55	9103.42	9101.11
500 000	10915.10	10591.36	9813.09	9584.86	9513.16	9490.16	9482.72	9480.32
520 000	11351.70	11015.02	10205.62	9968.25	9893.69	9869.76	9862.03	9859.53
540 000	11788.31	11438.67	10598.14	10351.65	10274.21	10249.37	10241.34	10238.75
560 000	12224.91	11862.32	10990.66	10735.04	10654.74	10628.97	10620.65	10617.96
580 000	12661.51	12285.98	11383.19	11118.44	11035.27	11008.58	10999.96	10997.17
600 000	13098.12	12709.63	11775.71	11501.83	11415.79	11388.19	11379.27	11376.38
620 000	13534.72	13133.29	12168.23	11885.23	11796.32	11767.79	11758.58	11755.60
640 000	13971.33	13556.94	12560.76	12268.62	12176.85	12147.40	12137.89	12134.81
660 000	14407.93	13980.60	12953.28	12652.01	12557.37	12527.01	12517.20	12514.02
680 000	14844.53	14404.25	13345.81	13035.41	12937.90	12906.61	12896.51	12893.23
700 000	15281.14	14827.91	13738.33	13418.80	13318.42	13286.22	13275.81	13272.45
720 000	15717.74	15251.56	1413C.85	13802.20	13698.95	13665.82	13655.12	13651.66
740 000	16154.35	15675.21	14523.38	14185.59	14079.48	14045.43	14034.43	14030.87
760 000	16590.95	16098.87	14915.90	14568.99	14460.00	14425.04	14413.74	14410.09
780 000	17027.55	16522.52	15308.42	14952.38	14840.53	14804.64	14793.05	14789.30
800 000	17464.16	16946.18	15700.95	15335.77	15221.06	15184.25	15172.36	15168.51
820 000	17900.76	17369.83	16093.47	15719.17	15601.58	15563.86	15551.67	15547.72
840 000	18337.36	17793.49	16485.99	16102.56	15982.11	15943.46	15930.98	15926.94
860 000	18773.97	18217.14	16878.52	16485.96	16362.64	16323.07	16310.29	16306.15
880 000	19210.57	18640.80	17271.04	16869.35	16743.16	16702.67	16689.60	16685.36
900 000	19647.18	19064.45	17663.57	17252.75	17123.69	17082.28	17068.91	17064.58
920 000	20083.78	19488.10	18056.09	17636.14	17504.22	17461.89	17448.21	17443.79
940 000	20520.38	19911.76	18448.61	18019.53	17884.74	17841.49	17827.52	17823.00
960 000	20956.99	20335.41	18841.14	18402.93	18265.27	18221.10	18206.83	18202.21
980 000	21393.59	20759.07	19233.66	18786.32	18645.79	18600.70	18586.14	18581.43
1000 000	21830.20	21182.72	19626.18	19169.72	19026.32	18980.31	18965.45	18960.64
Coefficient	.021830196	.021182722	.019626184	.019169718	.019026321	.018980311	.018965450	.018960639

145

23.00% MONTHLY AMORTIZING PAYMENTS

AMOUNT	1 YEAR	2 YEARS	3 YEARS	4 YEARS	5 YEARS	6 YEARS	7 YEARS	8 YEARS
10 000	940.76	523.73	387.10	320.51	281.90	257.23	240.47	228.61
20 000	1881.53	1047.47	774.19	641.03	563.81	514.46	480.94	457.22
30 000	2822.29	1571.20	1161.29	961.54	845.71	771.69	721.42	685.84
40 000	3763.05	2094.93	1548.39	1282.06	1127.62	1028.92	961.89	914.45
50 000	4703.82	2618.67	1935.49	1602.57	1409.52	1286.16	1202.36	1143.06
60 000	5644.58	3142.40	2322.58	1923.09	1691.43	1543.39	1442.83	1371.67
70 000	6585.34	3666.13	2709.68	2243.60	1973.33	1800.62	1683.30	1600.28
80 000	7526.11	4189.86	3096.78	2564.12	2255.24	2057.85	1923.78	1828.90
90 000	8466.87	4713.60	3483.87	2884.63	2537.14	2315.08	2164.25	2057.51
100 000	9407.63	5237.33	3870.97	3205.15	2819.05	2572.31	2404.72	2286.12
110 000	10348.40	5761.06	4258.07	3525.66	3100.95	2829.54	2645.19	2514.73
120 000	11289.16	6284.80	4645.17	3846.18	3382.86	3086.77	2885.66	2743.34
130 000	12229.92	6808.53	5032.26	4166.69	3664.76	3344.00	3126.14	2971.95
140 000	13170.69	7332.26	5419.36	4487.21	3946.67	3601.24	3366.61	3200.57
150 000	14111.45	7856.00	5806.46	4807.72	4228.57	3858.47	3607.08	3429.18
160 000	15052.21	8379.73	6193.56	5128.24	4510.48	4115.70	3847.55	3657.79
170 000	15992.98	8903.46	6580.65	5448.75	4792.38	4372.93	4088.02	3886.40
180 000	16933.74	9427.20	6967.75	5769.26	5074.28	4630.16	4328.49	4115.01
190 000	17874.50	9950.93	7354.85	6089.78	5356.19	4887.39	4568.97	4343.63
200 000	18815.27	10474.66	7741.94	6410.29	5638.09	5144.62	4809.44	4572.24
210 000	19756.03	10998.39	8129.04	6730.81	5920.00	5401.85	5049.91	4800.85
220 000	20696.79	11522.13	8516.14	7051.32	6201.90	5659.08	5290.38	5029.46
230 000	21637.55	12045.86	8903.24	7371.84	6483.81	5916.32	5530.85	5258.07
240 000	22578.32	12569.59	9290.33	7692.35	6765.71	6173.55	5771.33	5486.69
250 000	23519.08	13093.33	9677.43	8012.87	7047.62	6430.78	6011.80	5715.30
260 000	24459.84	13617.06	10064.53	8333.38	7329.52	6688.01	6252.27	5943.91
270 000	25400.61	14140.79	10451.62	8653.90	7611.43	6945.24	6492.74	6172.52
280 000	26341.37	14664.53	10838.72	8974.41	7893.33	7202.47	6733.21	6401.13
290 000	27282.13	15188.26	11225.82	9294.93	8175.24	7459.70	6973.69	6629.75
300 000	28222.90	15711.99	11612.92	9615.44	8457.14	7716.93	7214.16	6858.36
320 000	30104.42	16759.46	12387.11	10256.47	9020.95	8231.40	7695.10	7315.58
340 000	31985.95	17806.92	13161.30	10897.50	9584.76	8745.86	8176.05	7772.80
360 000	33867.48	18854.39	13935.50	11538.53	10148.57	9260.32	8656.99	8230.03
380 000	35749.00	19901.86	14709.69	12179.56	10712.38	9774.78	9137.93	8687.25
400 000	37630.53	20949.32	15483.89	12820.59	11276.19	10289.24	9618.88	9144.48
420 000	39512.06	21996.79	16258.08	13461.62	11840.00	10803.71	10099.82	9601.70
440 000	41393.58	23044.26	17032.28	14102.65	12403.81	11318.17	10580.77	10058.92
460 000	43275.11	24091.72	17806.47	14743.68	12967.62	11832.63	11061.71	10516.15
480 000	45156.64	25139.19	18580.67	15384.71	13531.43	12347.09	11542.65	10973.37
500 000	47038.16	26186.65	19354.86	16025.74	14095.24	12861.56	12023.60	11430.60
520 000	48919.69	27234.12	20129.05	16666.76	14659.04	13376.02	12504.54	11887.82
540 000	50801.22	28281.59	20903.25	17307.79	15222.85	13890.48	12985.48	12345.04
560 000	52682.74	29329.05	21677.44	17948.82	15786.66	14404.94	13466.43	12802.27
580 000	54564.27	30376.52	22451.64	18589.85	16350.47	14919.40	13947.37	13259.49
600 000	56445.80	31423.98	23225.83	19230.88	16914.28	15433.87	14428.32	13716.71
620 000	58327.32	32471.45	24000.03	19871.91	17478.09	15948.33	14909.26	14173.94
640 000	60208.85	33518.92	24774.22	20512.94	18041.90	16462.79	15390.20	14631.16
660 000	62090.38	34566.38	25548.42	21153.97	18605.71	16977.25	15871.15	15088.39
680 000	63971.90	35613.85	26322.61	21795.00	19169.52	17491.71	16352.09	15545.61
700 000	65853.43	36661.32	27096.80	22436.03	19733.33	18006.18	16833.04	16002.83
720 000	67734.95	37708.78	27871.00	23077.06	20297.14	18520.64	17313.98	16460.06
740 000	69616.48	38756.25	28645.19	23718.09	20860.95	19035.10	17794.92	16917.28
760 000	71498.01	39803.71	29419.39	24359.12	21424.76	19549.56	18275.87	17374.51
780 000	73379.53	40851.18	30193.58	25000.15	21988.57	20064.03	18756.81	17831.73
800 000	75261.06	41898.65	30967.78	25641.18	22552.38	20578.49	19237.76	18288.95
820 000	77142.59	42946.11	31741.97	26282.21	23116.19	21092.95	19718.70	18746.18
840 000	79024.11	43993.58	32516.16	26923.24	23680.00	21607.41	20199.64	19203.40
860 000	80905.64	45041.04	33290.36	27564.27	24243.81	22121.87	20680.59	19660.62
880 000	82787.17	46088.51	34064.55	28205.29	24807.61	22636.34	21161.53	20117.85
900 000	84668.69	47135.98	34838.75	28846.32	25371.42	23150.80	21642.47	20575.07
920 000	86550.22	48183.44	35612.94	29487.35	25935.23	23665.26	22123.42	21032.30
940 000	88431.75	49230.91	36387.14	30128.38	26499.04	24179.72	22604.36	21489.52
960 000	90313.27	50278.38	37161.33	30769.41	27062.85	24694.19	23085.31	21946.74
980 000	92194.80	51325.84	37935.53	31410.44	27626.66	25208.65	23566.25	22403.97
1000 000	94076.33	52373.31	38709.72	32051.47	28190.47	25723.11	24047.19	22861.19
Coefficient	.094076326	.052373308	.038709720	.032051471	.028190471	.025723110	.024047194	.022861191

AMOUNT	9 YEARS	10 YEARS	15 YEARS	20 YEARS	25 YEARS	30 YEARS	35 YEARS	40 YEARS
10 000	219.97	213.55	198.17	193.70	192.31	191.87	191.73	191.69
20 000	439.95	427.10	396.33	387.40	384.63	383.75	383.47	383.38
30 000	659.92	640.64	594.50	581.10	576.94	575.62	575.20	575.06
40 000	879.89	854.19	792.67	774.80	769.25	767.49	766.93	766.75
50 000	1099.87	1067.74	990.83	968.50	961.56	959.37	958.66	958.44
60 000	1319.84	1281.29	1189.00	1162.20	1153.88	1151.24	1150.40	1150.13
70 000	1539.81	1494.83	1387.16	1355.90	1346.19	1343.11	1342.13	1341.81
80 000	1759.79	1708.38	1585.33	1549.60	1538.50	1534.98	1533.86	1533.50
90 000	1979.76	1921.93	1783.50	1743.30	1730.82	1726.86	1725.59	1725.19
100 000	2199.73	2135.48	1981.66	1937.00	1923.13	1918.73	1917.33	1916.88
110 000	2419.71	2349.03	2179.83	2130.70	2115.44	2110.60	2109.06	2108.57
120 000	2639.68	2562.57	2378.00	2324.40	2307.76	2302.48	2300.79	2300.25
130 000	2859.65	2776.12	2576.16	2518.10	2500.07	2494.35	2492.52	2491.94
140 000	3079.63	2989.67	2774.33	2711.80	2692.38	2686.22	2684.26	2683.63
150 000	3299.60	3203.22	2972.50	2905.50	2884.69	2878.10	2875.99	2875.32
160 000	3519.57	3416.76	3170.66	3099.21	3077.01	3069.97	3067.72	3067.00
170 000	3739.54	3630.31	3368.83	3292.91	3269.32	3261.84	3259.46	3258.69
180 000	3959.52	3843.86	3566.99	3486.61	3461.63	3453.72	3451.19	3450.38
190 000	4179.49	4057.41	3765.16	3680.31	3653.95	3645.59	3642.92	3642.07
200 000	4399.46	4270.96	3963.33	3874.01	3846.26	3837.46	3834.65	3833.76
210 000	4619.44	4484.50	4161.49	4067.71	4038.57	4029.33	4026.39	4025.44
220 000	4839.41	4698.05	4359.66	4261.41	4230.89	4221.21	4218.12	4217.13
230 000	5059.38	4911.60	4557.83	4455.11	4423.20	4413.08	4409.85	4408.82
240 000	5279.36	5125.15	4755.99	4648.81	4615.51	4604.95	4601.58	4600.51
250 000	5499.33	5338.70	4954.16	4842.51	4807.82	4796.83	4793.32	4792.20
260 000	5719.30	5552.24	5152.33	5036.21	5000.14	4988.70	4985.05	4983.88
270 000	5939.28	5765.79	5350.49	5229.91	5192.45	5180.57	5176.78	5175.57
280 000	6159.25	5979.34	5548.66	5423.61	5384.76	5372.45	5368.52	5367.26
290 000	6379.22	6192.89	5746.82	5617.31	5577.08	5564.32	5560.25	5558.95
300 000	6599.20	6406.43	5944.99	5811.01	5769.39	5756.19	5751.98	5750.63
320 000	7039.14	6833.53	6341.32	6198.41	6154.02	6139.94	6135.45	6134.01
340 000	7479.09	7260.63	6737.66	6585.81	6538.64	6523.68	6518.91	6517.39
360 000	7919.04	7687.72	7133.99	6973.21	6923.27	6907.43	6902.38	6900.76
380 000	8358.98	8114.82	7530.32	7360.61	7307.89	7291.18	7285.84	7284.14
400 000	8798.93	8541.91	7926.65	7748.01	7692.52	7674.92	7669.31	7667.51
420 000	9238.88	8969.01	8322.99	8135.41	8077.15	8058.67	8052.77	8050.89
440 000	9678.82	9396.10	8719.32	8522.81	8461.77	8442.42	8436.24	8434.26
460 000	10118.77	9823.20	9115.65	8910.22	8846.40	8826.16	8819.70	8817.64
480 000	10558.71	10250.29	9511.98	9297.62	9231.02	9209.91	9203.17	9201.01
500 000	10998.66	10677.39	9908.32	9685.02	9615.65	9593.65	9586.63	9584.39
520 000	11438.61	11104.49	10304.65	10072.42	10000.27	9977.40	9970.10	9967.77
540 000	11878.55	11531.58	10700.98	10459.82	10384.90	10361.15	10353.57	10351.14
560 000	12318.50	11958.68	11097.32	10847.22	10769.53	10744.89	10737.03	10734.52
580 000	12758.45	12385.77	11493.65	11234.62	11154.15	11128.64	11120.50	11117.89
600 000	13198.39	12812.87	11889.98	11622.02	11538.78	11512.38	11503.96	11501.27
620 000	13638.34	13239.96	12286.31	12009.42	11923.40	11896.13	11887.43	11884.64
640 000	14078.29	13667.06	12682.65	12396.82	12308.03	12279.88	12270.89	12268.02
660 000	14518.23	14094.15	13078.98	12784.22	12692.66	12663.62	12654.36	12651.39
680 000	14958.18	14521.25	13475.31	13171.62	13077.28	13047.37	13037.82	13034.77
700 000	15398.13	14948.35	13871.64	13559.02	13461.91	13431.12	13421.29	13418.15
720 000	15838.07	15375.44	14267.98	13946.42	13846.53	13814.86	13804.75	13801.52
740 000	16278.02	15802.54	14664.31	14333.82	14231.16	14198.61	14188.22	14184.90
760 000	16717.96	16229.63	15060.64	14721.23	14615.79	14582.35	14571.68	14568.27
780 000	17157.91	16656.73	15456.98	15108.63	15000.41	14966.10	14955.15	14951.65
800 000	17597.86	17083.82	15853.31	15496.03	15385.04	15349.85	15338.62	15335.02
820 000	18037.80	17510.92	16249.64	15883.43	15769.66	15733.59	15722.08	15718.40
840 000	18477.75	17938.02	16645.97	16270.83	16154.29	16117.34	16105.55	16101.78
860 000	18917.70	18365.11	17042.31	16658.23	16538.92	16501.08	16489.01	16485.15
880 000	19357.64	18792.21	17438.64	17045.63	16923.54	16884.83	16872.48	16868.53
900 000	19797.59	19219.30	17834.97	17433.03	17308.17	17268.58	17255.94	17251.90
920 000	20237.54	19646.40	18231.30	17820.43	17692.79	17652.32	17639.41	17635.28
940 000	20677.48	20073.49	18627.64	18207.83	18077.42	18036.07	18022.87	18018.65
960 000	21117.43	20500.59	19023.97	18595.23	18462.05	18419.82	18406.34	18402.03
980 000	21557.38	20927.68	19420.30	18982.63	18846.67	18803.56	18789.80	18785.40
1000 000	21997.32	21354.78	19816.63	19370.03	19231.30	19187.31	19173.27	19168.78
Coefficient	.021997322	.021354780	.019816635	.019370033	.013231298	.019187308	.019173269	.019168780

147

23.25% MONTHLY AMORTIZING PAYMENTS

AMOUNT	1 YEAR	2 YEARS	3 YEARS	4 YEARS	5 YEARS	6 YEARS	7 YEARS	8 YEARS
10 000	941.97	524.98	388.40	321.89	283.34	258.73	242.04	230.23
20 000	1883.94	1049.95	776.80	643.77	566.69	517.47	484.07	460.47
30 000	2825.91	1574.93	1165.20	965.66	850.03	776.20	726.11	690.70
40 000	3767.88	2099.90	1553.61	1287.54	1133.37	1034.94	968.15	920.94
50 000	4709.85	2624.88	1942.01	1609.43	1416.71	1293.67	1210.18	1151.17
60 000	5651.82	3149.85	2330.41	1931.32	1700.06	1552.40	1452.22	1381.41
70 000	6593.79	3674.83	2718.81	2253.20	1983.40	1811.14	1694.26	1611.64
80 000	7535.76	4199.80	3107.21	2575.09	2266.74	2069.87	1936.29	1841.88
90 000	8477.73	4724.78	3495.61	2896.97	2550.09	2328.61	2178.33	2072.11
100 000	9419.70	5249.75	3884.01	3218.86	2833.43	2587.34	2420.37	2302.35
110 000	10361.67	5774.73	4272.42	3540.75	3116.77	2846.08	2662.40	2532.58
120 000	11303.64	6299.70	4660.82	3862.63	3400.11	3104.81	2904.44	2762.81
130 000	12245.61	6824.68	5049.22	4184.52	3683.46	3363.54	3146.48	2993.05
140 000	13187.58	7349.65	5437.62	4506.40	3966.80	3622.28	3388.51	3223.28
150 000	14129.55	7874.63	5826.02	4828.29	4250.14	3881.01	3630.55	3453.52
160 000	15071.52	8399.60	6214.42	5150.18	4533.49	4139.75	3872.59	3683.75
170 000	16013.49	8924.58	6602.82	5472.06	4816.83	4398.48	4114.62	3913.99
180 000	16955.46	9449.55	6991.23	5793.95	5100.17	4657.21	4356.66	4144.22
190 000	17897.43	9974.53	7379.63	6115.83	5383.52	4915.95	4598.70	4374.46
200 000	18839.40	10499.50	7768.03	6437.72	5666.86	5174.68	4840.73	4604.69
210 000	19781.37	11024.48	8156.43	6759.61	5950.20	5433.42	5082.77	4834.92
220 000	20723.34	11549.45	8544.83	7081.49	6233.54	5692.15	5324.81	5065.16
230 000	21665.31	12074.43	8933.23	7403.38	6516.89	5950.88	5566.84	5295.39
240 000	22607.28	12599.40	9321.63	7725.26	6800.23	6209.62	5808.88	5525.63
250 000	23549.25	13124.38	9710.04	8047.15	7083.57	6468.35	6050.92	5755.86
260 000	24491.22	13649.35	10098.44	8369.04	7366.92	6727.09	6292.95	5986.10
270 000	25433.19	14174.33	10486.84	8690.92	7650.26	6985.82	6534.99	6216.33
280 000	26375.16	14699.30	10875.24	9012.81	7933.60	7244.56	6777.03	6446.57
290 000	27317.13	15224.28	11263.64	9334.69	8216.94	7503.29	7019.06	6676.80
300 000	28259.11	15749.25	11652.04	9656.58	8500.29	7762.02	7261.10	6907.04
320 000	30143.05	16799.20	12428.85	10300.35	9066.97	8279.49	7745.17	7367.50
340 000	32026.99	17849.15	13205.65	10944.12	9633.66	8796.96	8229.25	7827.97
360 000	33910.93	18899.10	13982.45	11587.90	10200.34	9314.43	8713.32	8288.44
380 000	35794.87	19949.05	14759.25	12231.67	10767.03	9831.90	9197.39	8748.91
400 000	37678.81	20999.00	15536.06	12875.44	11333.72	10349.36	9681.47	9209.38
420 000	39562.75	22048.95	16312.86	13519.21	11900.40	10866.83	10165.54	9669.85
440 000	41446.69	23098.90	17089.66	14162.98	12467.09	11384.30	10649.61	10130.32
460 000	43330.63	24148.85	17866.47	14806.76	13033.77	11901.77	11133.69	10590.79
480 000	45214.57	25198.80	18643.27	15450.53	13600.46	12419.24	11617.76	11051.26
500 000	47098.51	26248.75	19420.07	16094.30	14167.15	12936.71	12101.83	11511.73
520 000	48982.45	27298.70	20196.87	16738.07	14733.83	13454.17	12585.91	11972.19
540 000	50866.39	28348.65	20973.68	17381.84	15300.52	13971.64	13069.98	12432.66
560 000	52750.33	29398.60	21750.48	18025.62	15867.20	14489.11	13554.05	12893.13
580 000	54634.27	30448.55	22527.28	18669.39	16433.89	15006.58	14038.13	13353.60
600 000	56518.21	31498.50	23304.09	19313.16	17000.57	15524.05	14522.20	13814.07
620 000	58402.15	32548.45	24080.89	19956.93	17567.26	16041.52	15006.27	14274.54
640 000	60286.09	33598.41	24857.69	20600.70	18133.95	16558.98	15490.34	14735.01
660 000	62170.03	34648.36	25634.49	21244.48	18700.63	17076.45	15974.42	15195.48
680 000	64053.97	35698.31	26411.30	21888.25	19267.32	17593.92	16458.49	15655.95
700 000	65937.91	36748.26	27188.10	22532.02	19834.00	18111.39	16942.56	16116.42
720 000	67821.85	37798.21	27964.90	23175.79	20400.69	18628.86	17426.64	16576.88
740 000	69705.79	38848.16	28741.71	23819.56	20967.37	19146.32	17910.71	17037.35
760 000	71589.73	39898.11	29518.51	24463.34	21534.06	19663.79	18394.78	17497.82
780 000	73473.67	40948.06	30295.31	25107.11	22100.75	20181.26	18878.86	17958.29
800 000	75357.61	41998.01	31072.11	25750.88	22667.43	20698.73	19362.93	18418.76
820 000	77241.55	43047.96	31848.92	26394.65	23234.12	21216.20	19847.00	18879.23
840 000	79125.49	44097.91	32625.72	27038.42	23800.80	21733.67	20331.08	19339.70
860 000	81009.43	45147.86	33402.52	27682.20	24367.49	22251.13	20815.15	19800.17
880 000	82893.37	46197.81	34179.32	28325.97	24934.18	22768.60	21299.22	20260.64
900 000	84777.32	47247.76	34956.13	28969.74	25500.86	23286.07	21783.30	20721.11
920 000	86661.26	48297.71	35732.93	29613.51	26067.55	23803.54	22267.37	21181.57
940 000	88545.20	49347.66	36509.73	30257.28	26634.23	24321.01	22751.44	21642.04
960 000	90429.14	50397.61	37286.54	30901.06	27200.92	24838.48	23235.52	22102.51
980 000	92313.08	51447.56	38063.34	31544.83	27767.60	25355.94	23719.59	22562.98
1000 000	94197.02	52497.51	38840.14	32188.60	28334.29	25873.41	24203.66	23023.45
Coefficient	.094197017	.052497508	.038840142	.032188599	.028334290	.025873412	.024203664	.023023451

148

MONTHLY AMORTIZING PAYMENTS · 23.25%

AMOUNT	9 YEARS	10 YEARS	15 YEARS	20 YEARS	25 YEARS	30 YEARS	35 YEARS	40 YEARS
10 000	221.65	215.27	200.08	195.71	194.36	193.94	193.81	193.77
20 000	443.32	430.55	400.15	391.41	388.73	387.89	387.62	387.54
30 000	664.95	645.82	600.23	587.12	583.09	581.83	581.43	581.31
40 000	886.60	861.09	800.30	782.83	777.46	775.78	775.25	775.08
50 000	1108.25	1076.37	1000.38	978.53	971.82	969.72	969.06	968.85
60 000	1329.90	1291.64	1200.45	1174.24	1166.19	1163.66	1162.87	1162.62
70 000	1551.55	1506.91	1400.53	1369.94	1360.55	1357.61	1356.68	1356.39
80 000	1773.20	1722.19	1600.60	1565.65	1554.91	1551.55	1550.48	1550.15
90 000	1994.85	1937.46	1800.68	1761.36	1749.28	1745.49	1744.30	1743.92
100 000	2216.50	2152.74	2000.75	1957.06	1943.64	1939.44	1938.11	1937.69
110 000	2438.15	2368.01	2200.83	2152.77	2138.01	2133.38	2131.92	2131.46
120 000	2659.79	2583.28	2400.90	2348.48	2332.37	2327.33	2325.73	2325.23
130 000	2881.44	2798.56	2600.98	2544.18	2526.74	2521.27	2519.55	2519.00
140 000	3103.09	3013.83	2801.05	2739.89	2721.10	2715.21	2713.36	2712.77
150 000	3324.74	3229.10	3001.13	2935.60	2915.47	2909.16	2907.17	2906.54
160 000	3546.39	3444.38	3201.20	3131.30	3109.83	3103.10	3100.98	3100.31
170 000	3768.04	3659.65	3401.28	3327.01	3304.19	3297.05	3294.79	3294.08
180 000	3989.69	3874.92	3601.35	3522.71	3498.56	3490.99	3488.60	3487.85
190 000	4211.34	4090.20	3801.43	3718.42	3692.92	3684.93	3682.41	3681.62
200 000	4432.99	4305.47	4001.50	3914.13	3887.29	3878.88	3876.23	3875.39
210 000	4654.64	4520.74	4201.58	4109.83	4081.65	4072.82	4070.04	4069.16
220 000	4876.29	4736.02	4401.66	4305.54	4276.02	4266.76	4263.85	4262.93
230 000	5097.94	4951.29	4601.73	4501.25	4470.38	4460.71	4457.66	4456.70
240 000	5319.59	5166.56	4801.81	4696.95	4664.74	4654.65	4651.47	4650.46
250 000	5541.24	5381.84	5001.88	4892.66	4859.11	4848.60	4845.28	4844.23
260 000	5762.89	5597.11	5201.96	5088.37	5053.47	5042.54	5039.09	5038.00
270 000	5984.54	5812.39	5402.03	5284.07	5247.84	5236.48	5232.90	5231.77
280 000	6206.19	6027.66	5602.11	5479.78	5442.20	5430.43	5426.72	5425.54
290 000	6427.84	6242.93	5802.18	5675.48	5636.57	5624.37	5620.53	5619.31
300 000	6649.49	6458.21	6002.26	5871.19	5830.93	5818.32	5814.34	5813.08
320 000	7092.79	6888.75	6402.41	6262.60	6219.66	6206.20	6201.96	6200.62
340 000	7536.08	7319.30	6802.56	6654.02	6608.39	6594.09	6589.58	6588.16
360 000	7979.38	7749.85	7202.71	7045.43	6997.12	6981.98	6977.21	6975.70
380 000	8422.68	8180.39	7602.86	7436.84	7385.85	7369.87	7364.83	7363.24
400 000	8865.98	8610.94	8003.01	7828.25	7774.57	7757.75	7752.45	7750.77
420 000	9309.28	9041.49	8403.16	8219.67	8163.30	8145.64	8140.07	8138.31
440 000	9752.58	9472.03	8803.31	8611.08	8552.03	8533.53	8527.70	8525.85
460 000	10195.88	9902.58	9203.46	9002.49	8940.76	8921.42	8915.32	8913.39
480 000	10639.18	10333.13	9603.61	9393.91	9329.49	9309.30	9302.94	9300.93
500 000	11082.48	10763.68	10003.76	9785.32	9718.22	9697.19	9690.56	9688.47
520 000	11525.78	11194.22	10403.91	10176.73	10106.95	10085.08	10078.19	10076.01
540 000	11969.08	11624.77	10804.06	10568.14	10495.68	10472.97	10465.81	10463.55
560 000	12412.37	12055.32	11204.21	10959.56	10884.40	10860.86	10853.43	10851.08
580 000	12855.67	12485.86	11604.36	11350.97	11273.13	11248.74	11241.05	11238.62
600 000	13298.97	12916.41	12004.51	11742.38	11661.86	11636.63	11628.68	11626.16
620 000	13742.27	13346.96	12404.66	12133.79	12050.59	12024.52	12016.30	12013.70
640 000	14185.57	13777.51	12804.82	12525.21	12439.32	12412.41	12403.92	12401.24
660 000	14628.87	14208.05	13204.97	12916.62	12828.05	12800.29	12791.54	12788.78
680 000	15072.17	14638.60	13605.12	13308.03	13216.78	13188.18	13179.17	13176.32
700 000	15515.47	15069.15	14005.27	13699.45	13605.51	13576.07	13566.79	13563.86
720 000	15958.77	15499.69	14405.42	14090.86	13994.23	13963.96	13954.41	13951.39
740 000	16402.07	15930.24	14805.57	14482.27	14382.96	14351.84	14342.03	14338.93
760 000	16845.37	16360.79	15205.72	14873.68	14771.69	14739.73	14729.66	14726.47
780 000	17288.66	16791.33	15605.87	15265.10	15160.42	15127.62	15117.28	15114.01
800 000	17731.96	17221.88	16006.02	15656.51	15549.15	15515.51	15504.90	15501.55
820 000	18175.26	17652.43	16406.17	16047.92	15937.88	15903.39	15892.52	15889.09
840 000	18618.56	18082.98	16806.32	16439.34	16326.61	16291.28	16280.14	16276.63
860 000	19061.86	18513.52	17206.47	16830.75	16715.33	16679.17	16667.77	16664.16
880 000	19505.16	18944.07	17606.62	17222.16	17104.06	17067.06	17055.39	17051.70
900 000	19948.46	19374.62	18006.77	17613.57	17492.79	17454.95	17443.01	17439.24
920 000	20391.76	19805.16	18406.92	18004.99	17881.52	17842.83	17830.63	17826.78
940 000	20835.06	20235.71	18807.07	18396.40	18270.25	18230.72	18218.26	18214.32
960 000	21278.36	20666.26	19207.22	18787.81	18658.98	18618.61	18605.88	18601.86
980 000	21721.66	21096.80	19607.37	19179.22	19047.71	19006.50	18993.50	18989.40
1000 000	22164.96	21527.35	20007.52	19570.64	19436.44	19394.38	19381.13	19376.94
Coefficient	.022164955	.021527352	.020007524	.019570637	.019436436	.019394384	.019381125	.019376936

149

AMOUNT	1 YEAR	2 YEARS	3 YEARS	4 YEARS	5 YEARS	6 YEARS	7 YEARS	8 YEARS
10 000	943.18	526.22	389.71	323.26	284.78	260.24	243.61	231.86
20 000	1886.36	1052.44	779.42	646.52	569.57	520.48	487.21	463.72
30 000	2829.53	1578.66	1169.12	969.78	854.35	780.72	730.82	695.59
40 000	3772.71	2104.87	1558.83	1293.04	1139.14	1040.97	974.42	927.45
50 000	4715.89	2631.09	1948.54	1616.30	1423.92	1301.21	1218.03	1159.31
60 000	5659.07	3157.31	2338.25	1939.56	1708.71	1561.45	1461.64	1391.17
70 000	6602.25	3683.53	2727.96	2262.82	1993.49	1821.69	1705.24	1623.03
80 000	7545.42	4209.75	3117.66	2586.08	2278.28	2081.93	1948.85	1854.90
90 000	8488.60	4735.97	3507.37	2909.34	2563.06	2342.17	2192.45	2086.76
100 000	9431.78	5262.19	3897.08	3232.60	2847.85	2602.41	2436.06	2318.62
110 000	10374.96	5788.41	4286.79	3555.86	3132.63	2862.65	2679.67	2550.48
120 000	11318.14	6314.62	4676.50	3879.12	3417.42	3122.90	2923.27	2782.34
130 000	12261.31	6840.84	5066.20	4202.38	3702.20	3383.14	3166.88	3014.21
140 000	13204.49	7367.06	5455.91	4525.64	3986.99	3643.38	3410.48	3246.07
150 000	14147.67	7893.28	5845.62	4848.91	4271.77	3903.62	3654.09	3477.93
160 000	15090.85	8419.50	6235.33	5172.17	4556.56	4163.86	3897.69	3709.79
170 000	16034.03	8945.72	6625.04	5495.43	4841.34	4424.10	4141.30	3941.65
180 000	16977.20	9471.94	7014.74	5818.69	5126.13	4684.34	4384.91	4173.52
190 000	17920.38	9998.16	7404.45	6141.95	5410.91	4944.59	4628.51	4405.38
200 000	18863.56	10524.37	7794.16	6465.21	5695.70	5204.83	4872.12	4637.24
210 000	19806.74	11050.59	8183.87	6788.47	5980.48	5465.07	5115.72	4869.10
220 000	20749.92	11576.81	8573.58	7111.73	6265.27	5725.31	5359.33	5100.96
230 000	21693.09	12103.03	8963.28	7434.99	6550.05	5985.55	5602.94	5332.83
240 000	22636.27	12629.25	9352.99	7758.25	6834.84	6245.79	5846.54	5564.69
250 000	23579.45	13155.47	9742.70	8081.51	7119.62	6506.03	6090.15	5796.55
260 000	24522.63	13681.69	10132.41	8404.77	7404.41	6766.28	6333.75	6028.41
270 000	25465.81	14207.90	10522.12	8728.03	7689.19	7026.52	6577.36	6260.27
280 000	26408.98	14734.12	10911.83	9051.29	7973.97	7286.76	6820.97	6492.13
290 000	27352.16	15260.34	11301.53	9374.55	8258.76	7547.00	7064.57	6724.00
300 000	28295.34	15786.56	11691.24	9697.81	8543.54	7807.24	7308.18	6955.86
320 000	30181.70	16839.00	12470.66	10344.33	9113.11	8327.72	7795.39	7419.58
340 000	32068.05	17891.44	13250.07	10990.85	9682.68	8848.21	8282.60	7883.31
360 000	33954.41	18943.87	14029.49	11637.37	10252.25	9368.69	8769.81	8347.03
380 000	35840.76	19996.31	14808.91	12283.89	10821.82	9889.17	9257.02	8810.75
400 000	37727.12	21048.75	15588.32	12930.41	11391.39	10409.65	9744.24	9274.48
420 000	39613.48	22101.18	16367.74	13576.93	11960.96	10930.14	10231.45	9738.20
440 000	41499.83	23153.62	17147.15	14223.45	12530.53	11450.62	10718.66	10201.93
460 000	43386.19	24206.06	17926.57	14869.98	13100.10	11971.10	11205.87	10665.65
480 000	45272.54	25258.50	18705.99	15516.50	13669.67	12491.58	11693.08	11129.37
500 000	47158.90	26310.93	19485.40	16163.02	14239.24	13012.07	12180.30	11593.10
520 000	49045.25	27363.37	20264.82	16809.54	14808.81	13532.55	12667.51	12056.82
540 000	50931.61	28415.81	21044.23	17456.06	15378.38	14053.03	13154.72	12520.55
560 000	52817.97	29468.25	21823.65	18102.58	15947.95	14573.52	13641.93	12984.27
580 000	54704.32	30520.68	22603.07	18749.10	16517.52	15094.00	14129.14	13447.99
600 000	56590.68	31573.12	23382.48	19395.62	17087.09	15614.48	14616.36	13911.72
620 000	58477.03	32625.56	24161.90	20042.14	17656.66	16134.96	15103.57	14375.44
640 000	60363.39	33678.00	24941.31	20688.66	18226.23	16655.45	15590.78	14839.17
660 000	62249.75	34730.43	25720.73	21335.18	18795.80	17175.93	16077.99	15302.89
680 000	64136.10	35782.87	26500.15	21981.70	19365.37	17696.41	16565.20	15766.61
700 000	66022.46	36835.31	27279.56	22628.22	19934.94	18216.89	17052.41	16230.34
720 000	67908.81	37887.75	28058.98	23274.74	20504.51	18737.38	17539.63	16694.06
740 000	69795.17	38940.18	28838.39	23921.27	21074.08	19257.86	18026.84	17157.79
760 000	71681.53	39992.62	29617.81	24567.79	21643.65	19778.34	18514.05	17621.51
780 000	73567.88	41045.06	30397.23	25214.31	22213.22	20298.83	19001.26	18085.23
800 000	75454.24	42097.50	31176.64	25860.83	22782.78	20819.31	19488.47	18548.96
820 000	77340.59	43149.93	31956.06	26507.35	23352.35	21339.79	19975.69	19012.68
840 000	79226.95	44202.37	32735.48	27153.87	23921.92	21860.27	20462.90	19476.40
860 000	81113.31	45254.81	33514.89	27800.39	24491.49	22380.76	20950.11	19940.13
880 000	82999.66	46307.24	34294.31	28446.91	25061.06	22901.24	21437.32	20403.85
900 000	84886.02	47359.68	35073.72	29093.43	25630.63	23421.72	21924.53	20867.58
920 000	86772.37	48412.12	35853.14	29739.95	26200.20	23942.20	22411.74	21331.30
940 000	88658.73	49464.56	36632.56	30386.47	26769.77	24462.69	22898.96	21795.02
960 000	90545.09	50516.99	37411.97	31032.99	27339.34	24983.17	23386.17	22258.75
980 000	92431.44	51569.43	38191.39	31679.51	27908.91	25503.65	23873.38	22722.47
1 000 000	94317.80	52621.87	38970.80	32326.03	28478.48	26024.14	24360.59	23186.20
Coefficient	.094317798	.052621869	.038970804	.032326034	.028478481	.026024135	.024360592	.023186196

AMOUNT	9 YEARS	10 YEARS	15 YEARS	20 YEARS	25 YEARS	30 YEARS	35 YEARS	40 YEARS
10 000	223.33	217.00	201.99	197.72	196.42	196.02	195.89	195.85
20 000	446.66	434.01	403.98	395.43	392.83	392.03	391.78	391.70
30 000	669.99	651.01	605.97	593.15	589.25	588.05	587.67	587.55
40 000	893.32	868.02	807.95	790.86	785.67	784.06	783.56	783.40
50 000	1116.65	1085.02	1009.94	988.58	982.09	980.08	979.45	979.26
60 000	1339.99	1302.03	1211.93	1186.29	1178.50	1176.09	1175.34	1175.11
70 000	1563.32	1519.03	1413.92	1384.01	1374.92	1372.11	1371.23	1370.96
80 000	1786.65	1736.03	1615.91	1581.72	1571.34	1568.12	1567.12	1566.81
90 000	2009.98	1953.04	1817.90	1779.44	1767.76	1764.14	1763.01	1762.66
100 000	2233.31	2170.04	2019.88	1977.15	1964.17	1960.15	1958.90	1958.51
110 000	2456.64	2387.05	2221.87	2174.87	2160.59	2156.17	2154.79	2154.36
120 000	2679.97	2604.05	2423.86	2372.58	2357.01	2352.18	2350.68	2350.21
130 000	2903.30	2821.06	2625.85	2570.30	2553.42	2548.20	2546.57	2546.06
140 000	3126.63	3038.06	2827.84	2768.01	2749.84	2744.21	2742.46	2741.92
150 000	3349.96	3255.06	3029.83	2965.73	2946.26	2940.23	2938.35	2937.77
160 000	3573.29	3472.07	3231.82	3163.44	3142.68	3136.25	3134.24	3133.62
170 000	3796.63	3689.07	3433.80	3361.16	3339.09	3332.26	3330.13	3329.47
180 000	4019.96	3906.08	3635.79	3558.87	3535.51	3528.28	3526.03	3525.32
190 000	4243.29	4123.08	3837.78	3756.59	3731.93	3724.29	3721.91	3721.17
200 000	4466.62	4340.09	4039.77	3954.30	3928.35	3920.31	3917.80	3917.02
210 000	4689.95	4557.09	4241.76	4152.02	4124.76	4116.32	4113.69	4112.87
220 000	4913.28	4774.10	4443.75	4349.73	4321.18	4312.34	4309.58	4308.72
230 000	5136.61	4991.10	4645.73	4547.45	4517.60	4508.35	4505.47	4504.57
240 000	5359.94	5208.10	4847.72	4745.16	4714.01	4704.37	4701.36	4700.43
250 000	5583.27	5425.11	5049.71	4942.88	4910.43	4900.38	4897.25	4896.28
260 000	5806.60	5642.11	5251.70	5140.59	5106.85	5096.40	5093.14	5092.13
270 000	6029.93	5859.12	5453.69	5338.31	5303.27	5292.41	5289.03	5287.98
280 000	6253.27	6076.12	5655.68	5536.03	5499.68	5488.43	5484.92	5483.83
290 000	6476.60	6293.13	5857.66	5733.74	5696.10	5684.45	5680.81	5679.68
300 000	6699.93	6510.13	6059.65	5931.46	5892.52	5880.46	5876.70	5875.53
320 000	7146.59	6944.14	6463.63	6326.89	6285.35	6272.49	6268.48	6267.23
340 000	7593.25	7378.15	6867.61	6722.32	6678.19	6664.52	6660.27	6658.94
360 000	8039.91	7812.16	7271.58	7117.72	7071.02	7056.55	7052.05	7050.64
380 000	8486.57	8246.16	7675.56	7513.18	7463.86	7448.58	7443.83	7442.34
400 000	8933.24	8680.17	8079.54	7908.61	7856.69	7840.61	7835.61	7834.04
420 000	9379.90	9114.18	8483.51	8304.04	8249.52	8232.64	8227.39	8225.75
440 000	9826.56	9548.19	8887.49	8699.47	8642.36	8624.68	8619.17	8617.45
460 000	10273.22	9982.20	9291.47	9094.90	9035.19	9016.71	9010.95	9009.15
480 000	10719.88	10416.21	9695.45	9490.33	9428.03	9408.74	9402.73	9400.85
500 000	11166.55	10850.22	10099.42	9885.76	9820.86	9800.77	9794.51	9792.55
520 000	11613.21	11284.22	10503.40	10281.19	10213.70	10192.80	10186.29	10184.26
540 000	12059.87	11718.23	10907.38	10676.62	10606.53	10584.83	10578.07	10575.96
560 000	12506.53	12152.24	11311.35	11072.05	10999.37	10976.86	10969.85	10967.66
580 000	12953.19	12586.25	11715.33	11467.48	11392.20	11368.89	11361.63	11359.36
600 000	13399.85	13020.26	12119.31	11862.91	11785.04	11760.92	11753.41	11751.06
620 000	13846.52	13454.27	12523.28	12258.34	12177.87	12152.95	12145.19	12142.77
640 000	14293.18	13888.28	12927.26	12653.77	12570.70	12544.98	12536.97	12534.47
660 000	14739.84	14322.29	13331.24	13049.20	12963.54	12937.01	12928.75	12926.17
680 000	15186.50	14756.29	13735.21	13444.63	13356.37	13329.04	13320.53	13317.87
700 000	15633.16	15190.30	14139.19	13840.06	13749.21	13721.07	13712.31	13709.58
720 000	16079.82	15624.31	14543.17	14235.49	14142.04	14113.11	14104.09	14101.28
740 000	16526.49	16058.32	14947.14	14630.92	14534.88	14505.14	14495.87	14492.98
760 000	16973.15	16492.33	15351.12	15026.35	14927.71	14897.17	14887.65	14884.68
780 000	17419.81	16926.34	15755.10	15421.78	15320.55	15289.20	15279.43	15276.38
800 000	17866.47	17360.35	16159.08	15817.21	15713.38	15681.23	15671.21	15668.09
820 000	18313.13	17794.35	16563.05	16212.64	16106.22	16073.26	16062.99	16059.79
840 000	18759.80	18228.36	16967.03	16608.08	16499.05	16465.29	16454.77	16451.49
860 000	19206.46	18662.37	17371.01	17003.51	16891.88	16857.32	16846.55	16843.19
880 000	19653.12	19096.38	17774.98	17398.94	17284.72	17249.35	17238.33	17234.90
900 000	20099.78	19530.39	18178.96	17794.37	17677.55	17641.38	17630.11	17626.60
920 000	20546.44	19964.40	18582.94	18189.80	18070.39	18033.41	18021.89	18018.30
940 000	20993.10	20398.41	18986.91	18585.23	18463.22	18425.44	18413.67	18410.00
960 000	21439.77	20832.41	19390.89	18980.66	18856.06	18817.47	18805.45	18801.70
980 000	21886.43	21266.42	19794.87	19376.09	19248.89	19209.50	19197.23	19193.41
1000 000	22333.09	21700.43	20198.84	19771.52	19641.73	19601.54	19589.02	19585.11
Coefficient	.022333090	.021700432	.020198844	.019771518	.019641726	.019601535	.019589015	.019585108

151

AMOUNT	1 YEAR	2 YEARS	3 YEARS	4 YEARS	5 YEARS	6 YEARS	7 YEARS	8 YEARS
10 000	944.39	527.46	391.02	324.64	286.23	261.75	245.18	233.49
20 000	1888.77	1054.93	782.03	649.28	572.46	523.51	490.36	466.99
30 000	2833.16	1582.39	1173.05	973.91	858.69	785.26	735.54	700.48
40 000	3777.55	2109.86	1564.07	1298.55	1144.92	1047.01	980.72	933.98
50 000	4721.93	2637.32	1955.09	1623.19	1431.15	1308.76	1225.90	1167.47
60 000	5666.32	3164.78	2346.10	1947.83	1717.38	1570.52	1471.08	1400.97
70 000	6610.71	3692.25	2737.12	2272.46	2003.61	1832.27	1716.26	1634.46
80 000	7555.09	4219.71	3128.14	2597.10	2289.84	2094.02	1961.44	1867.95
90 000	8499.48	4747.18	3519.15	2921.74	2576.07	2355.77	2206.62	2101.45
100 000	9443.87	5274.64	3910.17	3246.38	2862.30	2617.53	2451.80	2334.94
110 000	10388.25	5802.10	4301.19	3571.02	3148.53	2879.28	2696.98	2568.44
120 000	11332.64	6329.57	4692.20	3895.65	3434.76	3141.03	2942.16	2801.93
130 000	12277.03	6857.03	5083.22	4220.29	3721.00	3402.79	3187.34	3035.42
140 000	13221.41	7384.50	5474.24	4544.93	4007.23	3664.54	3432.52	3268.92
150 000	14165.80	7911.96	5865.26	4869.57	4293.46	3926.29	3677.70	3502.41
160 000	15110.19	8439.42	6256.27	5194.20	4579.69	4188.04	3922.88	3735.91
170 000	16054.57	8966.89	6647.29	5518.84	4865.92	4449.80	4168.06	3969.40
180 000	16998.96	9494.35	7038.31	5843.48	5152.15	4711.55	4413.24	4202.90
190 000	17943.35	10021.82	7429.32	6168.12	5438.38	4973.30	4658.42	4436.39
200 000	18887.73	10549.28	7820.34	6492.76	5724.61	5235.06	4903.60	4669.88
210 000	19832.12	11076.74	8211.36	6817.39	6010.84	5496.81	5148.77	4903.38
220 000	20776.50	11604.21	8602.38	7142.03	6297.07	5758.56	5393.95	5136.87
230 000	21720.89	12131.67	8993.39	7466.67	6583.30	6020.31	5639.13	5370.37
240 000	22665.28	12659.14	9384.41	7791.31	6869.53	6282.07	5884.31	5603.86
250 000	23609.66	13186.60	9775.43	8115.95	7155.76	6543.82	6129.49	5837.36
260 000	24554.05	13714.06	10166.44	8440.58	7441.99	6805.57	6374.67	6070.85
270 000	25498.44	14241.53	10557.46	8765.22	7728.22	7067.32	6619.85	6304.34
280 000	26442.82	14768.99	10948.48	9089.86	8014.45	7329.08	6865.03	6537.84
290 000	27387.21	15296.46	11339.50	9414.50	8300.68	7590.83	7110.21	6771.33
300 000	28331.60	15823.92	11730.51	9739.13	8586.91	7852.58	7355.39	7004.83
320 000	30220.37	16878.85	12512.55	10388.41	9159.37	8376.09	7845.75	7471.82
340 000	32109.14	17933.78	13294.58	11037.69	9731.83	8899.59	8336.11	7938.80
360 000	33997.92	18988.70	14076.61	11686.96	10304.29	9423.10	8826.47	8405.79
380 000	35886.69	20043.63	14858.65	12336.24	10876.75	9946.60	9316.83	8872.78
400 000	37775.46	21098.56	15640.68	12985.51	11449.22	10470.11	9807.19	9339.77
420 000	39664.24	22153.49	16422.72	13634.79	12021.68	10993.62	10297.55	9806.76
440 000	41553.01	23208.42	17204.75	14284.06	12594.14	11517.12	10787.91	10273.75
460 000	43441.78	24263.34	17986.79	14933.34	13166.60	12040.63	11278.27	10740.73
480 000	45330.56	25318.27	18768.82	15582.61	13739.06	12564.13	11768.63	11207.72
500 000	47219.33	26373.20	19550.85	16231.89	14311.52	13087.64	12258.99	11674.71
520 000	49108.10	27428.13	20332.89	16881.17	14883.98	13611.14	12749.35	12141.70
540 000	50996.88	28483.06	21114.92	17530.44	15456.44	14134.65	13239.71	12608.69
560 000	52885.65	29537.98	21896.96	18179.72	16028.90	14658.15	13730.07	13075.68
580 000	54774.42	30592.91	22678.99	18828.99	16601.36	15181.66	14220.43	13542.66
600 000	56663.20	31647.84	23461.02	19478.27	17173.82	15705.17	14710.79	14009.65
620 000	58551.97	32702.77	24243.06	20127.54	17746.28	16228.67	15201.14	14476.64
640 000	60440.74	33757.70	25025.09	20776.82	18318.74	16752.18	15691.50	14943.63
660 000	62329.51	34812.62	25807.13	21426.09	18891.21	17275.68	16181.86	15410.62
680 000	64218.29	35867.55	26589.16	22075.37	19463.67	17799.19	16672.22	15877.61
700 000	66107.06	36922.48	27371.19	22724.65	20036.13	18322.69	17162.58	16344.60
720 000	67995.83	37977.41	28153.23	23373.92	20608.59	18846.20	17652.94	16811.58
740 000	69884.61	39032.34	28935.26	24023.20	21181.05	19369.70	18143.30	17278.57
760 000	71773.38	40087.26	29717.30	24672.47	21753.51	19893.21	18633.66	17745.56
780 000	73662.15	41142.19	30499.33	25321.75	22325.97	20416.71	19124.02	18212.55
800 000	75550.93	42197.12	31281.37	25971.02	22898.43	20940.22	19614.38	18679.54
820 000	77439.70	43252.05	32063.40	26620.30	23470.89	21463.73	20104.74	19146.53
840 000	79328.47	44306.98	32845.43	27269.58	24043.35	21987.23	20595.10	19613.51
860 000	81217.25	45361.90	33627.47	27918.85	24615.81	22510.74	21085.46	20080.50
880 000	83106.02	46416.83	34409.50	28568.13	25188.27	23034.24	21575.82	20547.49
900 000	84994.79	47471.76	35191.54	29217.40	25760.74	23557.75	22066.18	21014.48
920 000	86883.57	48526.69	35973.57	29866.68	26333.20	24081.25	22556.54	21481.47
940 000	88772.34	49581.62	36755.60	30515.95	26905.66	24604.76	23046.90	21948.46
960 000	90661.11	50636.54	37537.64	31165.23	27478.12	25128.26	23537.26	22415.45
980 000	92549.89	51691.47	38319.67	31814.50	28050.58	25651.77	24027.62	22882.43
1000 000	94438.66	52746.40	39101.71	32463.78	28623.04	26175.28	24517.98	23349.42
Coefficient	.094438659	.052746399	.039101707	.032463780	.028623039	.026175275	.024517975	.023349422

152

AMOUNT	9 YEARS	10 YEARS	15 YEARS	20 YEARS	25 YEARS	30 YEARS	35 YEARS	40 YEARS
10 000	225.02	218.74	203.91	199.73	198.47	198.09	197.97	197.93
20 000	450.03	437.48	407.81	399.45	396.94	396.18	395.94	395.87
30 000	675.05	656.22	611.72	599.18	595.41	594.26	593.91	593.80
40 000	900.07	874.96	815.62	798.91	793.89	792.35	791.88	791.73
50 000	1125.09	1093.70	1019.53	998.63	992.36	990.44	989.85	989.66
60 000	1350.10	1312.44	1223.44	1198.36	1190.83	1188.53	1187.82	1187.60
70 000	1575.12	1531.18	1427.34	1398.09	1389.30	1386.61	1385.79	1385.53
80 000	1800.14	1749.92	1631.25	1597.81	1587.77	1584.70	1583.75	1583.46
90 000	2025.15	1968.66	1835.15	1797.54	1786.24	1782.79	1781.72	1781.40
100 000	2250.17	2187.40	2039.06	1997.27	1984.72	1980.88	1979.69	1979.33
110 000	2475.19	2406.14	2242.96	2196.99	2183.19	2178.96	2177.66	2177.26
120 000	2700.21	2624.88	2446.87	2396.72	2381.66	2377.05	2375.63	2375.20
130 000	2925.22	2843.62	2650.78	2596.45	2580.13	2575.14	2573.60	2573.13
140 000	3150.24	3062.36	2854.68	2796.17	2778.60	2773.23	2771.57	2771.06
150 000	3375.26	3281.10	3058.59	2995.90	2977.07	2971.31	2969.54	2968.99
160 000	3600.28	3499.84	3262.49	3195.63	3175.55	3169.40	3167.51	3166.93
170 000	3825.29	3718.58	3466.40	3395.35	3374.02	3367.49	3365.48	3364.86
180 000	4050.31	3937.32	3670.31	3595.08	3572.49	3565.58	3563.45	3562.79
190 000	4275.33	4156.06	3874.21	3794.81	3770.96	3763.66	3761.42	3760.73
200 000	4500.34	4374.80	4078.12	3994.53	3969.43	3961.75	3959.39	3958.66
210 000	4725.36	4593.54	4282.02	4194.26	4167.90	4159.84	4157.36	4156.59
220 000	4950.38	4812.28	4485.93	4393.99	4366.38	4357.93	4355.33	4354.52
230 000	5175.40	5031.02	4689.83	4593.71	4564.85	4556.01	4553.30	4552.46
240 000	5400.41	5249.76	4893.74	4793.44	4763.32	4754.10	4751.26	4750.39
250 000	5625.43	5468.50	5097.65	4993.17	4961.79	4952.19	4949.23	4948.32
260 000	5850.45	5687.24	5301.55	5192.89	5160.26	5150.28	5147.20	5146.26
270 000	6075.46	5905.98	5505.46	5392.62	5358.73	5348.36	5345.17	5344.19
280 000	6300.48	6124.72	5709.36	5592.35	5557.21	5546.45	5543.14	5542.12
290 000	6525.50	6343.46	5913.27	5792.07	5755.68	5744.54	5741.11	5740.05
300 000	6750.52	6562.20	6117.18	5991.80	5954.15	5942.63	5939.08	5937.99
320 000	7200.55	6999.68	6524.99	6391.25	6351.09	6338.80	6335.02	6333.85
340 000	7650.59	7437.17	6932.80	6790.71	6748.04	6734.98	6730.96	6729.72
360 000	8100.62	7874.65	7340.61	7190.16	7144.98	7131.15	7126.90	7125.59
380 000	8550.65	8312.13	7748.42	7589.61	7541.92	7527.33	7522.84	7521.45
400 000	9000.69	8749.61	8156.23	7989.07	7938.87	7923.50	7918.77	7917.32
420 000	9450.72	9187.09	8564.05	8388.52	8335.81	8319.68	8314.71	8313.18
440 000	9900.76	9624.57	8971.86	8787.97	8732.75	8715.85	8710.65	8709.05
460 000	10350.79	10062.05	9379.67	9187.43	9129.69	9112.03	9106.59	9104.91
480 000	10800.83	10499.53	9787.48	9586.88	9526.64	9508.20	9502.53	9500.78
500 000	11250.86	10937.01	10195.29	9986.34	9923.58	9904.38	9898.47	9896.65
520 000	11700.90	11374.49	10603.10	10385.79	10320.52	10300.55	10294.41	10292.51
540 000	12150.93	11811.97	11010.92	10785.24	10717.47	10696.73	10690.35	10688.38
560 000	12600.96	12249.45	11418.73	11184.70	11114.41	11092.90	11086.28	11084.24
580 000	13051.00	12686.93	11826.54	11584.15	11511.35	11489.08	11482.22	11480.11
600 000	13501.03	13124.41	12234.35	11983.60	11908.30	11885.25	11878.16	11875.98
620 000	13951.07	13561.89	12642.16	12383.06	12305.24	12281.43	12274.10	12271.84
640 000	14401.10	13999.37	13049.97	12782.51	12702.18	12677.60	12670.04	12667.71
660 000	14851.14	14436.85	13457.79	13181.96	13099.13	13073.78	13065.98	13063.57
680 000	15301.17	14874.33	13865.60	13581.42	13496.07	13469.95	13461.92	13459.44
700 000	15751.21	15311.81	14273.41	13980.87	13893.01	13866.13	13857.86	13855.30
720 000	16201.24	15749.29	14681.22	14380.32	14289.96	14262.30	14253.79	14251.17
740 000	16651.27	16186.77	15089.03	14779.78	14686.90	14658.48	14649.73	14647.04
760 000	17101.31	16624.25	15496.84	15179.23	15083.84	15054.65	15045.67	15042.90
780 000	17551.34	17061.73	15904.66	15578.68	15480.79	15450.83	15441.61	15438.77
800 000	18001.38	17499.21	16312.47	15978.14	15877.73	15847.00	15837.55	15834.63
820 000	18451.41	17936.69	16720.28	16377.59	16274.67	16243.18	16233.49	16230.50
840 000	18901.45	18374.17	17128.09	16777.04	16671.62	16639.36	16629.43	16626.37
860 000	19351.48	18811.65	17535.90	17176.50	17068.56	17035.53	17025.36	17022.23
880 000	19801.52	19249.13	17943.71	17575.95	17465.50	17431.71	17421.30	17418.10
900 000	20251.55	19686.61	18351.53	17975.40	17862.45	17827.88	17817.24	17813.96
920 000	20701.58	20124.09	18759.34	18374.86	18259.39	18224.06	18213.18	18209.83
940 000	21151.62	20561.58	19167.15	18774.31	18656.33	18620.23	18609.12	18605.69
960 000	21601.65	20999.06	19574.96	19173.76	19053.28	19016.41	19005.06	19001.56
980 000	22051.69	21436.54	19982.77	19573.22	19450.22	19412.58	19401.00	19397.43
1000 000	22501.72	21874.02	20390.58	19972.67	19847.16	19808.76	19796.94	19793.29
Coefficient	.022501722	.021874016	.020390584	.019972670	.019847163	.019808756	.019796936	.019793292

Annual
Amortization
Schedules

YEARLY AMORTIZATION SCHEDULES
PRINCIPAL = $10,000

5.00%

15 YEAR TERM $79.08/Month

YEAR	PRINCIPAL	INT. PAID	PRIN. PAID
1	9540.61	489.57	459.39
2	9057.73	466.06	482.89
3	8550.13	441.36	507.59
4	8016.57	415.39	533.56
5	7455.71	388.09	560.86
6	6866.15	359.40	589.56
7	6246.43	329.23	619.72
8	5595.01	297.53	651.42
9	4910.26	264.20	684.75
10	4190.47	229.17	719.79
11	3433.86	192.34	756.61
12	2638.54	153.63	795.32
13	1802.53	112.94	836.01
14	923.74	70.17	878.78
15	0.00	25.21	923.74

Total Payout = $14234.29   Total Interest = $4234.29

30 YEAR TERM $53.68/Month

YEAR	PRINCIPAL	INT. PAID	PRIN. PAID
1	9852.46	496.65	147.54
2	9697.38	489.10	155.08
3	9534.36	481.17	163.02
4	9363.00	472.83	171.36
5	9182.87	464.06	180.13
6	8993.53	454.84	189.34
7	8794.50	445.16	199.03
8	8585.29	434.97	209.21
9	8365.37	424.27	219.92
10	8134.21	413.02	231.17
11	7891.21	401.19	242.99
12	7635.79	388.76	255.43
13	7367.29	375.69	268.49
14	7085.06	361.96	282.23
15	6788.39	347.52	296.67
16	6476.54	332.34	311.85
17	6148.74	316.38	327.80
18	5804.17	299.61	344.57
19	5441.96	281.98	362.20
20	5061.23	263.45	380.73
21	4661.01	243.97	400.21
22	4240.33	223.50	420.69
23	3798.11	201.97	442.21
24	3333.28	179.35	464.84
25	2844.66	155.57	488.62
26	2331.04	130.57	513.62
27	1791.14	104.29	539.90
28	1223.63	76.67	567.52
29	627.08	47.63	596.55
30	0.00	17.11	627.07

Total Payout = $19325.58   Total Interest = $9325.58

5.25%

15 YEAR TERM $80.39/Month

YEAR	PRINCIPAL	INT. PAID	PRIN. PAID
1	9549.61	514.27	450.39
2	9075.00	490.04	474.61
3	8574.86	464.52	500.14
4	8047.83	437.62	527.03
5	7492.45	409.27	555.38
6	6907.20	379.40	585.25
7	6290.48	347.93	616.72
8	5640.58	314.76	649.89
9	4955.74	279.81	684.85
10	4234.06	242.98	721.68
11	3473.57	204.16	760.49
12	2672.18	163.26	801.39
13	1827.68	120.16	844.49
14	937.77	74.74	889.91
15	0.00	26.88	937.77

Total Payout = $14469.80   Total Interest = $4469.80

30 YEAR TERM $55.22/Month

YEAR	PRINCIPAL	INT. PAID	PRIN. PAID
1	9858.99	521.64	141.00
2	9710.41	514.06	148.59
3	9553.83	506.06	156.58
4	9388.82	497.64	165.00
5	9214.95	488.77	173.88
6	9031.72	479.42	183.23
7	8838.64	469.56	193.08
8	8635.18	459.18	203.47
9	8420.77	448.24	214.41
10	8194.83	436.71	225.94
11	7956.74	424.55	238.09
12	7705.84	411.75	250.90
13	7441.45	398.25	264.39
14	7162.84	384.04	278.61
15	6869.25	369.05	293.59
16	6559.87	353.26	309.38
17	6233.85	336.62	326.02
18	5890.29	319.09	343.56
19	5528.26	300.61	362.03
20	5146.75	281.14	381.50
21	4744.73	260.62	402.02
22	4321.09	239.00	423.64
23	3874.66	216.22	446.43
24	3404.22	192.21	470.44
25	2908.48	166.91	495.74
26	2386.08	140.24	522.40
27	1835.58	112.15	550.50
28	1255.48	82.54	580.10
29	644.18	51.34	611.30
30	0.00	18.47	644.18

Total Payout = $19879.33   Total Interest = $9879.33

YEARLY AMORTIZATION SCHEDULES
PRINCIPAL = $10,000

5.50%

15 YEAR TERM $81.71/Month

YEAR	PRINCIPAL	INT. PAID	PRIN. PAID
1	9558.48	538.98	441.52
2	9092.05	514.08	466.43
3	8599.32	487.77	492.74
4	8078.79	459.97	520.53
5	7528.90	430.61	549.89
6	6947.99	399.59	580.91
7	6334.31	366.82	613.68
8	5686.02	332.21	648.29
9	5001.16	295.64	684.86
10	4277.66	257.01	723.49
11	3513.36	216.20	764.30
12	2705.94	173.08	807.42
13	1852.98	127.54	852.96
14	951.90	79.42	901.08
15	0.00	28.60	951.90

Total Payout = $14707.50   Total Interest = $4707.50

30 YEAR TERM $56.78/Month

YEAR	PRINCIPAL	INT. PAID	PRIN. PAID
1	9865.29	546.64	134.71
2	9722.98	539.04	142.31
3	9572.65	531.01	150.33
4	9413.83	522.53	158.81
5	9246.06	513.57	167.77
6	9068.82	504.11	177.24
7	8881.59	494.11	187.23
8	8683.79	483.55	197.80
9	8474.84	472.39	208.95
10	8254.10	460.61	220.74
11	8020.91	448.16	233.19
12	7774.56	435.00	246.35
13	7514.32	421.11	260.24
14	7239.40	406.43	274.92
15	6948.97	390.92	290.43
16	6642.16	374.54	306.81
17	6318.04	357.22	324.12
18	5975.64	338.95	342.40
19	5613.93	319.63	361.71
20	5231.81	299.23	382.12
21	4828.14	277.67	403.67
22	4401.70	254.90	426.44
23	3951.20	230.85	450.50
24	3475.29	205.44	475.91
25	2972.54	178.59	502.75
26	2441.42	150.23	531.11
27	1880.35	120.27	561.07
28	1287.63	88.63	592.72
29	661.48	55.19	626.16
30	0.00	19.87	661.48

Total Payout = $20440.40   Total Interest = $10440.40

5.75%

15 YEAR TERM $83.04/Month

YEAR	PRINCIPAL	INT. PAID	PRIN. PAID
1	9567.22	563.71	432.78
2	9108.89	538.16	458.33
3	8623.50	511.10	485.39
4	8109.45	482.44	514.05
5	7565.05	452.09	544.40
6	6988.52	419.95	576.54
7	6377.94	385.92	610.58
8	5731.31	349.87	646.63
9	5046.51	311.69	684.80
10	4321.28	271.26	725.23
11	3553.23	228.44	768.05
12	2739.83	183.10	813.40
13	1878.41	135.07	861.42
14	966.14	84.22	912.28
15	0.00	30.35	966.14

Total Payout = $14947.38   Total Interest = $4947.38

30 YEAR TERM $58.36/Month

YEAR	PRINCIPAL	INT. PAID	PRIN. PAID
1	9871.36	571.64	128.64
2	9735.12	564.05	136.24
3	9590.84	556.01	144.28
4	9438.04	547.49	152.80
5	9276.22	538.47	161.82
6	9104.84	528.91	171.37
7	8923.35	518.79	181.49
8	8731.14	508.08	192.21
9	8527.59	496.73	203.56
10	8312.01	484.71	215.57
11	8083.71	471.99	228.30
12	7841.93	458.51	241.78
13	7585.88	444.23	256.05
14	7314.71	429.12	271.17
15	7027.52	413.11	287.18
16	6723.39	396.15	304.14
17	6401.29	378.19	322.09
18	6060.18	359.18	341.11
19	5698.94	339.04	361.25
20	5316.36	317.71	382.58
21	4911.20	295.12	405.16
22	4482.11	271.20	429.08
23	4027.69	245.87	454.42
24	3546.45	219.04	481.25
25	3036.79	190.63	509.66
26	2497.00	160.54	539.75
27	1925.42	128.67	571.62
28	1320.06	94.92	605.36
29	678.95	59.18	641.11
30	0.00	21.33	678.96

Total Payout = $21008.62   Total Interest = $11008.62

YEARLY AMORTIZATION SCHEDULES
PRINCIPAL = $10,000

6.00%

15 YEAR TERM $84.39/Month

YEAR	PRINCIPAL	INT. PAID	PRIN. PAID
1	9575.83	588.46	424.17
2	9125.50	562.30	450.33
3	8647.40	534.52	478.10
4	8139.81	505.04	507.59
5	7600.91	473.73	538.90
6	7028.77	440.49	572.14
7	6421.35	405.20	607.43
8	5776.46	367.74	644.89
9	5091.79	327.96	684.67
10	4364.90	285.73	726.89
11	3593.17	240.90	771.73
12	2773.84	193.30	819.33
13	1903.98	142.77	869.86
14	980.47	89.12	923.51
15	0.00	32.16	980.47

Total Payout = $15189.42   Total Interest = $5189.42

30 YEAR TERM $59.96/Month

YEAR	PRINCIPAL	INT. PAID	PRIN. PAID
1	9877.20	596.66	122.80
2	9746.82	589.09	130.38
3	9608.41	581.04	138.42
4	9461.45	572.51	146.95
5	9305.44	563.44	156.02
6	9139.80	553.82	165.64
7	8963.94	543.60	175.86
8	8777.24	532.76	186.70
9	8579.02	521.24	198.22
10	8368.57	509.02	210.44
11	8145.15	496.04	223.42
12	7907.94	482.26	237.20
13	7656.11	467.63	251.83
14	7388.74	452.09	267.37
15	7104.89	435.60	283.86
16	6803.52	418.10	301.37
17	6483.57	399.51	319.95
18	6143.88	379.77	339.69
19	5783.24	358.82	360.64
20	5400.36	336.58	382.88
21	4993.86	312.96	406.50
22	4562.29	287.89	431.57
23	4104.11	261.27	458.19
24	3617.66	233.01	486.45
25	3101.21	203.01	516.45
26	2552.91	171.16	548.30
27	1970.79	137.34	582.12
28	1352.76	101.44	618.03
29	696.62	63.32	656.14
30	0.00	22.85	696.61

Total Payout = $21583.82   Total Interest = $11583.82

6.25%

15 YEAR TERM $85.74/Month

YEAR	PRINCIPAL	INT. PAID	PRIN. PAID
1	9584.32	621.68	415.68
2	9141.90	586.49	442.42
3	8671.03	558.03	470.88
4	8169.86	527.74	501.16
5	7636.46	495.51	533.40
6	7068.76	461.20	567.71
7	6464.53	424.68	604.22
8	5821.44	385.82	643.09
9	5136.99	344.45	684.45
10	4408.51	300.43	728.48
11	3633.17	253.57	775.34
12	2807.97	203.70	825.21
13	1929.68	150.62	878.29
14	994.90	94.13	934.78
15	0.00	34.00	994.91

Total Payout = $15433.61   Total Interest = $5433.61

30 YEAR TERM $61.57/Month

YEAR	PRINCIPAL	INT. PAID	PRIN. PAID
1	9882.82	621.68	117.18
2	9758.10	614.14	124.72
3	9625.36	606.12	132.74
4	9484.09	597.58	141.28
5	9333.72	588.50	150.36
6	9173.69	578.83	160.04
7	9003.36	568.53	170.33
8	8822.07	557.58	181.29
9	8629.13	545.91	192.95
10	8423.77	533.50	205.36
11	8205.21	520.30	218.57
12	7972.58	506.24	232.62
13	7725.00	491.27	247.59
14	7461.48	475.35	263.51
15	7181.02	458.40	280.46
16	6882.52	440.36	298.50
17	6564.82	421.16	317.70
18	6226.68	400.72	338.14
19	5866.80	378.97	359.89
20	5483.76	355.83	383.03
21	5076.09	331.19	407.67
22	4642.19	304.97	433.89
23	4180.39	277.06	461.80
24	3688.88	247.35	491.51
25	3165.76	215.74	523.12
26	2608.99	182.09	556.77
27	2016.41	146.28	592.58
28	1385.71	108.16	630.70
29	714.44	67.59	671.27
30	0.00	24.42	714.44

Total Payout = $22165.82   Total Interest = $12165.82

YEARLY AMORTIZATION
PRINCIPAL = $10,0[...]

6.50%

15 YEAR TERM $87.11/Month

YEAR	PRINCIPAL	INT. PAID	PRIN. PAID
1	9592.68	638.01	407.32
2	9158.08	610.73	434.60
3	8694.37	581.62	463.71
4	8199.61	550.57	494.76
5	7671.71	517.43	527.90
6	7108.46	482.08	563.25
7	6507.49	444.36	600.97
8	5866.27	404.11	641.22
9	5182.10	361.16	684.17
10	4452.11	315.34	729.99
11	3673.24	266.46	778.87
12	2842.20	214.29	831.04
13	1955.51	158.64	886.69
14	1009.44	99.25	946.08
15	0.00	35.89	1009.44

Total Payout = $15679.93   Total Interest = $5679.93

30 YEAR TERM $63.21/Month

YEAR	PRINCIPAL	INT. PAID	PRIN. PAID
1	9888.23	646.71	111.77
2	9768.97	639.22	119.26
3	9641.72	631.24	127.25
4	9505.96	622.71	135.77
5	9361.10	613.62	144.86
6	9206.54	603.92	154.56
7	9041.62	593.57	164.91
8	8865.67	582.52	175.96
9	8677.93	570.74	187.74
10	8477.61	558.17	200.31
11	8263.88	544.75	213.73
12	8035.84	530.44	228.04
13	7792.52	515.17	243.32
14	7532.91	498.87	259.61
15	7255.91	481.48	277.00
16	6960.37	462.93	295.55
17	6645.02	443.14	315.34
18	6308.56	422.02	336.46
19	5949.57	399.49	358.99
20	5566.53	375.44	383.04
21	5157.84	349.79	408.69
22	4721.78	322.42	436.06
23	4256.51	293.22	465.26
24	3760.09	262.06	496.42
25	3230.42	228.81	529.67
26	2665.27	193.34	565.14
27	2062.28	155.49	602.99
28	1418.91	115.11	643.38
29	732.44	72.02	686.46
30	0.00	26.04	732.44

Total Payout = $22754.45   Total Interest = $12754.45

6.75%

15 YEAR TERM $88.49/Month

YEAR	PRINCIPAL	INT. PAID	PRIN. PAID
1	9600.91	662.80	399.09
2	9174.04	635.02	426.88
3	8717.44	605.29	456.60
4	8229.05	573.50	488.39
5	7706.65	539.50	522.40
6	7147.88	503.12	558.77
7	6550.21	464.22	597.68
8	5910.92	422.60	639.29
9	5227.11	378.09	683.80
10	4495.70	330.48	731.41
11	3713.36	279.55	782.34
12	2876.54	225.08	836.81
13	1981.47	166.81	895.08
14	1024.06	104.49	957.40
15	0.00	37.83	1024.06

Total Payout = $15928.37   Total Interest = $5928.37

30 YEAR TERM $64.86/Month

YEAR	PRINCIPAL	INT. PAID	PRIN. PAID
1	9893.43	671.74	106.57
2	9779.43	664.32	114.00
3	9657.50	656.39	121.93
4	9527.07	647.90	130.42
5	9387.57	638.81	139.50
6	9238.35	629.10	149.22
7	9078.75	618.71	159.61
8	8908.03	607.60	170.72
9	8725.42	595.71	182.61
10	8530.10	583.00	195.32
11	8321.18	569.40	208.92
12	8097.71	554.85	223.47
13	7858.68	539.29	239.03
14	7603.01	522.65	255.67
15	7329.54	504.85	273.47
16	7037.03	485.80	292.51
17	6724.15	465.44	312.88
18	6389.48	443.65	334.67
19	6031.51	420.35	357.97
20	5648.62	395.43	382.89
21	5239.07	368.77	409.55
22	4801.00	340.25	438.07
23	4332.43	309.75	468.57
24	3831.24	277.12	501.20
25	3295.14	242.22	536.09
26	2721.72	204.90	573.42
27	2108.38	164.97	613.35
28	1452.32	122.27	656.05
29	750.59	76.59	701.73
30	0.00	27.73	750.59

Total Payout = $23349.53   Total Interest = $13349.53

YEARLY AMORTIZATION SCHEDULES
PRINCIPAL = $10,000

7.00%

15 YEAR TERM $89.88/Month

YEAR	PRINCIPAL	INT. PAID	PRIN. PAID
1	9609.02	687.61	390.98
2	9189.78	659.35	419.24
3	8740.23	629.04	449.55
4	8258.18	596.54	482.05
5	7741.28	561.70	516.90
6	7187.02	524.33	554.26
7	6592.69	484.26	594.33
8	5955.39	441.30	637.29
9	5272.03	395.23	683.36
10	4539.26	345.83	732.77
11	3753.52	292.86	785.74
12	2910.99	236.06	842.54
13	2007.54	175.15	903.45
14	1038.79	109.84	968.76
15	0.00	39.81	1038.79

Total Payout = $16178.91   Total Interest = $6178.91

30 YEAR TERM $66.53/Month

YEAR	PRINCIPAL	INT. PAID	PRIN. PAID
1	9898.42	696.78	101.58
2	9789.49	689.44	108.92
3	9672.70	681.56	116.80
4	9547.45	673.12	125.24
5	9413.16	664.07	134.30
6	9269.16	654.36	144.00
7	9114.74	643.95	154.41
8	8949.16	632.79	165.58
9	8771.62	620.82	177.55
10	8581.28	607.98	190.38
11	8377.09	594.22	204.14
12	8158.19	579.46	218.90
13	7923.47	563.64	234.73
14	7671.78	546.67	251.69
15	7401.89	528.47	269.89
16	7112.49	508.96	289.40
17	6802.17	488.04	310.32
18	6469.42	465.61	332.75
19	6112.61	441.56	356.81
20	5730.01	415.76	382.60
21	5319.75	388.10	410.26
22	4879.83	358.45	439.92
23	4408.11	326.64	471.72
24	3902.29	292.54	505.82
25	3359.91	255.98	542.38
26	2778.32	216.77	581.59
27	2154.68	174.73	623.64
28	1485.96	129.64	668.72
29	768.90	81.30	717.06
30	0.00	29.46	768.90

Total Payout = $23950.89   Total Interest = $13950.89

7.25%

15 YEAR TERM $91.29/Month

YEAR	PRINCIPAL	INT. PAID	PRIN. PAID
1	9617.00	712.44	383.00
2	9205.30	683.73	411.70
3	8762.73	652.87	442.57
4	8286.99	619.70	475.74
5	7775.59	584.04	511.40
6	7225.86	545.70	549.73
7	6634.92	504.49	590.94
8	5999.68	460.20	635.24
9	5316.83	412.58	682.85
10	4582.79	361.40	734.04
11	3793.73	306.37	789.06
12	2945.52	247.23	848.21
13	2033.74	183.65	911.79
14	1053.60	115.30	980.13
15	0.00	41.83	1053.60

Total Payout = $16431.53   Total Interest = $6431.53

30 YEAR TERM $68.22/Month

YEAR	PRINCIPAL	INT. PAID	PRIN. PAID
1	9903.21	721.83	96.79
2	9799.17	714.57	104.04
3	9687.33	706.77	111.84
4	9567.11	698.39	120.22
5	9437.88	689.38	129.23
6	9298.96	679.69	138.92
7	9149.62	669.28	149.33
8	8989.09	658.08	160.53
9	8816.53	646.05	172.56
10	8631.03	633.12	185.50
11	8431.63	619.21	199.40
12	8217.29	604.26	214.35
13	7986.87	588.20	230.41
14	7739.18	570.93	247.69
15	7472.93	552.36	266.25
16	7186.72	532.40	286.21
17	6879.06	510.95	307.66
18	6548.33	487.89	330.73
19	6192.81	463.09	355.52
20	5810.65	436.45	382.17
21	5399.84	407.80	410.81
22	4958.23	377.01	441.61
23	4483.52	343.90	474.71
24	3973.23	308.32	510.29
25	3424.69	270.07	548.54
26	2835.03	228.95	589.66
27	2201.17	184.75	633.86
28	1519.80	137.24	681.37
29	787.35	86.16	732.45
30	0.00	31.26	787.35

Total Payout = $24558.35   Total Interest = $14558.35

160

YEARLY AMORTIZATION SCHEDULES
PRINCIPAL = $10,000

7.50%

15 YEAR TERM $92.70/Month

YEAR	PRINCIPAL	INT. PAID	PRIN. PAID
1	9624.86	737.28	375.14
2	9220.60	708.16	404.26
3	8784.96	676.77	435.64
4	8315.50	642.95	469.46
5	7809.59	606.51	505.91
6	7264.41	567.23	545.18
7	6676.90	524.91	587.51
8	6043.78	479.30	633.12
9	5361.52	430.15	682.27
10	4626.28	377.18	735.23
11	3833.97	320.10	792.31
12	2980.15	258.59	853.82
13	2060.05	192.31	920.11
14	1068.51	120.88	991.54
15	0.00	43.90	1068.51

Total Payout = $16686.22   Total Interest = $6686.22

30 YEAR TERM $69.92/Month

YEAR	PRINCIPAL	INT. PAID	PRIN. PAID
1	9907.82	746.87	92.18
2	9808.48	739.72	99.34
3	9701.42	732.01	107.05
4	9586.06	723.69	115.36
5	9461.74	714.74	124.32
6	9327.77	705.09	133.97
7	9183.40	694.69	144.37
8	9027.83	683.48	155.58
9	8860.17	671.40	167.66
10	8679.50	658.39	180.67
11	8484.80	644.36	194.70
12	8274.99	629.25	209.81
13	8048.89	612.96	226.10
14	7805.24	595.40	243.65
15	7542.67	576.49	262.57
16	7259.71	556.10	282.95
17	6954.80	534.14	304.92
18	6626.20	510.47	328.59
19	6272.10	484.96	354.10
20	5890.52	457.47	381.59
21	5479.30	427.84	411.21
22	5036.16	395.92	443.14
23	4558.63	361.52	477.54
24	4044.01	324.45	514.61
25	3489.45	284.50	554.56
26	2891.84	241.44	597.61
27	2247.83	195.05	644.01
28	1553.83	145.05	694.00
29	805.94	91.18	747.88
30	0.00	33.12	805.94

Total Payout = $25171.72   Total Interest = $15171.72

7.75%

15 YEAR TERM $94.13/Month

YEAR	PRINCIPAL	INT. PAID	PRIN. PAID
1	9632.60	762.13	367.40
2	9235.69	732.62	396.91
3	8806.91	700.75	428.78
4	8343.69	666.31	463.22
5	7843.27	629.11	500.42
6	7302.66	588.92	540.61
7	6718.63	545.50	584.03
8	6087.69	498.59	630.94
9	5406.08	447.92	681.61
10	4669.73	393.18	736.35
11	3874.24	334.04	795.49
12	3014.86	270.15	859.38
13	2086.47	201.13	928.40
14	1083.51	126.57	1002.96
15	0.00	46.02	1083.51

Total Payout = $16942.96   Total Interest = $6942.96

30 YEAR TERM $71.64/Month

YEAR	PRINCIPAL	INT. PAID	PRIN. PAID
1	9912.23	771.93	87.77
2	9817.41	764.88	94.82
3	9714.98	757.26	102.43
4	9604.32	749.04	110.66
5	9484.77	740.15	119.55
6	9355.63	730.55	129.15
7	9216.11	720.17	139.52
8	9065.38	708.97	150.73
9	8902.55	696.86	162.83
10	8726.64	683.79	175.91
11	8536.60	669.66	190.04
12	8331.31	654.40	205.30
13	8109.52	637.91	221.79
14	7869.92	620.10	239.60
15	7611.08	600.85	258.84
16	7331.45	580.06	279.63
17	7029.36	557.61	302.09
18	6703.01	533.34	326.35
19	6350.45	507.13	352.56
20	5969.58	478.82	380.88
21	5558.11	448.23	411.46
22	5113.60	415.18	444.51
23	4633.30	379.48	480.21
24	4114.61	340.92	518.78
25	3554.17	299.25	560.44
26	2948.72	254.24	605.45
27	2294.64	205.62	654.08
28	1588.03	153.09	706.61
29	824.67	96.34	763.36
30	0.01	35.03	824.67

Total Payout = $25790.84   Total Interest = $15790.84

YEARLY AMORTIZATION SCHEDULES
PRINCIPAL = $10,000

8.00%

15 YEAR TERM $95.57/Month

YEAR	PRINCIPAL	INT. PAID	PRIN. PAID
1	9640.22	787.00	359.78
2	9250.57	757.14	389.65
3	8828.58	724.80	421.99
4	8371.57	689.77	457.01
5	7876.63	651.84	494.94
6	7340.60	610.76	536.02
7	6760.09	566.27	580.51
8	6131.39	518.09	628.70
9	5450.52	465.91	680.88
10	4713.13	409.39	737.39
11	3914.53	348.19	798.59
12	3049.66	281.91	864.88
13	2113.00	210.12	936.66
14	1098.60	132.38	1014.40
15	0.00	48.19	1098.60

Total Payout = $17201.74   Total Interest = $7201.74

30 YEAR TERM $73.38/Month

YEAR	PRINCIPAL	INT. PAID	PRIN. PAID
1	9916.46	796.98	83.54
2	9825.99	790.05	90.47
3	9728.01	782.54	97.98
4	9621.90	774.41	106.11
5	9506.99	765.60	114.92
6	9382.53	756.06	124.46
7	9247.74	745.73	134.79
8	9101.77	734.54	145.97
9	8943.68	722.43	158.09
10	8772.47	709.31	171.21
11	8587.05	695.10	185.42
12	8386.24	679.71	200.81
13	8168.76	663.04	217.48
14	7933.23	644.99	235.53
15	7678.16	625.44	255.06
16	7401.91	604.27	276.25
17	7102.73	581.34	299.18
18	6778.72	556.51	324.01
19	6427.82	529.62	350.90
20	6047.79	500.49	380.03
21	5636.23	468.95	411.57
22	5190.50	434.79	445.73
23	4707.78	397.79	482.72
24	4184.99	357.73	522.79
25	3618.81	314.34	566.18
26	3005.64	267.35	613.17
27	2341.57	216.45	664.07
28	1622.39	161.34	719.18
29	843.52	101.64	778.87
30	0.00	37.00	843.52

Total Payout = $26415.53   Total Interest = $16415.53

8.25%

15 YEAR TERM $97.01/Month

YEAR	PRINCIPAL	INT. PAID	PRIN. PAID
1	9647.71	811.88	352.29
2	9265.23	781.69	382.48
3	8849.97	748.91	415.26
4	8399.13	713.33	450.84
5	7909.66	674.69	489.47
6	7378.24	632.75	531.42
7	6801.28	587.21	576.96
8	6174.89	537.77	626.40
9	5494.81	484.09	680.07
10	4756.46	425.82	738.35
11	3954.84	362.55	801.62
12	3084.53	293.85	870.31
13	2139.63	219.28	944.89
14	1113.77	138.31	1025.86
15	0.00	50.40	1113.77

Total Payout = $17462.53   Total Interest = $7462.53

30 YEAR TERM $75.13/Month

YEAR	PRINCIPAL	INT. PAID	PRIN. PAID
1	9920.52	822.04	79.48
2	9834.23	815.23	86.29
3	9740.54	807.83	93.69
4	9638.83	799.81	101.71
5	9528.40	791.09	110.43
6	9408.50	781.63	119.89
7	9278.34	771.35	130.17
8	9137.02	760.20	141.32
9	8983.58	748.09	153.43
10	8817.00	734.94	166.58
11	8636.15	720.67	180.85
12	8439.80	705.17	196.35
13	8226.62	688.34	213.18
14	7995.17	670.07	231.45
15	7743.90	650.24	251.28
16	7471.09	628.71	272.81
17	7174.90	605.33	296.19
18	6853.33	579.95	321.57
19	6504.20	552.39	349.13
20	6125.16	522.48	379.04
21	5713.63	490.00	411.52
22	5266.84	454.73	446.79
23	4781.77	416.45	485.07
24	4255.13	374.88	526.64
25	3683.36	329.75	571.77
26	3062.59	280.75	620.77
27	2388.63	227.56	673.96
28	1656.91	169.80	731.72
29	862.49	107.10	794.42
30	0.00	39.03	862.49

Total Payout = $27045.60   Total Interest = $17045.60

YEARLY AMORTIZATION SCHEDULES
PRINCIPAL = $10,000

8.50%

15 YEAR TERM $98.47/Month

YEAR	PRINCIPAL	INT. PAID	PRIN. PAID
1	9655.08	836.77	344.92
2	9279.67	806.28	375.41
3	8871.08	773.10	408.59
4	8426.38	736.98	444.71
5	7942.37	697.67	484.01
6	7415.17	654.89	526.80
7	6842.21	608.33	573.36
8	6218.17	557.65	624.04
9	5538.97	502.49	679.20
10	4799.74	442.45	739.23
11	3995.16	377.11	804.58
12	3119.47	305.99	875.69
13	2166.37	228.59	953.10
14	1129.03	144.35	1037.34
15	0.00	52.66	1129.03

Total Payout = $17725.31   Total Interest = $7725.31

30 YEAR TERM $76.89/Month

YEAR	PRINCIPAL	INT. PAID	PRIN. PAID
1	9924.40	847.10	75.60
2	9842.13	840.42	82.28
3	9752.57	833.15	89.55
4	9655.11	825.23	97.47
5	9549.05	816.61	106.08
6	9433.57	807.24	115.46
7	9307.90	797.03	125.66
8	9171.13	785.92	136.77
9	9022.27	773.84	148.86
10	8860.25	760.68	162.02
11	8683.91	746.36	176.34
12	8491.99	730.77	191.93
13	8283.10	713.81	208.89
14	8055.74	695.34	227.35
15	7808.29	675.25	247.45
16	7538.97	653.37	269.32
17	7245.84	629.57	293.13
18	6926.80	603.66	319.04
19	6579.56	575.46	347.24
20	6201.63	544.76	377.93
21	5790.29	511.36	411.34
22	5342.60	475.00	447.70
23	4855.33	435.43	487.27
24	4324.99	392.36	530.34
25	3747.77	345.48	577.22
26	3119.54	294.46	628.24
27	2435.77	238.93	683.77
28	1691.57	178.49	744.21
29	881.58	112.71	809.99
30	0.00	41.11	881.58

Total Payout = $27680.89   Total Interest = $17680.89

8.75%

15 YEAR TERM $99.94/Month

YEAR	PRINCIPAL	INT. PAID	PRIN. PAID
1	9662.33	861.67	337.67
2	9293.91	830.91	368.43
3	8891.92	797.35	401.99
4	8453.31	760.73	438.61
5	7974.74	720.77	478.56
6	7452.58	677.18	522.16
7	6882.86	629.61	569.73
8	6261.23	577.71	621.63
9	5582.98	521.09	678.25
10	4842.94	459.30	740.04
11	4035.48	391.88	807.45
12	3154.47	318.33	881.01
13	2193.21	238.07	961.27
14	1144.38	150.51	1048.83
15	0.00	54.96	1144.38

Total Payout = $17990.08   Total Interest = $7990.08

30 YEAR TERM $78.67/Month

YEAR	PRINCIPAL	INT. PAID	PRIN. PAID
1	9928.12	872.16	71.88
2	9849.70	865.62	78.43
3	9764.13	858.47	85.57
4	9670.76	850.68	93.36
5	9568.89	842.17	101.87
6	9457.74	832.89	111.15
7	9336.47	822.77	121.28
8	9204.14	811.72	132.32
9	9059.77	799.66	144.38
10	8902.24	786.51	157.53
11	8730.36	772.16	171.88
12	8542.82	756.50	187.54
13	8338.20	739.42	204.62
14	8114.94	720.78	223.26
15	7871.34	700.44	243.60
16	7605.55	678.25	265.79
17	7315.55	654.04	290.00
18	6999.13	627.62	316.42
19	6653.89	598.80	345.24
20	6277.19	567.35	376.69
21	5866.19	533.03	411.01
22	5417.73	495.59	448.45
23	4928.43	454.74	489.30
24	4394.55	410.16	533.88
25	3812.04	361.53	582.51
26	3176.47	308.47	635.57
27	2483.00	250.57	693.47
28	1726.35	187.40	756.65
29	900.78	118.47	825.57
30	0.00	43.26	900.78

Total Payout = $28321.21   Total Interest = $18321.21

163

YEARLY AMORTIZATION SCHEDULES
PRINCIPAL = $10,000

9.00%

15 YEAR TERM $101.43/Month

YEAR	PRINCIPAL	INT. PAID	PRIN. PAID
1	9669.47	886.59	330.53
2	9307.93	855.58	361.54
3	8912.47	821.66	395.46
4	8479.92	784.57	432.55
5	8006.79	743.99	473.13
6	7489.28	699.61	517.51
7	6923.23	651.06	566.06
8	6304.07	597.96	619.16
9	5626.83	539.88	677.24
10	4886.06	476.35	740.77
11	4075.81	406.86	810.26
12	3189.54	330.86	886.26
13	2220.14	247.72	969.40
14	1159.80	156.78	1060.34
15	0.00	57.31	1159.81

Total Payout = $18256.80   Total Interest = $8256.80

30 YEAR TERM $80.46/Month

YEAR	PRINCIPAL	INT. PAID	PRIN. PAID
1	9931.68	897.23	68.32
2	9856.95	890.82	74.73
3	9775.21	883.81	81.74
4	9685.81	876.14	89.41
5	9588.01	867.75	97.79
6	9481.05	858.58	106.97
7	9364.05	848.55	117.00
8	9236.07	837.57	127.98
9	9096.09	825.57	139.98
10	8942.97	812.43	153.11
11	8775.50	798.07	167.48
12	8592.31	782.36	183.19
13	8391.94	765.18	200.37
14	8172.78	746.38	219.17
15	7933.05	725.82	239.73
16	7670.84	703.33	262.21
17	7384.02	678.74	286.81
18	7070.31	651.83	313.72
19	6727.16	622.40	343.15
20	6351.83	590.21	375.33
21	5941.28	555.00	410.54
22	5492.23	516.49	449.06
23	5001.05	474.37	491.18
24	4463.79	428.29	537.26
25	3876.14	377.89	587.65
26	3233.36	322.77	642.78
27	2530.28	262.47	703.08
28	1761.25	196.52	769.03
29	920.08	124.38	841.17
30	0.00	45.47	920.08

Total Payout = $28966.41   Total Interest = $18966.41

9.25%

15 YEAR TERM $102.92/Month

YEAR	PRINCIPAL	INT. PAID	PRIN. PAID
1	9676.48	911.51	323.52
2	9321.74	880.28	354.75
3	8932.75	846.04	388.99
4	8506.21	808.50	426.53
5	8038.51	767.33	467.70
6	7525.66	722.18	512.85
7	6963.31	672.68	562.35
8	6346.68	618.40	616.63
9	5670.52	558.88	676.15
10	4929.11	493.61	741.42
11	4116.12	422.05	812.98
12	3224.67	343.58	891.45
13	2247.17	257.53	977.50
14	1175.31	163.18	1071.85
15	0.00	59.72	1175.31

Total Payout = $18525.46   Total Interest = $8525.46

30 YEAR TERM $82.27/Month

YEAR	PRINCIPAL	INT. PAID	PRIN. PAID
1	9935.08	922.29	64.92
2	9863.90	916.03	71.18
3	9785.85	909.16	78.05
4	9700.26	901.62	85.59
5	9606.41	893.36	93.85
6	9503.50	884.30	102.91
7	9390.66	874.37	112.84
8	9266.93	863.48	123.73
9	9131.25	851.53	135.68
10	8982.48	838.44	148.77
11	8819.35	824.08	163.13
12	8640.47	808.33	178.88
13	8444.32	791.07	196.14
14	8229.25	772.13	215.08
15	7993.41	751.37	235.84
16	7734.81	728.61	258.60
17	7451.25	703.65	283.56
18	7140.31	676.28	310.93
19	6799.37	646.26	340.95
20	6425.51	613.36	373.86
21	6015.57	577.27	409.94
22	5566.06	537.70	449.51
23	5073.16	494.31	492.90
24	4532.68	446.73	540.48
25	3940.04	394.57	592.64
26	3290.19	337.36	649.85
27	2577.61	274.63	712.58
28	1796.26	205.85	781.36
29	939.48	130.43	856.78
30	0.00	47.73	939.48

Total Payout = $29616.31   Total Interest = $19616.31

YEARLY AMORTIZATION SCHEDULES
PRINCIPAL = $10,000

9.50%

15 YEAR TERM $104.42/Month

YEAR	PRINCIPAL	INT. PAID	PRIN. PAID
1	9683.38	936.45	316.62
2	9335.34	905.03	348.04
3	8952.75	870.48	382.59
4	8532.19	832.51	420.56
5	8069.89	790.77	462.30
6	7561.72	744.89	508.18
7	7003.10	694.46	558.61
8	6389.05	639.01	614.06
9	5714.05	577.56	675.00
10	4972.06	511.08	741.99
11	4156.43	437.44	815.63
12	3259.85	356.49	896.58
13	2274.28	267.51	985.56
14	1190.90	169.69	1083.38
15	0.00	62.17	1190.90

Total Payout = $18796.04   Total Interest = $8796.04

30 YEAR TERM $84.09/Month

YEAR	PRINCIPAL	INT. PAID	PRIN. PAID
1	9938.34	947.36	61.66
2	9870.55	941.24	67.78
3	9796.04	934.51	74.51
4	9714.13	927.12	81.91
5	9624.10	918.99	90.04
6	9525.13	910.05	98.97
7	9416.33	900.23	108.79
8	9296.74	889.43	119.59
9	9165.28	877.56	131.46
10	9020.77	864.52	144.51
11	8861.92	850.17	158.85
12	8687.31	834.41	174.62
13	8495.36	817.08	191.95
14	8284.36	798.03	211.00
15	8052.43	777.09	231.94
16	7797.47	754.07	254.96
17	7517.21	728.77	280.26
18	7209.14	700.95	308.08
19	6870.48	670.37	338.65
20	6498.22	636.76	372.26
21	6089.02	599.82	409.21
22	5639.20	559.21	449.82
23	5144.73	514.56	494.46
24	4601.20	465.49	543.54
25	4003.71	411.54	597.48
26	3346.93	352.24	656.78
27	2624.97	287.06	721.96
28	1831.35	215.41	793.62
29	958.97	136.64	872.38
30	0.00	50.06	958.96

Total Payout = $30270.75   Total Interest = $20270.75

9.75%

15 YEAR TERM $105.94/Month

YEAR	PRINCIPAL	INT. PAID	PRIN. PAID
1	9690.16	961.40	309.84
2	9348.73	929.80	341.43
3	8972.47	894.98	376.25
4	8557.85	856.61	414.62
5	8100.95	814.33	456.90
6	7597.45	767.74	503.50
7	7042.60	716.39	554.84
8	6431.18	659.81	611.43
9	5757.40	597.46	673.78
10	5014.92	528.75	742.49
11	4196.71	453.03	818.20
12	3295.07	369.59	901.64
13	2301.48	277.65	993.59
14	1206.57	176.32	1094.91
15	0.00	64.67	1206.57

Total Payout = $19068.53   Total Interest = $9068.53

30 YEAR TERM $85.92/Month

YEAR	PRINCIPAL	INT. PAID	PRIN. PAID
1	9941.44	972.43	58.56
2	9876.92	966.46	64.53
3	9805.81	959.88	71.11
4	9727.45	952.63	78.36
5	9641.10	944.64	86.35
6	9545.94	935.83	95.16
7	9441.08	926.13	104.86
8	9325.53	915.43	115.55
9	9198.19	903.65	127.34
10	9057.87	890.66	140.32
11	8903.24	876.35	154.63
12	8732.84	860.58	170.40
13	8545.06	843.21	187.78
14	8338.14	824.06	206.93
15	8110.11	802.96	228.03
16	7858.82	779.70	251.28
17	7581.92	754.08	276.91
18	7276.77	725.84	305.15
19	6940.51	694.72	336.26
20	6569.95	660.43	370.55
21	6161.61	622.64	408.34
22	5711.63	581.00	449.98
23	5215.76	535.11	495.87
24	4669.31	484.55	546.44
25	4067.15	428.82	602.16
26	3403.58	367.41	663.57
27	2672.34	299.74	731.24
28	1866.53	225.17	805.81
29	978.54	143.00	887.99
30	0.00	52.45	978.54

Total Payout = $30929.56   Total Interest = $20929.56

YEARLY AMORTIZATION SCHEDULES
PRINCIPAL = $10,000

10.00%

15 YEAR TERM $107.46/Month

YEAR	PRINCIPAL	INT. PAID	PRIN. PAID
1	9696.83	986.35	303.17
2	9361.91	954.61	334.92
3	8991.92	919.54	369.99
4	8583.19	880.80	408.73
5	8131.66	838.00	451.53
6	7632.85	790.72	498.81
7	7081.84	738.48	551.04
8	6473.06	680.78	608.74
9	5800.58	617.04	672.49
10	5057.67	546.62	742.91
11	4236.97	468.83	820.70
12	3330.33	382.89	906.64
13	2328.76	287.95	1001.57
14	1222.31	183.08	1106.45
15	0.00	67.22	1222.31

Total Payout = $19342.89   Total Interest = $9342.89

30 YEAR TERM $87.76/Month

YEAR	PRINCIPAL	INT. PAID	PRIN. PAID
1	9944.41	997.50	55.59
2	9883.00	991.68	61.41
3	9815.16	985.25	67.84
4	9740.22	978.14	74.94
5	9657.43	970.30	82.79
6	9565.97	961.63	91.46
7	9464.94	952.05	101.04
8	9353.32	941.47	111.62
9	9230.02	929.78	123.30
10	9093.80	916.87	136.22
11	8943.32	902.61	150.48
12	8777.06	886.85	166.24
13	8593.44	869.44	183.64
14	8390.57	850.21	202.87
15	8166.46	828.97	224.12
16	7918.87	805.50	247.58
17	7645.36	779.58	273.51
18	7343.21	750.94	302.15
19	7009.42	719.30	333.79
20	6640.68	684.35	368.74
21	6233.33	645.73	407.35
22	5783.32	603.08	450.01
23	5286.20	555.96	497.13
24	4737.01	503.90	549.18
25	4130.32	446.39	606.69
26	3460.10	382.87	670.22
27	2719.70	312.68	740.40
28	1901.77	235.16	817.93
29	998.19	149.51	903.58
30	-0.01	54.89	998.20

Total Payout = $31592.58   Total Interest = $21592.58

10.25%

15 YEAR TERM $109.00/Month

YEAR	PRINCIPAL	INT. PAID	PRIN. PAID
1	9703.38	1011.32	296.62
2	9374.89	979.45	328.49
3	9011.10	944.15	363.79
4	8608.22	905.06	402.88
5	8162.04	861.77	446.17
6	7667.92	813.82	494.12
7	7120.71	760.73	547.21
8	6514.70	701.93	606.01
9	5843.57	636.81	671.13
10	5100.32	564.69	743.25
11	4277.20	484.83	823.12
12	3365.64	396.38	911.56
13	2356.12	298.43	1009.52
14	1238.13	189.95	1117.99
15	0.00	69.81	1238.13

Total Payout = $19619.12   Total Interest = $9619.12

30 YEAR TERM $89.61/Month

YEAR	PRINCIPAL	INT. PAID	PRIN. PAID
1	9947.25	1022.57	52.75
2	9888.82	1016.90	58.42
3	9824.12	1010.62	64.70
4	9752.47	1003.67	71.65
5	9673.12	995.97	79.35
6	9585.24	987.44	87.88
7	9487.91	978.00	97.32
8	9380.13	967.54	107.78
9	9260.77	955.90	119.36
10	9128.58	943.13	132.19
11	8982.19	928.93	146.39
12	8820.07	913.20	162.12
13	8640.52	895.78	179.54
14	8441.69	876.48	198.84
15	8221.48	855.12	220.20
16	7977.62	831.46	243.87
17	7707.55	805.25	270.07
18	7408.46	776.23	299.09
19	7077.23	744.09	331.23
20	6710.41	708.50	366.82
21	6304.17	669.08	406.24
22	5854.28	625.43	449.89
23	5356.05	577.09	498.23
24	4804.28	523.55	551.77
25	4193.22	464.26	611.06
26	3516.49	398.60	676.72
27	2767.05	325.88	749.44
28	1937.08	245.35	829.97
29	1017.92	156.17	919.16
30	0.00	57.40	1017.92

Total Payout = $32259.65   Total Interest = $22259.65

YEARLY AMORTIZATION SCHEDULES
PRINCIPAL = \$10,000

10.50%

15 YEAR TERM \$110.54/Month

YEAR	PRINCIPAL	INT. PAID	PRIN. PAID
1	9709.82	1036.30	290.18
2	9387.66	1004.32	322.16
3	9030.00	968.82	357.66
4	8632.92	929.40	397.08
5	8192.08	885.64	440.84
6	7702.67	837.06	489.42
7	7159.31	783.12	543.35
8	6556.08	723.25	603.23
9	5886.37	656.77	669.71
10	5142.85	582.96	743.52
11	4317.40	501.02	825.45
12	3400.97	410.06	916.42
13	2383.56	309.06	1017.42
14	1254.02	196.94	1129.54
15	0.00	72.46	1254.02

Total Payout = \$19897.18   Total Interest = \$9897.18

30 YEAR TERM \$91.47/Month

YEAR	PRINCIPAL	INT. PAID	PRIN. PAID
1	9949.95	1047.64	50.05
2	9894.38	1042.12	55.57
3	9832.69	1036.00	61.69
4	9764.21	1029.20	68.49
5	9688.17	1021.65	76.04
6	9603.75	1013.27	84.42
7	9510.04	1003.97	93.72
8	9405.99	993.64	104.05
9	9290.48	982.17	115.51
10	9162.24	969.45	128.24
11	9019.86	955.31	142.37
12	8861.80	939.62	158.06
13	8686.31	922.20	175.48
14	8491.49	902.86	194.82
15	8275.20	881.39	216.29
16	8035.07	857.56	240.13
17	7768.47	831.09	266.59
18	7472.50	801.71	295.97
19	7143.91	769.10	328.59
20	6779.11	732.89	364.80
21	6374.11	692.68	405.00
22	5924.47	648.05	449.64
23	5425.28	598.50	499.19
24	4871.08	543.49	554.20
25	4255.81	482.41	615.27
26	3572.73	414.61	683.08
27	2814.37	339.33	758.36
28	1972.44	255.76	841.93
29	1037.72	162.97	934.72
30	0.00	59.96	1037.72

Total Payout = \$32930.61   Total Interest = \$22930.61

10.75%

15 YEAR TERM \$112.09/Month

YEAR	PRINCIPAL	INT. PAID	PRIN. PAID
1	9716.15	1061.28	283.85
2	9400.23	1029.22	315.92
3	9048.63	993.54	351.60
4	8657.31	953.82	391.32
5	8221.79	909.62	435.52
6	7737.07	860.42	484.72
7	7197.60	805.67	539.47
8	6597.20	744.73	600.41
9	5928.97	676.91	668.23
10	5185.26	601.43	743.71
11	4357.55	517.42	827.72
12	3436.33	423.92	921.21
13	2411.06	319.87	1025.27
14	1269.98	204.05	1141.08
15	0.00	75.16	1269.98

Total Payout = \$20177.06   Total Interest = \$10177.06

30 YEAR TERM \$93.35/Month

YEAR	PRINCIPAL	INT. PAID	PRIN. PAID
1	9952.53	1072.71	47.47
2	9899.69	1067.34	52.83
3	9840.89	1061.38	58.80
4	9775.45	1054.73	65.44
5	9702.61	1047.34	72.84
6	9621.55	1039.11	81.06
7	9531.33	1029.96	90.22
8	9430.92	1019.77	100.41
9	9319.16	1008.42	111.75
10	9194.79	995.80	124.38
11	9056.36	981.75	138.43
12	8902.30	966.11	154.06
13	8730.83	948.71	171.47
14	8540.00	929.34	190.83
15	8327.60	907.79	212.39
16	8091.22	883.80	236.38
17	7828.14	857.09	263.08
18	7535.34	827.38	292.80
19	7209.46	794.30	325.87
20	6846.78	757.49	362.68
21	6443.13	716.52	403.65
22	5993.88	670.93	449.25
23	5493.88	620.18	499.99
24	4937.41	563.70	556.47
25	4318.08	500.85	619.33
26	3628.79	430.89	689.29
27	2861.64	353.00	767.15
28	2007.83	266.37	853.81
29	1057.58	169.93	950.25
30	-0.01	62.59	1057.59

Total Payout = \$33605.33   Total Interest = \$23605.33

YEARLY AMORTIZATION SCHEDULES
PRINCIPAL = $10,000

11.00%

15 YEAR TERM $113.66/Month

YEAR	PRINCIPAL	INT. PAID	PRIN. PAID
1	9722.36	1086.28	277.64
2	9412.60	1054.15	309.76
3	9066.99	1018.31	345.61
4	8681.38	978.31	385.60
5	8251.16	933.69	430.23
6	7771.15	883.91	480.01
7	7235.59	828.36	535.56
8	6638.06	766.38	597.53
9	5971.38	697.24	666.68
10	5227.55	620.09	743.82
11	4397.66	534.02	829.90
12	3471.72	437.98	925.93
13	2438.64	330.83	1033.08
14	1286.01	211.29	1152.63
15	0.00	77.91	1286.01

Total Payout = $20458.74   Total Interest = $10458.74

30 YEAR TERM $95.23/Month

YEAR	PRINCIPAL	INT. PAID	PRIN. PAID
1	9954.99	1097.78	45.01
2	9904.77	1092.57	50.22
3	9848.73	1086.76	56.03
4	9786.22	1080.27	62.52
5	9716.46	1073.04	69.75
6	9638.64	1064.97	77.82
7	9551.81	1055.96	86.83
8	9454.94	1045.91	96.88
9	9346.85	1034.70	108.09
10	9226.26	1022.19	120.59
11	9091.71	1008.24	134.55
12	8941.59	992.67	150.12
13	8774.10	975.30	167.49
14	8587.22	955.92	186.87
15	8378.73	934.29	208.50
16	8146.10	910.16	232.62
17	7886.56	883.24	259.54
18	7596.98	853.21	289.58
19	7273.89	819.70	323.09
20	6913.42	782.31	360.47
21	6511.23	740.60	402.19
22	6062.50	694.06	448.73
23	5561.84	642.13	500.66
24	5003.25	584.20	558.59
25	4380.02	519.56	623.23
26	3684.67	447.44	695.35
27	2908.86	366.97	775.81
28	2043.27	277.20	865.59
29	1077.51	177.03	965.76
30	0.00	65.28	1077.51

Total Payout = $34283.64   Total Interest = $24283.64

11.25%

15 YEAR TERM $115.23/Month

YEAR	PRINCIPAL	INT. PAID	PRIN. PAID
1	9728.47	1111.28	271.53
2	9424.76	1079.11	303.70
3	9085.08	1043.12	339.69
4	8705.14	1002.88	379.94
5	8280.18	957.86	424.95
6	7804.88	907.51	475.31
7	7273.26	851.19	531.62
8	6678.65	788.20	594.61
9	6013.58	717.75	665.07
10	5269.71	638.95	743.87
11	4437.71	550.81	832.00
12	3507.13	452.23	930.58
13	2466.28	341.97	1040.85
14	1302.11	218.64	1164.17
15	0.00	80.70	1302.11

Total Payout = $20742.20   Total Interest = $10742.20

30 YEAR TERM $97.13/Month

YEAR	PRINCIPAL	INT. PAID	PRIN. PAID
1	9957.33	1122.84	42.67
2	9909.61	1117.79	47.73
3	9856.23	1112.13	53.38
4	9796.52	1105.81	59.70
5	9729.74	1098.73	66.78
6	9655.05	1090.82	74.69
7	9571.51	1081.97	83.54
8	9478.07	1072.07	93.44
9	9373.56	1061.00	104.51
10	9256.67	1048.62	116.89
11	9125.92	1034.77	130.74
12	8979.69	1019.28	146.24
13	8816.13	1001.95	163.56
14	8633.18	982.57	182.94
15	8428.57	960.90	204.62
16	8199.70	936.65	228.86
17	7943.73	909.53	255.98
18	7657.42	879.20	286.31
19	7337.18	845.28	320.23
20	6979.01	807.34	358.18
21	6578.39	764.90	400.61
22	6130.31	717.43	448.08
23	5629.14	664.34	501.17
24	5068.58	604.96	560.55
25	4441.61	538.54	626.97
26	3740.35	464.25	701.26
27	2956.00	381.16	784.35
28	2078.72	288.23	877.28
29	1097.49	184.28	981.23
30	0.00	68.02	1097.49

Total Payout = $34965.41   Total Interest = $24965.41

YEARLY AMORTIZATION SCHEDULES
PRINCIPAL = \$10,000

11.50%

15 YEAR TERM \$116.82/Month

YEAR	PRINCIPAL	INT. PAID	PRIN. PAID
1	9734.47	1136.29	265.53
2	9436.73	1104.09	297.73
3	9102.90	1067.99	333.84
4	8728.58	1027.51	374.32
5	8308.87	982.12	419.71
6	7838.27	931.23	470.60
7	7310.61	874.16	527.66
8	6718.96	810.18	591.65
9	6055.57	738.44	663.39
10	5311.74	657.99	743.83
11	4477.71	567.80	834.03
12	3542.55	466.66	935.16
13	2493.98	353.27	1048.56
14	1318.28	226.12	1175.71
15	0.00	83.55	1318.27

Total Payout = \$21027.42   Total Interest = \$11027.42

30 YEAR TERM \$99.03/Month

YEAR	PRINCIPAL	INT. PAID	PRIN. PAID
1	9959.56	1147.91	40.44
2	9914.22	1143.01	45.34
3	9863.38	1137.51	50.84
4	9806.38	1131.35	57.00
5	9742.47	1124.43	63.92
6	9670.80	1116.68	71.67
7	9590.45	1107.99	80.36
8	9500.35	1098.25	90.10
9	9399.32	1087.32	101.02
10	9286.05	1075.07	113.27
11	9159.04	1061.34	127.01
12	9016.62	1045.94	142.41
13	8856.94	1028.67	159.68
14	8677.90	1009.31	179.04
15	8477.15	987.60	200.75
16	8252.05	963.25	225.10
17	7999.66	935.96	252.39
18	7716.66	905.35	283.00
19	7399.35	871.04	317.31
20	7043.56	832.56	355.79
21	6644.62	789.42	398.93
22	6197.31	741.04	447.31
23	5695.77	686.80	501.55
24	5133.40	625.98	562.37
25	4502.84	557.79	630.56
26	3795.82	481.33	707.02
27	3003.07	395.60	792.75
28	2114.19	299.47	888.88
29	1117.53	191.69	996.66
30	0.01	70.83	1117.52

Total Payout = \$35650.49   Total Interest = \$25650.49

11.75%

15 YEAR TERM \$118.41/Month

YEAR	PRINCIPAL	INT. PAID	PRIN. PAID
1	9740.35	1161.31	259.65
2	9448.50	1129.11	291.85
3	9120.45	1092.90	328.05
4	8751.71	1052.21	368.74
5	8337.22	1006.47	414.48
6	7871.33	955.06	465.89
7	7347.64	897.27	523.68
8	6759.00	832.32	588.64
9	6097.35	759.30	661.66
10	5353.62	677.23	743.73
11	4517.64	584.98	835.98
12	3577.97	481.29	939.67
13	2521.74	364.73	1056.23
14	1334.50	233.72	1187.24
15	0.00	86.45	1334.51

Total Payout = \$21314.37   Total Interest = \$11314.37

30 YEAR TERM \$100.94/Month

YEAR	PRINCIPAL	INT. PAID	PRIN. PAID
1	9961.69	1172.98	38.31
2	9918.63	1168.23	43.06
3	9870.22	1162.89	48.40
4	9815.81	1156.88	54.41
5	9754.65	1150.13	61.16
6	9685.91	1142.55	68.74
7	9608.64	1134.02	77.27
8	9521.78	1124.44	86.86
9	9424.15	1113.66	97.63
10	9314.42	1101.55	109.74
11	9191.07	1087.94	123.35
12	9052.41	1072.64	138.65
13	8896.57	1055.44	155.85
14	8721.39	1036.11	175.18
15	8524.48	1014.38	196.91
16	8303.14	989.96	221.33
17	8054.35	962.50	248.79
18	7774.71	931.64	279.65
19	7460.37	896.96	314.33
20	7107.05	857.97	353.32
21	6709.90	814.14	397.15
22	6263.49	764.88	446.41
23	5761.70	709.51	501.78
24	5197.67	647.27	564.03
25	4563.69	577.30	633.99
26	3851.06	498.67	712.63
27	3050.04	410.27	801.02
28	2149.66	310.91	900.38
29	1137.61	199.23	1012.06
30	0.01	73.70	1137.59

Total Payout = \$36338.75   Total Interest = \$26338.75

YEARLY AMORTIZATION SCHEDULES
PRINCIPAL = $10,000

12.00%

15 YEAR TERM $120.02/Month

YEAR	PRINCIPAL	INT. PAID	PRIN. PAID
1	9746.14	1186.34	253.86
2	9460.08	1154.14	286.06
3	9137.74	1117.86	322.34
4	8774.52	1076.98	363.22
5	8365.28	1030.92	409.28
6	7904.04	979.01	461.19
7	7384.36	920.52	519.68
8	6798.77	854.61	585.59
9	6138.91	780.34	659.86
10	5395.36	696.66	743.55
11	4557.51	602.35	837.85
12	3613.41	496.09	944.11
13	2549.56	376.36	1063.84
14	1350.80	241.44	1198.77
15	0.00	89.40	1350.80

Total Payout = $21603.03   Total Interest = $11603.03

30 YEAR TERM $102.86/Month

YEAR	PRINCIPAL	INT. PAID	PRIN. PAID
1	9963.71	1198.05	36.29
2	9922.82	1193.44	40.89
3	9876.75	1188.26	46.08
4	9824.83	1182.42	51.92
5	9766.32	1175.83	58.50
6	9700.40	1168.41	65.92
7	9626.11	1160.05	74.29
8	9542.41	1150.63	83.71
9	9448.08	1140.01	94.32
10	9341.80	1128.05	106.28
11	9222.04	1114.57	119.76
12	9087.08	1099.38	134.95
13	8935.01	1082.27	152.07
14	8763.66	1062.98	171.35
15	8570.57	1041.25	193.09
16	8353.00	1016.76	217.58
17	8107.83	989.17	245.17
18	7831.56	958.07	276.26
19	7520.26	923.04	311.30
20	7169.48	883.55	350.78
21	6774.21	839.07	395.27
22	6328.82	788.94	445.40
23	5826.93	732.45	501.89
24	5261.39	668.80	565.54
25	4624.13	597.07	637.26
26	3906.05	516.25	718.08
27	3096.90	425.18	809.15
28	2185.12	322.56	911.77
29	1157.71	206.92	1027.41
30	0.00	76.62	1157.71

Total Payout = $37030.05   Total Interest = $27030.05

12.25%

15 YEAR TERM $121.63/Month

YEAR	PRINCIPAL	INT. PAID	PRIN. PAID
1	9751.81	1211.37	248.19
2	9471.46	1179.20	280.36
3	9154.76	1142.86	316.69
4	8797.02	1101.81	357.74
5	8392.91	1055.44	404.11
6	7936.41	1003.06	456.49
7	7420.75	943.90	515.66
8	6838.25	877.06	582.50
9	6180.24	801.55	658.00
10	5436.95	716.26	743.29
11	4597.31	619.92	839.64
12	3648.84	511.09	948.47
13	2577.43	388.15	1071.41
14	1367.15	249.28	1210.28
15	0.00	92.41	1367.15

Total Payout = $21893.38   Total Interest = $11893.38

30 YEAR TERM $104.79/Month

YEAR	PRINCIPAL	INT. PAID	PRIN. PAID
1	9965.64	1223.11	34.36
2	9926.82	1218.66	38.82
3	9882.97	1213.63	43.85
4	9833.44	1207.94	49.53
5	9777.49	1201.52	55.95
6	9714.29	1194.27	63.20
7	9642.89	1186.08	71.40
8	9562.24	1176.83	80.65
9	9471.14	1166.37	91.10
10	9368.22	1154.56	102.91
11	9251.97	1141.22	116.25
12	9120.65	1126.16	131.32
13	8972.31	1109.13	148.34
14	8804.74	1089.91	167.57
15	8615.45	1068.19	189.29
16	8401.63	1043.65	213.82
17	8160.09	1015.94	241.54
18	7887.25	984.63	272.85
19	7579.03	949.26	308.21
20	7230.87	909.31	348.16
21	6837.58	864.19	393.29
22	6393.31	813.21	444.27
23	5891.46	755.62	501.85
24	5324.56	690.58	566.90
25	4684.18	617.10	640.38
26	3960.80	534.09	723.38
27	3143.65	440.33	817.15
28	2220.59	334.41	923.06
29	1177.88	214.77	1042.71
30	0.01	79.61	1177.86

Total Payout = $37724.27   Total Interest = $27724.27

YEARLY AMORTIZATION SCHEDULES
PRINCIPAL = $10,000

12.50%

15 YEAR TERM $123.25/Month

YEAR	PRINCIPAL	INT. PAID	PRIN. PAID
1	9757.39	1236.41	242.61
2	9482.65	1204.29	274.74
3	9171.53	1167.91	311.12
4	8819.21	1126.71	352.32
5	8420.24	1080.06	398.97
6	7968.44	1027.23	451.80
7	7456.81	967.40	511.63
8	6877.44	899.65	579.37
9	6221.35	822.93	656.09
10	5478.38	736.06	742.97
11	4637.03	637.68	841.35
12	3684.27	526.27	952.76
13	2605.35	400.11	1078.92
14	1383.57	257.24	1221.78
15	0.00	95.46	1383.57

Total Payout = $22185.40   Total Interest = $12185.40

30 YEAR TERM $106.73/Month

YEAR	PRINCIPAL	INT. PAID	PRIN. PAID
1	9967.47	1248.18	32.53
2	9930.63	1243.87	36.84
3	9888.91	1238.99	41.72
4	9841.67	1233.47	47.24
5	9788.18	1227.21	53.50
6	9727.59	1220.13	60.58
7	9658.91	1212.11	68.60
8	9581.31	1203.02	77.69
9	9493.33	1192.74	87.97
10	9393.71	1181.09	99.62
11	9280.90	1167.90	112.81
12	9153.15	1152.96	127.75
13	9008.48	1136.04	144.67
14	8844.65	1116.88	163.82
15	8659.14	1095.19	185.52
16	8449.05	1070.63	210.08
17	8211.15	1042.81	237.90
18	7941.75	1011.31	269.40
19	7636.67	975.63	305.08
20	7291.19	935.24	345.47
21	6899.97	889.49	391.22
22	6456.95	837.68	443.02
23	5955.26	779.02	501.69
24	5387.14	712.59	568.12
25	4743.79	637.36	643.35
26	4015.26	552.17	728.54
27	3190.25	455.70	825.01
28	2256.00	346.46	934.25
29	1198.04	222.75	1057.96
30	-0.01	82.66	1198.05

Total Payout = $38421.28   Total Interest = $28421.28

12.75%

15 YEAR TERM $124.88/Month

YEAR	PRINCIPAL	INT. PAID	PRIN. PAID
1	9762.85	1261.46	237.15
2	9493.64	1229.39	269.21
3	9188.03	1192.99	305.62
4	8841.09	1151.66	346.94
5	8447.23	1104.75	393.85
6	8000.12	1051.49	447.11
7	7492.55	991.03	507.57
8	6916.34	922.40	576.21
9	6262.22	844.48	654.12
10	5519.65	756.03	742.57
11	4676.66	655.62	842.98
12	3719.69	541.63	956.97
13	2633.32	412.23	1086.38
14	1400.04	265.33	1233.28
15	0.00	98.56	1400.04

Total Payout = $22479.07   Total Interest = $12479.07

30 YEAR TERM $108.67/Month

YEAR	PRINCIPAL	INT. PAID	PRIN. PAID
1	9969.21	1273.24	30.79
2	9934.26	1269.08	34.95
3	9894.58	1264.35	39.68
4	9849.53	1258.99	45.05
5	9798.40	1252.90	51.14
6	9740.34	1245.98	58.05
7	9674.44	1238.13	65.90
8	9599.63	1229.22	74.81
9	9514.70	1219.10	84.93
10	9418.29	1207.62	96.41
11	9308.84	1194.58	109.45
12	9184.59	1179.78	124.25
13	9043.54	1162.98	141.05
14	8883.42	1143.91	160.12
15	8701.64	1122.26	181.78
16	8495.29	1097.68	206.36
17	8261.03	1069.77	234.26
18	7995.09	1038.10	265.94
19	7693.20	1002.14	301.90
20	7350.48	961.31	342.72
21	6961.42	914.97	389.06
22	6519.75	862.36	441.67
23	6018.35	802.64	501.39
24	5449.16	734.84	569.19
25	4803.00	657.87	646.16
26	4069.47	570.50	733.53
27	3236.75	471.31	832.72
28	2291.42	358.71	945.32
29	1218.27	230.88	1073.15
30	0.01	85.77	1218.26

Total Payout = $39120.96   Total Interest = $29120.96

YEARLY AMORTIZATION SCHEDULES
PRINCIPAL = $10,000

13.00%

15 YEAR TERM $126.52/Month

YEAR	PRINCIPAL	INT. PAID	PRIN. PAID
1	9768.22	1286.51	231.78
2	9504.45	1254.52	263.77
3	9204.27	1218.11	300.18
4	8862.65	1176.68	341.62
5	8473.89	1129.52	388.77
6	8031.45	1075.86	442.43
7	7527.95	1014.79	503.50
8	6954.95	945.29	573.00
9	6302.86	866.20	652.09
10	5560.75	776.19	742.10
11	4716.21	673.75	844.54
12	3755.10	557.18	961.11
13	2661.32	424.51	1093.78
14	1416.57	273.54	1244.75
15	0.00	101.72	1416.57

Total Payout = $22774.36   Total Interest = $12774.36

30 YEAR TERM $110.62/Month

YEAR	PRINCIPAL	INT. PAID	PRIN. PAID
1	9970.87	1298.04	29.13
2	9937.71	1294.28	33.16
3	9899.98	1289.71	37.73
4	9857.03	1284.50	42.94
5	9808.17	1278.57	48.87
6	9752.55	1271.83	55.61
7	9689.26	1264.15	63.29
8	9617.23	1255.41	72.03
9	9535.26	1245.47	81.97
10	9441.98	1234.16	93.28
11	9335.82	1221.28	106.16
12	9215.01	1206.63	120.81
13	9077.52	1189.95	137.49
14	8921.05	1170.97	156.47
15	8742.99	1149.37	178.06
16	8540.34	1124.80	202.64
17	8309.73	1096.82	230.61
18	8047.28	1064.99	262.45
19	7748.61	1028.77	298.67
20	7408.71	987.54	339.90
21	7021.89	940.62	386.82
22	6581.68	887.23	440.21
23	6080.71	826.47	500.97
24	5510.58	757.31	570.12
25	4861.76	678.62	648.82
26	4123.38	589.06	738.38
27	3283.09	487.14	840.30
28	2326.80	371.15	956.29
29	1238.51	239.15	1088.29
30	0.01	88.93	1238.50

Total Payout = $39823.18   Total Interest = $29823.18

13.25%

15 YEAR TERM $128.17/Month

YEAR	PRINCIPAL	INT. PAID	PRIN. PAID
1	9773.49	1311.57	226.51
2	9515.07	1279.67	258.42
3	9220.26	1243.27	294.81
4	8883.92	1201.74	336.34
5	8500.20	1154.37	383.71
6	8062.44	1100.32	437.76
7	7563.03	1038.67	499.42
8	6993.27	968.32	569.76
9	6343.25	888.07	650.01
10	5601.69	796.52	741.57
11	4755.67	692.07	846.02
12	3790.50	572.91	965.18
13	2689.37	436.96	1101.12
14	1433.16	281.87	1256.22
15	0.00	104.93	1433.15

Total Payout = $23071.26   Total Interest = $13071.26

30 YEAR TERM $112.58/Month

YEAR	PRINCIPAL	INT. PAID	PRIN. PAID
1	9972.44	1323.37	27.56
2	9940.99	1319.48	31.44
3	9905.12	1315.05	35.87
4	9864.19	1310.00	40.93
5	9817.50	1304.24	46.69
6	9764.24	1297.66	53.27
7	9703.47	1290.16	60.77
8	9634.14	1281.60	69.33
9	9555.04	1271.83	79.09
10	9464.81	1260.69	90.23
11	9361.87	1247.98	102.94
12	9244.42	1233.48	117.44
13	9110.44	1216.94	133.99
14	8957.58	1198.07	152.86
15	8783.19	1176.54	174.39
16	8584.24	1151.98	198.95
17	8357.27	1123.96	226.97
18	8098.33	1091.99	258.94
19	7802.92	1055.52	295.41
20	7465.89	1013.91	337.02
21	7081.40	966.44	384.49
22	6642.75	912.28	438.65
23	6142.32	850.50	500.43
24	5571.41	780.01	570.92
25	4920.07	699.60	651.33
26	4177.00	607.86	743.07
27	3329.27	503.20	847.73
28	2362.13	383.79	967.14
29	1258.78	247.57	1103.36
30	0.01	92.16	1258.77

Total Payout = $40527.85   Total Interest = $30527.85

YEARLY AMORTIZATION SCHEDULES
PRINCIPAL = $10,000

13.50%

15 YEAR TERM $129.83/Month

YEAR	PRINCIPAL	INT. PAID	PRIN. PAID
1	9778.65	1336.64	221.35
2	9525.51	1304.83	253.15
3	9235.99	1268.46	289.52
4	8904.87	1226.87	331.12
5	8526.18	1179.29	378.69
6	8093.09	1124.89	433.10
7	7597.77	1062.66	495.32
8	7031.28	991.50	566.49
9	6383.40	910.11	647.88
10	5642.45	817.02	740.96
11	4795.03	710.57	847.42
12	3825.86	588.82	969.17
13	2717.45	449.57	1108.41
14	1449.79	290.32	1267.66
15	0.00	108.19	1449.79

Total Payout = $23369.73   Total Interest = $13369.73

30 YEAR TERM $114.54/Month

YEAR	PRINCIPAL	INT. PAID	PRIN. PAID
1	9973.93	1348.43	26.07
2	9944.12	1344.68	29.81
3	9910.02	1340.40	34.10
4	9871.02	1335.50	39.00
5	9826.42	1329.90	44.60
6	9775.42	1323.49	51.01
7	9717.08	1316.16	58.34
8	9650.37	1307.78	66.72
9	9574.06	1298.19	76.30
10	9486.80	1287.23	87.26
11	9387.00	1274.69	99.80
12	9272.86	1260.35	114.14
13	9142.31	1243.95	130.54
14	8993.02	1225.20	149.30
15	8822.27	1203.75	170.75
16	8626.99	1179.22	195.28
17	8403.66	1151.16	223.33
18	8148.24	1119.07	255.42
19	7856.12	1082.38	292.12
20	7522.03	1040.41	334.09
21	7139.94	992.41	382.09
22	6702.95	937.51	436.99
23	6203.18	874.72	499.77
24	5631.61	802.92	571.57
25	4977.92	720.80	653.69
26	4230.30	626.88	747.61
27	3375.28	519.47	855.03
28	2397.40	396.62	977.87
29	1279.00	256.13	1118.37
30	-0.01	95.45	1279.05

Total Payout = $41234.84   Total Interest = $31234.84

13.75%

15 YEAR TERM $131.50/Month

YEAR	PRINCIPAL	INT. PAID	PRIN. PAID
1	9783.72	1361.71	216.28
2	9535.76	1330.02	247.96
3	9251.46	1293.69	284.29
4	8925.52	1252.04	325.94
5	8551.83	1204.29	373.69
6	8123.38	1149.54	428.44
7	7632.17	1086.77	491.21
8	7069.00	1014.81	563.18
9	6423.31	932.30	645.69
10	5683.03	837.70	740.28
11	4834.29	729.25	848.74
12	3861.21	604.90	973.08
13	2745.57	462.34	1115.64
14	1466.48	298.90	1279.09
15	0.00	111.50	1466.48

Total Payout = $23669.77   Total Interest = $13669.77

30 YEAR TERM $116.51/Month

YEAR	PRINCIPAL	INT. PAID	PRIN. PAID
1	9975.35	1373.48	24.65
2	9947.09	1369.87	28.26
3	9914.69	1365.73	32.40
4	9877.54	1360.99	37.15
5	9834.95	1355.54	42.59
6	9786.11	1349.30	48.83
7	9730.13	1342.15	55.99
8	9665.94	1333.95	64.19
9	9592.35	1324.54	73.59
10	9507.98	1313.76	84.37
11	9411.24	1301.40	96.73
12	9300.34	1287.23	110.91
13	9173.18	1270.98	127.15
14	9027.40	1252.35	145.78
15	8860.26	1230.99	167.14
16	8668.63	1206.51	191.63
17	8448.93	1178.43	219.70
18	8197.04	1146.25	251.89
19	7908.25	1109.34	288.79
20	7577.14	1067.03	331.10
21	7197.53	1018.52	379.61
22	6762.31	962.91	435.23
23	6263.32	899.15	498.99
24	5691.23	826.04	572.09
25	5035.32	742.23	655.91
26	4283.32	646.13	752.00
27	3421.14	535.96	862.17
28	2432.66	409.65	988.49
29	1299.36	264.83	1133.30
30	0.02	98.80	1299.34

Total Payout = $41944.05   Total Interest = $31944.05

YEARLY AMORTIZATION SCHEDULES
PRINCIPAL = $10,000

14.00%

15 YEAR TERM $133.17/Month

YEAR	PRINCIPAL	INT. PAID	PRIN. PAID
1	9788.69	1386.78	211.31
2	9545.83	1355.22	242.87
3	9266.69	1318.95	279.14
4	8945.87	1277.27	320.82
5	8577.14	1229.36	368.73
6	8153.33	1174.29	423.80
7	7666.24	1111.00	487.09
8	7106.41	1038.25	559.84
9	6462.96	954.65	643.44
10	5723.43	858.55	739.54
11	4873.45	748.11	849.98
12	3896.53	621.17	976.92
13	2773.72	475.28	1122.81
14	1483.22	307.59	1290.50
15	0.00	114.87	1483.22

Total Payout = $23971.35   Total Interest = $13971.35

30 YEAR TERM $118.49/Month

YEAR	PRINCIPAL	INT. PAID	PRIN. PAID
1	9976.70	1398.54	23.30
2	9949.91	1395.96	26.78
3	9919.13	1391.06	30.78
4	9883.75	1386.46	35.38
5	9843.08	1381.18	40.67
6	9796.34	1375.11	46.74
7	9742.62	1368.13	53.72
8	9680.88	1360.11	61.74
9	9609.92	1350.88	70.96
10	9528.36	1340.29	81.56
11	9434.63	1328.11	93.74
12	9326.89	1314.11	107.74
13	9203.06	1298.02	123.83
14	9060.74	1279.53	142.32
15	8897.16	1258.27	163.57
16	8709.16	1233.84	188.00
17	8493.08	1205.77	216.08
18	8244.73	1173.50	248.35
19	7959.29	1136.41	285.44
20	7631.22	1093.78	328.07
21	7254.16	1044.78	377.06
22	6820.79	988.47	433.37
23	6322.69	923.75	498.09
24	5750.21	849.37	572.48
25	5092.24	763.87	657.98
26	4336.00	665.61	756.24
27	3466.82	552.67	869.18
28	2467.84	422.86	998.98
29	1319.67	273.67	1148.17
30	0.03	102.20	1319.64

Total Payout = $42655.38   Total Interest = $32655.38

14.25%

15 YEAR TERM $134.86/Month

YEAR	PRINCIPAL	INT. PAID	PRIN. PAID
1	9793.57	1411.86	206.43
2	9555.72	1380.45	237.85
3	9281.67	1344.25	274.05
4	8965.92	1302.54	315.75
5	8602.11	1254.49	363.81
6	8182.94	1199.12	419.17
7	7699.97	1135.33	482.96
8	7143.51	1061.83	556.46
9	6502.36	977.15	641.15
10	5763.64	879.57	738.72
11	4912.49	767.15	851.15
12	3931.81	637.62	980.68
13	2801.89	488.37	1129.92
14	1500.01	316.41	1301.88
15	0.00	118.29	1500.01

Total Payout = $24274.43   Total Interest = $14274.43

30 YEAR TERM $120.47/Month

YEAR	PRINCIPAL	INT. PAID	PRIN. PAID
1	9977.97	1423.60	22.03
2	9952.60	1420.25	25.38
3	9923.35	1416.38	29.24
4	9889.66	1411.93	33.69
5	9850.85	1406.81	38.82
6	9806.12	1400.90	44.73
7	9754.59	1394.09	51.53
8	9695.21	1386.25	59.37
9	9626.80	1377.21	68.41
10	9547.98	1366.80	78.82
11	9457.17	1354.81	90.82
12	9352.53	1340.99	104.64
13	9231.97	1325.06	120.56
14	9093.06	1306.71	138.91
15	8933.01	1285.57	160.05
16	8748.60	1261.22	184.41
17	8536.13	1233.15	212.47
18	8291.32	1200.82	244.81
19	8009.26	1163.56	282.06
20	7684.27	1120.64	324.99
21	7309.82	1071.18	374.45
22	6878.39	1014.19	431.43
23	6381.30	948.53	497.09
24	5808.56	872.88	572.74
25	5148.66	785.72	659.90
26	4388.33	685.29	760.33
27	3512.29	569.58	876.04
28	2502.93	436.26	1009.36
29	1339.96	282.65	1162.97
30	0.00	105.67	1339.96

Total Payout = $43368.74   Total Interest = $33368.74

YEARLY AMORTIZATION SCHEDULES
PRINCIPAL = $10,000

14.50%

15 YEAR TERM $136.55/Month

YEAR	PRINCIPAL	INT. PAID	PRIN. PAID
1	9798.35	1436.95	201.65
2	9565.43	1405.68	232.92
3	9296.40	1369.57	269.03
4	8985.66	1327.86	310.74
5	8626.75	1279.69	358.91
6	8212.20	1224.04	414.56
7	7733.37	1159.77	478.83
8	7180.31	1085.54	553.06
9	6541.50	999.79	638.81
10	5803.66	900.76	737.84
11	4951.42	786.37	852.24
12	3967.06	654.24	984.36
13	2830.09	501.63	1136.97
14	1516.84	325.36	1313.24
15	0.00	121.76	1516.84

Total Payout = $24579.02   Total Interest = $14579.02

30 YEAR TERM $122.46/Month

YEAR	PRINCIPAL	INT. PAID	PRIN. PAID
1	9979.19	1448.65	20.81
2	9955.14	1445.43	24.04
3	9927.38	1441.70	27.77
4	9895.30	1437.39	32.07
5	9858.26	1432.42	37.05
6	9815.47	1426.68	42.79
7	9766.04	1420.04	49.42
8	9708.96	1412.38	57.09
9	9643.02	1403.53	65.94
10	9566.86	1393.31	76.16
11	9478.89	1381.50	87.97
12	9377.29	1367.86	101.60
13	9259.93	1352.11	117.36
14	9124.38	1333.92	135.55
15	8967.82	1312.90	156.57
16	8786.98	1288.63	180.84
17	8578.10	1260.59	208.88
18	8336.84	1228.21	241.26
19	8058.18	1190.80	278.66
20	7736.32	1147.60	321.87
21	7364.55	1097.70	371.77
22	6935.15	1040.06	429.40
23	6439.17	973.49	495.97
24	5866.30	896.60	572.87
25	5204.62	807.78	661.68
26	4440.35	705.20	764.27
27	3557.60	586.71	882.76
28	2537.98	449.85	1019.61
29	1360.29	291.78	1177.69
30	0.02	109.19	1360.27

Total Payout = $44084.01   Total Interest = $34084.01

14.75%

15 YEAR TERM $138.25/Month

YEAR	PRINCIPAL	INT. PAID	PRIN. PAID
1	9803.03	1462.04	196.97
2	9574.96	1430.94	228.07
3	9310.89	1394.93	264.08
4	9005.11	1353.23	305.77
5	8651.06	1304.95	354.05
6	8241.11	1249.05	409.95
7	7766.42	1184.32	474.68
8	7216.79	1109.37	549.63
9	6580.38	1022.59	636.41
10	5843.48	922.11	736.90
11	4990.23	805.76	853.25
12	4002.26	671.04	987.97
13	2858.30	515.04	1143.96
14	1533.72	334.42	1324.58
15	0.00	125.28	1533.72

Total Payout = $24885.07   Total Interest = $14885.07

30 YEAR TERM $124.45/Month

YEAR	PRINCIPAL	INT. PAID	PRIN. PAID
1	9980.33	1473.74	19.67
2	9957.56	1470.60	22.77
3	9931.20	1467.01	26.37
4	9900.67	1462.84	30.53
5	9865.32	1458.02	35.35
6	9824.39	1452.44	40.93
7	9777.00	1445.98	47.39
8	9722.13	1438.50	54.87
9	9658.59	1429.83	63.54
10	9585.02	1419.80	73.57
11	9499.83	1408.18	85.19
12	9401.19	1394.73	98.64
13	9286.98	1379.16	114.21
14	9154.73	1361.13	132.25
15	9001.61	1340.25	153.13
16	8824.31	1316.07	177.30
17	8619.01	1288.07	205.30
18	8381.30	1255.66	237.71
19	8106.05	1218.13	275.24
20	7787.35	1174.67	318.70
21	7418.32	1124.35	369.02
22	6991.03	1066.08	427.29
23	6496.28	998.61	494.76
24	5923.40	920.50	572.87
25	5260.08	830.05	663.33
26	4492.00	725.31	768.06
27	3602.69	604.04	889.33
28	2572.94	463.62	1029.75
29	1380.61	301.03	1192.34
30	0.01	112.78	1380.60

Total Payout = $44801.13   Total Interest = $34801.13

YEARLY AMORTIZATION SCHEDULES
PRINCIPAL = \$10,000

15.00%

15 YEAR TERM \$139.96/Month

YEAR	PRINCIPAL	INT. PAID	PRIN. PAID
1	9807.63	1487.13	192.37
2	9584.33	1456.21	223.30
3	9325.13	1420.31	259.20
4	9024.27	1378.64	300.86
5	8675.04	1330.28	349.23
6	8269.67	1274.14	405.37
7	7799.14	1208.97	470.53
8	7252.97	1133.33	546.17
9	6618.99	1045.53	633.97
10	5883.11	943.62	735.89
11	5028.92	825.32	854.18
12	4037.43	688.01	991.50
13	2886.54	528.62	1150.88
14	1550.65	343.61	1335.89
15	0.00	128.86	1550.65

Total Payout = \$25192.57   Total Interest = \$15192.57

30 YEAR TERM \$126.44/Month

YEAR	PRINCIPAL	INT. PAID	PRIN. PAID
1	9981.42	1498.76	18.58
2	9959.86	1495.77	21.56
3	9934.84	1492.31	25.03
4	9905.78	1488.28	29.05
5	9872.06	1483.61	33.72
6	9832.92	1478.19	39.14
7	9787.49	1471.90	45.43
8	9734.75	1464.59	52.74
9	9673.53	1456.12	61.22
10	9602.48	1446.28	71.06
11	9520.00	1434.85	82.48
12	9424.26	1421.59	95.74
13	9313.13	1406.20	111.13
14	9184.14	1388.34	128.99
15	9034.41	1367.60	149.73
16	8860.61	1343.53	173.80
17	8658.87	1315.60	201.74
18	8424.70	1283.17	234.17
19	8152.89	1245.52	271.81
20	7837.39	1201.83	315.51
21	7471.16	1151.11	366.23
22	7046.06	1092.24	425.10
23	6552.63	1023.90	493.43
24	5979.87	944.58	572.76
25	5315.05	852.50	664.83
26	4543.34	745.63	771.70
27	3647.58	621.57	895.76
28	2607.83	477.58	1039.75
29	1400.93	310.43	1206.90
30	0.01	116.42	1400.91

Total Payout = \$45519.98   Total Interest = \$35519.98

15.25%

15 YEAR TERM \$141.67/Month

YEAR	PRINCIPAL	INT. PAID	PRIN. PAID
1	9812.13	1512.23	187.87
2	9593.52	1481.49	218.61
3	9339.13	1445.72	254.38
4	9043.13	1404.09	296.01
5	8698.69	1355.66	344.44
6	8297.89	1299.30	400.80
7	7831.51	1233.72	466.38
8	7288.83	1157.41	542.69
9	6657.34	1068.62	631.48
10	5922.53	965.29	734.81
11	5067.49	845.06	855.04
12	4072.54	705.15	994.95
13	2914.79	542.35	1157.75
14	1567.61	352.92	1347.18
15	0.00	132.49	1567.61

Total Payout = \$25501.49   Total Interest = \$15501.49

30 YEAR TERM \$128.45/Month

YEAR	PRINCIPAL	INT. PAID	PRIN. PAID
1	9982.46	1523.81	17.54
2	9962.04	1520.94	20.41
3	9938.29	1517.60	23.75
4	9910.65	1513.71	27.64
5	9878.49	1509.19	32.16
6	9841.06	1503.93	37.43
7	9797.51	1497.80	43.55
8	9746.84	1490.68	50.67
9	9687.87	1482.38	58.97
10	9619.26	1472.74	68.61
11	9539.42	1461.51	79.84
12	9446.51	1448.45	92.90
13	9338.41	1433.24	108.11
14	9212.61	1415.56	125.80
15	9066.23	1394.97	146.38
16	8895.91	1371.02	170.33
17	8697.71	1343.15	198.20
18	8467.08	1310.72	230.63
19	8198.71	1272.98	268.37
20	7886.44	1229.07	312.28
21	7523.06	1177.98	363.37
22	7100.23	1118.52	422.83
23	6608.22	1049.34	492.01
24	6035.70	968.83	572.52
25	5369.51	875.15	666.20
26	4594.30	766.15	775.20
27	3692.26	639.31	902.04
28	2642.62	491.71	1049.64
29	1421.24	319.96	1221.39
30	0.00	120.12	1421.23

Total Payout = \$46240.51   Total Interest = \$36240.51

YEARLY AMORTIZATION SCHEDULES
PRINCIPAL = $10,000

15.50%

15 YEAR TERM $143.40/Month

YEAR	PRINCIPAL	INT. PAID	PRIN. PAID
1	9816.54	1537.33	183.46
2	9602.54	1506.78	214.01
3	9352.90	1471.15	249.64
4	9061.70	1429.59	291.20
5	8722.01	1381.10	339.69
6	8325.76	1324.54	396.24
7	7863.55	1258.57	462.22
8	7324.37	1181.61	539.18
9	6695.42	1091.84	628.95
10	5961.75	987.12	733.67
11	5105.92	864.96	855.83
12	4107.60	722.47	998.32
13	2943.05	556.25	1164.54
14	1584.61	362.35	1358.44
15	0.00	136.17	1584.62

Total Payout = $25811.83   Total Interest = $15811.83

30 YEAR TERM $130.45/Month

YEAR	PRINCIPAL	INT. PAID	PRIN. PAID
1	9983.44	1548.86	16.56
2	9964.11	1546.10	19.32
3	9941.57	1542.88	22.54
4	9915.28	1539.13	26.29
5	9884.61	1534.75	30.67
6	9848.84	1529.64	35.78
7	9807.10	1523.69	41.73
8	9758.42	1516.74	48.68
9	9701.63	1508.66	56.79
10	9635.39	1499.18	66.24
11	9558.12	1488.15	77.27
12	9467.98	1475.28	90.14
13	9362.84	1460.28	105.15
14	9240.19	1442.77	122.65
15	9097.11	1422.35	143.07
16	8930.22	1398.53	166.89
17	8735.53	1370.74	194.68
18	8508.44	1338.32	227.10
19	8243.53	1300.51	264.91
20	7934.51	1256.40	309.02
21	7574.04	1204.95	360.47
22	7153.56	1144.94	420.49
23	6663.06	1074.92	490.50
24	6090.90	993.26	572.16
25	5423.47	897.99	667.43
26	4644.92	786.87	778.55
27	3736.73	657.24	908.18
28	2677.34	506.02	1059.40
29	1441.55	329.64	1235.78
30	0.01	123.88	1441.54

Total Payout = $46962.61   Total Interest = $36962.61

15.75%

15 YEAR TERM $145.13/Month

YEAR	PRINCIPAL	INT. PAID	PRIN. PAID
1	9820.86	1562.43	179.14
2	9611.39	1532.09	209.48
3	9366.43	1496.61	244.96
4	9079.98	1455.12	286.45
5	8745.00	1406.60	334.97
6	8353.30	1349.86	391.71
7	7895.24	1283.51	458.06
8	7359.59	1205.93	535.64
9	6733.22	1115.20	626.37
10	6000.75	1009.10	732.47
11	5144.22	885.03	856.54
12	4142.60	739.95	1001.62
13	2971.33	570.30	1171.27
14	1601.66	371.90	1369.67
15	0.00	139.91	1601.66

Total Payout = $26123.54   Total Interest = $16123.54

30 YEAR TERM $132.46/Month

YEAR	PRINCIPAL	INT. PAID	PRIN. PAID
1	9984.36	1573.90	15.64
2	9966.08	1571.25	18.29
3	9944.69	1568.16	21.38
4	9919.69	1564.54	25.01
5	9890.45	1560.30	29.24
6	9856.25	1555.35	34.19
7	9816.27	1549.55	39.99
8	9769.51	1542.78	46.76
9	9714.83	1534.86	54.68
10	9650.89	1525.60	63.94
11	9576.12	1514.77	74.77
12	9488.68	1502.11	87.44
13	9386.44	1487.30	102.25
14	9266.87	1469.98	119.56
15	9127.06	1449.72	139.82
16	8963.56	1426.04	163.50
17	8772.37	1398.35	191.19
18	8548.79	1365.96	223.58
19	8287.35	1328.09	261.45
20	7981.62	1283.81	305.73
21	7624.10	1232.03	357.51
22	7206.03	1171.47	418.07
23	6717.15	1100.66	488.89
24	6145.45	1017.85	571.69
25	5476.92	921.01	668.53
26	4695.16	807.78	781.76
27	3780.98	675.36	914.18
28	2711.95	520.51	1069.03
29	1461.85	339.44	1250.10
30	0.00	127.69	1461.85

Total Payout = $47686.22   Total Interest = $37686.22

177

YEARLY AMORTIZATION SCHEDULES
PRINCIPAL = $10,000

16.00%

15 YEAR TERM $146.87/Month

YEAR	PRINCIPAL	INT. PAID	PRIN. PAID
1	9825.10	1587.54	174.90
2	9620.07	1557.41	205.03
3	9379.72	1522.09	240.35
4	9097.97	1480.69	281.75
5	8767.68	1432.15	330.29
6	8380.48	1375.25	387.19
7	7926.59	1308.55	453.89
8	7394.50	1230.35	532.09
9	6770.75	1138.69	623.75
10	6039.55	1031.24	731.20
11	5182.38	905.27	857.17
12	4177.54	757.61	1004.83
13	2999.60	584.50	1177.94
14	1618.74	381.58	1380.86
15	0.00	143.70	1618.75

Total Payout = $26436.61   Total Interest = $16436.61

30 YEAR TERM $134.48/Month

YEAR	PRINCIPAL	INT. PAID	PRIN. PAID
1	9985.24	1598.95	14.76
2	9967.94	1596.41	17.30
3	9947.65	1593.43	20.28
4	9923.88	1589.93	23.78
5	9896.00	1585.83	27.87
6	9863.33	1581.03	32.68
7	9825.02	1575.40	38.30
8	9780.12	1568.81	44.90
9	9727.48	1561.07	52.64
10	9665.78	1552.00	61.71
11	9593.44	1541.37	72.34
12	9508.64	1528.91	84.80
13	9409.24	1514.30	99.41
14	9292.71	1497.18	116.53
15	9156.10	1477.10	136.61
16	8995.96	1453.57	160.14
17	8808.23	1425.98	187.73
18	8588.17	1393.64	220.07
19	8330.19	1355.73	257.98
20	8027.77	1311.29	302.42
21	7673.25	1259.19	354.52
22	7257.66	1198.12	415.59
23	6770.48	1126.52	487.18
24	6199.37	1042.60	571.11
25	5529.87	944.21	669.50
26	4745.04	828.88	784.83
27	3825.00	693.67	920.04
28	2746.47	535.18	1078.53
29	1482.14	349.38	1264.33
30	0.00	131.57	1482.14

Total Payout = $48411.25   Total Interest = $38411.25

16.25%

15 YEAR TERM $148.62/Month

YEAR	PRINCIPAL	INT. PAID	PRIN. PAID
1	9829.25	1612.65	170.75
2	9628.59	1582.74	200.66
3	9392.79	1547.60	235.81
4	9115.68	1506.29	277.11
5	8790.02	1457.75	325.65
6	8407.33	1400.71	382.70
7	7957.60	1333.67	449.73
8	7429.09	1254.89	528.51
9	6808.00	1162.32	621.09
10	6078.13	1053.52	729.88
11	5220.40	925.67	857.73
12	4212.42	775.43	1007.97
13	3027.89	598.87	1184.54
14	1635.86	391.38	1392.03
15	0.00	147.54	1635.86

Total Payout = $26751.03   Total Interest = $16751.03

30 YEAR TERM $136.49/Month

YEAR	PRINCIPAL	INT. PAID	PRIN. PAID
1	9986.07	1623.99	13.93
2	9969.70	1621.55	16.37
3	9950.47	1618.69	19.24
4	9927.86	1615.32	22.61
5	9901.30	1611.36	26.56
6	9870.08	1606.70	31.22
7	9833.39	1601.24	36.69
8	9790.28	1594.81	43.11
9	9739.61	1587.26	50.66
10	9680.08	1578.38	59.54
11	9610.11	1567.95	69.97
12	9527.88	1555.70	82.22
13	9431.25	1541.29	96.63
14	9317.70	1524.37	113.55
15	9184.26	1504.48	133.44
16	9027.44	1481.10	156.82
17	8843.15	1453.63	184.29
18	8626.58	1421.35	216.57
19	8372.07	1383.42	254.51
20	8072.99	1338.83	299.09
21	7721.51	1286.45	351.48
22	7308.47	1224.88	413.04
23	6823.07	1152.53	485.39
24	6252.65	1067.50	570.42
25	5582.31	967.58	670.34
26	4794.56	850.16	787.76
27	3868.81	712.18	925.75
28	2780.91	550.02	1087.91
29	1502.44	359.45	1278.47
30	0.02	135.51	1502.41

Total Payout = $49137.65   Total Interest = $39137.65

YEARLY AMORTIZATION SCHEDULES
PRINCIPAL = $10,000

16.50%

15 YEAR TERM $150.37/Month

YEAR	PRINCIPAL	INT. PAID	PRIN. PAID
1	9833.32	1637.77	166.68
2	9636.95	1608.09	196.36
3	9405.62	1573.12	231.33
4	9133.10	1531.93	272.52
5	8812.05	1483.40	321.05
6	8433.83	1426.23	378.22
7	7988.26	1358.88	445.57
8	7463.36	1279.54	524.91
9	6844.98	1186.07	618.38
10	6116.49	1075.96	728.49
11	5258.27	946.24	858.21
12	4247.24	793.42	1011.03
13	3056.17	613.38	1191.07
14	1653.02	401.29	1403.16
15	0.00	151.44	1653.01

Total Payout = $27066.75   Total Interest = $17066.75

30 YEAR TERM $138.51/Month

YEAR	PRINCIPAL	INT. PAID	PRIN. PAID
1	9986.86	1649.04	13.14
2	9971.38	1646.70	15.48
3	9953.14	1643.94	18.24
4	9931.65	1640.69	21.49
5	9906.34	1636.86	25.31
6	9876.51	1632.36	29.82
7	9841.38	1627.05	35.13
8	9800.00	1620.79	41.39
9	9751.24	1613.42	48.76
10	9693.80	1604.74	57.44
11	9626.14	1594.51	67.67
12	9546.42	1582.46	79.72
13	9452.51	1568.27	93.91
14	9341.88	1551.55	110.63
15	9211.54	1531.84	130.33
16	9058.00	1508.64	153.54
17	8877.12	1481.30	180.88
18	8664.03	1449.09	213.09
19	8413.00	1411.14	251.04
20	8117.26	1366.44	295.74
21	7768.86	1313.78	348.40
22	7358.42	1251.74	410.44
23	6874.90	1178.65	483.52
24	6305.28	1092.55	569.62
25	5634.22	991.12	671.05
26	4843.67	871.63	790.55
27	3912.35	730.86	931.32
28	2815.19	565.02	1097.16
29	1522.67	369.65	1292.53
30	-0.02	139.49	1522.68

Total Payout = $49865.33   Total Interest = $39865.33

16.75%

15 YEAR TERM $152.13/Month

YEAR	PRINCIPAL	INT. PAID	PRIN. PAID
1	9837.30	1662.88	162.70
2	9645.15	1633.44	192.15
3	9418.23	1598.67	226.92
4	9150.25	1557.60	267.99
5	8833.76	1509.10	316.49
6	8460.00	1451.82	373.76
7	8018.59	1384.18	441.41
8	7497.30	1304.30	521.29
9	6881.67	1209.95	615.63
10	6154.82	1098.54	727.05
11	5296.00	966.96	858.62
12	4281.98	811.57	1014.02
13	3084.45	628.06	1197.53
14	1670.20	411.33	1414.25
15	0.00	155.38	1670.20

Total Payout = $27383.78   Total Interest = $17383.78

30 YEAR TERM $140.54/Month

YEAR	PRINCIPAL	INT. PAID	PRIN. PAID
1	9987.60	1674.08	12.40
2	9972.96	1671.83	14.64
3	9955.67	1669.18	17.29
4	9935.25	1666.05	20.42
5	9911.13	1662.36	24.12
6	9882.65	1657.99	28.48
7	9849.01	1652.84	33.64
8	9809.29	1646.75	39.72
9	9762.38	1639.56	46.91
10	9706.98	1631.07	55.40
11	9641.55	1621.05	65.43
12	9564.28	1609.21	77.27
13	9473.03	1595.22	91.25
14	9365.26	1578.71	107.77
15	9237.99	1559.20	127.27
16	9087.69	1536.17	150.30
17	8910.18	1508.97	177.51
18	8700.55	1476.85	209.63
19	8452.99	1438.91	247.57
20	8160.62	1394.10	292.37
21	7815.33	1341.19	345.28
22	7407.56	1278.70	407.77
23	6925.99	1204.91	481.57
24	6357.27	1117.75	568.72
25	5685.62	1014.83	671.65
26	4892.42	893.28	793.20
27	3955.67	749.72	936.75
28	2849.39	580.19	1106.28
29	1542.90	379.98	1306.49
30	-0.03	143.54	1542.94

Total Payout = $50594.24   Total Interest = $40594.24

YEARLY AMORTIZATION SCHEDULES
PRINCIPAL = $10,000

17.00%

15 YEAR TERM $153.90/Month

YEAR	PRINCIPAL	INT. PAID	PRIN. PAID
1	9841.20	1688.00	158.80
2	9653.19	1658.80	188.00
3	9430.62	1624.23	222.58
4	9167.11	1583.30	263.51
5	8855.15	1534.84	311.96
6	8485.82	1477.48	369.33
7	8048.57	1409.56	437.25
8	7530.92	1329.15	517.65
9	6918.08	1233.96	612.84
10	6192.53	1121.26	725.54
11	5333.57	987.84	858.96
12	4316.65	829.89	1016.92
13	3112.73	642.88	1203.92
14	1687.42	421.49	1425.31
15	0.00	159.39	1687.42

Total Payout = $27702.08   Total Interest = $17702.08

30 YEAR TERM $142.57/Month

YEAR	PRINCIPAL	INT. PAID	PRIN. PAID
1	9988.31	1699.12	11.69
2	9974.46	1696.97	13.84
3	9958.07	1694.42	16.39
4	9938.67	1691.01	19.40
5	9915.70	1687.84	22.97
6	9888.50	1683.61	27.20
7	9856.30	1678.61	32.20
8	9818.18	1672.69	38.12
9	9773.05	1665.68	45.13
10	9719.63	1657.38	53.43
11	9656.38	1647.56	63.25
12	9581.49	1635.93	74.88
13	9492.84	1622.16	88.65
14	9387.88	1605.85	104.96
15	9263.63	1586.55	124.26
16	9116.52	1563.70	147.11
17	8942.36	1536.65	174.16
18	8736.17	1504.63	206.19
19	8492.07	1466.71	244.10
20	8203.08	1421.82	288.99
21	7860.95	1368.68	342.13
22	7455.91	1305.76	405.05
23	6976.38	1231.28	479.53
24	6408.66	1143.10	567.71
25	5736.55	1038.70	672.11
26	4940.84	915.10	795.71
27	3998.81	768.78	942.03
28	2883.55	595.55	1115.26
29	1563.20	390.46	1320.35
30	0.05	147.66	1563.15

Total Payout = $51324.31   Total Interest = $41324.31

17.25%

15 YEAR TERM $155.68/Month

YEAR	PRINCIPAL	INT. PAID	PRIN. PAID
1	9845.02	1713.13	154.98
2	9661.08	1684.17	183.94
3	9442.78	1649.81	218.30
4	9183.70	1609.03	259.08
5	8876.23	1560.63	307.48
6	8511.31	1503.19	364.92
7	8078.22	1435.02	433.09
8	7564.22	1354.11	514.00
9	6954.20	1258.09	610.02
10	6230.22	1144.13	723.98
11	5370.99	1008.88	859.23
12	4351.24	848.36	1019.74
13	3141.00	657.86	1210.25
14	1704.66	431.77	1436.34
15	0.00	163.44	1704.66

Total Payout = $28021.63   Total Interest = $18021.63

30 YEAR TERM $144.60/Month

YEAR	PRINCIPAL	INT. PAID	PRIN. PAID
1	9988.97	1724.16	11.03
2	9975.88	1722.09	13.09
3	9960.35	1719.65	15.53
4	9941.92	1716.75	18.43
5	9920.04	1713.30	21.88
6	9894.07	1709.22	25.97
7	9863.25	1704.37	30.82
8	9826.68	1698.61	36.57
9	9783.27	1691.78	43.41
10	9731.76	1683.67	51.52
11	9670.62	1674.04	61.14
12	9598.06	1662.62	72.56
13	9511.94	1649.07	86.12
14	9409.74	1632.98	102.20
15	9288.44	1613.89	121.30
16	9144.49	1591.23	143.96
17	8973.64	1564.33	170.85
18	8770.87	1532.42	202.77
19	8530.23	1494.54	240.65
20	8244.63	1449.58	285.60
21	7905.67	1396.23	338.95
22	7503.40	1332.91	402.28
23	7025.97	1257.76	477.43
24	6459.35	1168.57	566.62
25	5786.89	1062.71	672.47
26	4988.79	937.09	798.09
27	4041.60	787.99	947.19
28	2917.47	611.05	1124.14
29	1583.33	401.04	1334.14
30	-0.05	151.81	1583.38

Total Payout = $52055.49   Total Interest = $42055.49

YEARLY AMORTIZATION SCHEDULES
PRINCIPAL = \$10,000

17.50%

15 YEAR TERM \$157.46/Month

YEAR	PRINCIPAL	INT. PAID	PRIN. PAID
1	9848.76	1738.25	151.24
2	9668.81	1709.55	179.94
3	9454.73	1675.41	214.08
4	9200.02	1634.79	254.71
5	8896.99	1586.46	303.03
6	8536.46	1528.96	360.53
7	8107.52	1460.55	428.94
8	7597.19	1379.17	510.33
9	6990.03	1282.34	607.16
10	6267.40	1167.13	722.36
11	5408.25	1030.07	859.42
12	4385.76	867.00	1022.49
13	3169.26	672.99	1216.50
14	1721.93	442.17	1447.32
15	0.00	167.55	1721.94

Total Payout = \$28342.41   Total Interest = \$18342.41

30 YEAR TERM \$146.63/Month

YEAR	PRINCIPAL	INT. PAID	PRIN. PAID
1	9989.60	1749.19	10.40
2	9977.23	1747.22	12.37
3	9962.51	1744.87	14.72
4	9945.00	1742.08	17.51
5	9924.17	1738.76	20.83
6	9899.38	1734.80	24.79
7	9869.89	1730.10	29.49
8	9834.81	1724.51	35.09
9	9793.06	1717.85	41.74
10	9743.40	1709.93	49.66
11	9684.32	1700.50	59.09
12	9614.02	1689.29	70.30
13	9530.38	1675.96	83.63
14	9430.88	1660.09	99.50
15	9312.50	1641.21	118.38
16	9171.65	1618.74	140.85
17	9004.08	1592.02	167.57
18	8804.72	1560.22	199.37
19	8567.52	1522.40	237.19
20	8285.32	1477.39	282.20
21	7949.58	1423.85	335.74
22	7550.13	1360.14	399.45
23	7074.89	1284.35	475.24
24	6509.48	1194.18	565.41
25	5836.78	1086.89	672.70
26	5036.45	959.26	800.33
27	4084.26	807.40	952.19
28	2951.40	626.73	1132.86
29	1603.58	411.78	1347.81
30	0.03	156.04	1603.55

Total Payout = \$52787.71   Total Interest = \$42787.71

17.75%

15 YEAR TERM \$159.25/Month

YEAR	PRINCIPAL	INT. PAID	PRIN. PAID
1	9852.42	1763.38	147.58
2	9676.39	1734.94	176.02
3	9466.46	1701.02	209.94
4	9216.07	1660.57	250.39
5	8917.44	1612.33	298.63
6	8561.28	1554.79	356.17
7	8136.48	1486.17	424.79
8	7629.84	1404.32	506.64
9	7025.58	1306.70	604.26
10	6304.90	1190.27	720.69
11	5445.35	1051.41	859.55
12	4420.19	885.80	1025.16
13	3197.51	688.28	1222.68
14	1739.24	452.69	1458.27
15	0.00	171.72	1739.24

Total Payout = \$28664.40   Total Interest = \$18664.40

30 YEAR TERM \$148.67/Month

YEAR	PRINCIPAL	INT. PAID	PRIN. PAID
1	9990.20	1774.23	9.80
2	9978.51	1772.34	11.69
3	9964.56	1770.09	13.94
4	9947.93	1767.40	16.63
5	9928.10	1764.20	19.84
6	9904.44	1760.37	23.66
7	9876.22	1755.82	28.22
8	9842.57	1750.38	33.65
9	9802.44	1743.89	40.14
10	9754.57	1736.16	47.87
11	9697.47	1726.94	57.09
12	9629.38	1715.94	68.09
13	9548.17	1702.82	81.21
14	9451.31	1687.17	96.86
15	9335.79	1668.51	115.52
16	9198.01	1646.25	137.78
17	9033.68	1619.70	164.33
18	8837.69	1588.04	195.99
19	8603.93	1550.28	233.75
20	8325.14	1505.24	278.79
21	7992.63	1451.52	332.51
22	7596.06	1387.46	396.58
23	7123.07	1311.04	472.99
24	6558.95	1219.91	564.12
25	5886.14	1111.22	672.81
26	5083.69	981.58	802.45
27	4126.63	826.97	957.06
28	2985.16	642.57	1141.46
29	1623.77	422.63	1361.40
30	0.06	160.32	1623.71

Total Payout = \$53520.92   Total Interest = \$43520.92

YEARLY AMORTIZATION SCHEDULES
PRINCIPAL = $10,000

18.00%

15 YEAR TERM $161.04/Month

YEAR	PRINCIPAL	INT. PAID	PRIN. PAID
1	9856.00	1788.50	144.00
2	9683.83	1760.33	172.17
3	9477.97	1726.65	205.85
4	9231.85	1686.39	246.12
5	8937.59	1638.24	294.27
6	8585.76	1580.68	351.83
7	8165.11	1511.85	420.65
8	7662.16	1429.56	502.94
9	7060.84	1331.18	601.33
10	6341.88	1213.55	718.96
11	5482.29	1072.91	859.60
12	4454.54	904.76	1027.75
13	3225.74	703.71	1228.80
14	1756.57	463.33	1469.17
15	0.00	175.94	1756.57

Total Payout = $28987.58   Total Interest = $18987.58

30 YEAR TERM $150.71/Month

YEAR	PRINCIPAL	INT. PAID	PRIN. PAID
1	9990.76	1799.26	9.24
2	9979.71	1797.45	11.05
3	9966.50	1795.29	13.21
4	9950.71	1792.71	15.79
5	9931.83	1789.62	18.88
6	9909.25	1785.93	22.58
7	9882.26	1781.51	26.99
8	9849.99	1776.23	32.27
9	9811.40	1769.92	38.59
10	9765.27	1762.37	46.13
11	9710.11	1753.34	55.16
12	9644.16	1742.55	65.95
13	9565.32	1729.65	78.85
14	9471.04	1714.23	94.27
15	9358.33	1695.79	112.71
16	9223.57	1673.74	134.76
17	9062.44	1647.38	161.12
18	8869.80	1615.86	192.64
19	8639.47	1578.17	230.33
20	8364.08	1533.12	275.38
21	8034.83	1479.25	329.26
22	7641.17	1414.84	393.66
23	7170.49	1337.83	470.67
24	6607.75	1245.76	562.74
25	5934.93	1135.68	672.83
26	5130.48	1004.06	804.44
27	4168.86	846.70	961.81
28	3018.73	658.55	1149.95
29	1643.82	433.60	1374.90
30	-0.04	164.64	1643.86

Total Payout = $54255.07   Total Interest = $44255.07

18.25%

15 YEAR TERM $162.84/Month

YEAR	PRINCIPAL	INT. PAID	PRIN. PAID
1	9859.50	1813.63	140.50
2	9691.11	1785.73	168.39
3	9489.28	1752.30	201.83
4	9247.37	1712.22	241.91
5	8957.43	1664.19	289.94
6	8609.91	1606.61	347.52
7	8193.39	1537.61	416.52
8	7694.16	1454.90	499.23
9	7095.80	1355.77	598.36
10	6378.63	1236.96	717.17
11	5519.05	1094.55	859.58
12	4488.79	923.87	1030.26
13	3253.96	719.29	1234.84
14	1773.92	474.09	1480.03
15	0.00	180.21	1773.92

Total Payout = $29311.93   Total Interest = $19311.93

30 YEAR TERM $152.75/Month

YEAR	PRINCIPAL	INT. PAID	PRIN. PAID
1	9991.29	1824.30	8.71
2	9980.85	1822.57	10.44
3	9968.34	1820.49	12.51
4	9953.35	1818.01	14.99
5	9935.38	1815.03	17.97
6	9913.84	1811.46	21.54
7	9888.02	1807.19	25.82
8	9857.08	1802.06	30.94
9	9819.99	1795.92	37.09
10	9775.53	1788.55	44.45
11	9722.25	1779.72	53.28
12	9658.40	1769.14	63.86
13	9581.86	1756.46	76.54
14	9490.12	1741.27	91.74
15	9380.16	1723.05	109.95
16	9248.38	1701.22	131.79
17	9090.42	1675.05	157.96
18	8901.10	1643.68	189.32
19	8674.19	1606.09	226.91
20	8402.22	1561.03	271.97
21	8076.25	1507.03	325.97
22	7685.54	1442.30	390.70
23	7217.26	1364.72	468.28
24	6656.00	1271.74	561.27
25	5983.28	1160.29	672.72
26	5176.99	1026.71	806.29
27	4210.59	866.61	966.40
28	3052.30	674.71	1158.29
29	1664.01	444.72	1388.29
30	0.05	169.05	1663.96

Total Payout = $54990.12   Total Interest = $44990.12

YEARLY AMORTIZATION SCHEDULES
PRINCIPAL = $10,000

18.50%

15 YEAR TERM $164.65/Month

YEAR	PRINCIPAL	INT. PAID	PRIN. PAID
1	9862.93	1838.76	137.07
2	9698.25	1811.14	164.69
3	9500.37	1777.95	197.87
4	9262.62	1738.08	237.75
5	8976.96	1690.17	285.66
6	8633.73	1632.60	343.23
7	8221.34	1563.43	412.40
8	7725.83	1480.32	495.50
9	7130.47	1380.47	595.36
10	6415.14	1260.49	715.34
11	5555.65	1116.34	859.49
12	4522.95	943.13	1032.70
13	3282.15	735.02	1240.81
14	1791.29	484.97	1490.86
15	0.00	184.53	1791.29

Total Payout = $29637.42   Total Interest = $19637.42

30 YEAR TERM $154.79/Month

YEAR	PRINCIPAL	INT. PAID	PRIN. PAID
1	9991.79	1849.33	8.21
2	9981.93	1847.67	9.86
3	9970.09	1845.69	11.85
4	9955.85	1843.30	14.23
5	9938.75	1840.43	17.10
6	9918.20	1836.98	20.55
7	9893.51	1832.84	24.69
8	9863.84	1827.87	29.67
9	9828.20	1821.89	35.64
10	9785.37	1814.71	42.83
11	9733.91	1806.08	51.46
12	9672.09	1795.71	61.83
13	9597.80	1783.25	74.29
14	9508.54	1768.28	89.26
15	9401.29	1750.29	107.25
16	9272.44	1728.68	128.86
17	9117.61	1702.71	154.83
18	8931.58	1671.51	186.03
19	8708.07	1634.02	223.51
20	8439.51	1588.98	268.56
21	8116.83	1534.86	322.68
22	7729.13	1469.83	387.70
23	7263.29	1391.70	465.83
24	6703.58	1297.82	559.71
25	6031.08	1185.03	672.50
26	5223.05	1049.51	808.03
27	4252.19	886.67	970.86
28	3085.68	691.02	1166.51
29	1684.09	455.94	1401.59
30	0.05	173.49	1684.04

Total Payout = $55726.00   Total Interest = $45726.00

18.75%

15 YEAR TERM $166.47/Month

YEAR	PRINCIPAL	INT. PAID	PRIN. PAID
1	9866.29	1863.90	133.71
2	9705.24	1836.55	161.05
3	9511.26	1803.62	193.98
4	9277.62	1763.96	233.65
5	8996.20	1716.18	281.42
6	8657.23	1658.63	338.97
7	8248.95	1589.32	408.28
8	7757.18	1505.84	491.77
9	7164.85	1405.28	592.33
10	6451.41	1284.16	713.45
11	5592.07	1138.27	859.33
12	4557.02	962.55	1035.05
13	3310.32	750.90	1246.70
14	1808.69	495.97	1501.63
15	0.00	188.91	1808.69

Total Payout = $29964.04   Total Interest = $19964.04

30 YEAR TERM $156.84/Month

YEAR	PRINCIPAL	INT. PAID	PRIN. PAID
1	9992.27	1874.36	7.73
2	9982.96	1872.78	9.31
3	9971.74	1870.87	11.22
4	9958.23	1868.58	13.51
5	9941.95	1865.82	16.27
6	9922.35	1862.49	19.60
7	9898.74	1858.48	23.61
8	9870.31	1853.65	28.44
9	9836.06	1847.84	34.25
10	9794.80	1840.83	41.26
11	9745.11	1832.40	49.69
12	9685.26	1822.24	59.85
13	9613.16	1810.00	72.09
14	9526.33	1795.26	86.83
15	9421.74	1777.50	104.59
16	9295.77	1756.11	125.98
17	9144.03	1730.35	151.74
18	8961.27	1699.33	182.76
19	8741.13	1661.96	220.13
20	8475.99	1616.94	265.15
21	8156.62	1562.72	319.37
22	7771.95	1497.42	384.67
23	7308.62	1418.76	463.33
24	6750.55	1324.02	558.07
25	6078.36	1209.90	672.19
26	5268.72	1072.45	809.64
27	4293.52	906.89	975.20
28	3118.91	707.48	1174.61
29	1704.12	467.29	1414.80
30	0.02	177.99	1704.10

Total Payout = $56462.69   Total Interest = $46462.69

YEARLY AMORTIZATION SCHEDULES
PRINCIPAL = $10,000

19.00%

15 YEAR TERM $168.29/Month

YEAR	PRINCIPAL	INT. PAID	PRIN. PAID
1	9869.58	1889.03	130.42
2	9712.10	1861.97	157.48
3	9521.95	1829.30	190.15
4	9292.36	1789.86	229.59
5	9015.13	1742.23	277.22
6	8680.40	1684.72	334.73
7	8276.22	1615.28	404.18
8	7788.20	1531.43	488.02
9	7198.94	1430.19	589.26
10	6487.43	1307.95	711.51
11	5628.33	1160.34	859.11
12	4591.00	982.12	1037.33
13	3338.47	766.93	1252.53
14	1826.11	507.09	1512.36
15	0.00	193.35	1826.10

Total Payout = $30291.77   Total Interest = $20291.77

30 YEAR TERM $158.89/Month

YEAR	PRINCIPAL	INT. PAID	PRIN. PAID
1	9992.72	1899.39	7.28
2	9983.92	1897.88	8.79
3	9973.30	1896.05	10.62
4	9960.48	1893.85	12.82
5	9945.00	1891.19	15.48
6	9926.30	1887.98	18.69
7	9903.73	1884.10	22.57
8	9876.48	1879.42	27.25
9	9843.57	1873.76	32.91
10	9803.83	1866.94	39.74
11	9755.85	1858.69	47.98
12	9697.92	1848.74	57.93
13	9627.97	1836.72	69.95
14	9543.51	1822.21	84.46
15	9441.33	1804.69	101.98
16	9318.39	1783.53	123.14
17	9169.71	1757.99	148.68
18	8990.18	1727.14	179.53
19	8773.40	1689.90	216.77
20	8511.66	1644.93	261.74
21	8195.62	1590.63	316.04
22	7814.02	1525.07	381.60
23	7353.25	1445.90	460.77
24	6796.90	1350.32	556.35
25	6125.12	1234.90	671.77
26	5313.99	1095.54	811.13
27	4334.59	927.27	979.40
28	3152.02	724.09	1182.58
29	1724.11	478.77	1427.90
30	-0.01	182.55	1724.13

Total Payout = $57200.13   Total Interest = $47200.13

19.25%

15 YEAR TERM $170.11/Month

YEAR	PRINCIPAL	INT. PAID	PRIN. PAID
1	9872.79	1914.16	127.21
2	9718.81	1887.40	153.98
3	9532.44	1854.99	186.38
4	9306.84	1815.78	225.60
5	9033.77	1768.30	273.07
6	8703.24	1710.84	330.53
7	8303.16	1641.29	400.08
8	7818.90	1557.11	484.27
9	7232.73	1455.20	586.17
10	6523.21	1331.86	709.51
11	5664.40	1182.56	858.81
12	4624.87	1001.84	1039.53
13	3366.59	783.10	1258.28
14	1843.54	518.32	1523.05
15	0.00	197.83	1843.54

Total Payout = $30620.58   Total Interest = $20620.58

30 YEAR TERM $160.94/Month

YEAR	PRINCIPAL	INT. PAID	PRIN. PAID
1	9993.14	1924.42	6.86
2	9984.84	1922.97	8.30
3	9974.78	1921.22	10.05
4	9962.62	1919.11	12.17
5	9947.89	1916.55	14.73
6	9930.06	1913.45	17.83
7	9908.49	1909.70	21.58
8	9882.37	1905.16	26.12
9	9850.76	1899.66	31.61
10	9812.49	1893.01	38.27
11	9766.17	1884.96	46.32
12	9710.11	1875.21	56.06
13	9642.25	1863.42	67.86
14	9560.11	1849.14	82.14
15	9460.68	1831.85	99.43
16	9340.33	1810.93	120.35
17	9194.66	1785.60	145.67
18	9018.34	1754.95	176.32
19	8804.91	1717.85	213.43
20	8546.57	1672.94	258.34
21	8233.87	1618.58	312.70
22	7855.37	1552.78	378.50
23	7397.23	1473.13	458.15
24	6842.68	1376.73	554.55
25	6171.44	1260.03	671.24
26	5358.95	1118.79	812.49
27	4375.49	947.82	983.46
28	3185.08	740.87	1190.40
29	1744.19	490.38	1440.90
30	0.09	187.18	1744.10

Total Payout = $57938.28   Total Interest = $47938.28

YEARLY AMORTIZATION SCHEDULES
PRINCIPAL = $10,000

19.50%

15 YEAR TERM $171.95/Month

YEAR	PRINCIPAL	INT. PAID	PRIN. PAID
1	9875.93	1939.30	124.07
2	9725.39	1912.82	150.54
3	9542.72	1880.70	182.67
4	9321.07	1841.71	221.65
5	9052.12	1794.41	268.95
6	8725.77	1737.01	326.35
7	8329.77	1667.37	396.00
8	7849.27	1582.86	480.50
9	7266.22	1480.32	583.05
10	6558.75	1355.89	707.47
11	5700.29	1204.91	858.45
12	4658.64	1021.71	1041.66
13	3394.68	799.41	1263.95
14	1860.99	529.67	1533.69
15	0.00	202.37	1860.99

Total Payout = $30950.46   Total Interest = $20950.46

30 YEAR TERM $162.99/Month

YEAR	PRINCIPAL	INT. PAID	PRIN. PAID
1	9993.54	1949.44	6.46
2	9985.70	1948.06	7.84
3	9976.19	1946.39	9.51
4	9964.64	1944.36	11.54
5	9950.63	1941.90	14.01
6	9933.64	1938.91	17.00
7	9913.01	1935.28	20.62
8	9887.99	1930.88	25.02
9	9857.62	1925.54	30.37
10	9820.78	1919.06	36.85
11	9776.07	1911.20	44.71
12	9721.82	1901.65	54.25
13	9655.99	1890.08	65.83
14	9576.12	1876.03	79.87
15	9479.20	1858.98	96.92
16	9361.60	1838.30	117.60
17	9218.89	1813.20	142.70
18	9045.74	1782.75	173.16
19	8835.63	1745.80	210.11
20	8580.68	1700.96	254.95
21	8271.33	1646.55	309.35
22	7895.96	1580.53	375.37
23	7440.48	1500.42	455.48
24	6887.80	1403.22	552.68
25	6217.17	1285.27	670.63
26	5403.42	1142.16	813.75
27	4416.01	968.50	987.41
28	3217.89	757.78	1198.13
29	1764.07	502.09	1453.82
30	0.00	191.83	1764.07

Total Payout = $58677.12   Total Interest = $48677.12

19.75%

15 YEAR TERM $173.79/Month

YEAR	PRINCIPAL	INT. PAID	PRIN. PAID
1	9879.01	1964.43	120.99
2	9731.84	1938.25	147.17
3	9552.82	1906.41	179.02
4	9335.06	1867.67	217.76
5	9070.17	1820.54	264.88
6	8747.97	1763.22	322.20
7	8356.05	1693.50	391.92
8	7879.31	1608.69	476.74
9	7299.41	1505.53	579.90
10	6594.03	1380.04	705.39
11	5736.00	1227.40	858.03
12	4692.30	1041.72	1043.70
13	3422.74	815.87	1269.56
14	1878.46	541.14	1544.28
15	0.00	206.97	1878.46

Total Payout = $31281.39   Total Interest = $21281.39

30 YEAR TERM $165.05/Month

YEAR	PRINCIPAL	INT. PAID	PRIN. PAID
1	9993.92	1974.47	6.08
2	9986.51	1973.15	7.40
3	9977.51	1971.55	9.00
4	9966.56	1969.60	10.95
5	9953.24	1967.23	13.32
6	9937.04	1964.35	16.20
7	9917.33	1960.84	19.71
8	9893.36	1956.58	23.97
9	9864.19	1951.39	29.16
10	9828.72	1945.08	35.47
11	9785.57	1937.40	43.15
12	9733.09	1928.07	52.49
13	9669.24	1916.71	63.84
14	9591.58	1902.89	77.66
15	9497.12	1886.09	94.46
16	9382.22	1865.65	114.91
17	9242.44	1840.78	139.77
18	9072.43	1810.54	170.02
19	8865.62	1773.75	206.81
20	8614.06	1728.99	251.56
21	8308.07	1674.56	306.00
22	7935.85	1608.34	372.21
23	7483.10	1527.80	452.76
24	6932.37	1429.82	550.73
25	6262.46	1310.64	669.91
26	5447.58	1165.68	814.87
27	4456.37	989.34	991.21
28	3250.67	774.85	1205.70
29	1784.06	513.74	1466.61
30	0.08	196.57	1783.98

Total Payout = $59416.59   Total Interest = $49416.59

YEARLY AMORTIZATION SCHEDULES
PRINCIPAL = \$10,000

20.00%

15 YEAR TERM \$175.63/Month

YEAR	PRINCIPAL	INT. PAID	PRIN. PAID
1	9882.02	1989.57	117.98
2	9738.15	1963.69	143.87
3	9562.72	1932.12	175.43
4	9348.80	1893.64	213.92
5	9087.94	1846.70	260.85
6	8769.86	1789.47	318.08
7	8382.00	1719.69	387.87
8	7909.04	1634.60	472.96
9	7332.31	1530.83	576.72
10	6629.06	1404.31	703.25
11	5771.53	1250.02	857.54
12	4725.85	1061.88	1045.67
13	3450.77	832.47	1275.08
14	1895.94	552.73	1554.83
15	0.00	211.61	1895.94

Total Payout = \$31613.34   Total Interest = \$21613.34

30 YEAR TERM \$167.10/Month

YEAR	PRINCIPAL	INT. PAID	PRIN. PAID
1	9994.27	1999.49	5.73
2	9987.29	1998.24	6.99
3	9978.77	1996.70	8.52
4	9968.38	1994.84	10.39
5	9955.71	1992.56	12.67
6	9940.27	1989.78	15.44
7	9921.44	1986.39	18.83
8	9898.47	1982.26	22.96
9	9870.47	1977.22	28.00
10	9836.32	1971.08	34.15
11	9794.68	1963.58	41.64
12	9743.91	1954.45	50.77
13	9682.00	1943.31	61.91
14	9606.50	1929.73	75.50
15	9514.44	1913.16	92.06
16	9402.19	1892.97	112.26
17	9265.30	1868.34	136.88
18	9098.39	1838.31	166.91
19	8894.86	1801.69	203.53
20	8646.67	1757.04	248.19
21	8344.03	1702.58	302.64
22	7975.00	1636.19	369.03
23	7525.00	1555.23	450.00
24	6976.28	1456.50	548.72
25	6307.17	1336.12	669.11
26	5491.27	1189.32	815.90
27	4496.37	1010.32	994.90
28	3283.19	792.05	1213.18
29	1803.86	525.89	1479.34
30	-0.03	201.33	1803.89

Total Payout = \$60156.67   Total Interest = \$50156.67

20.25%

15 YEAR TERM \$177.48/Month

YEAR	PRINCIPAL	INT. PAID	PRIN. PAID
1	9884.96	2014.71	115.04
2	9744.33	1989.12	140.63
3	9572.42	1957.85	171.90
4	9362.29	1919.62	210.13
5	9105.43	1872.89	256.87
6	8791.43	1815.76	313.99
7	8407.61	1745.93	383.82
8	7938.44	1660.57	469.18
9	7364.91	1556.23	573.52
10	6663.85	1428.68	701.07
11	5806.87	1272.77	856.98
12	4759.30	1082.19	1047.57
13	3478.76	849.21	1280.54
14	1913.44	564.43	1565.32
15	0.00	216.31	1913.44

Total Payout = \$31946.30   Total Interest = \$21946.30

30 YEAR TERM \$169.16/Month

YEAR	PRINCIPAL	INT. PAID	PRIN. PAID
1	9994.61	2024.52	5.39
2	9988.01	2023.32	6.59
3	9979.96	2021.85	8.06
4	9970.10	2020.06	9.85
5	9958.06	2017.87	12.04
6	9943.34	2015.19	14.72
7	9925.35	2011.92	17.99
8	9903.36	2007.92	21.99
9	9876.47	2003.02	26.89
10	9843.60	1997.05	32.87
11	9803.43	1989.74	40.17
12	9754.32	1980.80	49.11
13	9694.29	1969.88	60.03
14	9620.91	1956.53	73.38
15	9531.21	1940.21	89.70
16	9421.56	1920.26	109.65
17	9287.52	1895.88	134.04
18	9123.68	1866.07	163.84
19	8923.40	1829.63	200.28
20	8678.57	1785.09	244.82
21	8379.31	1730.64	299.27
22	8013.48	1664.09	365.82
23	7566.30	1582.73	447.18
24	7019.67	1483.28	546.63
25	6351.47	1361.71	668.20
26	5534.67	1213.11	816.80
27	4536.22	1031.46	998.45
28	3315.72	809.41	1220.50
29	1823.79	537.98	1491.93
30	0.07	206.19	1823.72

Total Payout = \$60897.32   Total Interest = \$50897.32

YEARLY AMORTIZATION SCHEDULES
PRINCIPAL = $10,000

20.50%

15 YEAR TERM $179.33/Month

YEAR	PRINCIPAL	INT. PAID	PRIN. PAID
1	9887.83	2039.85	112.17
2	9750.38	2014.56	137.45
3	9581.95	1983.58	168.43
4	9375.65	1945.62	206.40
5	9122.63	1899.09	252.92
6	8812.69	1842.09	309.93
7	8432.91	1772.23	379.79
8	7967.51	1686.62	465.39
9	7397.22	1581.72	570.30
10	6698.37	1453.18	698.84
11	5842.01	1295.66	856.36
12	4792.63	1102.63	1049.39
13	3506.71	866.10	1285.92
14	1930.94	576.25	1575.77
15	-0.01	221.07	1930.95

Total Payout = $32280.24   Total Interest = $22280.24

30 YEAR TERM $171.22/Month

YEAR	PRINCIPAL	INT. PAID	PRIN. PAID
1	9994.92	2049.54	5.08
2	9988.70	2048.40	6.22
3	9981.08	2046.99	7.62
4	9971.74	2045.28	9.34
5	9960.29	2043.17	11.45
6	9946.26	2040.59	14.03
7	9929.07	2037.43	17.19
8	9908.01	2033.55	21.06
9	9882.20	2028.81	25.81
10	9850.57	2022.99	31.63
11	9811.81	2015.86	38.76
12	9764.32	2007.12	47.49
13	9706.12	1996.42	58.20
14	9634.80	1983.30	71.32
15	9547.40	1967.22	87.39
16	9440.31	1947.52	107.09
17	9309.08	1923.39	131.23
18	9148.27	1893.81	160.81
19	8951.21	1857.56	197.06
20	8709.74	1813.14	241.48
21	8413.83	1758.71	295.90
22	8051.73	1692.02	362.60
23	7606.90	1610.28	444.33
24	7062.41	1510.13	544.49
25	6395.20	1387.40	667.21
26	5577.60	1237.01	817.60
27	4575.70	1052.72	1001.89
28	3347.98	826.90	1227.72
29	1843.53	550.16	1504.45
30	-0.03	211.06	1843.56

Total Payout = $61638.52   Total Interest = $51638.52

20.75%

15 YEAR TERM $181.20/Month

YEAR	PRINCIPAL	INT. PAID	PRIN. PAID
1	9890.64	2064.99	109.36
2	9756.30	2040.01	134.34
3	9591.28	2009.32	165.02
4	9388.57	1971.63	202.72
5	9139.55	1925.32	249.02
6	8833.65	1868.44	305.90
7	8457.87	1798.57	375.77
8	7996.27	1712.74	461.61
9	7429.22	1607.30	567.05
10	6732.65	1477.78	696.57
11	5876.98	1318.67	855.68
12	4825.85	1123.27	1051.13
13	3534.63	883.12	1291.22
14	1948.47	588.18	1586.16
15	0.00	225.88	1948.47

Total Payout = $32615.16   Total Interest = $22615.16

30 YEAR TERM $173.28/Month

YEAR	PRINCIPAL	INT. PAID	PRIN. PAID
1	9995.22	2074.56	4.78
2	9989.35	2073.47	5.87
3	9982.14	2072.13	7.21
4	9973.29	2070.48	8.86
5	9962.40	2068.46	10.88
6	9949.04	2065.98	13.37
7	9932.62	2062.92	16.42
8	9912.45	2059.17	20.17
9	9887.68	2054.57	24.78
10	9857.24	2048.91	30.43
11	9819.86	2041.95	37.39
12	9773.93	2033.41	45.93
13	9717.51	2022.92	56.42
14	9648.21	2010.04	69.30
15	9563.08	1994.21	85.13
16	9458.50	1974.76	104.58
17	9330.03	1950.87	128.47
18	9172.22	1921.53	157.81
19	8978.36	1885.48	193.86
20	8740.23	1841.20	238.14
21	8447.70	1786.81	292.53
22	8088.34	1719.99	359.35
23	7646.91	1637.91	441.43
24	7104.65	1537.08	542.26
25	6438.52	1413.21	666.13
26	5620.24	1261.06	818.28
27	4615.05	1074.15	1005.19
28	3380.26	844.55	1234.79
29	1863.42	562.50	1516.84
30	0.11	216.03	1863.31

Total Payout = $62380.22   Total Interest = $52380.22

187

YEARLY AMORTIZATION SCHEDULES
PRINCIPAL = $10,000

21.00%

15 YEAR TERM $183.06/Month

YEAR	PRINCIPAL	INT. PAID	PRIN. PAID
1	9893.39	2090.12	106.61
2	9762.10	2065.45	131.28
3	9600.44	2035.07	161.67
4	9401.35	1997.65	199.09
5	9156.19	1951.57	245.16
6	8854.29	1894.83	301.90
7	8482.51	1824.96	371.77
8	8024.70	1738.92	457.82
9	7460.92	1632.96	563.77
10	6766.67	1502.48	694.25
11	5911.74	1341.80	854.93
12	4858.95	1143.94	1052.79
13	3562.49	900.28	1296.45
14	1965.99	600.23	1596.50
15	0.00	230.74	1966.00

Total Payout = $32951.02   Total Interest = $22951.02

30 YEAR TERM $175.34/Month

YEAR	PRINCIPAL	INT. PAID	PRIN. PAID
1	9995.50	2099.58	4.50
2	9989.97	2098.54	5.54
3	9983.15	2097.26	6.82
4	9974.75	2095.68	8.40
5	9964.41	2093.74	10.34
6	9951.68	2091.35	12.73
7	9935.99	2088.40	15.68
8	9916.68	2084.77	19.31
9	9892.91	2080.30	23.78
10	9863.62	2074.80	29.28
11	9827.56	2068.02	36.06
12	9783.16	2059.67	44.41
13	9728.48	2049.40	54.68
14	9661.14	2036.74	67.34
15	9578.22	2021.16	82.92
16	9476.10	2001.97	102.11
17	9350.35	1978.33	125.75
18	9195.50	1949.23	154.85
19	9004.81	1913.39	190.69
20	8769.99	1869.26	234.82
21	8480.82	1814.91	289.17
22	8124.73	1747.99	356.09
23	7686.22	1665.57	438.51
24	7146.23	1564.08	540.00
25	6481.26	1439.11	664.97
26	5662.38	1285.21	818.87
27	4653.99	1095.69	1008.39
28	3412.22	862.31	1241.77
29	1883.05	574.91	1529.17
30	-0.03	221.00	1883.08

Total Payout = $63122.40   Total Interest = $53122.40

21.25%

15 YEAR TERM $184.93/Month

YEAR	PRINCIPAL	INT. PAID	PRIN. PAID
1	9896.08	2115.26	103.92
2	9767.78	2090.90	128.29
3	9609.41	2060.82	158.37
4	9413.90	2023.68	195.51
5	9172.56	1977.84	241.35
6	8874.63	1921.25	297.93
7	8506.84	1851.40	367.79
8	8052.81	1765.16	454.02
9	7492.33	1658.71	560.48
10	6800.44	1527.29	691.89
11	5946.32	1365.07	854.12
12	4891.93	1164.80	1054.39
13	3590.33	917.58	1301.61
14	1983.54	612.40	1606.79
15	0.01	235.66	1983.53

Total Payout = $33287.82   Total Interest = $23287.82

30 YEAR TERM $177.40/Month

YEAR	PRINCIPAL	INT. PAID	PRIN. PAID
1	9995.77	2124.60	4.23
2	9990.55	2123.61	5.22
3	9984.10	2122.39	6.45
4	9976.14	2120.87	7.96
5	9966.31	2119.01	9.83
6	9954.18	2116.70	12.13
7	9939.21	2113.86	14.97
8	9920.72	2110.35	18.49
9	9897.90	2106.02	22.82
10	9869.73	2100.66	28.17
11	9834.96	2094.06	34.78
12	9792.03	2085.91	42.93
13	9739.03	2075.84	52.99
14	9673.61	2063.42	65.42
15	9592.86	2048.08	80.76
16	9493.16	2029.14	99.69
17	9370.09	2005.77	123.07
18	9218.17	1976.91	151.92
19	9030.62	1941.29	187.55
20	8799.10	1897.32	231.52
21	8513.30	1843.03	285.80
22	8160.49	1776.02	352.82
23	7724.95	1693.30	435.54
24	7187.29	1591.18	537.66
25	6523.56	1465.11	663.72
26	5704.22	1309.49	819.35
27	4692.76	1117.38	1011.46
28	3444.15	880.22	1248.61
29	1902.78	587.46	1541.37
30	0.00	226.06	1902.77

Total Payout = $63865.04   Total Interest = $53865.04

YEARLY AMORTIZATION SCHEDULES
PRINCIPAL = $10,000

21.50%

15 YEAR TERM $186.81/Month

YEAR	PRINCIPAL	INT. PAID	PRIN. PAID
1	9898.70	2140.40	101.30
2	9773.34	2116.34	125.36
3	9618.21	2086.57	155.13
4	9426.23	2049.72	191.98
5	9188.66	2004.13	237.57
6	8894.66	1947.70	294.00
7	8530.84	1877.88	363.82
8	8080.60	1791.47	450.23
9	7523.44	1684.54	557.16
10	6833.95	1552.21	689.49
11	5980.69	1388.45	853.25
12	4924.79	1185.80	1055.90
13	3618.11	935.02	1306.68
14	2001.08	624.67	1617.03
15	0.00	240.62	2001.08

Total Payout = $33625.52   Total Interest = $23625.52

30 YEAR TERM $179.47/Month

YEAR	PRINCIPAL	INT. PAID	PRIN. PAID
1	9996.02	2149.62	3.98
2	9991.09	2148.68	4.93
3	9985.00	2147.51	6.10
4	9977.45	2146.06	7.54
5	9968.11	2144.27	9.34
6	9956.56	2142.05	11.55
7	9942.26	2139.31	14.30
8	9924.57	2135.91	17.69
9	9902.67	2131.71	21.90
10	9875.57	2126.51	27.10
11	9842.04	2120.07	33.53
12	9800.54	2112.11	41.50
13	9749.19	2102.25	51.35
14	9685.64	2090.05	63.55
15	9607.00	2074.96	78.64
16	9509.68	2056.28	97.32
17	9389.24	2033.17	120.43
18	9240.21	2004.57	149.04
19	9055.77	1969.17	184.44
20	8827.53	1925.36	228.24
21	8545.08	1871.16	282.45
22	8195.56	1804.07	349.53
23	7763.01	1721.06	432.54
24	7227.74	1618.33	535.28
25	6565.33	1491.20	662.41
26	5745.60	1333.87	819.73
27	4731.18	1139.18	1014.42
28	3475.83	898.26	1255.35
29	1922.33	600.10	1553.50
30	-0.13	231.14	1922.46

Total Payout = $64608.12   Total Interest = $54608.12

21.75%

15 YEAR TERM $188.69/Month

YEAR	PRINCIPAL	INT. PAID	PRIN. PAID
1	9901.26	2165.54	98.74
2	9778.78	2141.79	122.49
3	9626.83	2112.33	151.95
4	9438.33	2075.78	188.50
5	9204.49	2030.43	233.84
6	8914.39	1974.18	290.09
7	8554.52	1904.40	359.87
8	8108.08	1817.83	446.44
9	7554.25	1710.44	553.83
10	6867.19	1577.22	687.05
11	6014.87	1411.95	852.32
12	4957.53	1206.93	1057.35
13	3645.84	952.59	1311.69
14	2018.63	637.07	1627.21
15	0.00	245.65	2018.63

Total Payout = $33964.13   Total Interest = $23964.13

30 YEAR TERM $181.53/Month

YEAR	PRINCIPAL	INT. PAID	PRIN. PAID
1	9996.25	2174.64	3.75
2	9991.61	2173.74	4.65
3	9985.84	2172.62	5.76
4	9978.69	2171.24	7.15
5	9969.82	2169.52	8.87
6	9958.82	2167.38	11.00
7	9945.17	2164.74	13.65
8	9928.24	2161.45	16.93
9	9907.23	2157.38	21.01
10	9881.17	2152.32	26.06
11	9848.84	2146.06	32.33
12	9808.73	2138.28	40.11
13	9758.97	2128.63	49.76
14	9697.25	2116.66	61.72
15	9620.68	2101.82	76.57
16	9525.69	2083.40	94.99
17	9407.85	2060.55	117.84
18	9261.66	2032.20	146.19
19	9080.31	1997.04	181.35
20	8855.34	1953.41	224.97
21	8576.25	1899.30	279.09
22	8230.03	1832.16	346.22
23	7800.52	1748.88	429.51
24	7267.70	1645.56	532.82
25	6606.71	1517.39	660.99
26	5786.72	1358.39	819.99
27	4769.48	1161.15	1017.24
28	3507.55	916.45	1261.93
29	1942.06	612.90	1565.49
30	0.00	236.33	1942.06

Total Payout = $65351.59   Total Interest = $55351.59

YEARLY AMORTIZATION SCHEDULES
PRINCIPAL = $10,000

22.00%

15 YEAR TERM $190.58/Month

YEAR	PRINCIPAL	INT. PAID	PRIN. PAID
1	9903.77	2190.68	96.23
2	9784.10	2167.24	119.67
3	9635.28	2138.09	148.82
4	9450.21	2101.83	185.07
5	9220.05	2056.75	230.16
6	8933.83	2000.69	286.22
7	8577.89	1930.96	355.94
8	8135.24	1844.26	442.65
9	7584.76	1736.43	550.48
10	6900.18	1602.33	684.57
11	6048.85	1435.57	851.33
12	4990.14	1228.19	1058.71
13	3673.52	970.29	1316.61
14	2036.19	649.57	1637.34
15	0.00	250.72	2036.19

Total Payout = $34303.61   Total Interest = $24303.61

30 YEAR TERM $183.60/Month

YEAR	PRINCIPAL	INT. PAID	PRIN. PAID
1	9996.48	2199.66	3.52
2	9992.10	2198.80	4.38
3	9986.65	2197.73	5.45
4	9979.87	2196.41	6.78
5	9971.45	2194.76	8.43
6	9960.97	2192.70	10.48
7	9947.94	2190.15	13.03
8	9931.73	2186.98	16.21
9	9911.58	2183.03	20.15
10	9886.51	2178.12	25.06
11	9855.34	2172.01	31.17
12	9816.58	2164.42	38.76
13	9768.38	2154.98	48.20
14	9708.44	2143.24	59.94
15	9633.89	2128.63	74.55
16	9541.18	2110.48	92.71
17	9425.89	2087.89	115.29
18	9282.52	2059.81	143.37
19	9104.22	2024.88	178.30
20	8882.49	1981.45	221.73
21	8606.75	1927.44	275.74
22	8263.83	1860.27	342.91
23	7837.39	1776.73	426.45
24	7307.06	1672.85	530.33
25	6647.54	1543.67	659.51
26	5827.37	1383.01	820.17
27	4807.41	1183.22	1019.96
28	3538.99	934.76	1268.42
29	1961.59	625.78	1577.40
30	-0.06	241.53	1961.65

Total Payout = $66095.45   Total Interest = $56095.45

22.25%

15 YEAR TERM $192.47/Month

YEAR	PRINCIPAL	INT. PAID	PRIN. PAID
1	9906.22	2215.82	93.78
2	9789.31	2192.69	116.91
3	9643.56	2163.85	145.75
4	9461.87	2127.90	181.70
5	9235.35	2083.08	226.51
6	8952.97	2027.21	282.38
7	8600.94	1957.56	352.03
8	8162.08	1870.73	438.86
9	7614.97	1762.49	547.11
10	6932.92	1627.54	682.05
11	6082.63	1459.31	850.29
12	5022.62	1249.59	1060.01
13	3701.16	988.13	1321.47
14	2053.75	662.19	1647.41
15	0.00	255.85	2053.75

Total Payout = $34643.95   Total Interest = $24643.95

30 YEAR TERM $185.67/Month

YEAR	PRINCIPAL	INT. PAID	PRIN. PAID
1	9996.69	2224.68	3.31
2	9992.56	2223.86	4.13
3	9987.41	2222.84	5.15
4	9980.99	2221.57	6.42
5	9972.98	2219.99	8.00
6	9963.00	2218.01	9.98
7	9950.57	2215.55	12.44
8	9935.06	2212.48	15.51
9	9915.73	2208.66	19.33
10	9891.63	2203.89	24.10
11	9861.58	2197.95	30.04
12	9824.13	2190.53	37.45
13	9777.44	2181.30	46.69
14	9719.23	2169.78	58.21
15	9646.66	2155.42	72.57
16	9556.20	2137.52	90.47
17	9443.42	2115.21	112.78
18	9302.82	2087.39	140.60
19	9127.54	2052.71	175.28
20	8909.04	2009.48	218.51
21	8636.63	1955.59	272.40
22	8297.04	1888.40	339.59
23	7873.69	1804.64	423.35
24	7345.91	1700.21	527.77
25	6687.96	1570.04	657.95
26	5867.72	1407.75	820.24
27	4845.17	1205.44	1022.55
28	3570.41	953.22	1274.77
29	1981.21	638.80	1589.19
30	0.04	246.82	1981.17

Total Payout = $66839.67   Total Interest = $56839.67

190

YEARLY AMORTIZATION SCHEDULES
PRINCIPAL = $10,000

22.50%

15 YEAR TERM $194.36/Month

YEAR	PRINCIPAL	INT. PAID	PRIN. PAID
1	9908.61	2240.95	91.39
2	9794.40	2218.13	114.21
3	9651.68	2189.61	142.73
4	9473.31	2153.97	178.37
5	9250.40	2109.43	222.91
6	8971.82	2053.77	278.58
7	8623.68	1984.20	348.14
8	8188.61	1897.27	435.08
9	7644.88	1788.62	543.72
10	6965.39	1652.84	679.50
11	6116.21	1483.16	849.18
12	5054.97	1271.11	1061.23
13	3728.73	1006.10	1326.24
14	2071.31	674.92	1657.43
15	-0.01	261.03	2071.31

Total Payout = $34985.13   Total Interest = $24985.13

30 YEAR TERM $187.73/Month

YEAR	PRINCIPAL	INT. PAID	PRIN. PAID
1	9996.88	2249.69	3.12
2	9992.99	2248.91	3.89
3	9988.12	2247.94	4.87
4	9982.04	2246.73	6.08
5	9974.44	2245.21	7.60
6	9964.94	2243.31	9.50
7	9953.07	2240.94	11.87
8	9938.23	2237.97	14.84
9	9919.69	2234.27	18.54
10	9896.52	2229.64	23.17
11	9867.56	2223.85	28.96
12	9831.37	2216.62	36.19
13	9786.15	2207.58	45.23
14	9729.63	2196.29	56.52
15	9659.00	2182.18	70.63
16	9570.73	2164.54	88.27
17	9460.41	2142.49	110.31
18	9322.55	2114.95	137.86
19	9150.27	2080.52	172.29
20	8934.96	2037.50	215.31
21	8665.89	1983.73	269.07
22	8329.62	1916.54	336.27
23	7909.38	1832.57	420.24
24	7384.20	1727.63	525.18
25	6727.88	1596.48	656.32
26	5907.66	1432.59	820.22
27	4882.62	1227.77	1025.04
28	3601.61	971.80	1281.01
29	2000.71	651.91	1600.90
30	0.04	252.14	2000.67

Total Payout = $67584.24   Total Interest = $57584.24

22.75%

15 YEAR TERM $196.26/Month

YEAR	PRINCIPAL	INT. PAID	PRIN. PAID
1	9910.95	2266.09	89.05
2	9799.39	2243.58	111.56
3	9659.63	2215.38	139.76
4	9484.54	2180.05	175.09
5	9265.18	2135.79	219.35
6	8990.38	2080.34	274.80
7	8646.12	2010.87	344.27
8	8214.82	1923.85	431.29
9	7674.50	1814.82	540.32
10	6997.60	1678.24	676.90
11	6149.58	1507.13	848.02
12	5087.20	1292.76	1062.38
13	3756.26	1024.20	1330.94
14	2088.87	687.76	1667.38
15	0.00	266.27	2088.88

Total Payout = $35327.13   Total Interest = $25327.13

30 YEAR TERM $189.80/Month

YEAR	PRINCIPAL	INT. PAID	PRIN. PAID
1	9997.07	2274.71	2.93
2	9993.40	2273.97	3.67
3	9988.80	2273.04	4.60
4	9983.04	2271.88	5.76
5	9975.82	2270.42	7.22
6	9966.78	2268.59	9.04
7	9955.45	2266.31	11.33
8	9941.25	2263.44	14.19
9	9923.47	2259.86	17.78
10	9901.20	2255.36	22.28
11	9873.29	2249.73	27.91
12	9838.33	2242.68	34.96
13	9794.53	2233.84	43.80
14	9739.66	2222.77	54.87
15	9670.92	2208.90	68.74
16	9584.80	2191.52	86.12
17	9476.91	2169.75	107.89
18	9341.76	2142.48	135.16
19	9172.43	2108.31	169.33
20	8960.30	2065.51	212.13
21	8694.55	2011.88	265.75
22	8361.62	1944.71	332.93
23	7944.52	1860.55	417.09
24	7422.00	1755.11	522.53
25	6767.38	1623.02	654.62
26	5947.29	1457.54	820.09
27	4919.89	1250.24	1027.40
28	3632.77	990.52	1287.11
29	2020.29	665.16	1612.48
30	0.20	257.54	2020.09

Total Payout = $68329.12   Total Interest = $58329.12

191

YEARLY AMORTIZATION SCHEDULES
PRINCIPAL = $10,000

23.00%

15 YEAR TERM $198.17/Month

YEAR	PRINCIPAL	INT. PAID	PRIN. PAID
1	9913.23	2291.23	86.77
2	9804.27	2269.03	108.97
3	9667.42	2241.15	136.85
4	9495.55	2206.13	171.86
5	9279.72	2162.16	215.84
6	9008.66	2106.94	271.06
7	8668.24	2037.58	340.42
8	8240.73	1950.48	427.52
9	7703.82	1841.09	536.90
10	7029.55	1703.72	674.28
11	6182.75	1531.00	846.80
12	5119.29	1314.53	1063.46
13	3783.72	1042.43	1335.56
14	2106.44	700.71	1677.29
15	-0.01	271.55	2106.44

Total Payout = $35669.94   Total Interest = $25669.94

30 YEAR TERM $191.87/Month

YEAR	PRINCIPAL	INT. PAID	PRIN. PAID
1	9997.24	2299.72	2.76
2	9993.78	2299.02	3.46
3	9989.44	2298.13	4.35
4	9983.98	2297.02	5.46
5	9977.13	2295.62	6.85
6	9968.52	2293.87	8.61
7	9957.71	2291.67	10.81
8	9944.13	2288.90	13.58
9	9927.08	2285.49	17.05
10	9905.67	2281.06	21.41
11	9878.77	2275.58	26.89
12	9845.00	2268.70	33.77
13	9802.59	2260.06	42.41
14	9749.32	2249.21	53.27
15	9682.43	2235.58	66.90
16	9598.41	2218.47	84.01
17	9492.91	2196.97	105.51
18	9360.41	2169.97	132.50
19	9194.00	2136.01	166.40
20	8985.00	2093.50	208.98
21	8722.57	2040.02	262.45
22	8392.96	1972.87	329.60
23	7979.02	1888.54	413.94
24	7459.17	1782.63	519.85
25	6806.31	1649.62	652.86
26	5986.41	1482.57	819.90
27	4956.72	1272.79	1029.69
28	3663.57	1009.33	1293.15
29	2039.55	678.46	1624.02
30	0.01	262.93	2039.55

Total Payout = $69074.31   Total Interest = $59074.31

23.25%

15 YEAR TERM $200.08/Month

YEAR	PRINCIPAL	INT. PAID	PRIN. PAID
1	9915.46	2316.37	84.54
2	9809.03	2294.48	106.43
3	9675.05	2266.92	133.99
4	9506.37	2232.22	168.68
5	9294.00	2188.54	212.36
6	9026.65	2133.55	267.35
7	8690.06	2064.32	336.58
8	8266.32	1977.16	423.74
9	7732.85	1867.43	533.47
10	7061.24	1729.29	671.61
11	6215.72	1555.38	845.52
12	5151.25	1336.43	1064.47
13	3811.14	1060.79	1340.11
14	2124.01	713.77	1687.13
15	0.01	276.90	2124.01

Total Payout = $36013.54   Total Interest = $26013.54

30 YEAR TERM $193.94/Month

YEAR	PRINCIPAL	INT. PAID	PRIN. PAID
1	9997.41	2324.74	2.59
2	9994.15	2324.06	3.26
3	9990.04	2323.22	4.11
4	9984.87	2322.16	5.17
5	9978.36	2320.82	6.51
6	9970.17	2319.13	8.19
7	9959.86	2317.01	10.31
8	9946.87	2314.34	12.99
9	9930.52	2310.98	16.35
10	9909.94	2306.74	20.58
11	9884.03	2301.41	25.91
12	9851.41	2294.70	32.62
13	9810.34	2286.26	41.07
14	9758.64	2275.64	51.70
15	9693.55	2262.23	65.09
16	9611.60	2245.38	81.95
17	9508.43	2224.16	103.17
18	9378.55	2197.45	129.88
19	9215.04	2163.81	163.51
20	9009.18	2121.47	205.85
21	8750.02	2068.17	259.16
22	8423.75	2001.06	326.27
23	8013.00	1916.57	410.76
24	7495.88	1810.21	517.12
25	6844.85	1676.30	651.03
26	6025.24	1507.72	819.61
27	4993.39	1295.48	1031.85
28	3694.35	1028.28	1299.04
29	2058.92	691.90	1635.43
30	0.01	268.41	2058.92

Total Payout = $69819.78   Total Interest = $59819.78

YEARLY AMORTIZATION SCHEDULES
PRINCIPAL = $10,000

23.50%

15 YEAR TERM $201.99/Month

YEAR	PRINCIPAL	INT. PAID	PRIN. PAID
1	9917.64	2341.50	82.36
2	9813.70	2319.92	103.94
3	9682.52	2292.68	131.18
4	9516.97	2258.31	165.55
5	9308.04	2214.93	208.93
6	9044.36	2160.18	263.68
7	8711.58	2091.09	332.78
8	8291.61	2003.89	419.98
9	7761.58	1893.84	530.03
10	7092.67	1754.95	668.91
11	6248.48	1579.67	844.19
12	5183.07	1358.46	1065.41
13	3838.49	1079.28	1344.58
14	2141.57	726.95	1696.92
15	0.00	282.29	2141.57

Total Payout = $36357.92   Total Interest = $26357.92

30 YEAR TERM $196.02/Month

YEAR	PRINCIPAL	INT. PAID	PRIN. PAID
1	9997.56	2349.75	2.44
2	9994.49	2349.11	3.07
3	9990.61	2348.31	3.88
4	9985.72	2347.29	4.90
5	9979.54	2346.01	6.18
6	9971.74	2344.39	7.80
7	9961.90	2342.34	9.84
8	9949.48	2339.76	12.42
9	9933.81	2336.51	15.67
10	9914.03	2332.40	19.78
11	9889.06	2327.22	24.96
12	9857.56	2320.68	31.51
13	9817.79	2312.42	39.76
14	9767.61	2302.00	50.18
15	9704.28	2288.85	63.33
16	9624.36	2272.26	79.92
17	9523.49	2251.32	100.87
18	9396.19	2224.88	127.30
19	9235.53	2191.53	160.66
20	9032.78	2149.43	202.76
21	8776.89	2096.30	255.89
22	8453.96	2029.25	322.94
23	8046.40	1944.63	407.56
24	7532.04	1837.83	514.36
25	6882.91	1703.05	649.14
26	6063.67	1532.95	819.24
27	5029.77	1318.28	1033.91
28	3724.93	1047.35	1304.83
29	2078.19	705.44	1646.75
30	-0.07	273.93	2078.26

Total Payout = $70565.53   Total Interest = $60565.53

23.75%

15 YEAR TERM $203.91/Month

YEAR	PRINCIPAL	INT. PAID	PRIN. PAID
1	9919.77	2366.64	80.23
2	9818.05	2345.36	101.51
3	9689.84	2318.45	128.42
4	9527.37	2284.40	162.47
5	9321.83	2241.33	205.54
6	9061.79	2186.83	260.04
7	8732.80	2117.88	328.99
8	8316.59	2030.66	416.21
9	7790.02	1920.30	526.57
10	7123.84	1780.69	666.18
11	6281.03	1604.06	842.81
12	5214.76	1380.60	1066.27
13	3865.78	1097.89	1348.98
14	2159.14	740.23	1706.64
15	0.00	287.74	2159.13

Total Payout = $36703.05   Total Interest = $26703.05

30 YEAR TERM $198.09/Month

YEAR	PRINCIPAL	INT. PAID	PRIN. PAID
1	9997.71	2374.76	2.29
2	9994.81	2374.15	2.90
3	9991.15	2373.39	3.66
4	9986.51	2372.41	4.64
5	9980.65	2371.19	5.86
6	9973.23	2369.63	7.42
7	9963.84	2367.66	9.39
8	9951.97	2365.17	11.88
9	9936.94	2362.03	15.02
10	9917.93	2358.04	19.01
11	9893.88	2353.00	24.05
12	9863.46	2346.63	30.42
13	9824.97	2338.56	38.49
14	9776.27	2328.35	48.70
15	9714.66	2315.44	61.61
16	9636.72	2299.11	77.94
17	9538.11	2278.44	98.61
18	9413.36	2252.30	124.75
19	9255.53	2219.22	157.83
20	9055.85	2177.37	199.68
21	8803.24	2124.43	252.62
22	8483.64	2057.46	319.60
23	8079.31	1972.72	404.33
24	7567.77	1865.52	511.54
25	6920.61	1729.89	647.16
26	6101.86	1558.30	818.75
27	5066.04	1341.22	1035.83
28	3755.57	1066.59	1310.47
29	2097.65	719.13	1657.92
30	0.16	279.56	2097.49

Total Payout = $71311.52   Total Interest = $61311.52

Glossary

Acceleration Clause Statement used in a mortgage or installment note giving the lender the right to demand all monies owed to be immediately due and payable upon the occurrence of a certain event, such as failure to pay an installment or anything else threatening the security of the loan. Also known as a **Call-Back Clause**.

Adjustable-Rate Mortgage (ARM) Loan offered at a lower initial interest rate, with the risk that the rate may rise later on. The first-year interest rate is usually indexed to the prime rate or the one-year US Treasury Bill rate. The rate is usually adjusted annually, with a cap on both the annual increase and a cap over the duration of the loan. Also known as a **Variable-Rate Mortgage (VRM)**.

Amortization Repayment of a debt in equal installments, applied to the principal and interest of the loan over a specific period of time to arrive at a balance of zero.

Assets Anything owned by a company or an individual that may be sold to repay debts.

Balloon Loan Loan requiring a series of payments that do not fully repay the loan, and where the balance must be paid out all at once at the end of the loan term in a lump sum. This balance is called a Balloon Payment. Also known as a **Balloon Note**.

Bridge Loan Short-term loan given on one property in order to purchase another. Monies from the sale of the first property must be used to pay off the loan or may also be converted to a second mortgage on the newly acquired property.

Cap Amount specifically negotiated in a mortgage contract that specifies an upper limit to the amount of interest charged in the monthly loan payment and also, possibly, a limit to the total rate of interest charged over the full term of the loan.

Closing Consummation of a real estate transaction between the buyer and the seller to the point when all documents are recorded and title has passed to the buyer.

Closing Costs Expenses incurred by both the buyer and seller in closing on a real estate transaction.

Collateral Personal or real property offered as security for a loan.

Conventional Loan Loan made by a lending institution which is not insured by a government program such as the FHA or VA. Also known as a **Permanent Loan**.

Depreciation Declining value of real or personal property. The loss from the original value is fixed by age and deterioration.

Direct Reduction Mortgage Loan where fixed amounts are paid on the principal while the amount paid on the interest varies according to the outstanding balance. Also known as an **Unequal Installment Mortgage**.

Equity Sum representing an owner's free and clear interest in real property.

Existing Mortgage Balance of a loan on real property.

Fannie Mae Private corporation trading in the discounted purchase of first mortgages. Also known as **FNMA**.

Federal Housing Administration (FHA) Agency of the

Department of Housing and Urban Development which insures first mortgages on homes.

First Mortgage Mortgage on real property whose rights are primary to all others; also, the first mortgage recorded on real property.

Fixed-Rate Mortgage Conventional mortgage with an interest rate and monthly payment that do not change over the duration of the loan.

Flexible Payment Mortgage (FPM) Loan with unequal payments which considers a borrower's current financial position and potential to manage larger payments in the future.

Government National Mortgage Association (GNMA) Federal association, working with the FHA, which purchases FHA loans in a secondary capacity. Also known as **Ginnie Mae**.

Graduated-Payment Mortgage (GPM) Variation on a fixed-rate interest mortgage. The rate of interest is fixed for the duration of the loan, with initially low monthly payments which gradually increase over the first 5 to 10 years of the loan and then level off.

Growing-Equity Mortgage (GEM) Fixed-rate interest mortgage with no interest rate adjustment, where payments increase annually in order to pay off the loan over a shorter period of time.

Interest Payment made for the use of borrowed money.

Interest Rate Annual percentage of the balance on a loan, which is charged as a fee for the use of the money.

Loan Specific sum of money lent on a promise to repay all monies, including interest.

Mortgage Legal document which secures real property in the name of a lender until a loan is fully repaid.

Mortgage Broker Middleman who brings borrowers and lenders together for a fee.

Mortgagee Lender—the party who holds the mortgage.

Mortgagor Borrower—the party who willingly gives the mortgage.

Personal Property Any property that is not deemed real property.

Points Fee(s) charged by lenders to originate a loan, payable over and above monthly interest payments and referring to a specific percentage of the original amount of the principal. Also known as **Discount Points**.

Principal Original or outstanding balance on a mortgage or loan.

Prime Rate Lowest interest rate charged by banks or other commercial lenders on short-term loans.

Real Estate Land and anything permanently attached to the land, such as buildings and fences, as well as anything attached to those buildings, such as plumbing and heating mechanisms. Real estate is (in most states) synonymous with **Real Property**.

Roll-Over Mortgage (ROM) Variation on a variable-rate mortgage where the interest rate is renegotiated at the end of a specific period or the loan must be paid off without a penalty.

Shared Appreciation Mortgage (SAM) Variation on a fixed-rate mortgage where the borrower obtains a lower interest rate by agreeing to share part of the increased value of the property with the lender when the property is sold.

Veteran's Administration (VA) Federal government agency guaranteeing repayment of home mortgages made to eligible veterans.

Telephone Numbers

Telephone Numbers

Telephone Numbers

Telephone Numbers

Notes

Notes